CCNP Enterprise Wireless Design
ENWLSD 300-425
and Implementation
ENWLSI 300-430

Official Cert Guide: Designing & Implementing Cisco Enterprise Wireless Networks

JEROME HENRY, CCIE No. 24750

ROBERT BARTON, CCIE No. 6660

DAVID HUCABY, CCIE No. 4594

Cisco Press

CCNP Enterprise Wireless Design ENWLSD 300-425 and Implementation ENWLSI 300-430 Official Cert Guide: Designing & Implementing Cisco Enterprise Wireless Networks

Jerome Henry
Robert Barton
David Hucaby

Published by:
Cisco Press
Hoboken, New Jersey

1 2020

Library of Congress Control Number: 2020909660

ISBN-13: 978-0-13-660095-4

ISBN-10: 0-13-660095-6

Warning and Disclaimer

This book is designed to provide information about the CCNP Enterprise Wireless Design ENWLSD 300-425 and Enterprise Wireless Implementation ENWLSI 300-430 exams. Every effort has been made to make this book as complete and as accurate as possible, but no warranty or fitness is implied.

The information is provided on an "as is" basis. The authors, Cisco Press, and Cisco Systems, Inc. shall have neither liability nor responsibility to any person or entity with respect to any loss or damages arising from the information contained in this book or from the use of the discs or programs that may accompany it.

The opinions expressed in this book belong to the author and are not necessarily those of Cisco Systems, Inc.

Trademark Acknowledgments

All terms mentioned in this book that are known to be trademarks or service marks have been appropriately capitalized. Cisco Press or Cisco Systems, Inc., cannot attest to the accuracy of this information. Use of a term in this book should not be regarded as affecting the validity of any trademark or service mark.

Special Sales

For information about buying this title in bulk quantities, or for special sales opportunities (which may include electronic versions; custom cover designs; and content particular to your business, training goals, marketing focus, or branding interests), please contact our corporate sales department at corpsales@pearsoned.com or (800) 382-3419.

For government sales inquiries, please contact governmentsales@pearsoned.com.

For questions about sales outside the U.S., please contact intlcs@pearson.com.

Feedback Information

At Cisco Press, our goal is to create in-depth technical books of the highest quality and value. Each book is crafted with care and precision, undergoing rigorous development that involves the unique expertise of members from the professional technical community.

Readers' feedback is a natural continuation of this process. If you have any comments regarding how we could improve the quality of this book, or otherwise alter it to better suit your needs, you can contact us through email at feedback@ciscopress.com. Please make sure to include the book title and ISBN in your message.

We greatly appreciate your assistance.

Editor-in-Chief: Mark Taub

Alliances Manager, Cisco Press: Arezou Gol

Director, ITP Product Management: Brett Bartow

Executive Editor: Nancy Davis

Managing Editor: Sandra Schroeder

Development Editor: Ellie Bru

Project Editor: Mandie Frank

Copy Editor: Bart Reed

Technical Editor: Samuel Clements

Editorial Assistant: Cindy Teeters

Designer: Chuti Prasertsith

Composition: codeMantra

Indexer: Timothy Wright

Proofreader: Donna Mulder

Americas Headquarters
Cisco Systems, Inc.
San Jose, CA

Asia Pacific Headquarters
Cisco Systems (USA) Pte. Ltd.
Singapore

Europe Headquarters
Cisco Systems International BV Amsterdam,
The Netherlands

Cisco has more than 200 offices worldwide. Addresses, phone numbers, and fax numbers are listed on the Cisco Website at **www.cisco.com/go/offices.**

Cisco and the Cisco logo are trademarks or registered trademarks of Cisco and/or its affiliates in the U.S. and other countries. To view a list of Cisco trademarks, go to this URL: www.cisco.com/go/trademarks. Third party trademarks mentioned are the property of their respective owners. The use of the word partner does not imply a partnership relationship between Cisco and any other company. (1110R)

Credits

About the Authors

Jerome Henry, CCIE No. 24750, is a Principal Engineer in the Office of the Wireless CTO at Cisco Systems. Jerome has more than 15 years' experience teaching technical Cisco courses, in more than 15 countries and four languages, to audiences ranging from bachelor's degree students to networking professionals and Cisco internal system engineers. Focusing on his wireless and networking experience, Jerome joined Cisco in 2012. Before that time, he was consulting and teaching about heterogeneous networks and wireless integration with the European Airespace team, which was later acquired by Cisco to become its main wireless solution. He then spent several years with a Cisco Learning Partner, developing networking courses and working on training materials for emerging technologies.

Jerome is a certified wireless networking expert (CWNE No. 45), has developed multiple Cisco courses, and authored several wireless books and video courses. Jerome holds more than 150 patents, is a member of the IEEE, where he was elevated to Senior Member in 2013, and also represents Cisco in multiple Wi-Fi Alliance working groups. With more than 10,000 hours in the classroom, Jerome was awarded the IT Training Award Best Instructor silver medal. He is based in Research Triangle Park, North Carolina.

Robert Barton, CCIE No. 6660, is a Distinguished Architect with Cisco and has worked in the wireless field for over 20 years, assisting with some of the largest Wi-Fi deployments globally. He graduated from the University of British Columbia with a degree in engineering physics and is a registered professional engineer. Rob holds dual CCIEs, in Routing and Switching and Security, and is a CCDE. Rob also holds patents in the areas of wireless communications, IoT, segment routing, and AI/machine learning. Rob is also a regular presenter at Cisco Live and has been inducted into Cisco's Distinguished Speaker Hall of Fame. Rob is located in Vancouver, Canada, where he lives with his wife and two teenage children.

David Hucaby, CCIE No. 4594, CWNE No. 292, is a lead network engineer for University of Kentucky HealthCare, where he focuses on wireless networks in a large medical environment. David holds bachelor's and master's degrees in electrical engineering. He has been authoring Cisco Press titles for 20 years. David lives in Kentucky with his wife, Marci, and two daughters.

About the Technical Reviewers

Samuel Clements is a Mobility Practice Manager for Presidio (www.presidio.com), a VAR in the United States. He is CCIE #40629 (Wireless) and CWNE #101 and is active in all things Wi-Fi. You can find him blogging at www.sc-wifi.com or on Twitter at @samuel_clements. When he's not doing Wi-Fi things, he's spending time in Tennessee with his wife, Sara, and his two children, Tristan and Ginny.

Dedications

Jerome Henry:

In many ways, this century (and probably the previous ones) resembles Wi-Fi. Every few years, new developments fundamentally change the way we work and communicate. Each time we look back a few years, we realize that today we have more information to absorb and more new technologies to understand. What was concluded as impossible is now experimented with or achieved sooner and faster than we thought. As you open this book, dear reader, to prepare for the CCNP exam, you know that this step may look steep today, but it will soon be just a memory of a time you knew less and could do less. Your will to excel and deepen your knowledge is what you, dear reader, give to us, the authors, as a reason to continue sharpening our expertise and share what we have learned on the way. So this book is for you, dear reader, and your aspiration to excellence. As my family blazon says, "sic itur ad astro"—this is how you reach for the stars!

Robert Barton:

When you come to the end of a long book project, it's an interesting experience to step back and reflect on your memories of the many hours spent over weekends, evenings, and holidays to accomplish a work such as this. For me, my enduring memory will be a connection to the early days of the coronavirus stay-at-home period, trying to balance all the unexpected new demands of life with finishing a book. During this time of change we found ways to support each other—physically, emotionally, and spiritually. For this, I dedicate our book to the three most important people in my life—my beautiful wife, Loretta, and my two boys, Adrian and Matthew.

David Hucaby:

As always, my work is dedicated to my wife and my daughters, for their love and support, and to God, who has blessed me with opportunities to learn, write, and work with so many friends—abundant life indeed!

Acknowledgments

My dear wife, Corinne, often says that she knows "that look," she knows "that pace," when I walk back and forth in the corridor of our home leading to my office. She knows when I am not satisfied with a sentence, critical of an explanation that I do not find clear enough, or unhappy with an example or an analogy that does not quite work like it should. Each time, she patiently throws me a question to help me verbalize the problem and, in the end, puts her finger on what was missing. This book would not have been possible without her patience. "Patience made human" is also how I see Brett Bartow, who helped us navigate the complexity of changing exam scopes, and Ellie Bru, who week after week herded us, her authors, corrected our mistakes, and patted our backs to help us stay at the level of quality she expected. If this book is not a collection of dis-organized notes on pieces of napkins, it is thanks to them. And, of course, flying with three pilots only works if each of them mixes excellence in their domain, acceptance that another one may be covering the left or the right field, and a permanent re-assessment of who is where, who has covered what, and who has left what gap or ground to complete. I could not dream of better co-pilots than Rob and Dave—two top guns who were kind enough to accept me and enjoy this flight together.

—*Jerome Henry*

Writing a book can be a monumental undertaking. As we started writing this book in mid-2019, we set out with a firm plan that went through more changes than any of us ever expected. However, for every challenge and curve ball we encountered, we adapted, came together as a team, and rose to the challenge. I am forever grateful to have worked with such incredible co-authors like Jerome and David. Together, we elevated our game and brought out the best in each other. I am truly appreciative to have worked with you both—like Proverbs says, "There is accomplishment through many advisers." You set the bar higher than I could have imagined, and in the end, we crafted an exceptional piece of work together. Thank you, guys!! I would also like to express my deep appreciation to Ellie Bru for her enduring patience, especially for keeping us focused during the hard-est days of the coronavirus stay-at-home period—when work got crazy and our chapter deadlines seemed to loom every day. The sloth emojis and memes really helped illuminate a bright spot of humor during those toughest days.

—*Robert Barton*

I am very grateful to Brett Bartow for giving me the opportunity to work on this project. An unexpected blessing was for two wireless projects to merge into one, allowing me to write alongside Jerome Henry and Rob Barton—two legends and now two friends! They have been great to work with, patient to help me when I needed it, and gracious to make me feel welcome on the team. Ellie Bru has been an awesome development editor and has kept us motivated all along the way with encouragement and funny GIFs. Nancy Davis joined us late in the game and has been a welcome addition to the editorial staff. Many thanks to Samuel Clements for his fine technical editing and review. I have graduated from reading his blog to reading his comments and suggestions. Finally, I would like to thank Eldad Perahia for graciously explaining some complex concepts when I was stuck.

—*David Hucaby*

Contents at a Glance

Reader Services

Register your copy at www.ciscopress.com/title/9780136600954 for convenient access
to downloads, updates, and corrections as they become available. To start the registration
process, go to www.ciscopress.com/register and log in or create an account.* Enter the
product ISBN 9780136600954 and click Submit. When the process is complete, you will
find any available bonus content under Registered Products.

*Be sure to check the box that you would like to hear from us to receive exclusive dis-
counts on future editions of this product.

Contents

Icons Used in This Book

 vBond

 Switch

 Server

 VSS

 Laptop

 vManage

 Router

 File Server

 Route Switch Processor

 WWW Server

 vSmart

 vEdge

 Cloud

 Wireless Router

Command Syntax Conventions

The conventions used to present command syntax in this book are the same conventions used in the IOS Command Reference. The Command Reference describes these conventions as follows:

- **Boldface** indicates commands and keywords that are entered literally as shown. In actual configuration examples and output (not general command syntax), boldface indicates commands that are manually input by the user (such as a **show** command).

- *Italic* indicates arguments for which you supply actual values.

- Vertical bars (|) separate alternative, mutually exclusive elements.

- Square brackets ([ ]) indicate an optional element.

- Braces ({ }) indicate a required choice.

- Braces within brackets ([{ }]) indicate a required choice within an optional element.

Introduction

Congratulations! If you are reading this Introduction, then you have probably decided to obtain a Cisco certification. Obtaining a Cisco certification will ensure that you have a solid understanding of common industry protocols along with Cisco's device architecture and configuration. Cisco has a high market share of network infrastructure of routers, switches, and firewalls, with a global footprint.

Professional certifications have been an important part of the computing industry for many years and will continue to become more important. Many reasons exist for these certifications, but the most popularly cited reason is credibility. All other factors being equal, a certified employee/consultant/job candidate is considered more valuable than one who is not certified.

Cisco provides three levels of certifications: Cisco Certified Network Associate (CCNA), Cisco Certified Network Professional (CCNP), and Cisco Certified Internetwork Expert (CCIE). Cisco made changes to all three certifications, effective February 2020. The following are the most notable of the many changes:

- The exams will include additional topics, such as programming.

- The CCNA certification is not a prerequisite for obtaining the CCNP certification.

- CCNA specializations will not be offered anymore.

- The exams will test a candidate's ability to configure and troubleshoot network devices in addition to answering multiple-choice questions.

- The CCNP is obtained by taking and passing a Core exam and a Concentration exam.

- The CCIE certification requires candidates to pass the Core written exam before the CCIE lab can be scheduled.

CCNP Enterprise candidates need to take and pass the Implementing and Operating Cisco Enterprise Network Core Technologies ENCOR 350-401 examination. Then they need to take and pass one of the following Concentration exams to obtain their CCNP Enterprise:

- 300-410 ENARSI: Implementing Cisco Enterprise Advanced Routing and Services (ENARSI)

- 300-415 ENSDWI: Implementing Cisco SD-WAN Solutions (ENSDWI)

- 300-420 ENSLD: Designing Cisco Enterprise Networks (ENSLD)

- 300-425 ENWLSD: Designing Cisco Enterprise Wireless Networks (ENWLSD)

- 300-430 ENWLSI: Implementing Cisco Enterprise Wireless Networks (ENWLSI)

- 300-435 ENAUTO: Automating and Programming Cisco Enterprise Solutions (ENAUTO)

This book helps you study for the CCNP ENWLSD 300-425 and ENWLSI 300-430 exams. The time allowed to take each test is 90 minutes to complete about 60 questions. Testing is done at Pearson VUE testing centers.

Be sure to visit www.cisco.com to find the latest information on CCNP Concentration requirements and to keep up to date on any new Concentration exams that are announced.

Goals and Methods

The most important and somewhat obvious goal of this book is to help you pass the Designing Cisco Enterprise Wireless Networks ENWLSD 300-425 and Implementing Cisco Enterprise Wireless Networks ENWLSI 300-430 exams. In fact, if the primary objective of this book was different, then the book's title would be misleading; however, the methods used in this book to help you pass the ENWLSD 300-425 and ENWLSI 300-430 exams are designed to also make you much more knowledgeable about how to do your job. While this book and the companion website together have more than enough questions to help you prepare for the actual exam, the method in which they are used is not to simply make you memorize as many questions and answers as you possibly can.

One key methodology used in this book is to help you discover the exam topics you need to review in more depth, to help you fully understand and remember those details, and to help you prove to yourself that you have retained your knowledge of those topics. So, this book does not try to help you pass by memorization, but helps you truly learn and understand the topics. Designing and implementing enterprise wireless networks are two of the concentration areas you can focus on to obtain the CCNP certification, and the knowledge contained within is vitally important to consider yourself a truly skilled Enterprise Wireless Networks engineer. This book will help you pass the ENWLSD 300-425 and ENWLSI 300-430 exams by using the following methods:

- Helping you discover which test topics you have not mastered

- Providing explanations and information to fill in your knowledge gaps

- Supplying exercises and scenarios that enhance your ability to recall and deduce the answers to test questions

Who Should Read This Book?

This book is not designed to be a general wireless networking topics book, although it can be used for that purpose. This book is intended to tremendously increase your chances of passing the Designing Cisco Enterprise Wireless Networks ENWLSD 300-425 and Implementing Cisco Enterprise Wireless Networks ENWLSI 300-430 CCNP specialization exams. Although other objectives can be achieved from using this book, the book is written with one goal in mind: to help you pass the exams.

Strategies for Exam Preparation

The strategy you use to study for the ENWLSD or ENWLSI exam might be slightly different than strategies used by other readers, mainly based on the skills, knowledge, and experience you already have obtained. For instance, if you have attended the ENWLSD or ENWLSI course, then you might take a different approach than someone who learned based on job experience alone.

Regardless of the strategy you use or the background you have, the book is designed to help you get to the point where you can pass the exam with the least amount of time required. For instance, there is no need for you to practice or read about IP addressing and subnetting if you fully understand it already. However, many people like to make sure they truly know a topic and thus read over material they already know. Several book features will help you gain the confidence you need to be convinced that you know some material already and to also help you know what topics you need to study more.

The Companion Website for Online Content Review

All the electronic review elements, as well as other electronic components of the book, exist on this book's companion website.

How to Access the Companion Website

To access the companion website, which gives you access to the electronic content with this book, start by establishing a login at www.ciscopress.com and registering your book. To do so, simply go to www.ciscopress.com/register and enter the ISBN of the print book: 9780136600954. After you have registered your book, go to your account page and click the Registered Products tab. From there, click the Access Bonus Content link to get access to the book's companion website.

Note that if you buy the Premium Edition eBook and Practice Test version of this book from Cisco Press, your book will automatically be registered on your account page.

Simply go to your account page, click the Registered Products tab, and select Access Bonus Content to access the book's companion website.

How to Access the Pearson Test Prep (PTP) App

You have two options for installing and using the Pearson Test Prep application: a web app and a desktop app. To use the Pearson Test Prep application, start by finding the registration code that comes with the book. You can find the code in these ways:

- **Print book:** Look in the cardboard sleeve in the back of the book for a piece of paper with your book's unique PTP code.

- **Premium Edition:** If you purchase the Premium Edition eBook and Practice Test directly from the Cisco Press website, the code will be populated on your account page after purchase. Just log in at www.ciscopress.com, click Account to see details of your account, and click the digital purchases tab.

- **Amazon Kindle:** For those who purchase a Kindle edition from Amazon, the access code will be supplied directly from Amazon.

- **Other Bookseller eBooks:** Note that if you purchase an eBook version from any other source, the practice test is not included because other vendors to date have not chosen to vend the required unique access code.

> **NOTE** Do not lose the activation code because it is the only means with which you can access the QA content with the book.

Once you have the access code, to find instructions about both the PTP web app and the desktop app, follow these steps:

Step 1. Open this book's companion website, as shown earlier in this Introduction under the heading "How to Access the Companion Website."

Step 2. Click the Practice Exams button.

Step 3. Follow the instructions listed there both for installing the desktop app and for using the web app.

Note that if you want to use the web app only at this point, just navigate to www.pearsontestprep.com, establish a free login if you do not already have one, and register this book's practice tests using the registration code you just found. The process should take only a couple of minutes.

> **NOTE** Amazon eBook (Kindle) customers: It is easy to miss Amazon's email that lists your PTP access code. Soon after you purchase the Kindle eBook, Amazon should send an email. However, the email uses very generic text, and makes no specific mention of PTP or practice exams. To find your code, read every email from Amazon after you purchase the book. Also do the usual checks for ensuring your email arrives, like checking your spam folder.

> **NOTE** Other eBook customers: As of the time of publication, only the publisher and Amazon supply PTP access codes when you purchase their eBook editions of this book.

How This Book Is Organized

Although this book could be read cover to cover, it is designed to be flexible and allow you to easily move between chapters and sections of chapters to cover just the material you need more work with. Chapters 1 through 9 cover wireless design topics that are relevant for the ENWLSD 300-425 exam, while Chapters 10 through 17 cover topics related to implementing wireless networks for the ENWLSI 300-430 exam.

The core chapters, Chapters 1 through 17, cover the following topics:

- **Chapter 1, "Wireless Design Requirements"** This chapter covers important wireless aspects of customer networks, access points, and client devices that can drive an effective network design.

- **Chapter 2, "Conducting an Offsite Site Survey"** This chapter describes how to prepare for an offsite site survey, by looking at common verticals requirements, determining obstacles' signal absorption, and conducting a predictive site survey.

- **Chapter 3, "Conducting an Onsite Site Survey"** This chapter discusses the onsite survey process, including the survey tools and the survey methodology. This chapter also provides recommendations on survey settings for data, voice, and location services.

- **Chapter 4, "Physical and Logical Infrastructure Requirements"** This chapter discusses the physical infrastructure, such as power and cabling, mounting, and grounding. The chapter also discusses the logical infrastructure components that support wireless services.

- **Chapter 5, "Applying Wireless Design Requirements"** This chapter discusses the behavior of specific applications and traffic types being carried over a wireless network, along with the network design guidelines and best practices for each.

- **Chapter 6, "Designing Radio Management"** This chapter explains Radio Resource Management (RRM) and how you can leverage it to automatically manage AP transmit power levels and channel assignments, along with adjustments for changing RF conditions.

- **Chapter 7, "Designing Wireless Mesh Networks"** This chapter introduces wireless mesh technology and details how mesh networks are designed. The chapter reviews mesh components and architecture and key design recommendations for outdoor mesh environments.

- **Chapter 8, "Designing for Client Mobility"** This chapter covers wireless client mobility, or the roaming process, along with ways to make it more efficient and seamless.

- **Chapter 9, "Designing High Availability"** This chapter introduces the features and strategies you can leverage to improve wireless LAN controller availability in case of equipment or link failure.

- **Chapter 10, "Implementing FlexConnect"** This chapter looks at branch office wireless deployments with a focus on FlexConnect. The chapter discusses how FlexConnect groups can be implemented as well as key features of FlexConnect. This chapter also discusses Office Extend APs (OEAP).

- **Chapter 11, "Implementing Quality of Service on a Wireless Network"** This chapter begins with a review of wireless QoS standards and how these are implemented in Cisco wireless controllers. The chapter also looks at key QoS capabilities such as Application Visibility and Control (AVC).

- **Chapter 12, "Implementing Multicast"** This chapter explains multicast traffic delivery in a wireless network, along with the features that can make it more efficient. Also covered are methods to handle multicast DNS as well as video stream delivery.

- **Chapter 13, "Location Services Deployment"** This chapter discusses how location is achieved using Wi-Fi technologies. This chapter also explains how to deploy location engines, such as CMX/MSE and DNA Spaces, and how to use them to track clients, interferers, and rogues.

- **Chapter 14, "Advanced Location Services Implementation"** This chapter explains how to make the most of your location engine, by implementing advanced features such as location-aware guest services and wireless intrusion protection systems (WIPSs). This chapter also discusses the implementation of Analytics and Presence services.

- **Chapter 15, "Security for Wireless Client Connectivity"** This chapter discusses wireless client authentication methods, such as Extensible Authentication Protocol (EAP). The chapter also discusses guest wireless access and how bring your own devices (BYODs) can be securely onboarded to a network.

- **Chapter 16, "Monitoring and Troubleshooting WLAN Components"** This chapter covers report and alarm management on Cisco Prime Infrastructure and DNA Center (DNAC). This chapter also discusses how to troubleshoot client connectivity and performance on the wireless LAN controller (WLC), Prime Infrastructure, and DNAC.

- **Chapter 17, "Device Hardening"** This chapter looks at how the security of wireless devices can be improved by controlling access to the wireless infrastructure and how APs can authenticate to a network.

Certification Exam Topics and This Book

The questions for each certification exam are a closely guarded secret. However, Cisco has published exam blueprints that list which topics you must know to *successfully* complete the exam. Table I-1 lists each exam topic listed in the blueprint along with a reference to the book chapter that covers the topic. These are the same topics you should be proficient in when designing and implementing Cisco Enterprise wireless networks in the real world.

Table I-1 ENWLSD 300-425 and ENWLSI 300-430 Exam Topics and Chapter References

Exam	Exam Topic	Chapter(s) in Which Topic Is Covered
ENWLSD 300-425	1.1 Collect design requirements and evaluate constraints	1
ENWLSD 300-425	1.2 Describe material attenuation and its effect on wireless design	2

Exam	Exam Topic	Chapter(s) in Which Topic Is Covered
ENWLSD 300-425	1.3 Perform and analyze a Layer 1 site survey	3
ENWLSD 300-425	1.4 Perform a pre-deployment site survey	3
ENWLSD 300-425	1.5 Perform a post-deployment site survey	3
ENWLSD 300-425	1.6 Perform a predictive site survey	2
ENWLSD 300-425	1.7 Utilize planning tools and evaluate key network metrics (Ekahau, AirMagnet, PI, Chanalyzer, Spectrum Analyzer)	2
ENWLSD 300-425	2.1 Determine physical infrastructure requirements such as AP power, cabling, switch port capacity, mounting, and grounding	4
ENWLSD 300-425	2.2 Determine logical infrastructure requirements such as WLC/AP licensing requirements based on the type of wireless architecture	4
ENWLSD 300-425	2.3 Design radio management	6
ENWLSD 300-425	2.4 Apply design requirements for these types of wireless networks	5
ENWLSD 300-425	2.5 Design high-density wireless networks and their associated components (campus, lecture halls, conference rooms)	5
ENWLSD 300-425	2.6 Design wireless bridging (mesh)	7
ENWLSD 300-425	3.1 Design mobility groups based on mobility roles	8
ENWLSD 300-425	3.2 Optimize client roaming	8
ENWLSD 300-425	3.3 Validate mobility tunneling for data and control path	8
ENWLSD 300-425	4.1 Design high availability for controllers	9
ENWLSD 300-425	4.2 Design high availability for APs	9
ENWLSI 300-430	1.1 Deploy FlexConnect components such as switching and operating modes	10
ENWLSI 300-430	1.2 Deploy FlexConnect capabilities	10
ENWLSI 300-430	1.3 Implement Office Extend	10
ENWLSI 300-430	2.1 Implement QoS schemes based on requirements including wired-to-wireless mapping	11
ENWLSI 300-430	2.2 Implement QoS for wireless clients	11
ENWLSI 300-430	2.3 Implement AVC including Fastlane (only on WLC)	11
ENWLSI 300-430	3.1 Implement multicast components	12
ENWLSI 300-430	3.2 Describe how multicast can affect wireless networks	12

Exam	Exam Topic	Chapter(s) in Which Topic Is Covered
ENWLSI 300-430	3.3 Implement multicast on a WLAN	12
ENWLSI 300-430	3.4 Implement mDNS	12
ENWLSI 300-430	3.5 Implement Multicast Direct	12
ENWLSI 300-430	4.1 Deploy MSE and CMX on a wireless network	13
ENWLSI 300-430	4.2 Implement location services	13
ENWLSI 300-430	5.1 Implement CMX components	14
ENWLSI 300-430	5.2 Implement location-aware guest services using custom portal and Facebook Wi-Fi	14
ENWLSI 300-430	5.3 Troubleshoot location accuracy using Cisco Hyperlocation	14
ENWLSI 300-430	5.4 Troubleshoot CMX high availability	14
ENWLSI 300-430	5.5 Implement WIPS using MSE	14
ENWLSI 300-430	6.1 Configure client profiling on WLC and ISE	15
ENWLSI 300-430	6.2 Implement BYOD and guest	15
ENWLSI 300-430	6.3 Implement 802.1X and AAA on different wireless architectures and ISE	15
ENWLSI 300-430	6.4 Implement Identity-Based Networking on different wireless architectures (VLANs, QoS, ACLs)	15
ENWLSI 300-430	7.1 Utilize reports on PI and Cisco DNA-C	16
ENWLSI 300-430	7.2 Manage alarms and rogues (APs and clients)	16
ENWLSI 300-430	7.3 Manage RF Interferers	16
ENWLSI 300-430	7.4 Troubleshoot client connectivity	16
ENWLSI 300-430	8.1 Implement device access controls (including RADIUS and TACACS+)	17
ENWLSI 300-430	8.2 Implement access point authentication (including 802.1X)	17
ENWLSI 300-430	8.3 Implement CPU ACLs on the controller	17

Each version of the exam can have topics that emphasize different functions or features, and some topics can be rather broad and generalized. The goal of this book is to provide the most comprehensive coverage to ensure that you are well prepared for the exam. Although some chapters might not address specific exam topics, they provide a foundation that is necessary for a clear understanding of important topics. Your short-term goal might be to pass this exam, but your long-term goal should be to become a qualified CCNP Enterprise wireless engineer.

It is also important to understand that this book is a "static" reference, whereas the exam topics are dynamic. Cisco can and does change the topics covered on certification exams often.

This exam guide should not be your only reference when preparing for the certification exam. You can find a wealth of information available at Cisco.com that covers each topic in great detail. If you think you need more detailed information on a specific topic, read the Cisco documentation that focuses on that topic.

Note that as CCNP Enterprise wireless network technologies continue to evolve, Cisco reserves the right to change the exam topics without notice. Although you can refer to the list of exam topics in Table I-1, always check Cisco.com to verify the actual list of topics to ensure you are prepared before taking the exam. You can view the current exam topics on any current Cisco certification exam by visiting the Cisco.com website, choosing Menu, clicking Training & Events, and then selecting from the Certifications list. Note also that, if needed, Cisco Press might post additional preparatory content on the web page associated with this book at www.ciscopress.com/title/9780136600954. It's a good idea to check the website a couple of weeks before taking your exam to be sure that you have up-to-date content.

Part I

Wireless Design (ENWLSD)

CHAPTER 1

Wireless Design Requirements

This chapter covers the following topics:

> **Following a Design Process:** This section describes the framework of a formal design process that Cisco recommends for the lifecycle of a network.
>
> **Evaluating Customer Requirements:** This section gives an overview of common parameters you should investigate with the end customer prior to beginning a wireless network design and site survey.
>
> **Evaluating Client Requirements:** This section discusses wireless device specifications and how you can interpret them as guidelines for a wireless design.
>
> **Choosing AP Types:** This brief section describes the basic AP types and how you can apply them to a wireless design.
>
> **Evaluating Security Requirements:** This section covers some design considerations related to security requirements in a wireless network.
>
> **AP Deployment Models:** This section describes the basic guidelines for deploying APs in network designs that focus on generic data, real-time applications, and location-based services.

This chapter covers the following ENWLSD exam topics:

- 1.1 Collect design requirements and evaluate constraints
    - 1.1.a Client density
    - 1.1.b Real-time applications
    - 1.1.c AP type
    - 1.1.d Deployment type (data, location, voice, video)
    - 1.1.e Security

Have you ever gone to a new location—perhaps an airport, hotel, restaurant, hospital, or even someone's home—and hoped you could use a wireless network with a device you were carrying? Think about the process you went through. First, you had to find a wireless network in that location, attempt to join it, and then attempt to use it. Hopefully you were successful and the network performed adequately during the time you used it. What applications did you use at the time? How many other people were using the same network along with you? Most likely you were a guest on the network, so you may have suffered through a less-than-enjoyable experience. Now suppose you were using a medical device that controlled a life support or patient safety function. Would your expectations change? You would probably want the wireless network to be very fast, very reliable, and very available in every possible location.

Wireless networks might appear to be simple and ubiquitous to the casual user, but they can be quite complex behind the scenes. In order to properly support all wireless users, a wireless network must be properly designed and implemented. In this chapter, you learn more about formal network design processes, as well as what important information you should gather from customers regarding their wireless network. You also learn how to evaluate several types of requirements and constraints that will help guide you toward an effective wireless design.

"Do I Know This Already?" Quiz

The "Do I Know This Already?" quiz allows you to assess whether you should read this entire chapter thoroughly or jump to the "Exam Preparation Tasks" section. If you are in doubt about your answers to these questions or your own assessment of your knowledge of the topics, read the entire chapter. Table 1-1 lists the major headings in this chapter and their corresponding "Do I Know This Already?" quiz questions. You can find the answers in Appendix D, "Answers to the 'Do I Know This Already?' Quizzes and Review Questions."

Table 1-1 "Do I Know This Already?" Section-to-Question Mapping

Foundation Topics Section	Questions
Following a Design Process	1
Evaluating Customer Requirements	2
Evaluating Client Requirements	3–5
Choosing AP Types	6
Evaluating Security Requirements	7
AP Deployment Models	8–10

1. Which one of the following describes a formal design process often used in the lifecycle of a network?

    a. FRA

    b. IEEE

    c. PPDIOO

    d. PBR

2. When you meet with a customer to gather information about an upcoming wireless project, which one of the following things will be most helpful as you prepare to perform a site survey?

    a. The scope of the project

    b. A list of buildings and locations that need wireless service

    c. Floor plans of buildings that need wireless service

    d. Diagrams of the wired network infrastructure

3. Suppose you collect information about the wireless devices that will be used at a customer's site. Which one of the following specifications will determine which bands you should enable in your wireless design?

   a. 802.11b/g/n

   b. Data rates: 6–54Mbps

   c. Antenna gain: 2.0 dBi

   d. Sensitivity: –90 dBm

4. Which one of the following wireless client specifications is helpful in designing the size of an AP cell?

   a. The antenna gain

   b. The receiver sensitivity

   c. The number of spatial streams

   d. The data rates supported

5. A high-density area in a wireless design is determined by which one of the following things?

   a. More clients are using the 5GHz band than the 2.4GHz band.

   b. A small number of clients in an area are using high-bandwidth applications.

   c. A higher number of clients associate with each AP in an area.

   d. A higher amount of RF coverage is needed in an area.

6. Which one of the following applications would be the most appropriate use for an AP model that has internal antennas?

   a. A location where a relatively wide coverage area is desired

   b. A location where coverage is needed toward one side of the AP

   c. A location where a patch antenna's pattern is required

   d. A location where an omnidirectional antenna is not desirable

7. Suppose a customer wants potential users to enter a username and password before being granted access to the wireless network. Which of the following items could you add to the list of requirements for your wireless design to meet the customer's requirement?

   a. RADIUS servers

   b. AAA servers

   c. ISE servers

   d. AES servers

8. In a data deployment model, which one of the following statements is true?

   a. Strict jitter requirements must be met.

   b. Strict latency requirements must be met.

   c. Strict packet loss requirements must be met.

   d. No specific requirements must be met.

9. Suppose a customer wants to use an application that requires jitter to be less than 30 milliseconds. Which one of the following AP deployment models is indicated for the wireless network design?

   a. Data deployment model

   b. Voice deployment model

   c. Location deployment model

   d. There is not enough information given to determine a deployment model.

10. Which one of the following parameters is used to estimate a client device's location in a wireless network?

    a. Wireless MAC address

    b. Ping response times

    c. Phase differential

    d. Received signal strength

Foundation Topics

Following a Design Process

Like any other complex network, a wireless network design should be approached by following a formal design process. Even if you have built a simple wireless network at home with one access point, you have likely gone through several different steps in a design process. For example, you probably began by determining that your home needed a wireless network, and then you set aside money to buy the AP and picked a date to do the work. You probably decided to install the AP in a central location to give RF coverage over the most living space. You might have thought about which 802.11 features you would like to use. Next, you installed and configured the AP, and then you and your family enjoyed using the new wireless network. Finally, perhaps a neighbor began using the same channel as your AP, so you had to move yours to a different channel to improve its performance.

The process just described follows a well-known Cisco lifecycle process that applies to both simple and very large, complex networks alike. The *PPDIOO* process is named from the first letter of its six phases: Prepare, Plan, Design, Implement, Operate, Optimize. As the left portion of Figure 1-1 illustrates, PPDIOO begins with the Prepare phase, where an organization usually determines a business case and a high-level design for a new network. As an example, suppose a new wing will be added to an existing building, and the new wing will need a wireless network to support the business's users and devices. This requirement leads into the Plan phase, which involves examining details about the site, determining any existing network to be upgraded or migrated, and identifying a set of network requirements. The Plan phase leads into the Design phase, where a detailed network design specification is developed. The detailed design usually specifies the equipment and features needed to provide the appropriate level of availability, reliability, scalability, performance, and security to support the business operations.

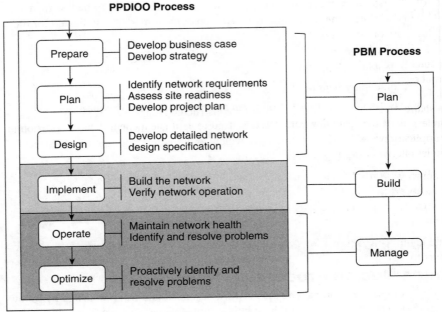

Figure 1-1 *The PPDIOO and PBM Lifecycle Processes*

Once a detailed design is produced, the Implement phase can begin, and the network can be built according to the design specifications. This is followed by the Operate phase, where the network implementation is put into production and maintained and monitored on a day-to-day basis. Any faults or problems should be detected and remediated too. Finally, the Optimize phase is used to replace reactive problem resolution with a more proactive approach to minimize future issues and outages. Notice that the Optimize phase also leads back into the Prepare phase so that recurring problems or other shortcomings, as well as network upgrades, can be addressed as continuous improvements. In other words, the sequence of six phases becomes an organized cycle of activities.

Cisco also uses the Plan-Build-Manage (PBM) process, illustrated in the right portion of Figure 1-1. The concept is identical to that of PPDIOO, but the process is simplified into three phases instead of six.

As you work through the chapters of this book, you will learn how to leverage your wireless expertise and knowledge as you participate in various wireless design activities. For example, you might meet with a customer to gather requirements as part of the Prepare phase. You could perform site surveys as part of the Plan and Design phases. In fact, Chapters 1–9 are devoted to Design phase–oriented work, whereas Chapters 10–15 focus on the Implement phase. Chapters 16 and 17 involve tasks like verifying, optimizing, monitoring, troubleshooting, and hardening—tasks that usually take place in the Operate and Optimize phases.

Evaluating Customer Requirements

The first step toward building a wireless network is to figure out exactly what you are trying to build. In other words, you need to develop a plan that is based on some requirements. While it is possible to build a wireless network at home by simply standing up one wireless

AP with its default configuration, that approach will likely not be useful in a corporate environment. After all, you should position the AP in a location where wireless coverage is needed and where it can serve the most users. In most cases, you will need many APs, even thousands of them, to cover every area where the customer expects its wireless users to be.

The plan quickly gets more complicated when you consider all of the variables involved with one customer, which might be completely different from the variables found with another customer. For instance, physical facilities are not the same everywhere. Buildings are usually unique in shape, size, and layout. They might be constructed from different materials, which affect wireless signals in different ways. Each business might use different wireless devices, different applications, and different functions, which could require appropriate adjustments to the wireless network design and configuration.

The best approach is to begin by meeting with and interviewing the customer. Gather information about the scope of the wireless project. Is the goal to build a new network or upgrade or expand an existing one? Find out if the project should address any existing wireless problems or support increasing numbers of users.

You should identify which locations, campuses, buildings, rooms, and areas where the customer wants to offer wireless service. This information will allow you to estimate the number of wireless LAN controllers, APs, and other devices needed to provide wireless coverage. It will also let you estimate the total floor area so that you know how long it will take to walk every area to perform site survey work. You will use site surveys to determine where each AP should be located and to verify the resulting coverage once the APs become operational. You can learn more about site surveys in Chapter 2, "Conducting an Offsite Site Survey," and Chapter 3, "Conducting an Onsite Site Survey," in this book.

Learning more about the project scope will also reveal information about the underlying wired network infrastructure. After all, you will need to connect wireless controllers and APs to a wired data network. If the customer has multiple sites or buildings, you may need to add some connecting infrastructure to your design. You can learn more about the wired network needed to support wireless service in Chapter 4, "Physical and Logical Infrastructure Requirements."

Find out more about the customer's user community and note types of users and their general job functions. Which areas do they frequent? What wireless devices do they use? Which applications are critical to the users' functions? The answers to these general questions will lead into more detailed information gathering, explained in the next sections.

Be sure to ask the customer to provide drawings of each building and floor area where wireless coverage will be needed. Electronic versions of the drawings will be invaluable as you perform site surveys. Printed versions will be useful when you mark AP locations, need to measure distances, check building materials, and jot down noteworthy things to remember about the sites.

If possible, tour the facilities so you can see every area that will need wireless coverage. Take notes and photos of typical areas to be covered. Note any special requirements and aesthetic constraints. For example, some large classrooms or auditoriums may need coverage, but APs might need to be located on high ceilings or in unexpected locations. Sometimes the customer might not want APs or antennas to be seen at all in buildings with historic or special significance. Warehouses might require unique AP locations due to shelving and stored materials. Lobbies and open walkways might need coverage if users travel through those areas and need wireless service. Keep in mind that every building and floor is unique and could require unique approaches to wireless coverage.

As you inspect the facilities and plans, make sure you understand the customer's expectations for each area too. For example, you might notice that one building has several large classrooms and a large lobby area. If you toured the building at a time when those areas were empty, you might not realize that the customer expects every classroom to support streaming video over the wireless network and that the lobby must support large numbers of people as they move between classes. Likewise, a healthcare customer might show you a large emergency department and an outdoor area where ambulances arrive. Unless you ask, you might not realize that the customer expects the outdoor area to have full wireless coverage for emergency staff, each carrying a wireless phone, as they move in and around a large number of ambulance vehicles. Ask about the need to cover stairwells, elevators, outside entrances, and other gathering places.

Vehicles are one example of large objects that can change location over time. You might also encounter helicopters on a rooftop helipad, forklifts in a warehouse or manufacturing facility, movable shelves full of books in a library, large doors, stacks of inventory, and so on. All of these things are objects that can attenuate or block wireless signals. Even if you know about them ahead of time and can plan the wireless coverage accordingly, they might move later on and affect another location that you did not anticipate.

You should become aware of the type of wireless coverage that the customer expects in each area. Some areas might need basic wireless coverage for users who are located throughout, while other areas receive multitudes of users who are densely packed and expect a high level of network performance. In other words, always evaluate each area according to RF coverage versus capacity. These topics are covered in greater detail in Chapter 5, "Applying Wireless Design Requirements."

Evaluating Client Requirements

It might seem obvious that the focus of a wireless design is to provide wireless coverage in all desired areas. The coverage should take the client or user population into account so that network performance is acceptable to all users, even the ones in densely populated areas. With these criteria, along with thorough site survey work, you should be able to choose the number and location of APs that are necessary.

Notice that the coverage is based on the number of "clients," as if all wireless clients are identical in feature sets and functions. This is usually not the case. A typical corporate site can have many different types and models of wireless client devices. For example, users might have a range of laptops and tablets made by various manufacturers. They might also carry wireless phones. You might also find wireless cameras, industrial control devices, medical devices, security devices, and so on. To participate in the wireless network, all devices must be compatible with the IEEE 802.11 standard. However, each device type and model can have very different capabilities and specifications. For this reason, an effective wireless design must also address client device requirements.

The IEEE 802.11 standard is very complex and consists of several thousand pages. Every wireless device must adhere to fundamental definitions like the 802.11 frame format, clear channel assessment, and so on, but may not support every possible feature defined in the standard. For example, some client devices may support 802.11a and 802.11n but not 802.11ac. Generally, an AP can support a wide range of 802.11 features because it acts as the hub for a mixed bag of clients. Not every feature is enabled or configured on an AP, but you may have to include and tune them as part of your wireless design. As you enable, disable, or tune each feature, you should make sure that doing so does not isolate or exclude any client devices the customer wants to support.

When you meet with a customer to begin a wireless design, you should gather information about all of the wireless devices used in each facility. Find out the device type (laptop, phone, RFID tag, and so on), manufacturer, and model number and then collect a list of technical specifications. The specifications, which can often be found on a product data sheet, list things like 802.11 support, RF capabilities, supported security suites, quality of service requirements, and so on. The information you collect will serve a twofold purpose:

- You can verify that your wireless design and configuration will support each device type in use

- You can identify the least capable of the supported devices, which will define some minimum design requirements

As an example, suppose you have consulted a customer and learned of four types of wireless devices being used in the enterprise. The customer is a healthcare provider using mobile surveillance cameras, voice communicators, wireless phones, and embedded wireless modules, among many other devices. (The embedded module is typically found in things like hospital beds and factory equipment.) In this scenario, all four devices are critical to the organization's mission, so your wireless design must support them completely. Other common devices, such as laptops and tablets are in use too, but their specifications are not shown for simplicity. Tables 1-2 through 1-4 list many of the device specifications you have collected.

Examining Client 802.11 Capabilities

Table 1-2 lists many of the specifications related to 802.11 functions. For example, notice that all four device types support both the 2.4 and 5GHz bands. If a device supported only one band, you would have to make sure that your design offered that band for use. As it stands, you should be able to design with dual-band APs to accommodate any device type.

Next, you might compare the values shown in the "802.11" row to see which 802.11 amendments each device type supports. Two of the devices support a/b/g/n, while the other two add support for ac. This information becomes important if you decide to disable specific data rates to improve performance and adjust the cell size of the APs. Fortunately, none of the devices requires only 802.11b, so you might think about disabling the slowest corresponding data rates. The information listed in the "Data Rates" row can also guide your rate tuning efforts.

Table 1-2   Example Wireless Device 802.11 Specifications

	Mobile Surveillance Camera	Voice Communicator	Wireless Phone	Embedded Wireless Module
Bands Supported	2.4GHz, 5GHz	2.4GHz, 5GHz	2.4GHz, 5GHz	2.4GHz, 5GHz
802.11	a/b/g/n/ac	a/b/g/n	a/b/g/n/ac	a/b/g/n

	Mobile Surveillance Camera	Voice Communicator	Wireless Phone	Embedded Wireless Module
Channels				
2.4GHz	1 to 13	11 channels	1 to 13	1 to 13
5GHz	36–48, 52–64, 100–140, 144, 149–161	20 channels	36–48, 52–64, 100–140, 149–165	All, but DFS not recommended
Channel Width	2.4GHz: 20, 40MHz 5GHz: 20, 40, 80MHz	2.4GHz: 20MHz 5GHz: 20, 40MHz	2.4GHz: 20MHz 5GHz: 20, 40, 80MHz	Unspecified
Data Rates	Unspecified	Unspecified		
802.11b			1–11Mbps	1–11Mbps
802.11g			6–54Mbps	6–54Mbps
802.11a			6–54Mbps	6–54Mbps
802.11n			MCS 0–7	MCS 0–6
802.11ac			MCS 0–8	N/A
802.11k	Not supported	Supported	Unspecified	Unspecified
802.11r (FT)	Not supported	Supported	Supported	Unspecified
802.11w	Not supported	Supported	Unspecified	Unspecified

Notice that each device type supports a specific list of channels on each band. On 2.4GHz, the voice communicator can work with channels 1 through 11, which may mean the device can be used only in the United States. The 5GHz channel specifications listed are not very consistent across the devices. Your basic wireless design can simply include 5GHz support, but you will probably have to decide which U-NII bands to enable based on the list of channels supported. This becomes important if a device supports channels that your design might have disabled. The device will still find APs operating on valid channels, but it may spend valuable time scanning the disabled channels to look for APs there. This wasted time can make roaming from one AP to another much longer, disrupting the user experience.

One unique difference among the devices can be found in the list of channels. The embedded wireless module can support all 5GHz channels but includes a note that discourages use of any Dynamic Frequency Selection (DFS) channel. DFS channels carry a special requirement that the AP and all clients using a channel must abandon it temporarily if a radar signal is detected. The process of abandoning a channel and moving to a different one takes valuable time, which would disrupt communications. Therefore, if you had planned on enabling all of the U-NII-1, U-NII-2, U-NII-2 Extended, and U-NII-3 bands to take advantage of the greatest number of available channels, you might be disregarding the recommendation. Instead, you should consider disabling the U-NII-2 and U-NII-2 Extended bands to avoid using the DFS channels.

You should also pay attention to the data rates supported by each device type. As you will learn later in this book, you will want to disable some of the lowest data rates on the APs to limit the size of their RF coverage or cell areas. As long as each device type can still support the remaining higher data rates that you will leave enabled, it should operate successfully. However, you might have some legacy or unique devices that require some lower data rates. If you disable those rates, the devices will not be able to operate at all.

You might also compare device support for the 802.11k and r amendments, which offer more efficient roaming between APs. The 802.11w amendment includes support for securing management frames over the wireless network. If you decide to enable support for these features, you should make sure that the wireless devices also support them.

Examining Client RF Capabilities

Wireless devices can also differ according to their RF capabilities, as shown by the sample devices in Table 1-3. For example, the transmit power level of one device might be very different from that of another device. This variation is usually due to the form factor involved. If a device is relatively small, such as a wireless phone or voice communicator, its battery is probably small too. The device may limit its transmit power to a lower level so that it can conserve its battery power throughout the day.

Table 1-3 Example Wireless Device RF Specifications

	Mobile Surveillance Camera	Voice Communicator	Wireless Phone	Embedded Wireless Module
Spatial Streams	2×2	Unspecified	Unspecified	1×1
Antenna Gain	Unspecified	Unspecified	2.4GHz: 2.4 dBi 5GHz: 3.0 dBi	Unspecified
Transmit Power (max, U.S.)	Unspecified	16 dBm	2.4GHz: 13 dBm 5GHz: 12 dBm	2.4GHz: 13 dBm 5GHz: 15 dBm
Sensitivity **2.4GHz**	–70 dBm			
11Mbps		–85 dBm	–91 dBm	–91 dBm
54Mbps		–71 dBm	–77 dBm	–78 dBm
5GHz (20MHz)				
6Mbps		–90 dBm	–94 dBm	–85 dBm
54Mbps		–73 dBm	–76 dBm	–73 dBm
802.11ac MCS7		–70 dBm	–74 dBm	–70 dBm
802.11ac MCS8		N/A	–70 dBm	–65 dBm

The maximum transmit power is an important specification to examine, as it defines the RF coverage area that extends from the device toward the APs. Ideally, the device and AP transmit power levels should be equal or symmetric so that the signals can travel and be received in both directions. Normally your wireless designs will focus on the coverage area of each AP. Any site surveys you perform will also measure the AP cell areas. You should also consider RF coverage provided by each device type, so that you can confirm that signals from the devices will be received intelligibly at the APs.

The size and shape of the device can also influence the construction and location of its antenna. Laptop antennas are usually mounted inside the display "lid," which can offer more space for the antenna, more of an upright orientation, and more antenna gain. The antennas on smaller devices are likely crowded in with other electronics and components, where they cannot even be exposed or extended. This can result in an antenna gain that is very low—even zero or a negative dBi value!

You should also be aware that a device's form factor can affect its performance due to the way it is held. A person's head or body can attenuate RF signals, particularly if the AP is on one side and the device is on the other. One example is a wireless phone held against a person's head during a call. Another is a seated person using a laptop in a classroom.

As you work through the wireless design process, you will need to choose the minimum signal level that defines the extent of the AP cells. When a client device is located near the edge of an AP cell, it must be able to receive the AP's signal at a level that is above the threshold its receiver requires to interpret the signal. That threshold is known as the *receiver sensitivity*.

Notice how the receiver sensitivity specifications are listed in Table 1-3. The values are not consistent across all of the device types simply because each one uses different circuitry and antennas to receive signals. The values also differ according to the 2.4 and 5GHz data rates listed in the leftmost column. As a rule of thumb, increasing data rates use more complex methods to encode and modulate the signal. This, in turn, requires higher *signal-to-noise ratios (SNRs)* and received signal levels that are higher than the sensitivity threshold. As you work on a wireless design, you should compare the receiver sensitivity values of all the devices that will be supported. Be sure to use the values listed for the minimum data rate your network will support. Then choose the lowest sensitivity value and use that as the minimum signal level at the AP cell boundaries.

Examining Client Security Capabilities

Recall that the 802.11 standard defines two methods of authentication: open and WEP. That means every client device should support both methods. WEP has been long deprecated due to its security weakness. Open authentication is used as a simple test to verify that a client is an 802.11 device. That might make you think that all client devices inherently have a complete support for wireless security. However, open authentication can also be used in concert with 802.1x port-based security and the Extensible Authentication Protocol (EAP) to offer a wide range of authentication methods. In other words, all wireless clients are not created equally.

As an example, look at the security specifications listed for each device type in Table 1-4. Each device can support a dizzying list of wireless security measures, yet that list is not consistent across all of the devices. The customer will likely want to leverage the most robust security mechanisms to protect the wireless network, but that method must also be supported on all of the devices that will use the network. Notice that the embedded wireless module has capabilities for WPA2-Personal and WPA2-Enterprise but no support for digital certificates. You should be aware of that limitation, as it could narrow the range of possible security mechanisms.

Table 1-4   Example Wireless Device Security and QoS Specifications

	Mobile Surveillance Camera	Voice Communicator	Wireless Phone	Embedded Wireless Module
Security	WPA (AES), WPA2 (AES), 802.1x (EAP), WPA-Enterprise, WPA2-Enterprise, EAP-TLS, EAP-PEAP, EAP-TTLS (PAP, CHAP, MSCHAP, MSCHAPv2)	None, WEP, TKIP, AES-CCMP, WPA/WPA2 Personal and Enterprise, LEAP, PEAP, MSCHAPv2, EAP-FAST, EAP-TLS	WPA/WPA2 Personal and Enterprise, EAP-FAST, PEAP-GTC, PEAP-MSCHAPv2, EAP-TLS	WPA/WPA2 Personal and Enterprise; PEAP-MSCHAPv2; no support for certificates
QoS	WMM supported	Unspecified	802.11e, WMM	Unspecified

After looking through the values listed in Tables 1-2 through 1-4, you may have noticed that many entries are listed as "unspecified." You may find those parameters missing entirely from the device specifications. Just because something is not listed, do not assume that it is not important or necessary. When the manufacturer does not report a specification, or when the customer does not have useful information about a device, you should spend more time and effort to discover the missing values. The more you know about the devices in use, the more complete and effective your wireless design will be.

Examining Client Density

By analyzing client device specifications, you can design a wireless network that supports the full range of devices. In effect, you are determining how the network will affect the clients. You should also consider how the clients will affect the network, especially in places where many clients will gather in close proximity to each other.

Client density is essentially the number of devices per AP. Where a single client is associated to an AP, it may take advantage of the full bandwidth available through the AP. No other device is present to contend for the airtime on the AP's channel. As more clients join an AP, they must all compete for the available airtime on the channel. The more active the clients are on the channel, the less airtime is available for any of them to use. The end results are poor performance and unsatisfactory user experience.

A good wireless design should provide RF coverage everywhere it is needed. It should also consider client density so that it can support the desired capacity through each AP. In other words, the design should provide an adequate number of APs such that the user population is distributed across the APs, giving more capacity to each. You can learn more about the balance between coverage and capacity in Chapter 5.

Choosing AP Types

As you work on a wireless design, your main task will be deciding how many APs will be needed and the physical location for each one of them. In indoor locations, APs will usually be mounted on ceilings or high on walls. You will likely encounter a wide variety of ways that buildings are constructed. For example, some will have a continuous ceiling surface throughout a floor, while others may have ceilings that are open to floors above and below.

Some buildings may be historical or have strict rules about aesthetics. In some cases, you will not be able to mount an AP exactly where you would like. In other cases, the customer will not want an AP to be visible or to become a distraction.

As you gather information from the customer, be sure to note any restrictions or preferences regarding AP appearance and mounting. Remember that each AP will need a wired network connection and will need to be powered by Power over Ethernet (PoE). Someone will need to install network cabling to the AP's location, with the assumption that the cabling will not exceed the usable distance from a network switch. Because PoE is necessary to power the APs, the network switches must be capable of offering PoE. You can learn more about AP cabling and PoE requirements in Chapter 4.

As you select a location for each AP, you will also need to select an AP model. Cisco offers several different model tiers, grouped according to how robust the feature set is. Most importantly, APs are made in two styles to support either internal integrated antennas or external antennas.

AP models with internal antennas normally have omnidirectional antennas that cover the surrounding area. You can mount these APs on ceilings to cover wireless clients on the floor area below. If you need to provide coverage in a certain direction or in a more focused area, you should select an AP model that has connectors for an external antenna. An external antenna can also be useful where the AP must be mounted some distance away from its antenna. There are many different antenna types available from Cisco and other vendors, so you can select an antenna with the appropriate gain and pattern to pair with the AP.

The offsite and onsite site survey processes described in Chapters 2 and 3 will be invaluable for determining the RF coverage area and specific antenna patterns. In areas with a high user density, you will likely need APs with external antennas to focus the AP cell and reduce the number of clients.

Evaluating Security Requirements

Beyond offering connectivity, wireless designs should also meet expectations for security. Wired networks have some level of inherent security because the data transmissions are contained within wires. Wireless networks transport data over the air, in a variety of directions, allowing other devices within range to eavesdrop or intervene.

During the design process, you should consult the customer and consider the following things:

- How will you secure access to the wireless network?

- How will you secure data traveling over a wireless LAN?

- Will you need to protect wireless users from each other?

- How will you protect wireless users from everyone else?

Securing access to a WLAN involves applying some authentication method to screen the users and devices that try to join. You can also apply an authorization method to determine what the users can access as well as an accounting method to collect an audit trail of user activity. *Authentication*, *authorization*, and *accounting* are the three A's in AAA. RADIUS servers and Cisco ISE can easily integrate into your network design to perform the AAA services.

Securing wireless data involves encryption and message integrity checks, to protect the data from being revealed to eavesdroppers and to protect it from being altered, respectively. The most robust security methods are usually best because they offer protection that is very difficult to defeat or exploit.

Normally, traffic from one wireless user to another must flow through an AP. By default, Cisco wireless LAN controllers (WLCs) allow traffic to pass between users on a WLAN in a peer-to-peer fashion. You can enable peer-to-peer blocking if the customer requires protection between wireless users on the WLAN.

Protecting wireless users from non-wireless users involves a wireless intrusion protection system (WIPS). Cisco WLCs offer a rich set of WIPS signatures that are used to match against traffic passing over a WLAN. If a signature is matched, a wireless protection policy is triggered to report suspicious activity and take some sort of action to protect the wireless users.

During the wireless design process, you should list the WLANs that the customer wants, along with the security suite that will be required for each WLAN. For example, a WLAN meant for corporate users working from corporate devices might require WPA2-Enterprise with AES, 802.1x with EAP-TLS, and digital certificates. Another WLAN offered to wireless phone devices might require WPA2-Personal with AES. A guest WLAN meant for corporate visitors might require web authentication with MAC address filtering. Each WLAN can have a unique set of security requirements that you must identify and specify as part of the wireless design.

AP Deployment Models

The type of client hardware and the density of the devices are important drivers for a wireless design. But the client can impact wireless performance in other ways beyond its specifications alone. For example, suppose two identical laptops are associated to a single AP. They probably share identical hardware, identical wireless adapters, and identical operating systems and driver software. Yet if one laptop sits idle while the other one runs software that performs massive file transfers, they will not affect the airtime equally.

To gauge the impact on the wireless network, you have to understand more about the applications that will run on the client devices. A dense population of bandwidth-intensive applications might starve users of available bandwidth. Similarly, you should gauge the impact that the wireless network might have on the applications. Consider the types of applications that will be used, the types of traffic involved, and any other network performance requirements. The goal is to design the network so that it can support each application adequately on each user's device. The greatest impact will come from the way you deploy the APs in your design.

Data Deployment Model

At a minimum, with no prior knowledge of the enterprise or its users, you can expect to find generic TCP/IP data on a wireless network. Applications such as email, web browsing, social media, and file transfers can be found in most settings. Such applications do not carry any specific service-level expectations; users simply expect a timely response from the network and the systems behind it. However, you should always strive to design a wireless network to avoid extensive congestion that would disrupt UDP flows and TCP connections.

To support generic data traffic, a basic coverage-only wireless design may be sufficient to keep most users satisfied. For basic RF coverage, the APs can have relatively large cell sizes or coverage areas. That translates into a "data" AP deployment model with a lower number of APs covering an area. Crowded venues may require more dense wireless support, if only to distribute the airtime and bandwidth to users who may be downloading or viewing identical content for a class.

The main factor in a data deployment is the minimum data rate supported by each AP. Lower data rates can be successfully used at greater distances from the AP because simpler modulation and coding methods are used to carry the data over the air. Such signals are easier to interpret at the receiving end, even in the presence of noise. Higher data rates use more complex methods and are more sensitive to the signal and noise levels. Therefore, they are dependable when the signal is stronger, nearer to the AP.

Figure 1-2 illustrates the data deployment model in two scenarios. In Design A, a low data rate of 6Mbps is acceptable, while Design B raises the rate to 24Mbps. Notice that the AP cell sizes are considerably larger in Design A than in Design B. That means only four APs can cover the area in Design A. To cover the same area in Design B, eight APs are required. With the focus on RF coverage, a low minimum data rate translates to a lower number of APs required. As the minimum data rate is raised, more APs are needed.

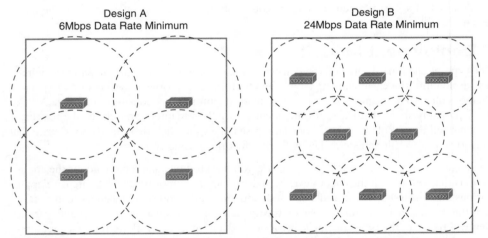

Figure 1-2 *Example Data AP Deployments Comparing Minimum Data Rates*

Reducing the AP cell size has one more effect. The number of clients associated to each AP is reduced, even if the clients are densely packed into the area. Therefore, a higher density of users can best be served by a higher density of APs. AP cell size and density are topics that are covered in greater detail in Chapter 5.

Voice/Video Deployment Model

If the application must send and receive data in a timely manner, it is known as a real-time application. Examples include voice over IP (VoIP), videoconferencing, and collaboration. You might have noticed a pattern—real-time applications involve voice and video; non-real-time applications include ordinary data.

Real-time applications require special consideration as you design, configure, and operate a wireless network. The following effects need to be minimized so that voice and video sessions can be heard and seen consistently, without interruption or corruption:

- **Latency:** The amount of time required to deliver a packet or frame from a transmitter to a receiver

- **Jitter:** The variance of the end-to-end latency experienced as consecutive packets arrive at a receiver

- **Packet loss:** The percentage of packets sent that do not arrive at the receiver

Even minor congestion can disrupt applications that require communication in real time. Wireless devices that support voice or video communication will usually have a limit on the acceptable amount of jitter. As well, these devices will need seamless roaming so that the voice or video calls are not dropped or interrupted as the clients move around.

Voice applications are usually the most sensitive to adverse network conditions. This is because the audio at one end of the call must be encoded and transmitted at fairly regular intervals and without excessive delay. The audio will be buffered and reassembled into the original audio stream at the receiver. If the stream of frames is interrupted enough, the audio will sound strangely metallic or full of clicks and pops at the other end of the call. The audio might even be unintelligible. Video applications are sensitive, too, because portions of the visual field must be sent and received in real time. The goal is to update any changes in the video image quickly enough that the viewer at the far end sees continuous and fluid video stream. Brief delays or interruptions might not be as noticeable in a video stream as they are in an audio stream.

As an example, suppose a hospital intends to start using a mobile surveillance camera so that staff can keep watch over some patients. The camera device is designed to send live video and audio streams over the wireless network, qualifying it as a real-time application. Some of the relevant specifications for the camera device are listed in Table 1-5.

Table 1-5   Example Network Requirements for a Mobile Camera Device

Bandwidth	1.5Mbps
Latency	Less than 150 ms
Jitter	Less than 30 ms
Packet loss	Less than 5%

To minimize the factors that affect real-time applications, any adverse conditions in a wireless environment must be controlled. For example, a source of interference can cause packet errors that interrupt a voice or video stream. As packets are lost, they can be retransmitted and delayed, increasing latency and jitter. Other factors like poor radio frequency (RF) coverage, high channel utilization, and excessive collisions can also impede good data throughput and integrity. A real-time application can also experience problems if the client device takes too long to roam between APs. During the roaming process, wireless frames might get lost or delayed.

An AP deployment model that is focused on voice and video application traffic is not too different from a data deployment. Figure 1-3 shows a typical AP layout over an empty area. The AP cells are sized according to the receiver sensitivity levels of the voice devices at an acceptable data rate. With an emphasis on efficient roaming and thorough coverage, cells are commonly designed to support a minimum mandatory data rate of 12 or 24Mbps, with boundaries at −67 dBm.

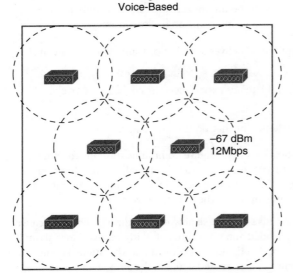

Figure 1-3   *An Example Voice/Video AP Deployment*

Location Deployment Model

Sometimes *real-time location services (RTLS)* are needed to automatically determine the physical location of wireless devices. RTLS can be used to track assets like healthcare equipment, to track rogue devices that might be causing problems on the network, to locate sources of wireless interference, and to track the locations of wireless clients within a building or campus.

A device is located by measuring its RSSI from several APs that can receive its signal, then using the multilateration technique to compute its physical location relative to the receiving APs. With 802.11-based devices, APs can easily receive frames transmitted by a device and relay the signal information on to an application that performs the location computations. If a single AP is used to determine a device's location, as shown in the left portion of Figure 1-4, the distance from the AP to the device can be estimated by the RSSI and attenuation from free space path loss. However, the device could be located anywhere along a circle surrounding the AP because the RSSI would likely be constant anywhere on that circle. If more APs are added to the computation, as in the right portion of Figure 1-4, the number of possible locations can be greatly narrowed. Ideally, a wireless design should have enough APs distributed across the covered area such that a signal from any device location can be received by at least three APs.

If an object has no 802.11 capability, a small 802.11 RFID tag can be attached to it. The tag periodically transmits an 802.11 probe request frame to announce itself to any listening APs, allowing its location to be computed. Usually RFID tags transmit at the lowest mandatory data rate so that their signals can reach the greatest number of APs. Depending on their capabilities, some tags can send a payload of information to local-based servers to relay data about embedded sensors, the status of push buttons, and so on.

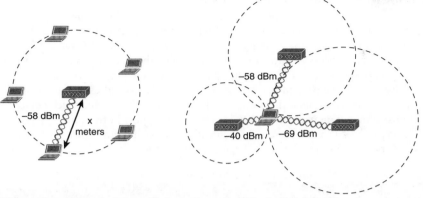

Key Topic

Figure 1-4 *Determining the Location of a Wireless Device*

NOTE   Be aware that RTLS is not a real-time application in the sense that streams of pack-ets must be delivered efficiently. The "real-time" portion of its name means that objects can be detected and located in near real time. RTLS does not bring any latency, jitter, or packet loss requirements of its own and has very low bandwidth requirements, which could be nota-bly different from the requirements needed to support real-time voice applications.

Typical location-based AP deployment models do not focus on any requirements other than RF coverage out to the edges of the floor area and device detection by multiple APs. Figure 1-5 shows a typical AP deployment. The APs are distributed in a familiar pattern over the cover-age area, but notice that some of the APs are located around the perimeter of the coverage area. Even when a tracked device is located near an outer wall, its location can be computed accurately. The addition of APs around the perimeter causes a location-based model to require more APs than other deployment models.

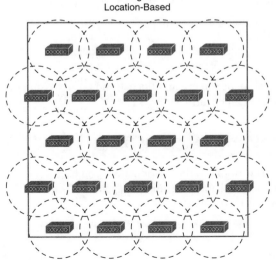

Design D
Location-Based

Figure 1-5 *An Example Location-Based AP Deployment*

AP Deployment Model Summary

You can use Table 1-6 to review the important attributes of each AP deployment model. Suppose a customer wants to use a combination of wireless devices that do not fit one specific model, such as laptops and tablets, along with wireless phones and RFID tags. Which model should drive your wireless design? You can combine all three to form a hybrid model that can support all of the devices. For example, all three models require RF coverage, so the APs should be distributed in a pattern that covers the entire area. To address the RFID tags, make sure to place some APs around the perimeter. To address both data and voice devices, you should choose a minimum mandatory data rate that can support both device types adequately and then size the AP cells accordingly. You will learn much more about the design process as you work through the remaining chapters of this book.

Table 1-6   AP Deployment Models and Their Attributes

Deployment Model	Attributes
Data	■ Focused on RF coverage only ■ No specific application requirements
Voice/Video	■ Focused on timely traffic delivery ■ Depends on thorough coverage and roaming efficiency
Location	■ APs are positioned to compute client location via multilateration ■ More APs are needed around the perimeter of floor area ■ Not focused on timely traffic delivery

Summary

This chapter described the main considerations needed as you begin to formulate a design for a wireless network. More precisely, you have learned the following:

- How a formal design and lifecycle process can produce more organized and successful results

- How different customers can have differing requirements for a wireless network

- How wireless client devices and applications can place important requirements and constraints on a wireless design

- How wireless security is a crucial aspect of a wireless design

- How the layout of APs and their physical locations can influence and properly support data, voice and video, and location-based applications

Exam Preparation Tasks

As mentioned in the section "How to Use This Book" in the Introduction, you have a few choices for exam preparation: the exercises here, Chapter 18, "Final Preparation," and the exam simulation questions in the Pearson Test Prep Software Online.

Review All Key Topics

Review the most important topics in this chapter, noted with the Key Topic icon in the outer margin of the page. Table 1-7 lists these key topics and the page numbers on which each is found.

Table 1-7 Key Topics for Chapter 1

Key Topic Element	Description	Page Number
Figure 1-1	PPDIOO and PBM lifecycle processes	8
Paragraph	Collecting wireless client information	11
Paragraph	Wireless client form factors	14
Paragraph	Client density	15
Paragraph	AP types and antennas	16
List	Wireless client security criteria	16
Paragraph	Data AP deployment model	18
List	Parameters affecting voice and video applications	19
Figure 1-4	Location-based AP deployment	21

Define Key Terms

Define the following key terms from this chapter and check your answers in the glossary:

client density, jitter, latency, packet loss, PBM, PPDIOO, real-time location services (RTLS), receiver sensitivity, signal-to-noise ratio (SNR)

CHAPTER 2

Conducting an Offsite Site Survey

This chapter covers the following topics:

The Effect of Material Attenuation on Wireless Design: This section covers the main materials that you may encounter in standard buildings where Wi-Fi is deployed and their effect on the Wi-Fi coverage.

Common Deployment Models for Different Industries: This section provides an overview of common requirements found for Wi-Fi networks in enterprises, healthcare, hospitality, hotspots, warehousing, manufacturing, retail, and education.

Designing with Regulations in Mind: This section provides a summary of the rules found in the FCC and ETSI domains for RF Wi-Fi transmissions.

Choosing the Right Survey Type: This section lists the different types of offsite and onsite surveys.

A Survey of Wireless Planning Tools: This section introduces the main site survey tools types as well as lists the main players.

Conducting a Predictive Site Survey: This section details the steps required to conduct a predictive site survey with Cisco Prime Infrastructure (PI).

This chapter covers the following ENWLSD exam topics:

- 1.2 Describe material attenuation and its effect on wireless design

- 1.6 Perform a predictive site survey

- 1.7 Utilize planning tools and evaluate key network metrics (Ekahau, AirMagnet, PI, Chanalyzer, Spectrum Analyzer)

Radio frequency (RF) propagation depends on the environment, and if you do not know the environment, you cannot possibly design your network properly. This does not mean that you should rush onsite with site survey tools. The site survey starts before traveling, by assessing elements that will help you save time and be more efficient once you are in the building to survey. Proper preparation may even save you the trip entirely. This chapter will cover the key elements of the preparation phase, starting by looking at building materials but also common coverage requirements for most industries and the impact of regulations on your design. You will then learn about the main survey tools for onsite or offsite evaluations. You will then learn how to perform a predictive site survey.

"Do I Know This Already?" Quiz

The "Do I Know This Already?" quiz allows you to assess whether you should read this entire chapter thoroughly or jump to the "Exam Preparation Tasks" section. If you are in doubt about your answers to these questions or your own assessment of your knowledge of the topics, read the entire chapter. Table 2-1 lists the major headings in this chapter and their corresponding "Do I Know This Already?" quiz questions. You can find the answers in Appendix D, "Answers to the 'Do I Know This Already?' Quizzes and Review Questions."

Table 2-1 "Do I Know This Already?" Section-to-Question Mapping

Foundation Topics Section	Questions
The Effect of Material Attenuation on Wireless Design	1–2
Common Deployment Models for Different Industries	3
Designing with Regulations in Mind	4
Choosing the Right Survey Type	5
A Survey of Wireless Planning Tools	6
Conducting a Predictive Site Survey	7

1. Which level of attenuation would you expect from drywall (or plasterboard wall)?

   a. About 1 to 2 dB

   b. About 3 to 4 dB

   c. About 6 to 8 dB

   d. About 10 to 12 dB

2. A wireless associate claims to have measured a 25 dB attenuation behind a concrete wall and asserts that the common reference table indicates 12 dB is wrong. What can you tell the associate?

   a. The associate may have measured the attenuation from the middle of the room instead of right behind the wall, thus leading to the discrepancy.

   b. The table is only indicative. Local differences may be found, and this is why surveys are important.

   c. The table is old. Newer walls have metal reinforcement that increases the attenuation.

   d. The table indicates the one-way attenuation, but Wi-Fi communication is bidirectional, so 24 to 25 dB is correct.

3. What is the primary purpose of coverage in a hospital?

   a. Staff mobile devices

   b. Medical machines

   c. Patient and guest Wi-Fi

   d. All of the above

   e. Can't say without more information

4. What is the maximum EIRP in U-NII-3 for the FCC domain?

   a. 100 mW

   b. 23 dBm

   c. 200 mW

   d. 30 dBm

5. You are asked to provide an indication of the number of access points (APs) for a new office without going onsite. What kind of survey best describes this type of estimation?

   a. Predictive site survey

   b. Layer 1 sweep

   c. Passive survey

   d. Proactive survey

6. A junior associate sees on your laptop a program called Chanalyzer and asks what it is used for. What would you answer?

   a. Predictive Active site surveys

   b. Layer 1 sweeps

   c. Layer 3 sweeps

   d. Position APs on a floor plan for channel planning

7. Customers ask in which areas of the building they can deploy their APs based on the result of your predictive survey. What would you answer?

   a. Only in open spaces

   b. Only in open spaces and cubicle areas

   c. Only in hallways and high ceiling areas

   d. None of the above

Foundation Topics

The Effect of Material Attenuation on Wireless Design

One of the first elements you should collect in preparation of a site survey is a map of the area to cover, along with scale and an idea of the building and material encountered. Covering an office building is not the same as covering a warehouse, and knowing the line of business and activity type of your customer will also provide precious information about potential issues and limitations.

Even before going onsite, you should have a clear idea of the type of coverage needed (Chapter 3, "Conducting an Onsite Site Survey," will help you make this assessment), data, real-time applications, and location-based services. You should also get to know the type of building you are designing for. This knowledge will help you approximate the number of APs needed. Knowing the number of APs will help you plan the time it will take to survey the facility.

Each AP cell area is limited because RF signals get attenuated as distance increases from the AP. The loss of signal strength is more pronounced as the signal passes through different objects. Therefore, knowing the expected obstacles will help you estimate each cell size.

AP radio signals are expressed in dBm. *dB* stands for decibels, a unit to measure relative power on a logarithmic scale, and *m* stands for milliwatt. Thus, the dBm scale measures the transmitted or received power, using 1 milliwatt as the reference value. Because the dB scale uses logarithms, it is not linear (which means that dividing or multiplying the value by 2 does not mean half or twice the power). Instead, doubling the power is represented by a gain of 3 dB (and, symmetrically, halving the power is represented by a loss of 3 dB). Multiplying the power by 10 is represented by adding 10 dB, and dividing by the power by 10 is represented by subtracting 10 dB. For example, a transmit power of 20 mW can be represented as 13 dBm. This is because you start from a 1 mW reference, which is 0 dBm, as you have nothing more or less than the reference starting point. You then multiply that reference power by 10, thus reaching 10 mW (or [0 + 10] dBm), and you double that power, thus reaching 20 mW (or [0 + 10 + 3] dBm).

> **NOTE** When you want to express the AP power, you use the milliwatt reference, thus stating, for example, "the AP radio is set to 13 dBm." When you evaluate the effect of an obstacle on your signal, you simply express the attenuation on the decibel scale (not the dBm scale), because the unit of reference (milliwatt) is the same on both sides and becomes irrelevant. Expressing gain or attenuation in "dBm" would be considered wrong.

Each obstacle and each material absorbs some of the signal. In the Cisco world, there is a common reference table, represented in Table 2-2.

Table 2-2   Common Obstacles and Their Estimated Attenuation Values

Object in Signal Path	Signal Attenuation Through the Object
Plasterboard wall	3 dB
Glass wall with metal frame	6 dB
Cinderblock wall	4 dB
Office window	1–3 dB
Metal door	6 dB
Brick wall	8 dB
Concrete wall	12 dB
Phone and body position	3–6 dB
Phone near field absorption	Up to 15 dB

Although you should know this table, you also have to keep in mind several additional elements:

- Do not take these values as absolutes. You will find other tables, from other vendors, with slightly or widely different references. Do not think that one vendor is right and the other is wrong; they just used different walls for reference.

- Different countries have different building practices. A brick wall that represents 8 dB attenuation in one country may be labeled as 12 dB attenuation in another, because the brick is different—thicker, with additive isolating material, with or without inner air chambers, and so on.

- Even within a particular region, attenuation may change over time. For example, a plaster wall in a dry and air-conditioned location may display less attenuation than the same wall in midseason when the air (and the wall) humidity level is higher.

- These attenuation values are usually measured far from the wall. There is a major difference between near field attenuation and far field attenuation. If you position your AP in the middle of a medium-sized room and then go to the middle of the neighboring room, you may measure an attenuation matching Table 2-2. However, if you move your laptop or measuring device just near the wall separating both rooms, the attenuation may suddenly become much higher, by 15 dB (as per the table), but may be also dramatically more (as much as 55 dB). This is because the attenuation affects the measuring device near field. In simple terms, the wall absorbs most of the energy received by your device.

Therefore, use Table 2-2 as a reference point but not as an absolute reference. Also keep in mind that each site surveyed will have different levels of multipath distortion, signal loss, and signal noise.

Common Deployment Models for Different Industries

These environmental constraints are also associated with standard practices. For example, hotels usually do not require high-density coverage in guest rooms, and this is because they expect a limited number of guests in each room. By contrast, schools usually expect a high density of devices in each classroom. Knowing the common requirements for standard verticals will help you pass the exam and will also help you ask the right questions when facing a new project.

Enterprise Office

In an enterprise office, mobile users require the same accessibility, security, quality of service (QoS), and high availability as wired users. Most of the time, you will be facing an existing network that needs to be upgraded for more performance, a higher user density, or more throughput. The office environment is ever-changing by nature. New applications and new devices may appear at any time when the business needs them, and the network is expected to be ready to support them from day 1. Enterprise Wi-Fi environments show two main trends:

- **Increase in devices:** Workers commonly get laptops (wired and fixed stations become less common), and users also bring phones and tablets. The wireless space becomes crowded with devices that associate and may consume airtime and bandwidth, even when idle. You need to determine with your client what types of devices are allowed to connect to the wireless network and evaluate the associated bandwidth requirements.

- **Increase in mobility needs:** Enterprise office users are traditionally thought of as not very mobile. In this context, "not very mobile" refers to what is called "nomadic roaming." Users work from one station, then move to another station and expect the connection to be available at their new location. The efficiency of the roaming (active communication while moving from one AP to the next) is not a big concern in that case, even if some applications are running in the background while the user moves. Many data-oriented applications are tolerant to changes in the throughput. However, these habits are changing. Real-time communication tools (video calls or conferences) have become common, and people pace or walk, looking for a quieter spot, while using these tools. You should evaluate this trend and treat these environments as requiring high efficiency (real-time application quality) everywhere.

During the initial discussion with your customer, you need to approach the possibility of future changes, and at a minimum make sure that your customer understands the possibilities of your deployment in each area. Your survey and the design specifications must clearly state the expected user density and the expected average throughput in every covered area. You should also explain to your customer that a wireless network is designed for a target throughput, and that adding throughput is not just about adding more APs later. Adding more throughput would typically mean conducting a new site survey. If any change of user density is expected, it is better to take this possibility into account early.

Office environments often have difficult areas, such as lobby areas designed with large atriums. Providing coverage there is expected but might prove challenging, because the atrium is an open space. The signal from many APs around the atrium, on different floors, may bleed through and travel far in the open space. The result may be that too many APs are detected from the atrium area. You may have to plan ahead and take this difficulty into consideration, by positioning the APs far from the atrium area, keeping only one or two APs specifically to cover the open space.

Another type of issue may be encountered in large meeting rooms or auditoriums, where you may expect a very high density of users, sometimes several hundreds. Because of the size of this type of room, using standard APs with internal antennas is often not feasible. You may have to come up with creative solutions, such as directional antennas or a high density of APs set to low power.

Last, you may need to know if the office building is entirely owned by one single corporation or if your client occupies only a suite on one floor. If your client occupies only a suite on one floor, then you should expect RF neighbors you cannot control. They may use all possible channels and be set to maximum power. You should be ready to work around these limitations by measuring neighboring systems' signal levels and rethink your channel plan accordingly.

Small or Home Offices

Small or home offices may need a single AP, in which case onsite survey is unlikely to be needed (survey is needed as soon as a network has more than one AP). However, they may also suffer from the same challenges as offices in a shared building: neighbors and their RF systems. Be prepared to respond to requests to verify the RF environment. Cisco APs, even when designed for remote or small offices, can use Radio Resource management (RRM) to select the best channel and power level, but the process is not magical. In a high-density dwelling, your survey may conclude that there is simply no "good" channel to choose from, and the settings will only pick the "least worst" option.

Healthcare

Healthcare site surveys are often time-consuming, because almost every hospital is a multi-story building with numerous small rooms. The survey must be thought of as a three-dimensional exercise, which is intellectually difficult when working with two-dimensional floor plans. Hospitals also have special rooms, like trauma and X-ray areas, where the walls might be lead-lined and completely stop RF signals. Last, hospitals have restricted access policies to some areas. Typical examples are surgical rooms and clean rooms. It is often difficult to obtain access to these rooms, and when you do, you may not be allowed to carry your laptop. You may still be expected to provide wireless access inside these areas.

Healthcare environments often require the WLAN to support a large number of application types: paging, voice, a wide range of data applications (such as mobile carts and patient monitoring devices), and location services. These applications may be critical for keeping patients alive, and your design should ensure optimal signal to every corner of every room, even when all doors are closed.

Check the Wi-Fi client type. Healthcare environments are often a mix of very recent applications or devices and older devices (only supporting older protocols such as 802.11b/g) that simply cannot be changed or replaced easily and still need to work in the new WLAN. You should also expect competition for the RF space. Some devices may be Wi-Fi-capable and consume a lot of bandwidth (for example, portable X-ray machines, sending high-resolution images, sometimes in real time, echography machines, and electrocardiography [ECG] machines). These devices may also use the same spectrum as Wi-Fi but with other protocols and, therefore, become sources of interference for your system.

Hospitals also use laptops on wheels (also called workstations on wheels, or WoWs) that are pushed throughout the hospital. They may be transmitting while moving and therefore you need to design your network by taking roaming paths and required throughput into account. Hospitals also often provide public Internet access service for their patients and visitors. This service may compete with the staff network.

Another common use case for wireless in healthcare environments is location tracking for assets (for example, blood pumps, beds, wheelchairs, and other assets that need to be located quickly), wandering patients, and to associate nurse and patient locations for billing purposes.

A last concern is aesthetics. It is common to be asked to hide the APs from view. Hiding APs may prove challenging in hospitals that do not use ceiling tiles. You may find creative solutions, such as hiding the APs in the walls, but even this type of solution may be difficult to implement in an environment where noise is banned and drilling through walls is not acceptable.

Hospitality and Hotels

Hotels are much like hospitals in their building construction and configuration (that is, usually multiple floors with many rooms). Beyond guest Wi-Fi (which may include video streaming as a standard service), hotels have started using WLANs to support data collection devices for taking inventory of things such as minibars, staff location, equipment status, and more. Wi-Fi keeps being rated as one of the most important services a hotel can provide (far more important than free breakfast or parking). Beyond requiring the engineer to look at the survey three-dimensionally, hotels present additional concerns about throughput and security. The high number of walls separating guest rooms decreases the range of APs and thus increases the need for more APs. Hotels want to offer their guests fast, reliable Internet access, which means fewer users per AP. This can easily be achieved in rooms. However, hotels often have restaurants and retail and convention areas, where user density may be much higher. You should carefully evaluate the maximum number of guests in these areas as well as the applications they may be expected to need. Running new cables is much more expensive than adding a few extra APs. Also, these are usually public places and thus susceptible to theft and vandalism. A common requirement is to properly secure APs to ceilings or walls or to hide them above the ceiling.

Network security may also be a concern. The main preoccupation is often "zero support." The hotel guest should be able to connect to the wireless network without requiring external assistance, which means that connection security is often very limited to allow for compatibility with the largest possible number of devices (for example, no Layer 2 security and web authentication for usage tracking and billing, strong firewalling, and sometimes website filtering).

Hotels also have many of the same concerns as hospitals regarding aesthetics. APs may need to be hidden in the walls or ceiling, where possible, or behind elements of the furniture.

Hotspots

The word *hotspot* refers to any type of 802.11 wireless access in public areas that's usually intended for guests or patrons, although the service may be provided without any purchase expectation. There are close to 500 million of those networks worldwide. Some provide a free connection, while others are built to generate revenue. The quality of the wireless coverage needed and the investment in the wireless infrastructure may be different depending on the model. Make sure to examine with your customer the hotspot goals and expected results, including the type of application expected to be supported and the maximum user density.

Education

The user density and data device types may be different depending on the type of school you are requested to cover. In grade schools, wireless data devices are usually laptops provided by the school to the class. In middle schools, you may see a larger proportion of personal devices, such as smartphones or laptops. In high schools and university, personal devices will be common. Many students will carry several devices. Most of these devices will be configured to connect to the school network and will associate as soon as they are in range. They may then perform automatic updates and stay connected all day long, even if the student is not actively using them. The devices, by their density, may place a serious strain on the wireless infrastructure and may force you to set up a security policy by which each student has credentials, allowing one session at a time. You may also have to implement congestion policies. A common design is to account for 25 to 30 students (students, not devices) per AP, thus sometimes resulting in more than one AP per classroom.

School buildings present the same issues as large office buildings and hospitals. The survey needs to be conducted with 3D in mind, as signal will bleed through floors and ceilings. You are also likely to face large atriums and large auditoriums with high student density, where the issue will be too much signal from too many APs. Here, again, you may need to use directional antennas to increase the AP density without creating too much interference.

Another concern in education is that students may be curious and sometimes destructive. An antenna mounted to the ceiling in a hallway and an AP with a flashing light can attract attention. In most cases, educational facilities must have the equipment installed in the most inconspicuous manner possible. National Electrical Manufacturers Association (NEMA) enclosures with enclosed locks can help prevent tampering or theft. You can use these enclosures in locations where APs cannot be hidden easily or in a truly high-risk area.

Retail

Retail, just like hospitality, has Wi-Fi needs for two populations: staff and customers. For staff, wireless data collection devices offer real-time updates to the store databases and the ability to place registers and printers throughout the store for special events (such as a sidewalk or tent sale) without having to worry about cabling. Some stores may conduct inventory at night (sometimes with high device density at that time). These inventory devices may be barcode scanners (possibly limited to 802.11b/g) or 802.11a/b/g/n/ac tablets. Some may use

VoWLAN during daytime operations, thus requiring real-time application quality coverage throughout the entire building. Some may consider guest Wi-Fi as critical to their business, but usually with data throughput. You should spend some time understanding the store's practices.

Stores must also often comply with specific regulations, such as those from the Payment Card Industry (PCI). These requirements may create additional constraints in the type of encryption and the characteristic of the Wi-Fi cells deployed for the staff. Another concern within the retail industry is the close proximity of the store to other RF devices. Some locations might stock and display RF devices in the store, such as satellite systems, baby monitors, and cordless phones. Others may use non-Wi-Fi cameras or cordless phone systems. Many of these devices might operate in the 2.4GHz range, and some might operate in the 5GHz range. APs should not be installed next to this type of equipment because they typically have a higher transmitter power. Retail stores might also be located in malls or strip malls where other Wi-Fi users might be operating.

Last, keep in mind that coverage may be needed on loading docks or inside trucks at the loading dock. Depending on the WLAN design, there might be enough RF coverage extending to the outside of the buildings to accommodate this need, but it should be factored into the design. You need to observe the customer behavior. If the staff scans goods from inside the trucks while loading or unloading, you need to plan for coverage accordingly. Trucks may have a metallic trailer, and providing coverage inside the truck might require a directional antenna. The goods may absorb the signal, so you might need to place your APs strategically to work around the absorption issue. Here again, observing customer habits is key to a good design.

Warehousing

The same coverage concerns for retail should be factored in for warehouse coverage. There might be a limited number of users during the day, but when a shipment comes in (or multiple shipments come in at the same time), many or all users might be operating at the same time. Coverage areas are generally large, subject to a lot of multipath distortion or RF interference because of concrete floors, metal roofing, and metal shelving. Cell size is more important than data rates because warehouse applications are generally transaction driven, with small packet sizes. Cell coverage overlap needs to be from 10 to 15 percent. The usage is not very high, but the users are highly mobile and must roam often.

There is no way of determining the distance of a signal without knowing the type of inventory. Different types of stock either reflect or absorb the radio frequency. It is important to talk with all people expected to use the WLAN. A forklift driver, for example, can have an accurate assessment of how stock levels vary over time (and what goods should be expected). A warehouse at a 50 percent stocking level has a much better RF footprint than the same warehouse has at 100 percent. Goods such as lead-based paint will reflect the signal, while paper or pet food will absorb the signal and reduce the usable cell size. If widespread information gathering is not possible, the plan should compensate for the potential increase in stock.

Additionally, some warehouses need their Wi-Fi network to operate primarily when inventory is full (for forklift and product retrieval) and other warehouses need their Wi-Fi network to operate primarily when inventory levels are low (for inventory reordering procedures), and some warehouses need both. Make sure to communicate with your customer to understand how the Wi-Fi network is expected to be used in order to design around the warehouse environment when it will be expected to operate. Not all use cases will warrant a functional Wi-Fi network when inventory levels are full.

Warehouses and distribution centers typically have maximum exposure to the elements. You should evaluate if APs may need protection boxes (and if protection is against dust, humidity, chemicals, temperatures, or other factors). You should also assess the space needed to mount the APs and their antennas (away from moving forklifts and other vehicles).

Manufacturing

Manufacturing presents the general same challenges as warehousing, with a few additional considerations. Machines and conveyor belts can be sources of RF interferences. Chain link fences may be deployed in some locations to block most (or all) RF signals. Distances to switches and power, high ceilings, or moving objects (forklifts or robots) may make AP and antenna positioning difficult. The factory plan may be changed at intervals to produce different items, and the Wi-Fi network is expected to adapt. And most importantly, any interruption costs a lot of money. Redundancy should be built in to make sure that the network and the Wi-Fi coverage are always available.

Designing with Regulations in Mind

The IEEE 802.11 working group designs the 802.11 standard. When several vendors decide to implement a common set of 802.11 features together, the Wi-Fi Alliance can create a certification program validating that all vendors implement the same features with the same logic.

The 802.11 protocol is more than 4,000 pages long and describes all possible modulations and frames matching each envisioned use case and exchange. During the design phase, the 802.11 working group interacts with the largest regulators to determine what type of RF signal shape (modulation) and power can or cannot be allowed in each targeted RF band. However, each country has its own regulations governing the RF spectrum, often limiting the scope of what the standard enables globally. It is common for several countries to use the same regulatory rules, also known as a regulatory domain. In the United States and several other countries, the Federal Communications Commission (FCC) determines what frequencies and transmission power levels can be used. Europe and some other countries follow the specifications of the European Telecommunications Standards Institute (ETSI). Rules for Japan are defined by the Ministry of Communication, and their applications are managed by the Telecom Engineering Center (Telec). Before implementing a wireless network, you must make sure that the AP transmissions comply with local regulations.

In most cases, access points are sold for a specific regulatory domain and only allow the channels that are legal in that domain. Although you do not need to know the rules for all countries, you should have an idea of which sub-bands and channels are allowed in the largest domains (FCC and ETSI), as represented in Figure 2-1, in comparison with two other domains.

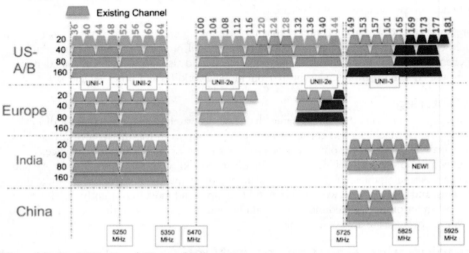

Figure 2-1 *5GHz Band Channel Allocation*

Channels 169 to 181 in the FCC domain and channel 144 in the ETSI domain are under discussion but not allowed yet.

In the United States, the 900MHz, 2.4GHz, and 5.8GHz bands are referred to as the ISM (Industrial, Scientific and Medical) bands and are regulated under FCC Part 15 rules. In addition, the 5GHz band is divided into several U-NII (Unlicensed National Information Infrastructure) bands in the United States and European Conference of Postal and Telecommunications Administrations (CEPT) bands in Europe. Japan has its own set of bands in both 2.4GHz and 5GHz. Although vendors must gain approval to sell devices emitting RF signal in these frequencies, customers do not need a license from the regulator to install and use these devices.

The regulation applies to which channels (defined by their center frequency) can be used, which signal (width, structure, and modulation) can be sent in these channels, and what power (amount of energy) is authorized. The FCC regulates the effective isotropic radiated power (EIRP), which is the total energy radiated out of the AP antennas on a particular channel. When you use an access point that has multiple radio chains (for example, with four possible spatial streams), the EIRP represents the combined energy of all chains. This means that each radio chain may transmit at higher or lower power, depending on which other radio chains are also transmitting. The AP makes that change automatically and dynamically on a per-frame basis.

The EIRP is calculated by adding the transmitter power (in dBm) to antenna gain (expressed in isotropic antenna or decibel referenced to isotropic antenna [dBi]) and subtracting any cable losses (in decibels):

EIRP = Tx power (dBm) + antenna gain (dBi) – cable loss (dB)

The FCC regulates transmissions by setting maximum limits to the EIRP, or the AP transmit power and associated maximal antenna gain, depending on the band:

- For the 2.4GHz band, the FCC allows an EIRP of 36 dBm for point-to-multipoint transmissions, with 30 dBm maximum transmitted power and 6 dBi maximum antenna gain and cable combination. A 1:1 ratio is allowed between these quantities. This means that if you reduce the transmit power by 1 dBm, you can increase the antenna gain by 1 dBi. The maximum allowed antenna gain is 16 dBi.

- For point-to-point links in the 2.4GHz band, the maximum EIRP is still the same (36 dBm with 30 dBm maximum transmit power and 6 dBi antenna + cable maximum), but a 3:1 ratio is allowed. For any reduction of 1 dBm transmit power, a 3 dBi gain at the antenna is allowed, up to 56 dBm EIRP maximum.

- In 5GHz, U-NII-1 band (channels 36 to 48) is allowed for outdoor transmissions with EIRP up to 36 dBm (4 watts). Indoors, the maximum allowed power is 50 mW (17 dBm) with a 6 dBi antenna maximum.

- U-NII-2A (channels 52 to 64) is also allowed both indoors and outdoors, with the same maximum power of 250 mW (24 dBm) and an EIRP of 1 watt (30 dBm) maximum.

- U-NII-2B is not allowed for unlicensed use.

- U-NII-2C (also called U-NII-2e, channels 100 to 144) is also allowed both indoors and outdoors, with a maximum power of 250 mW (24 dBm) and an EIRP of 1 watt (30 dBm) maximum. A Dynamic Frequency Selection (DFS) system must be in place to detect airport weather radars operating on the same frequency range and dynamically vacate the channel within 10 seconds when such a radar blast is detected. The affected frequency can't be reused for the following 30 minutes. In some countries using the FCC rules, the channels most frequently used by radars may be forbidden for Wi-Fi.

- U-NII-3 (channels 149 to 165) is also allowed both for indoor and outdoor use, with a maximum power of 250 mW (24 dBm) and an EIRP of 1 watt (30 dBm) maximum.

Instead of regulating the maximum transmit power or the EIRP, the ETSI domain only regulates the EIRP, sometimes with a maximum gain for the antenna. Sub-bands are called differently than in the FCC domain (U-NII names are provided for reference):

- In the 2.4GHz band, the maximum EIRP is 20 dBm indoors and outdoors, with a transmit power of 17 dBm maximum with a 3 dBi antenna. Professional installers can increase the antenna gain by 1 dBi for every 1 dBm decrease of the transmit power (1:1 rule).

- In the 5GHz band, U-NII-1 and U-NII-2A jointly form RLAN Band 1. U-NII-1 is Sub-band 1 and is only allowed for indoor transmissions. EIRP is 200 mW (23 dBm).

- U-NII-2A is RLAN Band 1, Sub-band 2, and is allowed both indoors and outdoors. Devices must implement DFS. They can also implement Transmit Power Control (TPC) to attempt to limit their power to the minimum needed for a successful transmission (thus limiting interferences with radars and other systems). Devices that do not implement TPC are restricted to an EIRP of 100 mW (20 dBm), and 200 mW (23 dBm) if they implement TPC.

- U-NII-2B is not a valid band (and not allowed for unlicensed communications).

- U-NII-2C (called RLAN Band 2) is allowed for both indoor and outdoor operations (but note that channel 144 is not allowed in most ETSI countries). Maximum EIRP is 1 watt (30 dBm) for devices implementing TPC and DFS. Devices that do not implement TPC (but implement DFS) are restricted to an EIRP of 500 mW (27 dBm), or 100 mW (20 dBm) if they implement neither TPC nor DFS.

- U-NII-3 (called Band 3) is not allowed yet for indoor or outdoor Wi-Fi (this band is only allowed for short-range devices). However, conversations are ongoing, in an attempt to allow Wi-Fi in this band, with an intended EIRP limit of 14 dBm.

Table 2-3 summarizes these limits:

Table 2-3   Wi-Fi RF Regulations for the FCC and ETSI Domains

Band (Domain)	Rules
2.4GHz (FCC)	36 dBm (4W) EIRP (P2MP), with 30 dBm (1 W) Tx / 6 dBi, 1:1 ratio.
	36 dBm (4 W) EIRP (P2P) with 30 dBm (1 W) Tx / 6 dBi, 3:1 ratio.
U-NII-1 (FCC)	Outdoors: Max EIRP 36 dBm (4 W).
	Indoors: Max Tx 17 dBm (50 mW), 6 dBi.
U-NII-2A (FCC)	Max EIRP 30 dBm (1 W), max Tx 24 dBm (250 mW).
U-NII-2B (FCC)	Not allowed for unlicensed use.
U-NII-2C (FCC)	Max EIRP 30 dBm (1 W), max Tx 24 dBm (250 mW).
	DFS required.
U-NII-3 (FCC)	Max EIRP 30 dBm (1 W), max Tx 24 dBm (250 mW).
2.4GHz (ETSI)	Max EIRP 20 dBm (100 mW), max Tx 17 dBm (50 mW) on 3 dBi.
	1:1 rule.
Band 1 (ETSI), Sub-band 1 (U-NII-1)	Max EIRP 23 dBm (200 mW).
Band 1 (ETSI), Sub-band 2 (U-NII-2A)	Max EIRP 23 dBm (200 mW) with TPC.
	Max EIRP 20 dBm, (100 mW) without TPC.
	DFS required.
Band 2 (ETSI) (U-NII-2C)	Max EIRP 30 dBm (1 W) with DFS and TPC.
	Max EIRP 27 dBm (500 mW) with DFS and no TPC.
	Max EIRP 20 dBm (100 mW) without TPC and DFS.
Band 3 (ETSI) (U-NII-3)	Under discussion. Not allowed for Wi-Fi yet. Target 14 dBm (25 mW).

The rules are many, and you are supposed to know them for the exam. Most importantly, you need to keep in mind that your design and survey should incorporate the regulatory settings matching the country where the network is to be deployed. Do not use "default" settings or "U.S. settings" when designing a network for a European country (and vice versa). Always look for the settings that activate the appropriate regulatory domain in your AP, WLC, survey laptop, or site survey software. Otherwise, your conclusions may be invalid (and as a professional, you may be liable if the system you designed exceeds the local maximums).

The rules you have to comply with go beyond the RF regulations. During the site survey itself, you may have to comply with local safety rules by wearing a protective hard hat, gloves, safety glasses, and so on, or overall in some areas you may require an escort or help operating some equipment (such as cherry pickers or even ladders in some locations). Check with your local safety agency (for example, the Occupational Safety and Health Act agency, or OSHA, in the United States, or the European Agency for Safety and Health at Work in Europe) before showing up for a site survey in an environment you are not familiar with. Local regulations can also put constraints on your AP positions (for example, restricting APs from being installed in elevator shafts or in enclosed areas with limited air volume). Bodies regulating buildings can usually help assess these restrictions in your state or country.

Choosing the Right Survey Type

You may have been told that "a site survey" was needed, but you should know that there is more than one type. Depending on the project, you may choose one type or another or perform more than one survey. Surveys can be divided in two types: offsite and onsite.

Offsite surveys are not performed onsite, but usually prior to (or instead of) a site visit. Their goal is to evaluate the building blueprint and estimate the number of APs needed. This task is important, because most onsite surveyors evaluate the position of 10 to 12 APs per day. Knowing the estimated AP count will help you plan the number of days onsite. These surveys are of two sub-types:

- **Blueprint study:** In this phase, you study the floor plans to identify areas that require specific focus: hard-to-cover areas because of their shape, building material, or obstacles (such as machines); areas of higher user density; areas difficult to access or survey and where AP deployment may be challenging; large atriums, and so on. You can also identify areas that have the same structure. If you can confirm this information onsite, surveying one area can expedite the survey of the other area, by starting from the same design.

- **Predictive survey:** In this phase, you use a tool to position APs on a map representing each floor to cover. In some cases, you can account for the obstacles (such as walls) that you expect to find onsite, expected service (voice and so on), and user density. Although the result is unlikely to be representative of the final position of the APs, you can use these tools to estimate an AP count and identify areas where special antennas may provide the coverage you need.

There are also multiple types of onsite surveys, and you should likely conduct most of them:

■ **Walkthrough:** In this phase, you walk through the facility and visually inspect the location. This phase is important to complement the blueprint study and identify areas that require special consideration. The walkthrough is also a very important phase to observe users' behaviors when available (for example, people cutting through a meeting room, thus indicating roaming paths that you did not see from the blueprint, people pacing when on calls or video conferences, and so on). You can also use this time to exchange and gain useful insight on how these users expect the Wi-Fi network to operate.

■ **Layer 1 site survey:** Sometimes called Layer 1 sweep, this phase aims at detecting the (non-Wi-Fi) RF activity in the facility. Even if you are covering an office building, you should always perform this survey, because you are likely to always discover non-Wi-Fi devices that will compete for your spectrum. Discovering sources of interference early allows you to address the issue before it blocks your design. You can inquire about the interferers and maybe have them removed, or at least account for them in your channel plan and your performance projections.

■ **Layer 2 site survey:** This is what most people think of when referring to site survey, but there are two sub-types: passive surveys (also called validation surveys), where you assess the presence of existing Wi-Fi networks in the environments, and AP-on-a-stick (APoS) surveys (sometimes called active surveys), where you install temporary APs and evaluate their coverage area. We will cover them more in detail in Chapter 3.

■ **Post-deployment site survey:** In this phase, the Wi-Fi network you designed has been deployed, and you test the coverage and performance. This phase is also critical to the success of your design and is covered in Chapter 12, "Implementing Multicast."

A Survey of Wireless Planning Tools

Hundreds of tools claim to help you design your Wi-Fi network. They tend to offer multiple functions, and you will see people using a single tool for all tasks. However, keep in mind that these tools should be divided in two categories with different goals:

■ **Offsite predictive tools:** These tools allow you to upload a map, specify its scale, and project the number of access points needed. Some tools are generic; others allow you to choose the AP vendor and model, the user density, draw obstacles, specify the target application, set the expected AP height, and so on. Some of these tools come in the form of an application running on a laptop or tablet (local install), some others require a server installation (LAN server), while others are completely online (cloud and web access). It is clear that sharing the project is easier as you move toward "fully online" categories.

■ **Onsite survey tools:** These tools allow you to run Layer 1 or Layer 2 (validation or APoS) surveys, often with a specific wireless adapter. They can sometimes emulate other clients (for example, major smartphone or tablet vendors and models). Chapter 3 provides more details.

To become a Cisco networking professional, you should know a few names and have some exposure to their functions:

- **Ekahau Pro:** This is a professional tool with all the functions described so far, and it comes as an application you install on a laptop. Although primarily intended for onsite surveys, Ekahau Pro incorporates a planning mode (supporting obstacles, application types, user density, and AP models—most Cisco APs are supported and known). A lighter version exists for tablets (Ekahau Survey for iPads). A cloud version is also available (Ekahau Cloud) to share projects.

- **Cisco Prime Infrastructure:** This is a network management tool, installed on a LAN server. It provides a planning mode detailed at the end of this chapter. You can also use it to evaluate the performances of your coverage. It does not integrate onsite survey functions.

- **Yagna RF Wi-Fi site planner:** This is an online planning tool, supporting most Cisco APs, obstacles, application types, user densities, and more. It integrates with Google maps and can also generate a bill or material (BoM).

These are the main players in a Cisco environment. There are, of course, other tools, likely very valuable, such as Airmagnet Survey Pro (a competitor to Ekahau Pro, also laptop-based), VisiWave Site Survey, Acrylic Wi-Fi heat maps, and SolarWinds Wi-Fi heat map. These last three products target laptop installation and can provide site survey, planning, and analysis features.

You will also find multiple simpler tools running on a phone or a tablet that are intended to display the name of detected APs with their signal strength and sometimes their direction. These tools can be very valuable for post-deployment site surveys.

Conducting a Predictive Site Survey

As a wireless professional, you should know how to conduct an onsite and an offsite survey. If your network incorporates Cisco networking devices and Cisco Prime Infrastructure, you can use this tool to estimate the number of APs needed in a location, before going for the onsite survey phase. This predictive planning is performed as follows:

Step 1. From the Cisco Prime Infrastructure dashboard, click the left menu and select **Maps**.

Step 2. Select the campus or building of your choice.

Step 3. Select the floor plan of your choice.

Step 4. In the upper-right area of the dashboard, click **Tools** and choose **Planning Mode**. Planning Mode opens a new window. The floor plan is surrounded by a dashed blue line, representing the area where new APs are needed. You can click the edge of the line and then move the line while maintaining the click so as to resize the area.

Step 5. From the upper menu, choose **Add APs**.

Step 6. From the left menu, you can choose the AP naming convention, the AP type, the antennas, the protocols to support, the minimum throughput expected at the edge of the cell, and the type of service expected: data, voice, location (or location with additional APs in Monitor mode).

Step 7. Click **Calculate** to compute the number of APs expected to be needed to provide the selected services. You can observe that voice requires more APs than data/coverage and location more APs than voice.

Step 8. By selecting **Advanced options**, you can set a safety margin, which increases the overlap between cells as you go, from Aggressive to Safe or Very Safe (or 7920_enabled for Voice).

Step 9. Click **Apply to map**. You should see the APs on the floor, as shown in Figure 2-2.

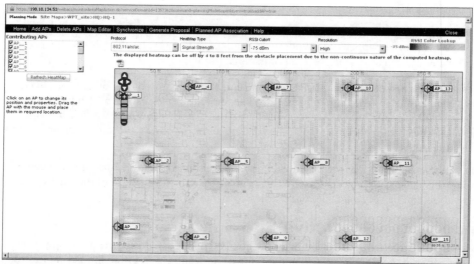

Figure 2-2 *Predictive Survey Output in Prime Infrastructure*

Note Before going into Planning mode, you can edit your map to add obstacles (walls and such). Although these obstacles are accounted for when displaying the AP heat map in Planning mode, they are not accounted for when computing the heat map. You can also add these obstacles from within Planning mode by clicking Map Editor.

The goal of Planning mode is to seed your map with APs. It is not intended to be a recommendation on where to position the APs. Once the APs are displayed on the map, you should spend time displaying various levels of cutoff values and moving the APs to locations that logically make sense for the intended floor plan.

If your floor plan is already managed and has APs, you can click Synchronize to take these APs into account in your planning. You can also generate a proposal document with the planned APs by clicking generate Proposal.

Summary

This chapter described the main considerations needed to prepare for an onsite survey and run an offsite survey. More precisely, you have learned the following:

- How construction material and obstacles affect your RF signal

- How different industries and verticals have specific but common requirements for wireless deployments

- How regulations affect the transmission power of your APs, the antenna you are allowed to use, and also how your survey can be conducted

- How site survey tools are divided into local install, local LAN server, and cloud categories

- How the term *site survey* is in fact a combination of multiple possible tasks

- How to perform a predictive site survey using Cisco Prime Infrastructure

References

For additional information, refer to these resources:

Cisco Campus LAN and Wireless LAN Design Guide: https://www.cisco.com/c/dam/en/us/td/docs/solutions/CVD/Campus/CVD-Campus-LAN-WLAN-Design-Guide-2018JAN.pdf

Cisco Enterprise Mobility 8.1 Design Guide: https://www.cisco.com/c/en/us/td/docs/wireless/controller/8-1/Enterprise-Mobility-8-1-Design-Guide/Enterprise_Mobility_8-1_Deployment_Guide.html

Cisco Wireless LAN Design Guide for High Density Client Environments in Higher Education: https://www.cisco.com/c/en/us/products/collateral/wireless/aironet-1250-series/design_guide_c07-693245.html

Cisco Dorm Deployment Guide: https://www.cisco.com/c/en/us/td/docs/wireless/technology/mesh/8-4/b_Dorm_deployment_guide.html

Cisco Prime Infrastructure: https://www.cisco.com/c/en/us/products/cloud-systems-management/prime-infrastructure/index.html

Cisco Prime Infrastructure Planning mode: https://www.cisco.com/c/en/us/td/docs/net_mgmt/prime/infrastructure/3-2/user/guide/bk_CiscoPrimeInfrastructure_3_2_0_User-Guide/bk_CiscoPrimeInfrastructure_3_2_0_UserGuide_chapter_0111.html

Ekahau Pro: https://www.ekahau.com/products/ekahau-site-survey/overview/

Yagna Predictive WiFi Site Survey: https://www.yagnaiq.com/wifi-site-planner/

Exam Preparation Tasks

As mentioned in the section "How to Use This Book" in the Introduction, you have a few choices for exam preparation: the exercises here, Chapter 18, "Final Preparation," and the exam simulation questions in the Pearson Test Prep Software Online.

Review All Key Topics

Review the most important topics in this chapter, noted with the Key Topic icon in the outer margin of the page. Table 2-4 lists these key topics and the page numbers on which each is found.

Table 2-4   Key Topics for Chapter 2

Key Topic Element	Description	Page Number
Paragraph	dB and dBm	26
Table 2-2	Common obstacles and their attenuation	27
Figure 2-1	5GHz channels in common regulatory domains	34
Table 2-3	Power limits in common regulatory domains	36
List	The main site survey tools	39

Define Key Terms

Define the following key terms from this chapter and check your answers in the glossary:

Federal Communications Commission (FCC), European Telecommunication Standards Institute (ETSI), Telecom Engineering Center (Telec), AP on a stick (APoS), validation survey, predictive survey, Layer 1 sweep, decibel (dB), decibel milliwatt (dBm)

CHAPTER 3

Conducting an Onsite Site Survey

This chapter covers the following topics:

Performing a Walkthrough Survey: This section will help you assess the environment and discover, before the actual survey, areas that need special attention.

Performing a Layer 1 Survey: This section will show you how to detect non-802.11 transmitters, map their position, and assess their possible impact on your WLAN design.

Performing a Layer 2 Survey: This section will guide you through the site survey process, from the methodology to sample tools, for data coverage, voice or real-time application, and location deployments.

Performing a Post-Deployment Onsite Survey: This section will show you how to verify the deployment and make sure that the APs offer the performances projected during the pre-deployment survey.

This chapter covers the following ENWLSD exam topics:

- 1.3 Perform and analyze a Layer 1 site survey
- 1.4 Perform a pre-deployment site survey
- 1.5 Perform a post-deployment site survey

Once you have performed an offsite site survey, you likely have an estimation of possible access point positions and densities. Now, it is time to go onsite and perform an actual site survey. A common saying among wireless professionals is "you should do an onsite site survey every time you plan to deploy more than one AP." This is because an offsite survey, although extremely valuable, cannot account for the realities of the environment and their influence on RF propagation.

However, you should not rush onsite with an AP on a tripod and start measuring cell sizes. The onsite survey process is composed of three phases, each of them aimed at saving your time for the phase that follows.

Therefore, this chapter will guide you through these different phases, starting with the walkthrough. This first phase can happen any time before the RF survey and aims at finding areas that will require particular care. These areas are often difficult to survey or likely to present challenges for your intended Wi-Fi coverage. The next phase is the actual survey, but its goal is not to design Wi-Fi cells. Rather, the Layer 1 survey phase is a critical step to determine the presence and position of any other RF transmitter that may affect your design or your future Wi-Fi coverage.

Then comes the actual Wi-Fi site survey that most experts refer to. In order for this phase to be fast, you need a systematic methodology, and this chapter will show you standard methods.

Last, once your network is deployed, you should go back onsite and verify the AP positions and configurations. You should also run specific tests to validate that the performance of the deployed network matches your design. This chapter will help you design and perform these tests.

"Do I Know This Already?" Quiz

The "Do I Know This Already?" quiz allows you to assess whether you should read this entire chapter thoroughly or jump to the "Exam Preparation Tasks" section. If you are in doubt about your answers to these questions or your own assessment of your knowledge of the topics, read the entire chapter. Table 3-1 lists the major headings in this chapter and their corresponding "Do I Know This Already?" quiz questions. You can find the answers in Appendix D, "Answers to the 'Do I Know This Already?' Quizzes and Review Questions."

Table 3-1 "Do I Know This Already?" Section-to-Question Mapping

Foundation Topics Section	Questions
Performing a Walkthrough Survey	1
Performing a Layer 1 Survey	2–3
Performing a Layer 2 Survey	4–5
Performing a Post-Deployment Onsite Survey	6

1. A customer has hired you to site-survey a factory but asks that you skip the walkthrough to save time and money. What would be your position?

   a. Walkthroughs are nice to have but can be skipped if the customer is familiar enough with the building.

   b. The walkthrough can simply be performed after the actual survey.

   c. Without a walkthrough, the survey will likely take longer and cost more money.

   d. The walkthrough is needed but can be performed by a local factory worker to save on cost and time.

2. During your Layer 1 sweep in an office building, you find RF traces near a desk showing low power as well as multiple spikes across the 2.4GHz band. Which transmitter is most likely to produce this pattern?

   a. A wireless security camera

   b. An old 802.11b access point

   c. A microwave oven

   d. A Bluetooth headset

3. An engineer reports the detection of a DECT phone on channels 4 to 5 and wonders what is the best way to design around the interferer. What would you answer?

   a. The phone may jump to other frequencies, and designing around it will be difficult.

   b. As the transmitter does not affect channels 1, 6, and 11 that Wi-Fi uses, it can be ignored.

   c. The admin needs to avoid channel 6 in this area.

   d. The admin should set the nearby AP to channel 6 so as to cover the interference.

4. Your junior associate wants to start surveying a cubicle space in an office building. Where should the associate position the first AP to start the AP-on-a-stick survey?

   a. At the corner of the building floor

   b. At the geometric center of the floor

   c. At the center of one cubicle block

   d. Over the corridor between two cubicle blocks

5. You need to perform a site survey for voice and real-time application support. What is the correct way to proceed?

   a. Perform a data site survey first. Then multiply the AP density by 1.3.

   b. Perform a data site survey, using a phone to measure the AP signal.

   c. Perform a voice survey, testing calls to evaluate each cell edge.

   d. Perform a standard survey, using voice RF parameters.

6. Which of the following is a good way to confirm good roaming performance during a post-deployment survey?

   a. Fewer than three channels scanned before the client associates to the next AP

   b. 50 ms or less between the last data packet on the previous AP and the first data packet on the next AP

   c. 30 ms or less between the probe request and the association request on the next AP

   d. Less than 10 percent packet loss in the roaming area between APs

Foundation Topics

Performing a Walkthrough Survey

Before jumping to your site survey equipment, and often before even conducting the offsite site survey described in Chapter 2, "Conducting an Offsite Site Survey," one of your first tasks is to go onsite and perform a walkthrough survey. This initial walkthrough is often a phase that is misunderstood by customers and networking professionals alike. You need to go to the site to survey, but without any site survey tool, just to assess what has to be done. The main purpose of the initial walkthrough may be summarized as "to answer questions that were not asked" (that is, to verify the required coverage by assessing the location with a professional look). Four types of areas can be identified, for each type of service needed (data, voice, or location, each with its relevant throughput target):

■ Areas where complete coverage and full performances are needed.

■ Areas where coverage is optional. Covering these areas is a plus, but no specific performance targets are set for these zones.

- Areas where coverage is not needed. There may be some signal and partial coverage in these areas as a side effect of the deployment in other areas, but these zones are not to be covered.

- Areas where coverage should not be present. There may be zones where coverage would be an issue. Typical areas may be parking lots, where visitors may try to eavesdrop or attack the network, research labs, and specific rooms in a healthcare environment, where the RF signal may disturb any existing Industrial, Scientific, and Medical (ISM) equipment.

Walking through the facility will allow you to identify precisely each of these areas. One additional benefit of the walkthrough is to verify the map you were provided. If the map is not recent, you may face unexpected surprises: wrong scale or wrong dimensions for some rooms, repurposed areas in which layout is now different from what the map indicates, or walls that were added or removed since the map was drawn. You do not need to verify the map and measure each room dimension down to the inch, but a quick look and comparison between what you see and what the map indicates will alert you if anything does not "look right."

Verifying the areas to cover is also an important objective. In most cases, your customer will have indicated on a map the zones where coverage was needed. This indication takes the form of a line surrounding the area to cover. This coverage area definition is usually not very precise, and many details are often left to be determined. For example, do you need to cover the stairwell? For data coverage, this type of area is typically optional. For voice coverage, users commonly expect to be able to place or receive a call while transiting between floors, and stairwell coverage, along with efficient roaming from the main floor area (stairwells often feature a heavy firewall door) is a must. This notion of roaming path is critical for the walkthrough survey. As you design AP positions, you will find that observing a map blueprint is not sufficient. You need to be onsite and observe the floor layout and people's behavior. You will see that people often use shortcuts through empty meeting rooms, avoid walking through certain areas (for example, open spaces where the local culture discourages disrupting people's work by walking through). These observations will cause you to rethink roaming paths and best AP positions.

User behavior is also critical when examining user density. From a map, you may see cubicles. But are users using wired connections for all of their devices and performing basic browsing tasks, or are they on the other end of the spectrum, in an all-wireless office, using wireless headsets, taking voice calls, and pacing around? Are the cubicle walls thin or thick? Are they high or low? Can you cover the area from one AP in the ceiling, or will you need a different strategy? The initial walkthrough will still be enough to alert you if the structure seems to be different from what the map indicated. A typical example is a sample area with plaster walls, whereas other areas, not to be surveyed, use thick glass windows instead of plaster walls. As a wireless professional, you immediately know that the multipath and absorption parameters will be very different in both areas and that they should both be surveyed. The map and your customer may simply see them both as "having walls."

Another goal of the structure examination is to evaluate constraints on AP placements. In many cases, APs will be installed at ceiling level. Thick concrete will be likely to provide some degree of RF isolation between floors, whereas thin structure with wood beams will most likely let the signal bleed from one floor to the next. This may cause devices on one floor to roam to the AP on the upper or lower floor, and such roaming may affect your ability to isolate floors or construct simple roaming paths, forcing you to think in three dimensions instead of on a floor-by-floor basis. Additionally, in buildings with decorative ceilings, positioning APs at ceiling level may not be possible, or it may be very expensive because the APs would need to be hidden above ceiling level and the decoration recreated. Some buildings also have hard ceilings of painted concrete, and positioning APs may be difficult or impossible, especially if there is a requirement to hide the AP or the Ethernet cable. Thick walls may introduce the same concerns for cabling. Some of these walls may have been built at a time when asbestos was used for insolation. There may be additional costs required to simply bring the cable to the AP intended location. Some buildings have atriums or high ceilings, too far from the floor level to provide good coverage without directional antennas and the risk of power mismatch between the AP and the clients. Last, there may be areas that will require special access considerations for the site survey, and the walkthrough should help you identify them. For example, many industrial environments have hazardous areas, because of chemicals or moving machinery, that require you to wear special attire or be accompanied by personnel. Some areas may not be always accessible (hospital cleanrooms or surgical blocks, occupied bedrooms in a hotel, and so on) and will require careful access-window planning.

During the walkthrough survey, you can also spot devices that may require closer examination, such as DECT phones, wireless cameras, and so on. In general, any device that seems to communicate with radio waves should be noted, so you can research what they are and what frequencies they use. This recommendation also applies to any detected AP. You need to know why this access point is here and if it is intended to stay. If you are planning for a wireless network upgrade, you need to clearly identify the existing deployment. The walkthrough can also help you assess the type of antennas and access points in use, which may provide useful information on specific building challenges that were identified during the previous survey.

During the walkthrough, another important item to monitor is the existing wired infrastructure. APs and Wireless LAN Controller (WLC) will connect to switches. These may be part of the deployment or upgrade plan. If you are expected to reuse some of the existing equipment, you will need to check for port availability and Power over Ethernet (PoE) budget. The walkthrough is a great time to reconcile the network map theory with the Intermediate Distribution Frame (IDF)'s reality. Another concern is cable length. The distance between the switch and the AP should not exceed 100 meters (328 feet). Distances may be short when calculated on a map, but a building is a three-dimensional environment. By looking at the switch positions, you may realize that some areas will be out of range because of the added distance due to high ceilings, pillars, or other obstacles. This environment may force you to install some mesh APs or request additional switches, in both cases adding to the deployment cost.

At the end of the walkthrough, you should have a clear initial idea on the complexity of the survey, but also on special considerations relative to the building structure or its occupancy that will have consequences on your WLAN design. The walkthrough can be performed at the beginning of the site survey phase. However, identified special conditions may force you to get special authorizations or equipment, and these may take time. As much as possible, it is therefore preferable to perform the walkthrough early in the design cycle, to ensure that your surveying time onsite will be as efficient as possible.

Performing a Layer 1 Survey

Once you have good information about the building particularities, and after you have performed an offsite survey to estimate possible AP locations, you are ready to go back onsite and survey the RF environment. This phase does not start with AP placement but with an evaluation of the RF environment itself. During the walkthrough, you may have visually identified non-802.11 devices. There are probably others, and most of them are likely not visible. The best way to assess their presence, and their possible impact on your WLANs, is to walk throughout the entire location while scanning the RF environment for any energy in the frequencies you plan to use. This activity is called a Layer 1 sweep, because you sweep the Physical Layer (the RF itself) in the frequencies you plan to use, without caring about what modulation and what protocol non-802.11 devices send. All that matters to you is the amount of energy they send (that is, how much they are likely to disrupt your WLAN).

However, this likelihood may not be easy to establish from a single sweep. Some non-802.11 devices are intermittent transmitters, sending different amounts of energy at different points in time. Therefore, the tool you need to use for this phase not only needs to detect RF energy, but it should also be able to inform you about the type of energy detected. At least it should identify the interferer's general type. At best, it will give you detailed information about the device, sometimes down to product name and characteristics. Armed with this information, you can evaluate the likely effect of the interferer on your WLAN. You can then decide if you can design around it or if you will need to find ways to remove it (for example, by replacing it with Wi-Fi-based equivalent objects).

L1 Sweep Tool Essentials

Many tools allow you to capture the raw RF and analyze the detected energy. These tools are grouped under the general name "spectrum analyzer." Many of them are laboratory devices, with a high-precision scanner, and are fairly expensive. They also offer many functions that are not needed for a simple site survey. You will also find programs that can run on a laptop and that can connect to a specialized card or device. When choosing such a tool, keep in mind that an application that uses your laptop Wi-Fi card will necessarily be limited by the low-level filter implemented by the card manufacturer, attempting to discard non-Wi-Fi waveforms. The application will have to extrapolate from the noise that was admitted through the low-level filters to attempt to guess what interferer and what energy may have reached the card from the energy that the filter admitted. Such an application will therefore produce less accurate results than an application that mandates specialized hardware to capture the entirety of the energy. Tools that require such a card include WiPry-Pro Spectrum Analyzer, WiFi Surveyor, CommView for WiFi, and MetaGeek Chanalyzer. You do not need to be an expert in any of these tools, but understanding their basic principles will go a long way when you perform a survey or analyze a source of interference.

In particular, Chanalyzer has the advantage of being able to capture from a specialized USB card but can also connect to a Cisco AP running CleanAir and capture raw data detected by the AP Spectrum Analysis Engine (SAgE). Although such a setup may not be the easiest for a site survey (because it supposes an AP, and thus a switch and a WLC, that you will have to power and carry around), it is definitely a solution that Cisco professionals are expected to know about. To enable such a mode, you can keep your AP in a normal (Local) mode, but you will then only be able to see that AP channel. If you want the AP to sweep the entire band, you need to set your AP to SE-Connect (in AireOS from **Wireless > AP > Select AP > General > AP Mode > SE-Connect**, and in C9800 from **Configuration > Wireless > Access Point > Select AP > General > AP Mode > SE-Connect**).

Then, on Chanalyzer, use the CleanAir menu and select **Connect to CleanAir AP**. Enter the AP name, the NSI key, and choose the slot (radio 0, 2.4GHz, radio 1, 5GHz or Monitor, to observe both radios) that you want to observe. This Network Spectrum Interface (NSI) key is a hash found in the WLC, on the AP General tab that you used to switch the AP to SE-Connect mode (the NSI key is also available in that same tab, if you choose to use the AP in local mode) and that encrypts the information exchanged with the AP. This method prevents eavesdroppers from intercepting and observing your exchanges with the AP. As you click Connect, you will see the energy reported by the radio(s) appear in the Chanalyzer GUI.

Whether you use Chanalyzer with an AP or a local module or another spectrum analyzer tool, you need to master some common concepts. The energy reported is commonly expressed in decibels. The decibel measures the power of a signal as a function of its ratio to another standardized value. The abbreviation for decibel is often combined with other abbreviations in order to represent the values that are compared. In the world of Wi-Fi, where energy is commonly expressed in milliwatts (mW), you will see the symbol dBm, representing the power level compared to 1 milliwatt (mW). A 0 dBm value is the same amount of energy as a direct 1 mW current. This would be an extremely high amount of energy for Wi-Fi. In most cases, you will see negative numbers (for example, –70 dBm and –80 dBm). On this negative scale, –80 dBm represents a smaller amount of energy than –70 dBm. The dBm scale is also used to express AP powers. For example, an AP set to a 1mW power level (this is pretty low) is set to a 0 dBm power level (because 1 mW is exactly the reference value, nothing more or nothing less). An AP set to 10 mW is set to 10 dBm, and an AP set to 20 mW is set to 13 dBm (10 dBs to get from 1 mW to 10 mW, then twice that power [that is, + 3 dB] to get to 20 mW; always start with the tens, then the threes).

When you compare two amounts of energy, expressed against the same reference unit, you remove the reference unit and only use the decibel term. For example, comparing interferer 1 detected at –70 dBm to interferer 2 detected at –80 dBm, you can say that interferer 2 is 10 dB weaker than interferer 1. The "milliwatt" symbol would not make sense here, as you are not comparing the energies against the 1 mW reference point, but you are comparing the interferers against one another. They happen to both be detected and measured against the mW reference point, but interferer 2 is 10 dB weaker than interferer 1, regardless of the unit against which they were measured. It is for the same reason that the signal's received signal strength indicator (RSSI) is expressed in dBm (compared to the energy obtained by receiving a direct 1 mW current), but the signal-to-noise ratio (SNR) is expressed in dB, because you compare the signal to the noise (not to the effect of a 1mW current). This comparison only makes sense if both signal and noise are expressed in the same unit (dBm), but their relative strength is independent from the unit in which they are both expressed.

The decibel scale is logarithmic and therefore its scale is not linear. An easy-to-remember rule is that adding 3 dB doubles the power. Removing 3 dBs halves the power. Adding 10 dB multiplies the power by 10 (and removing 10 dB divides the power by 10). This rule is an approximation, but it is sufficient to compare powers you measure. Thus, above interferer

2 is 10 dB weaker than interferer 1 and therefore 10 times weaker. If interferer 3 is detected at –76 dBm, it would be four times weaker (70–3 to get "twice," and –3 again to get "four times") than interferer 1, and a bit more than twice as powerful as interferer 2 (they are 4 dB apart, whereas "two times" would be 3 dB apart). This scale logic is valid irrespective of the unit you are comparing against (strictly dB, dBm, or dB measured against another reference).

Therefore, the amount of energy detected from each interferer will be presorted in your spectrum analysis tool with the power at which the energy was received (in dBm) and the frequency (in the spectrum) where the energy was detected, as shown in Figure 3-1. It is clear that a stronger signal will likely affect your WLANs more than a weaker signal. However, the effect is a bit more complex. Most RF devices send bursts of energy and then stop. For example, your Wi-Fi card will send a frame and then stop. Even within the frame transmission, your card sends small bursts of energy of slightly different intensity, to represent the 0s and the 1s. The complexity of this variation depends on the signal modulation (for example, BPSK or QPSK, DSSS or OFDM, and so on). The same logic applies to any RF transmitter. Therefore, your spectrum analyzer will also report another metric called the Duty Cycle. This metric shows, within each second, what the percentage of time was when the interferer was detected. If the interferer was detected for 20 ms over each second interval, then its duty cycle is 2 percent (1,000 milliseconds divided by 20). The interferer may have a strong energy (high reported dBm), but it will affect your network only 2 percent of the time. This may be less disrupting than a weaker interferer present 60 percent of the time. In the end, there is a fine balance between power strength and the amount of time where this power was detected that will determine the impact of the interferer on your WLAN. Smart spectrum analyzer tools will give you guidance on how to evaluate these metrics together. Most tools will also allow you to display the average amount of energy, the maximum amount observed, or a real-time plot. The plot is often called FFT, for Fast Fourier Transform, which is a method to represent the captured energy in both the frequency domain and the time domain.

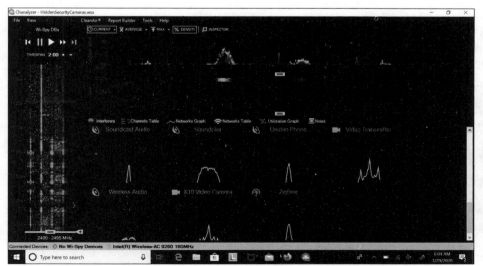

Figure 3-1   *View of a Wireless (Non-802.11) Camera in MetaGeek Chanalyzer*

NOTE   The 20 ms in our example may be grouped in a single burst or over many small bursts. Here, your ability to measure the duty cycle depends on the speed at which the spectrum analyzer card sweeps the band, and how granular it makes measurements. This is where the card price starts to matter, and you will read about resolution and rate. The resolution represents the amount of frequency, the channel size, that the card is able to capture at a time. If the card only captures 1MHz at a time, it may not see very narrow signals within that range (for example, a 12kHz signal), because they are too small to be distinguished from larger transmitters in that same chunk of the band, if both are transmitting at the same time. Therefore, a card with a good resolution will capture small chunks of band (for example, 72kHz) so as to be able to detect reliably narrow transmitters, even if they are sending energy in the same frequency as another larger transmitter. However, if your card needs to scan a 20MHz Wi-Fi channel, capturing only 72kHz may mean that the card might take a long time to sweep the entire channel, and its evaluation of the duty cycle may be coarse. The card may report a 10 percent duty cycle, but if it swept the channel once per second and averages over 10 seconds, its report will be less reliable than if it swept the channel 10 times during the last second. Therefore, cards will report the sweep rate, which is the amount of time in which they can sweep each chunk of frequency per second. This ability may depend on the width of the channel, and you may read metrics such as "10 sweeps per second over 40MHz."

Interferer Types and Effects

You do not need to be an RF expert to pass the CCNP exams. However, there are a few very common interferer types you will encounter often during your surveys. While managing your networks, you will also see them often in your WLC Monitor page or in Cisco Prime Infrastructure (see Chapter 16, "Monitoring and Troubleshooting WLAN Components," for more details on interferer management in deployed networks). In fact, they are so common that tools like Chanalyzer display their wave form in the main Interferers window. At the bottom of Figure 3-1, you see the shape of an 802.11b signal and the shape of an OFDM (802.11g/a/n/ac/ax) signal. A 20MHz-wide signal is shown in the 802.11g/n section. In the lower left part of the picture, you see a flat and wide signal, representing the same OFDM signal over 40MHz, as shown, along with other signals identified in Chanalyzer, in Figure 3-2.

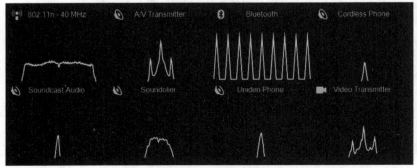

Figure 3-2   *Well-Known Signal Types in MetaGeek Chanalyzer*

802.11 transmitters are reported but are typically not considered as non-802.11 interferers. However, the following interferers are also common:

- **Bluetooth:** Present in 2.4GHz, BT transmitters are typical because of their spikes. There are frequency hoppers (they hop frequently between narrow channels spread across the entire 2.4GHz band). They are often low power. Many Bluetooth devices, or one very loud Bluetooth device, will negatively impact the wireless network. BLE (Bluetooth Low Energy) devices have an advertisement mode where only three channels outside of Wi-Fi channels 1, 6, and 11 are used. With BLE, you will see only three spikes until a connection is established, where all BT channels come back in use.

- **Video cameras (and A/V transmitters):** These transmitters become less and less common, as more cameras tend to use Wi-Fi. They are still present on the lower end of the video surveillance market. These cameras typically allow up to four channels that partially overlap with Wi-Fi channels in 2.4GHz, as show in Figure 3-1 (two cameras, affecting channels 4–5 and 8–9). Being continuous transmitters, their effect on Wi-Fi is typically severe.

- **Narrow transmitters:** In this category, you will find cordless phones, soundcast audio, and ZigBee. These transmitters use different protocols, but their channel is typically narrow (5MHz) and their Fast Fourier Transform (FFT)plots look similar, with a different signal strength. They all operate in the 2.4GHz band. Although some of these transmitters may use a fixed channel, allowing you to design around them, they also often implement some smart channel operations and may jump from one channel to another. They are therefore usually highly disruptive for the neighboring APs operating on the same band.

- **Microwave ovens:** Microwave ovens definitely interfere with Wi-Fi networks. The interference is short-lived but can be very complete. Microwaves typically impact channels 6 to 11, but mostly channel 11. Microwave ovens are prevalent in healthcare facilities. In many cases, older microwave ovens can be damaged and produce unhealthy levels of emissions. Leakage can be caused by a broken microwave oven door or simply by the seal being damaged or dirty.

- **Jammers:** Although they should not be expected in normal networks, jammers are cheap devices and easily bought online. Their characteristic is a continuous signal with a high duty cycle across the entire affected band. They may operate in 2.4GHz or 5GHz. The presence of a jammer signal is reflective of an attack against your network. Many jammers operate in the 2.4GHz band because this band is categorized as Industrial, Scientific, and Medical (ISM) and can be used by any transmitter (under some relaxed regulatory conditions). Most of the 5GHz band is not ISM, which makes it less susceptible to interferences from non-802.11 devices. However, different countries have different rules, and you may see in non-ISM 5GHz channels devices that were designed for a country where such operation is allowed.

Surveying for Interferers

As you perform your site survey, your first task is to walk the floor with a scanner and document any interferer detected. As your spectrum analyzer tool will report the signal strength, walk around to attempt to locate each interferer location. You may not visually locate the device (especially if it is embedded in another object or behind ceiling tiles), but you can document the location where the device was detected with the loudest signal. Also document the device type.

At the end of the process, you should have a map of the interferers, along with their expected severity and transmission profile. You can then evaluate their zone of impact as well as whether you can design your channel plan around the interferers or need to discuss with the Wi-Fi project sponsor to evaluate if the worst interferers can be removed (swapped for Wi-Fi-enabled, or Wi-Fi-friendly, equivalents).

Performing a Layer 2 Survey

Once you know what channels are available, your next step is to perform a Layer 2 site survey. This term is used to contrast against the Layer 1 sweep of the previous section, but its real meaning is simply a Wi-Fi survey (that is, a survey where you will determine the position of each intended AP).

The Site Survey Process

Depending on your user density model, you may design small cells or large cells. You may survey for simple data coverage, voice coverage, location, or all of them. Chapter 6, "Designing Radio Management," will help you make those decisions. However, regardless of your deployment model, the site survey principles are the same: Set a test AP to a target power level, enable all data rates and Modulation and Coding Schemes (MCS) (you will use your survey adapter to determine the data rate boundary), and then try to position the AP on the floor and estimate its coverage cell. If you use a Cisco AP, you can enable "Aironet IE" on the WLAN configuration. This allows your AP to send its name and power level in beacons and probe responses. Most professional survey tools can read these elements. They are very useful when you review your survey results.

In most cases, you will want to use a site survey tool. This tool allows you to upload a map of your floor, click your position on the map, and then capture the signal from one or all the detected APs. At the end of the process, the tool can display the resulting RF signal map. By moving APs around and combining such captures, you can evaluate the best AP position and density for your coverage intent. Several such tools exist. The main contenders are AirMagnet and Ekahau for professional surveys, but you will find many other products, including VisiWave, NetSpot, and MetaGeek Map-Plan. You are not supposed to be an expert in any of them to pass the CCNP exams, but some familiarity with AirMagnet or Ekahau Pro will go a long way in helping you understand questions about the general survey process.

All tools allow you to upload a floor map, define its scale, and also configure some target parameters, such as expected client count per cell or minimum cell signal or data rate. These elements are useful for the tool to define audio warnings where the matching thresholds are reached, thus helping you define cell edges more efficiently. Also keep in mind that you can perform two types of surveys:

- With AP-on-a-stick (APoS), you position an AP (usually on a tripod) and test the signal from the AP. This test can be done by simply listening to the AP messages (beacons and such) or by associating the wireless network card with the selected access point SSID (service set identifier) and then sending and receiving RF packets to and from the access point. The second method is only useful if you need to increase the number of 802.11 messages exchanged with the target AP.

- In a validation survey mode, the wireless network card does not associate to any particular access point or SSID. Instead, it simply listens to the 802.11 frames as you move through the site. At the end of the process, the site survey tool allows you to select which APs cell coverage you want to analyze.

> **NOTE**   The validation survey is sometimes called a "passive survey." The APoS survey is sometimes called an "active survey" (because you actively associate your adapter to an AP). However, these terms have different meanings in different tools. For example, in Ekahau Pro on a laptop, the Ekahau adapter (attached to your laptop USB port) never associates to an AP. However, you can use your laptop internal adapter to associate to the AP. If you do so, you can also activate an "active" mode to continuously ping the gateway, thus testing both the RF connection and the gateway connectivity performances at the same time.

3

You should start with the validation survey to assess the existing Wi-Fi environment before your deployment. This step is useful not only in detecting existing Wi-Fi APs on the floor of your survey but also in discovering neighboring networks and which channel plan and power level may have consequences on your design.

You will also perform a validation survey after your deployment is completed (to verify the coverage). During the initial Layer 2 survey phase of a new deployment, you will carry APoS surveys in most cases. The steps of this phase can be summarized as follows:

1. Determine the possible locations where an access point should be placed.

2. Place the access point in the most desirable location (APoS) and conduct as many surveys as needed to ensure that the access point intended coverage area is fully monitored, and that you did find the best location for that AP. In a survey tool, you may need to perform several surveys to examine the AP cell in multiple directions. Save the survey data at the end of each survey; you may end up merging (and associating) several survey data files for the access point at one location in order to get a full picture of the cell.

3. Repeat until the facility is covered.

4. Save the survey data at the end of each survey.

As your site survey should include overlaps between cells, it is best to use several access points in the process. Three APs is a common quantity. In places where carrying three APs is a challenge (each AP needs a power source, a pole, and so on, which adds to the overall volume of equipment to carry), you can use two or one access point instead. The difficulty in that case is to evaluate the overlap between cells.

To start your site survey, identify a large obstacle, such as the building edge or a large heavy wall through which signal will not bleed. Working from there, your job is to find the position of the first AP. Taking the edge of the building as an example, as illustrated in the left part of Figure 3-3, place the access point at location 1 to start. Perform a site survey to determine the signal strength of the coverage area. Mark where the data rate falls to the minimum acceptable value until you have traced a semicircular pattern on the floor, which will determine the coverage boundary. Move the original access point to a centrally located position on the coverage boundary 2, as shown on the right part of Figure 3-3, to create the first coverage area. The logic is that if you get coverage up to point 2 when the AP is at position 1, then you should get coverage down to point 1, which is the corner of the building, when the AP is at position 2. Position 2 is located along the coverage boundary determined when the AP was in position 1, preferably at equal distances from each building wall, which places the AP toward the center of the building.

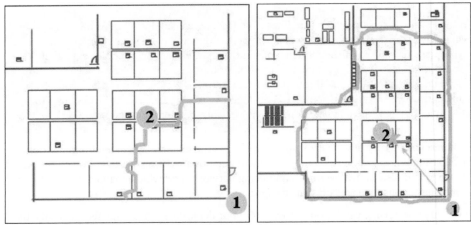

Figure 3-3   *The Site Survey Process—Positioning the First AP*

Once the AP is moved to position 2, perform a site survey to determine the signal strength of the new coverage area. Mark where the data rate falls to the minimum acceptable value until you have traced a circular pattern on the floor that will determine the coverage boundary. This is the position where the cell application performance would decrease to the point where your client device will search for a better AP. However, you should also continue capturing the AP signal beyond that point to evaluate the RF footprint of the AP. This will help you evaluate areas where APs on the same channel may interfere with each other.

This position 2 is expected to be the final position of the AP for this zone, and the coverage area should represent the expected useful coverage (the zone where a client can actively and efficiently perform data communication with the AP) when the final AP is deployed at this position. You may have to move the AP if the measured coverage area does not match your expectation because of obstacles or interfering objects.

Now place another access point adjacent to the first coverage area to determine another coverage area with appropriate overlap of the two areas, as shown in Figure 3-4. Continue through the facility until all areas needing coverage are accounted for and you have acquired the appropriate overlap between cells for client roaming purposes.

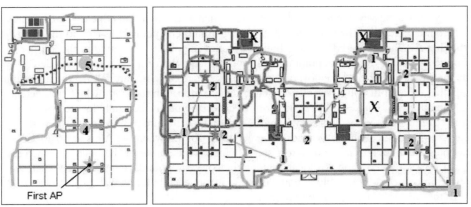

Figure 3-4   *The Site Survey Process—Positioning More APs*

Keep in mind the cell edge and the cell overlaps. If you decide that the cell edge is at −67 dBm, then this design means that at the position where the client detects the AP at −67 dBm, the client can also detect another AP at −67 dBm or higher. This does not mean, of course, that the client will roam at that point. Each client has its own internal algorithm and threshold structure to decide on roaming points. However, this design means that, as the client continues to move away from the first AP, the next AP signal becomes even stronger. At any point in space and time where the client decides to roam as you keep moving, the next AP will offer a good signal, sufficient for the client to make a fast roaming decision. Also keep in mind that the AP RF footprint does not stop at that cell edge. In theory, the AP signal reaches infinity. Practically speaking, the AP signal will be detectable way beyond the intended cell edge. You should continue surveying the AP coverage until you have assessed the full AP footprint (that is, to the point where the AP signal reaches the noise floor, typically around −94 dBm in a standard building).

If you work in an open space, or if the wall structure is fairly homogeneous, you can use shortcuts. In open space propagation, a common rule is "6 dB = twice the distance" and "the first meter loss is at least 50 dB with omnidirectional antennas." In other words, if you position an AP and set its power to 100 mW (20 dBm [that is, 10 dB to get from 1 mW to 10 mW, and another 10 dB to get from 10 to 100 mW]), you should expect at best −30 dBm at 1 meter from the AP (20−50). We say "at best" because imperfection in the antenna radiation pattern may cause the power to be even lower. Supposing an imperfect antenna and a signal at −36 dBm at 1 meter, you should then expect 6 dB less each time you double the distance (that is, −42 dBm at 2 meters, −48 dBm at 4 meters, −54 dBm at 8 meters, and so on). Keeping this ratio in mind can help you save time by converting distances into likely signal levels.

For example, suppose you deploy two APs in an open space. Suppose that you stand at the midpoint between these two APs, and you positioned them so that their signal reaches your client at −67 dBm at this position. If, from this point, you walk to any of the APs, you double the distance to the other AP (as you were standing midpoint). Therefore, that other AP's signal should now be around −73 dBm, or −67 − (−6). This also means that if you deploy one AP and then stand at that AP position while a colleague moves away another test AP, you can be confident that the other AP is at the right distance when you detect its signal at about −73 dBm. This model is, of course, only valid in open spaces. In most buildings, however, you will find walls and obstacles on your path that will make this shortcut more complex to apply, but the same principles can be applied with small variations. Refer to Chapter 2 for a list of common obstacles and their attenuation.

A more cautious approach is to position each AP individually and then systematically walk the floor around the AP so as to precisely find the cell edge. In most professional site survey tools, you can choose to emulate a particular client type. Then, as you walk, you can see the signal level in real time (or the data rate, the SNR, or other RF quantity you need to measure) for your target AP. To draw the contours of your AP heat map, click where you are on the map, walk a few steps, and then click your new position (some tools allow you to click a starting and ending points, then walk at a steady pace in a straight line between these two points, without having to click intermediate locations). In the end, the tool will display the heat map of the detected AP. Most of the those tools will also attempt to position the AP automatically, assuming that the direction of the strongest signal is likely to point to the AP. After repeating this exercise with a few APs, you can combine the views in a single heat map, as illustrated in Figure 3-5 for Ekahau Site Survey Pro.

Figure 3-5   *Ekahau Site Survey Pro*

Click the Survey tab to start the data collection, and click the Planning tab to work with existing data or make coverage predictions. From this mode, you can move the APs (green circles on the map) if the tool incorrectly assumed their position. You can see the recorded path in green, with green points that mark the positions that were clicked on the path. The current view includes all recorded APs (called "My Access Points"). You can add or remove APs to or from this list as you try and then keep or discard different AP positions. As you will likely carry fewer APs than the entire floor will need for full coverage, you will probably have to rename each AP as you move it to a new position. At the bottom of the screen, a real-time view of the RF environment allows you to monitor the current detected APs along with their channel and RF characteristics.

As you design your network, keep roaming in mind. If you expect your users to move while connected, you need to ensure optimal roaming conditions. This means that the client should always detect the next AP while moving. This principle is illustrated in Figure 3-6. A user walks along the path from points A to B and then C. APs are represented as green points. On the left side, as the user, associated to AP 1, turns at point B and walks toward point C, the elevator banks (represented by squares with crosses) on each side suddenly obfuscate the signal from AP 1. The client may have detected AP 2 before deciding to associate to AP 1, but AP 2 is now also not detectable. As a result, the client needs to undergo a panic scan before discovering and joining AP 3. This creates disruptions during the roaming phase. By contrast, on the right side, the client can jump to AP 2, because that AP is still accessible on the B-to-C segment. As the client scans to discover and join AP 2, it also discovers AP 3, which will be a possible jumping point when the user reaches the end of the corridor.

This principle illustrates that the view from the ceiling should match the view from the floor. As your client moves between APs, your design should ensure that a client associating to one AP always has RF reachability to the next AP on the path (even if that AP is farther away and therefore not chosen by the client). This principle has to work regardless of the walking direction. As you will learn in Chapter 8, "Designing for Client Mobility," the APs can send signals (using the 802.11v and 802.11k protocols) to help the client discover the next AP.

This means that the APs visible to the client should also be visible to the APs (thus making the view from the ground the same as the view from the ceiling, as much as possible).

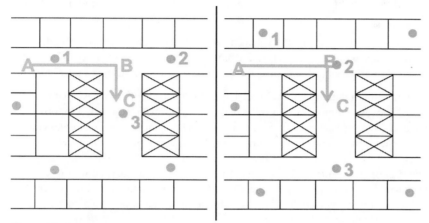

Figure 3-6 *Positioning the Next AP*

These general principles, along with the surveying method, should allow you to build your way through the floor, designing as you go to determine best AP location and AP density. At the end of the floor survey process, you should be able to build a complete view of the floor coverage by combining the heat maps of your different APs and their various expected best positions. You will use this outcome to produce a site survey report. This report lists the APs used, their power settings, channels, coverage target assumptions, and the expected resulting coverage heat map. This report will be used to deploy the APs. In most cases, it is also useful to take actual pictures of the spots (possibly marked with a piece of tape) where you project that the APs should be positioned.

Data vs. Voice vs. Location Deployments

The density of APs will depend on the application you intend to deploy. Data coverages are typically done with larger AP cells and low data rates at the edge, thus maximizing the cell size (and minimizing the AP count). Such deployment offers poor performance for time-sensitive applications (for example, voice). When designing for real-time applications, you will want smaller cells, with APs at lower power, so as to ensure that clients always have a high data rate. Chapter 5, "Applying Wireless Design Requirements," will give you additional details on these various requirements. In all cases, the survey process is to choose the target signal level at the cell edge, choose a target minimum data rate for that cell edge, and then position APs to find the cell contours. Here are some points to keep in mind:

- Start by deciding on the AP power level. This element primarily depends on the client type you expect in your cell. Most smartphones have power limited to 11 dBm or 14 dBm. Larger tablets and laptops can reach 16 or 20 dBm. If you know your target client, verify its capability. In most cases, the AP has a better receive sensitivity than the client, so you can set the AP power higher than the client. For a voice deployment, you can set the AP to 14 dBm, and 17 dBm for a data deployment. This value accounts for the fact that radio resource management (RRM) may be able to increase or decrease the AP power wherever needed.

- Think redundancy. If one AP gets disabled, you will want RRM tools to dynamically compensate for the gap by increasing the neighboring APs' power. Use the 6 dB rule to evaluate if you would still have coverage from neighboring APs, should one AP be disabled.

- Decide on the expected AP signal level (as measured by the client) at the cell edge. For data coverage only, a typical target is –72 dBm. For voice, it's –65 dBm to –67 dBm. As most indoor networks today expect to see voice traffic, –67 dBm is a good target.

- Decide the minimum data rate allowed to that cell edge location. For basic data coverage, 6Mbps is common. For voice or real-time application support, 12Mbps is common, and 24Mbps is expected if real-time video applications (for example, video conferencing) are your target. Here again, as most cells carry both data and voice, designing around 12Mbps minimum has become common even for data-only support, in anticipation of occasional voice activity. To ensure this boundary, configure your site survey tool to stop displaying the heat map below your data rate target (when displaying the data rate view). Most tools can emulate the signal level at which each client would use a particular data rate.

- Decide the minimum acceptable SNR for your cell. This parameter goes along with the RSSI and will dictate how close APs on the same channel can be to one another, as each AP will be a cause of noise (thus lower SNR) to the clients connecting to the other AP. A common value is 12 dB or more for basic data, and 25 dB or more for real-time applications.

NOTE   This SNR requirement means that if your cell edge is set to –67 dBm, at that position the noise floor should be at –92 dBm or lower, which is easily achieved in indoor environments. However, in high-density environments, you may have to position other APs in range on the same channel. In that case, the rule can be bent to 19 dBm isolation. This means that at the –67 dBm edge, the signal from the next AP on the same channel should be heard at –86 dBm or lower. This value is higher than the noise recommendation and is possible because the APs can recognize the 802.11 transmission and accommodate for it. This recommendation is for the next AP on the same channel. Of course, the neighboring AP will be heard much louder, as you want to ensure seamless roaming between APs. But that neighboring AP will be on a different channel.

These requirements are default templates for data and voice deployments. Your particular deployment needs may dictate different values. You will also find older recommendations that suggest to keep the 5GHz band for voice and real-time traffic and keep data in the 2.4GHz band. This scheme was valid at times when SSIDs were specialized (voice SSID, data SSID, and so on). Today, the same SSID carries all traffic. As such, you should design your WLAN in the 5GHz band, if it is allowed in your regulatory domain. Some deployments completely ignore the 2.4GHz band. Some others use it to carry IoT traffic (data from Wi-Fi sensors, with a different SSID than on 5GHz). Others use it as a backup, to allow coverage in zones where the 5GHz coverage may be weak. This logic is based on the fact that antenna sizes (for clients and APs) have a direct inverse relationship with the frequency of the signal. The 2.4GHz signal uses antennas about twice as large as the 5GHz signal, and therefore 2.4GHz transmissions appear to be about twice as powerful as 5GHz transmissions (as 2.4GHz antennas collect about twice as much energy as 5GHz antennas because they are about twice as large). A direct effect is that 2.4GHz cells expand to larger areas than 5GHz cells and can still provide coverage at distances where the 5GHz signal is too weak to be used. This gain is often accompanied by more noise, more interference, and more collisions, and this is why a larger 2.4GHz cell is only a backup in these scenarios. However, a 5GHz-only design is more common.

For location deployments, a few considerations need to be added:

■ Location uses trilateration, which means that you need several APs around each point of your floor so that a location engine in the infrastructure can combine the signal these APs receive from each client and compute the client location. For each point of the floor, you need at least three surrounding APs, in different directions (in different "quadrants"), and preferably four or more. At least three of these APs should be less than 70 feet (21 meters) away and should read any client signal coming from this point with a level of –75 dBm or more (–72 dBm recommended).

■ As much as possible, try to scatter the APs. In other words, do not set the APs in a long straight line. For example, in a hospital or a hotel where there are bedrooms and a central corridor, do not put the APs in a line in the corridor. Rather, try to position the APs in the rooms. This scatter disposition helps the trilateration computation.

■ As much as possible, try to create a "convex hull." This means that there should be APs at the edge of the floor, so as to make sure that the first recommendation applies everywhere and that each point where location is needed is surrounded by APs. Deploying APs near the building walls may not make sense from a pure data or voice coverage standpoint. For this reason, the APs at the edge are often set to Monitor mode. In this mode, the APs do not support any client service, and they only receive the client signals. In most cases, you would perform a survey for data or voice and then add at the edge of the floor additional APs set to Monitor mode.

■ Do not put your AP antennas too high. As the antennas get higher, the minimum distance from the client to the antenna increases. All clients start to appear as "far" regardless of their actual position, and the location accuracy gets degraded. A common recommendation is to place the antennas no higher than 20 feet (6 meters) above the clients' location. A typical ceiling height is 10 feet (3 meters), which is a good height. The maximum height recommendation is primarily intended for large indoor spaces, like warehouses or atriums.

These considerations are illustrated in Figure 3-7 and apply for location services based on RSSI (that is, when the infrastructure uses the client signal for location purposes). The convex hull is set for the upper part of the floor.

For other location technologies, like Fine Timing Measurement (FTM), Bluetooth Low Energy (BLE), and Angle of Arrival (AoA), other considerations may apply. Although these modes are too advanced for the CCNP exam, make sure to look up the vendor documentation if you plan on deploying these other location solutions.

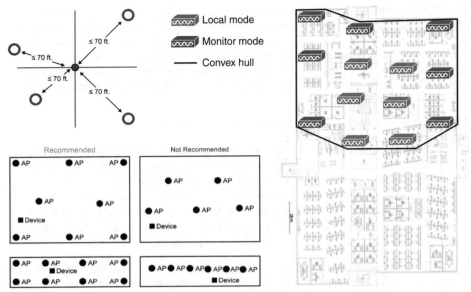

Figure 3-7   *Location Deployment Recommendations*

Performing a Post-Deployment Onsite Survey

Once your recommendations have been applied, there should be APs positioned on the floor at correct locations. However, deployment complexities are always possible (for example, A/C conduit behind a ceiling tile, preventing cabling from reaching your exact intended AP position). Additionally, you likely surveyed with a subset of the APs eventually deployed. Therefore, once installation is complete, you should always come back onsite and perform a post-deployment survey to verify coverage and performances.

Start by conducting a validation survey of the entire deployed environment (divided into several shorter surveys, if necessary) and compare the results to those generated during the pre-deployment survey. They should look nearly identical. Pay special attention to the areas that you identified, during the walkthrough or the survey, as difficult areas. These are typically areas where positioning APs and ensuring proper coverage are challenging (high ceiling, presence of strong multipath sources, and so on). A visual review of the deployment should help you identify those APs. The post-deployment survey will also reveal them by showing areas where coverage is inconsistent. In all these identified areas, perform a client performance test with a "poor" client, as defined later in this chapter, testing for the client and AP RSSI and SNR.

If the client performances do not match your expectations for those difficult areas, you may use several factors to mitigate the issue. One first and obvious possible action is to determine if the AP can be moved to a more "RF-friendly" location. In many cases, APs were deployed by insufficiently trained personnel, and the mis-location of the AP has no other cause than the installer being unaware of the detrimental effect of the environment on the AP performances. Relocating the AP may not be a major issue in that case. In some other cases, the AP location results from a conscious decision, based on aesthetical issues or other constraints, and the AP cannot be moved anymore. The second possible action is to work with the AP power level to help mitigate the performance issues. If the AP is behind an obstacle, manually raising the AP power level may help the AP signal get through the obstacle. Increasing the AP power level is not the best option, though, as "good configuration does not compensate for poor deployment," as the saying goes. As you increase the AP power, you also increase the issues related to reflections and multipath. The result is that the AP signal may be stronger at the client level, but multipath issues may be worse. Increasing the power also does not change the AP Rx sensitivity, and your client link may become asymmetric.

Testing real applications, with a real client, allows you to verify that the real-world network traffic (for example, physical data rate, packet loss or packet retry, uplink or downlink data) meets user requirements. Survey by SSID and by AP to ensure that smooth roaming is taking place. Walk both sides of all access points to ensure you stay connected. This task should preferably be done with a typical client or the client expected to perform the most poorly. ("Most poorly" in this context means the client that displays the lowest performances.) This can be measured by positioning several clients next to one another, connected to the same AP. The client displaying the lowest RSSI from the AP and the lowest data rate is likely the best candidate for testing. You should also attempt to measure the performances of the application most sensitive to roaming delays. This is typically a real-time application (for example, voice). A good test procedure is as follows:

- Associate with each access point in the WLAN.

- Make stationary calls and verify the audio quality.

- Verify that you can make roaming phone calls with good-quality audio and no disconnections.

- Place multiple calls, especially in areas that are designated for high-density use.

Make sure to test and identify rate-shifting points. During your site survey, you determined roaming paths and know that wireless client data rates are going to shift down as clients move away from the access points. If your deployment uses delay-sensitive applications, you may want to test how going through these rate-shifting points affects the client performances. You probably will not test each rate-shifting point for each AP but will focus on specific areas where rate shifting might be an issue. Those are any areas where brutal rate shifting is expected. For example, if a roaming path goes through self-closing doors, you know that the data rate will shift down brutally as soon as the door closes (if the connected AP is still on the other side of the door). The same issue may occur at any location where a sudden change in the AP signal is expected. This change may be due to the physical layout of the facility (angle in a corridor, pillar or wall section between the client and the AP, and so on). The change may also be due to the environment (areas with sources of multipath, reflection, or interferences). For delay-sensitive applications, you may want to test those areas and verify the roaming delay in both directions to ensure that the user experience will be seamless even through those difficult areas. In some cases, you may have to reconsider some APs' position or power level (for example, reducing an AP's power in order to make the client attempt to roam sooner).

NOTE   You cannot manipulate the clients' parameters. Most clients will start scanning for the next AP when the current AP signal falls below a target threshold. What you can do is measure the client behavior, determine the threshold, and set the AP to bring the roaming phase to an area where connection interruption will be shorter. Each client is different, but you will find common behaviors. For example, Apple iOS phones scan when the AP signal falls below –70 dBm. Samsung phones and most laptops (including macOS) scan when the AP signal falls below –75 dBm. Most clients need the alternate AP signal to be at least 6 to 8 dB better than the current AP to make the roaming decision.

As you test roaming, you can measure performances. Beyond measuring RSSI, SNR, and retries, the most accurate way to evaluate roaming efficiency is to measure the interval between the last data packet on the previous AP and the first data packet on the next AP. A roaming delay of 50 ms or less will likely not be noticed by any client or application. A delay of 100 ms may be detected by an audio application (causing one or a few packets to be lost and resulting in a short metallic texture to the sound or a click). Longer delays are obviously more impactful.

At the end of the post-deployment survey, you should be able to validate if the deployment matches your expectations. Document discrepancies so as to set correct expectations but also to plan for the next phase of the network lifecycle and future upgrades.

Summary

This chapter examined the process of an onsite site survey and its different phases. In this chapter you have learned the following:

- How to perform a walkthrough survey to identify problematic areas

- How to perform a Layer 1 survey and how to detect, map, and evaluate the effect of non-802.11 transmitters

- How to perform a Layer 2 site survey for data, real-time applications, and location coverage

- How to perform a post-deployment site survey and assess the network performances

References

For additional information, refer to these resources:

Cisco site survey guidelines: https://www.cisco.com/c/en/us/support/docs/wireless/5500-series-wireless-controllers/116057-site-survey-guidelines-wlan-00.html

VoWLAN site survey and validation: https://www.cisco.com/c/en/us/td/docs/wireless/technology/vowlan/troubleshooting/vowlan_troubleshoot/8_Site_Survey_RF_Design_Valid.html

Location-based services RF design: https://www.cisco.com/en/US/docs/solutions/Enterprise/Mobility/emob30dg/Locatn.html

Cisco WLANs for iOS design guide: https://www.cisco.com/c/dam/en/us/td/docs/wireless/controller/technotes/8-6/Enterprise_Best_Practices_for_iOS_devices_and_Mac_computers_on_Cisco_Wireless_LAN.pdf

Cisco 8821 design guide (coverage and redundancy recommendations): https://www.cisco.com/c/dam/en/us/td/docs/voice_ip_comm/cuipph/8821/english/Deployment/8821_wlandg.pdf

Exam Preparation Tasks

As mentioned in the section "How to Use This Book" in the Introduction, you have a few choices for exam preparation: the exercises here, Chapter 18, "Final Preparation," and the exam simulation questions in the Pearson Test Prep Software Online.

Review All Key Topics

Review the most important topics in this chapter, noted with the Key Topic icon in the outer margin of the page. Table 3-2 lists these key topics and the page numbers on which each is found.

Table 3-2   Key Topics for Chapter 3

Key Topic Element	Description	Page Number
Paragraph	Perform a walkthrough survey	46
Paragraph	Layer 1 essentials	49
Paragraph	Interferer types and effects	52
Paragraph	The site survey process	54
Figure 3-3	Positioning the first AP	56
Paragraph	Data vs. voice vs. location deployments	59

Define Key Terms

Define the following key terms from this chapter and check your answers in the glossary:

Layer 1 sweep

CHAPTER 4

Physical and Logical Infrastructure Requirements

This chapter discusses the following topics:

Physical Infrastructure Requirements: Powering an access point with Power over Ethernet (PoE) has several variants, including delivering power directly from a switch or through a power injector. However, PoE itself comes in several flavors that have cabling infrastructure dependencies. This section discusses the main types of PoE, including PoE, PoE+, UPoE, and UPoE+, and the types of cables that support them. In addition, as modern 802.11 standards begin to push beyond 1Gbps, traditional Ethernet connections over twisted pair cable is no longer enough to support the maximum performance capabilities of the access point. This section discusses the improved performance characteristics of mGig and the network requirements necessary. This section also discusses AP mounting and grounding strategies.

Logical Infrastructure Requirements: This section discusses the logical elements of a wireless network, such as the communication flow of the CAPWAP control and data channels as they traverse the network, and their implications on the underlying physical infrastructure. In addition, this section discusses controller and AP licensing mechanisms.

This chapter covers the following ENWLSD exam topics:

- 2.1 Determine physical infrastructure requirements such as AP power, cabling, switch port capacity, mounting, and grounding

- 2.2 Determine logical infrastructure requirements such as WLC/AP licensing requirements based on the type of wireless architecture

The focus of wireless network design often revolves around the RF aspects of the deployment—and indeed, as discussed throughout this book, RF design is the foundation of any successful wireless network and almost always involves a robust site survey. However, there are key infrastructure components that are just as important in any wireless design exercise. These are generally grouped into two major classes: the physical infrastructure components and logical infrastructure components.

The physical infrastructure includes components of the physical networking gear. This involves the physical gear itself, as well as how the access points are cabled, powered, mounted, and even grounded. This design aspect goes far beyond just the access points and the controller. For example, if a switch is used to deliver PoE to an AP, the switch must be able to accommodate the power requirements of the AP. If it cannot, either the AP will not power on or certain capabilities (such as secondary radios) will not work.

Additionally, the reachability of the APs over standard Ethernet cabling becomes a design criterion as distances from the switch grow and as higher data rates are used. When the existing cable plant cannot support the distances demanded by the placement of APs, suboptimal AP placement may be used, which in turn may lead to poor RF coverage. Understanding the design requirements of the physical infrastructure is a crucial aspect of developing a successful wireless design.

The second infrastructure aspect is the logical network—in other words, the path the communication flows take through the network, regardless of the underlying physical infrastructure. Controller-based wireless networks use CAPWAP (Control And Provisioning of Wireless Access Points), both as a control channel as well as to encapsulate client data traffic, effectively tunneling client traffic directly from the AP to the controller, and vice versa. This gives the logical appearance that the APs and controller are Layer 2 adjacent, when in reality they may be traversing many hops of the underlying physical network. Understanding the behavior and function of these logical elements introduces important considerations when developing the infrastructure side of the wireless design.

This chapter focuses on these two infrastructure aspects, beginning with the physical infrastructure and followed by the logical infrastructure.

"Do I Know This Already?" Quiz

The "Do I Know This Already?" quiz allows you to assess whether you should read this entire chapter thoroughly or jump to the "Exam Preparation Tasks" section. If you are in doubt about your answers to these questions or your own assessment of your knowledge of the topics, read the entire chapter. Table 4-1 lists the major headings in this chapter and their corresponding "Do I Know This Already?" quiz questions. You can find the answers in Appendix D, "Answers to the 'Do I Know This Already?' Quizzes and Review Questions."

Table 4-1 "Do I Know This Already?" Section-to-Question Mapping

Foundation Topics Section	Questions
Physical Infrastructure Requirements	1–4
Logical Infrastructure Requirements	5–6

1. An access point has been deployed with full features, including dual radios and hyper-location. The AP requires 38W of power. Which of the following Power over Ethernet capabilities should you recommend be used?

   a. PoE

   b. PoE+

   c. UPOE

   d. UPOE+

2. A group of new Wi-Fi 6 (IEEE 802.11ax) APs has just been installed in a building to replace the older Wi-Fi 5 (802.11ac wave 1) APs. What is a design consideration you need to be aware of when deploying the physical infrastructure?

   a. Mounting of the new APs to reflect changes in the 802.11ax RF radiation pattern.

   b. An increase of power will be required. The switch will need to be upgraded to support either UPOE or UPOE+.

    c. The number of Wi-Fi 6 APs required will be less than the older APs thanks to better performance and coverage patterns.

    d. The switch connected to the APs may need to be upgraded to support mGig.

3. For security reasons, the building facilities team abides by a policy that no devices (APs included) may be visible from the office floor. As an alternative, the network team is looking to deploy the APs above the suspended ceiling. What should they be aware of?

    a. Positioning APs above the ceiling will result in significant RF degradation, so a new site survey may be required.

    b. This configuration is not supported by Cisco.

    c. Specialized mounting brackets will be needed.

    d. The APs should be positioned as close to the T-bar rails as possible.

4. When deploying higher throughput wireless technologies in Local mode, what design aspect must be considered related to possible oversubscription of the physical infrastructure?

    a. Uplink capabilities of the access switch should be considered.

    b. Physical connections between the access switch and AP should be considered.

    c. Performance of the backbone network connecting to the controller should be aligned with overall wireless performance demands.

    d. Performance capabilities of the controller should be considered.

    e. All of the above.

5. What interfaces on a physical controller (such as the WLC 5520) are used to communicate to key services such as ISE and CMX? (Choose two.)

    a. The service port

    b. The Management Interface

    c. The virtual port

    d. Any LAN interface port on the controller

    e. The AP-Manager interface

6. Which Cisco wireless licensing model involves pooling of licenses?

    a. Right-to-Use (RTU) licensing

    b. Perpetual licensing

    c. Term licensing

    d. Product Activation Key (PAK) licensing

    e. Smart Licensing

Foundation Topics

Physical Infrastructure Requirements

The physical infrastructure of a wireless network includes all physical elements, including the access points, controllers, switches and routers, and any other physical network devices that facilitate communication between the wireless users and the network they are trying to access. In addition to networking devices, the physical infrastructure includes power delivery, cabling, mounting, and grounding of access points.

PoE and PoE+

Power over Ethernet (PoE) is a widely used infrastructure technology that allows DC power to be provided to an endpoint over a twisted pair Ethernet cable. Power is passed from power sourcing equipment (PSE), such as a PoE-capable switch, over the existing twisted pair Ethernet cable that carries data communications to powered devices (PDs), such as IP phones, video cameras, wireless access points, point-of-sale machines, access control card readers, LED luminaires, and many more. Through the use of PoE, external powering of endpoints is not required, thus greatly reducing the cost and effort required to deploy electrical power throughout the infrastructure. Typically, for a company to deploy electrical cabling in the ceiling requires a certified electrician to perform the task, whereas the deployment of Ethernet cables (which can run PoE) can be done by anyone, thus greatly simplifying the job of deploying access points wherever they need to go.

The power requirements of endpoints varies based on their power consumption requirements, which is typically a function of the physical function, application, and complexity of the device. For example, basic IP phones might draw approximately 6W of power, whereas contemporary LED lighting fixtures can draw up to 50W for routine operation. Wireless APs draw different power levels depending on which features are enabled and how many radios are concurrently active. For example, the Cisco 3800 typically draws ~30W with all features turned on.

Power delivery over Ethernet twisted pair is based on the IEEE 802.3af (2003) standard and delivers up to 15.4W of DC power per port of the PSE; however, due to power dissipation in the cable, only 12.95W of this is available to the PD.

After the initial introduction of PoE in 2003, endpoints were soon demanding greater power than 802.3af could deliver. Thus, in 2009, IEEE 802.3at was standardized, known as PoE Plus (PoE+). PoE+ delivers up to 30W of DC power per port, ensuring 25.5W of power to a PD due to power dissipation.

In both of these cases, PoE delivers power over two of the four twisted pairs of Class D/Category 5e or better cabling. The PSE uses only signal pairs—that is, the pairs formed by pins 1 and 2 and pins 3 and 6—to transport power from the PSE to the PD and leaves the spare pairs idle (consisting of pins 4 and 5 and pins 7 and 8). Note that PoE does not affect the network performance of Ethernet links to the PD.

UPOE and UPOE+

In recent years the enterprise workspace has continued to evolve, resulting in increasing numbers of devices and workloads converging onto the IP network. This has fueled increasing demand for higher PD power draw, far in excess of what PoE and PoE+ can offer (more than 25.5W).

To meet this demand, Cisco has developed extended PoE capabilities, including Universal PoE (UPOE), capable of delivering 60W per port, and Universal PoE Plus (UPOE+), which is capable of delivering up to 90W per port. Note that while PoE and PoE+ have been standardized by the IEEE, UPOE and UPOE+ are Cisco proprietary. In 2018, the IEEE defined 802.3bt as a standard to deliver up to 90W (sometimes referred to as PoE++).

The network's ability to deliver higher levels of power to endpoints has, in turn, significantly expanded the PoE-capable endpoint landscape. Thanks to these higher PoE capabilities, a wide variety of devices with higher power requirements can now be powered over Ethernet without requiring separate electrical wiring. These include video endpoints, LED lighting fixtures, digital signage, compact switches, and, of course, larger and more robust access points.

802.3bt, UPOE, and UPOE+ all use the same cabling standard as PoE/PoE+; however, instead of delivering power over just two of the twisted pairs, these higher power embodiments of PoE utilize all four twisted pairs of standard Ethernet cabling (Category 5e or better). They does this by using two PSE controllers to power both the signal pairs and the spare pairs. Figure 4-1 presents the difference between PoE/PoE+ and Cisco UPOE/UPOE+.

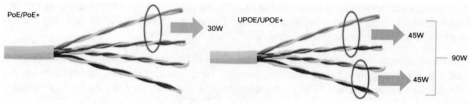

Figure 4-1 *Comparing PoE/PoE+ with UPOE/UPOE+*

In the case of PoE, PoE+, or UPOE, the minimum Ethernet cable type is Category 5e. In the case of UPOE+, Category 6a is required at a minimum. Regardless of the method of power over Ethernet, the maximum cable distance remains the same at 100 meters.

It is also important to note that support for the type of PoE desired depends on the capabilities of the Ethernet switch. For example, older switches may only support PoE/PoE+; however, modern switches (such as the Catalyst 9300) support UPOE, and certain higher-end switches support UPOE+ (such as the Catalyst 9400).

Table 4-2 summarizes the various PoE options available to power network devices.

Table 4-2 A Summary of Power over Ethernet Standards and Capabilities

	PoE	PoE+	UPOE	UPOE+	PoE++ (802.3bt class 4)
Minimum Cable Type	Cat5e	Cat5e	Cat5e	Cat6a	Cat6a
IEEE Standard	IEEE 802.3af	IEEE 802.3at	Cisco proprietary	Cisco proprietary	IEEE 802.3bt
Maximum Power per PoE Port	15.4W	30W	60W	90W	100W (class 4)
Maximum Power to PD	12.95W	25.5W	51W	71W	71W
Twisted Pairs Used	Two pairs	Two pairs	Four pairs	Four pairs	Four pairs
Distance	<100 meters	<100 meters	<100 meters	<100 meters	<100 meters

Power Injectors

PoE delivered by an access switch is a natural choice to power APs in most wireless deployments. This greatly reduces the wiring required and allows flexible AP placement throughout a building. That being said, there are still use cases where PoE delivered by the access switch is not practical, and power injectors must be considered. For example, there may be places where the switch simply doesn't support the necessary PoE mode, or perhaps the switch has no available PoE-capable ports, or it may even have a severely limited power budget due to too many other PDs. In some cases, certain APs with full features enabled may have greater power demands than a legacy PoE switch can offer. In these situations, using a power injector is a simple and often appealing alternative.

Power injectors generally have two Ethernet inputs: one connected to the upstream switch and another connected to the PD (that is, the access point). The power injector is also plugged into a power source via the 48V DC power supply, which then injects power into the two pairs, supporting PoE and PoE+.

Cisco power injectors are offered in two form factors. The first variant supports copper Category 5e or better cables both on the input and output (connected to the switch and to the access point). In this case, maximum cable distance from switch to AP remains at 100 meters—that is, the power injector does not function as a repeater and increase the maximum transmission distance over the twisted pair cable.

The second variant is a fiber optic link between the switch and the power injector. In this case, the power injector functions as a media converter and injects power onto the twisted pair cable that connects to the access point. Using single-mode fiber allows the power injector to be placed up to 2 kilometers from the switch, making it a practical option for places where the AP is far away, such as large factories, warehouses, and other places with sparse wiring closets.

Figure 4-2 illustrates the two power injector options for Cisco access points.

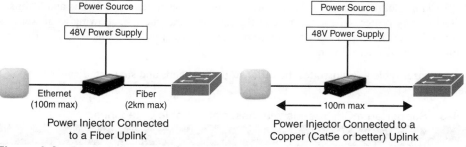

Figure 4-2   *Power Injector Deployment Options*

MultiGigabit

With increasing performance speeds of 802.11ac Wave 2 (Wi-Fi 5) and more recently 802.11ax (Wi-Fi 6), the maximum theoretical wireless throughput of an access point is pushing well beyond the 1Gpbs capability of traditional Ethernet access, potentially making the single wired uplink between the AP and switch a chokepoint.

To solve this problem, Cisco has championed the development of MultiGigabit (mGig) technology that delivers speeds of 2.5Gbps, 5Gbps, or 10Gbps on existing cables. The NBASE-T Alliance (created in 2014) initially led the standards development of MultiGigabit over Ethernet, but it was eventually merged with the Ethernet Alliance in April 2019 and is now marketed as mGig by Cisco. In addition to traditional Ethernet speeds over Category 5e cable, Cisco mGig supports speeds of 2.5Gbps, 5GBps, and 10Gbps. The technology also supports PoE, PoE+, and Cisco UPOE.

The main characteristics mGig are as follows:

- **Variable speeds:** Cisco mGig technology supports auto-negotiation of multiple speeds on switch ports (100Mbps, 1Gbps, 2.5Gbps, and 5bps on Cat 5e cable, and up to 10Gbps over Cat 6a cabling).

- **Flexible cable types:** mGig supports a wide range of cable types, including Cat 5e, Cat 6, and Cat 6a or above.

- **PoE power:** The technology supports PoE, PoE+, and UPOE (up to 60W) for all the supported speeds and cable types, providing access points with additional power for advanced features, such as hyperlocation and modularity.

Figure 4-3 illustrates the use of mGig between a capable access switch and an access point.

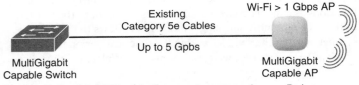

Figure 4-3 *MultiGigabit Connection to an Access Point*

Cisco 3800 and 4800 series access points (802.11ac Wave 2) and Cisco Catalyst 9100 series APs (Wi-Fi 6 / 802.11ax) support Cisco mGig technology at speeds of 2.5Gbps and 5Gbps. This technology protects the investment in the cabling infrastructure, allowing for newer and faster wireless technologies to be transported over the same physical Ethernet infrastructure without becoming a chokepoint.

To summarize, Table 4-3 illustrates the different mGig speeds and supported cable categories.

Table 4-3 Supported mGig Speeds with Associated Cable Categories

	1G	2.5G	5G	10G
Cat5e	Yes	Yes	Yes	N/A
Cat6	Yes	Yes	Yes	Yes (up to 55m)
Cat6a	Yes	Yes	Yes	Yes

Mounting Access Points

Wireless deployments often require a variety of different AP mounting options depending on the physical attributes and accessibility of each location. To address this, Cisco offers several different mounting bracket options. In addition, several third-party vendors provide mounting brackets and enclosures for less common scenarios.

This section discusses the three most common options for mounting Cisco APs:

- Ceiling and wall mounting

- Mounting below ceiling tiles

- Mounting above ceiling tiles

Ceiling and Wall Mounting Access Points

When mounting on a horizontal or vertical surface, you can use one of the two standard mounting brackets:

- **AIR-AP-BRACKET-1**: This mounting option features a low profile, making it a popular choice for ceilings.

- **AIR-AP-BRACKET-2**: This is a universal mounting bracket that is often used if the AP will be mounted on the wall or placed in a NEMA (National Electrical Manufacturers Association) enclosure.

Figure 4-4 illustrates the two mounting bracket options.

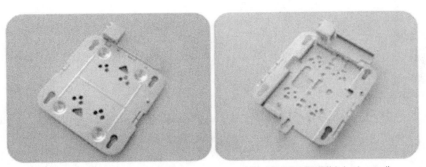

AIR-AP-BRACKET-1 (low profile)   AIR-AP-BRACKET-2 (universal)

Figure 4-4   *Cisco Access Point Mounting Bracket Options*

When wall mounting is desired, the installer should understand that walls can be a physical obstacle to the RF signal; therefore, maintaining 360-degree coverage can be compromised by the wall if the AP is not placed correctly. If the wall is an outside wall and/or if the goal is to transmit the signal in a narrower beam (such as down a food aisle in a grocery store), a directional antenna may be a better choice, assuming the external antenna model of an AP is used.

In most cases, it is recommended to avoid wall-mounting APs with internal antennas, as the antenna orientation of these APs is optimally designed for ceiling mount, providing RF coverage in a 360-degree pattern to the space below the floor. If the AP is wall mounted, it is recommended to use either a right-angle mount (where the AP is still oriented downward) or external antennas that project the RF energy into the space as expected. For this reason, it is generally recommended to mount indoor APs on the ceiling rather than on a wall.

Mounting Access Points Below a Suspended Ceiling

To facilitate mounting APs below a suspended ceiling, specialized mounting brackets are available that clip onto the rail of a T-bar ceiling. Figures 4-5 and 4-6 illustrate the mounting bracket for these types of ceilings.

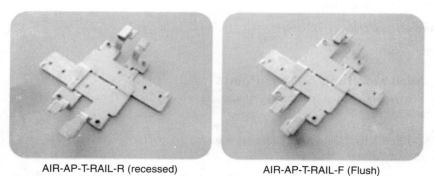

AIR-AP-T-RAIL-R (recessed)   AIR-AP-T-RAIL-F (Flush)

Figure 4-5   *T-Bar Ceiling Mounting Bracket Options*

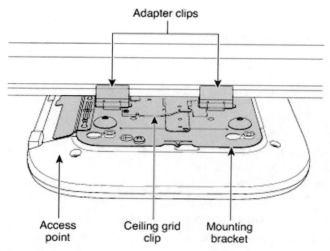

Adapter clips

Access
point

Ceiling grid
clip

Mounting
bracket

Figure 4-6   *Mounting an AP on a T-Bar Ceiling*

Mounting Access Points Above the Ceiling Tiles

Mounting access points below the ceiling tiles is the preferred option; however, in some cases, wireless engineers may prefer to position the access points so that nothing is visible from the ground, or there may be a building facilities policy that prohibits any device from attaching to the suspended ceiling. Mounting above the ceiling tiles may also be preferred for aesthetic reasons, or it may be done as a way to reduce theft in vulnerable areas (such as public hotspots where theft or damage may be a problem). In such circumstances, Cisco indoor access points (such as the Catalyst 9120i and 9120e) are rated for installation in the plenum area above the suspended ceiling (UL-2043), allowing them to be attached to the T-bar mesh but suspended above the tile.

Figure 4-7 illustrates a mounting schematic for an AP above the ceiling tiles.

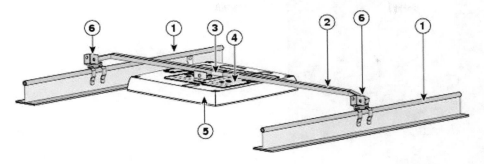

1	Suspended ceiling T-rail	4	Mounting bracket
2	Box hanger	5	Access point
3	Box hanger clip	6	T-rail clip

Figure 4-7   *Mounting the Access Point Above the Ceiling Tiles*

When mounting the AP above the ceiling tiles, it is important to remember that the tiles must not be conductive, as this would have a degrading effect on the RF performance of the AP and may interfere with wireless LAN features that depend on uniform coverage, such as voice and location services. Additionally, the AP should be mounted as close to the center of the ceiling tile as possible and away from any possible obstructions that could interfere with RF performance.

Grounding and Securing Access Points

Grounding is not always required for indoor installations because access points are classified as low-voltage devices and do not contain internal power supplies. However, electrical grounding is always recommended for outdoor access points. It is always best to check with local electrical standards to determine if grounding is necessary.

Although grounding is not mandatory for most indoor access points, it is required in certain scenarios. For example, in unground scenarios such as mining operations, indoor access points that are mounted too close to an electromagnetic source of interference may reboot suddenly or suffer hardware damage (such as APs deployed near a fluorescent light). This may occur even if the AP is not physically touching the electrical source but is just in close proximity to the electromagnetic source of interference. Grounding this access point or the mounting bracket helps prevent this issue from occurring. It is recommended that a certified electrical technician verify whether the installation requires grounding.

Figure 4-8 shows an outdoor access point with the grounding connector.

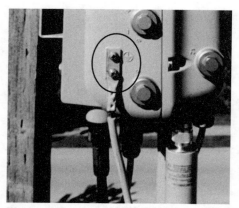

Figure 4-8   *An Outdoor Access Point with Electrical Grounding (Photo Credit: Ian Procyk)*

Logical Infrastructure Requirements

The path in which traffic flows through a network appears differently depending on your point of view. For example, from a network technician's point of view, a packet travels through the network in a hop-by-hop path across each physically connected device. However, from a wireless end user's perspective, if traffic is tunneled in an overlay, the user may only see one hop between an access point and the controller, when in reality numerous physical hops were encountered along the path of the underlying network. This is the difference between the physical and logical network.

Traffic also flows differently depending on the deployment model chosen: autonomous access points act as direct links between the wireless and the wired sides of the network, whereas centrally controlled access points in Local mode must forward all wireless client traffic to the controller over an encapsulated CAPWAP tunnel. In FlexConnect mode, some WLANs may be locally switched at the AP, while others may be centrally switched on the controller.

The following section will explore some of the logical infrastructure characteristics of a wireless network, including flow of the CAPWAP channels, logical connections to services supporting the wireless infrastructure such as AAA and DHCP servers, and finally the licensing options that are available to support the wireless deployment.

CAPWAP Flow

CAPWAP is a logical network connection between access points and a wireless LAN controller. CAPWAP is used to manage the behavior of the APs as well as tunnel encapsulated 802.11 traffic back to the controller.

CAPWAP sessions are established between the AP's logical IP address (gained through DHCP) and the controller's **management interface**. (In older versions of AireOS, the CAPWAP session terminated on the **ap-manager** interface; however, this has been changed to the management interface in more recent versions of AireOS.)

Whether in Local or FlexConnect mode, CAPWAP sessions between the controller and AP are used to manage the behavior of the AP. When in Local mode, CAPWAP is additionally used to encapsulate and tunnel all wireless client traffic so that it can be centrally processed by the controller. CAPWAP sessions use UDP for both the control and data channels, as follows:

- **CAPWAP Control Channel:** Uses UDP port 5246

- **CAPWAP Data Channel:** Uses UDP port 5247 and encapsulates (tunnels) the client's 802.11 frames

- Figure 4-9 illustrates the different CAPWAP channels between an AP and a controller.

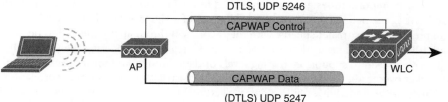

Figure 4-9   *CAPWAP Control and Data Plane Channels*

If there is a firewall or router with access control lists (ACLs) along the logical path between the AP and the controller, it is important to ensure that rules are in place to allow both the CAPWAP control and data channel ports through the firewall so that the AP and controller are able to communicate correctly. A complete list of recommended firewall rules can be found here:

https://www.cisco.com/c/en/us/support/docs/wireless/5500-series-wireless-controllers/113344-cuwn-ppm.html

As the number of APs grows, so does the number of CAPWAP tunnels terminating on the controller. Figure 4-10 illustrates the logical connection of multiple CAPWAP sessions over the physical infrastructure.

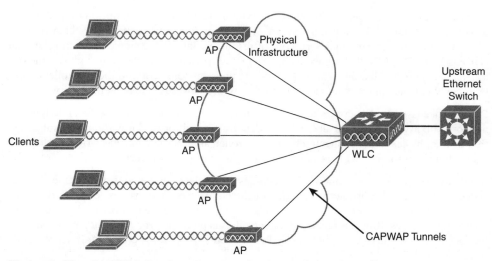

Figure 4-10   *CAPWAP Sessions Between the APs and the Controller*

NOTE   In Autonomous mode, the AP switches all traffic locally and CAPWAP is not used. In FlexConnect mode, wireless client traffic is switched locally while control of the AP is managed over the CAPWAP control channel. Only centrally controlled APs in Local mode use both the CAPWAP control and data channels. FlexConnect mode may use a hybrid— some WLANs may be locally switched while others are centrally switched, where the data traffic comes back to the controller over the CAPWAP data channel. In either case, FlexConnect APs are still managed by the CAPWAP control channel.

Considering that all APs in Local mode use CAPWAP to tunnel 802.11 client traffic back to the controller, an important design criterion related to traffic load must be considered. With 802.11ac Wave 2, the maximum theoretical throughput of a single AP is ~1.3Gbps. 802.11ax (Wi-Fi 6) promises even greater speeds, with the theoretical throughput expected to be in excess of 10Gbps from a single AP (based on multiple streams). Considering the CAPWAP data channel will need to support increasing levels of data throughput (not to mention framing and packet overhead), the demands of the logical infrastructure have a direct correlation to capabilities of the underlying physical infrastructure. In this vein, careful analysis must be taken at various places in the network to determine if the performance demands of the wireless network can be met. This includes the following design aspects:

- The physical connection between the AP and the access switch (evaluate if mGig is required)

- An estimation of oversubscription of the uplink of the access switch to the network

- Backbone capacity of the core network

- WAN connection speeds if the controllers are centralized and APs are in Local mode

- Network access speeds to the controller

- Performance capabilities of the controller

From a design perspective, the theoretical maximum bandwidth consumption of an AP is usually never attained. However, if enough APs are simultaneously generating a high volume of traffic, a controller can quickly run out of resources. Take the example of a controller that is licensed for 500 APs. If these were all Wi-Fi 6 APs passing an excessively high volume of traffic, the aggregate bandwidth capacity of the physical connection to the controller could be quickly exhausted, meaning more controllers wither fewer APs may be necessary.

Performance issues at the controller may manifest in two possible ways: (1) the underlying network's ability to aggregate all CAPWAP data traffic and forward it without oversubscription of the physical links connected to the controller, and (2) the controller's own performance limitations in being able to process the volume of data it is receiving.

If either of these two cases emerges, certain design changes can be considered. One change is decentralizing and splitting the function of the controllers such that less data is being managed by a single controller. Another option is to simply reduce the number of APs that each controller manages. If decentralizing the controllers is preferred, the roaming path must also be considered. While roaming between APs connected to the same controller is simple and should be seamless, if clients roam to an AP connected to a different controller, the roaming path will involve intercontroller communication and greater network complexity.

Another area where oversubscription may be an issue is on the access switch where the APs are physically connected. Take the example of an access switch with several dozen APs connected with mGig, all running Wi-Fi 6. If the clients associated to these APs are generating large amounts of aggregate data, the throughput demands could quickly exhaust even a 10Gbps uplink from the access switch. Thus, it is imperative to assess not only how many APs are being deployed (and how many of each type), but also careful calculation must be made to determine if the uplink capacity of the access switches can accommodate expected traffic demands, including how much oversubscription is acceptable. If it is found that the oversubscription rate is excessive, then either multiple uplinks will be needed (which requires port channeling) or a fewer number of APs should be deployed on each access switch.

> **NOTE** Oversubscription of centrally controlled APs over the WAN can be addressed using FlexConnect mode, which is discussed in detail in Chapter 10, "Implementing FlexConnect."

AAA and DHCP Services Logical Path

Another area where the logical path requires careful consideration is the path between the controller and the key services, such as the AAA and DHCP servers. Services such as AAA (ISE), DHCP, DNS, MSE/CMX, DNA Spaces, and many more may be placed at locations throughout the network that have firewalls protecting them. Understanding the logical path between these services will often require opening of firewall rules for the service to interface with the controller.

As with CAPWAP, the controller's **management interface** is used to communicate with AAA servers, as well as a host of other services, including MSE/CMX, directory servers, other controllers, and more.

For DHCP, controllers proxy communication to the DHCP sever on behalf of clients using the controller's IP address in the VLAN associated to the WLAN of those clients.

Table 4-4 summarize the ports that must be open to allow the controller to communicate with key services.

Table 4-4 Summary of AAA and DHCP Services and Ports Used for the Wireless Infrastructure

Service	Port
RADIUS Authentication	UDP port 1812 (some older versions use UDP port 1645)
RADIUS Authorization	UDP port 1813 (some older versions use UDP port 1646)
DHCP Server	UDP port 67
DHCP Client	UDP port 68

Licensing Overview

In addition to purchasing the controller itself, Cisco wireless deployments require licenses to activate the use of the access points. The following section provides a summary of how Cisco wireless controllers and APs are licensed.

Cisco AireOS wireless controllers support two types of licensing models: Right to Use (RTU) licensing and Smart Licensing.

Right to Use Licensing

Right to Use (RTU) licensing is an honor-based licensing mechanism that allows AP licenses to be enabled on AireOS controllers (such as the 5520 and 8500 series controllers) with end user license agreement (EULA) acceptance. The RTU license scheme simplifies the addition, deletion, and transfer of AP licenses and does not require specialized license keys or product activation key (PAK) licenses.

With RTU licensing, there are three types of licenses:

- **Permanent licenses:** The AP count is programmed into nonvolatile memory at the time of manufacturing. These licenses are not transferable from one controller to another.

- **Adder access point count licenses:** These are additional licenses that can be activated through the acceptance of the agreement. These licenses are also transferable between controllers and types of AireOS controllers.

- **Evaluation licenses:** These are used for demo and/or trial periods and are valid for 90 days, and they default to the full capacity of the controller. The evaluation license activation is performed through the AireOS command-line interface (CLI).

Smart Licensing

In addition to the RTU licensing model, AireOS controllers support Smart Licensing. Smart Licensing is a cloud-based flexible licensing model that simplifies the way licenses are managed across an organization rather than on a per-controller basis. The intent of Smart Licensing is to make it easier to manage and deploy Cisco software licenses from a central repository without having to track how licenses are used on individual products.

Instead of using product activation keys (PAKs) or RTU licensing, Smart Licenses establish a central pool of AP software licenses in a customer-defined Smart Account that can be used across the enterprise and across all controllers or APs. Smart Licensed products self-register upon configuration and activation with a single token, removing the need to register products individually with separate PAKs or to accept a license agreement. Thus, instead of licensing each individual controller for the number of APs that the administrator anticipates it to manage, the pool of licenses can be shared across all controllers in the enterprise and be used as needed. This approach has a distinct advantage over legacy licensing models by greatly simplifying and optimizing the use of licenses.

In the RTU model, one controller may be licensed for far more APs than it is currently managing, whereas another controller may not have enough licenses for what it needs. Smart Licensing eliminates the overhead and waste by simply putting all AP licenses in a central pool that can be managed and budgeted for as the need arises. As new APs are added or moved across the organization, the administrator no longer needs to determine the current license count on a per-controller basis—only the Smart Licensing pool of AP licenses needs to be monitored and maintained. This not only provides better utilization of licenses but also it makes it easier to procure and deploy licenses as the organization grows.

To use Smart Licensing, the following steps must be followed:

Step 1. Create a Smart Account:

    a. Create a Smart Account at the following link: https://software.cisco.com/software/company/smartaccounts/home#accountcreation-account.

    b. Go to Cisco Software Central at software.cisco.com.

    c. An editable profile appears.

    d. An email is automatically sent to the customer Smart Account administrator.

Step 2. Register the Cisco controller using the Smart Account.

    a. For existing customers, deposit existing licenses, if any, into the Smart Account.

    b. For a new purchase, purchase a Cisco DNA license for access points connecting to the Cisco Catalyst controller.

Step 3. Configure the license level on the controller, as desired.

> **NOTE** Unlike AireOS controllers, Catalyst 9800 controllers require mandatory Smart Licensing. While no licenses are required to boot up the controller, in order to connect any access points, Cisco DNA licenses managed through Smart Licensing are required for each access point that connects to the controller.

Summary

This chapter focused on both the physical and logical infrastructure requirements of wireless LAN deployments. In this chapter you have learned the following:

- The various PoE options available for different APs as well as the capabilities and function of each PoE mechanism.

- How higher-performance wireless standards, such as 802.11ac Wave 2 (Wi-Fi 5) and 802.11ax (Wi-Fi 6), can be supported through mGig

- AP mounting options, including above and below a tile ceiling mount and wall mount options

- The importance of grounding APs in certain situations

- The need to consider the logical path and its impact on the underlying physical infrastructure, including the CAPWAP control and data channels as well as AAA and DHCP services

- Different types of licensing models available for different Cisco Wireless LAN controllers, including RTU licensing and Smart Licensing, which is as a method of pooling licenses across the enterprise

References

For additional information, refer to these resources:

Cisco Enterprise Wireless—Intuitive Wi-Fi Starts Here: https://www.cisco.com/c/dam/en/us/products/collateral/wireless/nb-06-wireless-wifi-starts-here-ebook-cte-en.pdf

Catalyst 9120 Access Point Deployment Guide: https://www.cisco.com/c/en/us/products/collateral/wireless/catalyst-9100ax-access-points/guide-c07-742311.html

Network World—Best Practices When Cabling an Access Point: https://www.networkworld.com/article/3290459/what-are-the-best-practices-when-cabling-for-wi-fi.html

Power over Ethernet: Empowering Digital Transformation: https://www.cisco.com/c/dam/en/us/products/collateral/switches/catalyst-9000/nb-06-upoe-plus-wp-cte-en.pdf

Transform the Workspace with Cisco MultiGigabit Ethernet White Paper: https://www.cisco.com/c/en/us/solutions/collateral/enterprise-networks/catalyst-multigigabit-switching/white-paper-c11-733705.html

Cisco Smart Licensing Overview: https://www.cisco.com/c/dam/en/us/products/collateral/software/smart-accounts/q-and-a-c67-741561.pdf

Exam Preparation Tasks

As mentioned in the section "How to Use This Book" in the Introduction, you have a few choices for exam preparation: the exercises here, Chapter 18, "Final Preparation," and the exam simulation questions in the Pearson Test Prep Software Online.

Review All Key Topics

Review the most important topics in this chapter, noted with the Key Topic icon in the outer margin of the page. Table 4-5 lists these key topics and the page numbers on which each is found.

Table 4-5   Key Topics for Chapter 4

Key Topic Element	Description	Page Number
Table 4-2	Summary of Power over Ethernet Standards and Capabilities	70
Table 4-3	Supported mGig Speeds with Associated Cable Categories	72
Figure 4-9	CAPWAP Control and Data Plane Channels	77
Table 4-4	Summary of AAA and DHCP Services and Ports Used for the Wireless Infrastructure	79

Define Key Terms

Define the following key terms from this chapter and check your answers in the glossary:

PoE, PoE+, UPOE, UPOE+, Power Sourcing Equipment (PSE), Powered Device (PD), Power Injector, Cisco MultiGigabit, Right to Use (RTU), End User License Agreement (EULA), Smart Licensing

CHAPTER 5

Applying Wireless Design Requirements

This chapter covers the following topics:

Defining AP Coverage: This section explains an AP cell and the parameters that define usable wireless coverage inside the cell.

Expanding Coverage with Additional APs: This section explains the design process of using multiple AP cells to provide wireless coverage and service over a larger area.

Designing a Wireless Network for Data: This section explains the strategy behind developing an AP deployment to support generic data applications.

Designing a Wireless Network for High Density: This section covers design strategies to provide effective wireless coverage in areas with a high density of users.

Designing a Wireless Network for Voice and Video: This section explains design guidelines and special considerations for AP deployments that must support real-time applications.

Designing a Wireless Network for Location: This section covers design goals for AP deployments that support wireless device location in near real time.

This chapter covers the following ENWLSD exam topics:

- 2.4 Apply design requirements for these types of wireless networks

- 2.4.a Data

- 2.4.b Voice and video

- 2.4.c Location

- 2.4.d Hyperlocation

- 2.5 Design high-density wireless networks and their associated components (campus, lecture halls, conference rooms)

Wireless networks in the enterprise should be carefully designed so that they effectively support their target user communities. To build such a network, you must first understand how to control and tune a single AP's coverage cell. You can then apply the same principles to more APs to expand the wireless coverage over a greater area. The APs must operate their cells independently yet coexist and not interfere with each other. In this chapter, you will learn more about these design concepts as well as tailoring designs to support high client density and the unique characteristics of wireless applications.

"Do I Know This Already?" Quiz

The "Do I Know This Already?" quiz allows you to assess whether you should read this entire chapter thoroughly or jump to the "Exam Preparation Tasks" section. If you are in doubt about your answers to these questions or your own assessment of your knowledge of the topics, read the entire chapter. Table 5-1 lists the major headings in this chapter and their corresponding "Do I Know This Already?" quiz questions. You can find the answers in Appendix D, "Answers to the 'Do I Know This Already?' Quizzes and Review Questions."

Table 5-1 "Do I Know This Already?" Section-to-Question Mapping

Foundation Topics Section	Questions
Defining AP Coverage	1–5
Expanding Coverage with Additional APs	6
Designing a Wireless Network for Data	7
Designing a Wireless Network for High Density	8
Designing a Wireless Network for Voice and Video	9
Designing a Wireless Network for Location	10

1. To successfully receive a signal and interpret data from it, which of the following statements must be true about the receiver's sensitivity level?

   a. The received signal strength must be greater than the sensitivity level.

   b. The sensitivity level must be greater than the received signal strength.

   c. The sensitivity level must be less than the noise floor.

   d. The sensitivity level must be greater than the SNR.

2. Which one of the following parameters is measured as the main criteria to determine the boundary of an AP's coverage cell?

   a. Receiver sensitivity level

   b. Noise floor

   c. RSSI

   d. SNR

3. Which one of the following is a commonly used signal strength that defines the boundary of an AP cell?

   a. 20 dBm

   b. 67 dBm

   c. 0 dBm

   d. –20 dBm

   e. –67 dBm

4. The SNR is correctly measured according to which one of the following statements?

   a. The AP's transmit power level minus the noise floor

   b. The receiver's sensitivity level minus the noise floor

   c. The noise floor minus the AP's transmit power level

   d. The RSSI minus the noise floor

5. Regarding a wireless client in relation to an AP, which one of the following statements is not true?

    a. As the client moves away from the AP, the AP's signal strength decreases.

    b. As the client moves away from the AP, the usable data rate decreases.

    c. As the client moves toward the AP, the SNR increases (assuming the noise floor stays constant).

    d. As the client moves toward the AP, the usable data rate decreases.

6. When multiple APs are located with overlapping cells to cover a large area, some of them will likely be configured to use the same channel. At the cell boundary of an AP, the RSSI of that AP should be separated from the RSSI of neighboring APs using the same channel. Which one of the following identifies the correct amount?

    a. At least 19 dB higher than the neighbors.

    b. At least 19 dB lower than the neighbors.

    c. At least −82 dBm greater than the neighbors.

    d. It does not matter; neighboring APs can use the same channel without impact.

7. Suppose you want to design an AP deployment to support generic applications and their data. Which one of the following correctly describes a best practice design goal at AP cell boundaries?

    a. The RSSI of the AP should be −67 dBm at the highest mandatory or supported data rate.

    b. The RSSI of the AP should be −67 dBm at the lowest mandatory or supported data rate.

    c. The SNR of the AP should be −67 dBm at any data rate.

    d. The RSSI of the AP should equal the noise floor.

8. Suppose you are working on a wireless design that will support a high density of clients in a large classroom. You begin by adjusting an AP's transmit power level down to its lowest setting, but you find that the AP's cell is still too large for your design. What is the next logical step to take with the AP?

    a. Use an external omnidirectional antenna.

    b. Use an external patch antenna.

    c. Install a second AP next to the first one and use the same channel on each.

    d. Enable the lowest data rate to reduce the cell size.

9. Which of the following statements are valid design goals for an AP deployment that will support voice over Wi-Fi calls? (Choose all that apply.)

    a. Make 12Mbps the lowest mandatory data rate.

    b. Design for call capacity per AP.

    c. Use every possible 5GHz non-overlapping channel.

    d. Consider avoiding 5GHz DFS channels.

10. Suppose you need to design a wireless network to support location-based applications. Which one of the following is a correct strategy?

    a. Tracked devices must be associated to the APs on the same floor.

    b. Make sure at least one AP can receive a tracked device's signal at any location.

   c. Make sure the tracked device can be received at a minimum signal strength
   of –72 dBm.

   d. Make sure the tracked device can receive at least one AP's signal above –72 dBm.

Foundation Topics

Defining AP Coverage

The main goal of designing a wireless network is to bring the network to the users over the air or free space. That may sound like an easy task until you begin to think about all of the variables that might be involved. A wired network removes many variables by keeping data transmission bounded inside cables of a known construction and length. If a device connects to one end of a cable with an active network device at the other end, the connection is likely to be usable. Even the data transmission rate or bandwidth is predictable by design. In contrast, wireless data is unbounded because it is transmitted over the air using radio frequency (RF) signals, with very little to keep the signals contained or unaffected by their surroundings.

A wireless network design begins with using an access point (AP) to offer a usable signal to potential client devices. What constitutes a usable signal? The signal must be present where the clients are located so that it can be received intelligibly. Also, the clients must be able to send a usable signal back to the AP so that data can flow in both directions. There are other factors, too, that will be discussed as this section progresses.

Figure 5-1 illustrates how a single AP can be used to provide wireless service over a given area. This is usually known as the AP's *cell*. In 802.11 standard terms, an AP's wireless service is known as a basic service set (BSS) and its cell as a basic service area (BSA). If a client is located inside the cell boundary, such as at location A, the client has a usable signal from the AP. If the client is outside the boundary, the signal is probably not going to be usable and the service will not be acceptable. This concept is easy to see in a drawing, but what defines the cell boundary in the first place?

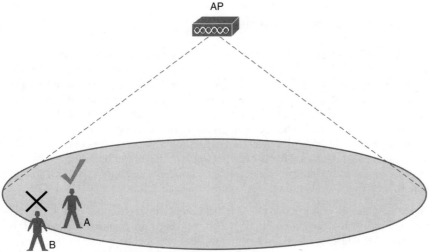

Figure 5-1   *The Effective Cell Area of a Wireless AP*

TIP The cell area shown in Figure 5-1 is based on an AP with an omnidirectional antenna, which produces a more or less circular pattern at floor level. The AP cells illustrated in this chapter are perfect circles for the sake of simplicity. Actual cell patterns in the real world are rarely that uniform and vary in shape, depending on the surrounding physical objects.

Considering Receive Sensitivity

The AP's transmit power level is a major factor in determining the usable range of its signal, defining the boundary of its cell area. Every client device has a receiver that has a *sensitivity level* or a threshold that divides intelligible, useful signals from unintelligible ones. As long as a signal is received with a power level that is greater than the sensitivity level, chances are that the data from the signal can be understood correctly. You might have experienced a similar scenario when you tried to hear a friend say something from a long distance away. As long as the friend spoke loudly enough, you were likely to understand every word the friend said. If you couldn't understand everything, you were probably too far away.

Figure 5-2 shows an example of how the signal strength at a receiver might change over time, in relation to the receiver's sensitivity level of –82 dBm. When the *received signal strength indicator* (RSSI) of the AP's signal falls below –82 dBm at the client's receiver, the AP's signal is no longer usable.

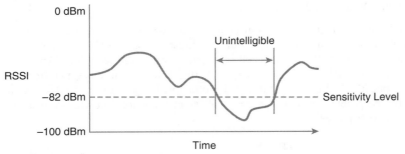

Figure 5-2 *An Example of Receiver Sensitivity Level*

Therefore, an AP's cell boundary, as shown in Figure 5-1, is actually formed by connecting all of the points around the AP where the RSSI of the AP's signal falls to some arbitrary threshold. Even though it might seem logical to use the receiver sensitivity as the threshold, that is seldom done in practice. Instead, wireless designers usually want a more graceful transition as client devices move away from an AP and approach the cell boundary. The threshold is usually chosen with some amount of cushion or margin above the receiver sensitivity level. In addition, you might have a difficult time selecting a threshold that represents one common sensitivity level of all client devices. That is because wireless clients can be produced by a variety of manufacturers with a variety of electronic components and antennas. Even among identical devices, sensitivity levels can vary. A commonly used cell boundary is –67 dBm.

Even though wireless design concepts involve AP cell boundaries, remember that RF signals do not just stop abruptly at a certain point. The RF signal keeps propagating further and further away from the AP, while its signal strength diminishes exponentially due to free space path loss. That means the cell boundary simply marks the point where the received signal strength equals an arbitrary threshold. If you measured the RSSI at a point further away from the AP, the signal would still exist but at a lower level.

This concept is shown in Figure 5-3, where concentric circles represent the RSSI of the AP's signal. As an example, the wireless user is standing near a point at which the AP's signal has fallen off to around −67 dBm. Once the signal extends further, it eventually diminishes to −90 dBm and below. At that point, the signal strength is so low that it begins to blend in with the ambient noise present in the environment on the same frequency. This is known as the *noise floor*, where Wi-Fi client receivers can no longer discriminate between legitimate signals and signals from random noise.

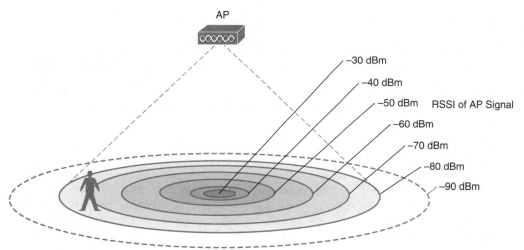

Figure 5-3 *Signal Attenuation Through Free Space*

It is easy to ignore noise as long as the noise floor is well below what you are trying to hear. For example, two people can whisper in a library effectively because there is very little competing noise. Those same two people would become very frustrated if they tried to whisper to each other in a crowded sports arena.

Considering the Signal-to-Noise Ratio

Receiving an RF signal is no different; its signal strength must be greater than the noise floor by a decent amount so that it can be received and understood correctly. The difference between the signal and the noise is called the *signal-to-noise ratio (SNR)*, measured in dB. A higher SNR value is preferred.

Figure 5-4 shows the RSSI of an example signal compared with the noise floor that is received. The RSSI averages around −54 dBm. On the left side of the graph, the noise floor is −90 dBm. The resulting SNR is the difference between −54 dBm and −90 dBm, or 36 dB. Toward the right side of the graph, the noise floor gradually increases to −65 dBm, reducing the SNR to 11 dB. The signal is so close to the noise that it might not be usable for data transmission.

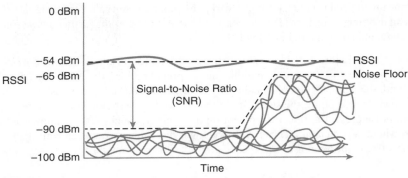

Figure 5-4 *An Example of a Changing Noise Floor and SNR*

Therefore, the SNR is also a factor that determines the usable cell boundary. Even though effective communication might be possible with a received signal that is stronger than the receiver's sensitivity threshold, the signal strength must also be stronger than the noise by some amount. Otherwise, even a strong signal could be corrupted by the noise. The acceptable SNR ultimately determines the maximum data rate that a transmitter and a receiver can successfully use.

As a general rule, low data rates require a low minimum SNR because their modulation and coding schemes (MCS) are relatively simple and are made to tolerate noisy and error-prone environments. Higher data rates are possible with more complex MCS methods, but progressively higher SNR conditions are required. More complex MCS techniques carry data more efficiently by varying the transmitted RF signal's amplitude and phase with higher granularity. The only way a receiver can successfully recognize and interpret the small signal variations is if the noise level is relatively low.

To get a feel for the relationship between minimum data rate and SNR, refer to the example wireless client specifications listed in Table 5-2. For simplicity, the table covers the nine MCS techniques that a transmitter and receiver can use with 802.11ac over a 20MHz channel. Because the receive sensitivity and minimum SNR values are measured at the client device, the values can vary depending on the specific device hardware capabilities. Notice that the lowest data rate (6.5Mbps) also has the lowest receive sensitivity and the lowest SNR requirements. That means a wireless client could maintain the lowest data rate as it travels far away from an AP. The highest data rate requires a much higher minimum signal strength and SNR, so a client would be limited to a closer range to the AP.

Table 5-2 Example Client Device Receive Sensitivity and SNR Specifications

Minimum Data Rate 802.11ac VHT 20MHz Channel	Modulation and Coding Scheme	Receive Sensitivity	Minimum SNR
6.5Mbps	MCS0	–93 dBm	7 dB
13Mbps	MCS1	–90 dBm	10 dB
19.5Mbps	MCS2	–87 dBm	13 dB
26Mbps	MCS3	–84 dBm	16 dB
39Mbps	MCS4	–81 dBm	19 dB

Minimum Data Rate 802.11ac VHT 20MHz Channel	Modulation and Coding Scheme	Receive Sensitivity	Minimum SNR
52Mbps	MCS5	–76 dBm	24 dB
58.5Mbps	MCS6	–75 dBm	25 dB
65Mbps	MCS7	–74 dBm	26 dB
78Mbps	MCS8	–70 dBm	30 dB

You might be surprised to learn that the minimum SNR also increases substantially as the channel width increases. Table 5-3 lists the receive sensitivity and minimum SNR for the same example device used in Table 5-2 by increasing channel width. Notice that when the channel width doubles from 20MHz to 40MHz, the minimum SNR increases from 7 to 10 dB. Assuming the transmit power level remains constant, the noise floor must be increasing for some reason. The increase of 3 dB means that the acceptable noise floor has doubled. The same thing happens when the channel width is doubled from 40MHz to 80MHz—the noise floor doubles again.

Table 5-3   Example Client Device Receiver Sensitivity and SNR Affected by Channel Width

Channel Width 802.11ac MCS 0	Minimum Data Rate	Receive Sensitivity	Minimum SNR
VHT 20MHz	6.5Mbps	–93 dBm	7 dB
VHT 40MHz	13Mbps	–90 dBm	10 dB
VHT 80MHz	30Mbps	–87 dBm	13 dB

Why would the noise floor raise just because the channel width increases? After all, the noise floor is generally ambient noise that should exist across all channels in a band. The main reason is something called thermal noise that is produced by the movement of electrons in the Wi-Fi receiver electronics. Thermal noise is proportional to temperature and bandwidth, and it is cumulative across all frequencies in the channel. In fact, the thermal noise energy doubles with each doubling of the channel width. The increase in thermal noise also causes an equal rise in receive sensitivity, as any received signal must overcome the noise to be intelligible.

As you design AP cells in a Wi-Fi network, you should design for a specific minimum data rate, which will then determine the minimum RSSI and SNR required. Consider channel width as part of the design, too. Wider channels may support more throughput, but remember that they also introduce RSSI and SNR adjustments that you must compensate for.

Further AP Cell Considerations

The data rate (and MCS method) used by a transmitting and a receiving device can vary over time. The goal is to always try to use the highest data rate possible, depending on the RF conditions between the devices. To complicate things, the transmitter, the receiver, or both might be mobile. As they move around, the SNR and RSSI conditions will likely change from one moment to the next. If the devices are located in a noisy environment, where a low SNR or a low RSSI might result, a lower data rate might be preferable. If not, a higher data rate is better.

Suppose a client device begins by using a very high data rate to communicate with an AP. If the client notices that the AP stops acknowledging some of the data sent, because the data was not received or was corrupted, it can then decide to try a lower data rate instead. The same is true of the AP as it transmits data to a client device. Each one can dynamically shift the rate up or down as needed—hence, the term *dynamic rate shifting (DRS)*. Because the data rate can change, you should only be concerned with designing an AP cell that can support a minimum required data rate. If the conditions allow, any higher data rate can be used as a bonus.

To properly design a wireless network, you should be concerned with determining the usable area of an access point's coverage cell. You can control the AP's transmit power level to expand or reduce the cell size, as long as the end result produces RF coverage that supports all client devices you expect to find within that area, and any data rates above a minimum. That means you must identify the potential client device types and determine their receiver sensitivity specifications, as well as their maximum transmit power levels. As an example, the specifications for a wireless phone device state the following:

To ensure acceptable voice quality, the device should always have a signal of –67 dBm or higher when using 5GHz or 2.4GHz, while the device meets the access point's receiver sensitivity required signal level for the transmitted data rate. A minimum SNR of 25 dB (–92 dBm noise level with –67 dBm signal level) should be maintained.

Notice that the requirements also included a statement about the client device's signal being sufficiently strong to meet the AP's receiver sensitivity at the desired data rate. Wireless communication is always two-way, so you must consider the AP's signal at the client device location, as well as the client's signal at the AP's location. As long as both are satisfied, the two can communicate effectively.

APs and clients often have very different transmit power level capabilities, simply because APs are designed to have more powerful transmitters, better antennas, and better receivers than typical client devices. As a result, the two can end up using transmit power levels that are not identical or symmetrical in each direction. The most noticeable result is an asymmetry in the data rates used, as shown in Figure 5-5. For example, if the AP can reach a client with a strong signal and a high SNR, then the AP can use a high data rate successfully toward the client. The client, on the other hand, might reach the AP with a weaker signal and a lower SNR, resulting in a lower successful data rate.

Sometimes a client might use a transmit power level that is higher than that of the AP. This can cause the client's signal to extend into neighboring cells on the same channel and contribute to co-channel interference. It can also be inefficient because the client will use more of its battery power than is necessary.

Figure 5-6 illustrates an extreme and disruptive case of asymmetric transmit power levels. The transmit power level of the AP is much greater than that of the client; the client can receive and interpret the AP's signal, but the AP cannot receive and interpret the client's much weaker signal above the required receive sensitivity and SNR. Because the client's transmit power level is too low, it becomes isolated from the AP.

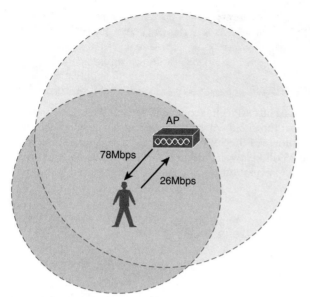

Figure 5-5 *Asymmetric Transmit Power Levels and Data Rates*

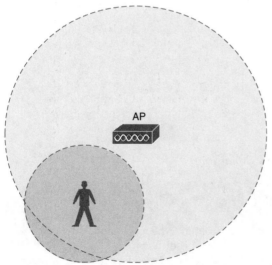

Figure 5-6 *Asymmetric Transmit Power Levels Isolating a Client*

Dynamic Transmit Power Control (DTPC) is a Cisco proprietary method that APs can use to advertise their own transmit power levels so that compatible clients can adjust their transmit power levels accordingly, up to the maximum available. AP advertisements are sent in beacon and probe response frames, inside a Cisco vendor-specific information element. Clients must support Cisco Compatible Extensions (CCX) to participate in the dynamic power adjustments. DTPC is enabled by default on Cisco wireless LAN controllers (WLCs), and Cisco recommends that it always be enabled.

TIP   Be aware that DTPC is different from Transmit Power Control (TPC). DPTC is used to adjust client transmit power levels to match that of an AP. TPC is part of the 802.11h standard and is used by APs to instruct clients to lower their power levels if a radar signal is detected on a DFS channel.

The best-practice guidelines for designing any AP cell recommend setting the cell boundary at –67 dBm, as shown in Figure 5-7. That threshold will suit most client devices and will support most reasonably high data rates, provided the SNR is 25 dB or above. That also means that the noise floor is expected to be 25 dB below –67 dBm, or –92 dBm. The noise floor in most common environments meets that expectation.

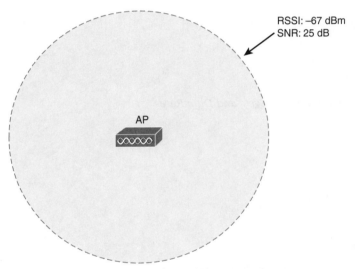

Figure 5-7   *Best-Practice AP Cell Boundary Conditions*

NOTE   You should be aware that RF signals propagate differently based on their frequency. As a signal travels through free space, its signal strength will be attenuated exponentially over the distance traveled. In addition, higher frequencies are attenuated more than lower ones, through free space and through walls and objects. This difference ultimately affects AP cell sizes. Most APs have dual radios that will create two independent RF cells—one on a channel in the 2.4GHz band and another on a channel in the 5GHz band. If both radios are configured to transmit at the same power level, the effective or usable 2.4GHz cell area will be somewhat larger than the 5GHz cell.

Expanding Coverage with Additional APs

Traditionally, wireless designers have focused on simply providing RF coverage to a given area so that data can be communicated. This goal usually results in a design that has a

minimal number of APs covering a maximum amount of area. It is also a goal that empha-
sizes connectivity to clients in all locations, rather than acceptable performance to each
client.

Coverage-based designs begin by placing an AP in a location where it can cover the most
area, as shown in Figure 5-8. Ideally, the AP's transmit power level should be set to provide
an appropriate coverage cell based on the guidelines presented in the previous sections. The
AP must also be assigned a channel to use. It might be tempting to configure the AP to
run at the highest possible transmit power level to maximize the RF cell area, but first consider the results of such a decision. Your goal should be to design the cell size based on the
receive sensitivity and SNR for a desired minimum data rate, as well as the number of wireless clients to be served by the AP. If the transmit power level is set at the maximum, the
−67 dBm cell boundary will likely be pushed out far away from the AP. That will maximize
the area covered, which might also maximize the number of clients, if many are present
within the cell area. That, in turn, may act to minimize performance for the users who are
contending for airtime on the AP's channel.

Running at maximum transmit power also constrains the design itself. Sometimes you may
need some flexibility to raise or lower the transmit power to tune the cell size. You will not
be able to raise the power level further because it is already at the maximum. Clients using
DTPC to adjust their own transmit power levels may always use a high level to try and match
that of the AP. That may unnecessarily lower the client runtimes on their batteries.

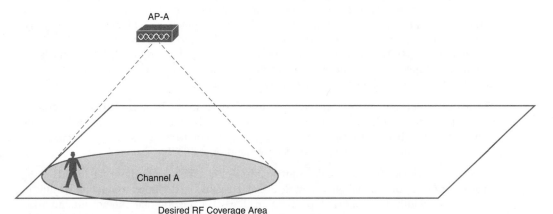

Figure 5-8 *RF Coverage Design Begins with a Single AP*

If one AP at the desired transmit power level does not cover the entire desired area, more
APs can be added to the design as needed until the area is sufficiently covered. In Figure 5-9,
a total of four APs has been used to cover the rectangular area. Notice how the AP coverage
cells are slightly overlapped. As a best practice, you should always position each AP such
that its cell overlaps the cells of the nearest neighboring APs by about 10 to 20 percent. The
overlap is necessary to provide continuous RF coverage for wireless client devices as they
roam from one AP's cell into another, without experiencing a loss of an acceptable signal.

Should you worry about the cell overlap causing interference between adjacent APs? Absolutely! In a best-practice design, adjacent APs should not be configured to use the same
channel. Instead, as client devices move, they should roam from one AP to another and from

one channel to another. As long as you carefully select the channel numbers for each AP and try to keep identical channel numbers from touching or overlapping, you will minimize the chance for co-channel interference.

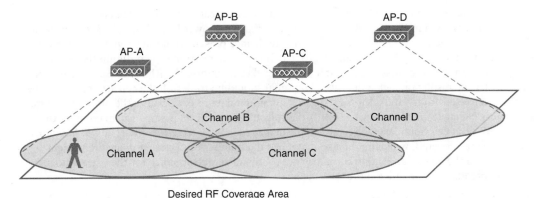

Desired RF Coverage Area

Figure 5-9   *Additional APs Complete the RF Coverage Design*

The channel layout process can become quite a difficult puzzle if your design includes many APs. The puzzle is most difficult in the 2.4GHz band because there are not many non-overlapping channels available for use. The general guideline is to stick with only channels 1, 6, and 11 and to stagger them in more or less a diamond-shaped pattern. For example, APs A through D in Figure 5-9 could be configured to use channels 1, 6, 11, and 1, respectively. Although 802.11n introduced 40MHz channel aggregation to bond two 20MHz channels together in the 2.4GHz band, it simply is not possible to have multiple 40MHz channels to assign to multiple APs without overlap. For that reason, you should always stick with the default 20MHz channel width for all 2.4GHz AP radios.

The 5GHz band is much less restrictive because all of its many 20MHz channels are considered to be non-overlapping. After all, each channel is 20MHz wide, and channels that are four channel numbers apart (the common case in most countries) are spaced 20MHz apart. For example, channels 36, 40, 44, and 48 have the proper 20MHz spacing.

Even so, a best practice is to avoid assigning adjacent channels to neighboring APs. The strongest portion of a signal on a specific 20MHz channel is designed to operate within the 20MHz bandwidth but is allowed to have a much weaker portion that extends into additional bandwidth on each side. The 802.11 standard defines a spectral mask that constrains every Wi-Fi signal, as shown in Figure 5-10. Notice how the sideband portions of signals on adjacent 20MHz channels actually do overlap each other, although at a very low signal strength. For this reason, it is best to keep neighboring APs on nonadjacent channels, where the channel numbers are at least eight apart.

You can also aggregate 5GHz channels together to form channels that are 40, 80, and even 160MHz wide. Be aware that your choice of channel width does affect the overall number of channels that will be available for use. For example, there are up to 24 available 20MHz channels in the United States. Aggregating those into 40MHz channels leaves you with only 11 channels to assign to APs in an area. Aggregating further into 80MHz leaves only five; aggregating into 160MHz leaves only two channels in the whole band.

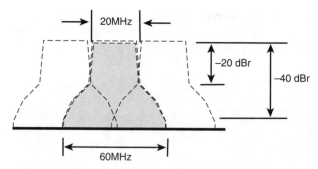

dBr: Signal strength relative to the maximum value

Figure 5-10   *802.11 Spectral Mask and Adjacent Channel Overlap*

Of the many 20MHz channels available, do not forget that many of them are located in the U-NII-2 and U-NII-2 Extended bands, which are subject to DFS constraints. If a radar signal is detected on a DFS channel, the AP and its clients must stop using it and move to a different channel. Abandoning a channel like that can be very disruptive to wireless applications, so you should verify that no radar signals are present on any DFS channels you plan to use.

As you assign channel numbers to each AP in a design, you should also pay attention to the way channel numbers repeat or are reused throughout an area. APs using the same channel not only can interfere with each other if their cells are adjacent and touch, but they can still interfere if they are not spaced far enough apart from each other. Consider the simple example shown in Figure 5-11, where channel 40 (20MHz wide) has been assigned to AP-A and reused some distance away by AP-C. The –67 dBm cell boundaries of each are shown by dashed outlines. At their boundaries, the cells of AP-A and AP-C do not touch or overlap.

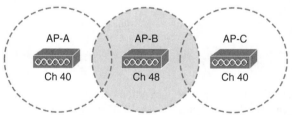

Figure 5-11   *An Example of Repeating Channel Layout*

It is entirely possible for AP-C's signal to extend into the cell of AP-A, simply because the signal continues to propagate past the –67 dBm boundary, losing signal strength along the way. If the signal is still above some level inside AP-A's cell, it could interfere with AP-A and its clients being able to use the channel. To prevent that from happening, you should follow the best-practice guideline to maintain a level of channel separation between APs sharing the same channel.

Figure 5-12 shows the scenario from Figure 5-11 with AP-B and its cell removed for clarity, as it does not impact either AP-A or AP-C on channel 40. At the –67 dBm boundary of AP-A, the signal strength from AP-C should be at least 19 dB below that of AP-A. By keeping a 19 dB level of separation, the neighboring AP's signal strength is pushed below –67 dBm minus 19 dB, or –86 dBm. The 802.11 standard requires every device to test its channel with the clear channel assessment (CCA) mechanism to make sure the channel is clear before transmitting. CCA uses a threshold of –82 dBm; as long as signals from neighboring APs are below it, those APs will not interfere with or contend for airtime on the channel inside the –67 dBm cell boundary.

> **TIP**   It is often difficult to maintain the 19 dB channel separation between APs in the 2.4GHz band, simply because there are too few channels to distribute across APs. No matter how you assign channels 1, 6, and 11 to APs, you will have to reuse a channel closer to itself than desired. The 5GHz band is much less restrictive due to the large number of channels that are available.

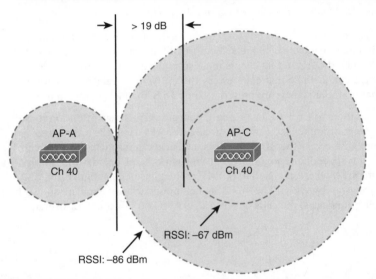

Figure 5-12   *Best Practice for Channel Separation*

With 23 available channels, the number of non-overlapping aggregated channels gets smaller as the channel width gets larger. For example, there are only eleven 40MHz channels, five 80MHz channels, and two 160MHz channels available.

Designing a Wireless Network for Data

In Chapter 1, "Wireless Design Requirements," you learned about a few different AP deployment models and how to determine when to apply each model to a network design. Beginning with this section, you will learn how to apply the deployment model and specific design criteria to ensure that your wireless design meets best-practice guidelines.

Suppose you need to work up a design in an area where there are only ordinary data applications in use. In other words, there are no voice, video, or location-based applications. Also, there is no pressing need to support large user populations in the coverage areas. Your goal should be to design for wireless coverage and acceptable performance.

First, consider the data rates that the APs will offer, with an eye toward disabling lower, less efficient data rates that can starve the available airtime on a channel. Determine if the network will need to support any legacy 802.11b-only client devices. If so, disable the lowest rates of 1, 2, 5, 6, and 9Mbps, while enabling 11Mbps and all rates above it. If no legacy devices are required, a common practice is to keep 12Mbps as the minimum (and only) basic data rate, with all higher rates supported. Clients and APs will try to use higher rates if the RF conditions support it.

NOTE   Does disabling low data rates change an AP's cell size? After all, lower data rates tend to be intelligible farther away from an AP than higher data rates. An AP's signal strength stays constant, regardless of the data rates offered. A proper design should tune data rates first, and then the survey is based on the minimum required data rate. Fortunately, a threshold of −67 dBm is high enough to support most any data rate. Even though disabling lower data rates does reduce the effective or usable cell size of an AP, the cell boundary will not move enough to interfere with the design constraints.

5

As you perform a survey, try to keep the AP power reduced to half that of the maximum transmit power you expect to find in any client. This will provide a margin or buffer that you can leverage if you need to adjust any AP transmit power levels, while staying within the capabilities of most client devices. This is also helpful if you plan to use Cisco Radio Resource Manager (RRM) to automatically and dynamically make AP power level adjustments.

Make sure your survey considers both signal strength and SNR throughout the coverage area. Be aware that RSSI is a relative measurement that can vary from one device to another. This is especially important if your survey device is not identical to any of the expected client devices. You should compare the RSSI reported by the survey device with values reported by actual client devices at the same location. Then you can adjust your survey measurements to reflect client devices accordingly.

Strive to have AP cell coverage extend to −67 dBm at the lowest data rate enabled. As a frame of reference, a signal strength of −85 dBm or below is considered poor and unlikely to sustain a client association; anything −55 dBm or greater is exceptional. The usable data rate is always determined by the device's receiver sensitivity, which is a function of RSSI and SNR.

You should also consider padding the minimum receive sensitivity threshold by 10 dB and the SNR by 10 dB to compensate for variations between devices and normal changes in the RF environment. A 10 percent packet loss is acceptable for a data-only design.

Designing a Wireless Network for High Density

A design based on RF coverage focuses on defining and maximizing the effective AP cell size for an area, based on any one client device. In other words, the main criteria is if a wireless client can see coverage and join the wireless network wherever it might be located within the coverage area, as shown in the left portion of Figure 5-13. What might happen if more and more users arrive and gather in a relatively small area, perhaps within the cell area of a single AP? They will all have to compete for the available airtime because they all share the same channel that is hosted by the basic service set (BSS) of the AP. In addition, they will all have to share the available bandwidth through the AP and its wired connection to the network infrastructure, as shown in the right portion of Figure 5-13.

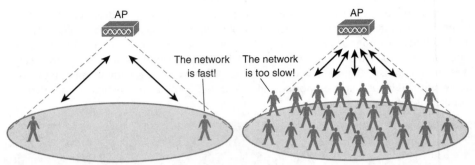

Figure 5-13 *Coverage Design as Planned (left) and with a High Density of Users (right)*

The best way to provide better wireless performance to a high density of users is to distribute those users across multiple APs and channels. That approach requires careful planning and a design that utilizes additional APs to cover the area. However, rather than adding APs that each cover a large area, each AP's cell size must be reduced to include only a desired number of users or a very small area.

This is straightforward to visualize in an area with dense, fixed seating. Figure 5-14 shows an example of a large auditorium-style classroom. A traditional RF coverage design has placed only two APs in the room, as shown. If the classroom is full, each AP might have 150 or more users associated and competing for airtime on the channel.

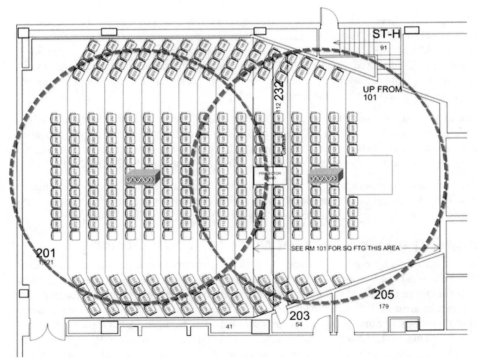

Figure 5-14 *A High Density of Users in an RF Design Based on Coverage*

Figure 5-15 illustrates a better approach that considers the high *client density* in the room. Notice how much smaller each AP cell is in comparison with the cells from Figure 5-14. This time if the room is full of people, each AP might carry around 25 associated clients. With the client load greatly reduced, each AP's channel will be much less utilized, giving users a greater chance to access the medium and have a better network experience.

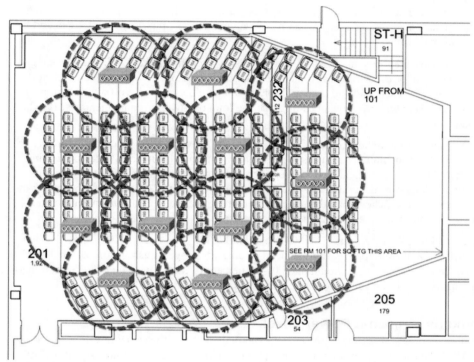

Figure 5-15 *A High Density of Users in a High-Density RF Design*

Areas with high user densities, such as theaters, auditoriums, and classrooms, are easy to predict because of their high-density seating. Buildings with fixed or modular office space usually have a lower user density because of their layout and seating arrangements. Open areas such as lobbies, retail space, and airport terminals have less obvious seating and standing arrangements, so you might have to observe them at different times to gauge the user density. Beyond user density, you should also consider that the average user carries several different wireless devices. Though users might not be actively using all of their devices at the same time, all of them may stay associated to the wireless network but have little traffic demands.

Drawing smaller circles on a floor plan is an easy task because it does not involve live APs and a real physical environment. How can you reduce the cell size of an AP that is actually mounted in one of the locations you designate? You can take the following two actions to tune the cell size appropriately:

- Limit the AP's transmit power level.

- Select an appropriate antenna for the AP.

Each of these actions is described further in the sections that follow. As you read through the remainder of the chapter, think about the overall strategy of setting and adjusting AP parameters to support a dynamic user population. These are processes you can work through manually during a wireless design, which are effective only when you use the data provided by the site surveys described in Chapter 2, "Conducting an Offsite Site Survey," and Chapter 3, "Conducting an Onsite Site Survey." Controlling transmit power and assigning channels are complex puzzles to solve during a wireless design. Chapter 6, "Designing Radio Management," goes even further by explaining how the puzzle can be refined and tuned automatically.

Once you have identified areas where a high density of clients is expected, your design goal should be to tailor the wireless coverage to support client capacity. Size up the bandwidth requirements for each user and then multiply by the number of users you want to support on each AP. That will give you an estimate of the total bandwidth requirements expected through each AP.

Locate each AP and adhere to the guidelines from the previous section to size each cell such that it will limit the number of users appropriately. You will also need to focus on making the small AP cells as efficient as possible. Keep 12Mbps as the only mandatory data rate, while disabling every data rate below it. Every data rate above 12Mbps should be configured as a supported rate. The higher data rates will improve channel contention and overall efficiency to support more clients and their applications.

You should focus on leveraging the 5GHz band in high-density areas, making sure that AP channels are non-overlapping. You will need to take advantage of using more channels within a small dense area. AP cells should have 10–15 percent overlap. Leverage DTPC to automatically influence the transmit power levels of compatible clients.

Limiting the Transmit Power Level

Recall that an AP's signal strength gets exponentially lower as the signal travels away from the AP. If the transmit power level is configured to a lower value, that lower signal strength will get even lower away from the AP. Therefore, you can control the AP's cell size to a certain extent by lowering the transmit power level. Figure 5-16 illustrates this concept by showing the relative cell size bounded by an RSSI of −67 dBm at decreasing transmit power levels of 20, 14, 8, and 2 dBm.

Cisco access points have at most eight transmit power level values, beginning with the maximum power allowed for the band in use, with each successive value decreasing the power level by about 3 dB or half. Even at the lowest power level setting, the cell size still might not be small enough to match your design goal—especially if you are using an AP model with integrated omnidirectional antennas. Recall that an omnidirectional antenna emits the RF energy more or less equally in all directions. Because the energy is not focused in any particular direction, coverage over a wide area is by design. When such an AP is mounted on the ceiling, most of the RF energy propagates out away from the AP to form a shape similar to a donut or torus.

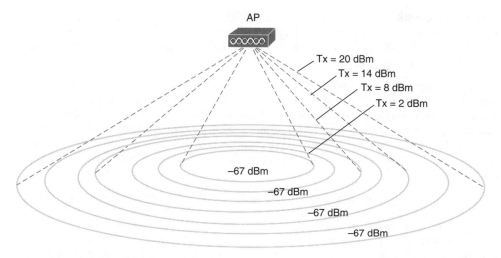

Figure 5-16 *Lowering an AP's Transmit Power Level Decreases Its Cell Size*

Leveraging APs and Antennas

You can tailor the cell size even further by using an AP model that is connected to an external antenna. *Patch antennas* are directional in nature and focus the RF energy toward a single direction. This means you can cover a small area by mounting a patch antenna on the ceiling above that area. The antenna's directional focus gives it a higher gain and the AP a smaller cell size. Patch antennas are available in various gain values and beam widths. Figure 5-17 illustrates a comparison between an AP with integrated omnidirectional antennas and 5 dBi gain, an AP connected to an external patch antenna with 7 dBi gain, and an AP with an external patch antenna with 11 dBi gain. Assume that each AP is transmitting at the same power level and then notice that as the gain increases, the angle of the antennas' beam decreases and the AP cell size also decreases.

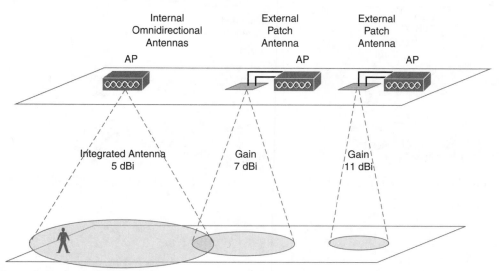

Figure 5-17 *The Effects of Antenna Gain on AP Cell Size*

Therefore, you could leverage APs with patch antennas in a crowded classroom or auditorium to produce a matrix of very small cells. This approach would reduce the number of users in each AP's cell, lower contention for opportunities to transmit over the AP's channel, and maximize the users' experience over the network.

Cisco also offers some AP models that support an extra radio that can be used to complement the RF coverage of the traditional dual-band radios. This feature is called Flexible Radio Architecture (FRA) and includes one dedicated 5GHz radio and one flexible radio that can operate on either 2.4 or 5GHz, but not both. The dedicated 5GHz radio has internal omnidirectional antennas and forms a normal "macro" cell with a broad coverage pattern. When the flexible radio is operating on the 2.4GHz band, it also produces a macro cell.

When the flexible radio is operating on 5GHz instead, its internal antennas have a narrow beam width and form a relatively smaller "micro" cell, as shown in the left portion of Figure 5-18. This is known as macro/micro mode, with the flexible radio micro cell operating at the lowest transmit power level. The end result is two 5GHz cells, in a "cell within a cell" pattern, with each radio operating on a different channel. With one access point, you can address normal RF coverage over an area and overlay a smaller cell to distribute the user load in an area that has a high density of users. Alternatively, the flexible radio can be connected to an external antenna, as in the right portion of Figure 5-18, such that both 5GHz radios provide independent macro-sized cells in roughly the same area. This is known as macro/macro mode. Again, with one AP and one external antenna, you can distribute a high density of users across two cells and two different channels.

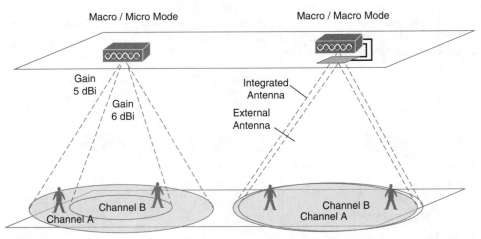

Figure 5-18 *Leveraging Flexible Radio Assignment to Offer High-Density Coverage*

> **NOTE** In the macro/micro FRA mode, both the fixed macro radio and the flexible micro radio operate on 5GHz channels. This means that the AP has no active radio operating on 2.4GHz. How then can you provide 2.4GHz coverage if you need it? Usually you do not need every AP to provide a 2.4GHz channel in a high-density capacity design, simply because the APs will be spaced closely together. You have only three non-overlapping channels to work with in the 2.4GHz band; if the APs are close together, their signals might extend far enough to overlap other APs using the same channels, causing co-channel interference. Instead, you can usually disable the 2.4GHz radios in most of the APs and get useful coverage from a few nearby APs that can offer 2.4GHz channels.

You should also be aware that the ceiling height where an AP or a patch antenna is mounted affects the resulting cell size toward the floor where users are located. Figure 5-19 shows a comparison between an antenna that is mounted 8 feet above the floor with the same antenna model that is mounted 10 feet above the floor. Assume that the antenna gain and the transmit power levels stay the same in both scenarios. The higher an antenna is mounted, the larger its footprint will be projected onto the floor. This concept becomes important in high-density areas with very high ceiling height. In those cases, you might need higher gain antennas to maintain a small AP cell area.

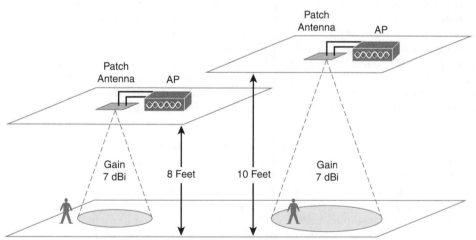

Figure 5-19   *The Effects of Antenna Mounting Height on AP Cell Size*

Designing a Wireless Network for Voice and Video

At this point in the chapter, it should be obvious that a good wireless design hinges on providing RF coverage in the locations where it is needed or expected. By clever placement and careful tuning, you can make the network even more usable for greater numbers of users. In addition to considering the physical environment, you should also look at the applications and the traffic types that will be used over the wireless network.

Most devices will make use of "normal" data that has no special requirements or expectations other than what the users consider to be decent responsive throughput. If the application must send and receive data in a timely manner, it is known as a real-time application.

Examples include voice over IP (VoIP), videoconferencing, and collaboration. You might have noticed a pattern—real-time applications involve voice and video; non-real-time applications include ordinary data. Real-time applications require special consideration as you design, configure, and operate a wireless network. The following effects need to be minimized so that voice and video sessions can be heard and seen consistently, without interruption or corruption:

- **Latency:** The amount of time required to deliver a packet or frame from a transmitter to a receiver

- **Jitter:** The variance of the end-to-end latency experienced as consecutive packets arrive at a receiver

- **Packet loss:** The percentage of packets sent that do not arrive at the receiver

To keep these factors minimized, the adverse conditions in a wireless environment must be controlled. For example, a source of interference can cause packet errors that interrupt a voice or video stream. As packets are lost, they can be retransmitted and delayed, increasing latency and jitter. Other factors like poor radio frequency (RF) coverage, high channel utilization, and excessive collisions can also impede good data throughput and integrity.

When you need an AP deployment that supports voice and video, your goal should be to design for wireless coverage and call capacity. AP cells should be overlapped by about 20 percent to streamline client roaming and handoff from one AP to another. Any delay or interruption will be very noticeable to users on an active call, so devices should be able to find candidate APs well ahead of time as the users move around. As the previous sections recommended, the RSSI of each AP should be –67 dBm or higher at the boundary of its cell, and the SNR should be 25 dB or greater. When you perform an active site survey to validate the network's performance, packet loss or the packet error rate (PER) should be no greater than about 1 percent.

As you plan the band and channel assignment for each AP, try to leverage the 5GHz band as much as possible. There are more non-overlapping channels there and much less chance of interference from non-Wi-Fi devices. A common practice is to use the U-NII-1 and U-NII-3 channels, while avoiding U-NII-2 and U-NII-2 Extended channels because of DFS requirements. If a radar signal is detected by an AP using a DFS channel, the AP and its clients must abandon the channel and move elsewhere. Such an event is very disruptive to voice and video sessions. You should consider using the DFS channels only if there is no detectable radar activity.

Dynamic rate shifting (DRS) and roaming events can also affect real-time applications. For example, when a mobile client or AP decides that it is time to shift to a lower data rate, it must have detected some problems with the higher data rate. Those problems usually include retransmissions due to a low RSSI or low SNR. This means that many wireless frames during the voice or video connection were likely lost before the condition can be improved with a rate shift. Careful AP layout, cell overlap, and data rate tuning can help mitigate DRS disruptions.

Likewise, when a wireless client decides that it is time to roam from one AP to another, it must take time to find a viable AP to roam toward. The client might also need to exchange credentials with the new AP, taking more time away from the voice or video data stream.

To minimize those disruptive events, you should look to leverage 802.11 features such as 802.11r, k, and v that streamline roaming and authentication.

Your design should address efficiency within AP cells. Lower data rates require more time to transmit a frame, so the channel stays busy longer. A better approach is to limit transmissions to use higher data rates so that stations transmit a frame and get off the air sooner, allowing other stations an opportunity to use the channel. That ultimately affects latency and jitter—parameters that are critical for acceptable voice and video performance. You should configure 12Mbps as the lowest and only mandatory data rate, while disabling all rates below that. All data rates greater than 12Mbps should be configured as supported so that they can be used by any device and application as RF conditions permit.

An effective design should take call capacity into account. For example, voice calls use bidirectional RTP streams to transport audio. Each call uses two separate streams, but they cannot be transmitted simultaneously because of channel contention. At a 24Mbps data rate, up to 27 simultaneous bidirectional RTP streams can exist, or up to 13 calls. A 6Mbps data rate can support only 13 streams or 6 calls. Therefore, the maximum number of calls depends on the data rate used, as well as the channel utilization.

Designing a Wireless Network for Location

Sometimes *real-time location services (RTLS)* are needed to automatically determine the location of wireless devices. RTLS can be used to track assets like healthcare equipment, to track rogue devices that might be causing problems on the network, to locate sources of wireless interference, and to track the locations of wireless clients within a building or campus. A device is located by triangulating the RSSI from several APs that can receive its signal.

If location-based services are required, your design goal should be to provide good RF coverage and an effective AP layout. APs should be positioned such that multiple APs can receive a signal from a device to be located. A minimum of three APs should be able to receive a client's signal, while four or more APs are preferred. You should think of every possible client location having at least one AP in each surrounding quadrant.

To derive a fairly accurate location, multiple APs must receive the client device or tag at an RSSI above a minimum signal level of –75 dBm. When you perform a site survey, you should use a threshold of –72 dBm, which will give a 3 dB buffer over the absolute minimum.

To minimize location computation errors, all of the receiving APs should not be located too close to the target client device. However, at least one AP should be within 70 feet of the client location. AP antennas should not be mounted too high above client locations. Otherwise, the client signals may be weak at the receiving AP, causing the client to appear to be located much farther away than it actually is. Ideally, omnidirectional antennas should be mounted around 10 feet high, while directional antennas can be mounted somewhat higher.

Keep in mind that the traffic necessary to locate devices essentially moves in one direction—from the device to any APs that are within range. When a wireless device is probing or already associated to an AP, it is obvious that the device must be near that AP. However, that does not give an accurate assessment of its location. Instead, any APs that receive management frames such as probe requests from the device measure its RSSI and report this information upstream to a wireless management platform, where the device's location is computed. Some normal wireless devices will be quite active on the network, while others like location tags will sleep most of the time and periodically wake up to send a probe request and announce their location.

Location-based applications do not add any requirements for wireless efficiency. Instead, the emphasis is on placing APs to maximize the accuracy of the location algorithms. To do that, you should locate the APs in a staggered fashion within a floor of a building, separating the APs in two directions rather than locating them along straight lines. The main idea is to have a minimum of three APs pick up the device's signal in any arbitrary location. The outermost APs should be placed near the perimeter of the building to improve the computed results when devices are located near the outer walls.

Summary

This chapter described the main considerations needed to apply design requirements to specific wireless network environments. More precisely, you have learned the following:

- How AP coverage can be determined and planned

- How wireless coverage can be scaled by adding and configuring more APs appropriately

- How scenarios requiring generic data transport can be addressed

- How environments with a high density of wireless clients can be effectively supported

- How voice and video applications require special treatment in a wireless network

- How a wireless network can support real-time location services

Exam Preparation Tasks

As mentioned in the section "How to Use This Book" in the Introduction, you have a few choices for exam preparation: the exercises here, Chapter 18, "Final Preparation," and the exam simulation questions in the Pearson Test Prep Software Online.

Review All Key Topics

Review the most important topics in this chapter, noted with the Key Topic icon in the outer margin of the page. Table 5-4 lists these key topics and the page numbers on which each is found.

Table 5-4 Key Topics for Chapter 5

Key Topic Element	Description	Page Number
Figure 5-2	Receiver sensitivity level	88
Figure 5-4	Noise floor and SNR	90
Figure 5-7	Best-practice AP cell boundary conditions	94
Figure 5-12	Best practice for channel separation between neighboring APs	98
Figure 5-13	Coverage design	100
Figure 5-15	An example of high-density RF design	101

Key Topic Element	Description	Page Number
List	Actions for tuning AP cell size	101
Figure 5-17	Adjusting AP cell size with antenna gain	103
Figure 5-18	Flexible radio assignment	104
List	Parameters affecting real-time applications	106

Define Key Terms

Define the following key terms from this chapter and check your answers in the glossary:

asymmetric transmit power levels, cell, client density, dynamic rate shifting, Flexible Radio Architecture, jitter, latency, noise floor, omnidirectional antenna, packet loss, patch antenna, real-time location services, received signal strength indicator, sensitivity level, signal-to-noise ratio

5

CHAPTER 6

Designing Radio Management

This chapter covers the following topics:

Understanding RRM: This section describes the algorithms that can monitor and adjust radio frequency parameters automatically in a wireless network.

Localizing RRM with RF Profiles: This section explains how RRM can be configured globally or customized for specific areas or buildings.

Optimizing AP Cell Sensitivity with RxSOP: This section covers a Cisco feature that can reduce AP cell size to increase performance and lessen co-channel interference in highly dense wireless networks.

This chapter covers the following ENWLSD exam topics:

- 2.0 Wired and Wireless Infrastructure

- 2.3 Design radio management

- 2.3.a RRM

- 2.3.b RF Profiles

- 2.3.c RxSOP

In Chapter 5, "Applying Wireless Design Requirements," you learned how to size access point (AP) cells appropriately by changing the transmit power levels and leveraging appropriate antennas. You also learned how important a proper channel layout is to promote efficient roaming and minimize co-channel interference. You probably also realized how difficult these tasks are when you have to tune the radio frequency (RF) parameters manually across a large number of APs.

In this chapter, you will learn about Radio Resource Management (RRM), a flexible and automatic mechanism that Cisco Wireless LAN controllers can use to make your life much easier.

"Do I Know This Already?" Quiz

The "Do I Know This Already?" quiz allows you to assess whether you should read this entire chapter thoroughly or jump to the "Exam Preparation Tasks" section. If you are in doubt about your answers to these questions or your own assessment of your knowledge of the topics, read the entire chapter. Table 6-1 lists the major headings in this chapter and their corresponding "Do I Know This Already?" quiz questions. You can find the answers in Appendix D, "Answers to the 'Do I Know This Already?' Quizzes and Review Questions."

Table 6-1 "Do I Know This Already?" Section-to-Question Mapping

Foundation Topics Section	Questions
Understanding RRM	1–9
Localizing RRM with RF Profiles	10
Optimizing AP Cell Sensitivity with RxSOP	11

1. Which one of the following protocols is used by APs to learn of other nearby APs?

   a. TPC

   b. NDP

   c. 802.11 neighbor announcement frames

   d. 802.11 beacon frames

2. Which two of the following statements are true about NDP messages?

   a. NDP messages are sent only on an AP's operating channel.

   b. NDP messages are sent on every channel that an AP supports.

   c. NDP messages are transmitted using the AP's normal transmit power level.

   d. NDP messages are transmitted using the AP's maximum supported transmit power level.

3. When RRM collects AP neighbor data from NDP messages that are received, it organizes APs into RF neighborhoods. Which one of the following is the correct criteria for forming an RF neighborhood?

   a. Any two APs appearing in each other's neighbor list at any RSSI value

   b. Any two APs appearing in each other's neighbor list at RSSI greater than –80 dBm

   c. Any two APs appearing in each other's neighbor list that are in the same RF group

   d. Any two APs appearing in each other's neighbor list but not in any other neighbor lists

4. The TPC algorithm is used for which one of the following purposes?

   a. To adjust the transmission control protocol rate

   b. To detect problems in transmission perimeter coverage

   c. To adjust the transmitting primary channel

   d. To adjust the transmit power level

5. If RRM decides to change an AP's transmit power level, which one of the following correctly identifies the action to be taken?

   a. The AP's transmit power level will be changed immediately to the desired value the next time TPC runs.

   b. The AP's transmit power level will be raised or lowered by one 3 dB increment as needed each time TPC runs.

   c. The AP's transmit power level will be changed immediately to the desired value the next time DCA runs.

   d. The AP's transmit power level will be raised or lowered by one 3 dB increment as needed each time DCA runs.

6. If the DCA algorithm detects that an AP is experiencing interference or excessive noise, what might it do to mitigate the problem?

   a. Increase the AP's transmit power level.

   b. Decrease the AP's transmit power level.

   c. Change the AP's channel number.

   d. Direct the client to a different band.

7. Which one of the following runs the DCA algorithm?

   a. RF group leader

   b. Master controller

   c. Each controller

   d. Cisco Prime Infrastructure or DNA Center

8. Suppose the 5GHz radio in one of several APs in a building has failed. Which one of the following algorithms should be able to detect the failure?

   a. CCA

   b. DCA

   c. Dead radio detection

   d. Coverage hole detection

9. Which two of the following choices are the correct criteria used by the FRA algorithm?

   a. 2.4GHz coverage overlap

   b. 5GHz coverage overlap

   c. An AP's COF value

   d. An AP's transmit power level value

10. Suppose you have designed a wireless network to leverage RRM for automated tuning. You have assembled a list of RRM, TPC, and DCA settings that will be applied to all APs in the RF group. However, the APs in one building on your campus need to use only a specific set of channel numbers and a different lowest mandatory data rate. Which one of the following strategies would be best for you to follow?

   a. Manually configure each AP in the one building with the specific RF settings needed.

   b. Create an RF profile that is tailored for the one building and then apply it to an AP group containing the building's APs.

   c. Disable RRM on APs in the one building.

   d. The one building cannot receive customized RRM settings, so it must conform to the global parameters used everywhere else.

11. Suppose you discover that there are some issues in high-density areas of your network caused by high channel utilization and co-channel interference between APs using the same 5GHz channel. Which one of the following design decisions could you take to alleviate the problem?

   a. Raise the TPC maximum transmit power level limit value.

   b. Disable the channels that show co-channel interference in the global DCA channel list.

    c.   Disable more 5GHz channels and try to steer clients toward the 2.4GHz band instead.

    d.   Use RxSOP with a carefully chosen threshold.

Foundation Topics

Understanding RRM

Suppose you need to provide wireless coverage in a rectangular-shaped building. For simplicity, assume that the building has one floor and no interior walls or other objects that would affect RF propagation. Using the information you have learned from this book, you decide to use six APs and locate them such that they form a staggered, regular pattern. The pattern shown in Figure 6-1 should create optimum conditions for roaming and channel use. (The building dimensions have not been mentioned, just to keep things simple.)

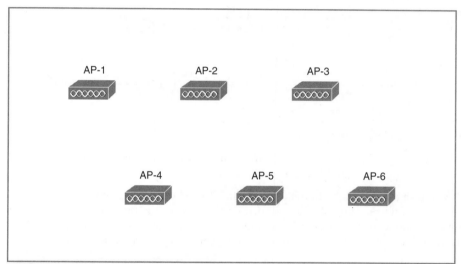

Figure 6-1   *A Hypothetical AP Layout*

So far, you have considered the layout pattern and an average cell size, but you still have to tackle the puzzle of selecting the transmit power level and channel number for each AP. The transmit power level will affect the final cell size, and the channel assignment will affect co-channel interference and roaming handoff. At this point, if all the APs are powered up, they might all end up transmitting on the same channel at maximum power (100 mW, for example). Figure 6-2 shows one possible scenario; each of the AP cells overlaps its neighbors by about 50 percent, and all the APs (and their clients) are fighting to use channel 36!

Where do you begin to prevent such mayhem? Because the AP locations are already nailed down, you can figure out the transmit power level that will give the proper cell overlap. Then you can work your way through the AP layout, choosing an alternating pattern of channel numbers. The example with six APs might not present a daunting task, but a large building with many APs on many floors is an entirely different situation.

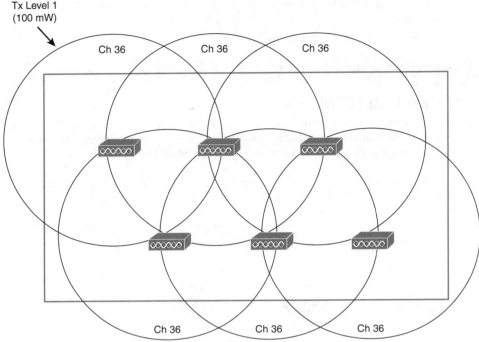

Figure 6-2 *Poorly Configured RF Coverage*

Do not forget to repeat the transmit power and channel assignment tasks for both 2.4 and 5GHz bands, as most APs have dual-band radios.

Also, if you plan on using 802.11n or 802.11ac with channel widths greater than 20MHz, do not forget to reserve the extra channels needed for that. Remember that only the 5GHz band is capable of supporting wide channels. Also remember that your choice of channel width also affects the available number of non-overlapping channels you can assign to the APs.

Suppose you happen to notice one day that an AP has failed. You could always reconfigure its neighboring APs to increase their transmit power level to expand their cells and cover the hole left by the failed AP.

One day in the future, you might identify an area where a higher density of users begins to gather. If you decide to introduce additional APs to distribute the client load, you will need to revisit the entire configuration again to make room for new cells and channels. As a result, you will probably need to rework the channel assignment on all of the APs to accommodate the new APs and their channels.

Did your life as the wireless LAN administrator just become depressing and tedious? Cisco *Radio Resource Management (RRM)* can handle all these tasks regularly and automatically. RRM consists of several algorithms that can look at a large portion of a wireless network and work out an optimum transmit power level and channel number for each AP. If conditions that affect the RF coverage change over time, RRM can detect that and make the appropriate adjustments dynamically. The sections that follow explain each of the mechanisms and algorithms used by RRM.

Discovering the RF Neighborhood with NDP

As you work through a wireless design, you have the ability to see the AP locations on a map and interpret the spatial relationships between each AP and its neighbors. You can even draw the cell boundaries or view them in a site survey map to gauge the cell overlap. RRM cannot use maps and drawings to make its calculations. Even if it could, the maps might not accurately depict the dynamic RF conditions in an area. Instead, RRM must collect real RF data from one AP to another and infer how each AP is situated with respect to its neighbors.

RRM uses the *Network Discovery Protocol (NDP)* to advertise each AP's presence. If an AP's advertisements are received by other APs, those APs must be in proximity to each other. In Figure 6-3, AP-1 is transmitting NDP messages to announce itself. Each of the other APs is able to receive AP-1's advertisement and measure its received signal strength—one of the components necessary for RRM calculations.

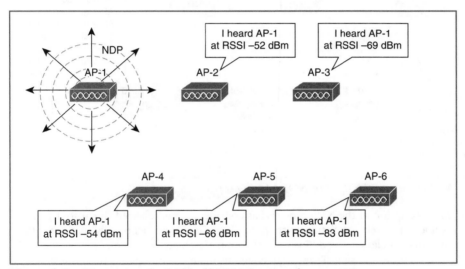

Figure 6-3   *Measuring the RSSI of NDP Messages from an AP*

NDP advertisements are sent to the multicast address 01:0B:85:00:00:00, which is recognized by all other Cisco APs. The messages are transmitted at the highest power allowed for the channel and band. By using the maximum power level, RRM can always know the strength of the signal as it leaves the AP's antenna. Then when that signal is received by other neighboring APs, RRM can use the RSSI to gauge the free space path loss between the transmitting and receiving APs. If the currently assigned Tx power level (lower than the maximum) was used instead, RRM could have a difficult time interpreting the results. In addition, relatively distant APs might not be able to receive the NDP frame at all.

NDP advertisements are transmitted using the lowest data rate possible in the band—regardless of whether or not that data rate has been enabled for use. For example, 1Mbps is always used in the 2.4GHz band and 6Mbps in the 5GHz band. By using the lowest data rate, the advertisements are more likely to be intelligible farther away from the transmitting AP and in noisy environments.

Now consider that each AP transmits its own NDP advertisements, and each AP listens to receive advertisements from any neighboring APs. Over time, each AP can collect the advertisements it receives and report the results to the wireless LAN controller (WLC), as long as the advertisements come from APs that are members of the same administrative group as the receiving AP. RRM can then compute any adjustments to the transmitting AP's power level to tune its cell size appropriately. Figure 6-4 shows example results gathered by the APs in an area; for simplicity, only AP-4 and AP-6 are shown.

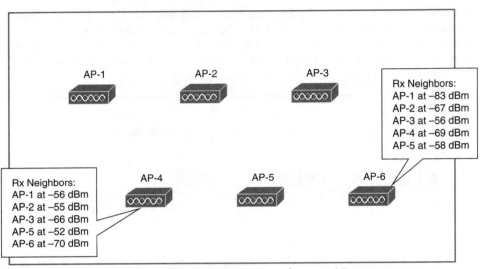

Figure 6-4   *Measuring the RSSI of NDP Messages from an AP*

So far, this description of the NDP process has considered only received signal strength, which assumes that every AP is transmitting on the same channel. Hopefully that is not the case in an actual wireless network! Instead, RRM must evaluate the interaction between APs on the channels they are using. Then it can compute and make changes to both transmit power levels *and* channel assignments.

To reach neighboring APs that might be operating on any arbitrary channel, each AP must transmit its NDP advertisement on every channel it is configured to support. It does this by waiting for an idle period on the current channel and then quickly tuning to a different channel and sending the NDP frame there. It must work through the entire set of channels over a period of 180 seconds. DFS channels are the exception; an NDP frame will be sent on a DFS channel only if the AP is currently the channel master and has determined that no radar signals are present.

Each AP must include its normal operating channel number in its NDP advertisement so that other APs will know its channel assignment. Figure 6-5 shows an over-the-air packet capture of NDP advertisements that were transmitted by a single AP. Notice the Channel column and how the AP has cycled through the channels sequentially over time. It even cycled through the 2.4 and 5GHz bands.

Packet	Source	Destination	BSSID	Channel	Signal dBm	Data Rate	Size	Delta Time	Protocol
1	B8:38:61:94:9A:50	01:0B:85:00:00:00		1	-57	1.0	108		00-0B-85-CC-CD
2	B8:38:61:94:9A:50	01:0B:85:00:00:00		1	-59	1.0	80	0.007000	00-0B-85-CC-CD
3	B8:38:61:94:9A:50	01:0B:85:00:00:00		6	-43	1.0	108	0:01:00.005432	00-0B-85-CC-CD
4	B8:38:61:94:9A:50	01:0B:85:00:00:00		6	-43	1.0	80	0.008000	00-0B-85-CC-CD
5	B8:38:61:94:9A:50	01:0B:85:00:00:00		11	-58	1.0	108	0:01:00.053435	00-0B-85-CC-CD
6	B8:38:61:94:9A:50	01:0B:85:00:00:00		11	-57	1.0	80	0.008000	00-0B-85-CC-CD
7	B8:38:61:94:9A:50	01:0B:85:00:00:00		36	-61	6.0	108	13.988800	00-0B-85-CC-CD
8	B8:38:61:94:9A:50	01:0B:85:00:00:00		36	-61	6.0	80	0.011001	00-0B-85-CC-CD
9	B8:38:61:94:9A:50	01:0B:85:00:00:00		40	-67	6.0	108	9.024516	00-0B-85-CC-CD
10	B8:38:61:94:9A:50	01:0B:85:00:00:00		40	-67	6.0	80	0.016001	00-0B-85-CC-CD
11	B8:38:61:94:9A:50	01:0B:85:00:00:00		44	-62	6.0	108	9.024516	00-0B-85-CC-CD
12	B8:38:61:94:9A:50	01:0B:85:00:00:00		44	-63	6.0	80	0.016001	00-0B-85-CC-CD
13	B8:38:61:94:9A:50	01:0B:85:00:00:00		48	-58	6.0	108	9.007515	00-0B-85-CC-CD
14	B8:38:61:94:9A:50	01:0B:85:00:00:00		48	-57	6.0	80	0.011001	00-0B-85-CC-CD

Figure 6-5   *Example NDP Advertisements Across Bands and Channels*

Figure 6-6 illustrates the scenario from Figure 6-4 with channel information added. Now each AP is able to build a list of neighboring APs complete with received signal strength and channel number information. Notice how the neighbor lists also contain data that can indicate co-channel interference. For example, AP-4 is operating on channel 52 and its neighbor list shows AP-3 also operating on channel 52 with a reasonably strong signal strength. Once the APs send their neighbor lists to the WLC, RRM can compute any adjustments needed to form a more effective channel assignment layout.

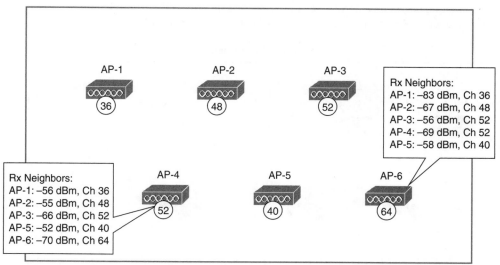

Figure 6-6   *Collecting RSSI and Channel Information from NDP Neighbors*

Each AP maintains a list of NDP advertisements received from up to 34 neighbors. To maintain some stability in the data, entries are automatically pruned and removed if no NDP message has been received from a neighbor after 15 minutes has elapsed.

NDP advertisements contain the following information about the sending AP:

- **Radio ID:** Designates which radio (2.4GHz, 5GHz) sent the frame

- **Group ID and hash:** Designates the logical group name where the AP is a member

- **Encryption:** Key information if the NDP message is encrypted

- **IP address:** The address of the WLC where RRM algorithms are running

- **AP channel:** Normal operating channel

- **Message channel:** Channel used to transmit the NDP message

- **Message power:** Transmit power level (dBm) used to transmit the NDP message

- **Antenna pattern:** The transmitting antenna pattern used

NOTE Every Cisco lightweight AP is expected to send periodic NDP advertisements. If a beacon frame is received from an AP that has not sent an NDP advertisement, the wireless intrusion detection system (WIDS) running on the Cisco WLC will flag that AP as a rogue device.

RF Groups

RRM works by monitoring a number of APs and working out optimal RF settings for each one. The APs that are included in the RRM algorithms are under a common administrative control and are considered members of a single logical *RF group*. For example, all of the APs that belong to an enterprise can be contained in a single RF group. Figure 6-7 shows an example of an RF group called "Enterprise" that contains nine APs.

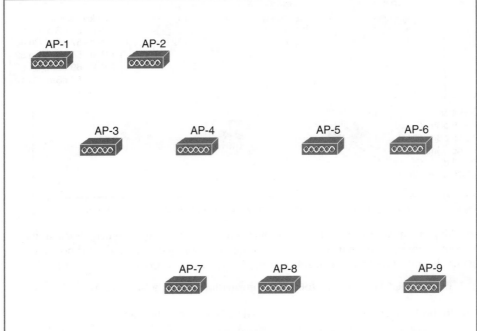

Figure 6-7 *An Example RF Group and Member APs*

By default, an RF group contains all the APs that are joined to a single controller because only one RF group name can be configured on it. If you have multiple controllers, you can include all of their associated APs in the group by configuring the same RF group name on each controller. All of the controllers must be able to communicate with each other through the normal wired network infrastructure.

An RF group can span multiple controllers, but only one of them can run the RRM algorithms for all of the APs involved in the RF group. That means one controller must be elected as the *RF group leader*. The group leader can be elected automatically or through static configuration. In an automatic election, the WLCs exchange information about each other. The WLC with the highest-performing platform and the greatest AP license will become the group leader. If there is a tie among identical controllers, the one with the highest IP address will win the election.

NOTE   A single RF group can contain up to 20 WLCs. Depending on the WLC platform, a single RF group can contain up to 6,000 APs.

Because there is no RF interaction between AP radios on the 2.4GHz band and radios on the 5GHz band, RRM can treat each band independently. In fact, each band has its own separate instance of RRM and its own RF group leader. After the group leader elections, you may see a single controller acting as group leader on both bands, or one controller as group leader on 2.4GHz and another as group leader on 5GHz.

Each AP in the RF group will then send its AP neighbor list updates to the RF group leader, where the RRM algorithms will be run. RRM bases its calculations on the degree that APs will interact or interfere with each other. Therefore, it has to identify all of the APs that might be affected by a transmit power or channel change. If a change is made to one AP, other neighboring APs could be impacted and need adjusting, too, causing their neighbors to be impacted, and so on. In other words, any RF change can have a cascading effect across all APs in a geographic area.

RRM organizes all APs contained in an RF group into *RF neighborhoods*, or sets of APs that are in close RF proximity to each other. The criteria is simple: Any two APs that appear in each other's AP neighbor list will become members of the same RF neighborhood, as long as the RSSI is –80 dBm or greater. An AP is removed from the neighborhood only if the RSSI of its received NDP messages drops below –85 dBm.

The idea is to develop an RF neighborhood by adding APs that are heard by other APs. The neighborhood expands from one AP to another until the NDP messages are too weak to meet the criteria. An RF group can expand across floors in a building, as long as an AP's signal can propagate through the floor or ceiling and be received by another AP located there.

Figure 6-8 illustrates the RF group and neighborhood concepts. All nine APs are part of the RF group "Enterprise" because they are all under the same administrative control. AP-1 through AP-6 all become members of RF neighborhood "A" because each one can be heard by another member of the neighborhood at an RSSI of –80 dBm or above. AP-7 and AP-8 form a separate RF neighborhood; they have a close RF proximity to each other but not to any members of RF neighborhood "A." Likewise, AP-9 becomes the sole member of RF neighborhood "C" because it is not close enough to be heard by any APs in the other two neighborhoods.

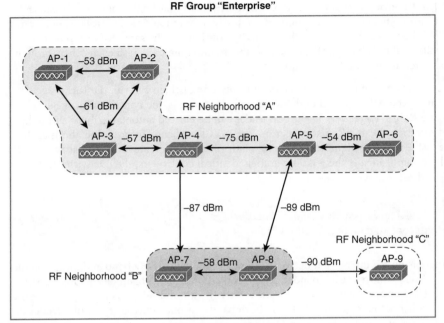

Figure 6-8 *An RF Group and Its RF Neighborhoods*

Once RF groups and RF neighborhoods have been defined, RRM can proceed with its analysis and computations. Each RF neighborhood can be handled independently because any transmit power or channel changes made to one will be too far away to affect any other.

Transmit Power Control (TPC)

The RRM algorithms are designed to keep the entire wireless network as stable and efficient as possible. The transmit power control (TPC) algorithm is one facet of RRM that focuses on one goal: setting each AP's transmit power level to an appropriate value so that it offers good coverage for clients while avoiding interference with neighboring APs that are using the same channel.

Figure 6-9 illustrates the TPC process. APs that were once transmitting too strongly and overlapping each other's cells too much are adjusted for proper coverage, reducing the cell size more appropriately to support clients.

Likewise, if any AP cells are too small and cannot effectively overlap their neighbors' cells, TPC will attempt to increase the transmit power levels to expand the cell size.

Controllers have no knowledge of the physical location of each AP. By looking at Figure 6-9, you can see that the APs are arranged in a nice evenly spaced pattern, but the controller cannot see that. When an AP joins a controller, it advertises only its MAC address, IP address, and some basic information to the controller. The AP is able to know its own transmit power level and can build a list of other neighboring APs as it receives NDP advertisements from them. From the AP's point of view, it can gauge how other APs are impacting its own cell but not how it is impacting others.

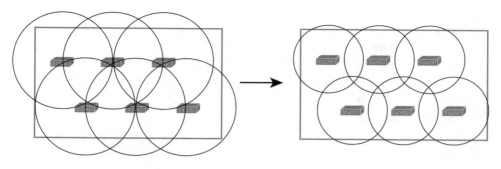

Before TPC   After TPC

Figure 6-9   *Basic Concept of the TPC Algorithm*

However, the TPC algorithm is able to compute the impact that each AP has on its neighbors because it runs on the RF group leader. Recall from the "Discovering the RF Neighborhood with NDP" section that the group leader maintains a database of the list of neighbors that each AP has overheard. To find out how strongly one AP is being received in other AP cells, the group leader can search the neighbor lists for the AP and respective RSSI values.

If an AP is being received too strongly in other AP cells, the TPC algorithm can configure a lower transmit power level on that AP. Likewise, if other APs have measured its signal as too weak, TPC can raise the AP's power level appropriately. Cisco has designed TPC to choose the neighbor that received the third strongest RSSI from an AP as the criteria. With NDP advertisements transmitted at the maximum transmit power level, the third strongest RSSI should be –70 dBm, as illustrated by Figure 6-10.

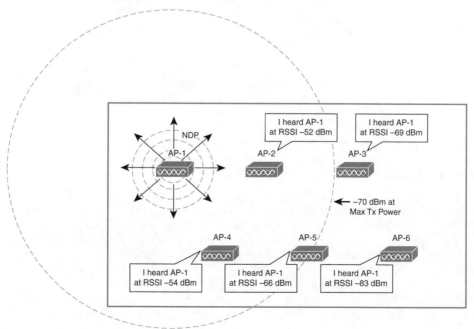

Figure 6-10   *TPC Selects the AP That Has Received the Third Strongest NDP Message from AP-1*

To gauge how far AP-1 is capable of reaching into other AP cells, the neighbor list of AP-5 is used because it has the third strongest RSSI recorded for AP-1. The goal is for AP-1 to be received at –70 dBm at AP-5's location, but it has been received at –66 dBm instead. That means AP-1's transmit power level can be lowered by 4 dBm from the maximum.

This same calculation is performed for every AP in the RF group, using the following formula:

Tx_Ideal = Tx_max + (Threshold – RSSI_3rd)

Suppose AP-1's maximum transmit power is 15 dBm. Then the ideal transmit power would be 15 dBm + (–70 dBm – –66 dBm), or 15 dBm minus 4 dBm. From Figure 6-11, you can compare the maximum power cell boundary at AP-5 with TPC's ideal boundary, shown as a shaded circle, where AP-1's transmit power level has been reduced to 11 dBm and the cell is bounded where the signal strength is –67 dBm.

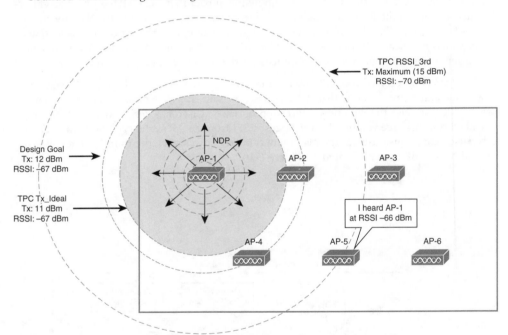

Figure 6-11 *Basic Concept of the TPC Algorithm*

TIP Be aware that the maximum transmit power an AP can use depends on which band it is currently operating in. The regulatory domain determines the maximum value that can be used. For example, in the United States, Wi-Fi devices are limited to 15 dBm in the U-NII-1 band (channels 36–48), 17 dBm in U-NII-2 (channels 52–64) and U-NII-2 Extended (channels 100–140), and 23 dBm in U-NII-3 (channels 149–165). Even though TPC does not consider channel numbers, the maximum transmit power values used in its calculations actually depend on which channels (and bands) the APs are using at the time the TPC algorithm runs.

This discussion has focused on the TPC algorithm, but do not forget that you must still begin with a thorough design that specifies AP locations and transmit power levels that place the –67 dBm cell boundaries where you need them to be. As an example, suppose AP-1 is located correctly in the design of Figure 6-11, and its transmit power level is set at 12 dBm. This value has been chosen because it is half (3 dB less than) the maximum power level of 15 dBm, leaving some flexibility to adjust greater or lower if needed. The design goal cell boundary is also shown in the figure. Fortunately, TPC's notion of the ideal transmit power is very close to the designer's notion, producing similar cell boundaries.

Keep in mind that a good design with appropriate AP locations and spacing affects RRM's TPC results. As long as APs are located with a reasonable space between them, TPC can produce expected results that are also reasonable. RRM will try to adjust AP transmit power levels to compensate for any holes or excessive overlap if it can. However, if you begin with APs that are located too far apart, where their cells might not overlap even at maximum power, TPC can only do so much to compensate for the design problems. After all, APs have a limited range of transmit power level values. An AP cannot transmit any greater than its maximum power level or any less than its minimum. In other words, even though RRM is automatic, it is not magical.

Once the ideal transmit power has been calculated for each AP in the RF group, TPC can begin making the necessary adjustments. Rather than make large, sudden changes in AP transmit power levels, TPC tries to maintain stability by making only incremental changes of 3 dB each time it runs. By default, TPC runs every 10 minutes. Suppose an AP's transmit power level needs to decrease 12 dB to reach the ideal value. TPC will lower the level by 3 dB the next time it runs, followed by another 3 dB during each of the next three cycles.

TIP To add more stability to the wireless network, you can configure the TPC interval to a greater value. For example, some environments that depend on critical services, such as mobile voice communication, might benefit from keeping RRM changes to a minimum during work shifts. In that case, you could configure the TPC interval to be 8 or 12 hours instead of the default 10 minutes.

Why does TPC use 3 dB increments to raise or lower AP transmit power? Cisco APs use a power level index that correlates to an actual value in dBm, as listed in Table 6-2. A power level of 1 always denotes the maximum allowable power level, which varies by band. Notice that some bands use eight power levels, while others use only six or five. Each increment of the power level index changes the power level by 3 dB, effectively doubling or halving the power.

Table 6-2 Example Cisco AP Transmit Power Level Value Correlation

Power Level	2.4GHz Ch 1–13	U-NII-1 Ch 36–48	U-NII-2 Ch 52–64	U-NII-2 Ext Ch 100–140	U-NII-3 Ch 149–161
1	23 dBm	15 dBm	17 dBm	17 dBm	23 dBm
2	20 dBm	12 dBm	14 dBm	14 dBm	20 dBm
3	17 dBm	9 dBm	11 dBm	11 dBm	17 dBm
4	14 dBm	6 dBm	8 dBm	8 dBm	14 dBm
5	11 dBm	3 dBm	5 dBm	5 dBm	11 dBm

Power Level	2.4GHz Ch 1–13	U-NII-1 Ch 36–48	U-NII-2 Ch 52–64	U-NII-2 Ext Ch 100–140	U-NII-3 Ch 149–161
6	8 dBm	—	2 dBm	2 dBm	8 dBm
7	5 dBm	—	—	—	5 dBm
8	2 dBm	—	—	—	2 dBm

By default, TPC determines the total transmit power level change needed for each AP in the RF group and then carries out those changes incrementally. You can also configure upper and lower limits to govern TPC's results. By default, TPC uses a maximum limit of 30 dBm and a minimum limit of –10 dBm. Notice that those values are outside the range that an AP can use, so the limits are effectively disabled. If you find that TPC is setting some APs with a transmit power level that is too high, you can configure a specific maximum value. Likewise, you can set a lower limit to prevent any APs from using a level that is weaker than expected. For consistency, remember to configure TPC identically on all controllers that might be members of the same RF group.

TIP   TPC can be a difficult concept to grasp. You can review its operation in greater detail in Appendix C, "RRM TPC Algorithm Example," which works through a step-by-step explanation of the algorithm in action in a real-world, high-density scenario.

Dynamic Channel Assignment (DCA)

When multiple APs are used in a wireless network, proper channel assignment is vital for efficient use of airtime and for client mobility. If neighboring APs use the same channel, they can interfere with each other. Ideally, adjacent APs should use different, non-overlapping channels. Working out a channel layout for many APs can be a difficult puzzle, but the DCA algorithm can work out optimum solutions automatically for all APs in an RF group.

Whenever a new AP first powers up, it uses the first non-overlapping channel in each band—channel 1 for 2.4GHz and channel 36 for 5GHz. Consider a simplistic scenario where all APs are new and powered up for the first time. You would end up with a building full of overlapping cells competing for the use of 2.4GHz channel 1. The DCA algorithm works to correct this situation by finding a channel that each AP in the RF group can use without overlapping or interfering with other APs. The basic process is shown in Figure 6-12. Like TPC, DCA works out one channel layout for the 2.4GHz band and another layout for the 5GHz band.

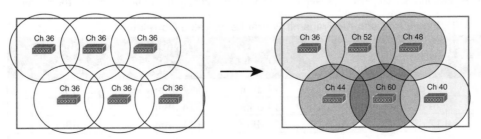

Before DCA   After DCA

Figure 6-12   *Basic Concept of the DCA Algorithm*

By default, DCA uses the complete list of channels available to a regulatory domain, with the exception of channels subject to DFS restriction. You can choose to include DFS channels as well. DCA also considers the channel width as it plans a channel assignment. By default, it will use 20MHz, but you can configure a different fixed channel width. As well, DCA can leverage Dynamic Bandwidth Selection (DBS) as an additional criteria to maximize throughput by changing the channel width in a dynamic fashion. DBS examines the mix of clients on an AP and decides if they and neighboring APs are compatible with a wider channel and could benefit from additional throughput.

DCA does not just solve the channel layout puzzle once for all APs. The algorithm runs every 10 minutes by default, so that it can detect any conditions that might require an AP's channel to change. APs in the RF group are monitored for the metrics listed in Table 6-3 that can influence the channel reassignment decision.

Table 6-3   Metrics Affecting DCA Decisions

Metric	Default State	Description
RSSI of neighboring APs	Always enabled	If DCA detects co-channel interference, it may move an AP to a different channel.
802.11 interference	Enabled	If transmissions from APs and devices that are not part of the wireless network are detected, DCA may choose to move an AP to a different channel.
Non-802.11 noise	Enabled	If excessive noise is present on a channel, DCA may choose to avoid using it.
AP traffic load	Disabled	If an AP is heavily used, DCA may not change its channel to keep client disruption to a minimum.
Persistent interference	Disabled	If an interference source with a high duty cycle is detected on a channel, DCA may choose to avoid using it.

Each of these metrics is combined into a single *cost metric (CM)* that reflects the potential performance that is possible on each channel. Notice that each metric is related to something that either interferes with or competes for airtime on a channel. The CM is something similar to an SNR measurement, with the addition of an interference component. A low CM reflects poor channel performance. The best performance is possible when an AP and a reasonable number of clients have exclusive use of an otherwise quiet channel.

The DCA algorithm tends to look at each AP individually to find the ones with the lowest CM and the worst RF conditions—ones that might be improved by moving them to a better channel. Changing the channel of even one AP can affect many other APs if there are no other viable alternative channels available. Suppose the worst AP is moved to a channel that shows an improved CM, but that action ends up forcing another neighboring AP to a channel that is worse than its original. Such a channel change was probably not wise after all because it did not result in an overall improvement.

To take a more holistic approach, DCA also considers how a channel change to one AP might affect all of that AP's nearest neighbors, as found in its NDP neighbor list. Channels might need to change for some of those neighbors as well, as a result. DCA also considers the effect of the channel change on the neighbors of the AP's neighbors, but none of those will be allowed to undergo a channel change. The idea is to gauge any improvement in the local area around the worst AP but move forward with a channel change plan only if the greater area around the AP would see an improvement or stay the same. DCA's goal is to make improvements, if possible, without impacting all APs in the entire RF group.

Figure 6-13 gives a simple view of the process, where the worst AP is located at the center, and shaded areas contain the AP's neighbors and neighbors of the neighbors. The darkest shaded area shows the extent of the channel decision, based on the CM of the single AP at the center. Notice that there are many other APs outside the shaded area that are also part of the same RF group but are not considered. Once DCA works on the worst AP, that AP and its neighbors are removed from further channel decisions. DCA then moves on and alternates between other random APs and APs with the worst CM until all APs in the RF group have been examined.

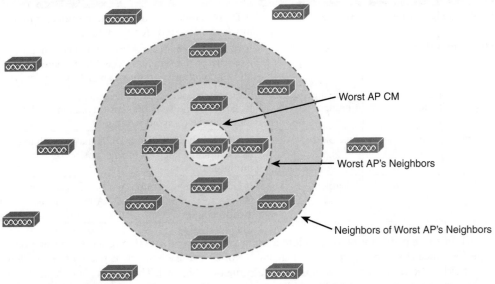

Figure 6-13   *Channel Change Decision Process at the AP with the Worst CM Value*

The end result of DCA is a channel layout that takes a variety of conditions into account. The channel layout is not just limited to the two dimensions of a single floor space in a building; it also extends to three-dimensional space because the RF signals from one floor can bleed through to another. As long as the APs on different floors belong to the same RF group, co-channel interference between them should be minimized.

The DCA algorithm uses a sensitivity threshold to keep channel changes under control. Some conditions such as the interference or traffic load on an AP can vary widely and quickly over time, causing the CM values to increase or decrease. Such abrupt changes could cause DCA to make frequent channel assignment changes. To prevent that from happening, the difference between the proposed CM and current CM must be greater than the sensitivity threshold before a change can be recommended by DCA. You can configure the sensitivity to low, medium (the default), or high.

Channel layout is a puzzle that may require several iterations to solve. For this reason, the controller that is the RF group leader will undergo an RRM startup mode after it is elected. During startup mode, DCA ignores the sensitivity threshold and any checks of neighbors of AP neighbors to calculate CM values. The assumption is that the RF group leader has just come online and needs to build the channel assignments from scratch. The startup mode consists of 10 DCA iterations at 10-minute intervals, or a total of 100 minutes before the channel layout reaches a steady state.

From then on, DCA will continue to run at regular intervals (default 10 minutes), but you can configure a different interval or run it manually on demand, if needed. For example, environments that depend on wireless phones might need to maximize network stability with a DCA interval of 8 or 12 hours. You can also configure an anchor time to fix the DCA schedule around a specific time of day. Keep in mind that channel changes can be disruptive to real-time applications.

NOTE   After APs have been added or removed from a network, or if the AP channel width has been changed globally, Cisco recommends a best practice of manually putting DCA into its startup mode. This will allow the RF group leader to aggressively build a fresh channel assignment without carrying over knowledge of previous conditions.

6

Event-driven RRM (ED-RRM) takes this a step further; DCA can be automatically triggered based on RF events that occur in real time and can take action with a channel change within 30 seconds. The Cisco CleanAir feature provides the triggers for ED-RRM and can be based on detected signals from an interfering transmitter or a rogue AP. If ED-RRM is enabled and an interfering device is detected on a channel, DCA is triggered and will try to avoid the channel in question. Once ED-RRM has flagged a channel, DCA will avoid using that channel again for 3 hours.

Coverage Hole Detection

The TPC algorithm normally adjusts AP transmit power levels to make cell sizes appropriate. Sometimes you might find that your best intentions at providing RF coverage with a good AP layout still come up short. For example, TPC can gauge appropriate coverage where there are many neighboring APs throughout an area but not many neighbors toward the edge of a coverage area. If clients venture out to the edge, they might find an AP that has its transmit power level set too low, which TPC cannot easily detect. You might also have an AP radio that happens to fail, causing a larger coverage hole. How would you discover such conditions? You could make a habit of surveying the RF coverage often. More likely, your wireless users will discover a weakness or hole in the coverage and complain to you about it.

RRM offers an additional algorithm that can detect coverage holes and take action to address them. *Coverage hole detection mitigation (CHDM)* can alert you to a hole that it has discovered and it can increase an AP's transmit power level to compensate for the hole.

Coverage hole detection is useful in two cases:

- Extending coverage in a weak area

- Rapidly healing a coverage hole caused by an AP or radio failure sooner than the TPC algorithm can detect and correct

The CHDM algorithm does not run at regular intervals like TPC and DCA do. Instead, it monitors the RF conditions of wireless clients and decides when to take action. In effect, the algorithm leverages your wireless users who are out in the field and tries to notice a problem before they do.

Every controller maintains a database of associated clients and their RSSI and signal-to-noise ratio (SNR) values. It might seem logical to think that a low RSSI or SNR would mean a client is experiencing a hole in coverage. Assuming the client and its AP are using similar transmit power levels, if the AP is receiving the client at a low level, the client must also be receiving the AP at a low level. This might not be true at all; the client might just be exiting the building and getting too far away from the AP. The client might also have a "sticky" roaming behavior, where it maintains an association with one AP until the RSSI falls to a very low level before reassociating elsewhere.

Coverage hole detection tries to rule out conditions that are experienced by small numbers of clients and signal conditions due to client roaming behavior. The process begins by discovering individual clients whose RSSI falls below a threshold for a minimum of 5 seconds, causing a number of failed or lost frames. Voice clients must fall below –75 dBm and data clients below –80 dBm. Because single clients and a short duration are used as criteria, these events are called pre-coverage holes, as they may be precursors to holes having a greater impact. Each event is reported to the controller so that it can be logged, tracked, and located.

A full-blown coverage hole is detected when some number and percentage of clients, all associated to the same AP, have RSSI values that fall below a threshold for a longer duration—all while staying associated to the same AP. By default, the following conditions must all be met for a coverage hole to be detected:

- The condition must affect at least three clients associated to a single AP
- The affected clients must make up at least 25 percent of clients on the AP

Unlike TPC and DCA, which operate on the entire RF group, coverage hole detection runs on a per-AP radio basis. Also, each controller runs CHDM independently. Once a coverage hole has been detected, CHDM can mitigate the effects of the hole by incrementing the AP's transmit power level by one step. This doubles the power level of the AP and keeps the power level change minimized to avoid creating co-channel interference and working against the efforts of the TPC algorithm.

Flexible Radio Assignment (FRA)

With a properly designed wireless network, the TPC algorithm can tune the transmit power level of each AP to optimize cell coverage and minimize co-channel interference. Recall that TPC runs on the 2.4 and 5GHz bands independently. Wireless designs usually determine AP placement based on the 5GHz AP cell boundaries because the 5GHz band offers more non-overlapping channels to use in high-density areas. Once an AP has been mounted, each of its radios (and internal antennas) has a coverage cell that is centered around the AP's location. If the AP has one 2.4GHz radio and one 5GHz radio, you might think the two cells would be superimposed to cover the same area, assuming the same transmit power level is used for each. However, each signal is subject to free space path loss, which is frequency dependent. That means at the same transmit power level, a 2.4GHz signal will reach its –67 dBm boundary quite a bit farther away from the AP than a 5GHz signal will.

If a design is based on 5GHz cell sizes, the end result is properly overlapped 5GHz cells with greatly overlapped 2.4GHz cells. Notice the difference between 5GHz and 2.4GHz cells in Figure 6-14. Because of the excessive overlap, some of the 2.4GHz cells can be considered to be redundant, as they add no unique coverage. Instead, they can make co-channel inter-ference worse. Figure 6-15 shows overlapped coverage of several 2.4GHz radios. Consider the highlighted AP cell in the left portion of the figure and then notice the RF coverage in the right portion with that AP removed. Even with the AP absent, the area is still almost adequately covered. That means the 2.4GHz radio could be turned off or disabled with no noticeable impact.

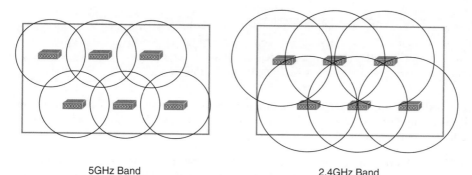

5GHz Band   2.4GHz Band

Figure 6-14   *Comparing Cell Size Between 5GHz and 2.4GHz AP Radios*

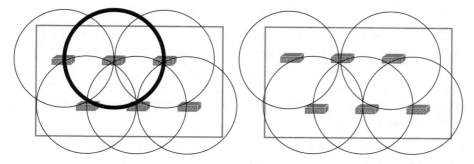

2.4GHz Coverage with Redundant AP   2.4GHz Coverage without the Redundant AP

Figure 6-15   *The Effects of Removing a Redundant 2.4GHz AP Radio*

RRM offers the *Flexible Radio Assignment (FRA)* algorithm, which can detect redundant 2.4GHz radios and repurpose them in the 5GHz band instead. FRA works with Cisco APs that offer one 5GHz radio and one flexible (XOR) radio, which can operate as a 2.4GHz radio, a 5GHz radio, or a monitoring radio.

FRA uses the NDP neighbor list data to compute a *Coverage Overlap Factor (COF)* for each 2.4GHz AP radio. The COF indicates percentage of an AP's cell area that has overlap-ping signals from other APs that are –67 dBm or stronger. If the COF meets or exceeds a threshold defined as low (100%), medium (95%), or high (90%), the radio is flagged as redun-dant and can be reassigned to a different role to make it more useful. Once a radio becomes redundant, FRA will not allow any of the other radios that overlapped it to become redun-dant too.

A redundant 2.4GHz flexible (XOR) radio will normally be reassigned to 5GHz duty, where it will overlap the AP's other 5GHz radio cell. The new overlap will not be destructive because the two 5GHz radios will be assigned to different channels so that they can share the load of associated clients. The additional 5GHz coverage is especially beneficial in high-density coverage areas. The cell size of each 5GHz radio depends on the AP model; some models support a macro/macro arrangement, where the two radios produce similarly sized cells. Other models support a macro/micro scheme, where one 5GHz radio produces a smaller cell footprint than the other, in a cell-within-a-cell arrangement. If the 5GHz coverage is already sufficient, then the redundant radio will be reassigned to a monitor role instead.

> **NOTE**   Once a flexible (XOR) radio has been reassigned from 2.4GHz to 5GHz, it will continue to operate that way. You can manually configure it to revert back to 2.4GHz operation if needed. Also, if the CHDM algorithm detects a 2.4GHz coverage hole at the AP's location, it will immediately revert the radio back to 2.4GHz operation.

When two AP cells overlap each other on different channels, it might be difficult to get wireless clients evenly distributed across the two radios. FRA can use the following three different methods to influence which BSS clients are able to join:

- **802.11v BSS transition**—If a client is 802.11v-capable, the AP will send the client a neighboring AP list containing only the target BSS, followed by an 802.11 deauthentication message. This effectively forces the client off its previous BSS so it can attempt to join the only advertised neighbor BSS. This method is enabled by default.

- **802.11k site report**—If a client requests an 802.11k site report to determine available BSSs, the AP will respond with a site report containing only the target BSS. This method is enabled by default.

- **802.11 probe suppression**—When probe requests are received on both 5GHz BSSs, the AP can respond from the target BSS and stay silent from the non-optimal BSS. This method is disabled by default.

In a macro/micro cell scenario, FRA also monitors client RSSI so it can steer clients toward the macro or micro BSS based on signal strength thresholds.

You can influence FRA actions through Client Network Preference, choosing to prefer either connectivity or throughput. Preferring connectivity will tend to keep the network stable, by preventing redundant radios from switching bands if more than three clients are present at the time DCA runs. Preferring throughput will allow FRA to reassign redundant radios to the other band regardless of the number of clients present.

Localizing RRM with RF Profiles

RRM can be enabled and configured on a WLC globally and independently for the 2.4 and 5GHz bands. Global configuration allows you to quickly make adjustments to all APs in an RF group at once. In large enterprises or geographically dispersed networks, you may need to tune RRM operation in one area differently from others. On a global scale, there is no easy way to accomplish that.

A common practice is to create logical AP groups on a WLC and assign specific APs to their respective groups. For example, a large campus might consist of many buildings. If each building has its own AP group, then RRM parameters can be applied on a per-group or per-building basis. AP groups can also contain a unique list of WLANs to be offered. Even within a building, you might have auditoriums or large classrooms where high densities of clients are expected. You could map those APs into their own AP group and treat them separately from other APs in the building.

You can also tailor RRM parameters to specific needs by configuring them in *RF profiles*, which then get applied to AP groups. This gives great flexibility for localized RF tuning and policy definition. An RF profile contains the following parameter definitions:

- 802.11 data rates and MCS support

- TPC power level limits and thresholds

- DCA channel list and channel width

- CHDM thresholds

- RxSOP threshold (covered in the next section)

- Client density and distribution options

By defining RF profiles and applying them to AP groups, you can customize TPC, DCA, and CHDM algorithms for APs that are members of an AP group. Figure 6-16 shows an example of an enterprise RF group that uses AP groups and RF profiles to tune RRM for each building. The global 5GHz RRM parameters have been configured to use one mandatory data rate of 12Mbps. All possible channels and 5GHz bands have been enabled for use by DCA. The TPC transmit power level limits have been left at the defaults of 30 and –10 dBm. The global RRM values will be applied to all APs that are not members of a specific AP group. Also, the global settings define the values that are inherited by all AP groups. The APs in two buildings have been mapped to an AP group for each building, MainBuilding and BuildingA, while APs in large auditoriums are members of an AP group called MainAuditoriums. A specific RF profile has been defined and applied to each AP group. Notice the settings listed in bold type that are unique in each RF profile and customized for each AP group.

NOTE   As you work out a wireless design, keep in mind that every RF profile must first inherit its parameters from the global RRM settings. For example, that means you can only make changes to channel numbers in an RF profile that have been enabled globally. Parameters that have been disabled globally will not be available to use in any RF profile.

6

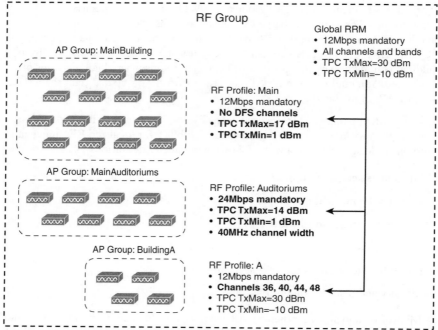

Figure 6-16   *Example AP Groups and RF Profiles Applied to Buildings*

Optimizing AP Cell Sensitivity with RxSOP

In Chapter 5, you learned how neighboring APs can interfere with each other if they share the same channel and their signal strength is above a threshold. The Clear Channel Assessment (CCA) threshold is one mechanism used by wireless stations to determine if a channel is busy. If a station has a frame to transmit, it must first check to see if the channel is busy. A signal received above the CCA threshold of –82 dBm (2.4GHz channel) or –85 dBm (5GHz channel) indicates that the channel is busy, so the station about to transmit must wait until the channel is clear. The more this happens, the greater the channel utilization will be, using up more and more of the airtime.

Ideally, a wireless design should space APs far enough apart to have an appropriate cell size and cell overlap, but neighboring APs assigned to the same channel should not be able to receive either other's signal above the CCA threshold. In practice, this is not always possible, especially in high-density areas. Even with low transmit power levels and directional antennas, the APs might still be close enough to contend for airtime unnecessarily.

Beyond the edge of an AP's cell, conditions can become difficult for client devices too. Clients normally roam from AP to AP as they move about. When a client leaves a coverage area, there are no more APs to roam to, so communication continues until either the AP or the client has an RSSI that falls below the receiver sensitivity. In other words, clients can try to use an AP's cell past the planned boundary.

Cisco offers the *Receiver Start of Packet Threshold Detection (RxSOP)* feature, which can solve both of these problems. RxSOP applies an RSSI threshold as wireless frames are received by an AP. If the signal strength is above the threshold, the frame is received and demodulated normally. If it is below the threshold, the AP simply ignores the rest of the frame as noise.

RxSOP can be useful in the case of distant APs sharing the same channel. Where the 802.11 CCA threshold would normally prevent an AP from ignoring weak transmissions from a distant AP, RxSOP defines a second-higher threshold that can filter them out. In effect, RxSOP puts "earmuffs" on the AP's ears to dampen out signals that are almost too weak to use. The end result is increased efficiency because the AP no longer has to wait for weak signals to finish transmitting before it can use the channel. Where channel utilization was once high because of weak competing devices, RxSOP filtering can open up more airtime and lower the utilization.

Figure 6-17 illustrates the effect of an RxSOP threshold on received signals at an AP. AP-1 and AP-3 share the same channel 36, even though they are separated by some distance. The graph shows how AP-1's signal strength attenuates over the distance from AP-1's location to a point past AP-3. Suppose AP-3 needs to transmit a frame but performs the mandatory CCA check to see if channel 36 is busy. If AP-1 is already transmitting, its signal strength stays above the CCA threshold of –85 dBm even past AP-3, forcing AP-3 to defer and wait. If an RxSOP threshold of –78 dBm is added to the scenario, AP-1's signal strength falls below that threshold just past AP-2. Therefore, if AP-3 uses RxSOP, the transmission from AP-1 will fall below the threshold at AP-3's location. AP-3 will be free to drop AP-1's frame and begin to transmit, provided no other stronger signals are received and in progress.

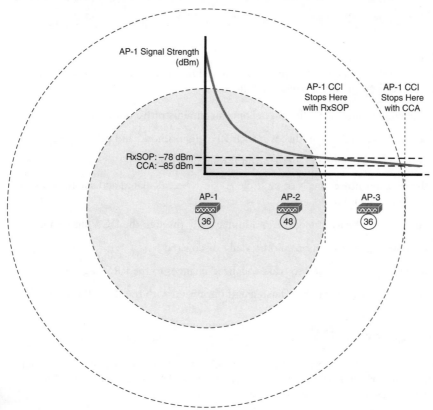

Figure 6-17   *The Effects of Setting an RxSOP Threshold*

The RxSOP threshold also serves to reduce AP cell size, addressing distant clients that do not undergo a clean break as they travel outside the RF coverage. Once client signals fall below the RxSOP threshold, the AP no longer spends time processing the client's frames. This tends to force clients off the Wi-Fi network sooner, giving them a better chance to switch over to cellular service instead, if they are able.

By default, RxSOP is disabled on all APs in an RF group. You can enable and tune RxSOP globally for an entire RF group, but it is usually best to leverage it more locally through the use of an RF profile and AP groups. Through the WLC GUI, you can set the RxSOP threshold as Low, Medium, High, or Auto, on a per-band basis. Table 6-4 lists the settings and their corresponding RSSI values in dBm.

Table 6-4 RxSOP Threshold Settings and RSSI Values

Band	High	Medium	Low	Auto
2.4GHz	−79 dBm	−82 dBm	−85 dBm	Radio default
5GHz	−76 dBm	−78 dBm	−80 dBm	Radio default

NOTE You should use caution and careful planning if you decide to implement an RxSOP threshold in a network. If you set the threshold too high, AP cell sizes could become much smaller than expected. That can open up coverage holes between APs and leave wireless clients stranded with no connectivity. It is best to start with a low threshold, test the results, and then decide if the threshold needs to be increased further.

Summary

This chapter described the main concepts needed to configure and manage individual AP radios. More precisely, you have learned the following:

- How managing radios manually can become an administrative burden

- How controllers and APs can discover their RF neighborhood and other nearby APs

- How radio management can be organized through RF groups

- How the transmit power levels of multiple APs can be calculated and set automatically with the TPC algorithm

- How channels can be assigned to APs automatically through the DCA algorithm

- How RF coverage holes can be automatically discovered

- How RF profiles can be used to make localized changes to the RRM algorithms

- How AP cell sensitivity can be adjusted and optimized with the RxSOP feature

Exam Preparation Tasks

As mentioned in the section "How to Use This Book" in the Introduction, you have a couple of choices for exam preparation: the exercises here, Chapter 18, "Final Preparation," and the exam simulation questions in the Pearson Test Prep Software Online.

Review All Key Topics

Review the most important topics in this chapter, noted with the Key Topic icon in the outer margin of the page. Table 6-5 lists these key topics and the page numbers on which each is found.

Table 6-5   Key Topics for Chapter 6

Key Topic Element	Description	Page Number
Figure 6-3	Measuring the RSSI of NDP messages from an AP	115
Figure 6-8	An RF group and its RF neighborhoods	120
Figure 6-9	Basic concept of the TPC algorithm	121
Figure 6-10	TPC and the third strongest NDP message	121
Table 6-2	Example AP transmit power level numbers	123
Figure 6-12	Basic DCA operation	124
List	Coverage hole detection criteria	128
Paragraph	FRA coverage overlap percentage criteria	129
List	RF configuration parameters available in RF profiles	131
Figure 6-17	Effects of setting an RxSOP threshold	133

Define Key Terms

Define the following key terms from this chapter and check your answers in the glossary:

cost metric (CM), Coverage hole, coverage hole detection mitigation (CHDM), coverage overlap factor (COF), dynamic bandwidth selection (DBS), dynamic channel assignment (DAC), event-driven RRM (ED-RRM), Flexible Radio Assignment (FRA), neighbor discovery protocol (NDP), radio resource management (RRM), RF group, RF group leader, RF profile, RxSOP, transmit power control (TPC)

6

CHAPTER 7

Designing Wireless Mesh Networks

This chapter covers the following topics:

> **Mesh Network Architecture and Components:** This section provides an overview of wireless mesh technology, including an introduction to the main components of a mesh network and the roles they play.

> **Site Preparation and Planning:** This section discusses key aspects of deploying a mesh in an outdoor environment, including available frequency bands, dynamic frequency selection (DFS), and AP mounting considerations.

> **Mesh Convergence and Traffic Flows:** This section discusses how mesh networks converge using the Cisco Adaptive Wireless Path Protocol (AWPP), as well as the available fast convergence options. This section also discusses how different traffic types are bridged through the mesh.

> **Cisco Wi-Fi Mesh Configuration:** This section provides an overview of the necessary configuration steps when deploying a Cisco Wi-Fi mesh network.

> **Daisy-Chaining Wireless Mesh Links:** This section discusses how the mesh may be extended through daisy chaining and shows the configuration steps to enable this model.

> **Workgroup Bridges:** This section highlights one key use case of mesh networks, the Workgroup Bridge (WGB). This section defines the function of the WGB and specific design and configuration considerations when using this technology.

This chapter covers the following ENWLSD exam topics:

- 2.6 Design wireless bridging (mesh)

- 2.6.a Modes of operation

- 2.6.b Ethernet bridging

- 2.6.c WGB and roaming

Wi-Fi is often thought of strictly in the context of indoor networks servicing mobile clients and devices; however, another major application of Wi-Fi is in mesh environments to provide network extension capabilities, both indoor and outdoor. For example, in a large open-pit mine where the topography is constantly changing and vehicles are in constant motion, it is impractical to build a wired network to reach all the remote communication nodes. Wi-Fi mesh is an easy way to simultaneously provide backbone transport to remote communication hubs as well as offer local wireless access to mobile clients, such as autonomous vehicles.

Wireless mesh has a host of different applications across many industries and is widely deployed in public city Wi-Fi networks, stadiums, factories, oil and gas refineries, pipelines, university campus networks, and many more.

This chapter will introduce the subject of Wi-Fi mesh technology and will take a close look at the key architectural components. Aspects of mesh convergence will be considered, as well as fundamentals of how traffic is bridged over the mesh. Facets of site preparation that are unique to outdoor environments will be discussed, including guidance on which frequency bands and channels can be used and which ones need to be avoided, how to correctly mount outdoor mesh access points, which antennas to use, and some practical reminders related to conducting an outdoor site survey. Different modes of mesh operation will be discussed, including how to design and deploy the network for Ethernet bridging and backhaul. Finally, the Workgroup Bridge (WGB), a key use case in mesh, will be discussed in detail, including some of the most common applications.

"Do I Know This Already?" Quiz

The "Do I Know This Already?" quiz helps you determine your level of knowledge on this chapter's topics before you begin. Table 7-1 details the major topics discussed in this chapter and their corresponding quiz sections.

Table 7-1 "Do I Know This Already?" Section-to-Question Mapping

Foundation Topics Section	Questions
Mesh Network Architecture and Components	1
Site Preparation and Planning	2
Mesh Convergence and Traffic Flows	3
Cisco Wi-Fi Mesh Configuration	4
Daisy-Chaining Wireless Mesh Links	5
Workgroup Bridges	6

1. Which component is the root of a Wi-Fi mesh?

    a. WGB

    b. The controller

    c. RAP

    d. MAP

2. How many 160MHz channels are available for deployment in outdoor mesh networks?

    a. One in the 5GHz spectrum

    b. One in the 2.4GHz spectrum

    c. Two in the 5GHz spectrum

    d. Three in the 5GHz spectrum

3. How are wired clients connected to MAPs bridged through the mesh network?

   a. They are encapsulated in CAPWAP and emerge on the configured VLAN on the controller.

   b. Wired clients are not supported on a wireless mesh.

   c. Wired traffic is not encapsulated in CAPWAP and is directed to the wired switch connected to the RAP.

   d. Wired traffic is encapsulated in a special mesh frame header that is handled by the controller and then switched to the matching VLAN.

4. What mode must all mesh APs be configured in to support mesh functions? (Choose two.)

   a. Local mode

   b. Bridge mode

   c. Flex+Bridge mode

   d. FlexConnect mode

5. What problem does backhaul bridging / daisy chaining overcome? (Choose two.)

   a. Allows the mesh to be used for point-to-point links

   b. Overcomes the limitation of a using a single channel in the mesh tree

   c. Extends the size of the mesh tree

   d. Allows the mesh to support Workgroup Bridges

6. What is the function of a Workgroup Bridge?

   a. A Mesh AP in Local mode

   b. A Mesh AP in Bridge mode

   c. An AP that acts as a client to the mesh network

   d. An AP that supports daisy chaining

Foundation Topics

Mesh Network Architecture and Components

One of the best ways to provide reliable wireless network access for outdoor environments is with 802.11 wireless mesh. Figure 7-1 provides an example of such a deployment in an open-pit mine where the APs are deployed in an industrial setting. Unlike traditional office Wi-Fi networks, where every access point is directly connected to an Ethernet port, mesh networking allows access points to be linked to one another without the use of wired network connections, both to service clients and provide backhaul connections to other APs that connect into a wired network.

In addition to supporting 802.11 mobile clients, wireless mesh networks also offer the ability to support directly connected wired clients as well as devices connected through a Workgroup Bridge (WGB), which is a networking device that both acts as a client to the wireless network and provides physical Ethernet connectivity to locally attached devices.

Figure 7-1 illustrates a Wi-Fi mesh deployed in an open-pit mine that is able to service clients across a region where there is no physical Ethernet infrastructure.

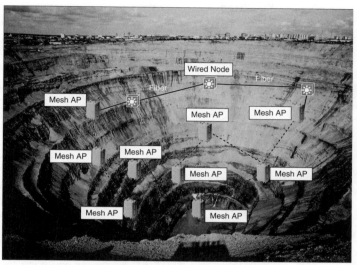

Figure 7-1 *Wi-Fi Deployment Example in an Open-Pit Mine*

At a high level, the components of a Wi-Fi mesh network are as follows:

- **Mesh access points:** Mesh access points function in a similar way to regular APs; however, in addition to supporting mobile clients, they have an added capability to mesh together and provide wireless backhaul services between APs, thus extending the coverage of the wireless network far beyond the wired boundaries. These APs are also generally environmentally hardened to cope with severe conditions, including moisture, extreme hot and cold weather, and vibrations.

- **Wireless LAN controller (WLC):** Although using a WLC to manage the mesh APs is not mandatory (APs may be deployed in Local mode, FlexConnect mode, or using Mobility Express, which is a controller on the AP), it is generally the simplest way to manage a mesh network and offer the widest array of services to both clients and backhaul nodes. Note that autonomous mode APs can also be deployed as wireless bridges, but strictly speaking, this is not considered a mesh.

- **Prime Infrastructure / DNA Center:** Similar to non-mesh wireless networks, Prime Infrastructure and DNA Center are recommended as management options to facilitate RF prediction, policy provisioning, network optimization, troubleshooting, user tracking, security monitoring, and wireless LAN systems management.

> **NOTE** In a production mesh environment, other components are typically deployed, including ISE, CMX / DNA Spaces, Active Directory, and so on. However, for simplicity, only the three listed components are presented in this chapter.

Mesh Access Points

Wireless mesh access points are similar in many ways to non-mesh APs, with the exception they are generally hardened devices, typically use externally mounted antennas, support wired Ethernet clients, and support wireless access as well as backhaul at the same time (although on different channels). Figure 7-2 illustrates some Cisco mesh APs.

1572IC   1572EAC

1540

1562E   1562I

Figure 7-2   *Examples of Cisco Outdoor Mesh APs*

In addition to supporting an extended temperature range for harsh environments, Cisco mesh access points follow the IP (International Protection) code for device hardening, which is based on the IEC 60529 standard for ingress protection. This code classifies the degree of environmental protection provided by the enclosure against things such as dust, water, intrusion, and so on. Naturally, these provide a strong measure of hardening against environmental factors, which plays a key role in harsh industrial environments such as mining, manufacturing, and others. The majority of Cisco mesh access points are rated as either IP65 or IP67. The first number in the IP rating refers to solid ingress protection, such as dust. The numbers rate from 0 (no protection) to 6 (dust tight). For example, the "6" in IP67 refers to the highest level of certified protection, which means the enclosure is dust tight. The second number in the certification refers to protection against liquid ingress, such as water or other chemicals. This number ranges from 0 (no protection) to 9K (powerful high-temperature water jets). The "7" in IP67 refers to protection of the device submerged in up to a maximum of 1 meter of water.

Figure 7-3 illustrates the degree of hardening certified by the International Protection system.

International Protection System Marking (IPxx)

1st Digit	Protection Against Solid Ingress	2nd Digit	Protection Against Liquid Ingress
0	Non-protected (not rated)	0	Non-protected or rated
1	> 50 mm gap for entry	1	Vertically dripping water
2	> 12 mm gap for entry	2	Dripping water tilted at 15°
3	> 2.5 mm gap for entry	3	Spraying water at an angle up to 60°
4	1.0 mm gap for entry	4	Splashing water at any direction
5	Dust protected	5	Jets of water from any direction
6	Dust tight	6	Heavy seas or powerful jets of water
		6K	Powerful water jets with increased pressure
		7	Harmful ingress of water when immersed between a depth of 150 to 1000 mm (5.9 - 40 in)
		8	Continuous immersion in water
		9K	Powerful high-temperature water jets

Example: IP67 = 6 dust tight + 7 protection from liquids, immersible to specification

Figure 7-3   *A Summary of the International Protection System Marking Scheme*

Access Point Roles in a Mesh Network

In a wireless mesh network, access points are deployed in one of the two following infrastructure modes:

- **Root access point (RAP):** Mesh access points have wired connectivity to the network to backhaul traffic and are connected with an Ethernet port. These tend to be in elevated positions, close to a wired communications node. RAPs are the root of the mesh tree and support multiple child mesh APs, call MAPs.

- **Mesh access point (MAP):** Mesh access points backhaul client traffic via a wireless radio interface, ideally on a different band than the client devices. MAPs may mesh together but ultimately link to a RAP.

In addition to these infrastructure modes, a wireless client device may be deployed as a Workgroup Bridge (WGB). The WGB is a dedicated device for bridging wired Ethernet traffic onto the wireless mesh. The WGB is a leaf node of the mesh allowing wired connections to bridge traffic through the wireless mesh back to the campus network. Some models offer additional features such as support for multiple Ethernet devices, multiple VLAN, and NAT/PAT.

In summary, wireless mesh networks are made up of two key infrastructure nodes: mesh APs and root APs. Each mesh network must have at least one RAP, but may have many MAPs that associate with local mobile devices, provide connectivity to devices that are directly connected over an Ethernet interface, and provide wireless backhaul to the RAP. The RAPs are the root of the network and provide a connection point back to the wired network where the controller is accessible. The Workgroup Bridge, or WGB, is an optional component that functions as both a wireless client on the mesh and provides wired extension to remote devices.

Mesh Network Architecture Overview

While RAPs have a wired connection to the network that has reachability to the controller, the MAPs only have wireless connections and function as relays back to the RAP. MAPs must communicate among themselves to find the best parent link, ultimately connecting to a RAP that provides connectivity back to the wired network and the controller. Based on RF conditions, MAPs are able to dynamically find their best parent node (the RAP or another MAP) using the Cisco Adaptive Wireless Path Protocol (AWPP), which will be discussed in more detail later in this chapter.

Figure 7-4 illustrates a typical Cisco mesh network.

As shown in Figure 7-4, a standard mesh tree topology has a single RAP that connects a MAP tree. All mesh deployments must have one active RAP, which is the root of the tree providing access to the wired network (it is not possible to build a mesh out of only MAPs). MAPs may be distributed in such a way that they connect to either other mesh devices, such as the RAP, or higher-level MAPs (parents), and they may also have children, including other MAPs or client devices.

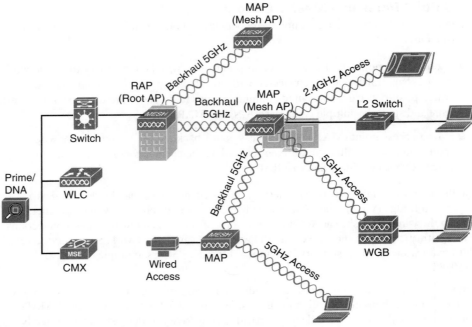

Figure 7-4   *A Typical Example of a Cisco Mesh Network*

It is also common to install a redundant RAP as a backup. In the case of a primary RAP failure, the MAPs will be orphaned and will automatically start scanning all channels in search of another RAP; once the MAPs have discovered the backup RAP, the mesh tree will reconverge. Installing a secondary RAP increases the initial cost, but interruption of connectivity is usually costlier than a second RAP. Using multiple RAPs is also a common technique used to load-balance the MAPs by creating different mesh trees (keep in mind the RAPs will need to be on different channels to avoid interference). As Wi-Fi is a half-duplex contention-based media and only one station can have access to the media at a time, each additional MAP reduces the available bandwidth of the other MAPs, regardless of the number of hops. In general, no more than 20 MAPs are connected to any given RAP.

As the mesh network also facilitates the extension of Ethernet bridging over wireless, the network must also participate in Spanning Tree to prevent loops. It is important to note that the RAP and MAPs themselves do not generate Spanning Tree Bridge Protocol Data Units (BPDUs). However, the RAP and MAPs forward BPDUs to upstream devices if they are received from other wired or wireless devices across the network.

Site Preparation and Planning

The deployment of wireless mesh networks introduces several challenges that are not typically encountered in traditional indoor environments. For example, if the mesh is used outdoors, the frequency bands need to be considered, including how to deal with potential risks such as interference with radar bands. In addition, strategies need to be considered how outdoor mesh APs should be mounted and what types of antennas should be used. These subjects are discussed in this section.

Supported Frequency Bands

While it is possible to use the 2.4GHz spectrum for wireless backhaul in mesh networks, due to the limited bandwidth and limited number of non-overlapping channels, the 5GHz spectrum is generally preferred (note that Cisco mesh APs support both 2.4GHz and 5GHz for backhaul). The 5GHz spectrum has the capacity for many more channels than 2.4GHz, and with 802.11ac there is support for ultra-wide 160MHz channels. However, the channels contained within 5GHz spectrum are not all equal and have different regulatory constraints depending on the band. FCC Part 15.407 divides the 5GHz spectrum into six different categories, called the Unlicensed National Information Infrastructure (U-NII) bands.

When 802.11a introduced Wi-Fi to the 5GHz spectrum, the U-NII-1 band was strictly allocated by the FCC for indoor use only; however, in 2014, the FCC relaxed this restriction by allowing the U-NII-1 band to be used both indoors and outdoors, with the stipulation that any antenna elevation angle greater than 30° from horizon must be limited to a maximum output power of 125mW EIRP. If the antenna is less than 30° from horizon, the maximum output power is limited to 30 dBm and the EIRP must be limited to 4W in the FCC domain.

The U-NII 2A band, from 5.250GHz to 5.350GHz, is more restricted than the U-NII 1 band in that it supports a maximum of 1W EIRP, but it does not have the same 30° from horizon restriction.

Between 5.350GHz and 5.470GHz there is a 120MHz protected band called the U-NII 2B band, which has been reserved by the FCC and cannot be used by Wi-Fi devices.

Figure 7-5 provides an illustrative chart of the 5GHz channels and frequencies allocated to each U-NII band.

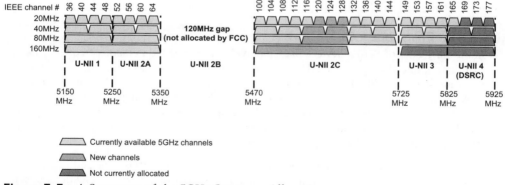

Figure 7-5 *A Summary of the 5GHz Spectrum Allocation*

Typically, wireless mesh will use wider channels on the backhaul to support greater aggregate performance. Thus, by combining allowed channels, it is possible to deploy up to six 80MHz non-overlapping channels, or up to two 160MHz non-overlapping channels. For example, the U-NII 1 and U-NII 2A bands may be combined to form a single 160MHz channel to achieve greater performance. While the 160MHz channel width obviously provides the highest possible throughput, the restriction of only having two non-overlapping channels must be considered when designing a mesh network (the other 160MHz channel is in the

U-NII 2C band from 5.470GHz to 5.630GHz). For example, if more than two mesh segments that are connected through daisy chaining are within interference range of each other, using 160MHz channels may not be possible without causing a significant amount of interference, and thus performance will suffer. If 160MHz channels are in use, it is also important to note that the maximum output power of the two available channels is different depending on the frequency (see Table 7-2).

Table 7-2 lists the various U-NII bands along with their bandwidth and associated maximum allowed output power and EIRP.

Table 7-2 5GHz U-NII Band Details in the FCC Domain

Band	Frequency Range	Bandwidth	Maximum Power	Maximum EIRP
U-NII 1	5.150–5.250GHz	100MHz	30 dBm (1W)	4W with 6 dBi antenna, 200W for fixed P2P with 23 dBi antenna*
U-NII 2	5.250–5.350GHz	100MHz	250mW	1W with 6 dBi antenna
U-NII 2B	5.350–5.470GHz	120MHz	N/A	N/A
U-NII 2C	5.470–5.725GHz	255MHz	250mW	1W with 6 dBi antenna
U-NII 3	5.725–5.850GHz	125MHz	1W	4W with 6 dBi antenna; no limit for P2P
U-NII 4 / DSRC	5.850–5.925GHz	75MHz	N/A	N/A

* Note: The U-NII 1 band is restricted to no more than 125mW EIRP if the antenna angle is greater than 30° from the horizon.

Dynamic Frequency Selection

In the early days of Wi-Fi, devices that employed radar operated in unique frequency bands that did not interfere with Wi-Fi. However, in recent years there has been a movement to open and share the radar bands with other types of wireless services, including Wi-Fi. Thus, as Wi-Fi mesh services are deployed (especially outdoors), there is a need to protect existing radar services against possible interference. To ensure protection of these services, regulatory bodies now require that devices wishing to share these newly opened sub-bands avoid interfering with both radar systems and satellite feeder links.

The IEEE 802.11h standard was developed to specifically address this issue and resulted in the Dynamic Frequency Selection (DFS) standard, used to avoid interference with radar services, and the radio transmit power control (TPC) standard, which is used to avoid interference with satellite feeder links.

DFS is a generalized method for that helps radio services in the 5GHz spectrum (such as Wi-Fi mesh, but it may also be extended to other types of wireless services) avoid interference with radar signals. DFS functions in the AP by scanning active channels for potential radar interference. If interference is detected, the AP stops transmitting for a minimum of 30 minutes on that channel. DFS then selects a different channel, but before transmitting it monitors the channel to ensure it is clear of any radar signals. If no radar is detected on the new channel for 1 minute, the radio may begin using this channel. Once an AP begins using the DFS band, it must continually monitor that band for possible radar signal interference.

From a deployment perspective, it is important to be aware of the DFS bands and to try and avoid using these bands for mesh backhaul links when possible to limit any possible interruption to the wireless backhaul between MAPs and the RAP.

Table 7-3 summarizes the DFS bands in the 5GHz spectrum.

Table 7-3   DFS Bands in the 5GHz Spectrum

Range	Channel	Frequency (MHz)
U-NII-1	36	5180
	40	5200
	44	5220
	48	5240
U-NII-2 DFS required	52	5260
	56	5280
	60	5300
	64	5320
U-NII-2e DFS required	100	5500
	104	5520
	108	5540
	112	5560
	116	5580
	120	5600
	124	5620
	128	5640
	132	5660
	136	5680
	140	5700
U-NII-3	149	5745
	153	5765
	157	5785
	161	5805
	165	5825

Antenna and Mounting Considerations for Outdoor Mesh

As with all 802.11 wireless networks, proper radio and network planning and engineering are required for optimal performance. This is especially true for wireless mesh networks that tend to have ever-changing environments (particularly outdoor environments). For example, higher-gain omnidirectional antennas do not always result in better client connectivity, especially when there is a significant change in elevation. An antenna is a passive device.

The amount of energy it radiates depends on the energy inserted into the antenna and the shape of the antenna. Various antennas can send energy in different directions, but the overall amount of energy sent stays the same. A classical comparison is an inflated balloon. A balloon can be squeezed so it gets larger in one direction, but the overall amount of air inside always stays the same.

Using antennas with higher gain means sending more energy in one direction and, thus, less energy in the other directions. A common high antenna doesn't get the gain because more energy is being pushed through the radio; rather, the gain improvement comes from changing the shape of the radiated energy. For example, an omnidirectional antenna roughly radiates energy in the shape of a sphere (low gain), whereas the energy radiated from a directional antenna focuses the energy into more of a cone shape in a particular direction. The result is a longer horizontal range but at the cost of a shorter vertical range. This is not a problem when the client and MAP antennas are at the same elevation, but it can create huge coverage gaps in open-pit mines where there is often a large elevation difference between the two.

Figure 7-6 illustrates an example of an autonomous vehicle in an open-pit mine whose omnidirectional antenna gain is too high and the client cannot communicate with the MAP below or the RAP above; therefore, antenna planning is a requirement for effective connectivity. Antenna types will depend on the mine topology and the device to which the Wi-Fi system is attached.

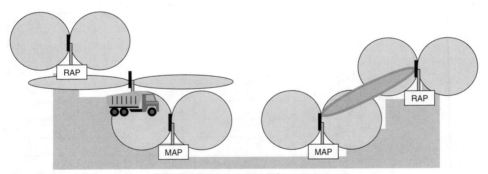

Figure 7-6   *Antennas and Coverage Limits in Three Dimensions*

The mounting location of an antenna in also an important consideration. 802.11 antennas need a clear line of sight to communicate, but they also need to be protected from hazards. A balance between line of sight and protection from rockfall or other hazards must be considered. Many installations will leverage multi-antennas in order to achieve optimal results.

Another consideration is how the RAPs are mounted on buildings. If the RAP is elevated too high on a building, the structure will cast an "RF shadow" below. Just like a visible light shadow, this is an area where the SNR will be very small and a client station may struggle to associate to the AP, whereas areas outside of the RF shadow zone will result in a much larger SNR with better overall wireless performance. It is therefore important to consider the mounting location, shape, and direction of the RAP's antenna, as well as to conduct a post-implementation site survey to ensure coverage is as expected. Figure 7-7 illustrates the typical RF shadowing effect when a RAP is mounted on a tall building.

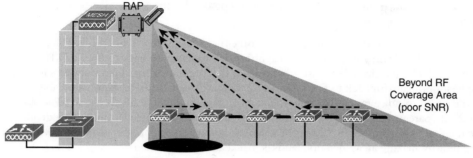

Figure 7-7 *The RF Shadowing Effect*

In summary, RAPs should be mounted using the following guidelines:

- Mount the RAP such that it has a good view of the area to be covered, using directional antennas if possible.

- Place RAPs and MAPs at a height that will not cast an RF shadow (this will require testing of the RF environment).

- Place MAPs and RAPs at the same height if possible.

- The minimum recommended SNR is 20–25 dB with an RSSI of –67 dBm for all data rates, utilizing 15 percent cell overlap.

- Do not install the MAPs in an area where structures, trees, or hills obstruct radio signals to and from the mesh APs. Also be aware of seasonal changes to vegetation that may change RF coverage.

Mesh Convergence and Traffic Flows

This section discusses how the mesh is formed and details the protocols involved in optimizing the mesh performance, beginning with the Adaptive Wireless Path Protocol (AWPP).

Adaptive Wireless Path Protocol

As large mesh networks are deployed, there may be many MAPs in the mesh tree that are several levels deep. Before a MAP can join the mesh, it first analyzes other members of the mesh that are part of the same Bridge Group Network (BGN) to look for suitable parents with which it can make a backhaul connection (either another MAP or the RAP). The method the MAP uses to discover its optimal parent and then make the backhaul connection is governed by the Cisco Adaptive Wireless Path Protocol (AWPP). AWPP is a process where a remote MAP dynamically finds the best parent to connect with and ultimately builds a path back to the RAP.

In a sense, AWPP is very similar to other routing protocols—but with the purpose of helping MAPs to find their optimal wireless backhaul path back to the root (the RAP). However, AWPP has some major differences with common IGPs, such as OSPF, ISIS, and BGP, that are using L3 addressing information to find the next best hop to a destination. Unlike these traditional routing protocols, AWPP uses RF and physical metrics as its decision criteria (also called the objective function).

After it powers on, a MAP begins soliciting other neighbor MAPs. During this solicitation phase, the MAP learns of its available neighbors that have a path back to the RAP. The MAP then measures a metric called "ease" that helps it determine which neighbor appears to have the best optimal path back to the RAP. Ease is primarily calculated based on a combination of the signal-to-noise ratio (SNR) and the number of hops to the RAP. As the MAP looks at candidate parents to build a backhaul link with, the initial ease value is adjusted by dividing the number of hops to the RAP. Once the MAP chooses its parent, it synchronizes with that neighbor by making an association, and the backhaul link is formed.

After a path is established, the MAP uses AWPP to continuously monitor the mesh backhaul link for changes in the RF conditions and will select a different parent if necessary. In this way, AWPP allows the mesh to not only be self-configuring but also self-healing. AWPP also performs a dampening function to ensure that the stochastic nature of the RF environment does not impact network stability and create a situation where child MAPs are constantly bouncing from one parent to another.

As an example, consider the mesh network depicted in Figure 7-8. In this mesh example, a new MAP has just been enabled that has three candidate RAPs to choose from. The APs are all part of Bridge Group Number 1 (BGN_1). Notice that the three RAPs have been configured on different 5GHz channels. Once the MAP powers on, it attempts to join one of the three available RAPs using AWPP.

This scenario will work as follows:

1. MAP-1 scans all available channels looking for a parent (either another MAP or a RAP) that is part of the same BGN. In this case, it sees all three RAPs as candidate parents.

2. Each candidate parent is examined for its SNR value and its hop count (a measure of how far away it is from the root). This results in an "ease" value.

3. By comparing the different ease values, the one with the highest value is chosen as the parent. In the case of Figure 7-8, RAP1 has the highest ease value (3500) and is selected as the parent. In this process, MAP-1 establishes a link to RAP1 on channel 60.

4. MAP-1 conducts a background scan of all potential parents to determine the best candidate backup parent if the current parent fails.

Once a parent-child relationship has been formed, mesh stability can be easily undermined if the MAP were to constantly bounce from one parent to another just because a new parent may have a slightly better ease value than the current one. A fluctuating ease value can actually be fairly common in wireless mesh environments due to the stochastic nature of RF, especially in outdoor environments that may be affected by moving vehicles and other external sources of interference. To deal with this, AWPP assigns the current parent a 20 percent bonus to its ease value to reduce the chance of flapping between parent nodes that may have a similar ease value. Although parent switching is generally transparent to CAPWAP and other applications using the mesh, stabilizing the parent relationship of MAPs in this way will contribute to improving the overall mesh performance.

RAP1 Is Selected as Parent

BGN	RAP Channels
BGN_1	60, 100, 140

MAP-1

Channel	AP	Link SNR	Ease
60	RAP1	35	**3500**
100	RAP2	24	2000
140	RAP3	10	1000

Figure 7-8   *A MAP Is Attempting to Join the Mesh Using AWPP*

AWPP also incorporates a loop-prevention mechanism by discarding routes that contain its own MAC address. In other words, routing includes the MAC address of each hop back to the RAP, so if any hops contain their own MAC address along the path, it would quickly be identified as a loop and that route would be discarded.

Once a child MAP has established an uplink with the RAP or another RAP, AWPP uses the Neighbor Discovery Request/Response (NDReq/NDResp) messages, which act as keep-alives to ensure the parent is still active and reachable. If there are consecutive losses of the NDResp messages, a parent is declared lost and the child MAP will attempt to find a new parent. To help speed the process of finding a new parent, the MAP maintains a list of neighbors on the current on-channel. When the current parent is lost, the MAP immediately attempts to roam to the next-best parent on the same channel. However, if no other neighbors (parents) are found on the same channel, the MAP must scan all channels to find another parent. Cisco mesh APs employ four different modes of configuring the keepalive times: Standard, Fast, Very Fast, and Noise-tolerant-fast. In Standard mode, the MAP scans all channels, making convergence relatively slow. In Fast and Very Fast modes, the scan is only on channels found in the same group, and the timers are tuned more aggressively.

The fourth method is Noise-tolerant-fast detection. This method is based on the failure to get a response for an AWPP neighbor request, which evaluates the current parent every 21 seconds. Each neighbor is sent a unicast request every 3 seconds, along with a request to the parent. Failure to get a response from the parent initiates either a roam if neighbors are available on the same channel or a full scan for a new parent.

Table 7-4 illustrates the expected convergence times of the four different convergence methods.

Table 7-4   Mesh Fast Convergence Options

	Parent Loss Detection/Keepalive Timers	Channel Scan/Seek	DHCP/CAPWAP Information	Time Per Hop (sec)
Standard	21 / 3 sec	Scan/seek all channels	Renew/restart CAPWAP	48.6
Fast	7 / 3 sec	Scan/seek only channels found in same bridge group	Maintain DHCP and CAPWAP	20.5

	Parent Loss Detection/Keepalive Timers	Channel Scan/Seek	DHCP/CAPWAP Information	Time Per Hop (sec)
Very Fast	4 / 2 sec	Scan/seek only channels found in same bridge group	Maintain DHCP and CAPWAP	15.9
Noise-tolerant-fast	21 / 3	Scan/seek only channels found in same bridge group	Maintain DHCP and CAPWAP	8–10

Traffic Flow Through the Mesh

In addition to providing wireless services to local clients, mesh APs also support local wired connections, which are bridged back through the mesh. Thus, in summary, traffic flow on a wireless mesh can be divided into the following three categories:

- CAPWAP traffic from wireless clients that flows between mesh AP and the controller (the standard CAPWAP control for local wireless clients)

- Wireless mesh data frames (for locally attached devices)

- AWPP traffic used between nodes to build the mesh

NOTE   Cisco mesh APs can also be deployed in FlexConnect bridging mode where all wireless traffic is locally switched at the AP; however, this section deals with mesh APs that are deployed in central controller mode. FlexConnect is discussed in Chapter 10, "Implementing FlexConnect."

The function of CAPWAP in a wireless mesh is virtually identical to that of a non-mesh AP. Similar to non-mesh APs, a CAPWAP tunnel is formed between the controller and all APs where all 802.11 traffic is bridged through the tunnel until it emerges from the controller on the desired VLAN. The only subtle difference in a mesh environment is that the CAPWAP packets are encapsulated inside a special bridge frame on the mesh backhaul until they emerge from the RAP and are then forwarded to the controller.

Unlike wireless access traffic, devices connected to the local Ethernet ports on a mesh AP do not use CAPWAP encapsulation and are not sent to the controller (such as video cameras attached to a MAP's Ethernet interface—see Figure 7-9). In this case, locally connected devices are forwarded to the RAP and then on to the default gateway of the VLAN where they are routed as regular IP packets.

The backhaul interfaces of mesh APs are referred to as primary interfaces, whereas other physical interfaces are referred to as secondary interfaces. In a mesh environment where VLAN trunking is needed for Ethernet bridging, the secondary Ethernet interfaces on MAPs are assigned to a VLAN individually (typically used for things like cameras or other devices that are directly connected to a MAP). In this case, the backhaul (primary interfaces) functions as VLAN trunks with all VLANs enabled, thus allowing segmentation of devices connected to secondary interfaces. Wireless client traffic and other untagged Ethernet bridged traffic utilize the native VLAN of the APs in the mesh. VLAN-tagged frames are tunneled through AWPP over wireless backhaul links.

Figure 7-9 illustrates a mesh network that supports both 802.11 clients associated to APs as well as wired devices that are directly attached to a MAP's Ethernet interface. Notice how the wireless client's 802.11 traffic is encapsulated in CAPWAP by the local MAP and is then forwarded through mesh to the RAP and on to the controller, whereas wired devices are simply switched through the mesh network until the traffic can be locally switched after emerging from the RAP. In either case, both the CAPWAP and locally connected traffic are switched as bridge frames through the mesh.

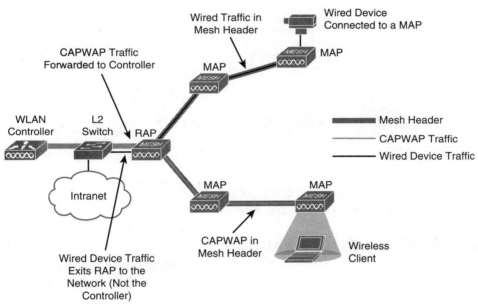

 Figure 7-9   *Traffic Flow of Wireless and Wired Traffic Through a Mesh Network*

Ethernet Bridging

A standard 802.11 data frame can use up to four MAC layer address fields, including the receiver, transmitter, destination, and source addresses. From the perspective of a MAP or a RAP, these are defined as follows:

- **Receiver:** The MAP or RAP receiving a frame from the child MAP (the MAC address of the local mesh AP).

- **Transmitter:** The MAC address of the child MAP that transmitted the frame.

- **Destination:** The ultimate destination of the frame being transmitted, typically the default gateway of the RAP.

- **Source:** The MAC address of the station where the frame originated, possibly behind the transmitter MAP.

Standard 802.11 frames transmitted between a wireless client and an AP typically use only three of these address fields because the transmitter and source addresses are the same (meaning there is no device behind the client). However, in a wireless mesh network where bridging is in use, all four address fields are needed—because the frame might have been generated by a device *behind* the transmitter.

For example, Figure 7-10 illustrates a MAP that originates a frame destined for a controller. From the perspective of the RAP, the receiver, transmitter, destination, and source addresses are shown. In this case, the source address is needed to know which MAP the frame originated from, not just where it was relayed from on the prior hop.

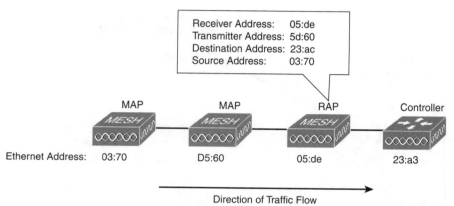

Figure 7-10 *Wireless Mesh Bridge Addressing Example*

Cisco Wi-Fi Mesh Configuration

When a mesh AP is first added to the network, it must be configured for the correct mode it will play. Cisco mesh APs can be configured to work in the following possible modes:

- **Local mode:** This is the traditional AP mode used in enterprise environments. In this mode, the AP can handle clients on its assigned channel as well as looking for rogue client beacons, noise floor measurements, interference, and IDS events. The AP is also able to scan for CleanAir interference on the channel in this mode.

- **FlexConnect mode:** In FlexConnect mode, the mesh AP is managed by the controller, but client traffic is locally switched instead of being sent back to the controller.

- **Monitor mode:** In this mode, the AP radios are in the receive state (they cannot accept client associations). The AP scans all the channels every 12 seconds for rogue client beacons, noise floor measurements, interference, IDS events, and CleanAir intruders.

- **Sniffer mode:** In this mode, the AP captures and forwards all packets on a channel to a remote device that decodes the packets with packet analyzer software such as Wireshark.

- **Flex+Bridge Mode:** In this mode, both the FlexConnect and Bridge mode configuration options are available on the access point.

■ **SE-Connect:** In Spectrum Expert mode, a user can connect Cisco Spectrum Expert to the AP to gain information about the RF spectrum around the AP. In this mode, the AP does not service clients.

> **NOTE**   Although the options listed here are possible on a Cisco mesh AP, for it to function as part of a mesh, the AP must be configured in either Bridge mode or Bridge+Flex mode, where the Bridge+Flex mode allows local switching of the mesh WLANs and Bridge mode utilizes centralized switching.

■ To configure the mesh AP for the right mode, go to the **Wireless > Access Point > (AP_NAME)** page on the WLC.

Figure 7-11 illustrates these various modes for an AP that is being added as a RAP.

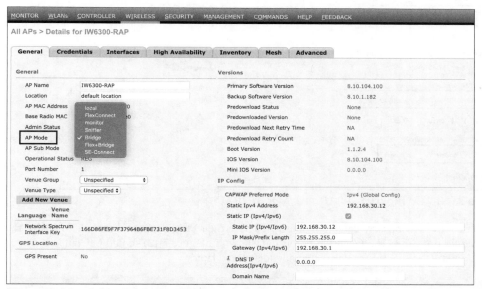

Figure 7-11   *Selecting the "Bridge" Mode for a Mesh AP So That It Can Be Configured as a RAP or a MAP*

Once the mesh AP has been assigned the correct mode as a bridge in the controller, it is necessary to identify what role the bridge will play. In Bridge mode, APs can be configured as either a MAP or a RAP. This is done by navigating to **Wireless > Access Point > (AP_NAME) > Mesh** on the WLC. In addition to the administrator being able to select the correct role, this menu also presents various options to configure the mesh AP. For example, if the RAP role is selected, the **VLAN Support** option may be selected. This option enables VLAN trunking on the Ethernet port that connects back to the wired network. A suboption also allows the administrator to select the correct native VLAN ID for the trunk.

If the mesh tree will use the 2.4GHz spectrum for backhaul instead of 5GHz, this option may also be selected. Note that because a mesh tree (the RAP and all MAPs) uses the same frequency, the same option must be selected for all nodes in a given mesh tree.

The exception to this is if the MAPs have multiple backhaul radios or daisy chaining is used (discussed later in this chapter).

Figure 7-12 illustrates the process of configuring a new mesh AP as a RAP.

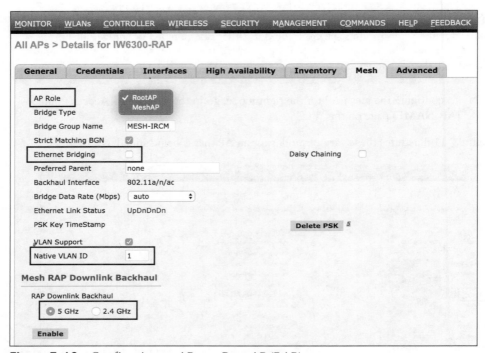

Figure 7-12   *Configuring an AP as a Root AP (RAP)*

For security reasons, by default all mesh APs have their Ethernet port disabled. To enable the Ethernet port, the Ethernet Bridging option (shown in Figure 7-12) should be enabled. This option is also required for daisy chaining (discussed later).

NOTE   When mesh APs ship from Cisco, they are configured as MAPs by default. To configure the AP as a RAP, it must be explicitly configured as a "RootAP" in the WLC page shown in Figure 7-12. If the MAP has an Ethernet cable connected and is up, it will use the Ethernet port as the primary backhaul, and secondarily it will use the wireless radio. This is useful because it gives the network administrator an opportunity to reconfigure the MAP as a RAP; however, if a MAP is left connected to the Ethernet port, it will not build a mesh. Once the Ethernet port is disconnected, it will begin looking for a suitable parent using AWPP. On the other hand, a RAP will always use the Ethernet port as its primary backhaul and will only use wireless for backhaul if the Ethernet port is in the down state.

While Figure 7-12 illustrates configuration details of a single mesh AP, many of the mesh capabilities can be configured globally from the **Wireless > Mesh** tab on the controller. This includes configuration options for **Range** (RAP to MAP range), **Mesh Backhaul RRM**,

Convergence (various options for mesh convergence), **Ethernet Bridging,** and **Security** (mesh security).

Once the mesh network has been deployed, a summary of the mesh configuration can be displayed with the **show mesh config** command from the CLI, as shown in Example 7-1.

Example 7-1   *Displaying the Mesh Configuration on a RAP*

```
(Cisco Controller)> show mesh config
Mesh Range................................... 12000
Backhaul with client access status.............. disabled
Background Scanning State...................... enabled
Mesh Security

Security Mode............................... EAP
External-Auth.............................. disabled
Use MAC Filter in External AAA server........ disabled
Force External Authentication................ disabled

Mesh Alarm Criteria
Max Hop Count.............................. 4
Recommended Max Children for MAP............. 10
Recommended Max Children for RAP............. 20
Low Link SNR............................... 12
High Link SNR.............................. 60
Max Association Number....................... 10
Association Interval........................ 60 minutes
Parent Change Numbers....................... 3
Parent Change Interval...................... 60 minutes

Mesh Multicast Mode........................... In-Out
Mesh Full Sector DFS.......................... enabled

Mesh Ethernet Bridging VLAN Transparent Mode..... enabled
```

Daisy-Chaining Wireless Mesh Links

In wireless mesh networks, a common deployment method is to dedicate the 5GHz radio for backhaul and the 2.4GHz radio for client connectivity. Many 802.11 wireless mesh networks can be deployed with access points that only support a single radio for each band. However, deploying in this mode (without the use of serial backhaul or back-to-back daisy chaining) has performance and throughput implications. Mesh networks are typically built with a tree structure. A RAP connects to the wired infrastructure and uses its 5GHz radio to connect one or several MAPs that form the first hop. Farther away, other MAPs backhaul traffic through the first-hop MAPs. All mesh APs in this scenario are on the same 5GHz channel. However, as the size of the mesh increases, sharing a single channel can become a bottleneck, even if wide 160MHz channels are used.

Wi-Fi is inherently half-duplex and relies on CSMA/CA for media access; thus, a MAP cannot simultaneously communicate with the upstream RAP or MAP (the MAP that leads toward the RAP) and a downstream MAP (a MAP further away from the RAP). Even if wider channels are used, only a single station (a client, WGB, MAP, or RAP) may transmit at a given time or risk a collision. The bigger the mesh gets, the single channel quickly becomes a limiting factor both to size of the mesh (number of MAP levels in the tree) and the overall performance of the backhaul links.

A MAP spends some of its time relaying traffic upstream, some of its time relaying traffic downstream, and some of its time relaying traffic for its own clients (typically in the 2.4GHz spectrum). As a consequence, each hop generates additional latency that increases at each level of the mesh. For example, a MAP that relays traffic from three child MAPs will proportionally spend more time relaying and less time forwarding its own client traffic, compared with a MAP that relays traffic from a single other MAP. In a multi-hop mesh, when a single radio is used to connect to both the upstream RAP and downstream MAPs, the available bandwidth is greatly reduced with each hop. For this reason, wireless mesh networks are generally recommended to be no larger than four hops in depth (although eight hops is technically supported).

The single 5GHz backhaul radio architecture also reduces range. Imagine a deployment with a RAP and two MAPs organized in a straight line (a two-hop deployment scenario). The first-hop MAP must use an omnidirectional antenna to reach the RAP on one side and the second-hop MAP on the other side. An omnidirectional antenna has a lower gain than a directional antenna. Such an architecture reduces the possible inter-AP distance, as most of the RF energy is wasted into the air without being focused at either the RAP or downstream RAP. An ideal configuration would include dedicated directional antennas for each direction of the link (for example, using a narrow beam width antenna for upstream connectivity to the RAP and an equally appropriate antenna to service the downstream MAPs).

Daisy chaining was designed as a method to overcome these limitations (also known as the back-to-back deployment model). In this scenario a virtual serial-backhaul MAP can be created with two mesh access points cabled together, as shown in Figure 7-13.

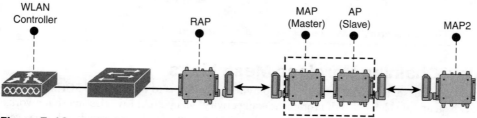

Figure 7-13 *MAP Daisy-Chaining Topology*

Upstream traffic is processed through one of the 5GHz APs, called the master, whereas downstream traffic is processed through the other AP's 5GHz radio, called the slave. Each AP has a directional antenna for increased range. In this model, traffic passes from one MAP to the other via the wired Ethernet connection. The result is better overall throughput, greatly increased range, and a larger mesh that doesn't rely on a single channel, thus avoiding many of the interference problems common in mesh deployments.

Figure 7-14 illustrates a multi-hop mesh using the daisy-chaining method, along with the expected performance based on 802.11n using Cisco mesh access points.

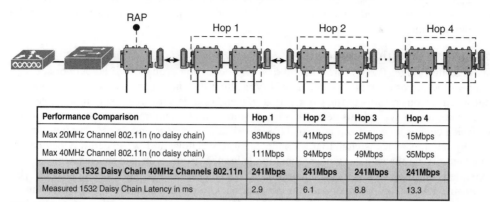

Performance Comparison	Hop 1	Hop 2	Hop 3	Hop 4
Max 20MHz Channel 802.11n (no daisy chain)	83Mbps	41Mbps	25Mbps	15Mbps
Max 40MHz Channel 802.11n (no daisy chain)	111Mbps	94Mbps	49Mbps	35Mbps
Measured 1532 Daisy Chain 40MHz Channels 802.11n	**241Mbps**	**241Mbps**	**241Mbps**	**241Mbps**
Measured 1532 Daisy Chain Latency in ms	2.9	6.1	8.8	13.3

Figure 7-14 *Daisy-Chaining MAPs in a Wireless Mesh Deployment*

To configure daisy chaining, the AP must be in MAP mode (a RAP should not be used for daisy chaining, as it is already the root of the mesh tree). To configure the MAP, from the WLC GUI, go to **Wireless > Access Point > (AP_NAME) > Mesh** (see Figure 7-15) and then check the **Daisy Chaining** check box. If the AP is used in a serial-backhaul solution, the **Preferred Parent** option must be selected. Note that daisy chaining should only be enabled on the slave, and the Master MAP should have daisy chaining disabled. If the MAP is configured as the master, then only the **Ethernet Bridging** option should be selected.

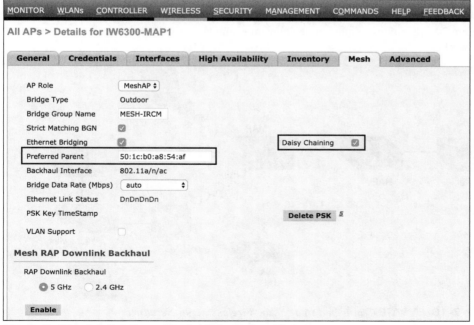

Figure 7-15 *Configuring a Mesh AP for Daisy Chaining*

Workgroup Bridges

In many cases it is necessary to extend Ethernet switching services for wired clients over the wireless mesh. Workgroup Bridges are designed for this purpose and will be discussed in the following section.

Workgroup Bridging Overview

Workgroup Bridges (WGBs) are a useful tool for connecting orphaned wired networks over a wireless mesh. For example, a city bus will typically use cellular backhaul when on the road, but when the bus returns to the work yard at the end of a day, it can connect to a wireless mesh network. A typical bus network is often quite complex and involves services for video surveillance, bus dispatch and control, GPS, the ticketing system, and so on. This network usually requires a local switch that is connected to the cellular and Wi-Fi gateway device. The network on the vehicle is like a mini mobile branch office. How can this network be extended over the wireless mesh and appear as an extension of the regular campus network? To enable seamless connectivity of this network back to the campus, the WGB acts as the wireless client to the mesh but also provides bridging services so the vehicle network, including any VLANs, is extended back to the campus.

Some typical WGB deployment examples include the following:

- Connection of a wired printer to the network

- Industrial deployments where it is not feasible or practical to run a cable to the wired device

- Vehicle deployments where the WGB provides connectivity from a car, bus, truck, or metro train to an outdoor wireless network

Figure 7-16 illustrates a common deployment example of a WGB connected to a mesh network.

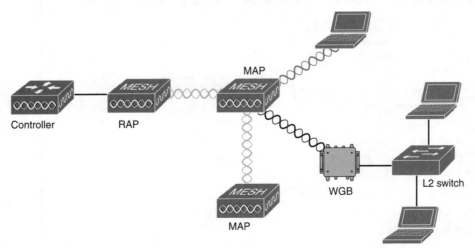

Figure 7-16 *A WGB Connected to a Cisco Wireless Mesh Network*

Unlike other components of a mesh, such as the RAP and MAPs, the WGB is not managed by the controller. From the controller's perspective, the WGB appears as a wireless client, not as an infrastructure device. The WGB may be either configured as an autonomous IOS device or an AP-COS platform AP (AP-COS is a controller-based operating system used on 802.11ac Wave 2 access points). From the wired side of the WGB, the MAC addresses of wired clients are learned and reported to the mesh infrastructure APs (MAPs or the RAP) using Internet Access Point Protocol (IAPP) messaging. The wired clients may be either directly connected to the WGB or attached through an intermediary L2 switch. The WGB, in turn, associates to the mesh AP and provides bridging for the wired clients into the network.

As with other wireless clients, the WGB is centrally authenticated by the mesh wireless infrastructure for security; however, the clients attached to the WGB are not. Rather, any wired clients attached to the WGB will inherit its AAA authentication and QoS attributes independent of the wireless mesh (which also may be central, but it is not part of the wireless onboarding process).

Configuring Workgroup Bridges

To configure the WGB, it is generally recommended to create a dedicated SSID specifically for the WGBs on the mesh network. In this sense, the WGB is much like any other client that must have an SSID supported by the APs, a VLAN ID on the controller, and a security profile between the WGB and the infrastructure. In addition to these configuration steps, the Aironet IE field must be enabled under the **WLAN > ID > Advanced** tab (see Figure 7-17).

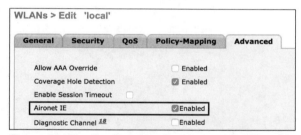

Figure 7-17 *Configuring the Aironet IE Allows the WGB to Associate to the Mesh AP*

It is often desirable to have multiple VLANs behind the WGB trunked through the wireless mesh. In this case, the VLAN ID that maps to the SSID of the WGB becomes the native VLAN, and other VLANs are simply trunked through the mesh over CAPWAP until they emerge from the controller.

Once the native VLAN is defined, configure the controller with the data-plane VLANs that will be trunked over the WGB through the wireless mesh. For example, Figure 7-18 illustrates a WLC that has WGBs associated to the mesh on "vlan11" (the native VLAN) but has two further data VLANs behind the WGB ("wgb_vlan44" and "wgb_vlan55"). On the WLC, these two interfaces are configured as VLANs, given an IP address, and attached to an uplink port.

In order to support VLAN trunking from the WGB, the device must also have 802.1q trunking configured between itself and the adjacent L2 switch. When the WGB receives an L2 trunked frame, it removes the dot1q header before sending the frame over the wireless link. In the reverse direction (downstream), the WGB identifies which VLAN the frame belongs to and adds the correct dot1q tag to identify the VLAN before sending it to the attached L2 switch.

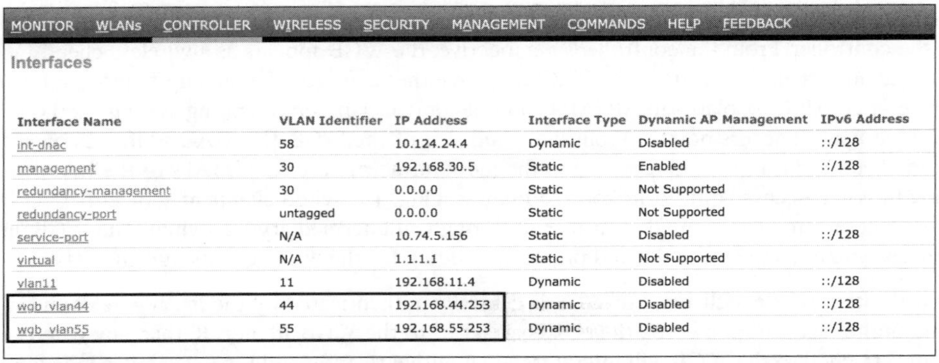

Interface Name	VLAN Identifier	IP Address	Interface Type	Dynamic AP Management	IPv6 Address
int-dnac	58	10.124.24.4	Dynamic	Disabled	::/128
management	30	192.168.30.5	Static	Enabled	::/128
redundancy-management	30	0.0.0.0	Static	Not Supported	
redundancy-port	untagged	0.0.0.0	Static	Not Supported	
service-port	N/A	10.74.5.156	Static	Disabled	::/128
virtual	N/A	1.1.1.1	Static	Not Supported	
vlan11	11	192.168.11.4	Dynamic	Disabled	::/128
wgb_vlan44	44	192.168.44.253	Dynamic	Disabled	::/128
wgb_vlan55	55	192.168.55.253	Dynamic	Disabled	::/128

Figure 7-18 *Configuring VLANs Trunked from a WGB Through the Wireless Mesh*

An example of the WGB wireless configuration to support VLAN trunking is shown in Example 7-2.

Example 7-2 *Configuring the WGB for Multi-VLAN Support*

```
! wireless portion of the configuration

WGB# config t
WGB# interface dot11radio 0.11
WGB# encapsulation dot1q 11 native

WGB# interface dot11radio 0.44
WGB# encapsulation dot1q 44
WGB# bridge-group 44

WGB# interface dot11radio 0.55
WGB# encapsulation dot1q 55
WGB# bridge-group 55

! wired interface portion of the configuration

WGB# interface gigabit 0.11
WGB# encapsulation dot1q 11 native

WGB# interface gigabit 0.44
WGB# encapsulation dot1q 44
WGB# bridge-group 44

WGB# interface gigabit 0.55
WGB# encapsulation dot1q 55
WGB# bridge-group 55

! enable WGB to inform WLC of the VLAN assignments

WGB# workgroup-bridge vlan-client
```

The final command shown in Example 7-2 (workgroup-bridge unified-vlan-client) is critical, as it allows the WGB to inform the WLC via IAPP which VLAN the clients should be assigned, allowing them to be bridged onto this VLAN as the frame emerges out of the controller.

Note that while a WGB may join the mesh if the Aironet IE is enabled (and it is authenticated), multi-VLAN support is disabled by default. To enable support for WGBs, use the following command:

>config wgb vlan enable

Summary

This chapter described Wi-Fi mesh bridging, including design considerations as well as configuration steps. In this chapter you have learned the following:

- The main components and roles of a Wi-Fi mesh network

- How a mesh network is architected

- Outdoor frequency band considerations

- Mesh AP mounting considerations

- Mesh convergence and traffic patterns

- Mesh AP configuration steps

- Daisy-chaining techniques to extend a mesh network

- How to configure a Workgroup Bridge

References

For additional information, refer to these resources:

Mesh Deployment Guide 8.8: https://www.cisco.com/c/en/us/td/docs/wireless/controller/technotes/8-8/b_mesh_88.pdf

Cisco Wireless Best Practices: https://www.cisco.com/c/en/us/td/docs/wireless/controller/technotes/8-6/b_Cisco_Wireless_LAN_Controller_Configuration_Best_Practices.html

WGB Roaming: Internal Details and Configuration: https://www.cisco.com/c/en/us/support/docs/wireless/aironet-1130-ag-series/113198-wgb-roam-config.html

WGB VLAN Configuration Guide: https://www.cisco.com/c/en/us/support/docs/wireless-mobility/service-set-identifier-ssid/211293-Configure-Work-Group-Bridge-WGB-Multip.html#WGBconfig

Autonomous Mesh AP Configuration Guide: http://www.cisco.com/c/en/us/td/docs/wireless/access_point/15_2_4_JA/configuration/guide/scg15-2-4_book.html

Operation of the U-NII Bands: https://www.naic.edu/~phil/rfi/u_niiband_802.11_aug16.pdf

Exam Preparation Tasks

As mentioned in the section "How to Use This Book" in the Introduction, you have a few choices for exam preparation: the exercises here, Chapter 18, "Final Preparation," and the exam simulation questions in the Pearson Test Prep Software Online.

Review All Key Topics

Review the most important topics in this chapter, noted with the Key Topic icon in the outer margin of the page. Table 7-5 lists these key topics and the page numbers on which each is found.

Table 7-5   Key Topics for Chapter 7

Key Topic Element	Description	Page Number
Figure 7-4	A Typical Example of a Cisco Mesh Network	142
Figure 7-5	A Summary of the 5GHz Spectrum Allocation	143
Table 7-4	Mesh Fast Convergence Options	149
Figure 7-9	Traffic Flow of Wireless and Wired Traffic Through a Mesh Network	151
Figure 7-13	MAP Daisy-Chaining Topology	156

Define Key Terms

Define the following key terms from this chapter and check your answers in the glossary:

root access point (RAP), mesh access point (MAP), daisy chaining, Adaptive Wireless Path Protocol (AWPP), ease, Dynamic Frequency Selection (DFS), AP-COS, Workgroup Bridge (WGB)

CHAPTER 8

Designing for Client Mobility

This chapter covers the following topics:

Roaming Review: This section reviews the process a wireless client uses to roam from one AP to another, as well as the different types of roaming supported by a Cisco wireless network.

Organizing Roaming Behavior with Mobility Groups: This section discusses how Cisco WLCs can be assigned to logical groups that support client roaming within an enterprise.

Optimizing AP Selection for Client Roaming: This section provides an overview of ways that wireless clients scan for available APs and select one for association. Several methods to make the AP selection more efficient are also covered.

Optimizing Security Processes for Roaming: This section explains the robust secure network (RSN) and its impact on wireless client roaming. It also covers five common methods to streamline the roaming process in the midst of robust security.

This chapter covers the following ENWLSD exam topics:

- 3.1 Design mobility groups based on mobility roles

- 3.2 Optimize client roaming

- 3.3 Validate mobility tunneling for data and control path

Wireless client devices are inherently mobile, so you should expect them to move around. This chapter discusses client mobility from the AP and controller perspectives. You should have a good understanding of client roaming so that you can design and configure your wireless network properly as it grows over time.

"Do I Know This Already?" Quiz

The "Do I Know This Already?" quiz allows you to assess if you should read this entire chapter. If you miss no more than one of these self-assessment questions, you might want to move ahead to the "Exam Preparation Tasks" section. Table 8-1 lists the major headings in this chapter and the "Do I Know This Already?" quiz questions covering the material in those headings so you can assess your knowledge of these specific areas. You can find the answers to the "Do I Know This Already?" quiz in Appendix D.

Table 8-1 "Do I Know This Already?" Section-to-Question Mapping

Foundation Topics Section	Questions
Roaming Review	1–3
Organizing Roaming Behavior with Mobility Groups	4–6
Optimizing AP Selection for Client Roaming	7–8
Optimizing Security Processes for Roaming	9–10

1. Which one of the following 802.11 management frames is used to initiate a roam from one AP to another?

   a. Authentication request

   b. Association request

   c. Roam request

   d. Reassociation request

2. Suppose AP-1 is joined to WLC-1 and AP-2 is joined to WLC-2. Both APs offer the SSID "Wi-Fi" and the same IP subnet. A client undergoes a roam from AP-1 to AP-2, then back to AP-1. Which one of the following roam types did the client undergo from AP-2 to AP-1?

   a. Intra-controller

   b. Inter-controller Layer 2

   c. Inter-controller Layer 3

   d. Autonomous

3. Suppose AP-1 is joined to WLC-1 and AP-2 is joined to WLC-2. Both APs offer the SSID "Wi-Fi," but each offers a different IP subnet. A client undergoes a roam from AP-1 to AP-2 and is able to keep using its original IP address. For this client roam, which of the following correctly identifies the roles played by WLC-2?

   a. Anchor controller, POA

   b. Anchor controller, POP

   c. Foreign controller, POA

   d. Foreign controller, POP

4. A single mobility group can have a maximum of how many controllers? (Choose one.)

   a. 10

   b. 24

   c. 50

   d. 72

5. When you configure mobility groups on Cisco WLCs, what is the maximum number of controllers that can belong to the same mobility domain?

    a. 10

    b. 24

    c. 50

    d. 72

6. To verify that mobility tunneling is working correctly over a CAPWAP tunnel between two WLCs, which one of the following CLI commands should you use?

    a. ping

    b. eping

    c. cping

    d. mping

7. Which one of the following statements is correct about active scanning?

    a. A client actively tunes its radio through a sequence of channels and waits to receive 802.11 beacon frames from APs.

    b. A client actively tunes its radio through a sequence of channels and transmits 802.11 probe request frames, then waits for replies from APs.

    c. A client tunes its radio through a sequence of channels and transmits 802.11 Action frames to discover APs that answer.

    d. An AP actively tunes its radio through a sequence of channels to discover any clients sending 802.11 beacon frames.

8. Which two of the following 802.11 amendments can be used to assist clients in finding candidate APs to roam toward?

    a. 802.11k

    b. 802.11r

    c. 802.11s

    d. 802.11v

    e. 802.11w

9. The 802.11r amendment is also known as which one of the following?

    a. Fast secure roaming

    b. Opportunistic Key Caching (OKC)

    c. Fast BSS Transition (FT)

    d. Fast Key Caching (FKC)

10. Suppose an 802.11r client initiates a roam with a target AP. Which one of the following correctly describes the step when the PTK and GTK are generated?

    a. When the client undergoes 802.1X/EAP authentication with a RADIUS server

    b. When the client and AP exchange 802.11 authentication and reassociation messages

    c. Right after the 802.1X/EAP authentication is completed

    d. During the normal 4-way handshake

Foundation Topics

Roaming Review

Perhaps the best way to begin a chapter about wireless mobility is to review client roaming in various scenarios. Before a client device can use a wireless network, it must join or associate itself with an AP by completing the following steps:

1. Discover an AP's presence by scanning channels to receive 802.11 beacon frames or by sending 802.11 probe request frames.

2. Authenticate itself to a specific AP at its BSSID address, using either open system or shared key authentication.

3. Associate with the AP by sending an 802.11 association request frame to the AP; if the AP is agreeable, it responds with an association response frame.

4. If the WLAN uses WPA2 or WPA3 and is a secured with a pre-shared key (PSK) or 802.1X, the client must authenticate itself with the PSK or through EAP and RADIUS.

Once fully associated, the client can communicate over the wireless network through that AP, as long as the client stays within the AP's cell. Wireless clients are free to move around, so a client device must remain aware of the quality of its current association so it can be ready to move its association to a different AP when necessary. Ideally, a client will move its association well ahead of time so that communication with the original AP does not become unusable before the roam occurs.

Figure 8-1 illustrates the basic roaming process. The client begins with an association to AP-1 while inside that cell. As the client moves away from AP-1, it notices that the RF conditions become less and less favorable for maintaining a good connection with AP-1. The client discovers AP-2's presence and a better signal, so it decides to try to roam there by sending an 802.11 reassociation frame to AP-2. If the reassociation is successful, the client's previous association with AP-1 is torn down. If AP-1 has any unsent data destined for the client, it relays that data to AP-2 over the wired network.

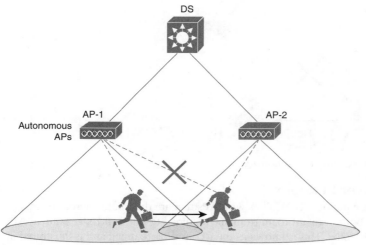

Figure 8-1 *A Basic Roam from One AP to Another*

The basic idea is to request an *association* when a fresh connection to an AP is needed and to request a *reassociation* when a roam from one AP to another is needed. The reassociation is designed to preserve network connectivity as much as possible, minimizing any disruption while the client transitions between two APs.

From the client's perspective, the roaming process is always the same between any two APs. However, the roaming mechanism can take many forms on the back end, depending on the wireless network architecture. The following sections provide a quick review.

Autonomous APs

When a network is built from autonomous APs, there are no back-end mechanisms to support roaming, as each AP acts independently. Therefore, the roaming operation is quite simple and straightforward and is the scenario shown in Figure 8-1. If the client moves from one IP subnet into another subnet as it roams between APs, it must take time to request a new IP address from a DHCP server through the new AP association.

Intra-Controller (Layer 2) Roam

Suppose the wireless network is made up of lightweight APs joined to a single WLC, as shown in Figure 8-2. Each AP maintains CAPWAP tunnels to the WLC to transport control and data traffic. When a client roams between AP-1 and AP-2, its associations are handled within the same controller. The controller simply has to update its table of client associations to reflect the change from AP-1 to AP-2. The SSID, security parameters, and IP subnet can all stay consistent, so the roam transition can be as efficient as possible. Because the client's IP address can remain the same, the roaming event occurs at Layer 2.

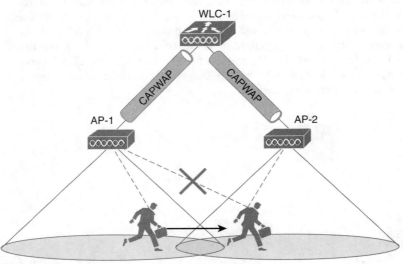

Figure 8-2   *A Basic Intra-Controller Roaming*

Inter-Controller (Layer 2) Roam

Larger networks may use multiple controllers with APs that are distributed across them. As a mobile client moves about, it might roam from an AP joined to one controller onto an AP joined to a different controller. This is known as inter-controller roaming and is illustrated in Figure 8-3. As the client moves from AP-1 to AP-2, its association is passed from WLC-1 to

WLC-2. Such a seamless handoff does require some cooperation between controllers behind the scenes, which is discussed further in the section "Organizing Roaming Behavior with Mobility Groups" in this chapter.

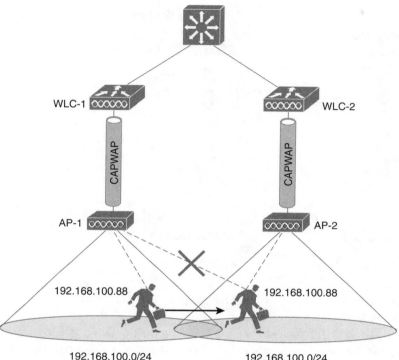

 Figure 8-3 *A Layer 2 Inter-Controller Roam*

Another important aspect to notice is what happens to the client's IP address. Both AP-1 and AP-2 offer the same SSID and the same IP subnet (192.168.100.0/24). As the client roams, it moves between AP cells but remains in the same subnet, so it can keep using the same IP address without stopping to request a new one from a DHCP server. This is also known as a Layer 2 inter-controller roam.

Inter-Controller (Layer 3) Roam

When multiple controllers are used in a network design, they might not always offer the same IP subnet on the same WLAN. That does not mean that clients cannot roam between APs hosted by different controllers. Inter-controller roaming can also support roams that cross Layer 3 boundaries. In Figure 8-4, a wireless client has roamed from AP-1 to AP-2, and from WLC-1 to WLC-2, where the APs are joined. Notice that the two APs support two different IP subnets and that the client was using 192.168.100.88 while it was associated with AP-1.

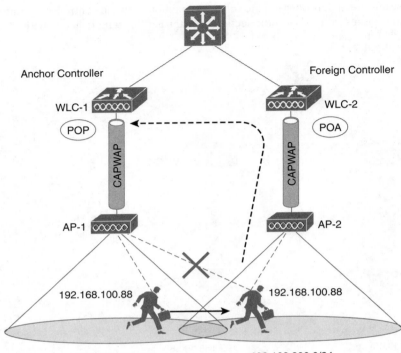

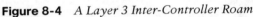

Figure 8-4   *A Layer 3 Inter-Controller Roam*

Now notice that the client is still using 192.168.100.88 after it reassociated with AP-2. Even though AP-2 (and WLC-2) does not directly offer the 192.168.100.0/24 subnet, the controllers have worked together to maintain connectivity with that subnet. A Layer 3 inter-controller roam is a cooperation between controllers that allows a subnet from one to be supported on another.

Behind the scenes, the controllers take on specific roles to support the roaming client. When the client first joins the wireless network, such as AP-1 in Figure 8-4, the controller hosting the client takes on the *anchor controller* role and provides the initial IP address for the client. When the client roams to a different AP that is joined to a different controller, the new controller takes on the *foreign controller* role. Because the foreign controller is not able to support the client's IP address directly, it builds an additional CAPWAP tunnel to the anchor controller just to transport traffic to and from the roamed client and its original IP address.

Layer 3 roaming also involves two other roles. The *point of attachment (POA)* refers to the AP and controller where a wireless client is currently associated. Therefore, the POA moves to follow a client as it roams. The *point of presence (POP)* refers to the controller where the client is seen to be. In other words, the POP is located at the point where the client's IP address can connect with the corresponding IP subnet and VLAN. When the client initially associates with the network, it obtains the IP address it will use and continue to use while undergoing Layer 3 roams, so its POP remains stationary. You can think of the POP as the client's anchor point (conveniently located at the anchor controller). The POA travels with the client but is always tethered to the POP. That also means the controller-to-controller CAPWAP tunnel will move to follow the client and its POA.

Cisco WLCs also support the following two special cases of Layer 3 inter-controller roaming:

- **Static IP tunneling:** This feature provides Layer 3 roaming for wireless clients that have statically configured IP addresses. As long as a controller directly connects to the corresponding IP subnet, it can become an anchor controller. Then foreign controllers will build CAPWAP tunnels to the anchor to transport traffic to and from the client's static IP address.

- **Guest anchor:** When a WLAN is defined on a controller, it can be flagged as a guest WLAN that will always be tunneled to a controller that serves as a static anchor point. In effect, clients associated to a guest WLAN will be connected to a guest VLAN connected to the anchor controller. In this way, all guest users can be contained at the guest anchor, regardless of their physical location.

Organizing Roaming Behavior with Mobility Groups

The previous section explained that wireless clients can roam between APs, even when the APs are joined to different wireless controllers. To make the roaming process consistent and transparent to the client, Cisco WLCs must work behind the scenes to keep track of roaming events and to hand off clients from one controller to another.

Defining the Mobility Hierarchy

If multiple controllers exist in a network, they must be configured into *mobility groups* or logical collections. As long as controllers are placed in the same mobility group, client roaming can be handled seamlessly between any of the controllers. You can place up to 24 controllers into a single mobility group. In Figure 8-5, four controllers belong to the mobility group called "Group1." Each controller maintains a list of mobility group members, each identified by MAC address and management IP address, along with the mobility group name. The figure also lists the group members from WLC-1's perspective. The first line of the mobility group list always refers to the local controller, which already knows its own group name assignment. Therefore, the group name is not shown in the first line of the list.

As clients roam, controllers must inform each other of the event. Even in the case of an intra-controller roam, where the client stays within the same controller, the controller must inform all other group members. Inter-controller roams involve two different controllers, so they must coordinate the roam and hand off clients from one to the other. Layer 3 roams require a further step, where anchor and foreign controllers must form a relationship and the extra CAPWAP tunnel required to transport the client's traffic between them.

Notice in Figure 8-5 that each of the four controllers has a "connection" to every other controller in the mobility group. The controllers in the group must form a full mesh of unicast connections so that they can communicate events and handshake with each other. Imagine what the full mesh diagram would look like if the maximum of 24 controllers were members of the same group! Fortunately, you can leverage IP multicast instead so that any of the controllers can send events to one multicast address and reach all controllers in the group simultaneously.

Mobility Group "Group1"

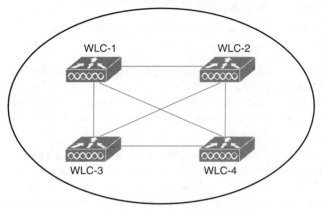

WLC-1 Mobility Group Members

```
00:00:00:01:01:01   192.168.199.101   none
00:00:00:02:02:02   192.168.199.102   none   Group1
00:00:00:03:03:03   192.168.199.103   none   Group1
00:00:00:04:04:04   192.168.199.104   none   Group1
```

Figure 8-5 *An Example Mobility Group of Four Wireless Controllers*

TIP You can learn more about configuring and using multicast on wireless controllers by reading Chapter 12, "Implementing Multicast."

In a design with many controllers, you can group them into multiple mobility groups, each containing up to 24 controllers. However, seamless roaming is supported between a maximum of three mobility groups that are organized as a *mobility domain*, up to a maximum of 72 controllers in total. You can have additional mobility groups that lie outside the mobility domain, but those are considered to be in their own mobility domain. If a client roams from one mobility domain to another, the roam will be disruptive to the user experience because it requires the client to start a new association, a new DHCP exchange, and a new authentication process.

Figure 8-6 illustrates the mobility group and domain relationships. Three mobility groups, "GroupA," "GroupB," and "GroupC," form one mobility domain, while "Group D" belongs to a different mobility domain. Only two controllers are shown in each mobility group for simplicity. Clients can roam between any controllers in any of the three groups, A through C, and preserve their connectivity. Roaming between controllers that lie in different mobility domains is still possible but will be disruptive to the user experience.

One interesting thing about mobility groups is the manner in which they are defined and configured. Each controller must have a complete list of itself and every other controller in the mobility domain, but the mobility domain itself is not explicitly defined. Consider the list of group members defined on WLC-A1 in Figure 8-6. WLC-A1 appears on the first line without a group name, followed by WLC-A2 with "GroupA." GroupB is defined as controllers WLC-B1 and WLC-B2, and GroupC as WLC-C1 and WLC-C2. Each of the other controllers must have its own list, too, so that each controller has the same concept of the mobility group memberships. Mobility group "GroupD" is never mentioned in the list because it lies outside the three-group maximum for the first mobility domain. Instead, it forms the only group that is part of the second mobility domain.

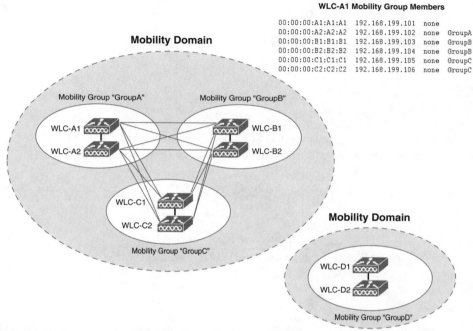

```
                                         WLC-A1 Mobility Group Members

                          00:00:00:A1:A1:A1  192.168.199.101  none
                          00:00:00:A2:A2:A2  192.168.199.102  none  GroupA
                          00:00:00:B1:B1:B1  192.168.199.103  none  GroupB
                          00:00:00:B2:B2:B2  192.168.199.104  none  GroupB
                          00:00:00:C1:C1:C1  192.168.199.105  none  GroupC
                          00:00:00:C2:C2:C2  192.168.199.106  none  GroupC
```

Figure 8-6 *An Example of the Mobility Group and Domain Hierarchy*

Exploring Mobility Operations

Each type of client roam involves a different communication exchange between controllers. Even before roaming the first time, a client must associate with an AP somewhere in the network. In Figure 8-7, the client has associated with AP-1 on WLC-1. Therefore, WLC-1 must announce the client's action so that all other controllers in the mobility domain will be aware of the event. This is done by sending a Mobility Announce message to every other controller—either by unicast to the full mesh of controllers or by a single multicast.

Now consider an intra-controller roam, as depicted in Figure 8-8. The client roams from AP-1 to AP-2, both joined to WLC-1. The controller is able to update the client's association change (technically a reassociation) internally, but it must also send a Mobility Announce message to update all other controllers.

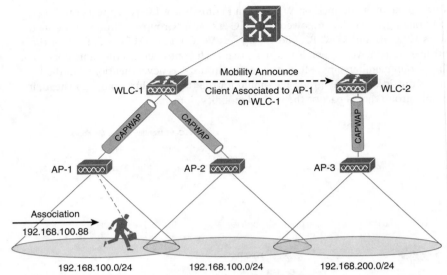

Figure 8-7 *Announcing a Client Association in a Mobility Domain*

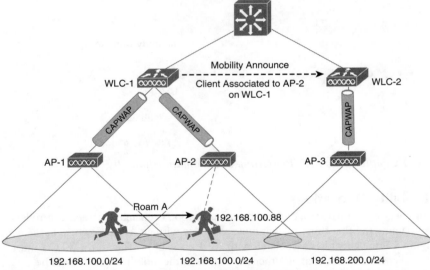

Figure 8-8 *Announcing an Intra-Controller Roam in a Mobility Domain*

Layer 3 inter-controller roams are a bit more complex because they involve an interaction between two different controllers and their roles. In Figure 8-9, the client has roamed from AP-2 to AP-3, moving from WLC-1 to WLC-2. The event begins with a Mobility Announce message from WLC-2 to inform all other controllers where the client is now reassociated or attached. WLC-1 must also communicate a Mobile Handoff event about the move from WLC-1 to WLC-2. Finally, the two controllers must take on the anchor and foreign controller roles to support the client's original IP address on an AP with a different subnet. This is done through an exchange of Mobile Anchor handshake messages.

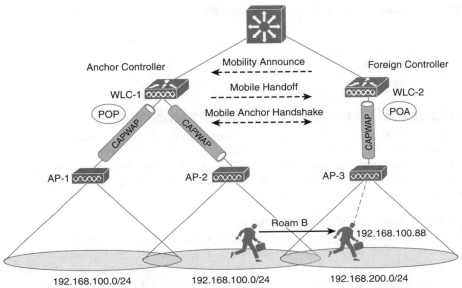

Figure 8-9 *Announcing an Inter-Controller Layer 3 Roam in a Mobility Domain*

Validating the Mobility Hierarchy and Tunneling

Cisco WLCs exchange mobility traffic with each other using various tunneling methods, depending on the controller platform. The most recent platforms, such as the Catalyst 9800, transport mobility control messages over encrypted CAPWAP tunnels. Client data traffic is also transported over CAPWAP tunnels, but encryption is optional. Legacy controller platforms that are based on AireOS software prior to release 8.5 transport mobility messages over Ethernet-over-IP (EoIP) tunnels (IP protocol 97) and UDP port 16666. AireOS platforms running release 8.5 or later support encrypted CAPWAP.

If a network consists of a mix of controller platforms, you should validate that mobility messaging actually works between them. Mobility messages cannot be exchanged at all between Catalyst 9800 and AireOS platforms unless the AireOS controllers are running release 8.8.111 or later, which introduced the Inter-Release Controller Mobility (IRCM) feature.

Also, the network may have a firewall or some problem that prevents the mobility messages from being delivered successfully. You can use the commands listed in Table 8-2 from the controller CLI to verify successful messaging connectivity. Test packets are sourced from the controller's management IP address and target the far end controller's management IP address. Example output from the **cping** command is shown in Example 8-1.

Table 8-2   CLI Commands for Testing Mobility Messaging Between Controllers

Description	Command Syntax
Test mobility messaging over CAPWAP	**cping** *ip-address*
Test mobility data over EoIP	**eping** *ip-address*
Test mobility control messaging over UDP port 16666	**mping** *ip-address*

Example 8-1   *Sample Output from Testing CAPWAP Mobility Messaging to WLC 192.168.250.10*

```
(Cisco Controller) >cping 192.168.250.10
Send count=3, Receive count=3 from 192.168.250.10
(Cisco Controller) >
```

Optimizing AP Selection for Client Roaming

As a wireless client device moves around, it must roam from one AP to another to maintain good connectivity. Because the clients, and not the APs, can be in motion, they must play the active role in finding and maintaining a usable signal. Therefore, the decision to roam is normally reserved for the client device. This section explores the decision process and various methods that can make it more efficient.

Optimizing the AP Scanning Process

Wireless clients usually use a proprietary algorithm to decide when it is time to roam. Imagine a client device that begins its association very near to an AP. RF conditions there should be good, with a high RSSI (both AP at the client and client at the AP) and a high SNR. The data rate will likely be higher and 802.11 frames will be received intact and uncorrupted.

Now imagine the client as it moves away from the AP, as shown in Figure 8-10. The RSSI will get lower and lower as the client gets near the AP-1's cell boundary. SNR will also reduce because of the lower signal strength. The data rate will fall, and more frames will be lost between the client and the AP. At some point along this path, the client should realize what is happening and try to find a new, better AP to join. Hopefully the client will do this well ahead of time—before the RF conditions get too low to stay connected to the AP, with enough time to allow for the roaming process itself to take place.

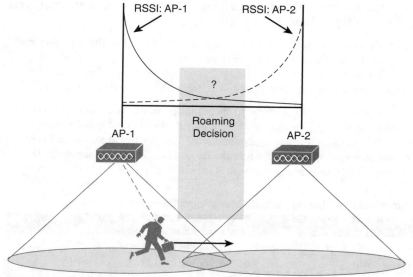

Figure 8-10   *RF Conditions as a Client Travels Between Two APs*

Generally a client device will monitor parameters such as the AP's RSSI, the SNR, data frame retries, and how the data rate is shifting before attempting to roam. The values and combination of these thresholds are usually proprietary and not configurable, and they can vary from one device to another. Some clients offer a "roaming aggressiveness" setting, which can modify the thresholds so that roaming occurs more or less frequently, but the setting values are usually generic terms such as low, medium, high, and so on.

With no outside assistance, a client device must attempt to discover any neighboring APs that might offer RF conditions that support a better connection. During times when the client radio is idle and has no data to transmit, it can scan through all of the available channels (and bands) and use one of the following methods to find candidate APs:

- **Passive scanning:** The client tunes its radio to a channel and waits a short time to receive 802.11 beacon frames from any AP and SSID.

- **Active scanning:** The client tunes its radio to a channel, transmits an 802.11 probe request frame, and then waits a period of time to receive any probe response frames from APs.

Passive scanning can be useful when a client needs to conserve battery power because it involves only receiving frames, rather than transmitting too. However, it requires the client to dwell longer on each scanned channel to wait for beacons, which are transmitted every 102 milliseconds. The client might have to wait even longer to receive a beacon that advertises the specific SSID that is needed.

In contrast, active scanning is a more efficient use of time because the client can request a specific SSID from listening APs. Probe responses are usually returned within about 10 milliseconds.

By default, client devices usually scan every possible channel in both the 2.4 and 5GHz bands. The time spent dwelling on each of many channels can cause the roaming process to become disruptive. For example, voice calls require a latency that is less than 150 milliseconds; if it takes longer than that to roam between APs, the audio quality can suffer. One solution is to reduce the total number of channels and bands to scan. Some environments may choose to disable all DFS channels on the controllers and APs. If that is done, then the same channels should be disabled on the clients as well, so that they do not waste time scanning channels that are not in use.

Optimizing with CCX Assistance

Client devices that support the Cisco Compatibility Extensions (CCX) can interact with a Cisco wireless network beyond the basic 802.11 operations. CCX can offer the following features to assist clients to roam more efficiently:

- **Roaming thresholds:** You can configure thresholds on the controller that get pushed out to clients supporting CCX version 4 or better. You can set the minimum AP RSSI (−85 dBm by default), roam hysteresis or how much greater a different AP's RSSI must be before a roam (default 3 dB), the threshold to trigger active scanning (default −72 dBm), and the maximum time for the client to complete a scan and roam (default 5 seconds).

- **Enhanced neighbor list:** As clients that support CCX version 2 or better associate with an AP, they share data about the APs they roamed from. The AP can then maintain a neighbor list to share with other clients as they associate. Compatible clients can use the list to make more efficient choices as they roam away from the AP.

- **Directed roam request:** A controller can send a request informing a client that it might benefit from roaming to a different AP from the one currently in use. The client must support CCX version 4 or better, and it may choose to follow the controller's guidance or ignore it.

> **TIP**   The CCX roaming threshold parameters can be configured per band, under **Wireless > 802.11a/n/ac > Client Roaming and Wireless > 802.11b/g/n > Client Roaming.**

Optimizing with 802.11k Assistance

A Cisco wireless network can support 802.11k, which is a standards-based method of assisted roaming. As long as the client also supports 802.11k, the APs and controllers can interact with it to suggest the need to roam, as well as a list of known-good candidate APs it can roam to. This interaction is performed with 802.11 action management frames. The following steps are taken in the assisted roaming process:

1. The AP where the client is currently associated determines that the client is moving away, as the client's RSSI is seen to be decreasing.

2. The AP informs the client that it should roam soon.

3. The client requests a list of neighboring APs from the associated AP.

4. The AP sends the client a list of neighboring APs that offer the same SSID, along with their channel numbers.

5. The client reassociates to the best AP in the neighbor list.

Notice that 802.11k places the decision to roam on the AP rather than the client. Granted, the client is still free to initiate the roam by requesting the list of candidate APs and requesting the actual reassociation, but the AP (and its controller) help with the decision process.

In fact, you might have noticed that the whole process never mentions the client using passive or active scanning to find APs. With 802.11k, the client does not need to scan on its own because the AP provides the list of candidate APs. This means the client does not have to tune its radio off-channel to scan other channels, nor does it have to expend battery power to transmit probe request frames to find APs.

In step 4, the AP sends a list of neighboring APs that is generated dynamically, rather than one that is maintained on the controller like the CCX enhanced neighbor list. The dynamic information comes from the RRM neighbor list that is collected from the NDP advertisements sent between APs. Indeed, the 802.11k standard is part of the RRM process definition.

The neighbor list sent by the AP contains up to six candidate APs the client can try. The APs are prioritized in the list according to the expected RSSI at the client location, the floor location, and the roaming history collected by the controller. The controller is able to leverage Cisco Prime Infrastructure to limit the list of neighbors to APs that are located on the same floor level as the client's current AP. The controller can also adjust the neighbor priorities to favor one AP over another, effectively load-balancing clients across APs by influencing which AP appears best for each client.

> **TIP**   You can configure 802.11k on a per-WLAN basis in the **WLANs > WLAN > Advanced** tab. By default, it is disabled. Once enabled, it can send neighbor lists only on the client's current band or on both bands.

Optimizing with 802.11v Assistance

The 802.11v amendment defines several wireless network management methods. BSS Transition can be used to influence client roaming behavior. For example, a client can send a "solicited request" to its associated AP to ask for a list of neighboring APs it might roam toward.

APs can also use 802.11v to send unsolicited requests to a client, in order to suggest that it is time for the client to roam or make a BSS transition. The client's signal strength at the AP might be getting low enough that it would actually fare better by reassociating to a different AP. Or the AP might suggest roaming as a means to lighten the client load on the current AP.

The unsolicited BSS transition requests are exactly that—the AP suggests, but does not mandate, a roam. The client is free to decide whether or not to roam; if not, the AP can continue monitoring the client and dissociate it if it does not eventually roam.

Through 802.11v, an AP can also control admission by refusing to let clients with weak RSSI to associate at all.

> **TIP**   802.11v can be enabled and configured on a per-WLAN basis in the **WLANs > WLAN > Advanced** tab.

Optimizing Security Processes for Roaming

This chapter began with a review of the four basic steps of the roaming process. The fourth step involves the interaction between the client, the AP, and perhaps a RADIUS server, to implement a secure wireless connection. Because of the complexity involved, that step can be the most time consuming. The following sections explain the problem and some solutions to make secure roaming more efficient. The solutions are commonly called "fast secure roaming" methods.

RSN in a Nutshell

The 802.11i amendment defined a robust security network (RSN) as a wireless network that leverages cryptography to secure the integrity and content of data passing between APs and their associated clients. The security measures require a hierarchy of cryptographic keys to be generated, derived, and then used during a wireless session. An RSN also requires WPA2 or WPA3 to implement the necessary key generation and mechanisms for robust security.

Recall that WPA2 and WPA3 have personal and enterprise modes that can authenticate wireless clients with a pre-shared key (PSK) and 802.1X, respectively. With a PSK, all wireless clients and APs allowed to participate in a WLAN are configured with the same key string. With 802.11X, EAP is leveraged so that an external RADIUS server can authenticate and authorize clients to connect.

8

Figure 8-11 shows an overview of the entire process when a client associates with a WLAN that is offered by an AP. Working from the top down, the client and AP must progress through the familiar 802.11 probe, open authentication, and association exchanges. This part of the process is normally quick and can be made more efficient through the features described in the previous sections.

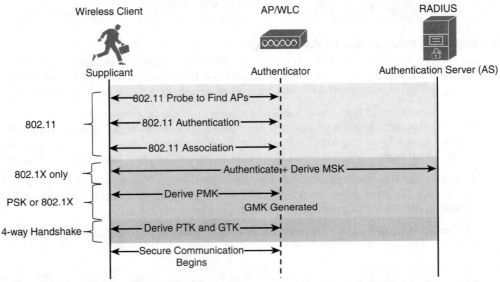

Figure 8-11 *Overview of Client Association in a Secure WLAN*

Once a client is associated with the AP, it must be authenticated and cryptographic keys generated for its session. An entire hierarchy of keys must be generated, beginning with the Master Session Key (MSK). If WPA2-Personal or WPA3-Personal is in use, then the MSK is derived from the pre-shared key. Otherwise, the MSK is derived during the EAP exchange as the client is authenticated by the RADIUS server. In turn, a Pairwise Master Key (PMK) is derived from the MSK and will be used to derive further keys involved with unicast communication and the client. Refer to Figure 8-12 for an overview of the key hierarchy, acronyms, and the order in which they are derived from each other.

The controller also generates a Group Master Key (GMK) that will be used to derive further keys to protect multicast and broadcast traffic. Because the GMK is used for broadcast and multicast traffic, it is meant for multiple clients at a time. Therefore, the GMK is generated independently of any client association, but keys derived from it will be shared with each client associated to the WLAN.

Once the master keys are ready, the client and the AP (actually its controller) must undergo an exchange of four EAP over LAN (EAPoL) frames. This is known as the *4-way handshake*, which is used to derive the pairwise (PTK) and group (GTK) temporal keys. These keys will become the basis for any further keys that are needed to protect the data integrity (MIC) and encrypt the data contents (AES) of wireless frames to and from the one specific client.

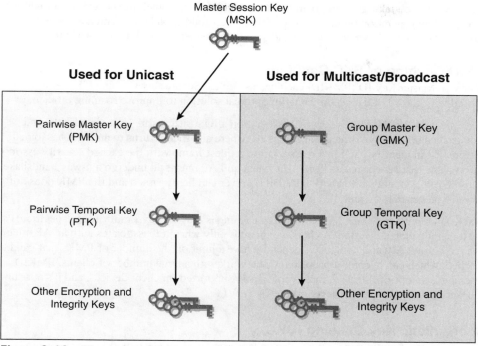

Figure 8-12 *Hierarchy of Cryptographic Keys Derived for an RSN Client*

The description here is meant to give an overview of the many keys involved in securing wireless traffic. Indeed, there are many keys and acronyms involved. Just remember that master keys produce temporal keys, that pairwise keys are specific to a client, and that group keys are used for multiple clients.

Then remember that the whole process of authenticating with 802.1X and generating keys is complex and lengthy. Why is that important? By default, 802.1X will block any data traffic going to or from the client until the client can be authenticated through EAP and its wireless session secured. In the meantime, the client must simply wait until communication can begin. That might not matter too much during an initial association with an AP, as data has not yet begun to flow anyway.

Any time a client roams to a different AP, it must go through the entire process shown in Figure 8-11 again because it must be authenticated at the new AP. New cryptographic keys must be generated again because they are not shared among APs. This process can take a second or more to complete. During that time, the client must wait and any data flow already in progress will be disrupted—something that becomes very noticeable to voice and real-time applications. In other words, such a roam is not seamless at all.

One other sometimes unexpected outcome is the impact that secure roaming has on the authentication resources. Consider a large university where many large classrooms are full of people. While classes are in session, large populations of users are sitting still and are mostly not roaming. Most classes begin and end at the same time, so all students go into motion at roughly the same time. This results in large bursts of authentications, which can tax the RADIUS resources.

The solution to making secure roaming more seamless is to somehow shorten the authentication and key generation processes. The sections that follow explain several approaches that you can leverage in a wireless design, along with the benefits and drawbacks of each.

PMKID Caching or SKC Caching

Pairwise Master Key ID (PMKID) caching, also called Secure Key Caching (SKC), was introduced with the 802.11i amendment as an optional solution to improve roaming efficiency.

The client and an AP form a security association after a successful 4-way handshake and key exchange process. If the client roams elsewhere and then returns to an AP it has joined before, it can identify itself in a reassociation request frame with the cached security association name that references its PMK. The client and AP must still undergo a 4-way handshake, but the full EAP interaction with a RADIUS server can be bypassed and the PMK does not have to be generated again.

PMKID Caching has some limitations. The caching is only locally significant to specific APs, so it is not a global solution. A client can benefit only when it reassociates with an AP it has visited before. APs and controllers generally have a limit on the number of PMKs that can be cached, which can become a problem in a network with a large number of clients. PMKID caching is an optional feature that is not widely supported on client devices, and it's not supported during inter-controller roams on Cisco WLCs.

Opportunistic Key Caching (OKC)

Opportunistic Key Caching (OKC), also called Proactive Key Caching (PKC), is very similar to PMKID Caching because one PMK is generated and cached per client. The PMK is cached for the lifetime of the client on the WLAN and is shared across all APs that are joined to the same controller.

OKC differs from PMKID because only one PMKID is needed per client. Clients can reassociate to any AP, with no prior association, as long as OKC has shared the client's PMK information ahead of time. OKC is limited by its support across platforms because it is not defined in the 802.11 standard.

Preauthentication

Preauthentication was also introduced in the 802.11i amendment. Its goal is to allow a client to associate with an AP and then instruct the AP to send enough information on to a list of neighboring APs so that they can preauthenticate the client even while it has not yet associated with them. The AP-to-AP communication occurs over the distribution system (DS). Each of the neighbor APs can run through the EAP authentication and PMK generation for the client ahead of time. Then, when the client moves and reassociates to one of the neighboring APs, it can bypass the time-consuming EAP and PMK steps and move directly into the 4-way handshake.

Preauthentication has more limitations than benefits. For example, it was never widely adopted and is not supported on Cisco APs or WLCs at all. RADIUS resources can become taxed as clients attempt preauthentication with multiple APs in an area.

CCKM

Cisco Centralized Key Management (CCKM) is a proprietary fast secure roaming method. A wireless client goes through the entire EAP authentication and 4-way handshake and then the controller caches the client's PMK for 1 hour. If the client roams back to the original AP or to a different AP on the same controller, the PMK is already cached, so only the PTK needs to be generated. That means the reassociated client can skip both the EAP and the 4-way handshake processes.

CCKM also works across multiple controllers and mobility groups because the controllers pass the client's credential information as part of the mobility handoff. However, it is Cisco proprietary and requires a client to run a CCX version that supports the specific EAP method in use. For example, WPA2 with 802.1X, AES, and EAP-TLS require CCX version 4 or 5.

802.11r: Fast BSS Transition (FT)

The 802.11r amendment defines a standards-based technique for fast transition between APs. The technique is similar to the other fast secure roaming techniques presented in this chapter, as client key material is shared among APs to preauthenticate the client. However, 802.11r leverages a clever twist to the roaming process itself to make the transition even more efficient.

A client capable of using 802.11r begins with a full AP association, as shown in Figure 8-13. The figure looks very similar to the normal AP association process from Figure 8-11, with two small changes. During the 802.11 authentication and association request/response exchanges, the client signals that it would like to use 802.11r by including RSN and FT information elements within the frame contents of its requests. If the AP also supports 802.11r FT, it includes those elements in its responses. The frames also contain information about the keys that will be involved in the client's secure session.

You might have noticed another change in the key derivations in the "PSK or 802.1X" portion of the figure. The 802.11r still depends on a hierarchy of cryptographic keys, but it expands on the scope and use. As a result, the key names are somewhat different from normal RSN keys. Every client still has an MSK, but the PMK is split in two. PMK-R0 is derived from the MSK, while PMK-R1 is derived from PMK-R0. The basic idea is to distribute a client's PMK material across multiple "key holders" within the network. For example, a client's PMK-R0 might be held by a controller while PMK-R1 is held by some APs. Each client still derives a PTK and a GTK with the PMK-R1 holder.

Like every other fast secure roaming scheme, the 802.11r initial association process is not very different from normal. The efficiency gains come from steps in the reassociation that can be bypassed. Figure 8-14 shows a typical 802.11r roam and reassociation. At the top of the figure, the client is associated with AP-1 for its data connection; at the bottom, the client has reassociated with AP-2. The step for 802.1X and EAP exchange has been bypassed, as well as the step for PMK generation. Did you notice that the 4-way EAPOL handshake for PTK and GTK keys is also missing?

8

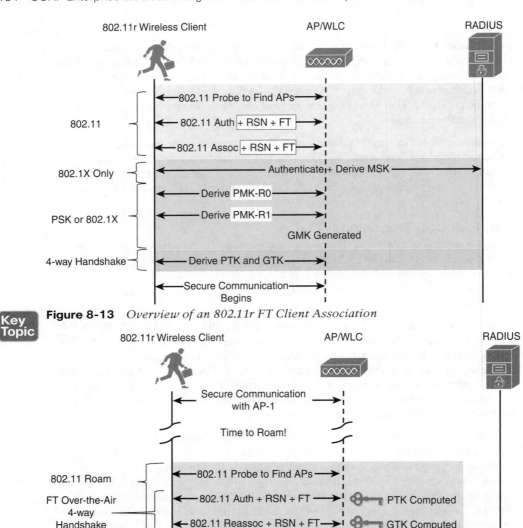

Figure 8-13   *Overview of an 802.11r FT Client Association*

Figure 8-14   *Steps Required During an 802.11r FT Client Roam*

The handshake is cleverly moved to coincide with the 802.11 open authentication and reassociation exchanges, which occur at the very beginning of every roam. Enough of the higher-level key information about the client's prior 802.1X and security association is shared across controllers and APs within the mobility domain, even before the client needs to roam anywhere.

Along with the normal 802.11 content, the client adds RSN and FT information elements into its authentication and reassociation request frames. The AP works with the same elements in its response frames. The client begins by presenting information about its PMK-R0 key and key holder; then the AP references the PMK-R1 key and holder. If the key information checks out, the client and AP can go ahead and generate the PTK and GTK keys—even while the client is authenticating and reassociating! Once the AP sends a reassociation response frame, the client can begin using a fully secured connection.

The FT process bypasses EAP and the usual 4-way handshake during reassociations for both PSK and 802.1X clients. To accomplish an efficient roam, a client can participate in an FT 4-way handshake in an over-the-air or over-the-DS exchange. With over-the-air, the client is free to contact the next AP directly for the FT 4-way handshake. In contrast, over-the-DS requires the currently associated AP to relay the FT 4-way handshake to the new AP over the DS or wired network. In practice, over-the-DS is rarely implemented and used by clients.

Because of the unique handshake and key structure, 802.11r can work only if both the client and the AP/controller can support it. In fact, the client must signal to the AP that it wants to use FT. What if a network has clients that are not capable of FT? The 802.11r amendment defines a mixed or hybrid mode that is supposed to work with FT and non-FT clients, but some legacy clients still are not able to understand the necessary information elements. Cisco WLCs also offer an adaptive mode that supports even clients that are not able to recognize the RSN information elements in frames.

Fast Secure Roaming Review

This chapter has covered a variety of common methods to improve roaming efficiency in a robust secure network. As you review and compare the methods, be sure you understand the process that a wireless client goes through to join a secure WLAN. Specifically, remember where the 4-way handshake lies in the order of steps, and remember that most of the methods try to bypass the time-consuming 802.1X/EAP authentication and PMK generation steps. You can also refer to Table 8-3 to review the benefits and limitations of each method.

Table 8-3   A Summary of Common Fast Secure Roaming Methods

Fast Secure Roaming Method	Roaming Benefits	Limitations
PMKID Caching, SKC	■ Bypasses 802.1X/EAP and PMK generation steps	■ Optional ■ Not widely supported ■ Does not work for inter-controller roams
Opportunistic Key Caching (OKC), Proactive Key Caching (PKC)	■ Bypasses 802.1X/EAP and PMK generation steps ■ One PMKID per client for lifetime on WLAN ■ PMK shared across all APs	■ Not defined in 802.11 standard ■ Not widely or consistently supported
Preauthentication	■ Bypasses 802.1X/EAP and PMK generation steps	■ Not widely adopted ■ Not supported on Cisco WLCs ■ Bursty EAP activity can tax RADIUS servers

Fast Secure Roaming Method	Roaming Benefits	Limitations
CCKM	■ Bypasses 802.1X/EAP, PMK generation, and 4-way handshake	■ Cisco proprietary ■ Requires client with CCX version that supports specific EAP method
802.11r, Fast BSS Transition (FT)	■ Standards based ■ Bypasses 802.1X/EAP, PMK generation, and 4-way handshake ■ Adaptive mode can work with FT-capable and non-FT clients	■ Requires support on client and AP/controller

Summary

This chapter described the main considerations needed to design a wireless network that maximizes client mobility and roaming. More precisely, you have learned the following:

■ How client roaming is handled by various controller topologies

■ How you can leverage logical mobility groups to organize controllers and their APs

■ How you can verify mobility communications between controllers

■ How wireless clients discover available APs and how the 802.11k and 802.11v features can make roaming more efficient

■ How various fast secure roaming features operate and can maximize roaming efficiency

Exam Preparation Tasks

As mentioned in the section "How to Use This Book" in the Introduction, you have a few choices for exam preparation: the exercises here, Chapter 18, "Final Preparation," and the exam simulation questions in the Pearson Test Prep Software Online.

Review All Key Topics

Review the most important topics in this chapter, noted with the Key Topic icon in the outer margin of the page. Table 8-4 lists these key topics and the page numbers on which each is found.

Table 8-4 Key Topics for Chapter 8

Key Topic Element	Description	Page Number
List	Client association process	167
Figure 8-2	Intra-controller roaming	168
Figure 8-3	Inter-controller roaming	169

Key Topic Element	Description	Page Number
Figure 8-4	Layer 3 roaming	170
Figure 8-6	Mobility domain and groups	173
Table 8-2	Commands for testing mobility messaging between controllers	175
Figure 8-11	Client association in a secure WLAN	180
Figure 8-13	802.11r client association process	184
Figure 8-14	802.11r fast transition roaming process	184

Define Key Terms

Define the following key terms from this chapter and check your answers in the glossary:

802.11k, 802.11r, 802.11v, anchor controller, association, CCKM, fast BSS transition (FT), foreign controller, inter-controller roaming, intra-controller roaming, Layer 2 roam, Layer 3 roam, mobility domain, mobility group, Opportunistic Key Caching (OKC), PMKID Caching, point of attachment (POA), point of presence (POP), preauthentication, proactive key caching (PKC), reassociation, SKC Caching

8

CHAPTER 9

Designing High Availability

This chapter covers the following topics:

Making Controller Connectivity More Resilient: This section describes a method of bundling multiple physical ports into a single logical link so that the wireless network can survive controller port failures.

Designing High Availability for APs: This section explains how APs can detect a controller failure, how they can join other controllers in an orderly fashion, and how they can automatically fall back to their original controllers after service has been restored.

Designing High Availability for Controllers: This section covers various approaches that can be used to offer redundant controllers and minimize the impact of a controller failure.

This chapter covers the following ENWLSD exam topics:

- 4.0 WLAN High Availability

- 4.1 Design high availability for controllers

  - 4.1.a Network availability through LAG

  - 4.1.b Stateful Switchover (SSO)

- 4.2 Design high availability for APs

  - 4.2.a AP prioritization

  - 4.2.b Fallback (assigning primary, secondary, and tertiary)

Cisco lightweight wireless access points normally need to be paired with a wireless LAN controller to provide a functional wireless network. If the controller fails for some reason, wireless service could be interrupted. This chapter discusses several features and mechanisms you can leverage to make wireless controllers more resilient and redundant, thus improving network availability for the end user.

"Do I Know This Already?" Quiz

The "Do I Know This Already?" quiz allows you to assess whether you should read this entire chapter thoroughly or jump to the "Exam Preparation Tasks" section. If you are in doubt about your answers to these questions or your own assessment of your knowledge of the topics, read the entire chapter. Table 9-1 lists the major headings in this chapter and their corresponding "Do I Know This Already?" quiz questions. You can find the answers in Appendix D, "Answers to the 'Do I Know This Already?' Quizzes and Review Questions."

Table 9-1 "Do I Know This Already?" Section-to-Question Mapping

Foundation Topics Section	Questions
Making Controller Connectivity More Resilient	1–3
Designing High Availability for APs	4–7
Designing High Availability for Controllers	8–10

1. Which of the following are likely reasons you would configure a LAG on a WLC?

    a. To bind two controllers together into a logical HA pair

    b. To make client roaming more efficient

    c. To load-balance traffic across multiple links

    d. To add redundancy to the WLC's distribution ports

2. When you configure multiple distribution ports on a WLC to form a single logical link, you are forming which one of the following?

    a. A MAP

    b. A LAG

    c. An SSO

    d. A CAPWAP

3. Suppose you have configured a LAG on a controller. Which one of the following lists the negotiation method that must be used between the switch and the controller to successfully bring up the LAG?

    a. PAgP

    b. LACP

    c. GLBP

    d. None; the LAG cannot be negotiated.

4. Which one of the following makes a controller failure most disruptive to connected clients?

    a. The controller must take time to find a replacement for itself.

    b. The clients must take time to find a new controller to join.

    c. The APs must take time to find a new controller to join.

    d. The clients must wait for the Spanning Tree Protocol to unblock the links from the APs to the new controller.

5. You can configure the priority value on an AP to accomplish which one of the following?

    a. To set the controller it will try to join first

    b. To define which APs will be preferred when joining a controller

    c. To set the SSID that will be advertised first

    d. To identify the least loaded controller to join

6. Which one of the following is the default AP priority value?

   a. Low

   b. Medium

   c. High

   d. Critical

7. By default, which one of the following methods and intervals does an AP use to detect a failed controller?

   a. ICMP, 60 seconds

   b. ICMP, 30 seconds

   c. CAPWAP keepalive, 60 seconds

   d. CAPWAP keepalive, 30 seconds

   e. CAPWAP discovery, 30 seconds

8. Suppose that an AP is joined to the WLC that is configured as the primary controller. At a later time, that controller fails and the AP joins its secondary controller. Once the primary controller is restored to service, which feature would allow the AP to rejoin it again?

   a. CAPWAP Rejoin

   b. AP Failover

   c. AP Priority

   d. AP Fallback

9. Suppose a wireless design consists of two controllers and a number of APs. The APs are distributed equally across the two controllers. Each AP is configured with one controller as primary and the other controller as secondary. Based on this information, which one of the following redundancy models is being used?

   a. No redundancy

   b. N+1 redundancy

   c. N+N redundancy

   d. N+N+1 redundancy

   e. SSO redundancy

10. Which one of the following controller redundancy designs is the least disruptive to APs and wireless clients when a controller fails?

    a. N+1 redundancy

    b. N+N redundancy

    c. N+N+1 redundancy

    d. SSO redundancy

Foundation Topics

A wireless network design is generally successful if the network is accessible in the places where users are located and the performance is satisfactory for the number of users gathered there. In other words, the network should be available, convenient, and efficient. At first glance, network availability might mean that a user can detect and join a live network.

Keeping a wireless network alive involves much more than providing RF coverage. Figure 9-1 illustrates the basic building blocks of a wireless network (labeled A through F), along with icons that denote possible failure points. Notice that each building block, including links between them, can potentially fail. To make the network highly available, you should consider ways to improve each component's resiliency.

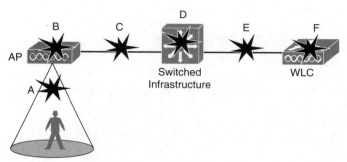

Figure 9-1 *Basic Wireless Network Building Blocks and Potential Failures*

Table 9-2 lists the potential failure points illustrated in Figure 9-1. Some components, such as switch redundancy (D), can be provided by following LAN switching network design best practices. Failures of the RF signal (A) and an AP (B) can be addressed manually, with a wireless design that places APs such that they completely overlap each other's cell coverage, or automatically, through the use of Radio Resource Management (RRM), which is covered in more detail in Chapter 6, "Designing Radio Management." Failures at the WLC level (E and F) can be mitigated by using design strategies presented in the sections that follow.

Table 9-2 Wireless Network Failure Points

	Component	Failure Mitigation
A	RF signal	Augment the coverage hole of missing RF with signals from neighboring APs.
B	AP	Augment RF coverage hole with signals from neighboring APs; could co-locate APs on different channels for full fault tolerance.
C	AP uplink	None; APs usually support only one wired Ethernet connection.
D	Switch	Leverage switch stacking or pairing for redundancy, multiple links between switch layers.
E	Controller uplink	Leverage multiple links between WLC and switches.
F	Wireless LAN controller	Design and configure WLC high-availability features, AP Fallback, and anchor controller redundancy.

TIP Because the exam objectives covered in this chapter all begin with "design," you should not expect to know how to configure the high-availability features on a WLC. Even so, each section ends with a tip that explains where you can find the relevant settings in a controller's GUI.

Making Controller Connectivity More Resilient

Wireless LAN controllers have several distribution system ports that make physical connections to an external wired or switched network. These ports carry most of the data coming to and going from the controller. For example, the CAPWAP tunnels (control and data) that extend to each of a controller's APs pass across the distribution system ports. Client data also passes from wireless LANs to wired VLANs over the ports. In addition, any management traffic using a web browser, Secure Shell (SSH), Simple Network Management Protocol (SNMP), Trivial File Transfer Protocol (TFTP), and so on, normally reaches the controller in-band through the ports.

> **TIP**   You might be thinking that "distribution system ports" is an odd name for what appear to be regular data ports. Recall that the wired network that connects APs together is called the distribution system (DS). With the split MAC architecture, the point where APs touch the DS is moved upstream to the WLC instead, through the distribution system ports.

Because the distribution system ports must carry data that is associated with many different VLANs, VLAN tags and numbers become very important. For that reason, the distribution system ports always operate in 802.1Q trunking mode. When you connect the ports to a switch, you should also configure the switch ports for unconditional 802.1Q trunk mode.

The distribution system ports can operate independently, each one transporting multiple VLANs to a unique group of internal controller interfaces. However, if the link to one port fails for some reason, the controller would lose connectivity for the VLANs being carried over the port. For resiliency, you can configure distribution system ports in redundant pairs. One port is primarily used; if it fails, a backup port is used instead.

To get the most use out of each distribution system port, you can configure all of them to operate as a single logical group, much like an EtherChannel or port-channel on a switch. Controller distribution system ports can be configured as a link aggregation group (LAG) such that they are bundled together to act as one larger link. In Figure 9-2, the four distribution system ports are configured as a single logical LAG.

With a LAG configuration, traffic can be load-balanced across the individual ports that make up the LAG. The switch will compute a hash based on parameters in a packet's IP header to decide which port to use to reach the WLC. For example, suppose an AP sends a CAPWAP packet to the WLC. The switch can use the source and destination IP addresses from the packet, as well as other methods, to select an egress port. As long as the switch is configured to use IP addresses as a load-balancing method, and as long as the IP addresses vary, the switch will be able to distribute traffic across the links in the LAG. The WLC uses a different method for its outbound traffic across the LAG—packets are sent over the same port they arrived on. When the WLC receives a CAPWAP packet from an AP, it un-encapsulates the contents and forwards the packet onto the corresponding VLAN. That VLAN is reached through the switch, so the controller sends the packet out the same port where the incoming CAPWAP packet was received. As long as the switch is evenly distributing the packets it sends to the controller, the controller will follow suit with traffic it sends back across the LAG links.

The LAG also offers resiliency; if one individual link fails for some reason, traffic will be automatically redirected to the remaining working links instead. Even if multiple links fail, traffic will continue to be forwarded in and out of the WLC as long as at least one working link remains.

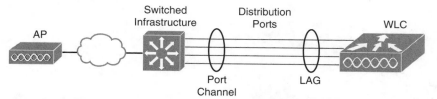

Figure 9-2 *Cisco WLC Distribution System Ports Configured as a Single LAG*

The LAG depicted in Figure 9-2 does increase the controller's availability by keeping it connected to the switch. However, the switch can become a single point of failure if it goes offline or has a faulty line card. A better design distributes the individual links of the LAG across multiple line cards in a single physical switch, across a stack of switches, or across a pair of switches configured as a single logical switch. The design shown in Figure 9-3 can survive a switch failure and individual link failures.

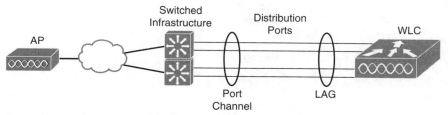

Figure 9-3 *Improving WLC Availability by Distributing Links of the LAG*

TIP Be aware that even though the LAG acts as a traditional EtherChannel, Cisco WLCs do not support any link aggregation negotiation protocol, like LACP or PAgP, at all. Therefore, you must configure the switch ports as an unconditional or always-on EtherChannel. You can configure and verify the LAG mode by going to **Controller > General > LAG Mode on next reboot.**

Designing High Availability for APs

Cisco lightweight wireless access points need to be paired with a wireless LAN controller to function. Each AP must discover and bind itself with a controller before wireless clients can be supported. An AP can discover and build a list of live candidate controllers through prior knowledge of WLCs, DHCP and DNS information, or by broadcasting on the local subnet to solicit controllers. Once an AP has discovered, selected, and joined a controller, it must stay joined to that controller to remain functional.

Now consider that a single controller might support as many as 1,000 or even 6,000 APs— enough to cover a very large building or an entire enterprise. If something ever causes the controller to fail, a large number of APs would fail along with it. In the worst case, where a single controller carries the enterprise, the entire wireless network would become unavailable. That might be catastrophic.

Fortunately, Cisco APs can discover multiple controllers—not just the one that it chooses to join. Figure 9-4 shows this scenario, where the AP has joined WLC-A. If the joined controller becomes unavailable, the AP can simply select the next least-loaded controller and request to join it, as Figure 9-5 depicts. That sounds simple, but it is not very deterministic.

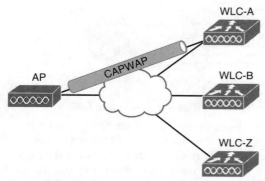

Figure 9-4   *An AP Joins One of Several Discovered Controllers*

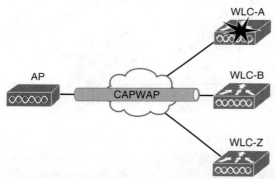

Figure 9-5   *An AP Joins a Different Controller After WLC-A Fails*

For example, if a controller full of 1,000 APs fails, all 1,000 APs must detect the failure, discover other candidate controllers, and then select the least loaded one to join. During that time, wireless clients can be left stranded with no connectivity. You might envision the controller failure as a commercial airline flight that has just been canceled; everyone who purchased a ticket suddenly joins a mad rush to find another flight out.

The most deterministic approach is to leverage the primary, secondary, and tertiary controller fields that every AP stores in nonvolatile memory. Even after a reboot or power failure, the AP will remember the controllers it has "primed" in its configuration. If any of these fields are configured with a controller name or address, the AP knows which three controllers to try in sequence before resorting to a more generic search. Be aware that a controller name is not the same as its DNS entry; rather, it is the name string configured on the individual controller.

> **TIP** When an AP boots and builds a list of potential controllers, it can use CAPWAP to build a tunnel to more than one controller. The AP will join only one controller, which it uses as the primary unit. By building a tunnel with a second controller ahead of time, before the primary controller fails, the AP will not have to spend time building a tunnel to the backup controller before joining it.

> **TIP** You can find the primary, secondary, and tertiary controller fields on an AireOS WLC by going to **Wireless > All APs**, selecting an AP's name, and then selecting the **High Availability** tab.

AP Prioritization

As a wireless network grows, you might have several controllers implemented just to support the number of APs that are required. Each WLC platform is rated to support a maximum number of APs and must be licensed for some number of concurrently joined APs. It is not enough just to have multiple controllers in a network, even if they can all handle the total number of APs in use. A good network design should also take failures and high availability (HA) into consideration. What if the controllers are all in use and full of APs? If one of the controllers fails, there would not be enough room to spare for a large group of additional, displaced APs to join in their time of need. In the commercial flight analogy, there might be other flights departing the airport soon after the cancellation. If those flights are already mostly full of passengers, many people will be left waiting at the gate.

Figure 9-6 illustrates an example network that does not offer enough capacity to fully survive a controller failure. In the "before" diagram, a group of 400 APs has joined controller WLC-A, and a group of 300 APs has joined WLC-B. Suppose each controller has a maximum capacity of 500 APs. As long as both controllers stay up and functional, the wireless network should work fine. In the "after" diagram, WLC-A has failed. All 400 APs that were previously joined to WLC-A will discover that WLC-B is alive, so they will all try to join it. WLC-B already has 300 APs, so it has room for only 200 more. That means the first 200 APs to request to join WLC-B will be able to, but 200 more will be left out in the cold with no controller to join at all. Once controller WLC-B has the maximum number of APs joined to it, it will reject any additional APs.

To provide some flexibility in supporting APs on an oversubscribed controller, where more APs are trying to join than a license allows, you can configure the APs with a priority value. All APs begin with a default priority of low. You can change the value to low, medium, high, or critical. A controller will try to accommodate as many higher-priority APs as possible. Once a controller is full of APs, it will reject an AP with the lowest priority to make room for a new one that has a higher priority.

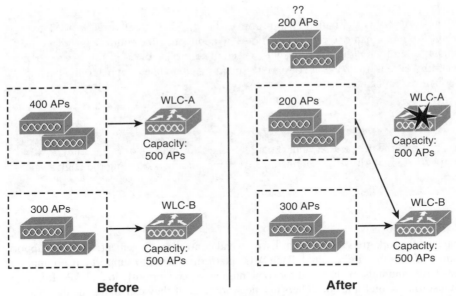

Figure 9-6   *The Result of Undersized Controllers During a Failure*

TIP   You can find the AP priority setting by going to **Wireless > All APs** and selecting an AP's name. Select the **High Availability** tab and look for the **AP Failover Priority** drop-down menu.

Detecting a Controller Failure

When HA is required, make sure you design your wireless network to support it properly. Fortunately, Cisco APs and controllers are built with HA in mind, so you have several strategies at your disposal. First, it is important to understand how APs detect a controller failure and what action they take to recover from it.

Once an AP joins a controller, it sends keepalive (also called heartbeat) messages to the controller over the wired network at regular intervals. By default, keepalives are sent every 30 seconds. The controller is expected to answer each keepalive as evidence that it is still alive and working. If a keepalive is not answered, an AP will escalate the test by sending four more keepalives at 3-second intervals. If the controller answers, all is well; if it does not answer, the AP presumes that the controller has failed. The AP then moves quickly to find a successor to join.

Using the default values, an AP can detect a controller failure in as little as 35 seconds. You can adjust the regular keepalive timer between 1 and 30 seconds and the escalated or "fast" heartbeat timer between 1 and 10 seconds. By using the minimum values, a failure can be detected after only 6 seconds.

> **TIP**   You can find the keepalive and fast heartbeat timer settings by going to **Wireless >
> Access Points > Global Configuration** and looking under the **High Availability** section of
> parameters.

AP Fallback

Normally, an AP will stay joined to a controller until it fails. If the AP has been configured
with primary and secondary controller information, it will join the primary controller first.
If the primary fails, the AP will try to join the secondary until it fails. Even if the primary
controller is put back into service, the AP will stay with the secondary. You can change that
behavior by enabling the AP Fallback feature—a global controller configuration parameter.
If AP Fallback is enabled (the default), an AP can try to rejoin its primary controller at any
time, whether its current controller has failed or not.

> **TIP**   You can find this feature setting under **Controller > General > AP Fallback**.

Designing High Availability for Controllers

Building a wireless network with one controller and some APs is straightforward, but it does
not address what would happen if the controller fails for some reason. Adding another controller or two could provide some redundancy, as long as the APs know how to move from
one controller to another when the time comes.

Redundancy is best configured in the most deterministic way possible, such that APs know
exactly what action to take if a controller fails, in the most efficient way possible. In other
words, the APs should be able to recover from a failure event with a minimal disruption to
the wireless users. The following sections explain how you can configure APs with primary,
secondary, and tertiary controller fields to implement various forms of redundancy. The sections present a progression from basic to robust. As you read through the sections, keep in
mind that redundant controllers should be configured consistently so that APs can move
from one controller to another and operate exactly as before.

> **TIP**   The following sections discuss WLC high availability for APs operating within an
> enterprise. For APs operating in FlexConnect mode, refer to Chapter 10, "Implementing
> FlexConnect," to learn more about how high availability works with FlexConnect.

N+1 Redundancy

The simplest way to introduce HA into a Cisco wireless network is to provide an extra
backup controller. This is commonly called N+1 or N:1 redundancy, where N represents
some number of active controllers and 1 denotes the one backup controller.

By having one backup controller, N+1 redundancy can withstand a failure of only one active
controller. As long as the backup controller is sized appropriately, it can accept all of a
failed controller's APs. However, once an active controller fails and all its APs rehome to the
backup controller, there will be no space to accept any other APs if a second controller fails.

9

Figure 9-7 illustrates N+1 redundancy with a two-controller network for simplicity. The network could have any number of active controllers but only one backup controller. WLC-A is the active controller and normally carries 100 percent of the network's APs. WLC-Z is the backup controller, which normally carries no APs at all. The backup controller sits idle until an active controller fails.

To configure N+1 redundancy, you configure the primary controller field on all APs with the name or IP address of an active controller (WLC-A, for example). The secondary controller field is set to the name or address of the backup controller (WLC-Z).

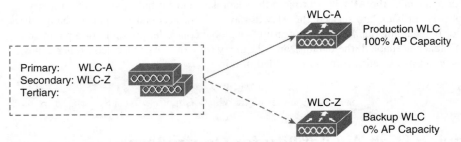

Figure 9-7   *A Design Using N+1 Controller Redundancy*

N+N Redundancy

N+1 design is simple, but it has a couple of shortcomings. First, the backup controller must sit idle and empty of APs until another controller fails. That might not sound like a problem, except that the backup unit must be purchased with the same AP license capacity as the active controller it supports. That means the active and backup controllers must be purchased at the same price. Having a full-price device sit empty and idle might seem like a poor use of funds.

Second, the backup controller must be configured identically to every other active controller it has to support. The idea is to make a controller failure as seamless as possible so the APs should not have any noticeable configuration differences when they move from one controller to another.

The N+N redundancy strategy tries to make better use of the available controllers. N+N gets its name from grouping controllers in pairs. If you have one active controller, you would pair it with one other controller; two controllers would be paired with two others, and so on. You might also see the same strategy called N:N or 1+1.

By grouping controllers in pairs, you can divide the active role across two separate devices. This makes better use of the AP capacity on each controller. Also, the APs' and clients' loads will be distributed across separate hardware while still supporting redundancy during a failure. N+N redundancy can support failures of more than one controller, but only if the active controllers are configured in pairs.

Figure 9-8 illustrates the N+N scenario consisting of two controllers: WLC-A and WLC-B. The APs are divided into two groups—one that joins WLC-A as primary controller and another that joins WLC-B as primary. Notice that the primary and secondary controllers are reversed between the two groups of APs. To support the full set of APs during a failure, each controller must not be loaded with more than 50 percent of its AP capacity.

Rather than having an extra controller sitting idle waiting for another controller to fail, N+N puts all of the controllers to use. However, it also requires more controllers and licenses than you actually need. N+N is an extremely reliable but extremely expensive solution.

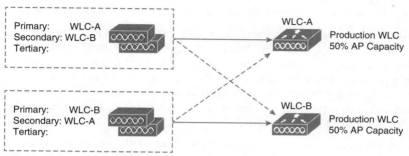

Figure 9-8 *A Design Using N+N Controller Redundancy*

N+N+1 Redundancy

What if a scenario calls for more resiliency than the N+N plan can provide? You can simply add one more controller to the mix, as a backup unit. As you might expect, this is commonly called N+N+1 redundancy and combines the advantages of the N+N and N+1 strategies.

Two or more active controllers are configured to share the AP and client load, while reserving some AP capacity for use during a failure. One additional backup controller is set aside as an additional safety net. Figure 9-9 shows a simple example using three controllers—two active (WLC-A and WLC-B) and one backup (WLC-Z). Like N+N redundancy, the two groups of APs are configured with primary and secondary controllers that are the reverse of each other. Each group of APs is also configured with a tertiary controller that points to the backup unit.

If one active controller fails, APs that were joined to it will move to the secondary controller. As long as the two active controllers are not loaded with over 50 percent of their AP capacity, either one may accept the full number of APs. N+N+1 goes one step further; if the other active controller happens to fail, the backup controller is available to carry the load. This means that the active controllers can be loaded to more than 50 percent each because the backup controller will be available to share the load when an active controller fails.

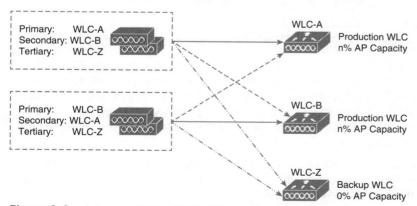

Figure 9-9 *A Design Using N+N+1 Controller Redundancy*

SSO Redundancy

The N+1, N+N, and N+N+1 strategies all address redundancy and fault tolerance, but each still relies on the basic controller discovery and join processes. In other words, APs require a certain amount of time to detect a failed controller and to seek out a new one to join. That process can be disruptive to wireless client devices that are using the network at the time.

You can use stateful switchover (SSO) redundancy on WLCs to maximize redundancy and minimize disruption. SSO groups controllers into HA pairs, where one controller takes on the active role while the other is in a hot standby mode. Only the active unit must be purchased with the appropriate license to support the AP count. The standby unit is purchased with an HA license, allowing it to be paired with an active unit of any license size. The standby unit never needs an actual license count because it inherits the licenses when it takes on the active role from another licensed controller.

Figure 9-10 depicts SSO redundancy. The APs can be configured with only a primary controller name that references the name or IP address of the active unit. The active and standby units keep their configurations synchronized so that the standby unit is always ready to take over if needed. In case the active controller fails, the standby controller becomes active and assumes the previous active unit's IP address. Therefore, the APs need to know about only the active unit. Because each active controller has its own hot standby controller, there really is no need to configure a secondary or tertiary controller on the APs unless you need an additional layer of redundancy. To achieve that extra redundancy, you could set up controllers in HA pairs and then configure the active controller of each pair as the primary, secondary, and tertiary controllers.

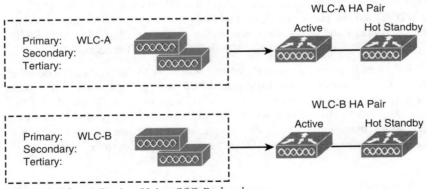

Figure 9-10   *A Design Using SSO Redundancy*

Each AP learns of the active unit in the HA pair during a CAPWAP discovery phase and then builds a CAPWAP tunnel to the active controller. The active unit keeps CAPWAP tunnels, AP states, client states, configurations, and image files all in sync with the hot standby unit. If the active unit fails, the hot standby unit quickly takes over the active role. The APs do not have to discover another controller to join; the controllers simply swap roles so the APs can stay joined to the active controller in the HA pair.

The APs do not even have to rebuild their CAPWAP tunnels after a failure. The tunnels are synchronized between active and standby, so they are always maintained. The SSO switchover occurs at the controllers—not at the APs.

The active controller also synchronizes the state of each associated client that is in the RUN state with the hot standby controller. If the active fails, the standby will already have the current state information for each client, making the failover process transparent to the end users. HA synchronization takes place over a special *redundancy port* that connects the active and hot standby units in an HA pair.

The hot standby controller monitors the active unit through keepalives that are sent every 100 ms. If a keepalive is not answered, the standby unit begins to send ICMP echo requests to the active unit to determine what sort of failure has occurred. For example, the active unit could have crashed, lost power, or had its network connectivity severed.

Once the hot standby unit has declared the active unit as failed, it assumes the active role. The failover may take up to 500 ms, in the case of a crash or power failure, or up to 4 seconds if a network failure has occurred.

SSO is designed to keep the failover process transparent from the AP's perspective, as well as the client's. In fact, the APs know only of the active unit; they are not even aware that the hot standby unit exists. The two controllers share a "mobility" MAC address that initially comes from the first active unit's MAC address. From then on, that address is maintained by whichever unit has the active role at any given time. The controllers also share a common virtual management IP address. Keeping both MAC and IP addresses virtual and consistent allows the APs to stay in contact with the active controller—regardless of which controller currently has that role.

Summary

This chapter described the main considerations needed to design a wireless network that maximizes availability for the end users. More precisely, you have learned the following:

- How wireless controllers can support multiple links to scale performance and tolerate faults

- How multiple wireless controllers can handle the AP load and offer greater availability if one fails

- How controller redundancy is classified according to the number of active and standby controllers

- How stateful switchover (SSO) can be leveraged to maximize controller redundancy and minimize disruption

Exam Preparation Tasks

As mentioned in the section "How to Use This Book" in the Introduction, you have a few choices for exam preparation: the exercises here, Chapter 18, "Final Preparation," and the exam simulation questions in the Pearson Test Prep Software Online.

Review All Key Topics

Review the most important topics in this chapter, noted with the Key Topic icon in the outer margin of the page. Table 9-3 lists these key topics and the page numbers on which each is found.

Table 9-3 Key Topics for Chapter 9

Key Topic Element	Description	Page Number
Figure 9-2	Multiple WLC ports configured as a single logical LAG	193
Paragraph	Assigning AP priorities	195
Paragraph	Using AP Fallback	197
Figure 9-10	SSO redundancy	200

Define Key Terms

Define the following key terms from this chapter and check your answers in the glossary:

AP Fallback, AP prioritization, N+1 redundancy, N+N redundancy, N+N+1 redundancy, SSO

Part II

Wireless Implementation (ENWLSI)

CHAPTER 10

Implementing FlexConnect

This chapter covers the following topics:

Remote Office Wireless Deployment Modes: This section provides an overview of the various deployment options for enterprise wireless in remote locations, including Local mode (using a local controller at the branch), FlexConnect, Mobility Express, and Office Extend.

FlexConnect Overview and Requirements: This section discusses the details of the FlexConnect architecture, including modes of operation and AP and WAN requirements.

Implementing FlexConnect with AireOS: This section discusses how FlexConnect is configured and implemented, including the configuration of local versus central switching, the function of FlexConnect groups, and how roaming is accomplished within Flex-Connect groups.

FlexConnect High Availability and Resiliency: This section provides an overview of FlexConnect survivability and high-availability options and how these are implemented.

FlexConnect ACLs: This section discusses the various uses of FlexConnect ACLs and how these are used to achieve split tunneling and map SSIDs to VLANs.

FlexConnect Smart AP Image Upgrades: This section discusses how AP software upgrades are accomplished using smart software upgrades in a FlexConnect environment.

Implementing FlexConnect with IOS-XE Controllers: This section introduces the IOS-XE controller and how FlexConnect may be implemented leveraging many of the same concepts introduced earlier in this chapter.

A Summary of FlexConnect Best Practices Recommendations: This section reviews the best practices discussed in this chapter, with application to both AireOS and IOS-XE controllers.

Office Extend: The final section gives an overview of the Office Extend mode for remote deployments and how these are configured in the wireless controller.

This chapter covers the following ENWLSI exam topics:

- 1.1 Deploy FlexConnect components such as switching and operating modes
- 1.2 Deploy FlexConnect capabilities
  - 1.2.a FlexConnect groups and roaming
  - 1.2.b Split tunneling and fault tolerance

- 1.2.c VLAN-based central switching and Flex ACL
- 1.2.d Smart AP image upgrade
- 1.3 Implement Office Extend

Deployment of enterprise wireless in branch offices introduces new challenges that are not encountered when deploying wireless in a centralized campus network. In a campus environment, the controller is typically deployed on a network that has reliable, high-bandwidth, and low-latency access to the APs it manages. In these environments, both the control plane traffic and the data plane traffic of the AP are managed by the controller. This has obvious architectural benefits in that it promotes centralization of policy and systematic control of client traffic entering or leaving the wireless network. Additionally, this mode allows the controller to dynamically optimize the AP's RF settings and interactions using radio resource management (RRM) and it provides a central way to manage QoS to the wireless network.

However, when wireless networks are expanded to branch or remote locations, the use of a centralized wireless controller is not always practical. This is primarily due to the increased latency, jitter, and packet loss caused by backhauling the wireless traffic over the WAN to a central location, not to mention possible issues with WAN circuit reliability. For example, if a remote office was to have only a handful of APs serving a few employees, bringing all client wireless back to a centralized point over the WAN would not only be inefficient, but it would also introduce latency issues that would negatively impact certain traffic types, especially real-time applications, including voice and video. Also, consider a situation where wireless clients at a remote branch need access to a local file server or printer at the same location. Using a centralized wireless controller means all application traffic inside the CAPWAP tunnel must be backhauled over the WAN to the controller, and it is then tromboned back again to the branch over the same WAN—essentially forcing data plane traffic to traverse the WAN twice (and doubling the latency) when the service was sitting nearby on the local LAN in the first place. Clearly, this is inefficient and can cause both user satisfaction and application performance issues, not to mention unnecessarily burdening the WAN with traffic it doesn't need to see.

This chapter discusses various methods to solve this problem, with a primary focus on FlexConnect. All relevant exam objectives are discussed, including FlexConnect architecture and capabilities, along with the basic requirements needed to deploy FlexConnect. In addition, this chapter introduces advanced implementation topics, including the use of ACLs to selectively map SSIDs to VLANs and map specific VLANs to be either locally or centrally switched (split tunneling). FlexConnect resiliency and high availability are also introduced, as well as how FlexConnect APs can be efficiently upgraded over the WAN. Both the AireOS controller and IOS-XE controller implementations are discussed.

The chapter concludes with a discussion of Office Extend as way to offer wireless services and extend the corporate enterprise network to a single AP.

"Do I Know This Already?" Quiz

The "Do I Know This Already?" quiz allows you to assess whether you should read this entire chapter thoroughly or jump to the "Exam Preparation Tasks" section. If you are in doubt about your answers to these questions or your own assessment of your knowledge of the topics, read the entire chapter. Table 10-1 lists the major headings in this chapter and their corresponding "Do I Know This Already?" quiz questions. You can find the answers in Appendix D, "Answers to the 'Do I Know This Already?' Quizzes and Review Questions."

Table 10-1   "Do I Know This Already?" Section-to-Question Mapping

Foundation Topics Section	Questions
Remote Office Wireless Deployment Modes	1
FlexConnect Overview and Requirements	2–3
Implementing FlexConnect with AireOS	4–5
FlexConnect High Availability and Resiliency	6–7
FlexConnect ACLs	8
FlexConnect Smart AP Image Upgrades	9
Implementing FlexConnect with IOS-XE Controllers	10
Office Extend	11–12

1. FlexConnect APs have been deployed in a remote branch office. Due to a network outage at the central site, the controller has become unavailable, forcing the APs to go into standalone mode. Which services are lost on the access points while in standalone mode?

   a. Client authentication services

   b. RRM

   c. Roaming

   d. No services are lost. The FlexConnect APs are designed to function in a semi-autonomous mode.

2. A company is looking to deploy 10 FlexConnect APs in a medium-sized branch location. The branch location will have a variety of wired video conference units, but otherwise the employees are expected to use wireless for data services. What are the minimum design requirements to be aware of?

   a. Minimum bandwidth should be 640Kbps and the latency should be less than 300 ms.

   b. Latency and bandwidth are not a concern because FlexConnect APs are designed to work autonomously from the controller.

   c. The minimum bandwidth should be 128Kbps and the latency should be less than 300 ms.

   d. In compliance with ITU-T recommendations for voice, one-way latency must be under 150 ms and jitter must be no more than 30 ms.

3. An engineer is planning to deploy a new FlexConnect AP. The AP is converted to FlexConnect mode, the native VLAN is configured, and the WLAN-to-VLAN mapping has been correctly configured. What critical configuration step has been overlooked?

   a. The AP must be rebooted.

   b. The AP must be added to a FlexConnect group.

   c. The FlexConnect WLAN has not been configured for local switching.

   d. VLAN trunking has not been enabled on the AP.

4. Seamless roaming is desired at a branch office. Which important feature must be configured to ensure this works correctly?

   a. 802.11r Fast Transition (FT)

   b. CCKM/OCK local key caching

   c. Local authentication

   d. FlexConnect groups

5. A FlexConnect group has been enabled on the branch wireless network. Due to limited WAN bandwidth, it was noticed that it takes longer than expected for clients to authenticate to the WAN. What are steps the engineering team can take to improve WLAN performance at the branch? (Choose two.)

   a. Turn on local authentication caching on the FlexConnect APs.

   b. Enable CAPWAP message aggregation.

   c. Configure the WLAN to use WPA-PSK.

   d. Enable local authentication for this WLAN.

   e. Extend the key refresh interval.

6. What is a key requirement to enable split tunneling on a FlexConnect AP?

   a. The centrally switched WLAN must have the locally switched option selected.

   b. NAT/PAT must be configured to allow centrally switched traffic to access the local VLAN.

   c. An ACL must be used for split tunneling to take effect.

   d. Split tunneling must be configured at the FlexConnect group level.

10

7. The Smart AP Image Upgrade option has been selected, but no master has been configured. What will happen?

   a. The image upgrade will fail and the APs will continue to wait until a master is properly configured.

   b. A master AP will be automatically selected based on the lowest MAC address.

   c. The APs will bypass the option until a master is configured and will simply download the new image from the controller directly.

   d. The APs will elect a master among themselves based on the lowest IP address.

8. How are Office Extend access points able to securely communicate with the controller?

   a. IPSec encryption of the CAPWAP tunnel must be enabled through the **security** page on the controller.

   b. DTLS is enabled by default on the OEAP.

   c. FlexVPN is enabled by default on the OEAP.

   d. Encryption is not natively supported—the CAPWAP tunnel must be externally protected through the use of a VPN router.

9. A new access point is going to be converted to OEAP mode. What step must be taken to convert the AP to OEAP mode?

   a. The AP must first be converted to FlexConnect mode, then to OEAP mode.

   b. An AP cannot be converted to OEAP mode in the field—OEAP must be configured from the factory.

   c. As with other AP modes, it is converted directly to OEAP mode from the **wireless** tab in the controller.

   d. An AP can only be converted to OEAP mode by overriding the default settings in the CLI.

Foundation Topics

Remote Office Wireless Deployment Modes

The alternative to deploying centrally controlled APs (where the data plane is switched by the controller) is to deploy the APs in one of four ways:

■ **Deploy a local controller at each branch:** While the deployment of local controllers at each branch will offer the exact same services to the branch that are available at the central location, there are certain downsides to this approach. For example, the deployment of a local controller at each branch will involve added cost and

management overhead, especially if redundant controllers are used. Continual mainte-
nance of software updates of a large number of controllers is also a disadvantage that
needs to be considered. For example, if a company has 6,000 branches, this implies
adding at least 6,000 new controllers to the network, including the network infrastructure required to connect the controllers at each branch location (note that controllers
can be deployed as either a standalone appliance or as a virtual machine on a server).
Practically speaking, if the number of APs required at a branch office is large, it might
make perfect sense to deploy a local controller—in fact, in some cases there may be
no alternative other than deploying a local controller at a large branch. However, if the
number of APs is low to moderate, using a controller per branch is generally considered suboptimal.

■ **FlexConnect at the branch:** FlexConnect is a hybrid architecture that offers a compro-
mise where the control plane of office APs is still managed by a centralized controller,
but the data can be locally switched at the AP on a per-SSID basis. This allows the AP
to deliver most of the same services available in centralized mode, but the controller
does not switch data plane traffic or terminate the data plane CAPWAP tunnels. As
the name implies, FlexConnect is flexible in that the administrator can choose which
SSIDs are locally switched versus which ones are centrally switched at the controller.
Note that the deployment of FlexConnect is the main focus of this chapter.

■ **Mobility Express at the branch:** An alternative to using a dedicated local controller
at each branch is to deploy the APs in Mobility Express (ME) mode. ME is essentially
the full controller functionality but deployed as software locally on an AP. In other
words, instead of deploying a standalone controller at the branch site, in ME mode
one of the APs takes on the role of controller for the other APs at the same location.
Similar to a dedicated controller, the ME master AP terminates the CAPWAP control
plane tunnels for the other APs and behaves much like a centralized controller supporting FlexConnect, with obvious performance limitations because the AP needs to
function as both a controller and an AP at the same time.

One disadvantage of ME is that it involves a certain amount of overhead, as each
branch will have an independent controller-on-AP that needs to be managed independently (meaning you are back to managing a different controller per branch—with the
advantage being that you don't need to purchase any dedicated controller hardware at
the branch offices).

10

NOTE   Mobility Express is not discussed in depth in this chapter.

■ **Office Extend on the APs:** In situations where a small branch office only requires
a single AP, Office Extend is a simple way to connect remote users to the corporate
network. As the name suggests, Office Extend is a way for the corporate network to
be extended to remote users via an encrypted VPN tunnel directly from the AP to the
controller.

It is clear that several options exist to extend wireless services to remote and branch offices. The decision of which to deploy involves several factors, including the following:

- Is communication between the branches and the corporate network reliable, and what is the latency profile?

- Do the branch users require real-time applications, such as voice and video, or are they limited to data-only communications?

- Does the organization have a lean IT team?

- What is the number of branches involved?

- How many employees are at each branch, and how many APs are required per branch?

- Do branch offices support local Internet access, or are the branches connected to the core network in a hub-and-spoke fashion?

Scalability of APs at a branch can often be a limiting decision as to which architecture to use. For example, Mobility Express supports either 50 or 100 APs, depending on the type of master AP used, and FlexConnect can support a maximum of 100 APs per group (but multiple groups may be used). Thus, if the size of the branch exceeds this number of APs, either a controller will be required at the branch, or multiple independent ME or FlexConnect groups will need to be deployed. The downside to deploying multiple independent ME or FlexConnect groups is that certain functions will be lost between groups. For example, in a large centralized campus, the controller supports functions such as RRM and seamless roaming between APs; however, if multiple ME and FlexConnect groups are in use, RRM and roaming will not be possible between group boundaries. In this case, the remote location is better served by a local controller.

FlexConnect and Mobility Express both offer similar services to remote branch APs, so when should one be used over the other? Generally, FlexConnect can be used in branch office scenarios when WAN connectivity to the controller is reliable and meets the minimum requirements for controlling FlexConnect APs. On the other hand, Mobility Express is typically used when the WAN is unreliable, the central controller is either too far away (the latency is high), or the bandwidth is so constrained that FlexConnect APs are not able to function correctly for a prolonged period. Mobility Express offers the advantage of having a full suite of controller capabilities local to the branch, running directly on one of the APs (meaning a standalone controller is not required). The downside of ME is that it involves the use of more controllers that must be managed and involves greater support from the IT staff.

The following section reviews the FlexConnect architecture and deployment requirements.

FlexConnect Overview and Requirements

FlexConnect is a method to connect APs and wireless users at a remote or branch office through the use of a centralized controller. Unlike centralized wireless deployments, where all wireless data plane traffic is sent to the controller via CAPWAP, FlexConnect allows wireless traffic to be locally switched and processed directly by the branch AP. In effect, local switching of traffic gives the FlexConnect AP some autonomy from the controller where services such as security, roaming, and QoS can be supported independently without oversight from the controller.

While FlexConnect is designed to locally switch certain SSIDs, it is also flexible in that some SSIDs can be centrally switched if desired. For example, if there is a requirement to have certain traffic switched centrally (such as traffic that needs to be processed through a central firewall), then these SSIDs may be brought back over CAPWAP and are centrally switched by the controller. The key point is that FlexConnect APs are able to support both locally and centrally switched WLANs on the same AP simultaneously.

Figure 10-1 illustrates a FlexConnect AP that locally switches traffic from a wireless client to a printer on one SSID, while a different client associated to a different SSID on the same AP sends all wireless traffic back to the controller at the corporate office where it is centrally switched.

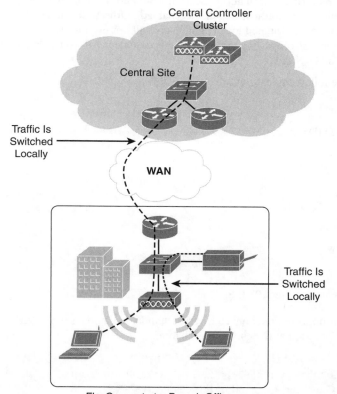

Figure 10-1 *A FlexConnect AP Deployed at a Branch Locally Switches One SSID While Another Is Centrally Switched*

Modes of Operation

FlexConnect APs operate in one of two modes: connected mode or standalone mode. Connected mode refers to a state when the AP is able to actively reach the controller (the CAPWAP control channel between controller and AP is up). Standalone is a fallback mode when the AP is no longer able to reach the controller.

The normal operation of FlexConnect APs should be connected mode, where the controller provides key services, including centralized authentication, client profiling, and RRM. It is expected that in most cases the AP will run in this mode; however, if the AP loses connectivity to the controller, it then goes into standalone mode. In standalone mode, the AP still functions, allowing packets to be locally switched and clients can still access the wireless network; however, certain high-touch services are temporarily lost, such as RRM and centralized authentication of clients.

For example, if there was a WAN disruption that prevented an AP from communicating with its controller, but Internet access was still available, the APs would simply revert to standalone mode during the service disruption and would continue to function normally, with the exception that new clients requiring central authentication would not be able to associate to the wireless network (unless local authentication was enabled). Otherwise, all locally switched traffic would continue to be switched locally and users will not even notice the change in AP mode. Note that it is also possible to configure FlexConnect APs to use local authentication in the event of a WAN failure.

While in standalone mode, the following features are not available to the AP:

- Client web authentication
- Any centrally switched SSIDs
- RRM
- IPv6 mobility
- Native profiling
- Policy classification
- Service Discovery Gateway
- Configuration updates
- Wireless intrusion prevention system (WIPS)

For a complete list of features supported in connected versus standalone mode, see the feature matrix in the "References" section at the end of this chapter.

NOTE   802.11ac Wave 2 and 802.11ax (Wi-Fi 6) APs have a different feature matrix, which can be found in the "References" section at the end of this chapter.

WAN Requirements for FlexConnect

Although FlexConnect APs are designed to switch traffic locally, they leverage key control capabilities from the controller, including configuration management and RRM. Similar to local mode, control of FlexConnect APs is accomplished through the CAPWAP control tunnel. Thus, for FlexConnect APs to function correctly in connected mode, they must meet minimum latency and bandwidth requirements, depending on how the AP is used. Table 10-2 summarizes the bandwidth and latency requirements for APs deployed supporting data-only clients, data + voice clients, and APs deployed in monitor mode.

Table 10-2   A Summary of FlexConnect WAN Requirements

Deployment Type	WAN Bandwidth (Min)	WAN RTT Latency (Max)	Max APs per Branch	Max Clients per Branch
Data	64Kbps	300 ms	5	25
Data	640Kbps	300 ms	50	1,000
Data	1.44Mbps	1 sec	50	1,000
Data + Voice	128Kbps	100 ms	5	25
Data + Voice	1.44Mbps	100 ms	50	1,000
Monitor	64Kbps	2 sec	5	N/A
Monitor	640Kbps	2 sec	50	N/A

As noted in Table 10-2, WAN bandwidth requirements are dependent on the number of APs and clients in use at the branch. The relationship between bandwidth and the number of APs is generally linear, meaning as the number of APs and clients increases, so follows the minimal bandwidth requirement. The minimum latency requirement is generally constant, depending on the wireless applications in use (for data only the minimum latency is 300 ms, and for data + voice the minimum latency is 100). If these requirements are not met, the APs may fall back into standalone mode and certain services will be lost until the network is restored to threshold limits.

When the FlexConnect APs are deployed in monitor mode, the latency requirements are eased since these APs do not need to centrally authenticate users and require less administrative overhead from the controller.

Implementing FlexConnect with AireOS

FlexConnect is a special mode that allows APs to switch traffic locally and to act in a semi-autonomous mode from the controller. At a high level, the steps involved in configuring a FlexConnect AP in an AireOS controller are as follows (configuration in an IOS-XE controller is discussed later):

1. Change the mode of the AP to FlexConnect mode.
2. Configure FlexConnect local switching on the AP.
3. Configure the native VLAN on the FlexConnect AP and the attached Ethernet switch and configure the correct WLAN-to-VLAN mapping.

These three steps will be discussed in the following sections.

Convert the AP to FlexConnect Mode

The first step is to change the AP mode to FlexConnect. In the AireOS controller menu, navigate to **Wireless > Access Point > (AP_NAME) > AP Mode** and choose **FlexConnect**. When the AP mode is changed from local to FlexConnect, it does not need to reboot (however, when it is changed back from FlexConnect to local mode, it requires a reboot and

10

displays the following error message: "Warning: Changing AP Mode will reboot the AP and will rejoin the controller after a few minutes. Are you sure you want to continue?").

Figure 10-2 illustrates how the AP mode is changed.

Figure 10-2   *Changing the AP to FlexConnect Mode*

Configure the Locally Switched WLANs

The second step is to configure local switching on the WLANs that will be used at the branch. Select the SSID that will be locally switched in the **WLANs > (WLAN Name) > Advanced** menu. Navigate to the FlexConnect menu and select **FlexConnect Local Switching**. This now enables the WLAN to be locally switched at the FlexConnect AP. Figure 10-3 illustrates this configuration step.

When an AP is configured in FlexConnect mode, it is expected that at least one WLAN will be locally switched. While centrally switched WLANs are inherited by default on the Flex-Connect AP, WLANs that are locally switched must be specifically configured as distinct from the centrally switched WLANs. In this way, a FlexConnect AP may simultaneously support both centrally and locally switched WLANs. In fact, it is also possible to create multiple SSIDs with the same name but with different switching profiles. This is common in guest scenarios where some sites may require locally switched SSIDs and other sites may want centrally switched SSIDs, both having the same SSID name.

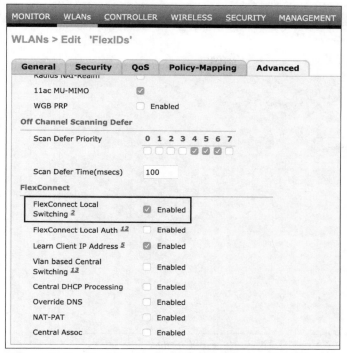

Figure 10-3   *Enabling Local Switching for the WLAN*

Configure the Native VLAN and WLAN-to-VLAN Mapping

Once a locally switched SSID/WLAN is configured, the next step is to configure the native VLAN of the AP and the local WLAN-to-VLAN mapping. When APs are configured in local mode, they simply bridge all 802.11 traffic back to the controller over CAPWAP and the controller is then responsible for mapping the WLAN to the correct VLAN where it is sent over an 802.1Q VLAN trunk connected to the controller's local switch. Thus, VLAN trunking is not required on APs in local mode.

However, in the case of FlexConnect, the locally switched traffic must emerge directly from the AP onto the correct VLAN, meaning the AP and its connected switch must both be configured for 802.1Q VLAN trunking. On the **Wireless** menu in the AireOS controller, a Flex-Connect sub-tab will appear for the AP once the mode has been changed to FlexConnect. This can be found by navigating to **Wireless > Access Point > (AP_NAME) > FlexConnect**. Figure 10-4 illustrates the FlexConnect sub-tab.

The first feature that must be configured is the **VLAN Support** option. This option enables 802.1Q trunking on the AP. Note that the VLAN IDs and trunk configuration on this page must be matched on the switch connecting to the AP (this includes the correct native VLAN, allowed VLAN IDs on the trunk, and trunking mode). Once the **Native VLAN** option has been configured, select the **VLAN Name Id Mappings** option. The VLAN Name ID Mappings configuration page is shown in Figure 10-5.

10

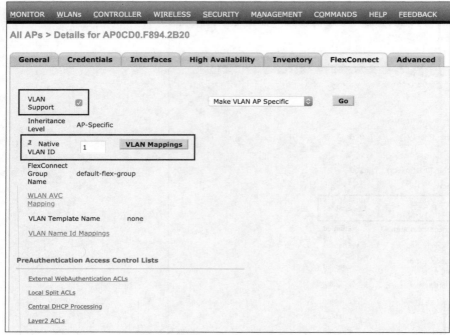

Figure 10-4 *Configuring the Native VLAN on the FlexConnect Sub-Tab*

From here, the specific WLAN-to-VLAN mappings can be configured. This involves mapping the WLAN ID to the correct VLAN ID that is used on the 802.1Q trunk. Repeat this configuration step for all locally switched VLANs (but not centrally switched WLANs). Also note in Figure 10-5 that a list of centrally switched WLANs is displayed for each AP. These are the WLANs that have been left in the centrally switched default state. To add any WLANs to the mapping, they must first be changed to "locally switched" in the **WLANs** configuration page, as discussed earlier.

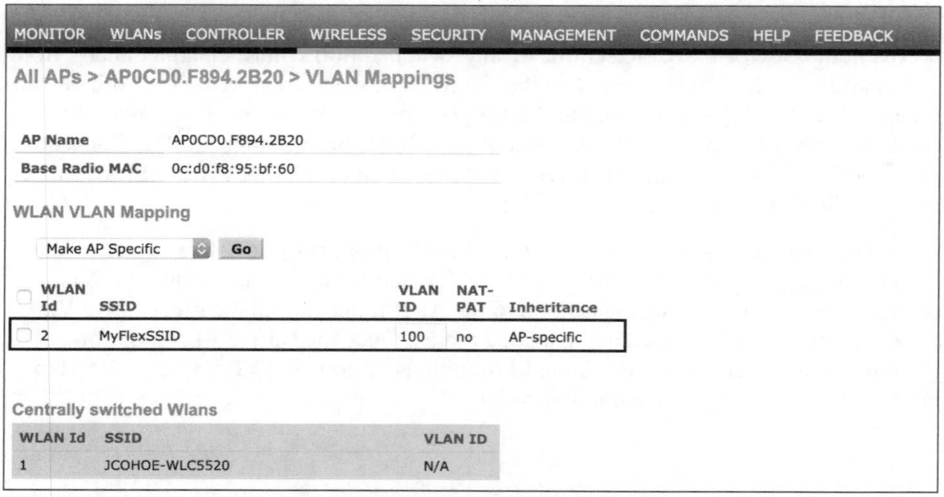

Figure 10-5 *Configuring the WLAN-to-VLAN Mapping*

Once the native VLAN and WLAN-to-VLAN mappings have been configured, the next step is to ensure the connected switch mirrors the VLAN trunking configuration. In Example 10-1, the native VLAN is left as 1 (which is the default), and only VLAN 100 is allowed on the trunk (VLAN 100 is the mapping of the locally switched WLAN).

Example 10-1   *Configuring the Matching VLAN Trunk Details on the Connected Switch*

```
interface GigabitEthernet1/0/13
 switchport trunk encapsulation dot1q
 switchport trunk allowed vlan 100
 switchport trunk native vlan <native VLAN number>
switchport mode trunk
```

By default, VLAN 1 is the default native VLAN in Cisco switches and does not need to be specifically configured. If a different VLAN is used for the native, then this must be configured, as shown in Example 10-1.

The configuration steps shown thus far need to be performed on a per-AP basis in the controller. However, if there are hundreds or thousands of APs in use, this approach clearly does not easily scale. The next section will discuss how FlexConnect groups are used to improve functionality and speed up bulk configuration tasks.

Implementing FlexConnect Groups

FlexConnect groups are responsible for sharing services between APs in the group. For example, the following services are shared within a FlexConnect group:

■ Cisco Centralized Key Management (CCKM) / Opportunistic Key Caching (OKC) fast roaming keys

■ Local/backup RADIUS server keys

■ Local EAP (Extensible Authentication Protocol) authentication

■ Smart Image upgrade

■ FlexConnect AVC (Application Visibility and Control)

■ AAA-Override for local switching

At a high level, FlexConnect groups are a way for APs in the group to inherit common configuration attributes without you having to configure each individual AP. They also play a key role in supporting seamless roaming between APs within the group. By way of contrast, for SSIDs in central switching mode (or on APs in local mode), the controller is responsible for sharing the CCKM/OCK keys between APs, thus supporting high-speed roaming between APs and overcoming the problem of client reauthentication each time a client roams. FlexConnect groups are designed to accomplish the same capability for locally switched WLANs.

To illustrate how FlexConnect works, consider how it handles CCKM/OCK key sharing. When a wireless client associates and authenticates to a WLAN, the RADIUS server allocates two keys—one for the client and one for the AP. As the client roams between APs, the key from the first AP is transferred to the next, so the client doesn't need to reauthenticate. When the AP is in connected mode, the controller stores these keys and pushes them to the new AP as the client roams. If this model were used for FlexConnect, two problems would be encountered. First, pushing keys to an AP over the WAN each time a client roams will likely introduce unacceptable latency that results in a slower roam times, making it noticeable on the client side, especially if real-time applications are in use. The second problem is when the controller becomes unavailable and the FlexConnect APs go into standalone mode. In this case, roaming will require reauthentication as the client attempts to move from one AP to another. However, because the controller is no longer available and reauthentication is not possible, the roam will fail (unless a local backup RADIUS server is deployed).

While in connected mode, the controller shares the keys with the APs in the FlexConnect group, creating a local roaming domain where the APs no longer need to retrieve the keys from the controller each time a client roams. This also solves the problem when the controller becomes unavailable and the APs are in standalone mode. In this case, the APs in the FlexConnect group already have the keys, and clients are able to roam seamlessly without the need to contact the controller. However, if an AP boots up in standalone mode where it has not yet seen the controller, it will not have access to the CCKM/OCK keys to become part of the roaming domain, and seamless roaming will not be possible until connected mode is restored for that AP.

> **NOTE**   The concept of AP groups should be fairly familiar to you by now. AP groups are a way to create a logical grouping of APs that deliver a similar set of Wi-Fi services. It is important to note that AP groups and FlexConnect groups are not mutually exclusive, meaning that a branch AP may be part of both an AP group and a FlexConnect group.

FlexConnect groups can be created in the **Wireless > FlexConnect Groups** menu. Figure 10-6 illustrates the creation of a new FlexConnect group called **FLEX-1**.

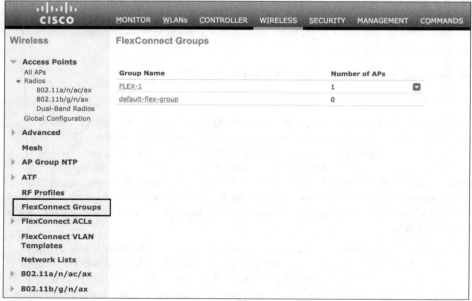

Figure 10-6   *Creation of a FlexConnect Group*

When first configured, all FlexConnect APs are part of a group called "default-flex-group." While certain configuration options can be configured in the default group, this group does not share authentication keys among other members of the group, meaning the group does not support seamless roaming, so it is recommended to create a FlexConnect group at each remote location.

Figure 10-7 illustrates the configuration options for a FlexConnect group.

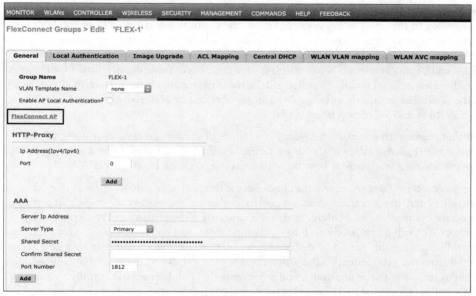

Figure 10-7 *Configuration of the FlexConnect Group*

In the FlexConnect configuration menu, the group can be given configuration characteristics that are inherited by all APs assigned to the same group. These include attributes for **Local Authentication**, **Image Upgrade**, **ACL mapping**, **Central DHCP**, **WLAN VLAN mapping**, and **WLAN AVC mapping**.

Once the FlexConnect group has been created and configured, the final step is to add APs to the group. This can be done by selecting the **FlexConnect AP** option on the **General** menu and then adding selected APs to the group (as shown in Figure 10-7). Only APs that have been configured in FlexConnect mode are listed as available options that can be added to the FlexConnect group (refer Figure 10-2), and APs may only be part of one FlexConnect group at a time.

Due to scalability limitations related to authentication key caching, FlexConnect groups are limited to no more than 100 APs per group. Additionally, the total number of configurable groups varies with the size and capacity of the controller used (for example, the WLC 5520 supports a maximum of 1,500 FlexConnect groups).

FlexConnect High Availability and Resiliency

The following section describes methods to ensure resiliency of FlexConnect in the event of WAN failure or other types of service degradation where access to the controller is impaired or lost.

FlexConnect Resiliency Scenarios

One of the most common FlexConnect failure scenarios is a complete loss or serious degradation of the WAN, thus impairing the CAPWAP control channel. When WAN connectivity is degraded to the point where connectivity to the controller is lost, FlexConnect APs at remote locations immediately go into standalone mode. While in standalone mode there is no impact to locally switched SSIDs; however, all clients that are part of centrally switched SSIDs will be disconnected. While wireless services can continue uninterrupted for clients already associated on locally switched SSIDs, the ultimate goal is to reestablish connectivity to the controller as quickly as possible so all services can be restored. Until then, services such as RRM and WIPS will be unavailable.

Another scenario that impacts resiliency is a failure of the central controller itself. Chapter 9, "Designing High Availability," discusses various controller high-availability scenarios, but it is worth taking a brief look at how these options interact with FlexConnect APs.

One common resiliency scenario for controllers is the N+1 scenario, where multiple active controllers may use a common backup controller that can be used in the event that any of the active controllers has a failure. In this scenario, when the primary controller fails, FlexConnect APs will immediately go into standalone mode and will begin looking for a backup controller. During this period of disconnection, all centrally switched clients will be disconnected from the FlexConnect APs. When the APs find a backup controller, they immediately begin to resync with the controller, and any clients that need access to centrally switched SSIDs will be reassociated. During this transition period, locally switched clients are not affected and will not even notice the service disruption.

Another common controller resiliency model is Stateful Switchover (SSO). In this mode, the controllers are deployed as a 1:1 pair, where the running state of the active controller is replicated to a dedicated backup controller. In this scenario, the AP database, including all information related to FlexConnect APs, their centrally switched SSIDs, and client run state, is actively synchronized on the backup controller. During the failure of the active controller to the stateful backup, FlexConnect APs remain in connected mode and do not enter standalone mode, meaning centrally switched SSIDs will not go down.

AAA Survivability

When a FlexConnect AP goes into standalone mode due to a WAN failure, actively connected clients continue to function and may roam seamlessly from one AP to another within the FlexConnect group. However, any new clients that wish to associate to the locally switched WLAN during this time will be unable to because the AAA server at the central location is unavailable.

One resiliency option to deal with this situation is to offer a backup AAA server at the remote location that is accessible by the FlexConnect group. Figure 10-8 illustrates this model.

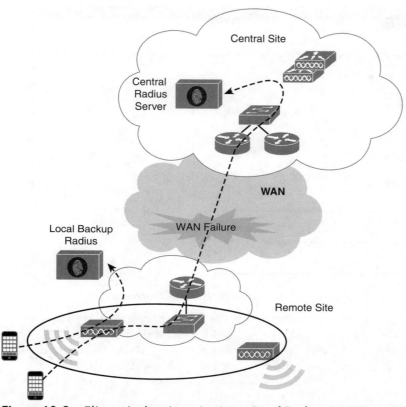

Figure 10-8 *Clients Authenticate Against a Local Backup AAA Server When the Central AAA Server Becomes Unavailable Due to a WAN Failure*

With local authentication enabled, the backup RADIUS server is only used when APs go into standalone mode—that is, when the APs are in connected mode, the local backup AAA server is not used. When the local backup AAA is used for authentication by FlexConnect APs, the authentication keys are distributed to all APs in the FlexConnect group in the same way they are when a centralized AAA server is used. In this way, even when a local backup RADIUS is in use, new clients are still be able to roam without being asked to reauthenticate.

Configuring AAA Survivability

Figure 10-9 illustrates how local authentication in the FlexConnect group may be configured. As can be noted in Figure 10-9, the **Enable AP Local Authentication** option needs to be selected first, then the primary AAA configuration is added. Also note that a secondary backup AAA server can be configured at the remote site if desired.

10

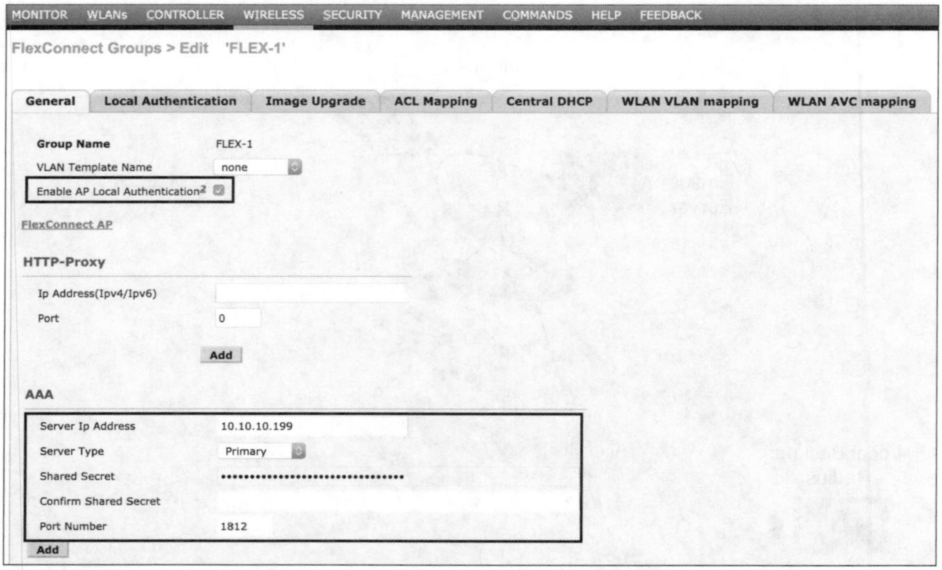

Figure 10-9   *Configuring Local Authentication in the FlexConnect Group*

NOTE   As previously discussed, the backup AAA server is only used when the WAN is down and the central AAA server is unavailable. Thus, while Flex APs are in connected mode, the central AAA server is used for all authentications. However, there may be cases where local authentication is desired, even when the WAN is up and the central RADIUS server is accessible. In cases like this, it is also possible to configure the FlexConnect APs to only use a local authentication server. To configure this in AireOS, select the option under **WLAN > (WLAN ID) > Advanced** and select the **FlexConnect Local Auth** option.

CAPWAP Message Aggregation

One final tool to help with branch resiliency is an option called "CAPWAP Message Aggregation." When the controller communicates to an AP to perform a certain control task, such as authenticating a client, making radio changes through RRM, or any other type of configuration changes, it is sent to the AP through the CAPWAP control channel. As part of CAPWAP's built-in resiliency mechanism, it uses an application-level acknowledgment for each message that is sent between the controller and each AP. However, in a very busy WLAN scenario where clients are continually roaming, rogues are being detected, and the RF environment is fluctuating, the performance of CAPWAP can suffer because each message needs to be acknowledged before the next can be sent. In a WAN that is already suffering latency and packet loss issues, this can further undermine the performance of the CAPWAP control traffic, causing a noticeable effect on wireless performance at the branch.

An efficient solution to this problem is to aggregate CAPWAP control messages for the APs. Figure 10-10 illustrates a "before and after" scenario of a controller that has CAPWAP message aggregation enabled.

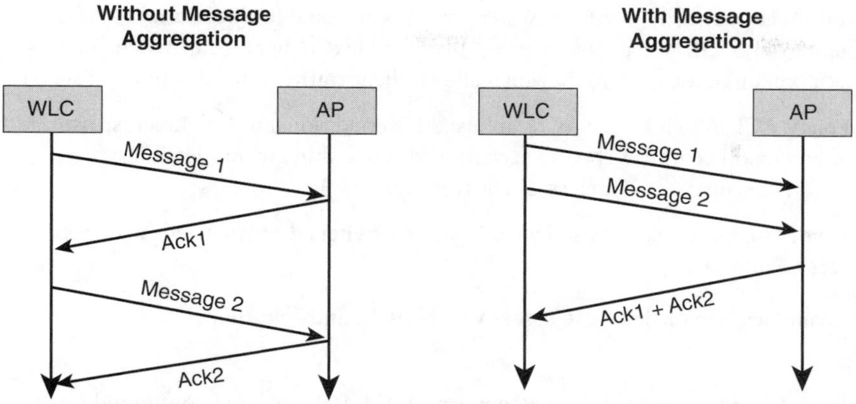

Figure 10-10 *A Before and After Comparison When CAPWAP Message Aggregation Is Enabled*

As can be seen in Figure 10-10, CAPWAP message aggregation allows multiple control messages to be sent in bulk from the controller to the AP, and then the AP returns a bulk acknowledgment back to the controller (for example, Ack 1 and Ack 2 are sent together rather than in separate messages). In a branch office with limited WAN connectivity, congestion of CAPWAP control messages can be one of the main causes of slow client authentication time. Thus, message aggregation has the effect of greatly improving both the transmission of the control messages and returning their acknowledgment; thus, it is recommended this feature be enabled at all times.

CAPWAP message aggregation may be enabled with the following command in AireOS (note that this feature is enabled by default in IOS-XE and is enabled by default in AireOS 8.6 and later):

```
config advanced capwap-message-aggregation enable
```

FlexConnect ACLs

A useful design characteristic of centralized wireless systems is that the controller can function in a central place to enforce security controls for all traffic as it leaves the network. For example, there may be certain SSIDs that require central security policy enforcement by a firewall. If using centrally switched SSIDs, wireless traffic can be mapped to a VLAN on the controller that is directly connected to a central firewall. In this way, a centralized method is employed both to protect the wireless clients and also to restrict what they can access. In a distributed model where FlexConnect APs at branches are configured for local switching, this level of control is decentralized and is more difficult to enforce. In order to provide security for locally switched networks, FlexConnect ACLs may be used.

FlexConnect ACLs are centrally configured on the controller and then automatically downloaded to the APs. An AireOS controller supports a maximum of 512 ACLs, and up to 96 ACLs can be downloaded to a single FlexConnect AP, with a maximum of 64 rules per ACL. FlexConnect ACLs may be used in four different ways:

- **VLAN ACLs:** These are primarily used as security ACLs that are applied on the ingress or egress direction on the wireless interface of the AP and may use either an IP address or a URL to match traffic.

10

- **Webauth/Webpassthrough ACLs:** Webauth ACLs are used for Webauth/Webpassthrough SSIDs that have been enabled for FlexConnect local switching. This is used as a pre-authentication ACL, which allows client traffic to reach a redirect server.

- **Web Policy ACLs:** Web Policy ACLs are used for conditional web redirect, splash page redirect, and central WebAuth scenarios (discussed in greater detail in Chapter 15, "Security for Wireless Client Connectivity").

- **Split Tunnel ACLs:** These are used when centrally switched traffic needs to access resources locally.

This section examines two of these use cases: VLAN ACLs and split tunnel ACLs.

VLAN ACLs

As with other ACLs on the controller, FlexConnect VLAN ACLs are first configured on the **Security** menu in the AireOS controller (they may also be configured from the **wireless** menu). Cisco controllers support both IPv4 and IPv6 security ACLs. Figure 10-11 illustrates the creation of a security ACL that will be used for FlexConnect.

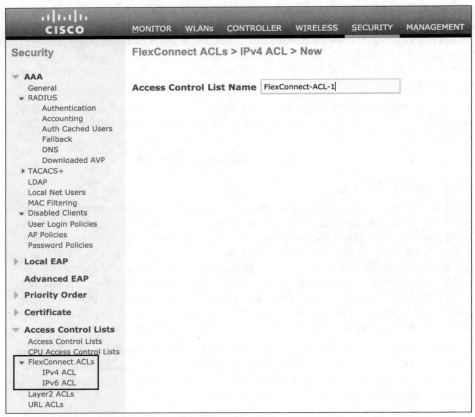

Figure 10-11 *The Creation of VLAN ACLs to Be Used for FlexConnect*

Figure 10-12 provides an example of an ACL with its associated rules that will be applied to a FlexConnect group. Note that both IP-based and URL-based rules may be added to an ACL.

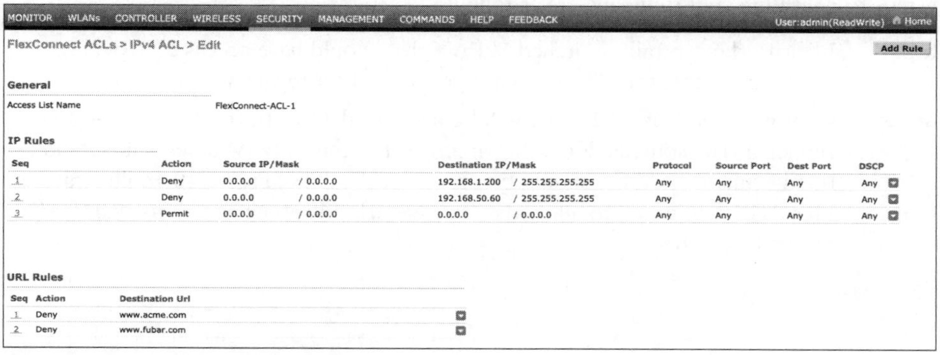

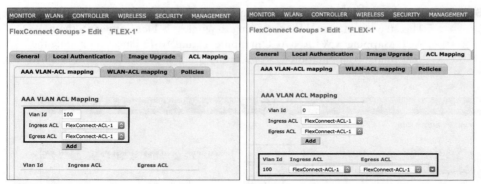

Figure 10-12 *The FlexConnect ACL Rules*

Once an ACL has been created, it needs to be added to a FlexConnect AP or the FlexConnect group. To add the VLAN ACL to a FlexConnect group in AireOS, navigate to **wireless > FlexConnect > (name) > ACL Mapping > AAA VLAN-ACL mapping**. From here, add the VLAN ID that the ACL is being added to and select the ingress and egress ACL options from the pull-down menu. Once this is done, click **Add** (see Figure 10-13).

Figure 10-13 *Adding the VLAN ACLs to a FlexConnect Group*

FlexConnect Split Tunneling (Using the Split ACL Mapping Feature)

Another common use case in FlexConnect is where clients are part of centrally switched WLAN but require access to local resources. Because these clients are centrally switched, they can't access these resources without having to traverse the CAPWAP tunnel over the WAN, be switched through the controller, and then return to the branch over the same WAN once again (incurring extra latency along the way). The FlexConnect split tunnel feature allows centrally switched clients to access local resources without having to traverse the CAPWAP tunnel.

With split tunneling enabled, an ACL is applied on the FlexConnect APs to examine matching packets to determine if they should be sent over the CAPWAP tunnel toward the controller or should exit the WLAN onto a specific local VLAN directly from the AP. To do this, split tunneling uses a NAT/PAT feature along with the ACL to bridge traffic directly onto the correct local LAN. Split tunneling uses the AP's management IP address as the NAT/PAT address.

The steps to configure split tunneling are as follows:

Step 1. Identify the centrally switched WLAN that should have access to a local service. Ensure that this WLAN is not configured for local switching.

Step 2. Configure the Flex ACLs that will be used to identify traffic that will be split-tunneled. The source address belonging to the centrally switched subnet and the destination address should be on the local subnet. Figure 10-14 illustrates a Flex ACL configured to allow the 192.168.10.0/24 subnet access to 10.0.10.5/32 on the local LAN.

Figure 10-14 *Configuring a FlexConnect ACL for Split Tunneling*

Step 3. Configure local split tunneling on a per-AP or per-FlexConnect group basis. This step is configured by navigating to **wireless > FlexConnect > (name) > ACL Mapping > WLAN-ACL mapping**. Figure 10-15 illustrates adding the split tunnel configuration to a Flex group.

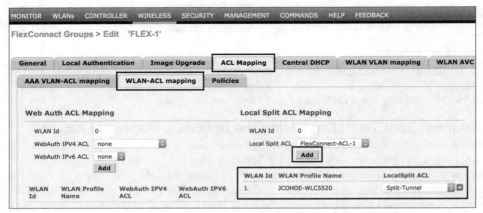

Figure 10-15 *Adding the Split Tunnel ACL to the FlexConnect Group*

FlexConnect Smart AP Image Upgrades

Upgrading APs over the WAN can be a challenge when there are a large number of APs and when the WAN bandwidth is constrained. For example, imagine a situation where a company has 1,000 branch offices, with an average of five FlexConnect APs per branch, totaling 5,000 remote APs. While each branch may not have a large number of APs, the process of upgrading all of the APs one at a time over a low-bandwidth WAN means the upgrade will take a very long time and will be prone to failure.

Consider also that upgrading multiple APs at a single branch involves sending the same image file multiple times over and over again to the same branch, potentially causing WAN link exhaustion.

An efficient way to upgrade remote APs is to use the Smart AP Image Upgrade feature. This feature uses a master AP in each FlexConnect group that acts as a proxy for the upgrade process for the other APs in the same group. When this feature is enabled, only the master AP in the FlexConnect group downloads the new image over the WAN. The remaining APs in the group then download the new image from the master over the local network without directly contacting the controller.

A FlexConnect group can have at most one master per model of AP. If the master is not selected manually, it will be automatically selected based on the lowest MAC address among the APs in the FlexConnect group.

Once the master has downloaded its new image, a maximum of three slave APs of the same model can concurrently download this image from their master. If more than three APs attempt to download from the master at the same time, they will use a random back-off timer that is greater than 100 seconds to retry the master at a later time. After a slave AP downloads the image, the AP informs the controller about the completion of the download. If a slave AP is unsuccessful in downloading the image from the master AP after a configured number of retries, it will reach out to the controller to attempt an image download directly.

To configure the Smart AP Upgrade feature in AireOS, navigate to the **wireless > FlexConnect Groups > (name) > Image Upgrade** page. Figure 10-16 illustrates the configuration of this feature.

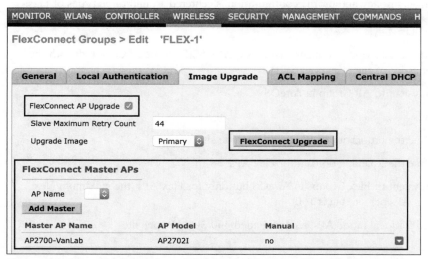

Figure 10-16 *Configuration of the Smart AP Image Upgrade Feature in a FlexConnect Group*

To summarize the example shown in Figure 10-16, the configuration is as follows:

- The FlexConnect AP Upgrade option must first be selected.

- Configure the slave maximum retry count. This is the number of times the slave will attempt to download the new image from the master. The default is 44, but this may be configured as desired.

- Select the upgrade image—the options are Primary, Backup, and Abort.

- From the AP Name option, select the AP that will be the master. In this example, one AP has been selected and all others in the FlexConnect group will be the slaves.

- Once this configuration has been applied, click FlexConnect Upgrade to perform the upgrade.

Implementing FlexConnect with IOS-XE Controllers

As this is the first chapter that discusses implementation, a quick overview of the IOS-XE wireless controller configuration principles is warranted. Cisco introduced the family of IOS-XE controllers in 2018. IOS-XE controllers come in a variety of form factors, including the Catalyst 9800. Unlike AireOS controllers, which have been in use for many years, IOS-XE controllers inherit many of the native modular configuration capabilities of IOS-XE, while maintaining very similar features to the traditional AireOS. While the feature capabilities of AireOS and IOS-XE are very similar, the configuration methodology has significant differences.

In the AireOS controller, most wireless policies are centered around the WLANs, AP Groups, Flex Groups, and RF Profiles. In the IOS-XE controller, these configuration elements are decoupled (making them more reusable) and are modularized (making them more flexible), similar to other IOS- and IOS-XE-based systems.

IOS-XE controller policy and profile configuration is centered around three types of tags:

- Policy Tags:

  - Define the broadcast domain (list of WLANs/SSIDs to be broadcasted) with the properties of the respective SSIDs

  - Equivalent to AP Group in AireOS

- Site Tags:

  - Define the properties of the central/remote site

  - Define the Roaming domain for Flex APs

  - Equivalent to Flex Groups in AireOS but only for Flex APs (the maximum Flex mode APs per site tag is 100)

  - Used for local mode APs, recommended 400/500 APs per site

■ RF Tags:

    ■ Define the RF properties of the group of APs

Through the use of tags, IOS-XE controllers allow you to configure which policies will be adopted on which sites and what RF characteristics will be implemented, with the tags allowing policies and RF characteristics to be reused on other wireless segments.

Figure 10-17 illustrates a summary of these configuration aspects in the IOS-XE controller.

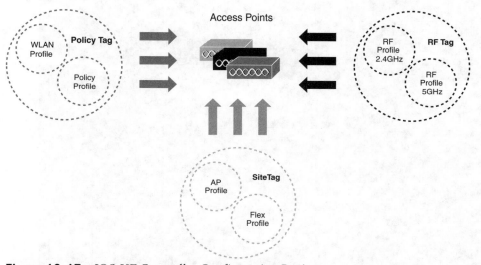

Figure 10-17   *IOS-XE Controller Configuration Basics*

The IOS-XE controller also supports configuration wizards that allow quick configuration of WLANs, APs, and sites.

To configure FlexConnect, navigate to the **Configuration > Wireless Setup > Basic** configuration page on the controller. This is illustrated in Figure 10-18.

After navigating to the **Configuration > Wireless Setup > Basic** page, use the following steps to configure a new site for FlexConnect:

Step 1.   Define the Location (such as a remote branch office location).

Step 2.   Select Flex for Location Type (the options are Local or Flex).

Step 3.   Select Client Density.

Step 4.   Enter the Native VLAN ID.

Step 5.   Add a AAA server (if not already added) and select it as the AAA for the remote location.

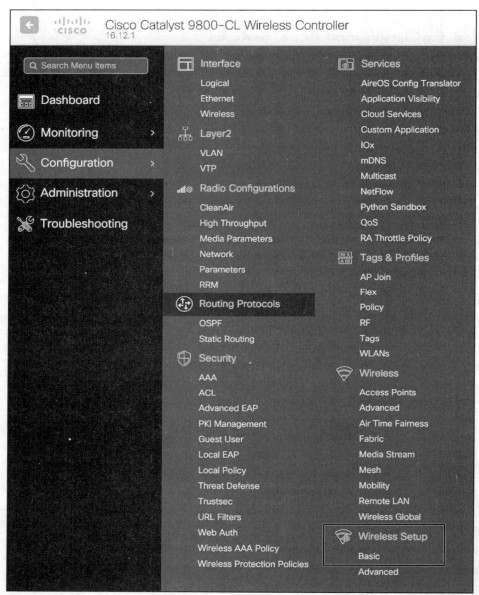

Figure 10-18 *Wireless Basic Configuration*

Figure 10-19 illustrates configuration of the new remote location under the **Configuration > Wireless Setup > Basic > General** tab.

Figure 10-19   *Configure the Site for FlexConnect*

Note the example in Figure 10-19 does not highlight the use tags because a configuration wizard is being used instead. The same configuration outcome can also be configured through the use of tags, but this is not shown for the sake of simplicity.

Once the site has been configured, navigate to the **Wireless Network** tab on the same page and follow these configuration steps (Figure 10-20 illustrates these configuration steps):

Step 1.   Create the WLAN (or add it if already defined).

Step 2.   Select a VLAN or a VLAN group—there will be a 1:1 mapping of VLANs to WLANs, and this needs to be configured for each locally switched WLAN used at the remote location.

Step 3.   Select Authentication and switching methods.

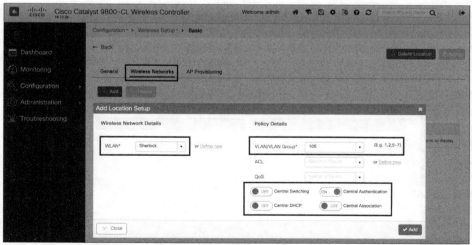

Figure 10-20   *Configuring the FlexConnect Location Details*

Once the Wireless Networks components have been configured, the next step is to add the correct APs to the site. Navigate to the **AP Provisioning** tab and select the APs you wish to add and then click **Apply**. Figure 10-21 illustrates this step.

Figure 10-21   *Adding the AP to the FlexConnect Group*

The final step in the configuration is to add the locally switched VLANs to the Flex profile. Navigate to **Configuration > Tags & Profiles > Flex**. Under this tab, select the remote location you want to configure (which is really the Flex profile name). Figure 10-22 illustrates this configuration step.

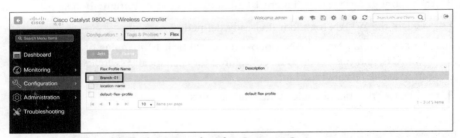

Figure 10-22   *Adding the AP to the FlexConnect Group*

From here, navigate to the **VLAN** tab and add the VLANs to the Flex profile. This is illustrated in Figure 10-23. Note each VLAN used.

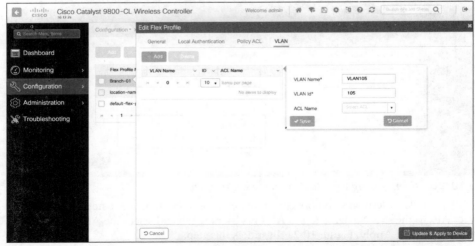

Figure 10-23   *Configuring the Locally Switched VLANs for the FlexConnect APs*

With this last step completed, the location and Flex profile are configured and are ready for service. This example used the basic configuration wizard; however, behind the scenes the Policy, RF, and Site tags have all been configured in the CLI. Example 10-2 illustrates the CLI output from the configuration steps previously shown (note only the relevant configuration items are displayed).

Example 10-2   *IOS-XE Controller CLI Configuration Output*

```
catalyst9800#show run
aaa group server radius radgrp_Branch-01
 server name rad_192.168.10.1

wireless profile flex Branch-01
 acl-policy preauth_v4
 local-auth radius-server-group radgrp_Branch-01
 native-vlan-id 221
 vlan-name VLAN105
  vlan-id 105

wireless profile policy Branch-01_WLANID_5
 no central association
 no central dhcp
 no central switching
 description Branch-01_Sherlock

wireless tag site Branch-01
 ap-profile Branch-01
 flex-profile Branch-01
 no local-site

wireless tag policy Branch-01
 wlan Sherlock policy Branch-01_WLANID_5

wireless tag rf Branch-01
 24ghz-rf-policy Typical_Client_Density_rf_24gh
 5ghz-rf-policy Typical_Client_Density_rf_5gh

wlan Sherlock 5 Sherlock

ap location name Branch-01
 description "221b Baker Street"
 tag policy Branch-01
 tag rf Branch-01
 tag site Branch-01

ap profile Branch-01
```

10

Example 10-3 illustrates the output from the **show wireless tag** CLI command.

Example 10-3   *A CLI Summary of the Wireless Tags Created Using the Configuration Wizard*

```
catalyst9800#show wireless tag policy all


Policy Tag Name : Branch-01
Description    :


Number of WLAN-POLICY maps: 0
WLAN Profile Name                   Policy Name
---------------------------------------------------------------------
Sherlock                            Branch-01_WLANID_5


Number of RLAN-POLICY maps: 0



catalyst9800#show wireless tag rf all


Tag Name            : Branch-01
Description         :
----------------------------------------
5ghz RF Policy      : Typical_Client_Density_rf_5gh
2.4ghz RF Policy    : Typical_Client_Density_rf_24gh


catalyst9800#show wireless tag site all


Site Tag Name       : Branch-01
Description         :
----------------------------------------
Flex Profile        : Branch-01
AP Profile          : Branch-01
Local-site          : No
Image Download Profile: default
```

A Summary of FlexConnect Best Practices Recommendations

The following list summarizes recommended best practices when deploying FlexConnect for remote and branch wireless networks:

■ Enable unique FlexConnect groups for each remote location.

■ If the number of APs at the remote location exceeds 100 APs, either configure multiple Flex groups or deploy a local wireless controller at the remote location.

- Ensure the wired switch VLANs match with the FlexConnect locally switched WLAN-to-VLAN mapping, including the native VLAN, which is used for CAPWAP traffic.

- Configure features at the FlexConnect group level such as the VLAN-WLAN mappings.

- Design the controllers for resiliency (either N+1 or SSO).

- Enable CAPWAP Message aggregation to accelerate AP to controller communications (if using AireOS versions prior to 8.6).

- Configure VLAN ACLs as necessary to implement security at the remote location.

- Enable split tunneling (split ACL mapping) as necessary for centrally switched WLAN clients that need to access local resources.

- Enable Smart AP image upgrade. Ideally, select and configure the master AP for image upgrades.

Office Extend

In some scenarios, no more than one access point is needed at a remote location. An example may be an employee's home office or a very small remote office requiring just a single AP. Although FlexConnect may still be used in these scenarios, a simpler approach is to deploy Office Extend AP (OEAP). This type of deployment is designed to extend the corporate office network to a single AP over the Internet through a VPN connection, making the extended wireless network appear as if it is directly connected to the corporate network.

OEAPs provide secure communications from the access point at a remote location to the central controller, seamlessly extending the corporate WLAN over the Internet to a remote location, such as a home residence, thus providing the same experience for users at the home office as they would expect at the corporate office. Datagram Transport Layer Security (DTLS) encryption is used between the AP and the controller to ensure all communication is encrypted and protected.

NOTE   OEAP is only supported on specific access point models. Please consult the AP data sheet to determine which models support OEAP functionality.

10

Office Extend works in the following way. A user is given an AP that is primed with the IP address of the central controller. Alternatively, the user can enter the IP address of the controller from the web configuration screen. The user connects the AP into the home or office router. Once the AP boots and gets a local address, it communicates over the Internet to the address of the controller and creates a secured DTLS tunnel.

The OEAP then downloads its configuration and begins advertising the corporate SSID, thus making the user's home or small office an extension of the corporate WLAN. Additionally, OEAPs have the ability to support local LAN ports, allowing the user to plug in a wired port that is also tunneled back to the controller. In addition, the user can enable an additional SSID for personal use, ensuring the corporate Wi-Fi network is not used for personal information.

To configure an AP as an OEAP, the AP first needs to be running in FlexConnect mode. From here, navigate to the **wireless > All APs > (name) > FlexConnect** page. Select the **Enable Office Extend AP** option. DTLS data encryption is enabled automatically when you enable the Office Extend mode for an access point.

Figure 10-24 illustrates how an AP may be converted to OEAP mode.

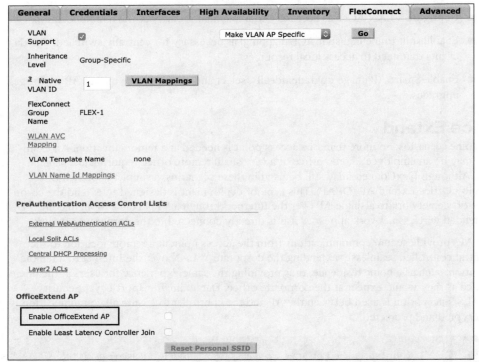

Figure 10-24   *Converting a FlexConnect into an OEAP (AireOS Configuration Shown)*

Once the AP has been converted to OEAP mode, the user can navigate to the OEAP's web GUI at https://<ip address of AP>, where the personal SSID may be configured.

Summary

This chapter discussed the deployment of wireless in remote branch offices, focusing on FlexConnect. In this chapter you have learned the following:

■   Various options to deploy APs at remote branch offices, including the use of a local controller, Mobility Express, FlexConnect, and Office Extend

- The operating modes of FlexConnect, including connected and standalone modes

- The minimum latency and bandwidth requirements needed to deploy FlexConnect APs

- Implementation steps required to deploy FlexConnect

- The need to configure FlexConnect groups to allow seamless high-speed roaming at a branch location

- How to configure FlexConnect for high availability

- FlexConnect ACL VLAN mapping and split tunneling configuration

- How to implement Smart AP Image Upgrade

- Implementation of Office Extend APs

References

For additional information, refer to these resources:

AireOS FlexConnect Configuration Guide: https://www.cisco.com/c/en/us/td/docs/wireless/controller/8-8/config-guide/b_cg88/flexconnect.html

FlexConnect Feature Matrix: http://www.cisco.com/c/en/us/support/docs/wireless/5500-series-wireless-controllers/112042-technote-wlc-00.html

Catalyst 9800 FlexConnect Configuration Guide: https://www.cisco.com/c/en/us/td/docs/wireless/controller/9800/config-guide/b_wl_16_10_cg/flexconnect.html#ID340

Office Extend Configuration Guide, AireOS 8.8: https://www.cisco.com/c/en/us/td/docs/wireless/controller/8-8/config-guide/b_cg88/configuring_officeextend_access_points.html

AireOS Mobility Express Configuration Guide: https://www.cisco.com/c/en/us/support/wireless/mobility-express/products-installation-and-configuration-guides-list.html

Exam Preparation Tasks

As mentioned in the section "How to Use This Book" in the Introduction, you have a few choices for exam preparation: the exercises here, Chapter 18, "Final Preparation," and the exam simulation questions in the Pearson Test Prep Software Online.

10

Review All Key Topics

Review the most important topics in this chapter, noted with the Key Topic icon in the outer margin of the page. Table 10-3 lists these key topics and the page numbers on which each is found.

Table 10-3 Key Topics for Chapter 10

Key Topic Element	Description	Page Number
Figure 10-1	FlexConnect architectural example	213
Table 10-2	A summary of FlexConnect WAN requirements	215
Figure 10-7	Configuration of a FlexConnect group	221
Figure 10-18	IOS-XE wireless configuration basics	232
List	Summary of implementation recommendations	236

Define Key Terms

Define the following key terms from this chapter and check your answers in the glossary:

FlexConnect, Mobility Express, Central Switching, Local Switching, Connected Mode, Standalone Mode, FlexConnect Groups, CAPWAP Message Aggregation, Split Tunneling, Smart Image Upgrade, OEAP

CHAPTER 11

Implementing Quality of Service on a Wireless Network

This chapter covers the following topics:

An Overview of Wireless QoS Principles: This section begins by examining some of the differences between traditional wired QoS and wireless, and it looks at how the unique challenges of wireless QoS led to the development of the 802.11e and WMM standards.

Implementing QoS Policies on the Wireless Controller: This section introduces you to how QoS is implemented on both the AireOS and IOS-XE controllers. This section discusses QoS profiles, how DSCP-to-802.11e User Priority (UP) mapping occurs, and how other QoS functions are implemented in the wireless controller.

Implementing QoS for Wireless Clients: QoS in the upstream direction begins on the client and determines how well real-time applications, such as voice and video, operate. This section examines how QoS marking is accomplished on various operating systems and how these markings are preserved through the wireless infrastructure.

Implementing Application Visibility and Control: This section examines how AVC can be implemented in the controller to identify applications within the packet to provide better QoS and security controls. This includes an overview of the Fastlane AutoQoS macro that helps to quickly deploy AVC and other QoS services in a best-practices manner.

This chapter covers the following ENWLSI exam topics:

- 2.1 Implement QoS schemes based on requirements including wired-to-wireless mapping
- 2.2 Implement QoS for wireless clients
- 2.3 Implement AVC including Fastlane (only on WLC)

Quality of service (QoS) is one of the most important cornerstones of any network deployment. Without QoS, applications will not function predictably and the user experience will suffer. There is nothing worse than being on a video conference and having your session interrupted by pixelation caused by bandwidth limitations, packet loss, or just poor network performance. Networks by their very nature are built to be oversubscribed—while it makes good engineering sense to design a network like this, the result is that inevitably a network link somewhere along the line will become congested and cause undesirable application performance issues.

While some applications are not latency sensitive (such as email), other are extremely sensitive to even minimal amounts of jitter and latency. Many companies have come to rely on real-time applications such as WebEx, Telepresence, and others to conduct their internal and external meetings. A network without QoS will suffer noticeably poor performance in times of congestion, especially for these real-time applications.

You are probably familiar with the saying that a chain is only as strong as its weakest link. If one of those links is weaker than the others, it is the most likely place the chain will break if put under strain. QoS is exactly like this—to be truly effective, it needs to be implemented end to end, at every hop along the way. If there is even one node that either isn't configured correctly for QoS or doesn't support it, that is your weak point in the chain, and application performance will be impacted. Wireless LAN by its very nature is stochastic and unpredictable, making it one of the most challenging places in the network to implement QoS—meaning without proper handling, it can easily become the weakest link in the chain.

This chapter begins with an overview of wireless QoS fundamentals and how the wireless standards have developed to bring QoS to this challenging medium. Next, you learn how to implement QoS on the both the AireOS and IOS-XE wireless LAN controllers. Following that, we examine QoS from the client's perspective and how QoS can be implemented to protect critical applications. Finally, you are introduced to AVC on the wireless controller and learn how Fastlane can be used to improve overall QoS capabilities of the wireless infrastructure.

"Do I Know This Already?" Quiz

The "Do I Know This Already?" quiz allows you to assess whether you should read this entire chapter thoroughly or jump to the "Exam Preparation Tasks" section. If you are in doubt about your answers to these questions or your own assessment of your knowledge of the topics, read the entire chapter. Table 11-1 lists the major headings in this chapter and their corresponding "Do I Know This Already?" quiz questions. You can find the answers in Appendix D, "Answers to the 'Do I Know This Already?' Quizzes and Review Questions."

Table 11-1 "Do I Know This Already?" Section-to-Question Mapping

Foundation Topics Section	Questions
An Overview of Wireless QoS Principles	1–4
Implementing QoS Policies on the Wireless Controller	5
Implement QoS for Wireless Clients	6
Implementing Application Visibility and Control	7

1. What is a unique characteristic of CSMA/CA?

    a. The AP uses a point coordination function to instruct the stations when to send.

    b. CSMA/CA is able to detect collisions after transmission.

    c. CSMA/CA avoids collisions by first asking permission of the AP to send.

    d. Every frame must be acknowledged by the receiving station.

2. How many Access Categories are defined by EDCA?

   a. Two

   b. Four

   c. Eight

   d. Unlimited

3. Which EDCA metric defines how long a station may continue transmitting?

   a. AIFSN

   b. CWmin

   c. CWmax

   d. TXOP

   e. TSpec

4. What is the primary role of the QoS profile in AireOS?

   a. Sets the DSCP trust boundary

   b. Allows customization of the EDCA parameters for QoS handling

   c. Sets the UP-to-DSCP and marking scheme

   d. Sets a maximum allowable DSCP value that can be used on the CAPWAP header and downstream UP value

5. To restrict traffic to a QoS level that uses DSCP and UP values of 0, what profile should be chosen?

   a. Platinum

   b. Gold

   c. Silver

   d. Bronze

6. What methods are available to control QoS on a wireless client? (Choose all that apply.)

   a. Microsoft Group Policy

   b. Apple Configurator

   c. Meraki MDM

   d. DNA-Center

7. Which of the following is *not* a feature of AVC?

   a. Remarking of DSCP

   b. Weighted Tail Drop

   c. Rate Limiting

   d. Traffic Drop

Foundation Topics

An Overview of Wireless QoS Principles

Wireless networks operate in a far less predictable manner than their wired counterparts, making reliable transport of latency-sensitive applications that much more challenging. Many longtime networking engineers will remember working with hubs—these were very basic half-duplex Ethernet devices where all the ports were part of the same collision domain, meaning no two stations could transmit at the same time without causing a collision. If one station were to transmit at the same time as another, a collision would occur, and both stations would need to back off for a random period of time in which they would try their transmissions again. In a hub environment, it was next to impossible to implement QoS of any kind—the environment was just too unpredictable and packet loss caused by collisions meant that real-time applications could never work reliably.

Today, hubs are next to extinct and have long since been replaced by Layer 2 switches that operate in full-duplex mode and use Content Addressable Memory (CAM) tables to ensure collisions do not occur. You may find it surprising that today's Wi-Fi (up to 802.11ac Wave 2) essentially acts like a hub environment. Similar to hubs, Wi-Fi is a half-duplex medium, and only one station can transmit at a time without causing a collision (that is, each AP operates in its own collision domain). In other words, if an AP can be compared to a hub, and considering QoS was nearly impossible with hubs, how can QoS possibly be implemented at all in a wireless network?

The primary role of QoS in wired networks is to manage congestion; however, in wireless networks, the role of QoS is broader and much more difficult. In a wireless network, the main objective is to manage and limit the number of collisions for high-priority applications, thereby improving the overall quality of experience (QoE) for end users.

In the early days of Wi-Fi, primarily 802.11a/b/g, there was no QoS mechanism whatsoever. However, over the years the 802.11 QoS toolset slowly matured, with continual progress being made by the IEEE 802.11e Working Group. In 2016, further WLAN QoS enhancements that were proposed by IEEE 802.11e were rolled into a new wider definition of the 802.11-2016 standard, which includes the current definitive standard for wireless QoS. However, it is important to keep in mind that while the IEEE 802.11 body sets the standards, they are not responsible for ensuring equipment vendors are compatible with this standard. To address this, the Wi-Fi alliance formed a wireless QoS compatibility standard (which is based on the 802.11e enhancements defined in the 802.11-2016 standard), called Wireless Multimedia (WMM).

In Wi-Fi networks, every station associated to a particular AP must share the medium with all the other stations, and only one station may transmit at a given time—including the AP itself. The result is that each station must contend with all the other stations for airtime. WLANs are not half-duplex by choice. Wireless is by definition a multiple-access, broadcast medium, meaning that if more than one station transmits at a given time, the two signals interfere with each other and the receiver will not be able to decipher what was transmitted.

This situation is quite familiar to many people in business environments. Have you ever been on a conference call when two people try to talk at the same time? Although our brains have the ability interpret even the subtlest of sounds, it is almost impossible to untangle more than one sound (or person speaking) at a time. The brain's limbic system is responsible for sorting out what we really want to listen to versus all other background sounds, but if more than one person speaks to us at the same time, all we hear is noise.

Now compare this with how a wireless AP communicates. Since the RF spectrum used by an AP and all its associated stations is shared, there is a physical limitation that only one station can transmit at a given time on a given channel without causing interference.

11

NOTE   The method of shared channel access described here primarily relates to 802.11a/b/g/n/ac. IEEE 802.11ax (Wi-Fi 6) introduces a new method of channel access that is much more structured and controlled by a scheduling and resource allocation mechanism in the AP. With 802.11ax, each client device is given a subset of the available channel called a Resource Unit (RU), meaning the approach to QoS is somewhat different. 802.11ax is described in more detail in Appendix A, "802.11ax."

QoS mechanisms in wired networks are chiefly responsible for managing which packet, according to its class, is transmitted next, especially during times of congestion. In a Wi-Fi network, the job of QoS is far more complicated. Because the wireless medium is both shared and half-duplex, the QoS mechanism must manage priority access to the RF channel for all end stations in an organized and predictable way.

The following section examines the fundamentals of 802.11 media access, which will lead to a discussion of how it has been adapted to support QoS. Although the first incarnation of 802.11 media access had no ability to support QoS, a good grasp of how it works will enable you to understand how the modifications introduced by 802.11e have made WLAN QoS a reality.

The Distributed Coordination Function

Media access in the early days of 802.11 (802.11a/b/g) was governed by a process called the Distributed Coordination Function (DCF). Although much has changed since the early days of DCF, it still remains a foundational topic for modern 802.11 media access operation. DCF, and its successor, the Enhanced Distributed Channel Access (EDCA), can be thought of as "the rules of the road" for how a station gains access to the medium to transmit a frame.

Wi-Fi networks are completely egalitarian, meaning that all stations have equal access to the medium. In fact, even the AP has the exact same level of priority access to the medium as client stations do. If no controls were imposed on media access and all stations could transmit at will, collisions would be uncontrollable—in fact, as more clients are associated to the AP and try to transmit, the probability of collisions dramatically increases. In turn, after each collision, as stations attempt to retransmit, the situation snowballs, causing even more collisions until the situation degrades to the point where the network is all but paralyzed.

A similar problem was encountered in the early days of wired Ethernet hubs. To address this situation, a system called Carrier Sense Multiple Access with Collision Detection (CSMA/CD) was developed. CSMA/CD is a set of transmission and retransmission rules where all stations that wish to transmit must first wait until the medium is idle before transmitting a frame—essentially a "listen before you transmit" model. Once a station confirms there are no other stations currently transmitting and the medium is clear, it will transmit. After transmission, the station continues to listen in case another station happened to transmit at the exact same time, causing a collision. If there is a collision, both sending stations must wait a random backoff period before resending the frame, and hopefully the next time they transmit there will not be a collision. If there is, they again wait for another random backoff period, but this time they exponentially increase their random backoff window.

Similar to hubs, wireless networks are also collisions domains; however, they have unique challenges that cannot be solved simply by applying CSMA/CD. In a wired hub, a transmitting station can detect collisions by continually listening to the wire for an energy signal that would indicate simultaneous transmission. However, wireless stations that are broadcasting into the air do not have this ability—unlike hubs, there is no possible way to detect a collision in the air simply by listening to the wireless medium. Further, wireless clients often experience the "hidden node" problem, where two transmitting clients cannot see each other when listening to see if the medium is idle (because they are either too far away from each other or an obstruction sits between them). This often results in both stations attempting to send at the same time as soon as the medium is free, thereby causing a collision.

In an effort to alleviate the collision problem in wireless networks, CSMA/CD was modified into Carrier Sense Multiple Access with *Collision Avoidance* (CSMA/CA). There are many similarities between CSMA/CD and CSMA/CD, including the "listen before you talk" method. The main difference comes in what happens after a transmission—instead of just listening to see if a collision occurred, CSMA/CA requires every frame to be acknowledged by the receiver. Thus, instead of listening to the medium to see if a collision occurred (which is not reliable in a wireless medium), the transmitting client will wait until an acknowledgment (ACK) is received from the receiving station to know that the transmission was successful before it moves to the next frame. If an ACK is not received, the station will know it must retransmit. It will then wait a random backoff period and then try to retransmit until it finally receives an ACK.

It is important to note that CSMA/CA can never fully guarantee that a collision won't occur; rather, it reduces the *probability* that a collision will occur by trying to avoid a future collision. CSMA/CA is something like stopping your car at a four-way stop. Although you might try very hard to avoid a collision by looking both ways carefully before driving into the intersection, you can never fully guarantee what other drivers will do. If you decide to step on the gas, there is always a slight possibility that another driver might do the same thing at the same time, meaning the possibility of a collision is always present. The same goes for wireless stations that operate using CSMA/CA—even though stations listen before sending, they can never fully guarantee a collision won't occur after the frame is transmitted.

DCF heavily leverages CSMA/CA for media access. As mentioned earlier, CSMA/CA provides a framework of "listen before you talk" for wireless stations. When a wireless station wants to transmit a frame, the first thing it does is wait a predetermined amount of time called the DCF Interframe Space (DIFS) timer—a period of 34 microseconds in 802.11. Once the DIFS period has expired and if the medium is still clear, the station transmits the frame. Note that all stations must wait the mandatory DIFS period before sending their frame—it is like a level set for all stations that want to transmit. If they all just started transmitting as soon as they had a frame in the queue, collisions would be unavoidable. However, by waiting the DIFS period, it gives a chance for stations to confirm that the media is indeed clear for transmission.

The DIFS is actually two timers in one—a period of 16 microseconds called the Short Interframe Space (SIFS) that occurs as soon as a station finishes transmitting. The SIFS is a short period that confirms the station is indeed finished transmitting. Once the SIFS is concluded, a further 18 microseconds of waiting follows (composed of two slot times, 9 microseconds each). Remember, in CSMA/CA, all frames must be acknowledged by the other side. This last part of the DIFS timer allows the receiver to send its ACK to confirm the transmission was successful. This period finishes the DIFS interval.

Once the DIFS is complete, the station generates a random number called the Contention Window (CW). The CW is a slot time value that must be counted down to zero, at which

11

point if the medium is still free the station begins to transmit. The initial CW value is a number chosen between 0 and 15 slot times (where each slot time is 9 microseconds) and is called the CWmin. Once the CW timer counts to zero, the station begins to transmit its frame. Figure 11-1 illustrates this process.

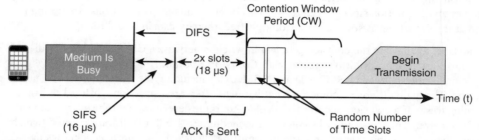

Figure 11-1 *Media Access with the DCF Process*

What about situations where a transmission is not acknowledged by the receiving station? In this case, either a collision occurred or interference was encountered. The client must try again, but with a modification to its CW. On the second attempt, the CWmin is doubled to 0–31 slot times (meaning a random countdown number is chosen between 0 and 31). If this is still not successful, the CW is doubled again to 63, and so on and so forth. This process continues until the CW is increased to 0–1,023 slot times, a value called the CWmax. This doesn't mean that the CW will be 1,023; rather, it simply increases the range of possible random numbers that may be chosen. Figure 11-2 illustrates this process.

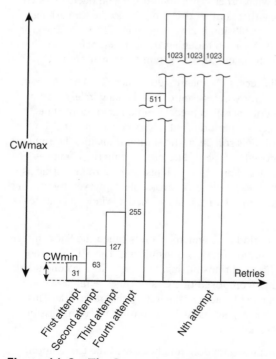

Figure 11-2 *The Contention Window Exponential Increase from CWmin to CWmax*

You might be wondering how long this algorithm will continue if a station does not receive an ACK from the receiving station. In 802.11, there is no predefined limit to the number of retries that a station may attempt; however, in a Cisco AP, the limit is 64 retries before the frame is dumped.

Putting this all together, Figure 11-3 illustrates the overall DCF decision process for a station that is attempting to transmit a frame onto the wireless medium.

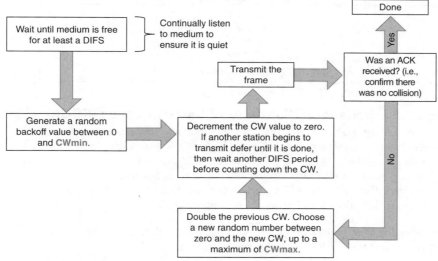

Figure 11-3   *The DCF Algorithm Block Diagram*

Based on the DCF algorithm described in Figure 11-3, consider an example of how this might apply when multiple stations are attempting to transmit frames at the same time and encounter contention. In the following example illustrated in Figure 11-4, there are five stations associated to the same AP. Stations A, B, C, D, and E are all trying to send frames at approximately the same time.

To begin, Station A is already sending an Ethernet frame. Stations B, C, and D all show up and want to transmit, but since Station A is in the midst of a transmission, they must all defer until the channel is clear (they know this by listening to the medium). Once Station A finishes its transmission, Stations B, C, and D detect that the medium is clear. First, they all wait the mandatory DIFS period. Once the DIFS period has expired, the remaining three stations generate a random number between 0 and CWmin. In this example, Station B generates the smallest random CW value. Once Station B counts down to zero, it immediately transmits its frame (assuming the medium is still clear).

As soon as Station B begins transmitting, Stations C and D hear the transmission and immediately pause their CW countdown timers. These stations must now defer/wait until Station B is finished before they can resume. Notice that during Station B's transmission, Station E suddenly shows up and wants to transmit as well, so now there are again three stations contending for access to the medium. Once Station B finishes, Stations C and D resume their countdown. Because Station D has the smallest CW timer, it reaches zero first and begins transmission while Stations C and E defer, and so the algorithm continues until everyone has had the opportunity to transmit their frames.

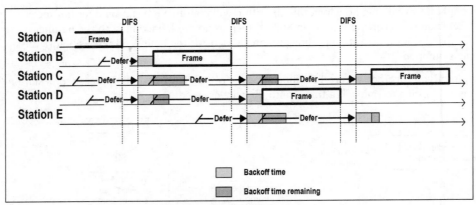

Figure 11-4 *An Example of the DCF Algorithm in Action*

Retrofitting DCF—Enhanced Distributed Channel Access (EDCA)

While DCF does a pretty good job at managing contention and media access, it has an obvious flaw—there is no differentiation of service for higher- or lower-priority applications. In short, there is no QoS in DCF. With the emergence of 802.11e and WMM, a media access algorithm that supports QoS was introduced, called the Enhanced Distributed Channel Access (EDCA) algorithm. While EDCA builds on the foundations of DCF, it introduced five major enhancements that allow Wi-Fi networks to support QoS:

- The establishment of four Access Categories (ACs), which are analogous to queues in a wired switch and allow differentiated service handling.

- Instead of a single DIFS for all traffic, 802.11e/WMM introduces different interframe spacing values for each AC, allowing more aggressive media access for high-priority traffic. This spacing timer is called the Arbitrated Interframe Space Number (AIFSN).

- Different contention window values for each AC (that is, different CWmin and CWmax values for each AC).

- Transmission Opportunity (TXOP) values for each AC.

- Call Admission Control (TSpec).

These five key enhancements of EDCA are discussed in the following sections.

Access Categories

EDCA is similar to DCF in many ways, especially in the way that it leverages CSMA/CA for media access. However, it diverges in use of Access Categories and the wait timers that help deal with contention. 802.11e EDCA and WMM specify four different ACs (from highest priority to least):

- Video (AC_VO)

- Voice (AC_VI)

- Best Effort (AC_BE)

- Background (AC_BK)

Unlike wired switches and routers that may have different numbers of transmit queues depending on the type of interface, link speed, manufacturer and device type, Wi-Fi devices by convention may only have four Access Categories. In fact, to meet WMM compliance, Wi-Fi devices must have these four ACs—no more and no less.

In order to distinguish different classes of service, the 802.11e Ethernet frame header incorporates a 3-bit field known as the 802.11e User Priority (UP) that offers up to eight different values; however, although eight UP values are possible, only four ACs are available for use. The 802.11e UP field is similar to the 802.1p CoS field used on wired 802.1q Ethernet trunks, but in this case UP is only used between wireless stations.

> **NOTE**   The UP value was only introduced as part of 802.11n, meaning there is no UP value in prior generations (802.11a/b/g).

Figure 11-5 illustrates the WMM AC-to-UP mapping on a Wi-Fi interface.

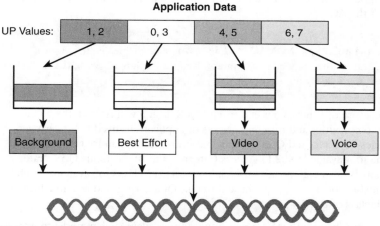

 Figure 11-5   *Access Categories and Their UP Mappings*

At this point, you may be wondering how a frame is marked with the correct UP value and thus put into the correct AC when it is being transmitted. This happens through a mapping of the IP packet's DSCP to the 802.11e UP value. In other words, as an IP packet enters the controller in the downstream direction (or arrives at an AP in the upstream direction), the controller examines the DSCP value and maps it to a corresponding UP value, which is then written into the 802.11 header. Table 11-2 summarizes the mappings of DSCP to WMM UP to AC.

 Table 11-2   Mapping of DSCP to WMM UP Value to Access Category

Traffic Type	DSCP	WMM UP Value	Access Category Mapping
Voice	46 (ef)	6	Voice (AC_VO)
Interactive Video	34 (af41)	5	Video (AC_VI)
Call Signaling	24 (cs3)	3	Best Effort (AC_BE)

11

Traffic Type	DSCP	WMM UP Value	Access Category Mapping
Transactional / Interactive Data	18 (af21)	3	Best Effort (AC_BE)
Bulk Data	10 (af11)	2	Background (AC_BK)
Best Effort	0 (be)	0	Best Effort (AC_BE)

Outside of the specific mapping values shown in Table 11-1, other DSCP-to-UP mappings are derived by taking the three most significant bits (MSB) of the DSCP field and using this to generate an UP value. For example, a DSCP value of 40 in binary is 101000. Taking the MSB of this is 101, which translates to a decimal value of 5. The 802.11e UP value of 5 would then be mapped to the Video AC (AC_VI). The mapping of DSCP to UP values is standardized by RFC 8325, which aligns to the implementation used by Cisco wireless LAN controllers.

As data is processed by each radio interface, the DSCP value is mapped to the corresponding UP value, which in turn assigns the frame to the correct Access Category. Once the frame is assigned to the appropriate AC, the Wi-Fi radio begins to transmit the frame according to the relative priority of the AC.

NOTE   One aspect of the 802.11e/WMM AC model shown in Table 11-2 is that voice is mapped to a value of 6, rather than 5, which is common for 802.1p CoS, showing that the two marking systems do not exactly align.

Another aspect to be aware of is how your end-to-end QoS design will fit with the wireless network. Due to the complexities and different classes of applications used in modern networks, many companies have adopted QoS designs that utilize more than four classes, making a challenge for the four available 802.11 Access Categories to fit a campus QoS strategy. Today, it is not uncommon to see companies use eight or even 12 class QoS systems. Each networking device must in some way adopt these different QoS classes and provide differential treatment to each class of traffic.

If your network uses more than four QoS classes, how can you adapt such a model to wireless networks? You might be thinking that four is a very small number of QoS classes, but remember that this limitation is something of an artifact from the 802.11e standard that was introduced in 2005. In the early 2000s, use of 4-class QoS models was fairly common. However, today the demands of modern applications have pushed this much higher. The result is that no matter how many QoS classes are in use in your network, in a wireless network this design is reduced to a 4-class model, as all QoS markings will be mapped to one of the four available wireless access categories.

Figure 11-6 illustrates a simple mapping scheme of a typical 8-class system to a wireless network.

As can be seen in Figure 11-6, an enterprise QoS class structure must be mapped to the four available ACs, regardless of how many classes are used in the enterprise model. This is done through the DSCP-to-UP mapping scheme. For example, if your enterprise uses two separate QoS classes for video—one for broadcast video and another for interactive video—these could both be mapped into the Video AC (AV_VI). Since UP values of 4 and 5 are mapped to this AC, it is important to ensure that only DSCP values that map to these 11e UP values are chosen for these application classes.

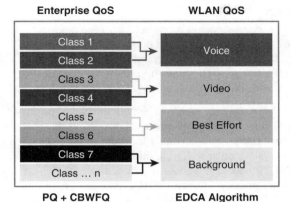

Figure 11-6 *Mapping an 8-Class QoS System to the Four Access Categories in a Wireless LAN*

Also, while most wired networks employ a priority queuing system for voice (and sometimes video) and rely on Class-Based Weighted Fair Queuing (CBWFQ) for everything else, in wireless networks there is no such thing as a priority queue. All Wi-Fi ACs are handled by the rules of EDCA.

Arbitrated Interframe Space Number (AIFSN)

One of the key limitations of DCF is that the DIFS value is the same for all traffic types, regardless of how latency-sensitive the data is. To address this, EDCA introduces different interframe spacing periods for each Access Category, called the Arbitration Interframe Spacing Number (AIFSN). The intention of assigning different interframe spacing values to each AC is that the higher-priority ACs are assigned a shorter initial wait period compared to the lower-priority ACs, thus giving high-priority traffic a much better probability of being transmitted first and reducing its probability of contention and retries (thus reducing latency and jitter). The AIFSN values defined in EDCA are shown in Table 11-3 (measured in slot times).

Table 11-3 AIFSNs per Access Category

AC Priority Queue	AIFSN Slot Times
Voice (AC_VO)	2
Video (AC_VI)	2
Best Effort (AC_BE)	3
Background (AC_BK)	7

By way of comparison, the DIFS used by DCF uses an interframe space of two slot times (the same value used by AC_VO in EDCA). Clearly, with the voice and video ACs having a much shorter AIFSN, you would expect latency-sensitive data to spend much less time in the contention algorithm and on average be sent before lower-priority traffic. While assigning differential AIFSNs to each AC goes a long way toward improving QoS, 802.11 is still a contention-based medium and collisions can occur. What varying AIFSNs accomplish is an improvement in the probability of higher-priority traffic being serviced first by giving it a statistical advantage over lower-priority traffic; however, AIFSNs do not guarantee that voice and other high-priority traffic will always be sent first, like you would expect from a strict priority queue on a wired switch.

Contention Window Enhancements

In legacy DCF environments, once the DIFS expires, each station backs off for a random contention window period. If collisions occur, the CW is doubled up to a value of CWmax. Similar to using a common DIFS for all traffic types, DCF in general gives no preferential CW treatment to higher-priority traffic, meaning all traffic types have the same statistical probability of dealing with contention.

Like AIFSNs, EDCA introduces different CW ranges for each AC, helping the higher-priority ACs compete more aggressively to transmit their frames in the presence of contention. This is particularly important for latency-sensitive traffic such as voice and video, which suffer if they have to wait the longer CWmax intervals. Similar to having different AIFSN values assigned to each AC, different CWmin and CWmax values are also assigned to each AC, providing a statistical advantage to the higher-priority ACs. The EDCA CW values are listed in Table 11-4.

Table 11-4   EDCA Contention Window Times for Each Access Category

	CWmin (slot times)	CWmax (slot times)
Legacy DCF CW Values (for comparison)	15	1,023
Voice (AC_VO)	3	7
Video (AC_VI)	7	15
Best Effort (AC_BE)	15	1,023
Background (AC_BK)	15	1,023

Note from Table 11-4 how AC_VO only backs off between 0 and 3 (CWmin) slot times and a maximum of 0 to 7 (CWmax) slot times. Note also how AC_BE and AC_BK are given the same CW times as DCF. Of course, since the CW is randomly generated, there is still a small probability that the lower-priority ACs could back off for a shorter period than a higher-priority AC; however, statistically speaking, the higher-priority ACs will experience much less contention than the lower-priority ones.

In summary, the AIFSN and CW timers work together to greatly improve the overall handling of high-priority traffic and its ability to successfully transmit, even in the presence of contention.

Transmission Opportunity (TXOP)

A fourth enhancement of 802.11e/WMM is contention-free access periods for stations to access the medium, called the Transmission Opportunity (TOXP). The TXOP is a set period of time when a wireless station may continue to send as many frames as possible without having to contend with other stations. Winning the EDCA contention algorithm in a busy WLAN is something like winning a contest—but imagine if a transmitting station were to only win the right to send one single frame at a time before going back and competing all over again before it can send the next frame. Obviously, this would severely impact latency-sensitive traffic and would be largely ineffective. Conversely, if the transmitting station were to be given unlimited access and continually send frames after it wins the contention algorithm, this could starve out other stations.

With EDCA's TXOP enhancement, each AC has a set time limit where it can continually transmit frames uninterrupted. Once the TXOP limit expires, it must give up access to the medium and go back and contend once again for its the next chance to transmit. Table 11-5 summarizes the TXOP values for each AC.

Table 11-5   EDCA Transmission Opportunity (TXOP) Values for Each Access Category

EDCA / WMM AC	TXOP (µs)	TXOP (Units)
Voice (AC_VO)	2,080	65
Video (AC_VI)	4,096	128
Best Effort (AC_BE)	2,528	79
Background (AC_BK)	2,528	79

Notice from Table 11-5 that AC_VO has a shorter TXOP value than any other AC. In fact, AC_VI's TXOP is double that of AC_VO, despite having a lower priority. The explanation is in how congestion is handled by the TXOP. Recall that voice traffic generally consumes only a small amount of bandwidth, requiring much less airtime. For example, as shown in Figure 11-7, only one voice packet is sent every 20 ms. Compare that to a 4K video stream where each video frame contains 8.3 million pixels, most of which are changing 30 times per second (much faster than voice). The sheer volume of data needed by video requires a larger TXOP to maintain an acceptable performance level. As for AC_BE and AC_BK, giving a larger TXOP than voice actually helps voice traffic by reducing the amount of time lower-priority traffic contends for the medium.

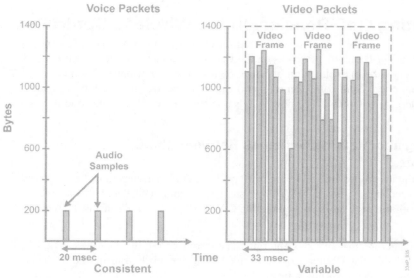

Figure 11-7   *Comparing Voice and Video Traffic Volumes for TXOP Use*

802.11 Transmission Specification (TSpec)

The last major QoS enhancement introduced by 802.11e/WMM is a method of Call Admission Control (CAC) called Traffic Specification (TSpec). TSpec allows real-time applications, such as voice calls, to be prioritized by reserving bandwidth on the AP before it begins transmission. To use this feature, TSpec must be configured on the AP and optionally on the client stations.

When running TSpec, a client station signals its traffic requirements (data rate, power save mode, frame size, and so on) to the AP using an ADD Traffic Stream (ADDTS) message. If the AP is running TSpec for that AC, it will respond back with either an acceptance or a rejection of the request. If the request is accepted, the AP will reserve the requested bandwidth for the client and the call may be made. If the AP is not able to accommodate the request, it will reply back that the ADDTS request has been declined and the client may try to transmit anyway without reserved bandwidth, or it may attempt to roam to another AP.

Figure 11-8 illustrates the function of TSpec.

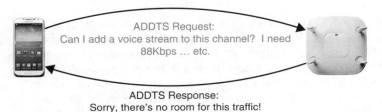

ADDTS Request:
Can I add a voice stream to this channel? I need
88Kbps ... etc.

ADDTS Response:
Sorry, there's no room for this traffic!

Figure 11-8   *The Function of TSpec*

As 802.11 networks have become faster and support wider channels, TSpec has become less critical for real-time applications. In general, the greatest improvements to QoS are seen through the EDCA timers, particularly the AIFSN, CW, and TXOP timers.

Implementing QoS Policies on the Wireless Controller

Before the wireless controller can be configured for QoS, it is important to understand how the mappings of DSCP to UP works on the CAPWAP tunnel, and vice versa. The next section will begin with an explanation of how QoS markings are managed, both in the downstream direction (from controller to client) and in the upstream direction (from client to controller). Next, you will see how QoS is implemented on the AireOS and IOS-XE controllers.

QoS Mapping and Marking Schemes Between the Client and Controller

In order to maintain proper QoS handling of IP packets, QoS markings must be preserved end-to-end. To accomplish this, a consistent system of mapping DSCP and UP values is required for both the original IP packet and the CAPWAP packet that tunnels the wireless traffic.

In the downstream direction (packets entering the controller from the wired network, which are passed into the CAPWAP tunnel down to the AP and are finally transmitted to the client), there are two QoS remarking steps involved:

Step 1.   An Ethernet frame is received over an 802.1q trunk at the controller from its upstream switch. The controller examines the DSCP marking on the IP packet and transcribes this to the DSCP field on the header of the CAPWAP packet.

Although the 802.1q trunk will likely carry an 802.1p CoS value, this is generally ignored because DSCP is the preferred method of QoS trust.

Note that in most cases the inner DSCP and the CAPWAP DSCP will be the same; however, some exceptions to this rule exist, which will be discussed later in this chapter.

Step 2.   When the AP receives an incoming CAPWAP packet, the DSCP value on the CAPWAP tunnel is examined and mapped to an 802.11e UP value. This is then transmitted over the air from the corresponding AC. The mapping of DSCP to UP in this case is based on the mapping table shown in Table 11-2. Figure 11-9 illustrates the downstream QoS remarking and mapping process.

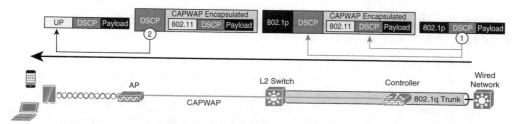

① The Ethernet frame is received over an 802.1q trunk by the WLC. The WLC uses the DSCP value of the IP packet and maps it to the outer DSCP of the CAPWAP tunnel.

② Once the Ethernet frame is received by the AP, it maps the DSCP value of the IP packet to the 802.11e UP value on the wireless frame. The frame is then sent to the client.

Figure 11-9 *QoS Mapping and Remarking in the Downstream Direction*

An important subtlety in this scheme is where the final downstream mapping of DSCP to UP is derived from. At the AP, the CAPWAP's DSCP value is used rather than the inner packet. In most cases, this is not an issue because the two DSCP values are exactly the same. However, there are important cases where the DSCP values on the CAPWAP header and the inner IP packet are in fact different, meaning the UP value that is selected will give a different QoS handling than what is marked on the inner packet.

In the upstream direction, the process is much the same but in reverse. The two steps in the upstream direction are as follows:

Step 1.   A client transmits a frame with the UP field marked on the 802.11 header, as well as the DSCP value on the IP packet header. When the frame arrives at the AP, it has the choice (defined by the administrator) to either inherently trust the DSCP value of the inner packet and map this to the CAPWAP header or to map the Layer 2 11e UP value to a DSCP value based on Table 11-2 and then map this to the CAPWAP header. The inner DSCP marking is preserved and does not change.

Step 2.   After the CAPWAP packet is decapsulated at the controller, the original IP packet is sent to the upstream switch over an 802.1q trunk. Again, even if QoS is used by default, it is ignored in place of the DSCP value. Figure 11-10 illustrates how the QoS markings are handled in the upstream direction.

11

① The client 802.11e frame is received by the AP. The AP maps the 802.11e UP value
  or original packet DSCP to the outer CAPWAP IP DSCP header (configurable).

② At the WLC end of the CAPWAP tunnel, the 802.11e frame is bridged to the Ethernet
  switch and original DSCP value is used on emerging packet.

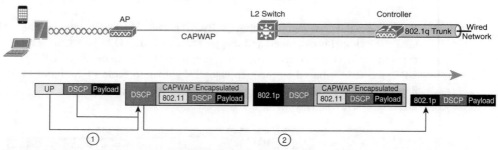

Figure 11-10 *QoS Mapping and Remarking in the Upstream Direction*

As discussed previously, the administrator has the choice to either trust DSCP or UP at the access point, but the recommended approach is to trust DSCP in the upstream direction.

> **NOTE**   If the client does not support WMM, there will be no 802.11e UP value marked into the frame (since 802.11e UP is only supported by WMM). In this case, the AP is forced to apply a default QoS setting to the traffic. This is described in more detail later in this chapter.

From the underlying IP transport network's perspective, the CAPWAP tunnel is simply a flow of IP packets that need to be handled with the appropriate level of QoS based on the DSCP marking in the IP header.

Handling QoS Marking in the WLAN

The AireOS controller implements QoS in four profiles, known as "precious metal" profiles. These profiles are something of a historical artifact in AireOS, with a loose mapping to the four WMM Access Categories; however, today there is no real correlation between the QoS profiles and the WMM ACs. The QoS profiles provide a method to tweak the QoS handling in a templated way and then have this mapped to a WLAN.

The fundamental purpose of the QoS profiles is to set a maximum DSCP marking limit on the CAPWAP tunnel and in turn the downstream 11e UP value. As discussed earlier, the inner IP packet's DSCP value is mapped directly to the DSCP value of the CAPWAP header; however, the precious metal profile can override this mapping function by capping the DSCP on the CAPWAP header to a maximum value. For example, if the Platinum profile is implemented, but a packet with a DSCP value of 56 enters the controller in the downstream direction, the CAPWAP DSCP value will be restricted to 46 while the inner IP packet's DSCP value will remain at 46. Table 11-6 summarizes the maximum DSCP value of each QoS profile.

Table 11-6   The Four QoS Profiles in AireOS Controllers

QoS Profile Name	Maximum DSCP Ceiling	Use Case
Platinum	46	Most commonly used. Recommended for most enterprise deployments.
Gold	34	Limited use.
Silver	0	Hotspots/guest users.
Bronze	10	Limited use.

In past literature, it was recommended to implement a separate WLAN for each class of service used in the wireless network and then apply a different QoS profile to these WLANs. For example, a common recommendation was to deploy wireless IP phones on a dedicated voice SSID and apply the Platinum profile. Clearly, this is no longer a practical way to implement a wireless network, as mobile phones, laptops, and anything else you can think of are Wi-Fi capable and most of them can be used for voice and video communications. The need to mix these types of devices on a single WLAN means dedicating a single voice WLAN, which is not practical. In light of this, it is generally recommended to use the Platinum profile for all enterprise applications, meaning the other profiles are rarely used. In some cases where you may want to limit the CAPWAP DSCP value, such as in a guest or a hotspot network, the Silver or Bronze profile may be used.

So how do these QoS profiles actually work? In the downstream direction, the QoS is handled by mapping the incoming packet's DSCP value to the CAPWAP DSCP (as illustrated in Figure 11-9). At the AP, the DSCP is mapped to the corresponding 802.11e UP value and is placed in the correct egress AC. As packets enter the controller, the DSCP makings are compared with the QoS profile applied to the WLAN. If the DSCP value exceeds the QoS profile's maximum allowable DSCP value, it will be downgraded to the maximum allowed value for that profile. For example, if a WLAN has the Gold profile implemented, the maximum DSCP allowed on the CAPWAP header is 34 (af41). If a packet enters the controller from the wired side with a DSCP of 46 (ef), the controller will downgrade the DSCP to 34 on the CAPWAP tunnel, and the packet will now be treated as a video packet (af41 is generally used for video packets in an IP network according to RFC 4594).

It is important to note that the mappings in the AP and the controller never impact the inner IP packet's DSCP value—the profile only limits the DSCP value on the CAPWAP header. If a packet enters the controller from the wired side with a DSCP lower than the default maximum of the QoS profile on that WLAN, then the original packet's DSCP value is simply transcribed to the CAPWAP header and is in turn used to map to the 802.11e UP value at the AP.

In the upstream direction, the AP maps the QoS fields in a very similar way to how the controller does it but in reverse. Since the 802.11e UP values are set by the client, the AP can either (1) compare the incoming 11e UP value with the maximum allowed UP value for the QoS profile on that WLAN and then map it to the corresponding DSCP on the CAPWAP header or (2) just copy the inner packet's DSCP value directly to the CAPWAP header (this is the preferred model). In either case, the DSCP value that is written on the CAPWAP header will be up to the maximum of the QoS profile.

11

By controlling the CAPWAP DSCP, the QoS profile also indirectly sets a maximum allowable 802.11e UP value for each WLAN. For example, if the profile is set to Gold, then by enforcing a maximum DSCP value of 34, a maximum UP value of 5 results at the AP. In the upstream direction, if a frame with an UP value of 6 is received by the AP, it will map the UP value to a DSCP of 34 on the upstream CAPWAP packet, essentially downgrading the QoS handling of that packet across the IP transport network. However, if the AP receives any lower UP values (1–5), these will just be mapped to the corresponding DSCP value shown in Table 11-2. Although this doesn't really constitute as a trust model, it does allow the AP and controller to establish a ceiling on the QoS levels that are accepted per WLAN.

Figure 11-11 illustrates the example of a controller where the Gold profile has been applied to the WLAN. Note what happens when voice packets enter the controller or AP marked with DSCP 46 (EF), either in the upstream or downstream direction.

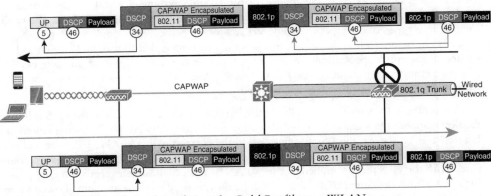

Figure 11-11 *The Effect of Applying the Gold Profile to a WLAN*

Consider another example where the QoS policy can be used to mark down traffic to best effort. This might be the case with a guest wireless network where all traffic should be remarked to DSCP 0. Although you cannot control the DSCP and 802.11e UP markings that originate from the client device, the AP can use the Silver QoS profile, which has a default maximum value of 0 to enforce the maximum DSCP on the CAPWAP header as well as the downstream UP value used on the WLAN.

It is important to note that the mappings shown in Table 11-2 are not customizable and the QoS profile ceilings are hardcoded. This means that certain situations may arise where the AP maps the UP value to a DSCP that is not aligned with the QoS policy in the campus network, thus affecting the handling of CAPWAP packets as they are transported across the IP backbone.

Implementing QoS on the AireOS Controller

To implement the QoS policies, navigate to **Wireless > QoS > QoS Profiles**. Figure 11-12 illustrates how the four "precious metal" QoS profiles are presented in the AireOS controller.

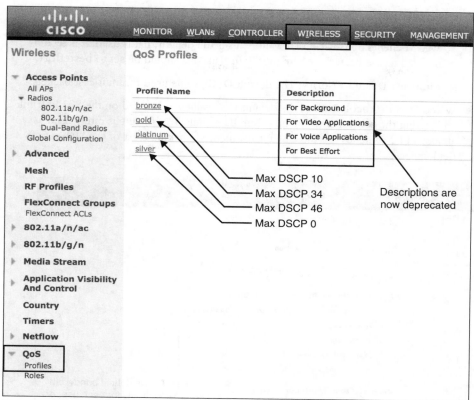

Figure 11-12 *The QoS Profile Configuration Menu in AireOS*

As noted in Figure 11-12, the description of each profile can be ignored, as this is nothing more than a historical artifact. The best-practice recommendation is to use the Platinum profile for enterprise deployments. By clicking each profile, you can configure certain aspects of the profile. This is shown in Figure 11-13. In this menu, the following QoS capabilities can be configured:

- **Per-User Bandwidth Contracts:** A bandwidth rate limiter/policer that is applied for each (useful for hotspots or guest networks).

- **Per-SSID Bandwidth Contracts:** A bandwidth rate limiter for the whole SSID (this is rarely used).

- **WLAN QoS Parameters:**

  - **Maximum Priority:** Sets the upper limit of the DSCP value on the CAPWAP header:

    Voice profile max DSCP = 46

    Video profile max DSCP = 34

    Best Effort profile max DSCP = 0

    Background profile max DSCP = 10

■ **Unicast Default Priority:** Sets the default DSCP value that will be used on the CAPWAP header if non-WMM clients are present (802.11a/b/g). Because non-WMM clients don't use an UP value, this is the default that is used. It is recommended to use **besteffort** here (DSCP 0). This one should be set to **besteffort**.

■ **Multicast Default Priority:** The default DSCP value used for multicast packets.

■ **Wired QoS Protocol:** Defines the default QoS values to be used on the 802.1q trunk connecting the controller to the upstream L2 switch. This feature is rarely used as almost all L2 switches use the DSCP trust method, making trust of the 802.1p QoS field unnecessary.

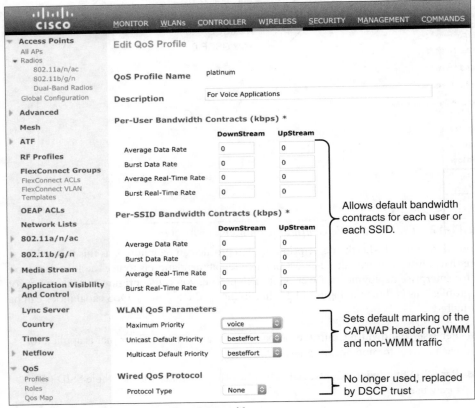

Figure 11-13 *Configuring the QoS Profile*

NOTE   Although design recommendations around per-user and per-SSID bandwidth controls varies depending on the network, it should be considered in places where there is a high density of users (such as in university campus networks) or in places where the AP's wired connection is bandwidth limited, such as at a remote site.

Once the QoS profile has been configured, the final step is to apply the profile to the WLAN. Figure 11-14 illustrates how the Platinum QoS policy is applied to **wlan-enterprise**.

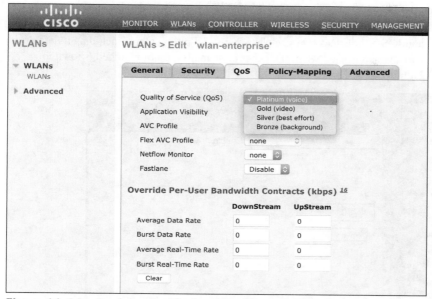

Figure 11-14 *Applying the Platinum Profile to a WLAN*

Implementing QoS on the IOS-XE Controller

The IOS-XE controller offers similar QoS functionality to the AireOS controller, but also inherits many of the well-known native QoS capabilities in IOS and IOS-XE. For example, the IOS-XE controller supports multilevel hierarchical QoS levels, starting with the physical port level, AP radio level, SSID level, and finally the individual user (see Figure 11-15).

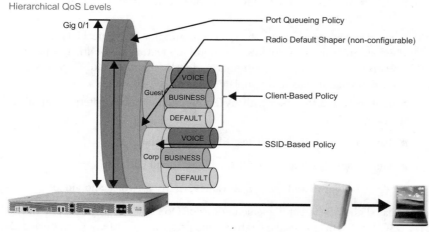

Figure 11-15 *Hierarchical QoS Policies in the IOS-XE Controller*

To configure a QoS policy in the IOS-XE controller, follow these steps:

Step 1. Navigate to **Configuration > Services > QoS** and click **Add**. Here you will be presented with a menu similar to Figure 11-16. In this menu there is an option to add class-maps that will define the QoS behavior for the policy. The underlying CLI syntax follows the same Modular QoS CLI (MQC) used in other IOS and IOS-XE devices that use class-maps and policy maps, including a default class, which is used when the other class-maps are not matched (shown in Figure 11-16).

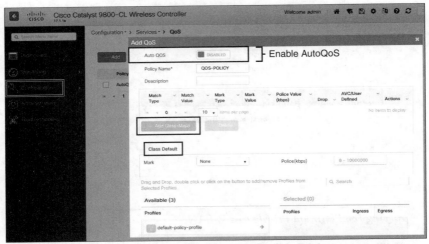

Figure 11-16 *Configuration of a QoS Policy in the IOS-XE Controller*

By clicking **Add** to create a class-map, you can define matching criteria that will trigger behavior of the policy and apply an action. For example, the class-map can be configured to match on either an **AVC** (Application Visibility and Control) or a **User Defined** criteria. If **User Defined** is selected, a matching criterion, such as **ACL** or incoming **DSCP**, can be selected. The action taken can be either to remark or to drop the packet.

You may also have noticed that the QoS configuration in Figure 11-17 allows for the configuration of AutoQoS. The AutoQoS feature is essentially a macro that generates the underlying configuration for different types of QoS profile. The AutoQoS feature has four template options, as follows:

- Enterprise (adds classes with AVC criteria for common enterprise applications)

- Fastlane (implements the latest EDCA parameters)

- Guest (sets DSCP to a default value of 0 for all packets)

- Voice (classifies and sets DSCP values strictly for voice and video)

Each has slightly different implementations of QoS that support best practices for DSCP-to-UP mappings, DSCP trust, and prioritization of common business applications through the use of AVC.

Figure 11-17   *Defining the QoS Policy*

NOTE   AireOS supports an AutoQoS macro called Fastlane. This will be discussed later in the chapter.

Step 2.   Once the policy has been created, add the new QoS policy to the correct policy profile and select the direction of traffic you would like it to be applied in (ingress or egress or both), as shown in Figure 11-18.

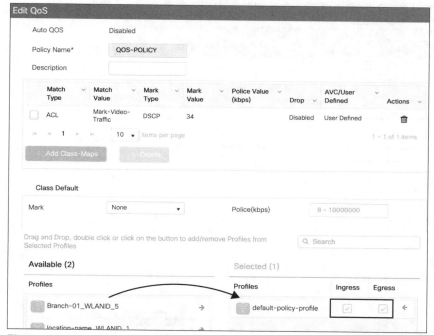

Figure 11-18   *Selecting a Policy Profile for the QoS Policy That Was Just Created*

Step 3.   In the final step, the policy needs to be added to the correct WLANs and APs. Figure 11-19 shows an example of adding the default-policy-profile to the correct WLAN.

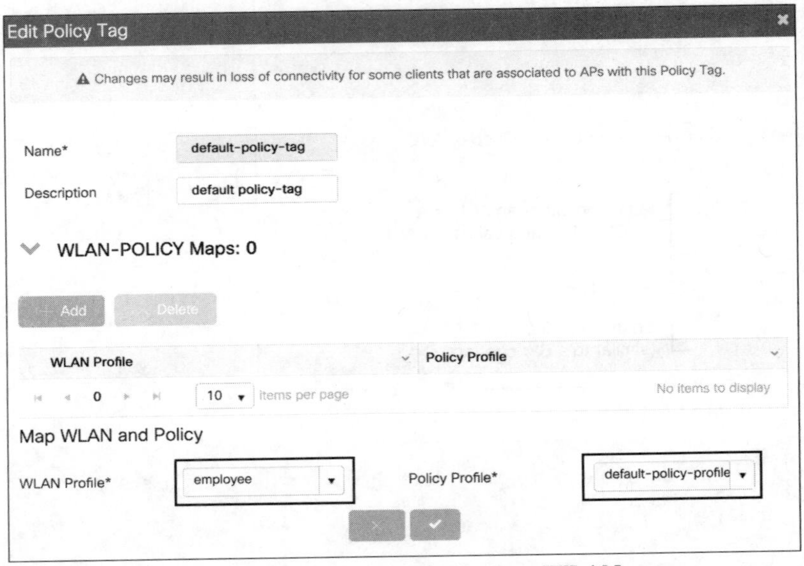

Figure 11-19   *Adding the Policy to the Correct WLAN*

In addition to creating QoS policies as described, it is also possible to implement a DSCP ceiling on the CAPWAP header, similar to using the four precious metal profiles in AireOS (Platinum/Gold/Silver/Bronze), as shown in Figure 11-20.

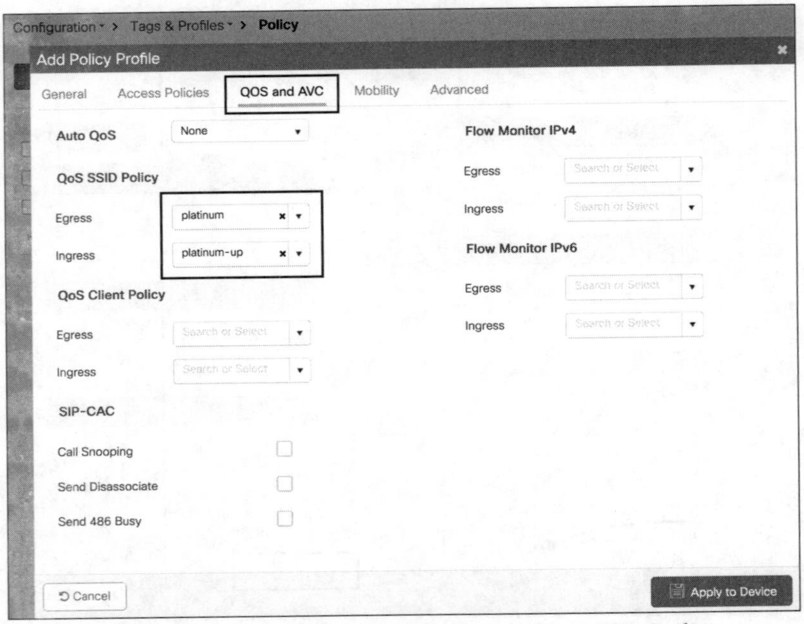

Figure 11-20   *Customizing the QoS Policy with a DSCP Ceiling*

Implementing QoS for Wireless Clients

If QoS is to be compared to a chain, which is only as strong as its weakest link, then wireless QoS from the client to the AP can easily be considered one of the weakest links in the chain. All wireless stations, from the AP to the client, must obey the same rules of EDCA. Each station must use the same access category schemes and follow the same AIFSN, CWmin, CWmax, and TXOP timers for a given WLAN. Media access only works if everybody obeys the same rules for contention. To ensure this happens, the EDCA parameters that clients will use are announced from the AP in wireless management frames. When a client station receives the AP's instructions for the EDC parameters, it must use them. In fact, if the client ignores the EDCA instruction set from the AP, the client cannot be considered Wi-Fi compliant. The following sections examine implementation considerations for the wireless client.

Implementing Client QoS Marking Schemes

For QoS in the upstream direction (from the client to AP) to be successful, not only must the EDCA parameters be correctly observed, but the client also needs to ensure the applications are properly classified and marked and are correctly mapped to the 802.11e UP value that will ensure the frame is sent from the right access category. If a client is not set up to correctly mark DSCP of the packets, or if the mapping of DSCP to UP is not correct, QoS in the upstream direction will not work as expected, or it may not work at all.

In most corporate wireless environments the DSCP marking of packets from an application is orchestrated centrally to prevent a client from incorrectly (or maliciously) misconfiguring the DSCP values and disrupting QoS functions on the network. For example, imagine the impact to a network if a client marked all BitTorrent traffic as high priority, such as DSCP ef (46). Not only would this compete with other voice traffic, it could potentially cause massive disruptions to backbone switches and routers.

In a Microsoft environment, DSCP values are generally controlled by central Group Policy. By default, Windows policy has a default DSCP value of 0; however, on a per-application basis, this can be overridden as desired by Group Policy. For example, a Group Policy Object can be defined to mark all voice traffic originating from webex.exe as DSCP 46. Figure 11-21 illustrates a centralized Group Policy scheme to mark MS Lync traffic.

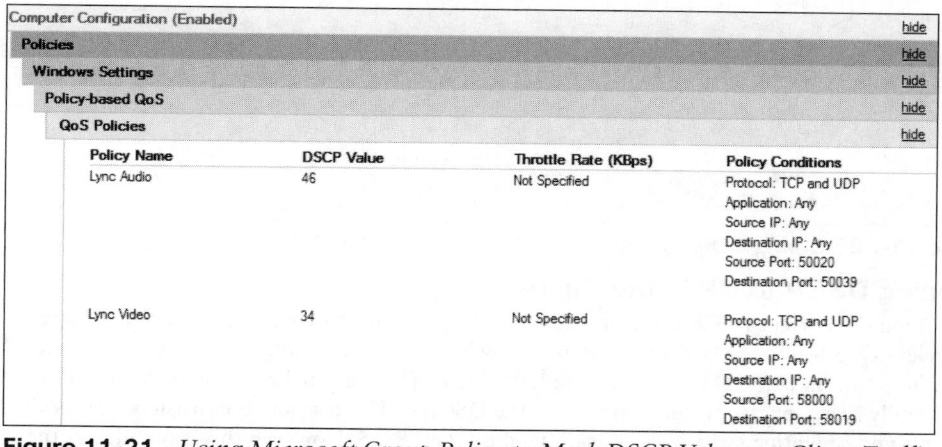

Computer Configuration (Enabled)			hide
Policies			hide
Windows Settings			hide
Policy-based QoS			hide
QoS Policies			hide
Policy Name	**DSCP Value**	**Throttle Rate (KBps)**	**Policy Conditions**
Lync Audio	46	Not Specified	Protocol: TCP and UDP
			Application: Any
			Source IP: Any
			Destination IP: Any
			Source Port: 50020
			Destination Port: 50039
Lync Video	34	Not Specified	Protocol: TCP and UDP
			Application: Any
			Source IP: Any
			Destination IP: Any
			Source Port: 58000
			Destination Port: 58019

Figure 11-21   *Using Microsoft Group Policy to Mark DSCP Values on Client Traffic*

11

For other operating systems, such as MacOS, iOS, and Android, the DSCP markings are natively set by the application and are implicitly trusted by the application (as opposed to marking all traffic to DSCP zero). While this is user-friendly, it also carries the risk that certain applications may incorrectly mark traffic that do not comply with the QoS design or class structure used in an organization. For example, if someone was to transmit a high volume of streaming media packets and give them the highest level of QoS, it could interfere with other applications that are using the same DSCP values but are trusted by the organization.

For these situations, an approach that is similar to Microsoft Group Policy can be used to administer the applications on end users' devices. Two such examples are Apple Configurator and the Meraki MDM (Mobile Device Manager). A tool like Meraki MDM allows an administrator to control not only which applications are used on a device but also what DSCP marking those devices may use. Either the MDM can trust the DSCP values natively used by these applications (since the applications are already assumed to be trusted by corporate IT) or it can remark the DSCP to some other value. All other applications will have their DSCP values remarked to zero. Figure 11-22 illustrates the QoS configuration menu in the Meraki MDM for a collection of applications.

Figure 11-22 *Configuring Client-Side QoS with the Meraki MDM*

Mapping DSCP to UP in the Client

Marking the correct DSCP value on a client is the one aspect that you can control; however, wireless QoS is ultimately decided by which WMM access category the frame is transmitted from, meaning the DSCP-to-802.11e UP value marked into the frame must be accurate. Generally speaking, we would expect that the DSCP-to-UP mapping is consistent across all clients and operating systems, as it is defined by RFC 8325. However, this is not always the case. One example is in Microsoft Windows, where the mapping of DSCP to UP does not follow the mapping standard (unlike Apple and Android).

In the case of Windows, the DSCP value is derived from the three most significant bits (MSB) of the DSCP value. For example, if DSCP 46 (ef) is marked into a voice packet, the binary value of the DSCP is 101110. Taking the three MSB of this DSCP value results in a binary value of 101. In decimal form this is 5, which becomes the UP value on the 802.11 frame. An UP value of 5 translates to AC_VI rather than AC_VO, meaning the voice packet will need to contend for access as if it was video, not voice. The mapping of DSCP to UP is something that is hardcoded into Windows and cannot be changed. Figure 11-23 illustrates a wireless sniffer trace of this effect.

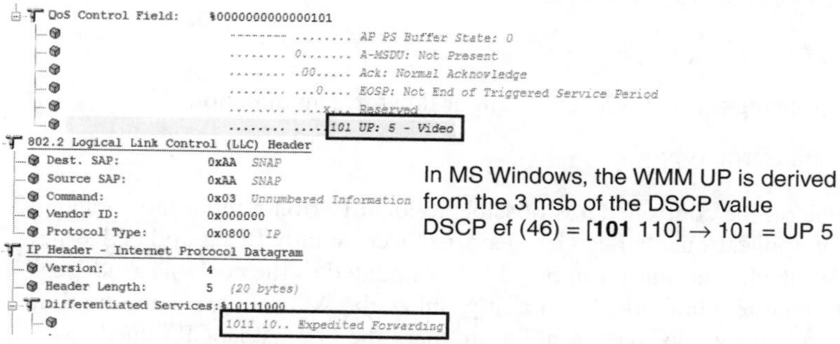

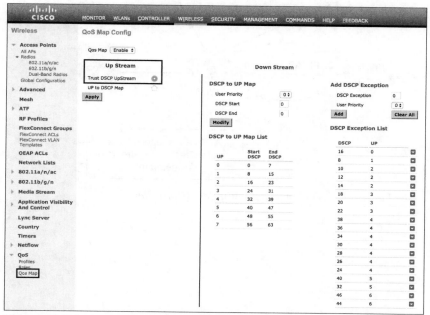

```
⊟  ☂  QoS Control Field:        %0000000000000101
    ⊢ ☺                         ---------- ........  AP PS Buffer State: 0
    ⊢ ☺                         ......... 0.......  A-MSDU: Not Present
    ⊢ ☺                         ......... .00.....  Ack: Normal Acknowledge
    ⊢ ☺                         ......... ...0....  EOSP: Not End of Triggered Service Period
    ⊢ ☺                         ......... ....x...  Reserved
    ⊢ ☺                         ......... ....101   UP: 5 - Video
  ☂  802.2 Logical Link Control (LLC) Header
    ⊢ ☺  Dest. SAP:             0xAA  SNAP
    ⊢ ☺  Source SAP:            0xAA  SNAP            In MS Windows, the WMM UP is derived
    ⊢ ☺  Command:               0x03  Unnumbered Information   from the 3 msb of the DSCP value
    ⊢ ☺  Vendor ID:             0x000000           DSCP ef (46) = [101 110] → 101 = UP 5
    ⊢ ☺  Protocol Type:         0x0800  IP
  ☂  IP Header - Internet Protocol Datagram
    ⊢ ☺  Version:               4
    ⊢ ☺  Header Length:         5  (20 bytes)
  ⊟ ☂  Differentiated Services:%10111000
    ⊢ ☺                         1011 10..  Expedited Forwarding
```

Figure 11-23 *Comparing the DSCP and UP Markings in a Windows OS*

As the frame arrives at the AP, the true QoS value of the inner packet should be reprioritized as voice, not video. If the controller were to trust the incoming UP value and translate this to a corresponding DSCP value on the CAPWAP header, it would translate UP 5 Ð DSCP 34, which is incorrect for voice. To overcome this, it is important to configure the AP to trust DSCP in the upstream direction rather than UP. This configuration option is illustrated in Figure 11-24 on an AireOS controller.

Figure 11-24 *Trusting Upstream DSCP from the Client*

Implementing Application Visibility and Control

Application Visibility and Control (AVC) is a technology that involves multiple components, including Network-Based Application Recognition Version 2 (NBAR2), Flexible NetFlow (FNF), and management tools that provide powerful application visibility and control capabilities based on stateful deep packet inspection (DPI).

With the Cisco AVC solution available on wireless controllers from AireOS 7.4 onward, it is possible to identify applications inside the packet and to have a measure of control over them. Types of control include the following:

- Marking of DSCP

- Rate-limiting/policing traffic in the upstream or downstream direction

- Dropping certain traffic types

Using the AVC engine on the controller, it is possible to identify over a thousand applications. The number of applications that can be identified is constantly being updated as new signatures become available, and these can be added or updated to the controller independently of an operating system upgrade. Importantly, unlike the WLAN QoS configuration that was discussed previously, AVC has the ability to mark the original DSCP value. Figure 11-25 illustrates the functionality of AVC in Cisco wireless controllers.

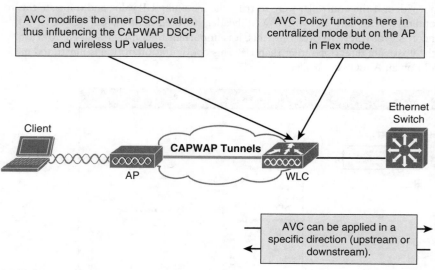

Figure 11-25   *The Function of AVC in a Cisco Wireless Controller*

With DSCP remarking capabilities, better QoS handling in the downstream direction can be achieved. Since AVC operates on the controller in centralized mode, the effect on wireless QoS is only in the downstream direction. Note that in FlexConnect mode, AVC operates in the AP, whereas in centralized mode it operates only on the controller. This also means that for upstream traffic, the effect of AVC for controlling traffic is only toward the wired network from the controller (meaning from the AP to the controller over the CAPWAP tunnel, AVC will have no effect in the upstream direction until it reaches the controller).

The following summarizes the interaction of AVC and QoS in the controller in both the upstream and downstream directions:

Upstream direction (from wireless client to wired network):

1. A packet is sent from a wireless client.

2. The DSCP is mapped to an 802.11e UP value and is transmitted to the AP.

3. The AP trusts the DSCP value on the incoming packet and maps this to the CAPWAP tunnel but does not touch the inner DSCP marking.

4. The controller receives the incoming packet via CAPWAP.

5. Using AVC, the controller examines the inner packet at the application layer and applies an AVC policy (such as remarking DSCP to the configured value).

6. The packet is sent to the wired network with the new DSCP value.

Downstream direction (from wired network to wireless client):

1. A packet is sent to the controller from the wired network.

2. Using AVC, the controller examines the IP packet and applies an AVC policy (such as rewriting the DSCP into the original packet header).

3. The controller compares this new DSCP value to the WLAN QoS profile and uses the lower of the two to write the DSCP value into the CAPWAP header (in other words, the profile's upper limit does not trump the AVC policy for the CAPWAP DSCP).

4. When the AP receives the packet, it examines the CAPWAP header and maps the DSCP value to an 802.11e UP value as per RFC 8325.

5. The packet is transmitted to the wireless client.

From a visibility and monitoring perspective, the controller can collect and display various wireless performance metrics, such as bandwidth usage for individual clients and applications. This reporting information can be displayed locally on the controller or exported through NetFlow to a management tool.

Through this technology, the controller has the ability to identify applications such as Oracle, SAP, Citrix, BitTorrent, MS Exchange, Skype, Facebook, and many others. Figure 11-26 illustrates the visibility offered by AVC (an IOS-XE controller is shown here).

11

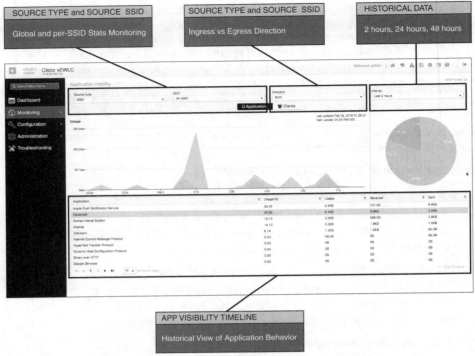

Figure 11-26   *AVC Visibility Shown on an IOS-XE Controller*

Implementing AVC on a Cisco Wireless Controller

To configure AVC in an AireOS controller, the following steps must be followed:

Step 1.   Create an AVC policy.

Step 2.   Create rules for the policy.

Step 3.   Attach the policy to the WLAN.

The following provides these steps in detail:

Step 1.   To create the AVC policy, navigate to **Wireless > Application Visibility and Control**. Under this menu, select **AVC Profiles** and create a new profile.

Step 2.   Once the profile is created, rules must be added. Profiles are composed of a series of rules that are used to first identify an application and then take an action. To make things simpler, the applications are collected into logical groupings. Figure 11-27 illustrates the voice-and-video application group.

Once you have identified the correct application group, the next step is to identify the specific application you want to create a rule for. Figure 11-28 illustrates how an application can be identified.

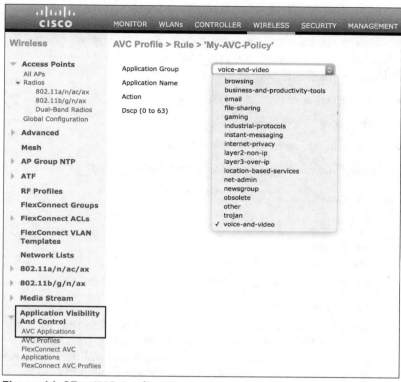

Figure 11-27   *AVC Application Groupings in a New Rule*

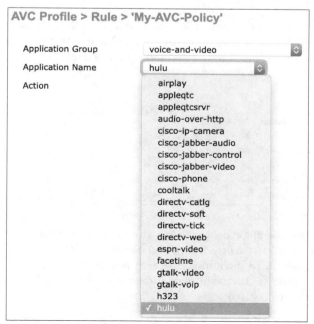

Figure 11-28   *Selecting the AVC Application Identifier for a Rule*

Once you select the application, a rule may be configured. Figure 11-29 illustrates how this may be done. AVC can either remark the DSCP, rate-limit the application through the controller, or drop the packets. Note in this example that the Mark option allows five different marking options:

- **Platinum** (packets are remarked to DSCP 46)

- **Gold** (packets are remarked to DSCP 34)

- **Silver** (packets are remarked to DSCP 0)

- **Bronze** (packets are remarked to DSCP 10)

- **Custom** (you can remark to whatever DSCP you choose)

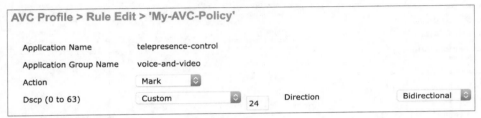

AVC Profile > Rule Edit > 'My-AVC-Policy'

Application Name	telepresence-control
Application Group Name	voice-and-video
Action	Mark
Dscp (0 to 63)	Custom 24 Direction Bidirectional

Figure 11-29   *Creating an AVC Policy Rule*

If packets are remarked with one of the precious metal profiles, the DSCP values will map to the 802.11e UP values discussed previously. If you choose a custom DSCP, this value is marked on the downstream CAPWAP tunnel and is in turn mapped to the appropriate 802.11e UP value according to RFC 8325. Also, you can select the direction (upstream or downstream) in which the rule is applied.

Figure 11-30 illustrates a series of rules that have been created on the controller. Note from this example that multiple rules have been created with different controls: some remark, another drops traffic, and another limits rate.

AVC Profile > Edit   'My-AVC-Policy'

Application Name	Application Group Name	Action	DSCP	Direction	Rate Limit (avg/burst rate)Kbps	
cisco-jabber-video	voice-and-video	mark	46	Bidirectional	NA	
telepresence-media	voice-and-video	mark	34	Bidirectional	NA	
telepresence-control	voice-and-video	mark	24	Bidirectional	NA	
hulu	voice-and-video	ratelimit	NA	NA	256 / 256	
twitter	browsing	drop	NA	NA	NA	

Figure 11-30   *Example of Different AVC Rules Created on the Controller*

As the list of rules grows, you might be wondering what about applications that are not covered by a rule in the list? To deal with this, a default rule can be added to remark any unidentified applications to a set value. In Figure 11-30, the application **class-default** used at the bottom of the list is used to catch all other traffic and remark it to DSCP 0.

Step 3. The final step is to add the policy to the correct WLAN. Two things are required: first enable AVC for the WLAN, and then attach the correct AVC profile. Figure 11-31 illustrates how to add the AVC profile your WLAN.

AVC Profile > Edit 'My-AVC-Policy'					
Application Name	**Application Group Name**	**Action**	**DSCP**	**Direction**	**Rate Limit (avg/burst rate)Kbps**
cisco-jabber-video	voice-and-video	mark	46	Bidirectional	NA
telepresence-media	voice-and-video	mark	34	Bidirectional	NA
telepresence-control	voice-and-video	mark	24	Bidirectional	NA
hulu	voice-and-video	ratelimit	NA	NA	256 / 256
twitter	browsing	drop	NA	NA	NA
class-default	other	mark	0	Bidirectional	NA

Figure 11-31 *Attaching the AVC Profile to a WLAN*

The prior steps demonstrated how AVC can be implemented on an AireOS controller, but it can also be implemented in a similar way on an IOS-XE controller—with a few improvements that are available when compared with AireOS. One example with IOS-XE is that it allows you to create custom AVC inspection policies. For example, you can create an AVC rule that matches on a specific value in the HTTP header, such as a URL. The customized policy is generated through use of regular expressions, as shown in Example 11-1.

Example 11-1 *Creating a Custom AVC Rule in IOS-XE*

```
C9800(config)# ip nbar custom my_http http url "latest/whatsnew.html"
C9800(config)# ip nbar custom my_http http host "www.anydomain.com"
C9800(config)# ip nbar custom my_http http url "latest/whatsnew" host
"www.anydomain.com"
```

Implementing AutoQoS with Fastlane

As you can see in this chapter, implementing QoS in a wireless LAN has many aspects. To make the task of configuring QoS easier, AutoQoS macros are supported in both AireOS and IOS-XE. In AireOS, the AutoQoS macro is called Fastlane. Fastlane helps you configure all the QoS features of the controller according to best practices in one click. This includes configuration of the Platinum profile, the DSCP-to-UP mappings, EDCA profiles, CAC features, as well as a generic best-practices AVC profile that uses a sampling of common business applications, called **AUTOQOS-AVC-PROFILE**.

Fastlane is enabled under the **WLAN > QoS** configuration menu, as shown in Figure 11-32.

11

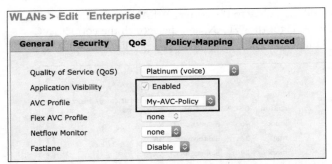

Figure 11-32   *Enabling Fastlane on an AireOS Controller*

As soon as Fastlane is enabled, the AutoQoS macro will execute and generate the QoS configuration. Example 11-2 shows the AVC profile that is created by Fastlane.

Example 11-2   *The AVC Profile Created by the Fastlane Command*

```
(Cisco Controller) >debug aaa tacacs enable


. . . snip . . .

avc profile AUTOQOS-AVC-PROFILE create
avc profile AUTOQOS-AVC-PROFILE rule add application cisco-phone-audio mark 46
avc profile AUTOQOS-AVC-PROFILE rule add application cisco-jabber-audio mark 46
avc profile AUTOQOS-AVC-PROFILE rule add application ms-lync-audio mark 46
avc profile AUTOQOS-AVC-PROFILE rule add application citrix-audio mark 46
avc profile AUTOQOS-AVC-PROFILE rule add application cisco-phone-video mark 34
avc profile AUTOQOS-AVC-PROFILE rule add application cisco-jabber-video mark 34
avc profile AUTOQOS-AVC-PROFILE rule add application ms-lync-video mark 34
avc profile AUTOQOS-AVC-PROFILE rule add application webex-media mark 34
avc profile AUTOQOS-AVC-PROFILE rule add application citrix mark 26
avc profile AUTOQOS-AVC-PROFILE rule add application pcoip mark 26
avc profile AUTOQOS-AVC-PROFILE rule add application vnc mark 26
avc profile AUTOQOS-AVC-PROFILE rule add application vnc-http mark 26
avc profile AUTOQOS-AVC-PROFILE rule add application skinny mark 24
avc profile AUTOQOS-AVC-PROFILE rule add application cisco-jabber-control mark 24
avc profile AUTOQOS-AVC-PROFILE rule add application sip mark 24
avc profile AUTOQOS-AVC-PROFILE rule add application sip-tls mark 24
avc profile AUTOQOS-AVC-PROFILE rule add application cisco-jabber-im mark 18
avc profile AUTOQOS-AVC-PROFILE rule add application ms-office-web-apps mark 18
avc profile AUTOQOS-AVC-PROFILE rule add application salesforce mark 18
avc profile AUTOQOS-AVC-PROFILE rule add application sap mark 18
avc profile AUTOQOS-AVC-PROFILE rule add application dhcp mark 16
avc profile AUTOQOS-AVC-PROFILE rule add application dns mark 16
avc profile AUTOQOS-AVC-PROFILE rule add application ntp mark 16
avc profile AUTOQOS-AVC-PROFILE rule add application snmp mark 16
avc profile AUTOQOS-AVC-PROFILE rule add application ftp mark 10
```

```
avc profile AUTOQOS-AVC-PROFILE rule add application ftp-data mark 10
avc profile AUTOQOS-AVC-PROFILE rule add application ftps-data mark 10
avc profile AUTOQOS-AVC-PROFILE rule add application cifs mark 10
avc profile AUTOQOS-AVC-PROFILE rule add application netflix mark 8
avc profile AUTOQOS-AVC-PROFILE rule add application youtube mark 8
avc profile AUTOQOS-AVC-PROFILE rule add application skype mark 8
avc profile AUTOQOS-AVC-PROFILE rule add application bittorrent mark 8
```

Summary

This chapter focused on implementing QoS in a wireless network. In this chapter you have learned the following:

- The fundamentals of how DCF was developed to support multiple-access media access in Wi-Fi systems

- Improvements made through EDCA to support QoS through the use of access categories and the various parameters that are used in each access category to offer differentiated services

- The upstream and downstream marking schemes used in a centralized wireless implementation

- How QoS is implemented in both the AireOS and IOS-XE wireless controllers

- How QoS is controlled on wireless clients and implications to upstream QoS handling over the wireless LAN

- The implementation of AVC in wireless networks, including Fastlane

References

For additional information, refer to these resources:

Enterprise Wireless Design Guide 8.5—QoS Chapter: https://www.cisco.com/c/en/us/td/docs/wireless/controller/8-5/Enterprise-Mobility-8-5-Design-Guide/Enterprise_Mobility_8-5_Deployment_Guide/ch5_QoS.html

RFC 8325: Mapping Diffserv to 802.11: https://tools.ietf.org/html/rfc8325

QoS Design and Deployment for Wireless LANs: https://www.ciscolive.com/c/dam/r/ciscolive/us/docs/2018/pdf/BRKRST-2515.pdf

AutoQoS on the Catalyst 9800: https://www.cisco.com/c/en/us/td/docs/wireless/controller/9800/config-guide/b_wl_16_10_cg/wireless-auto-qos.html

Wireless QoS on the Catalyst 9800: https://www.cisco.com/c/en/us/td/docs/wireless/controller/9800/config-guide/b_wl_16_10_cg/quality-of-service.html

802.11 QoS Tutorial: http://www.ieee802.org/1/files/public/docs2008/avb-gs-802-11-qos-tutorial-1108.pdf

Wireless QoS: Five-Part Series: http://www.revolutionwifi.net/revolutionwifi/2010/07/wireless-qos-part-1-background_7048.html

11

Exam Preparation Tasks

As mentioned in the section "How to Use This Book" in the Introduction, you have a few choices for exam preparation: the exercises here, Chapter 18, "Final Preparation," and the exam simulation questions in the Pearson Test Prep Software Online.

Review All Key Topics

Review the most important topics in this chapter, noted with the Key Topic icon in the outer margin of the page. Table 11-7 lists these key topics and the page numbers on which each is found.

Table 11-7 Key Topics for Chapter 11

Key Topic Element	Description	Page Number
Figure 11-5	Access Categories and their UP mappings	251
Table 11-2	Mapping of DSCP to WMM UP value to Access Category	251
Table 11-6	The four QoS profiles in AireOS controllers	259
Figure 11-12	The QoS profile configuration menu in AireOS	261
Figure 11-25	The function of AVC in a Cisco wireless controller	270
Example 11-2	The AVC profile created by the Fastlane command	276

Define Key Terms

Define the following key terms from this chapter and check your answers in the glossary:

Carrier Sense Multiple Access / Collision Avoidance (CSMA/CA), Distributed Coordination Function (DCF), contention, Enhanced Distributed Channel Access (EDCA), Access Category (AC), Arbitrated Interframe Space Number (AIFSN), Contention Window (CW), Transmission Opportunity (TXOP), Transmission Specification (TSpec), User Priority (UP), Wireless Multimedia (WMM), Diffserv Code Point (DSCP), Application Visibility and Control (AVC), Fastlane

CHAPTER 12

Implementing Multicast

This chapter covers the following topics:

> **Multicast Overview:** This section provides an overview of multicast traffic and how it is transported through both wired and wireless networks.
>
> **Implementing mDNS:** This section explains the mDNS mechanism that is used by Apple Bonjour and Google Chromecast to locate services dynamically. It also describes how to configure a Cisco WLC to act as an mDNS Bonjour gateway that can assist service discovery across network segments.
>
> **Implementing Multicast Direct:** This section describes the Multicast Direct feature and how it can be used to deliver multicast video streams more reliably and effectively in a wireless environment.

This chapter covers the following ELWSI exam topics:

- 3.1 Implement multicast components
- 3.2 Describe how multicast can affect wireless networks
- 3.3 Implement multicast on a WLAN
- 3.4 Implement mDNS
- 3.5 Implement Multicast Direct

Multicast traffic is typically sent by one source and received by a group of recipients that might be spread throughout a network. In addition, the recipients within the group might change over time. Examples of multicast traffic include video streams for instruction or entertainment, certain audio conference calls, and one-to-many PC file imaging applications.

Because not everyone on a network wants to receive the traffic from a multicast source, the network infrastructure must have some means of forwarding traffic to exactly the destinations that want to receive it. This chapter covers multicast from a wireless network perspective.

"Do I Know This Already?" Quiz

The "Do I Know This Already?" quiz allows you to assess whether you should read this entire chapter thoroughly or jump to the "Exam Preparation Tasks" section. If you are in doubt about your answers to these questions or your own assessment of your knowledge of the topics, read the entire chapter. Table 12-1 lists the major headings in this chapter and their corresponding "Do I Know This Already?" quiz questions. You can find the answers in Appendix D, "Answers to the 'Do I Know This Already?' Quizzes and Review Questions."

Table 12-1 "Do I Know This Already?" Section-to-Question Mapping

Foundation Topics Section	Questions
Multicast Overview	1–7
Implementing mDNS	8–9
Implementing Multicast Direct	10

1. When a multicast frame must be sent by an AP toward wireless clients, which of the following statements are true? (Choose all that apply.)

    a. The client recipient must return an ACK frame.

    b. The frame must be transmitted on a 20MHz channel.

    c. The frame must be transmitted at the data rate already in use for the client.

    d. The frame must be transmitted at the highest mandatory data rate.

2. To receive a multicast stream, a recipient host must first do which one of the following?

    a. Send an ICMP Request packet to the multicast source address.

    b. Send an IGMP Membership Report packet to the multicast source address.

    c. Send an IGMP Membership Report to the upstream router.

    d. Do nothing. Multicast traffic always reaches every host.

3. Which one of the following will maximize the efficiency of multicast traffic transport over a wireless network, where the recipients are at various locations?

    a. Use the default WLC multicast-unicast mode.

    b. Use the WLC multicast-multicast mode.

    c. Enable PIM on every WLC.

    d. Multicast traffic is not supported over a wireless network.

4. Suppose a WLC has been configured for multicast-multicast mode. Which one of the following actions must each AP take to participate in multicast traffic delivery?

    a. Merely join the WLC with a CAPWAP tunnel.

    b. Send CAPWAP packets with the WLC's multicast group address as the destination.

    c. Learn the WLC's CAPWAP multicast group address and then send an IGMP membership report to join that group.

    d. Enable a virtual interface that uses the CAPWAP multicast group address.

5. Which one of the following allows a WLC to determine if an AP has any active multicast recipients for a specific group address?

    a. Entries in its ARP table

    b. IGMP snooping

    c. A valid CAPWAP group address

    d. IGMP membership reports sent from the router

6. What is the correct function of an MGID?

   a. It identifies an AP participating in multicast delivery.

   b. It is an identifier assigned to each multicast source.

   c. It is an identifier assigned to each multicast interface on a WLC.

   d. It identifies each multicast group address and registered recipients.

7. Which one of the following is a true statement regarding multicast messaging on a WLC?

   a. A controller can send mobility messages to other controllers via a multicast group address.

   b. The mobility multicast group address must be the same as the CAPWAP multicast group address.

   c. To multicast mobility messages between controllers, each controller must have a unique multicast group address.

   d. All controllers in the same mobility group must have the same mobility multicast group address.

8. In order to assist Apple devices to discover online resources with the Bonjour protocol, which one of the following features should be configured?

   a. IGMP snooping

   b. Bonjour Direct

   c. mDNS snooping

   d. Multicast Direct

9. Which one of the following is uniquely used by LSS in replies to Bonjour requests for a specific resource?

   a. The complete list of all Bonjour advertisements that have been received from all network segments

   b. A list of only the resources learned on the list of neighboring APs

   c. A list of only the Bonjour advertisements for the same resource requested

   d. The address of the nearest mDNS router

10. Which one of the following is a unique characteristic of Multicast Direct?

   a. A WLC will direct all multicast streams toward its next-hop router.

   b. Specific multicast streams will be redirected toward wireless clients as unicast streams.

   c. Multicast streams from wireless clients will be directed toward an anchor controller.

   d. WLCs will provide an easy-to-use web-based interface to assist clients in receiving multicast traffic.

Foundation Topics

Multicast Overview

In a typical network, three basic types of IP traffic traverse the wired and wireless topologies:

- **Unicast:** Packets that are sent from one source host address to a single destination host address. A router or Layer 3 switch forwards them by finding the destination IP address in its routing table. A Layer 2 switch relies on the destination's MAC address only.

- **Broadcast:** Packets that are sent from one source host address to a broadcast destination address. The destination can be all hosts (255.255.255.255), a directed broadcast to a subnet (that is, 192.168.10.255), or some portion of a subnet. A router or Layer 3 switch will not forward these by default unless some method of relaying has been configured. A Layer 2 switch floods the packet out all ports on the destination VLAN.

- **Multicast:** Packets that are sent from one source host address to a special group-based destination address. The destination represents only the hosts that are interested in receiving the packets and no others. A router or Layer 3 switch does not forward these packets by default unless some form of multicast routing is enabled. A Layer 2 switch cannot learn the location of the destination multicast group address, so the packets are flooded to all ports on the destination VLAN by default.

Two extremes are covered here, as illustrated in Figure 12-1:

- A unicast, which travels from one host to another host

- A broadcast, which travels from one host to every host on a segment

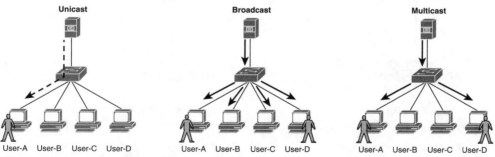

Figure 12-1 *Comparison of Unicast, Broadcast, and Multicast Delivery*

Multicast falls somewhere in the middle. The intention is to send packets from one host to only the users who want to receive them—namely, those known to belong in the designated *multicast group*. In Figure 12-1, only User-A and User-D are interested in receiving the multicast traffic. Ideally, the recipients of multicast packets could be located anywhere, not just on the local segment.

By default, a Layer 2 switch must flood broadcast and multicast packets to all of its interfaces that are mapped to the VLAN, in a best effort to reach every potential recipient. The same is true in a wireless network. Figure 12-2 compares broadcast or multicast delivery with an autonomous AP and a lightweight AP joined to a wireless LAN controller (WLC). Broadcast and multicast frames are transmitted into the AP's cell on the relevant WLAN, and it is up to the individual clients to receive and interpret them. When a WLC is involved, the broadcast or multicast packet is received by the WLC and then sent to the AP over a CAPWAP tunnel. Nevertheless, the two AP scenarios deliver the frame into the cell for all clients to receive.

> **TIP**   You should be aware of a few important aspects that the 802.11 standard defines about broadcast and multicast frames:
>
> ■ They are transmitted at the highest mandatory data rate. You should make sure that mandatory rate is usable at the edge of the AP cells.
>
> ■ They do not require an ACK.
>
> ■ They must be sent on the primary 20MHz channel so that all associated stations can receive them, regardless of what channel width is in use.

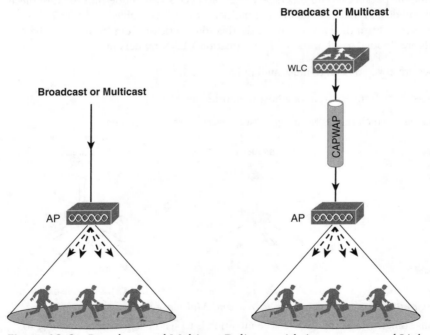

Figure 12-2   *Broadcast and Multicast Delivery with Autonomous and Lightweight APs*

Multicast traffic is generally unidirectional. Because many hosts will receive the same data, it makes little sense to allow one of the hosts to send packets back toward the source over the multicast mechanism. Instead, a receiving host can send return traffic to the source as a unicast. Multicast traffic is sent in a best-effort connectionless format, usually with UDP, but not with connection-oriented TCP.

Hosts that want to receive data from a multicast source can join or leave a multicast group dynamically. In addition, a host can decide to become a member of more than one multicast group at any time. The principal network task is then to figure out how to deliver multicast traffic to the group members without disturbing other uninterested hosts.

IP multicast traffic is routed, just like any other Layer 3 packets. The difference is in knowing where to forward the packets. Multicast IP packets can have many destination interfaces, depending on where the recipients are located. Routers use multicast routing protocols, such as Protocol Independent Multicast (PIM), to transport multicast packets from one router hop to another.

How does a router know of the recipients in a multicast group, much less of their locations? To receive multicast traffic from a source, every recipient must first join a common multicast group address. A host can join a multicast group by sending a request to its local router. This is done through the Internet Group Management Protocol (IGMP). To join a group, a host sends an IGMP Membership Report message to its local router. From then on, the router knows that the multicast group is active on the interface where the host connects. Hosts can also leave multicast groups at any time or age out if they do not answer periodic IGMP Queries.

Multicast Delivery in a Wireless Network

From Figure 12-2, you can see how multicast traffic is sent between the WLC and an AP, which are at each end of the split-MAC architecture. What goes into the controller comes out at the AP, even broadcast and multicast traffic. Most wireless networks are made up of multiple APs, so the scale of multicast delivery can grow too.

By default, a WLC operates in unicast mode (also called broadcast-unicast or multicast-unicast mode) to deliver multicast traffic to the APs that are joined to it. That means the controller must replicate the incoming multicast traffic and send it as a separate unicast connection to each AP over the CAPWAP tunnel that is already in place. Figure 12-3 shows a network with one WLC and three APs. For this example, the single multicast packet coming into the WLC must be copied three times and sent to AP-1, AP-2, and AP-3. This places the burden of replicating traffic on the WLC and its resources, rather than taking advantage of multicast's one-to-many inherent efficiency. Imagine a large network that has a WLC controlling 3,000 APs. The unicast replication could become very taxing on the controller!

A better solution is to configure the controller for multicast delivery mode (also known as multicast-multicast mode). A CAPWAP multicast group address is assigned to the controller, which will be used as the destination address for all multicast traffic that will be tunneled to each AP. Keep in mind that controllers are usually separated from their APs by layers of switches and routers. Therefore, the multicast delivery must also rely on IP multicast routing within the wired network infrastructure. Each AP must join its controller's multicast group before it can receive the multicast traffic.

Like any hosts that want to join a multicast group, the APs must learn of the CAPWAP multicast group address when joining the controller and then send IGMP membership report messages to join the group. Figure 12-4 illustrates this scenario, where three APs are requesting to join the CAPWAP group 239.1.1.9. The underlying wired network will use the IGMP requests to learn the location of each AP and will take care of replicating the multicast traffic to be delivered.

12

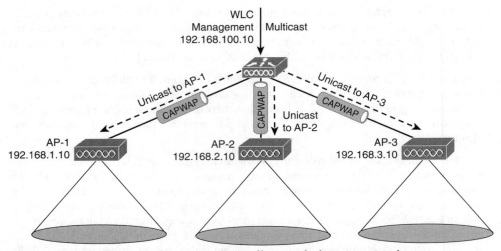

Figure 12-3   *Multicast Delivery in a Controller's Default Unicast Mode*

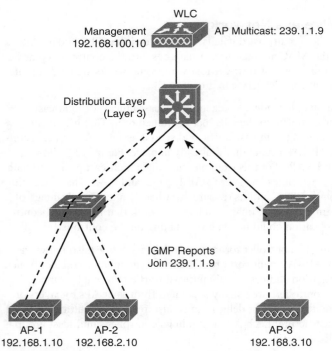

Figure 12-4   *APs Join a Controller's CAPWAP Multicast Group*

The result is shown in Figure 12-5. The controller can now relay incoming multicast traffic to all three of its APs by encapsulating it in CAPWAP with destination address 239.1.1.9. The burden on the controller is light because it just needs to relay traffic to a single multicast group destination.

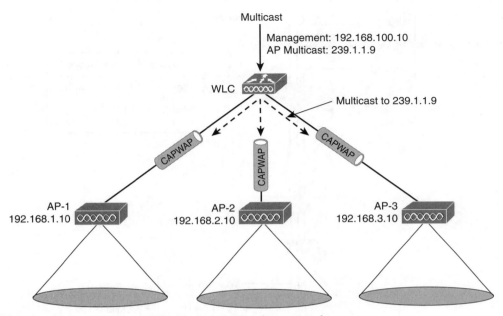

Multicast

Management: 192.168.100.10
AP Multicast: 239.1.1.9

WLC

Multicast to 239.1.1.9

CAPWAP   CAPWAP   CAPWAP

AP-1
192.168.1.10

AP-2
192.168.2.10

AP-3
192.168.3.10

Figure 12-5 *Multicast Delivery in WLC Multicast Mode*

Key Topic

When a multicast frame is sourced from a client on a WLAN, the AP sends it across the CAPWAP tunnel to WLC, which forwards it onto the wired network. The WLC must also create a copy the frame and send into the normal CAPWAP multicast group for delivery back into WLANs, where other wireless recipients may also be located.

The process is now straightforward, but how does the controller deliver multicasts that are destined for specific WLANs at the APs? After all, a single CAPWAP multicast group address is used to deliver multicast traffic to any WLAN necessary. To keep track, a controller maintains a Layer 2 table of multicast entries by mapping which of its interfaces should have multicast traffic sent to which of its WLANs.

Figure 12-6 provides an example. WLC interface wlan-a is configured to connect to VLAN 100, and any incoming multicast traffic should be forwarded to the WLAN named "WLAN-A." Each of these table entries is assigned an arbitrary multicast group ID (MGID) as an index. Then as the controller encapsulates a multicast packet into the CAPWAP tunnel, it includes a bitmap that instructs the APs about the destination WLANs. In other words, the same IP multicast group address might exist on more than one WLAN, if hosts have registered to join it there. The AP can transmit the multicast frame onto each of the relevant WLANs, which might exist on both bands supported by the AP's radios.

12

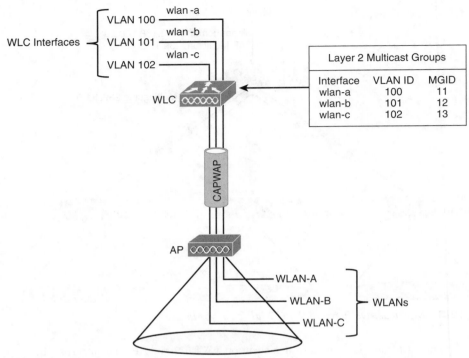

Figure 12-6 *Layer 2 Multicast Group Mapping Between a WLC and an AP*

IGMP Snooping

You may have noticed that IGMP is designed to inform Layer 3 routers about multicast groups and members. Layer 2 devices do not participate in routing or IGMP, so they cannot enjoy the luxury of on-demand multicast forwarding at all; the best information they have is the destination multicast address, and that signifies only that the frame needs to be flooded out all ports on the VLAN or transmitted into the AP's cell.

A feature called IGMP snooping allows a Layer 2 device to eavesdrop on IGMP membership reports that are sent by hosts. This allows a switch or a wireless controller to find out who is requesting which multicast group, without having to participate in IGMP at all.

Figure 12-7 illustrates how *IGMP snooping* works on a Layer 2 switch. In the left portion of the figure, connected hosts User-A and User-D that want to receive traffic sent to multicast group address 239.9.9.9 each send IGMP membership reports toward an upstream router. The Layer 2 switch cannot do anything with multicast routing, but it can intercept the IGMP messages to learn which interfaces have joined the multicast group. Then when traffic is sent from the multicast source to 239.9.9.9, shown in the right portion of the figure, the switch knows to forward that traffic out its interfaces where User-A and User-D are connected. The multicast traffic does not get forwarded out the other user interfaces.

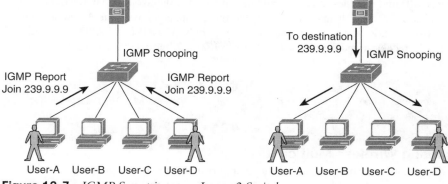

Figure 12-7   *IGMP Snooping on a Layer 2 Switch*

A wireless LAN controller can also leverage IGMP snooping to identify hosts that join multicast groups. The goal is not to forward multicast frames to those specific hosts, however, because that is not practical in a wireless LAN. Instead, the controller snoops to learn which wireless clients want to join which multicast groups on which APs. The multicast traffic will be forwarded to all APs over their CAPWAP tunnels via the CAPWAP multicast address. However, only the APs hosting clients that are registered for the multicast group will transmit that traffic onto the WLAN. The other APs will not.

Controllers maintain a Layer 3 multicast group table that is based on the IGMP snooping activity. Figure 12-8 shows an example scenario with three APs, all offering the WLAN named "Staff." Client-A and Client-B are associated with AP-1 and have sent IGMP membership reports to join multicast group 239.2.0.252. Client-C is associated with AP-3 and has joined the same multicast group address.

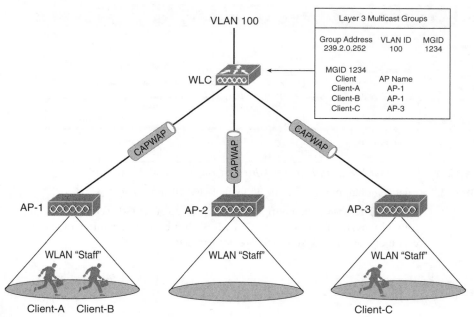

Figure 12-8   *WLC Data Collected by IGMP Snooping*

The controller's Layer 3 multicast table is also shown. Each entry in the list is assigned an arbitrary MGID and includes the group address and VLAN ID involved. MGID 1234 also contains a list of specific clients that have joined the group, along with the AP names where they are associated. From this table, you can see that only APs AP-1 and AP-3 will need to transmit frames destined for multicast group 239.2.0.252 because they have valid client recipients.

> **NOTE**   Cisco WLCs can also use *Multicast Listener Discovery (MLD)* to learn of IPv6 multicast recipients. MLD functions much like IGMP for IPv4, so it is not discussed here.

Implementing Wireless Multicast

Before the wireless network can successfully support multicast, the wired network infrastructure must be configured to support it. Once that occurs, the wired network can route the multicast traffic needed between WLCs and their APs.

The actual WLC multicast configuration process is fairly simple, using the following steps:

Step 1.   Enable multicast mode and assign an AP multicast group address.

Figure 12-9 shows the configuration on an AireOS WLC, found by selecting **CONTROLLER > General**. The AP Multicast Mode is changed from Unicast to Multicast; then the multicast address box appears and is assigned to 239.1.1.9. Figure 12-10 shows the same configuration step on an IOS-XE-based controller in the **Configuration > Services > Multicast** page.

You can use an address from the range 239.0.0.0 through 239.255.255.255, but avoid 239.0.0.x and 239.120.0.x. If you need to configure multiple controllers with multicast group addresses, make sure each one gets a unique address.

Figure 12-9   *Multicast Mode and Group Address Configuration in AireOS*

Step 2.   Enable global multicast mode and enable IGMP snooping.

Figure 12-11 shows the configuration step on an AireOS-based controller, found by navigating to **CONTROLLER > Multicast**. By default, global multicast mode and IGMP snooping are not enabled.

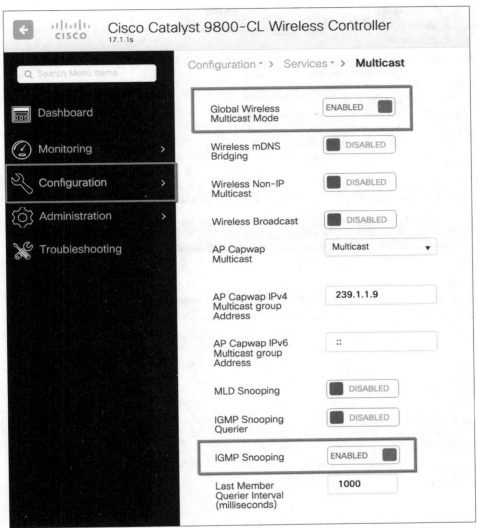

Figure 12-10 *Multicast Mode and Group Address Configuration in IOS-XE*

Once multicast and IGMP snooping are operational, you can view the multicast group information that a controller gathers from intercepted traffic. Navigate to **Monitoring > Multicast** to display the current list of Layer 3 and Layer 2 MGIDs, as shown in Figure 12-12. You can also select one of the Layer 3 MGIDs to display a list of specific clients that have joined the multicast group, along with the name of their associated APs.

12

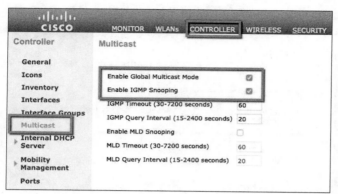

Figure 12-11 *Enabling Global Multicast Mode and IGMP Snooping in AireOS*

Group address	Vlan	MGID	IGMP/MLD
224.0.1.1	3626	15761	IGMP
224.0.1.1	3639	14903	IGMP
224.0.1.1	3654	14689	IGMP
224.0.1.60	3621	14666	IGMP
224.0.1.60	3625	14428	IGMP
224.0.1.60	3626	14664	IGMP
224.0.1.60	3629	13735	IGMP
224.0.1.60	3630	13754	IGMP
224.0.1.60	3633	14910	IGMP
224.0.1.60	3638	12473	IGMP
224.0.1.60	3639	14706	IGMP
224.0.1.60	3650	12904	IGMP
224.0.1.60	3654	15471	IGMP
224.0.1.60	3655	14408	IGMP
224.0.1.187	3614	14755	IGMP
224.0.1.187	3621	12958	IGMP
224.0.1.187	3622	16265	IGMP
224.0.1.187	3624	15249	IGMP

Figure 12-12 *Displaying IGMP Snooping Activity*

Multicast traffic has one other useful purpose in the WLC operation—controllers can use it to send messages about client mobility to each other all at once. Without multicast, the controllers configured in the same mobility group must build a full mesh of connections to each other. Each time a client roams, that event must be shared with all other controllers in the mobility group. As the number of controllers grows, so does the number of controller-to-controller connections and the number of replicated client mobility event messages. By using multicast, any controller can send a single message to all other controllers that are members of the same multicast group.

To leverage multicast in a mobility group, you should enable Multicast Messaging on each controller and assign it a multicast group address. The group address should be unique from other multicast group addresses in use on the network, but the same address should be configured on each controller in the mobility group. In Figure 12-13, an AireOS controller has been configured to use 239.1.0.1 to communicate mobility events with the other controllers. You can find these settings by navigating to **CONTROLLER > Mobility Management > Multicast Messaging.**

Figure 12-13 *Configuring Multicast Mobility Messaging in AireOS*

Implementing mDNS

To locate services on a network, Apple devices use the Bonjour protocol, which is based on multicast DNS (mDNS). Google Chromecast is also based on mDNS. Devices such as AppleTV, printers, file shares, and AirPlay periodically advertise their services via multicast. Other devices can learn about those resources by receiving the multicast advertisements or by sending multicast queries to look for services.

As long as a device is using the same IP subnet as a service resource, it can discover that resource. Bonjour mDNS advertisements use UDP port 5353 and are sent to multicast IPv4 group address 224.0.0.251 or IPv6 address FF02::FB. Because the 224.0.0.251 address is within the range of link local addresses, the multicast packets will stay within the same IP subnet and will not be routed across subnets.

This means a device will not be able to discover resources that reside on another subnet without some sort of intervention. In Figure 12-14, the wireless client is located on VLAN 100 and is trying to find the AppleTV that is located in the same room. Unfortunately, the AppleTV resides on VLAN 200 and a different WLAN. Therefore, the client cannot find the resource it needs.

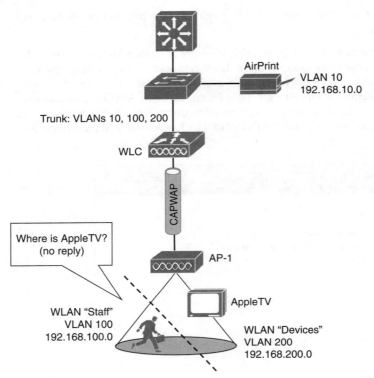

Figure 12-14 *Isolation of Apple Resources Due to Bonjour mDNS*

A Cisco WLC can act as an mDNS gateway and maintain a cache of Bonjour services that it overhears as they are advertised on VLANs that are directly connected to it. Then when wireless clients send an mDNS query to find a resource, the WLC will respond on behalf of the resources in its cache. In Figure 12-15, the WLC is able to respond to the client's request for an AppleTV based on an entry in its mDNS Bonjour cache. As long as there is a router between the client and AppleTV VLANs, the two can connect.

Suppose there are many AppleTVs located in conference rooms throughout an enterprise. A client requesting AppleTV service might end up receiving responses listing all of those resources, even ones located in other buildings or floors. A WLC can also offer Location Specific Services (LSS) to limit resource replies so that they are relevant to the client's physical location.

When LSS is enabled, each Bonjour advertisement is recorded along with the AP that relayed it. When a client requests a resource, the WLC will return only the relevant resources that are located near the list of neighboring APs.

A WLC can also learn of mDNS advertisements about resources that are available on wired network VLANs that do not directly connect. The mDNS AP feature allows an AP to snoop for mDNS advertisements it overhears on wired VLANs that connect to it. The AP then acts as a remote sensor and relays the advertisements to the WLC for its Bonjour cache.

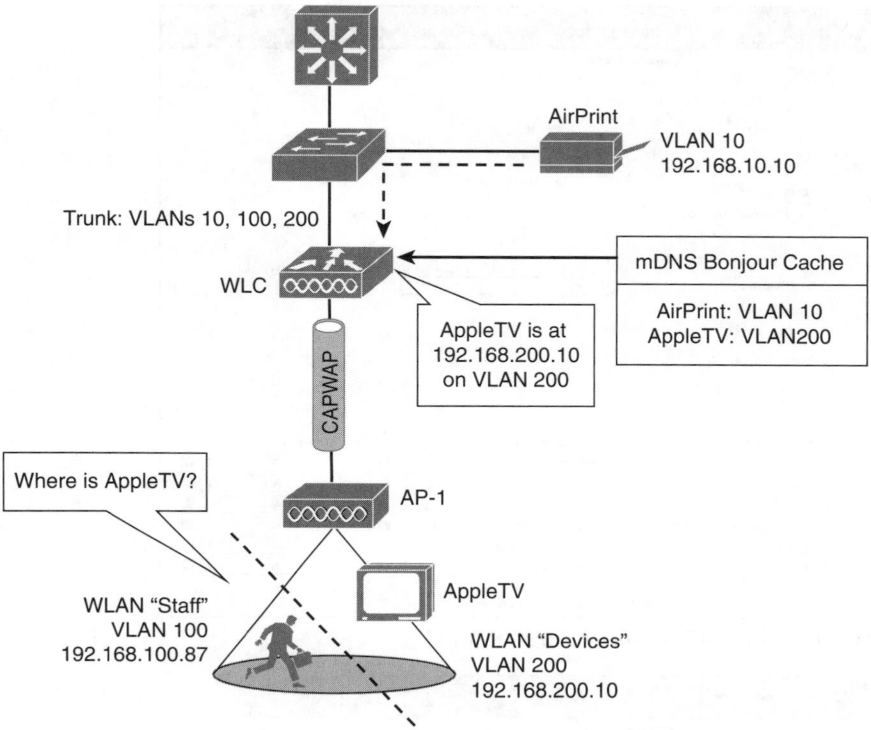

Figure 12-15   *mDNS Bonjour Gateway Links Apple Resources on Different Subnets*

To configure an AireOS controller to participate in mDNS, navigate to **CONTROLLER > mDNS > General** and then check the box next to **mDNS Global Snooping** to enable it, as shown in Figure 12-16. For an IOS-XE controller, go to **Configuration > Services > mDNS Gateway** and select **Transport**. Then choose **ipv4**, **ipv6**, or both, and click **Apply**.

> **TIP**   As you configure mDNS on a controller, you may find several different names for it: mDNS, mDNS gateway, Bonjour Gateway, and mDNS Snooping.

By default, mDNS is prepopulated with a list of service advertisements that it recognizes. The WLC will respond to queries for these services, as shown by the check boxes under Query Status. You can enable LSS for the services too. Under the Origin column, you can tell the controller to respond to queries sourced from wireless, wired, or both (all).

You can also define an mDNS profile that can be applied to specific WLANs by navigating to **CONTROLLER > mDNS > Profiles** on an AireOS controller. A default profile named default-mdns-profile contains a list of the six services shown at the bottom of Figure 12-16, which will be applied to all WLANs defined on the WLC. You can edit the profile, as shown in Figure 12-17. Notice that the profile will be applied to WLC interfaces, but the list of interfaces shown is blank. You can specify interfaces within the profile or bind the profile to specific interfaces in the next step.

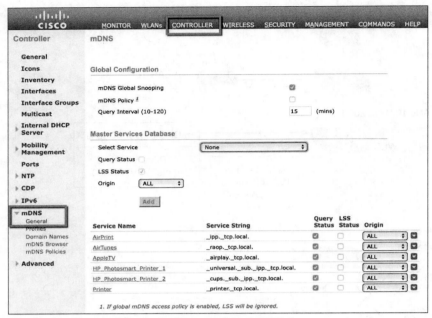

Figure 12-16   *Enabling mDNS on an AireOS WLC*

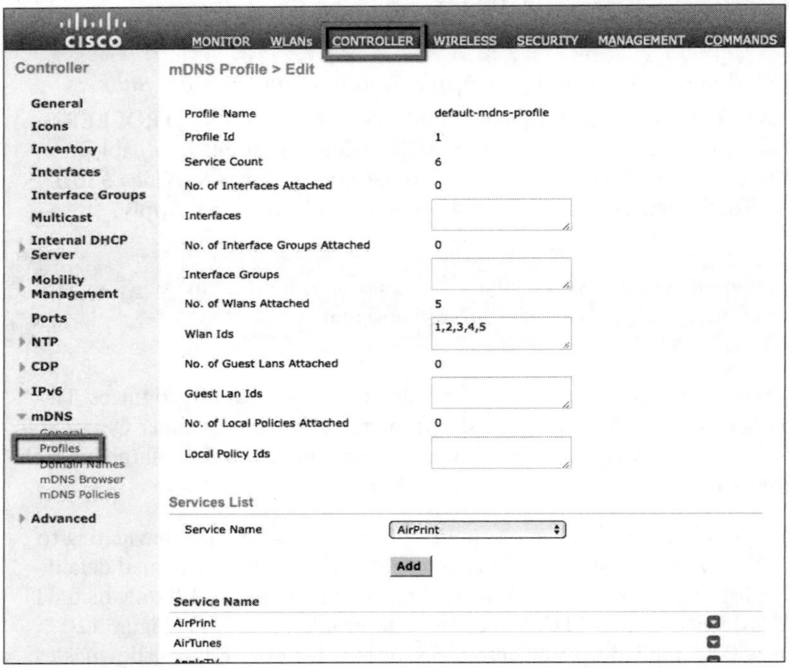

Figure 12-17   *Editing the Default mDNS Profile on an AireOS WLC*

Finally, you must enable mDNS on each WLAN that will use it. Navigate to **WLANs > WLANs** and edit the desired WLAN; then select the **Advanced** tab, as shown in Figure 12-18. Scroll down to the mDNS section and check the box next to **mDNS Snooping**. The mDNS Profile drop-down menu will appear and the default-mdns-profile will be selected.

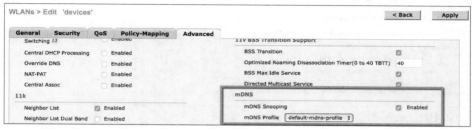

Figure 12-18 *Enabling mDNS Snooping on a WLAN*

Implementing Multicast Direct

Recall from earlier in this chapter that APs transmit multicast frames at the lowest mandatory data rate configured. Suppose a wireless client is associated with an AP and is positioned such that the RF conditions allow the AP to transmit unicast frames to the client at a 24Mbps data rate. If the lowest mandatory data rate is 6Mbps, then any multicast traffic will be sent at that lower rate rather than the higher usable rate.

The quality of multicast streams used by real-time applications like video can suffer due to the lower data rate constraint and a lack of QoS marking. Also, recall that 802.11 normally requires transmitted frames to be acknowledged by the receiver to confirm receipt. Such acknowledgements are not possible with multicast traffic, so some streamed frames can be lost undetected. However, the resulting loss in the video quality will not go undetected.

You can leverage the *Multicast Direct* feature to enable a WLC to intercept certain multicast streams upon ingress and convert them to unicast streams at the AP. By using unicast, the streams can be sent at better data rates (if possible), and the streams will become more reliable with acknowledgements feedback from the receiving clients. Remember that there could be multiple clients registered to receive the multicast stream, so the WLC will need to replicate the stream traffic into an individual unicast stream to each client.

> **TIP**   As you configure Multicast Direct, be aware that it is known by several different names: Multicast Direct, VideoStream, and Media Stream.

Use the following four steps to configure Multicast Direct on a WLC:

Step 1.   Enable Multicast Direct globally.

Navigate to **WIRELESS > Media Stream > General** and check the box next to **Multicast Direct feature**, as shown in Figure 12-19. The fields under Session Message Config are used to notify and assist the stream recipient in case there are problems with the stream.

12

Figure 12-19   *Enabling Multicast Direct*

Step 2.   Identify the multicast streams to intercept and convert.

Navigate to **WIRELESS > Media Stream > Streams** and click the **Add New** button to define a new stream template, as shown in Figure 12-20. This will tell the WLC which multicast streams to intercept and how to convert them to unicast. Define a name for the stream, the range of multicast group addresses that will be used, and the expected bandwidth for a typical stream. When traffic destined to any of those addresses is received, the WLC will reserve the resources you define. You can select a predefined resource template from the drop-down list. If the stream traffic exceeds the rate and packet size defined, then those packets will either be dropped or delivered as best effort.

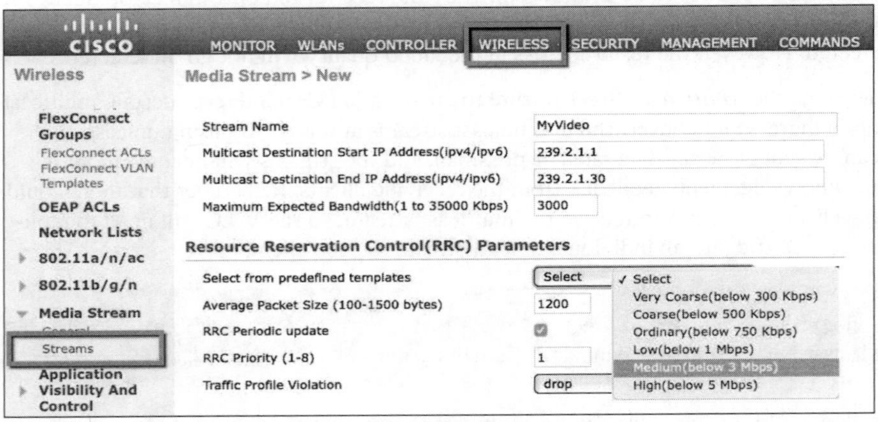

Figure 12-20   *Identifying Multicast Streams to Convert*

Step 3.   Enable Multicast Direct on a specific radio band.

Because Multicast Direct strives to maximize the quality of video streams, it relies on well-defined QoS mechanisms. The WLC can control how much load each type of media traffic (voice, video, and media streams) is allowed to use the wireless bandwidth at any given time. You will need to set the Multicast Direct parameters on each of the desired radio bands. For example, navigate to **WIRELESS > 802.11a/n/ac > Media** and select the **Media** tab, as shown in Figure 12-21.

TIP   If the radios in that band are already operational, you may have to disable them first, then make the Multicast Direct media changes, and then re-enable the radios.

Check the box next to **Unicast Video Redirect** to enable the multicast-to-unicast conversion. Then define the maximum bandwidth that will be allocated to the multicast direct streams, out of the total wireless bandwidth available at the AP. In the figure, the media streams are limited to 70 percent. The minimum client data rate is limited to 6Mbps by default.

In the **Media Stream - Multicast Direct Parameters** section, check the box next to **Multicast Direct Enable** to use the Multicast Direct feature. By default, there is no limit on the number of streams that can be sent through an AP radio or to an individual client. You can change these limits through the drop-down menus if needed. The **Best Effort QoS Admission** check box should remain unchecked unless you want additional streams to be allowed beyond the limit.

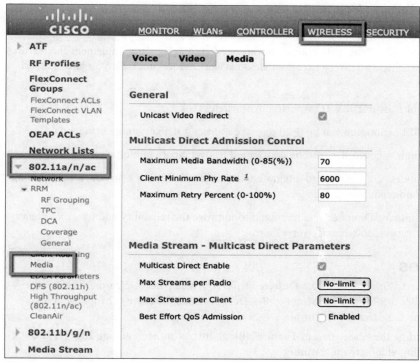

Figure 12-21   *Identifying Multicast Streams to Convert*

Step 4.   Enable Multicast Direct on each desired WLAN.

Multicast Direct relies on QoS mechanisms for the best stream delivery, so you must also set the WLAN QoS to **Gold (video)** and enable Multicast Direct. Navigate to **WLANs > WLANs** and select a WLAN to edit. Then make the settings shown in Figure 12-22.

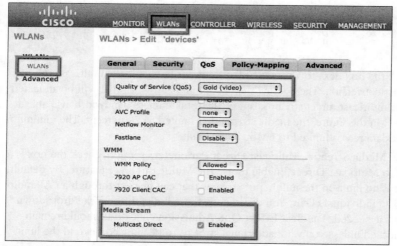

Figure 12-22   *Enabling Multicast Direct for a Specific WLAN*

Summary

This chapter described the main considerations needed to design and implement the features necessary for multicast delivery over a wireless network. More precisely, you have learned the following:

- How multicast traffic is transported over wireless

- How IGMP snooping can be used to make multicast delivery more efficient

- How wireless controllers can be configured to participate in multicast traffic delivery

- How wireless controllers can integrate with multicast DNS to assist devices in finding networked resources

- How Multicast Direct can be leveraged to improve the reliability and user experience of multicast video streams over wireless

References

Cisco Unified Wireless Multicast Design: https://www.cisco.com/c/en/us/td/docs/wireless/controller/8-5/Enterprise-Mobility-8-5-Design-Guide/Enterprise_Mobility_8-5_Deployment_Guide/ch6_Mcst.html

"Understanding the 'Videostream' Feature" (Blog): https://mrncciew.com/2012/12/24/understanding-videostream-feature/

Exam Preparation Tasks

As mentioned in the section "How to Use This Book" in the Introduction, you have a few choices for exam preparation: the exercises here, Chapter 18, "Final Preparation," and the exam simulation questions in the Pearson Test Prep Software Online.

Review All Key Topics

Review the most important topics in this chapter, noted with the Key Topic icon in the outer margin of the page. Table 12-2 lists these key topics and the page numbers on which each is found.

Table 12-2   Key Topics for Chapter 12

Key Topic Element	Description	Page Number
Figure 12-4	APs join a controller's CAPWAP multicast group	286
Figure 12-5	Multicast delivery in WLC multicast mode	287
Figure 12-8	WLC data collected by IGMP snooping	289
Figure 12-15	mDNS Bonjour gateway operation	295
Step list	Multicast Direct configuration steps	297

Define Key Terms

Define the following key terms from this chapter and check your answers in the glossary:

IGMP, Internet Group Management Report (IGMP), IGMP Snooping, Location Specific Services (LSS), LSS, mDNS, MGID, multicast, Multicast Direct, multicast DNS, multicast group, multicast group ID (MGID), Multicast Listener Discovery (MLD), PIM, Protocol Independent Multicast (PIM)

12

CHAPTER 13

Location Services Deployment

This chapter covers the following topics:

Indoor Location: This section covers the various available techniques to provide mobile device location from an infrastructure standpoint.

Deploying Location Services: This section discusses the roles of the various elements involved in indoor location services as well as how to connect them to each other.

Tracking Clients, RFID Tags, Rogues, and Interferers: This section illustrates how you can use the various location solutions to track the location of devices detected by your access points.

Customizing Location Services: This section shows how to fine-tune the location parameters.

This chapter covers the following ENWLSI exam topics:

- 4.1 Deploy MSE and CMX on a wireless network

- 4.2 Implement location services

  - 4.2.a Client tracking

  - 4.2.b RFID tag

  - 4.2.c Interferers

  - 4.2.d Rogue APs

  - 4.2.e Clients

Wi-Fi-based indoor location services are often misunderstood because they respond to challenges that are very different from outdoor location services. Outdoor location is mostly solved with GPS and only addresses a single use case (individual user location is displayed on an individual device map). GPS does not work well indoors, and the use cases are different: in some cases, users want to know their location, but they may also need to know the location of the access points (APs). The IT team may also need to know the location of mobile users or confirm the relative positions of the APs. As a result, where outdoor location solves a single use case, indoor location presents multiple solutions for multiple needs.

This chapter introduces the subject of Wi-Fi indoor location, as seen from the perspective of a network admin, and the need to monitor the Wi-Fi network and assess its performances. Part of such an assessment includes knowing the presence of rogue devices or interferers and being able to determine their position and zone of impact. Another part includes the ability to determine mobile device density and location. Such elements are critical to assess the network scale and efficiency and also to facilitate troubleshooting. This chapter covers the various location techniques available for indoor location, the various elements involved when location is computed by the Wi-Fi infrastructure, how these elements connect to one another, how they are deployed using Cisco Mobility Services Engine (MSE), Cisco Mobile Experience (CMX), or Cisco DNA Spaces, and how they can be customized to match the local network requirements.

"Do I Know This Already?" Quiz

The "Do I Know This Already?" quiz allows you to assess if you should read this entire chapter. If you miss no more than one of these self-assessment questions, you might want to move ahead to the "Exam Preparation Tasks" section. Table 13-1 lists the major headings in this chapter and the "Do I Know This Already?" quiz questions covering the material in those headings so you can assess your knowledge of these specific areas. You can find the answers to the "Do I Know This Already?" quiz in Appendix D.

Table 13-1 "Do I Know This Already?" Section-to-Question Mapping

Foundation Topics Section	Questions
Indoor Location	1–2
Deploying Location Services	3
Tracking Clients, RFID Tags, Rogues, and Interferers	4–5
Customizing Location Services	6

1. Which location parameter is most important?
   a. Precision
   b. Accuracy
   c. RSSI threshold
   d. SNR threshold

2. Which technique typically provides the best accuracy when deployed properly?
   a. RSSI trilateration
   b. Cell of origin
   c. Angle of Arrival
   d. FastLocate

3. Which elements are required to deploy DNA Spaces in cloud-only mode?
   a. APs, WLCs (running 8.7 or earlier, or with DNA Spaces Translator for 8.8 or later)
   b. APs, WLCs, on-premises MSE
   c. APs, WLCs, DNA Spaces Connector
   d. APs, DNA Spaces Connector

4. Which of the following options allows you to deploy floor maps on the MSE?
   a. Import from Cisco Prime Infrastructure
   b. Download from DNA Spaces
   c. Direct configuration on MSE
   d. Import from WLCs

5. What is a "heat map" on the activity map?
   a. A representation of the AP cell coverage
   b. A representation of location accuracy
   c. A representation of location precision
   d. A representation of device density

6. How many devices can be represented on a single floor plan activity map in CMX?
   a. 500
   b. 2,000
   c. 10,000
   d. 20,000

Foundation Topics

Indoor Location

With the advent of GPS, outdoor location has mostly been solved. GPS is integrated in most mobile devices, and second- and third-generation GPS systems provide an accuracy below 1 meter in good conditions. By contrast, GPS does not work well inside, and indoor location has not been solved yet. There are technical challenges that are difficult to overcome, and this chapter provides some examples. There is also a larger set of considerations to address:

- **The IT team may need to know individual mobile device location** to optimize associated technical resources ("Add more APs in this area"), business assets ("The line is too long; send more sales associates"), or facilitate troubleshooting ("The connection failed as the device entered the elevator").

- **Individual users may need to know their location (blue dot).** This need is similar to that of outdoor location but typically only appears in public venues. Users spend 90 percent of their time in known places (home, office, familiar public places visited often) and seldom need blue dot services in these locations.

- **The device that performs location may not be the device that needs location.** Indoor location can be achieved by either side (infrastructure detecting mobile devices and computing their location; mobile devices detecting known reference points and computing their blue dot position relative to these points). Collaboration is also possible (for example, infrastructure devices signaling their geo-position to mobile devices as well as mobile devices sending information helping the infrastructure to conclude on the mobile device location). Such cooperation needs to be built between endpoint and infrastructure vendors, while respecting both sides' needs (for example, end user privacy).

This complex constellation means that indoor location is a very active topic, with multiple elements that you are expected to understand. Working from the angle of the infrastructure IT team, you will be able to deploy a location solution while keeping in mind that your deployment only solves part of the equation.

Indoor Location Protocols

Wireless-based indoor location in general supposes a mobile device and a form of radio exchanges between that mobile device and some infrastructure elements. These exchanges allow the infrastructure or the mobile device to compute the device location or position.

> **NOTE**   Position usually refers to a relative distance (for example, "17 meters from AP2, at a 230-degree angle from the North direction"). Location usually refers to an absolute or relative point on Earth (for example, "right at the West entrance door of the shopping mall" or "at geo-position 37.419986 North, −121.919982 West").

When we refer to "indoor location" in this chapter, we always imply that some form of radio communication between devices is involved and that the location of some of the devices (commonly called "anchors") is known. Three main protocols and technologies are available for indoor location purposes:

- **Ultra-Wide Band (UWB):** Defined by the IEEE 802.15.4 group under 802.15.4a (currently revised to 802.15.4z), UWB relies on one side sending pulses with instructions on when to respond. The frames exchanged are marked with a timestamp, and time of flight (ToF) is computed to estimate range information. Although UWB can also be used to exchange data, its primary goal is ranging. As such, it leverages wide channels and is highly accurate (20 cm or less). However, no AP, smartphone, laptop, or other general-purpose device includes a UWB radio today compatible with ranging protocols. Thus, implementing UWB ranging would require both the infrastructure and the mobile devices to be equipped with a new additional radio compatible with UWB frequencies and protocols. This radio usage would be limited to indoor location, and UWB would work only if both sides had installed UWB radios. As the proportion of such UWB-location-capable Wi-Fi clients and APs is currently 0 percent, there is a chicken-and-egg problem. Infrastructure vendors have low incentive to install UWB chips as no clients can use them, and client vendors have low incentive to install UWB chips as they won't be usable against any infrastructure networks yet. As such, UWB is not widely used (and not incorporated into Cisco APs) yet. This situation may change if adoption is pushed conjointly by a large AP vendor and one or more large client vendors.

- **Bluetooth / Bluetooth Low Energy (BLE):** In 2015, the Bluetooth Standard version 4.2 extended the specification to low-energy communication, thus allowing a mobile device to exchange frames with surrounding objects for purposes others than establishing a master-slave relationship with a dependent object (for example, headset or printer). With BLE, the mobile device can use its Bluetooth (BT) radio to send connectionless messages to other objects, exchanging information such as transmission power, identification, or position. This exchange allows the device to compute its

13

relative distance (using the Tx power information and the RSSI trilateration technique described later) to several other BLE objects. The accuracy can be down to 1 or 2 meters, but the range is limited (typically 10 to 20 meters in most cases). Then an app can display a map with the known location of these objects and the relative position of the device. The objects can be dedicated beacon tags, but these are difficult to manage: their range is limited, they are usually battery operated, their battery needs to be monitored and replaced when needed, they can be stolen, and so on. A better solution is to integrate BLE beacons within powered and fixed objects (for example, APs). As the beacons are integrated within the AP, they have no battery limitation; they are also much harder to steal. Each BLE radio can also emulate several "virtual beacons." Today, most Cisco APs incorporate such BLE beacons. Most mobile devices also support Bluetooth, and many recent mobile devices support BT 4.2 or later, thus making support for BLE location very common. However, this solution requires an app to display the AP positions for blue dot service. The location is also primarily for blue dot service (most mobile devices will not reply to AP BLE messages). As such, action is on the client side (installing an app that is often venue specific) that usually does not answer the need for infrastructure-locating mobile devices.

■ **Wi-Fi:** As most mobile clients support Wi-Fi, 802.11 has long been expected to support indoor location. The 2012 revision of 802.11 started incorporating location features. The 2016 revision includes provisions by which an initiating station (ISTA) can exchange Fine Timing Measurements (FTM) messages with a responding station (RSTA) to perform ranging based on time of flight. An amendment (802.11az) is being specifically developed for this purpose, improving the security and the possible methods for such exchanges. The ISTA is usually understood as "the mobile device" and the RSTA as "the AP." As such, this protocol is primarily oriented toward blue dot service. The accuracy depends very much on the channel size (from 6 to 8 meters for 20MHz channels to 2 meters for 80MHz channels). The feature is still not widely deployed and also does not answer the need for infrastructure location, for which several techniques exist, as discussed next.

Infrastructure and 802.11-Based Location

As a Wi-Fi infrastructure vendor, Cisco has long been concerned primarily with the need of IT teams to locate mobile devices and has leveraged several techniques over the years. As a Cisco Networking Professional, you need to understand these various techniques, their interactions, and their limitations.

Cell of Origin Techniques

With these techniques, a station's 802.11 frames are detected by one or more APs. The station location is deemed to be near the AP that received the strongest signal (nearest AP) or near the AP to which the station associated (associated AP). Quite clearly, these techniques offer only limited accuracy. First, a cell may sometimes be up to 100 meters in radius or more, limiting location to a general area. The client may also be near an AP and yet associated to another AP. Even when the strongest signal technique is used, obstacles between the client and nearby APs (for example, elevator shaft) can make the strongest signal appear on a farther AP. In summary, cell of origin techniques are only used for "presence detection" (that is, reporting that a station is in a given area) or providing a rough count of stations in a given zone.

RSSI Trilateration Techniques

RSSI trilateration is undoubtedly the oldest technique implemented for infrastructure location. *Lateration* is a technical term used in navigation and geo-location techniques that comes from the Latin term *lateral*, which means "side." With lateration, you draw geometric figures that represent reference objects at known positions and mobile objects for which distance to the reference objects is known (regardless of the technique used to learn that distance). Then you measure the length of the sides of these figures (that is, the distances between the object you're trying to locate and the various known objects). This method allows you to learn the unknown object position. With trilateration, you use at least three reference points (APs in our case). Practically speaking, the 802.11 frames from a mobile station are detected by one or more APs (preferably three or more). The APs (or a location engine outside of the APs) then use the Received Signal Strength Indicator (RSSI), which is the signal strength at which the station frame was received on each AP, to estimate the distance between the station and the AP. When three or more APs perform such computation, and these APs' locations are known, and if these APs are deployed around the station (as explained in Chapter 3, "Conducting an Onsite Site Survey," and Chapter 6, "Designing Radio Management"), then the location of the station can also be determined. Such technique has several implications you have to keep in mind:

- The signal gets weaker with distance, which is the whole idea behind RSSI trilateration. However, this attenuation strongly depends on the environment. At the same distance, the signal will reach the AP at a stronger level if it crosses an open space environment than if it goes through multiple office walls. Therefore, when you deploy a Cisco location solution that uses trilateration techniques, you need to specify each floor environment type (for example, open space, light cubicles, or walled offices). The system uses this element of information to infer the average attenuation for such an environment (this technique is called RF fingerprinting).

- At a given distance, the received signal strength depends not only on the AP Receive chain sensitivity (which is known), but also on the client transmit power and Transmit chain characteristics, which are unknown. The AP therefore has to assume an average value for the client transmission characteristics. Of course, such estimation is never perfect, and this uncertainty always affects the accuracy of the estimated distance, thus mechanically limiting the accuracy that such a technique allows.

- Computing the distance to a single AP does not provide the station position. The client can be at any position on a circle around the AP, where the circle radius is the estimated distance. However, when three or more APs detect the client signal, its position can be estimated to be where the circles representing the distance to each detecting APs intersect, as shown in Figure 13-1. Each circle is only a range estimation, and their intersection provides a location probability estimation. As the number of detecting APs (and the number of detected frames from the station) increases, the location accuracy confidence increases.

13

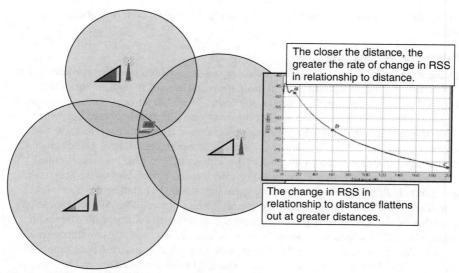

The closer the distance, the greater the rate of change in RSS in relationship to distance.

The change in RSS in relationship to distance flattens out at greater distances.

Figure 13-1 *RSSI Trilateration Illustration*

Angle of Arrival (AoA) Techniques

The limitations inherent in RSSI brought Cisco to use a new location technique inspired by radars: Angle of Arrival (AoA). Airport radars are positioned at known locations, and they use a rotating antenna to send radio waves and detect airplanes from the radio wave echoes. Because the antenna rotates, the radar can evaluate with high accuracy the angle at which the airplane is detected. When two or more radars work together, the distance to the airplane can be computed from the angle to each radar, as shown on the left side of Figure 13-2.

Indoors, however, Wi-Fi AP antennas do not rotate. Instead, Cisco has developed a ring positioned around the access point body, forming an array of 16 to 32 mini directional antennas. When a station signal reaches the AP, a Hyperlocation system evaluates the comparative angle at which the signal is received on each detecting antenna, as illustrated on the right side of Figure 13-2. These measurements are combined to estimate the station position, with an accuracy of 1 to 3 meters (90 percent of estimations), and in some cases less than 1 meter.

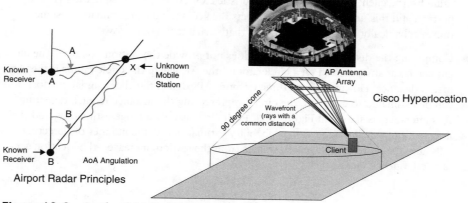

Figure 13-2 *Angle of Arrival Techniques*

One major strength of Hyperlocation is that a single AP is often sufficient to estimate the station location (and not just the client position). However, you need to install APs that either support the addition of a Hyperlocation ring (called Hyperlocation module) or already include that module. Additionally, when positioning your APs on a map (in your location engine), you need to very carefully document the AP (and the Hyperlocation module) position and orientation. Any imprecision can lead to wide inaccuracies in the location estimation.

802.11 Frames Used for Location

The AP must receive frames from a station so as to estimate the signal strength or angle, which means that the receiving AP must be on the correct channel. If the client transmits frames on a single channel, then only neighboring APs that are on that channel will contribute to the client location. In a standard deployment, APs on the same channel are not close to each other. In many cases, the network design mandates co-channel RF isolation, which means that only one or two APs are able to detect the client signal, limiting the accuracy that can be expected from leveraging this frame. An efficient way of mitigating this issue is to add APs to your deployment, set to Monitor mode, as described in Chapters 3 and 6. In this mode, the additional APs cannot provide client service, but they scan all channels, in turn, spending 1.1 second on each channel. Although these additional APs may not always be on the client channel, using them increases your chances of having more APs detecting the client signal. The client may also send frames on multiple channels at short intervals (for example, probe requests during scanning). Using such frames increases location accuracy as many neighboring APs may be contributing.

Receiving the client signal is useful but is only valid for location purposes if the sending client can be identified. Therefore, all techniques suppose the ability for each receiving AP to demodulate the client signal and read the transmitter MAC address. Therefore, the type of frame transmitted is critical:

- Broadcast management frames (for example, probe requests) are sent at a low data rate and high power and therefore can be detected by multiple APs, provided they are on the right channel. However, a station may only send these frames occasionally, which reduces the distance estimation interval and thus the location accuracy. Both associated and unassociated stations send broadcast frames, and their interval depends on the station state. An associated station may only need to send probe requests occasionally. For example, the station may only probe every 5 or 6 minutes, to keep an awareness of the AP environment. The station may also only scan a subset of all channels (those on which it previously detected APs). As the user stops actively using the device (screen off), the station may go to sleep and stop sending any traffic completely for a long time. For some devices (for example, Apple iOS), the station may only become active again if the user starts interacting again with the device (screen on). Until then, the device is no longer visible (from a location standpoint). If the user is active, as soon as the device reaches the edge of the cell, the associated station may probe at short intervals (multiple all-channels scans), thus providing a lot of samples from which to compute range. An unassociated station only sends probe requests when in awake mode and actively attempting to discover networks.

13

■ More and more stations hide their real MAC address by using locally administered MAC addresses when probing. Each 802.11 interface has a globally unique MAC address, which is composed of an Organizationally Unique Identifier (OUI) and a unique Network Interface Controller (NIC) identifier, as shown in Figure 13-3. When the station sends frames, the Transmitter Address (TA) field mentions the station's MAC address. When the station is associated and sends data traffic, this identifier needs to be stable. However, such a requirement disappears if the station is only trying to discover its environment. Therefore, in an attempt to increase the user privacy (and make the stable mapping between a device's signal and its associated user identity and location more difficult), more and more station vendors use a locally administered address for broadcast and discovery frames. In that case, the second bit of the first byte of the address is set to 1, and all the other bits can be random, as shown in Figure 13-3. The station only needs to maintain this address long enough to collect the responses it needs, and it may then change its address for the next query. From the infrastructure standpoint, there is no continuity between one request and the next, and the location engine cannot estimate if consecutive requests come from the same station or from several stations in the same approximate location. Associated stations often probe their current channel using their associated (stable) MAC address. Unassociated stations often use a locally administered address for each probe, thus making location possible but not useful for individual station location tracking.

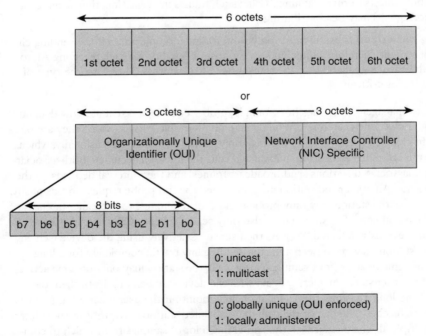

Figure 13-3 *The Structure of a MAC Address*

■ Unicast data frames are often sent at the highest possible data rate (MCS) and are therefore only properly demodulated by the AP to which the station is associated. These frames can be frequent, thus providing multiple distance estimations at close intervals. However, only one AP typically performs this estimation (the AP to which the client is associated). Using only these frames would not provide great location results. However, adding the unicast frames to the broadcast frames can greatly enhance the accuracy of the client position estimation. In a Cisco network, adding these unicast frames is called FastLocate.

These constraints result in different location performances, depending on the stations you are tracking, their associated state, and the configuration of your Cisco location system:

- With RSSI trilateration relying on broadcast frames (and a deployment matching the recommendations for location services, detailed in Chapter 5, "Applying Wireless Design Requirements"), you can expect an accuracy of 7 to 9 meters. This means that the estimated client position is within 7 to 9 meters of the actual client position, 90 percent of the time (that is, for 90 percent of estimations). There may be time lapses during which no estimation is available (because the station is not sending any broadcast frames). There may also be cases where the client changes its MAC address at each request, thus making the computed location unusable for individual station tracking. In that case, you can locate stations, but you do not know how many stations are present.

- With the addition of FastLocate, you enable tracking for unicast data frames. This mode increases the location accuracy, as it adds the contribution of frequent unicast frames to the broadcast frames. This mode is only possible for associated stations, and it brings the accuracy to 5 to 7 meters (for 90 percent of estimations). It also increases the efficiency of individual station tracking, as the client must use a stable MAC address (even if the address is locally administered) for its data communication throughout the entire session.

Precision vs. Accuracy

Precision and accuracy are two primary goals for location services. Accuracy evaluates how close the position estimation is to the actual station position (called "ground truth"). If a station is at an actual position, "A," and your estimation evaluates the station position as being 1 meter away from position "A," then your accuracy is higher than if your estimation evaluates the station position as being 5 meters away from the "A" ground truth position.

However, your system typically uses multiple consecutive frames before making a position estimation. Precision measures consecutive evaluations proximity to one another. If your consecutive estimations result in position points near each other, precision is high. You should note that high precision does not mean high accuracy (and vice versa). Your multiple samples can each result in evaluation points far from each other (low precision), but their average still results in a final position evaluation close to the station ground truth position (high accuracy).

Regardless of the technique you use, keep in mind that location does not happen in real time. In all cases, one or more APs must collect the client signal and then send it to a location engine. The location engine does not provide the result of location computation for each frame from each client. This is because Wi-Fi signals are stochastic. Multipath makes that signal or angle estimations only display limited stability indoors. Therefore, the location engine needs several samples for each client before computing an average and the associated likely position. If the location engine relies on broadcast frames (probe requests), it will wait for the completion of the client probe cycle to conclude on the client location. Most clients probe a few (or all) channels in sequence. The entire probing cycle can take up to 6 to 10 seconds, resulting in location estimations every 10 to 15 seconds while the client is probing. If the location engine also uses unicast data frames, the location estimation can happen more often if the client is actively transmitting. Table 13-2 compares these various infrastructure-based location techniques.

Table 13-2   Infrastructure-Based Location Technique Key Characteristics

Technique	RSSI Trilateration	FastLocate	AoA
Frames	Broadcast (management frames)	Any (broadcast and unicast frames)	Any (broadcast and unicast OFDM frames)
Max refresh rate	10–15 seconds	2–4 seconds	2–4 seconds
Accuracy	7–9 meters (90%)	5–7 meters (90%)	1–3 meters (90%)
Notes	Works with associated and unassociated stations. Inactive stations may not be detected for a long time.	Requires stations to be associated. Inactive stations may not be detected for a long time.	Works with associated and unassociated stations. Inactive stations may not be detected for a long time.

Deploying Location Services

Location is usually not computed directly within the AP (for example, because several APs may be needed to perform RSS trilateration). Even with Hyperlocation, more contributing APs provide finer location estimation. As such, several elements are interconnected in a Cisco location architecture:

- The APs collect the signal from the stations. With FastLocate, the APs can also trigger client frames, by sending 802.11n/ac/ax Block Ack Responses (BAR) to the client, which are acknowledged (thus causing the client to send a frame that can be evaluated at the AP). The APs then send the client information to the WLC or the location engine.

- The WLC receives from all APs the signal information for all detected stations. The WLC sorts the information by client MAC address and then sends the resulting table (client, detecting AP, detection time, RSSI) at intervals to a location system (MSE, CMX, or DNA Spaces). You should keep in mind that the WLC does not have maps, does not have information about individual APs location, and therefore cannot compute any client position. The WLC role is therefore only to forward the information received from the APs (RSSI value and/or Angle of Arrival).

- A location engine (CMX, MSE, DNA Spaces) receives at intervals client information (RSSI and/or AoA) from multiple APs through possibly multiple WLCs, then computes for each MAC address the corresponding mobile device position, based on the information received and the known location of the reporting APs.

If you use RSSI trilateration, the APs send the client information (RSSI) to the WLC through regular management and data forwarding messages, using the Control and Provisioning of Wireless Access Points (CAPWAP) protocol. CAPWAP is the general protocol used by Cisco APs and WLCs to exchange configuration information (using UDP port 5246) or forward client data (using UDP port 5247). The CAPWAP encapsulation always mentions the client RSSI. The WLC then forwards the concatenated client information to the location engine, using the Network Mobility Service Protocol (NMSP—not to be confused with Simple Network Management Protocol, SNMP). If your APs implement FastLocate, they forward the unicast frame information data (client MAC and RSSI) "directly" to the location engine. If your APs implement AoA, they can also "directly" forward to the location engine the angle values for the client signal. These various modes are represented in Figure 13-4.

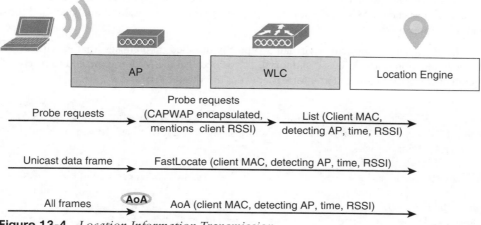

Figure 13-4   *Location Information Transmission*

NOTE   The word "directly" needs to be qualified, as it is a common trap for students. There is no IP connection established between an individual AP and the location engine. All traffic from the APs go to the WLC first. This is necessary, as many deployments do not allow direct IP connectivity between the AP subnets and the MSE subnet. The meaning of "directly" in the context of location is that the WLC receives FastLocate or AoA record reports from the APs. The WLC recognizes these reports from their header and cannot read them (they are encrypted with a key provided by CMX to avoid eavesdropping on the path). The WLC role is limited to decapsulating (removing the CAPWAP header), changing the MAC and IP sources to its own (instead of the AP's) and forwarding immediately the packet to the MSE. The WLC is just a transparent relay. By contrast, when receiving the RSSI information (with trilateration), the WLC collects the information and then builds a table of clients, APs, and signals that the WLC concatenates in a file at regular intervals, before sending the result to CMX. The WLC here plays an active part, building the table and deciding when to send it, instead of being a transparent relay.

13

Location Engines and Services

The general location principles summarized earlier imply that your deployment needs a central location engine. This engine implements one or more techniques to compute the best estimate for the location of detected 802.11 devices. In the literature, you will see the terms DNA Spaces, Connector, Mobility Services Engine (MSE), and Cisco Connected Mobile Experience (CMX). As a networking professional, you need to differentiate these elements.

MSE or CMX is often described as the location engine that is deployed on premises (that is, "not" in the cloud). Even among professionals, in a Cisco environment, you will hear people use the terms MSE and CMX interchangeably. Formally, however, the Mobility Services Engine (MSE) is the name given to the appliance where the location engine runs. The MSE can be a physical appliance (the older Cisco MSE 3355, or the newer Cisco MSEs 3365 and 3375) or a virtual appliance (running on VMware or Microsoft HyperV). Cisco Connected Mobile Experience (CMX) is the software package that runs on the MSE appliance and provides location services.

The MSE appliance (physical or virtual) is typically installed on premises (that is, with a LAN connection to the WLCs it supports). This is because the MSE is expected to receive frequent flows of measurement information from the various APs and WLCs.

> **NOTE**   One key limitation of the MSE (and of CMX) is that the solution is not designed to allow for easy upload of maps of your facilities. The expectation is that location is an extension of your network management tasks, performed on Cisco Prime Infrastructure (the network management platform). Therefore, the normal procedure is to use Cisco Prime Infrastructure to upload and initialize maps in MSE/CMX. In CMX, you create and edit zones. Then you use Cisco Prime Infrastructure to create campuses, buildings, and floors and to upload their associated map pictures. You also position the APs on the maps. Once this step is completed, you can upload these maps to your zones in CMX. However, you will see in the next section that there is a way to import maps (and WLCs) directly into MSE. This procedure is designed as an exception, only used when PI import is not possible.

In 2018, Cisco acquired a company called July Systems that produced a cloud-based location engine. This solution was integrated with CMX in 2019, allowing the Cisco location solution to offer both cloud and on-premises capabilities. The entire location solution set was renamed DNA Spaces. You can now subscribe to a cloud-based version of DNA Spaces or use an on-premises version of DNA Spaces that implements the CMX software suite on an MSE appliance. You can also use a hybrid cloud/on-premises solution where DNA Spaces (in the cloud) connects to an on-premises relay, which can be a simple connector appliance (called the DNA Spaces Connector) or a full MSE.

In the cloud-based version of DNA Spaces, you configure your WLCs (AireOS WLC or Catalyst 9800 controller) to use DNA Spaces as their location engine. This capability appears in AireOS 8.8 MR2 and later as well as C9800 16.10.1 and later.

Older controller versions do not support such direct connection. In this case, you can use an on-premises relay, DNA Spaces Connector. The Connector points to DNA Spaces in the Cloud and is seen by your controllers as a location engine (MSE). The Connector does not perform location computation directly but simply concatenates the WLC messages in a format consumable by DNA Spaces. In the other direction, the Connector converts the DNA Spaces messages into Network Mobility Services Protocol (NMSP) messages, which are the location protocol messages traditionally used between Cisco controllers and CMX. As the Connector also uses enhanced messaging, your WLC needs to run AireOS 8.0 or later to support this configuration.

You can also implement another solution, where CMX is deployed onsite and performs all location tasks. This is the traditional solution.

DNA Spaces (in the cloud) also adds interesting capabilities to those of on-premises CMX, such as vertical-specific dashboards and a rich API set that allows integration with enterprise systems. With these capabilities, you can use location information to dynamically act on building resources (for example, modulate air conditioning and heating, lighting, and so on, based on detected presence and user density). Therefore, you may want to add DNA Spaces to your CMX deployment. In that case, you can configure your CMX 10.5 or later to also point to DNA Spaces and export the location data you need in DNA Spaces. These various connection solutions are shown in Figure 13-5.

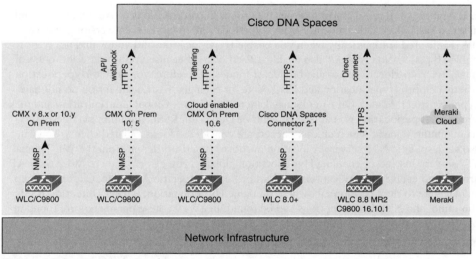

Figure 13-5   *Location Deployment Options*

Because the history of location is fairly rich, you should check software compatibility before choosing one solution to make sure that the location solution will work with your AP models and WLC platform and code release. The software compatibility matrix can be found here:

https://www.cisco.com/c/en/us/td/docs/wireless/compatibility/matrix/compatibility-matrix.html?referring_site=RE&pos=5&page=

https://www.cisco.com/c/en/us/solutions/collateral/enterprise-networks/connected-mobile-experiences/datasheet-c78-742287.html

13

Configuring APs and WLCs for Location Support

Your configuration will depend on the type of location data you want to send. In all cases, you should point both the WLC (and thus its associated APs) and your location engine to the same Network Time Protocol (NTP) server, so as to ensure time consistency. NTP is configured in AireOS from **Controller > NTP**, from **General Settings** in eWLC initial setup, and in the **Configuration > Tags & Profiles > AP Join** profiles once the eWLC is active.

In the MSE, the NTP server is configured during the initial setup. You can configure it again by calling, from the CLI, the **cmxctl config** script.

DNA Spaces does not require NTP configuration (it is enabled by default). However, you can use the **Location Hierarchy > More Actions** menu to define the time zone for each location and its associated WLCs. If you use a Connector, NTP is configured during the initial setup and in the upper menu once the Connector is active.

Next, enable support for FastLocate and/or Hyperlocation. RSSI trilateration does not require any specific configuration on the WLC. Your APs always collect client RSSI data and send it to the WLC. You just need to connect the WLC and the location engine as described in the following section.

FastLocate is configured globally or per AP group. In older versions of AireOS, you would only use FastLocate independently from Hyperlocation. In more recent versions, the feature is activated automatically when you enable Hyperlocation, and you would not want to enable Hyperlocation without also enabling FastLocate (because you would want to use all frames for Hyperlocation, not just broadcast frames). Therefore, you enable Hyperlocation to activate both Hyperlocation and FastLocate, or even just FastLocate if you do not have Hyperlocation modules. On AireOS, navigate to **Wireless > Global Configuration** and make sure that **Hyperlocation** is enabled. The **Packet Detection RSSI Minimum** parameter sets the minimum value at which unicast packets are considered for associated clients. You can also set a specific NTP server for location purposes (that is, different from the WLC global NTP server). Instead of enabling Hyperlocation globally, you can navigate to **WLANs > AP Groups** and enable Hyperlocation and FastLocate for a specific AP group. Click the group and navigate to the **Location** tab, where the same **Hyperlocation, Packet Detection RSSI Minimum**, and **NTP Server** options can be found. In eWLC, these parameters are found in the **Configuration > AP Join** profile, in the **AP > Hyperlocation** tab.

The last task is to point your WLC to CMX, DNA Spaces Connector, or DNA Spaces. This task is in fact started from these appliances, as detailed next. In your WLC, you can verify and complete the configuration from **Management > Cloud Services** in AireOS, where you will find the options **Server** (for DNA Spaces) and **CMX**. In the C9800, use **Configuration > Services > Cloud Services**.

Deploying DNA Spaces, MSE, and CMX

Once you have chosen a location engine, you may need an initial server installation and then the configuration of communication parameters between your WLCs and the location engine components. For each task, we will distinguish DNA Spaces (with or without Connector) and the on-premises MSE/CMX solution.

Initial Installation

If you buy a physical MSE appliance, your setup task is limited to physical mounting in a rack, providing an initial configuration, and optionally upgrading the CMX software package. If you install a virtual MSE, you need to follow the server sizing instructions and installation procedure detailed here: https://www.cisco.com/c/en/us/td/docs/wireless/mse/10-3/installation/guide/installation_guide_103/installing_a_cisco_mse_virtual_appliance.html.

The CMX software package is installed by default along with the MSE appliance. At initial deployment, the MSE will require you to connect to the appliance console (using a serial connection for older platforms, serial or USB connection for newer platforms, and the virtual console connection for virtual appliances) and then follow the initial setup script. You can also call this script at any time (to perform the initial configuration or modify one of its parameters) from the MSE CLI, using the **cmxctl config** command. The script will require you to configure an IP address for the MSE appliance and credentials for the default cmxadmin super user. You can also set the password for the root super user.

NOTE   Root is used to access the MSE CLI and configure the appliance. cmxadmin is the account used to manage the CMX service, through the CLI or the web interface.

You can install the appliance to provide presence services or location services (but not both). Presence provides device count per zone, typically for analytics purposes. Location provides individual device location. You would typically choose Presence for outdoor deployments and indoor low-density deployments. You would typically choose Location for most indoor deployments (standard and high density). You can also choose to install the MSE (physical or virtual) as a secondary server, providing high availability in combination with another, primary MSE server. In this case, your configuration is limited to informing the system about the primary server IP address and access credentials. Once the initial setup script completes, you can access the CMX system through HTTPS, using the configured IP address and cmxadmin credentials, and continue your configuration from there. You can also access the MSE CLI through SSH (or Telnet, if you choose to enable it).

If you choose the cloud-based version of DNA Spaces, then no specific installation is required, just a subscription from the website portal (https://dnaspaces.cisco.com).

CMX Deployment Configuration

You can use MSE and CMX with or without DNA Spaces, and we will examine both scenarios. In all cases, once MSE and CMX are installed, your first task is to import maps and WLCs. Maps are obtained from Cisco Prime Infrastructure (PI), so this part supposes that you have a Cisco PI installation in your network, where maps and WLCs are already present. Refer to the Cisco Prime Infrastructure User guide for more details (https://www.cisco.com/c/en/us/td/docs/net_mgmt/prime/infrastructure/3-2/user/guide/bk_CiscoPrimeInfrastructure_3_2_0_UserGuide.html) on the Cisco PI configuration procedure. You need to add your WLCs to Cisco Prime Infrastructure (they bring their APs along automatically). You also need to add the MSE from the **Services > Mobility Services > Mobility Services Engines** page, using the MSE IP address and the cmxadmin credentials.

You can then activate location services from Cisco Prime and export your maps. However, the Cisco Prime team may not be the location team. Therefore, you can also import the maps (and the WLCs) directly from CMX.

13

> **NOTE**   Although this procedure is available, keep in mind, as a CCNP candidate, that the normal process is to use Cisco Prime Infrastructure as described in the previous section. Direct import is expected to be an exception and only used when PI export is not directly possible.

Log in to CMX and click **Settings** at the top-right corner of the window. Choose the **Controllers and Maps Setup > Import** tab and enter Cisco Prime Infrastructure administrative username, password, and IP address. Then, to override the existing maps that currently exist in Cisco CMX while importing, check the **Delete & replace existing maps & analytics data** check box. If you import a map with a new campus, you need not check the **Delete & replace existing zones** check box. Cisco CMX will automatically process all the zones added in the map. Click **Import Controllers and Maps** and then click **Save** to apply.

If your Cisco PI IP address is not accessible from CMX, you need to manually export the maps from PI. From the Cisco PI web interface, choose **Site Maps** from the **Maps** menu. Then choose **Export Maps** and click **Go**. Select the map to be exported and click **Export**. The maps will be downloaded as a tar.gz archive. Then, from the MSE main dashboard, choose **Settings** and then choose **Controllers and Maps Setup > Advanced**. Under the **Maps** area, click **Browse** and choose the tar.gz file exported from Cisco PI. Click **Open** and then click **Upload**. Click **Save** to validate.

You may then also have to import WLCs manually. Under the **Controllers** area, enter your WLC IP address. Choose the **Applicable Services** (for location, choose Context Aware Services, or **CAS**). Enter the SNMP values configured on your WLC and then click **Add Controller**. Click **Save** to validate.

At this point, your CMX is ready to perform location tasks. If you use CMX without DNA Spaces, you can skip the next section.

DNA Spaces Deployment Configuration

With DNA Spaces Cloud, you need to configure your WLC to point to DNA Spaces. This is possible if your WLC runs AireOS code release 8.8 MR2 and later, or if your Cisco Catalyst 9800/eWLC runs IOS code release 16.10 and later. Start from the DNA Spaces dashboard. In the left menu, select **Setup > Wireless Networks > Connect your Wireless Network**. Several options are available, as shown in Figure 13-6.

If you are unsure of which option is best in your configuration, choose the **Get your wireless network connected with Cisco DNA Spaces > Add New** option to access a multi-option menu page. Alternatively, to connect your WLC directly, choose the **Connect WLC/ Catalyst 9800 Directly** option. Communication between the WLC and DNA Spaces supposes that your WLC accepts your DNA Spaces root certificate. Therefore, the first step is to install that root certificate on your WLC. Click the **View Certificate** option and import the certificate into your WLC using the procedure described here:

https://www.cisco.com/c/en/us/support/docs/wireless/dna-spaces/214668-dna-spaces-direct-connect-configuration.html

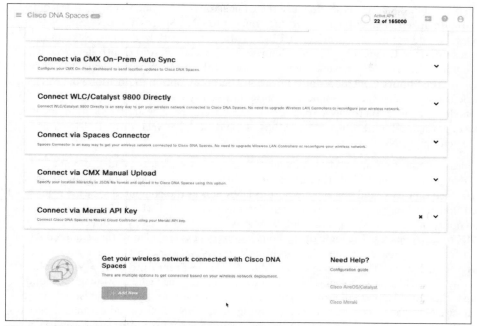

Figure 13-6 *DNA Spaces Connection Options*

Next, still in DNA Spaces, choose **Configure Token** and **View Token**. You will see an id-token value unique for your DNA Spaces account, along with a Customer path key, LB domain, and IP address values. Copy these elements. Then input these values in your controller. In AireOS, navigate to **Management > Cloud Services**, enter the server URL in the form https://{Customer Path Key}.{LB Domain} {LB IP Address}, and then enter the id-token value. In C9800, the same options are accessible from **Configuration > Services > Cloud Services > CMX Cloud**.

The last step is to associate the WLC to a location, by clicking **Import Controllers** in DNA Spaces. If connectivity was successfully achieved in the previous step, your WLC should appear in the list along with a count of the WLC APs. Select the WLC and click **Next** to choose the associated location. Click **Finish** to validate. You can also create locations at this stage.

When you choose this direct connection, your WLC will need 250Kbps of bandwidth to DNA Spaces. As location information can be bandwidth intensive, especially in real time, this WLC Cloud Connect mode limits the amount of data (and its frequency).

If you have an older version of AireOS or Catalyst 9800/eWLC where direct connection options to DNA Spaces are not available, or if you want to get location closer to real time, you can use Cisco DNA Spaces Connector. Start in DNA Spaces, in the select **Setup > Wireless Networks > Connect your Wireless Network** menu. Then choose **Connect via Spaces Connector > View Token** to copy the DNA Spaces token. You can also download the Connector OVA from the same general menu. Once the Connector OVA has been deployed as explained in the previous section, use the Connector GUI Settings menu (a gear icon) and **Configure Token** to enter the id-token and connect to DNA Spaces. On DNA Spaces Connector, you do not need to configure URLs, certificates, or path key values. Next, in DNA Spaces, from the **Connect via Spaces Connector** page, choose **Add Controller**. You will need your WLC IP address, name, and type, along with SNMP Write credentials. You can then use the **Import Controllers into Location Hierarchy** option to position your WLC in a particular site. Using such a Connector configuration may be useful even if your WLC supports direct connection to DNA Spaces, as the Connector provides faster location updates. However, this deployment mandates 4Mbps of bandwidth between Cisco DNA Spaces Connector and DNA Spaces.

A third option is to install CMX on premises, use CMX for location, and also point CMX to DNA Spaces in the Cloud. The advantage of this option is that location computation is performed on CMX, and you only export to DNA Spaces the computed location results and their updates. There are two ways of achieving this goal. With CMX 10.5, you export location notifications to DNA Spaces using Webhook. With CMX 10.6, you directly connect CMX to DNA Spaces. The logic of the connection process is similar to that explored so far. Start from DNA Spaces, in the select **Setup > Wireless Networks > Connect your Wireless Network** menu. Then choose **Connect via CMX On-Prem Auto Sync > View Token** to copy the DNA Spaces token. Then log in to Cisco CMX, navigate to **Manage > Cloud Apps**, click **Enable**, paste the token, and click **Save**. At this point, your CMX should try to contact DNA Spaces (you do not need to configure the DNA Spaces address in CMX; only the token is needed). Go back to DNA Spaces, navigate to **Setup > Wireless Networks > Connect via CMX On-Prem Auto Sync**, and click **Add CMX**. If your token configuration was successful, your CMX should appear in the list. Choose the location where you want to import CMX and click **Next**. Configure the display name and select the campus, building, and floors you want to add from CMX to the Location Hierarchy. Then, click **Import**. Your CMX should now be connected to DNA Spaces. You can use CMX for location tasks and augment it with DNA Spaces functionalities. To confirm that CMX is communicating with Cisco DNA Spaces, you can always go back to CMX and navigate to **Manage > Cloud Apps** to see the statistics of the CMX northbound notifications to DNA Spaces.

Tracking Clients, RFID Tags, Rogues, and Interferers

At this point, your APs, WLCs, and location engine(s) are connected. CMX and DNA Spaces integrate several services that you can activate either independently or as a superset of one another. Additional services will be examined in next chapter, while this chapter focuses on location tracking.

Tracking Mobile Devices with CMX

Location tracking is enabled in CMX through the **Detect and Locate** service. The service is activated automatically at installation, with a 120-day trial period. Remember that in order to use this service, you need to have imported maps and WLCs into CMX. Then, in the CMX main window, click **Detect and Locate** in the upper menu. You will then see the various maps of your deployment on the left menu, in what is called the activity map. You can then click individual campuses, outdoor areas, buildings, and floors. You can then view all the access points (APs) deployed in all the buildings of a campus or view the APs deployed on the individual floors of each building. You can also locate Wi-Fi clients (associated or not), Wi-Fi tags, Wi-Fi interferers, and Bluetooth Low Energy (BLE) tags, as shown in Figure 13-7.

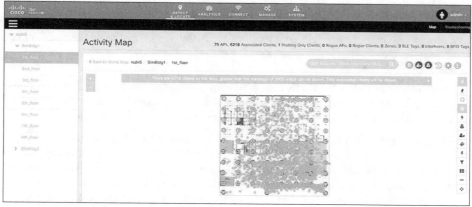

Figure 13-7 *Floor Activity Map in CMX*

> **NOTE** In CMX, maps are hierarchical. You can add maps starting from a campus or from a building level. If you start from a campus, you can then add buildings or outdoor areas. In buildings, you can then add floors and basements.

Once at the floor level, you can use the right menu to display or hide individual elements. In CMX parlance, wireless devices receive different names based on their interaction with your wireless network. Neighboring APs (those APs that are not known through a WLC added to CMX) are called rogue APs. Mobile devices that are known clients to your network (their MAC address was recorded on MSE while they were associated to one of your APs) and that are detected connecting to those rogue APs are called rogue clients. Some specific devices, called RFID tags, can be attached to non-Wi-Fi mobile objects and help locate these objects. There are multiple types of RFID tags. The Wi-Fi RFID tags are programmed to send a frame at specific intervals (or upon specific events or triggers, like button push or movement) to a well-known multicast MAC address. Because of their specific behavior, these devices are treated separately. Then, most other mobile devices emitting 802.11 frames will be considered "clients," regardless of whether they are associated or not. Cisco APs can also detect BLE tags. Other non-802.11 devices can also be detected, using Cisco CleanAir, if they send signals within the bands where APs are deployed. They are called interferers.

Clients are the items you will monitor most. The client category is represented with a location ( ) icon. Click the icon to show or hide all the client devices (connected or simply detected) that are being tracked by your Cisco CMX on that floor. Client devices are displayed either as red dots (probing clients) or green dots (connected clients). Clicking a connected client shows the AP that the client is associated with (blue lines) and the APs that are participating in the location calculation (red lines). Clicking an unassociated client displays the APs that are being used to detect the clients (red lines). Keep in mind that the displayed location is the "last computed location." Mobile devices that are not sending any frames (because they are in sleep mode, for example) cannot have their location refreshed. You can configure a timeout (see next section) after which a device that is no longer detected will stop being displayed on the map.

13

NOTE The maximum number of clients that can be displayed on a map at any given time is 2,000. If you have more devices on your map, CMX will first display the connected clients (up to 2,000).

You can also show or hide what CMX calls heat maps, using the flame icon (![flame icon]). This does not represent the AP heat map (AP signal strength at leach location) but rather the client concentration. Areas with a high concentration of client devices are marked bright red.

Rogue APs are represented as a human figure in suit and coat with a hat and glasses (![rogue AP icon]). Although the intent is to represent a hacker, keep in mind that APs that do not belong to your system are not all malicious, especially if they are at the edge or outside your coverage area. However, you should know about the rogue APs that are placed in the midst of your coverage area. Rogue APs are labeled as Unclassified, Malicious, Friendly, or Custom and are indicated by different colors on the activity map. Cisco CMX uses a predefined zone of impact (radius of 3.28 feet) for all rogue APs. This zone represents the expected coverage cell of the rogue AP. In most cases, the real coverage area will be much larger, but CMX cannot evaluate it. This happens because Cisco CMX cannot know the AP transmit power, which is needed to compute an actual projected zone of impact.

Rogue clients are represented differently from the rogue APs. The rogue client icon is a human figure with an X, representing a user not properly connected (![rogue client icon]). Recall that a rogue client was initially a client on your system but is now connected to a rogue AP. Rogue clients deserve your attention because, in a normal scenario, one of your clients should not roam automatically or manually to a rogue AP, if the client is successfully connected to one of your APs.

RFID tags are represented with a tag icon (![tag icon]). When you click a tag, the vendor-specific information related to the tags is displayed in raw format.

BLE tags are represented with a Bluetooth icon (![bluetooth icon]). Keep in mind that Cisco APs with BLE radios can detect BLE beacons natively. Other Cisco APs will detect beacons as an interferer. Just like for the other detected objects, you can click a BLE tag to display more information. If the beacon is chirping with an iBeacon profile, Cisco CMX displays the properties such as UUID and Major and Minor numbers. If the beacon is chirping with the Eddystone-UID profile, Cisco CMX displays properties such as Namespace and Instance-Id. If the beacon is chirping with the Eddystone-URL profile, Cisco CMX displays the HTTP resource URL being broadcasted by that beacon.

NOTE In CMX 10.4 and later, you can no longer manage the beacons from CMX. In previous versions, you could see the beacon message and manage (configure) some beacon types. In CMX 10.4 and later, beacon notifications are no longer provided. BLE beacons detected by Cisco CleanAir are displayed on Cisco CMX as interferers. BLE-related information is no longer available in the apidocs file. BLE beacons management functionality is moved to Beacons Management on Cloud.

Interferers are represented with a lightning icon (⚡). When you display the interferers, CMX also displays the zone of impact, which is the area where the interference is likely to disrupt your Wi-Fi communications. Click the icon to show or hide all the RF interferers that have been detected by the wireless network and their zone of impact.

For any aforementioned device, when the object is expected to be mobile, you can replay the history of the object location. When clicking the object on the map, or when using the search function in the upper-right part of the page (using the object MAC address), you can click the clock yellow icon to display the Client Playback pane. This pane is represented as a blue bar with start and end dates and times. You can customize the time window for which you want to trace the various locations. You can then click the Play icon to display on the map the various locations where the device was detected over the chosen time window. Keep in mind that location is not computed continuously, but each time data or frames are received from the device. Therefore, you will see the location replay as a succession of positions, not as a smooth displacement.

You can also display or hide your APs, which are collectively represented as an icon with a set of concentric circles (◎). APs are then displayed as circular objects, with a number in the center. This number indicates the number of clients connected to that specific AP. Inactive access points (red circle with a hyphen) are also detected when there is no RSSI probe packets coming to Cisco CMX. Inactive APs are detected usually when there are no devices present in the AP area, or when the WLC to which the AP is connected is not detected anymore by CMX. Clicking an AP shows the clients connected to it (blue lines), the probing clients that are detected by the AP (red lines), and additional information such as height, orientation, and X,Y location of the AP on the map.

For all these objects, you can use the filter icon (▼) to create a display filter and only display devices based on parameters such as connection status, manufacturer, and service set identifier (SSID).

The other icons available on the right menu provide display functions that are not related to the tracked object but to the floor itself. Inclusion & Exclusion regions, represented by four squares (▩), are useful to constrain location within or outside of specific areas. For example, in a shopping mall, you could choose to include common areas (hallways, food court, and so on) but exclude the areas within the stores that are not within your purview. In a factory, you could decide to exclude machines or places where Wi-Fi devices could not possibly be present. These areas are created in Cisco Prime Infrastructure. In Cisco CMX, you can view these regions but you cannot modify them. The inclusion regions are shown in green, and the exclusion regions are shown in grey. In a similar fashion, you can click the Thick Walls icon (represented as a thick line) to view any thick walls that have been created on prime infrastructure and included on the floor. Thick walls improve location by modeling areas of high RF signal attenuation with more accuracy.

You can also create and view zones, represented with an empty square icon (▢). These zones are useful when you want to create separate rules for different areas of the floor. For example, you could decide on different web portal appearances depending on where the users are. These functions will be covered in Chapter 15, "Security for Wireless Client Connectivity."

13

Last, you can click the GPS Markers icon (a diamond icon) to display the GPS markers. These are geo-position points manually added to the floor. When at least three GPS markers are placed on a floor, the system can use these to provide GPS coordinates, in addition to X,Y coordinates in client location API requests. The system can also use these points to align floors above one another. Cisco CMX shows the GPS markers as a green color when the GPS markers are valid ones.

Tracking Mobile Devices with DNA Spaces

The DNA Spaces interface was designed to resemble the CMX interface so as to ease configuration tasks. From the dashboard, you can access location functions by clicking the **Detect and Locate** tile in the main page. You are then redirected to a page that shows the managed campuses. Just like in CMX, you can then click a campus, building, and floor to access the activity map where clients are tracked. You can then use the left menu to access options similar to those of CMX, as shown in Figure 13-8.

Click the eye icon to show or hide clients, RFID tags, rogue APs, rogue clients, or interferers.

In the left menu, click the wheel to show or hide the heat map, which shows areas where user density is high. Click the square icon to show or hide zones. Click the radio wave icon to show or hide APs. Click the chain icon to show or hide clusters. When clustering is enabled, you see green circles around APs, which show how many clients are detected in each AP area. When you disable clustering, each client location is displayed individually, as in Figure 13-8.

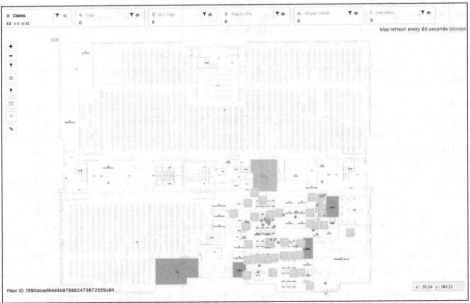

Figure 13-8 *DNA Spaces Activity Map Options*

Customizing Location Services

Although all the aforementioned elements are tracked by default, it is obvious that each of them is going to consume memory space. You may want to customize what is tracked and how long the memory of the object and its location are kept.

Customizing CMX Location Services

Customizing CMX location services is done through the **gear** icon at the top-right corner of the **System > Dashboard** window. Clicking this icon brings you to the **Settings** window displayed in Figure 13-9.

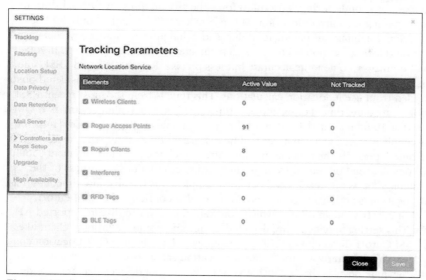

Figure 13-9   *CMX Settings*

The top menu represents the tracking parameters. Here, you can decide which device type to track and which to ignore.

In the **Filtering** tab, you regulate how interferers are tracked, using **Duty Cycle** parameters. Interferers do not send 802.11 frames but rather energy pulses that are measured over time. When energy is measured continuously, duty cycle is said to be 100 percent. In most cases, interferers will send energy pulses separated by quiet periods (the activity of a Wi-Fi device would be interpreted the same way if we were not able to read the 802.11 content). Sometimes, interferers are very short, bursty, and overwhelm Cisco CMX but then stop sending anything. With **Duty Cycle Cutoff**, you can decide the minimum time occupancy needed for an interferer to be reported. With **Severity Cutoff**, you can also decide how long a severe (strong signal) interferer needs to be seen to be reported.

You can also regulate the RSSI threshold at which clients will start being reported, using **RSSI Cutoff (Probing Only Clients)**. The default is −85 dBm. This parameter only applies to non-associated clients. Associated clients will always be reported when tracked. However, they are expected to disconnect when the signal becomes poor or unusable (often between −78 dBm and −82 dBm, depending on the client type), thus becoming non-associated. You can also ignore the non-associated clients by selecting **Exclude Probing Only Clients**. These filters can be combined with **Location MAC Filtering** to filter specific MAC addresses. For example, you can use this to filter out MAC addresses of employees' devices. After checking this, either you can specify a MAC address that you want to allow or disallow or you can choose to allow, disallow, or delete previously entered MAC addresses. You can also

13

combine these filters with **Location SSID Filtering.** Check this box so that the location service excludes all visitor devices associated to a particular SSID.

In the **Location Setup** tab, you can define how location is computed. Most items are beyond the scope of the CCNP Enterprise exam. However, some elements are of particular relevance. **Enable Location Filtering** is useful to force the system to use previous location estimates for estimating the current location. This parameter will be applied only for client location calculation. Enabling this parameter reduces location jitter for stationary clients and improves location tracking for mobile clients. This parameter is enabled by default. If you disable it, location may become more accurate but less precise. **Relative discard RSSI time** represents the time in minutes after which the RSSI measurement should be considered obsolete and discarded from use in location calculations. This time is from the most recent RSSI sample and not an absolute time. For example, if this value is set to 3 minutes, and two samples are received at 10 minutes and 12 minutes, both the samples will be retained. However, an additional sample received at 15 minutes will be discarded. By contrast, the **Absolute discard RSSI time** represents the time, in minutes, after which the RSSI measurement should be considered obsolete and discarded from use in location calculations regardless of the most recent sample. This is not the interval between samples; it is the absolute timeout after which a MAC location is no longer considered. You can also configure the **RSSI cutoff,** which is the RSSI cutoff value in dBm at which you want the server to discard reported AP measurements. This setting applies to any detected device and not just a probing client like the previous **RSSI Cutoff** (Probing Only Clients) parameter. Last, **Enable OW Location** configures the system to use outer walls (obstacles for location calculation. It is useful when you want to clearly separate devices that are inside your building from devices that are outside (for example, passing down the street, not inside near the external wall).

You can also set several **Movement Detection Parameters:**

- **Individual RSSI change threshold:** Enter a threshold in dBm beyond which you want individual RSSI movement recalculation to be triggered. For example, if a particular MAC address signal changes by 6 dB or more, recompute its location.

- **Aggregated RSSI change threshold:** Specify the aggregated RSSI movement recalculation trigger threshold. This element is the same as the previous but computed for all detecting APs. This is useful because signal change on a single AP may be caused by a moving obstacle (person or object between the mobile device and the AP). But if the signal changes on all detecting APs, then movement is more likely.

- **Many new RSSI change percentage threshold:** Specify the trigger threshold recalculation (as a percentage) for many new RSSI changes. This parameter determines how many of the new signals must be different to trigger a recomputation.

- **Many missing RSSI percentage threshold:** Specify the trigger threshold recalculation (as a percentage) for many missing RSSI changes. This parameter determines how many messages can be missing to signal a need for recomputation. For example, suppose you configure the system so that the aggregated RSSI threshold should be 6 dB. Eight APs are reporting this device. Your **Many new RSSI change percentage threshold** is 25 percent. As soon as 25 percent of the messages are received 6 dB away (up or down) from the previous estimation on each AP, the location recomputation starts. However, if a device moves, some APs may stop detecting the device. Suppose that only five APs report the device, still with a cumulated 6 dB difference. You can then use the **Many missing RSSI percentage threshold**, for example, with a 20 percent threshold (in general, you should not change these parameters anyway without Cisco technical guidance) to force the recomputation to occur as soon as two APs or more stop reporting the device. The combination of all these parameters allows for a finer tracking of moving devices.

The other parameters in the Location Setup menu apply to advanced settings beyond the CCNP Enterprise exam level (such as Use new location algorithm and User Default Heatmaps for Non-Cisco Antennas). Other advanced settings are specific to RFID tags and chokepoints. Chokepoints are specific RFID tag sensors typically installed at critical location points (above a door, for example). When an RFID tag is detected at close range, the chokepoint instructs the tag to send a specific message. This mechanism allows the IT admin to know that the RFID tag (and whatever it is attached to) went through the door and at what exact point in time.

All these tracked devices need to be remembered along with their location, which consumes a lot of disk space if not managed carefully. You should monitor your system often (from the **System** menu in the dashboard). If you see that your hard drive is filling up fast, you may want to reduce the amount of information stored by the system. In the **Data Retention** tab, you can set **Client History Pruning Interval (days)** to a value beyond which a client location is forgotten (deleted). The default value is 30 days. Similarly, you can also set **Rogues History Pruning Interval (days)** and **Analytics Raw Data Pruning Interval (days)**. The rogue default pruning interval is also 30 days, but the analytics raw data pruning default interval is a year (365 days), as the goal of analytics is to provide a view of trends, which allows for concatenation (thus using less memory than individual device location snapshots).

Customizing DNA Spaces Location Services

You can also customize what items should be tracked in DNA Spaces, from the left menu, by choosing **Configure > Tracking**. There, you can selectively choose to track or ignore clients, rogue access points, rogue clients, RFID tags, and interferers.

From the **Configure > Data Source** menu, you can activate or disable Hyperlocation, depending on your network capabilities.

From the **Configure > Filtering** page, you will find the same items as in the equivalent CMX page: **RSSI Cutoff for Probing Clients, Exclude Probing Clients only** (to ignore unassociated clients), **MAC Filtering** (which may be locally defined or pulled from CMX), and **SSID Location Filtering**, with the options to only consider ("**allow**") clients on a subset of SSIDs or to ignore ("**disallow**") a subset of SSIDs.

From the **Configure > Location Setup** page, you can configure the same RSSI thresholds as on the equivalent CMX page. A nice feature of this page is that the recommended values are displayed graphically, as illustrated in Figure 13-10.

13

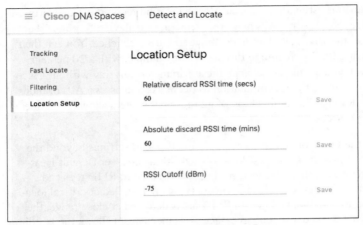

Figure 13-10 *DNA Spaces Location Setup Page*

Summary

This chapter described location services and how to deploy them with Cisco MSE, CMX, or DNA Spaces. In this chapter you have learned the following:

- The various available indoor location protocols and techniques

- How an 802.11 infrastructure performs mobile device location

- The roles of the APs, WLCs, and location engine for indoor location

- The various solution engines available with a Cisco location solution

- How to deploy DNA Spaces, MSE, and CMX

- How to track clients, RFID tags, rogues, and interferers

- How to customize the locations services

References

For additional information, refer to these resources:

Cisco CMX Configuration Guide: https://www.cisco.com/c/en/us/td/docs/wireless/mse/10-6/cmx_config/b_cg_cmx106.html

Cisco DNA Spaces Configuration Guide: https://www.cisco.com/c/en/us/td/docs/solutions/Enterprise/Mobility/DNA-Spaces/cisco-dna-spaces-config/dnaspaces-configuration-guide.html

Cisco Prime Infrastructure User Guide ("Cisco Mobility Services Engine and Services" chapter): https://www.cisco.com/c/en/us/td/docs/net_mgmt/prime/infrastructure/3-4/user/guide/bk_CiscoPrimeInfrastructure_3_4_0_UserGuide/bk_CiscoPrimeInfrastructure_3_4_0_UserGuide_chapter_0100111.html

Cisco DNA Spaces connection configuration examples: https://www.cisco.com/c/en/us/support/wireless/dna-spaces/products-configuration-examples-list.html

Exam Preparation Tasks

As mentioned in the section "How to Use This Book" in the Introduction, you have a few choices for exam preparation: the exercises here, Chapter 18, "Final Preparation," and the exam simulation questions in the Pearson Test Prep Software Online.

Review All Key Topics

Review the most important topics in this chapter, noted with the Key Topic icon in the outer margin of the page. Table 13-3 lists these key topics and the page numbers on which each is found.

Table 13-3   Key Topics for Chapter 13

Key Topic Element	Description	Page Number
Paragraph	RSSI trilateration techniques	307
Paragraph	Angle of Arrival techniques	308
Paragraph	Different ways to compute location and which options are possible together	
Paragraph	Precision vs. accuracy	311
List	Location architecture	312
Paragraph	DNA Spaces, MSE, and CMX	314
Figure 13-7	Tracking devices with CMX	320

Define Key Terms

Define the following key terms from this chapter and check your answers in the glossary:

DNA Spaces, MSE, CMX, RSSI trilateration, FastLocate, Hyperlocation, location precision, location accuracy, client (location context).

CHAPTER 14

Advanced Location Services Implementation

This chapter covers the following topics:

CMX and DNA Spaces Services and Licenses: This section provides an overview of the main services available on CMX and DNA Spaces. This section also discusses which services are core to the network administrator and which are the focus of specialized engineers.

Implementing Analytics: This section discusses how to use the analytics services available on both CMX and DNA Spaces and also contrasts the implementation differences between both platforms.

Implementing Guest Portals: This section shows how to configure location-specific portals for visitors and guests on CMX and DNA Spaces. The section also details the WLC guest WLAN configuration for AireOS and C9800.

Implementing WIPS on MSE: This section details how to configure MSE 8.0 for an adaptive wireless intrusion prevention system.

Ensuring Location Operational Efficiency: This section shows how to configure MSE high availability. It also details the steps to take to verify and optimize location accuracy.

This chapter covers the following ENWLSI exam topics:

- 5.1 Implement CMX Components

  - 5.1.a Detect and Locate

  - 5.1.b Analytics

  - 5.1.c Presence Services

- 5.2 Implement location-aware guest services using custom portal and Facebook Wi-Fi

- 5.3 Troubleshoot location accuracy using Cisco Hyperlocation

- 5.4 Troubleshoot CMX high availability

- 5.5 Implement WIPS using MSE

Location services are not limited to performing the location of individual devices. Most businesses need to manage resources based on the number of users likely to use these resources. This requirement means detecting mobile network users, counting them, understanding how they roam, identifying the areas where density peaks appear, measuring how long they stay in each zone, how much bandwidth they consume, and so on.

Therefore, an efficient location solution should do more than just locate devices. Based on this location information, the solution should offer various metrics about Wi-Fi users, along with functions to ease the task of managing Wi-Fi users.

This chapter introduces advanced location services, which are those services that leverage location information in order to provide additional functions. You will learn not only which additional functions, based on location, are available in Cisco CMX and DNA Spaces but also which ones are "must-knows" and which ones are beyond the expected scope of a networking professional and belong to the domain of specialized engineers. Among these services, you will learn how to manage analytics to better understand users and network patterns. You will also learn how to implement location-specific guest portals. This ability is particularly important in public spaces, where providing environmental information is expected for most Wi-Fi guest users. You will then learn how to implement wireless intrusion prevention by using location information to detect and mitigate Wi-Fi-based attacks. Location is the fundamental brick behind all these services. Therefore, in the last section of this chapter, you will learn how to ensure that location continues to be performed at the level of accuracy needed by your deployment.

"Do I Know This Already?" Quiz

The "Do I Know This Already?" quiz allows you to assess whether you should read this entire chapter thoroughly or jump to the "Exam Preparation Tasks" section. If you are in doubt about your answers to these questions or your own assessment of your knowledge of the topics, read the entire chapter. Table 14-1 lists the major headings in this chapter and their corresponding "Do I Know This Already?" quiz questions. You can find the answers in Appendix D, "Answers to the 'Do I Know This Already?' Quizzes and Review Questions."

Table 14-1 "Do I Know This Already?" Section-to-Question Mapping

Foundation Topics Section	Questions
CMX and DNA Spaces Services and Licenses	1
Implementing Analytics	2–3
Implementing Guest Portals	4
Implementing WIPS on MSE	5
Ensuring Location Operational Efficiency	6

1. Which of the following represents the MSE trial license allowance?

   a. All services, 120 days for 100 APs

   b. Location only, for 10 APs and 30 days

   c. One guest portal and one AP, 60 days

   d. Presence only, and all guest portals in read-only mode

2. Which license level is required on DNA Spaces to activate Location Analytics functions?

   a. Advance license

   b. Act license

   c. Analytics+ license

   d. Insight license

3. What is a "zone" in CMX Analytics?

   a. The coverage area of a single AP (that is, the AP cell)

   b. An area where location can be computed with good accuracy

   c. An area where devices are expected to be mobile (that is, a transition area)

   d. An area with a label, with no specific RF meaning

4. How does a C9800 redirect ACL to ensure that traffic targeting the MSE IP address is redirected to the MSE?

   a. With a specific permit instruction

   b. With a specific deny instruction

   c. With a final permit any wrapper

   d. With a final (implicit) deny any wrapper

5. Can you perform real-time WIPS with an AP in Monitor (no submode) mode?

   a. No, intrusion prevention is only active if the AP is set to WIPS mode, with Monitor submode.

   b. No, intrusion prevention requires the Local or Monitor mode with WIPS submode.

   c. Yes, intrusion prevention works seamlessly with all AP modes and submodes.

   d. Yes, you can if the AP is assigned to a WIPS zone in CMX.

6. To which MSE port does a WLC send AoA messages?

   a. The WLC does not send AoA messages; APs send them directly to MSE.

   b. TCP 16113

   c. UDP 2003

   d. The WLC does not send AoA messages; MSE pulls them from the WLC using NMSP.

Foundation Topics

CMX and DNA Spaces Services and Licenses

Chapter 13, "Location Services Deployment," primarily focused on location services. However, both CMX and DNA Spaces integrate multiple other components that a networking professional should be familiar with. This section does not describe all possible services, as some of them are considered "advanced" and the domain of specialized professionals. Additionally, new services appear all the time that you may see in the interfaces and not described here. Make sure to keep up-to-date with the exam blueprint to verify which services you are expected to master.

CMX Services and Licenses

CMX integrates several services that you can activate either independently or as a superset of one another. Some services are activated at installation time and come with an evaluation license. Other services require an activation license. Licenses are purchased and downloaded in an .lic file. To install a license file, navigate to **Manage > Licenses** and import the .lic file. You can install two types of licenses:

- A CMX Base license, which includes the CMX Connect, CMX Locate and Detect, and High Availability capabilities.

- A CMX Advanced license, which includes all CMX Base license capabilities, along with the CMX Analytics and DNA Spaces Connector capabilities.

The Locate and Detect capability is the function referred to as "location" in much of the literature and in Chapter 13. This service uses the data provided by Cisco WLCs and APs (RSSI and AoA) to calculate the location of wireless devices that are detected by the access points. The service is activated by default when you install CMX with a 120-day trial period. This temporary license is valid for all CMX services and 100 APs.

The Analytics service provides additional tools for analyzing Wi-Fi device locations. This service is called Analytics when leveraging the output of the Locate and Detect service, and Presence Analytics when using only nearest AP or associated AP location. When you install CMX, you need to specify if you want to enable location or presence (you cannot enable both). In small indoor deployments and most outdoor deployments, presence is sufficient. However, you need to enable location to use AoA or FastLocate and to obtain an accurate individual device location.

The Connect service provides a location-specific guest web portal interface to onboard visitors with Facebook or OAuth-based credentials. The service can be enabled with location or presence.

DNA Spaces Services and Licenses

DNA Spaces (Cloud) also implements a large set of services, some of which complement services available with on-premises CMX. Services are activated with licenses enabled directly within the DNA Spaces cloud interface. Two license types are available, each for 3-, 5-, or 7-year durations:

- **See:** The See license offers business metrics, Wi-Fi metrics, real-time metrics, location computation (RSSI trilateration), and location hierarchy visualization.

- **Act:** The Act license offers all the features available in the See license and also the Captive portal function (what MSE calls "Connect") with profile rules and Engage features (to send notifications to Wi-Fi users based on rules and the user location), an API to expose location to third-party applications (with Webhook), a partner stream feature (to stream data in and out of DNA Spaces), operational insights, and Hyperlocation if you also have an on-premises CMX (where this Hyperlocation is first computed).

The feature set partially overlaps with the CMX features described previously. The metric features provide the equivalent of what CMX describes as Analytics. Business metrics allow you to measure the impact of a particular marketing campaign on your Wi-Fi traffic. Real-time traffic shows the clients in real time in each location, and Wi-Fi metrics show the number of clients per location and SSID.

As a networking professional, you may be asked to help business owners determine which feature requires which solution combination and with which type of license. Table 14-2 can help you answer most of these questions. Note that the DNA Spaces solution is very fluid. Always verify on Cisco.com the latest license and feature combination.

Table 14-2 DNA Spaces and CMX Feature Combination

Feature	License	X/Y Location or Presence	CMX On-Prem. Required
Cisco DNA Center integration	See	X/Y	Yes
Cisco Prime Infrastructure integration	See	X/Y	Yes
Business insight	See	Presence	No
Hyperlocation	Act	X/Y	Yes
Captive portal	Act	Presence or X/Y	No
Engagement	Act	Presence or X/Y	No
Location personas	Act	Presence or X/Y	No
Operational insight	Act	X/Y	No
BLE Manager	Act	X/Y	Yes
Location Analytics	Act	X/Y	Yes
Partner Stream	Act	X/Y	Yes
Third party via API/Webhook	Act	X/Y	No

Implementing Analytics

Analytics is a critical component of the administrator toolbelt. As soon as location, or even presence, is computed, businesses need to know the user density so as to deploy network resources (or staff) accordingly. Analytics can be implemented on either CMX or DNA Spaces. There are basic differences between these platforms that you need to know and advanced functions that are not critical to the nonspecialist.

Implementing CMX Analytics

The CMX Analytics service is often confused with the Detect and Locate service, because Analytics relies on location information. Make sure to understand their differences. Detect and Locate provides the computed location for each detected device at individual moments in time. This information is stored in CMX database. The Analytics service then provides a set of data analytic tools packaged for analyzing Wi-Fi device locations. In other words, the service uses the location information (that is, it needs Detect and Locate to provide valid information) and functions as a data visualization engine that helps organizations use their network as a data source for business analysis to understand behavior patterns and trends, which can help them make decisions on how to improve visitor experience and boost customer service. Depending on the granularity of the information you need, you can obtain location through the CMX Presence function or through the full Location function. With Presence, devices' locations are approximated to the nearest AP (unassociated devices) or associated AP (associated devices). With Location, depending on which features you enabled, devices' locations are determined using RSSI trilateration and AoA, using the signal coming from broadcast messages or unicast messages (when FastLocate is activated).

Defining Zones

Whereas Detect and Locate typically starts from the idea of locating individual devices, Analytics functions at the zone level and for a specific time period. The zone can be any hierarchical block, campus, building, floor, or zone on a floor. You can access your zones from **Manage > Location**. In the left pane of the window that is displayed, you can click **Campus, Building, Floor**, or **Zone**, depending on the area you want to view. Click the curved arrow at the top-right corner of each item box to view details pertaining to that item. The curved arrow at the top-right corner of a floor box is called the *Go to map view* arrow. This arrow is available on the box of items at any level. For example, for a building, this opens the first floor. For a campus, this opens the first floor of the first building. You can then switch to other buildings and floors in that campus. When you click the top-right corner curved arrow and the map opens, you are in what CMX calls the Zone Editor. From there, in the right part of the screen, icons appear that allow you to create (a pen icon), delete (a trash can icon), or edit (a pen in a square icon) several objects:

- **Perimeters:** A perimeter defines the area where location is performed. With location inaccuracies, your clients may appear a few meters from their real position. At the edge of the coverage area, this may mean that some devices appear to be outside of the building, floating in the air. A common practice is to define the perimeter as the edge of floor area, preventing the devices from showing as being outside of that perimeter line (they will be shown inside, close to the perimeter line), thus avoiding that location inaccuracies display the devices in a location where they cannot be.

- **Inclusion areas:** An inclusion area defines a zone where devices can appear. Devices for which location is detected outside of the inclusion area will be snapped on the boundary. You can define only one inclusion region per floor. When there is no inclusion region defined in the floor maps, Cisco CMX creates a default inclusion region that is the same as the floor dimension.

- **Exclusion areas:** An exclusion area defines a zone where a device cannot be present. There can be multiple exclusion regions on a floor. Depending on your floor layout, you can use the inclusion areas, exclusion areas, or both to avoid displaying devices where they cannot be present. For example, in a factory where workers are limited to a small set of walking paths between large machines, you can define an associated inclusion area. If only a few locations are inaccessible, use exclusion areas.

- **Zones:** A zone is an area with a label. The zone does not need to have particular significance from an RF standpoint, and it commonly represents an area that makes sense for the network administrator (for example, "entrance and lobby" or "store XYZ").

When you create an object, you click at the corners of the matching polygon until the object covers the area you need. Then, when you edit the object, you can click any vertex to move it.

You can also double-click any point of a line to create a new vertex at this position (then move it if needed). You can also click inside the object (the mouse arrow changes to a hand) to move it.

Configuring Analytics Widgets

Analytics provides insights about clients in your different zones. For each of them, and for a given time period, the Analytics service allows for the visualization of six different types of location-related elements:

- **Device count:** For the target zone, this element displays the number of detected clients (associated or not). This widget is useful to understand the user density. As the function is correlated with a particular time period, you can also see a summary of how this count compares to the previous period, including the user count trend (up or down, compared to the previous period), how many users are new, and how many are repeat visitors.

- **Dwell time:** For the target zone, this element displays the average duration for which clients (associated or not) were detected. This widget is useful to distinguish zones where clients are just passing by from zones where clients stay for a longer time. The widget distinguishes new from repeat visitors, as their behavior may be different. For example, repeat visitors may go directly to a particular location, while new visitors may spend more time exploring transition areas. The function also displays the trend and comparison with previous periods.

- **Dwell time breakdown:** For the target zone, this element displays a more detailed view of the dwell time by durations. You can see the percentage of devices that were detected in the target zone for less than 5 minutes, between 5 and 20 minutes, 20 and 60 minutes, 60 to 120 minutes, or more than 120 minutes. Here again, you can see trends and comparisons with previous periods.

- **Associated user or probing only:** For the previous widgets, you can filter the view to only display devices that effectively associated to the network or that only probed (and never associated). In some versions of CMX, this function is also called Wi-Fi adoption, representing the number of clients that decided to adopt and join your Wi-Fi network. Here again, you can compare between periods. You can also visualize the visits or the devices. With the visit view, a device that is detected, then leaves the area (or stops being detected for a configurable timeout value), and then is detected again will be counted as visiting the zone twice. With the device view, you will see a count of unique MAC addresses, regardless of how many times they entered or left the zone.

- **Path:** This element analyzes the paths taken by visitors (or client devices) before and after visiting a focus location as well as provides a graphical representation of the paths. The green (left) side represents where a device is coming from (for example, immediately before entering the focus zone). The blue (right) side represents where a device goes (for example, immediately after exiting the focus zone). Hovering your cursor over the focus reveals a breakdown based on percentage of paths that either started or ended in the focus zone and the percentage of paths that either arrived or departed from the focus zone. Hovering your cursor over a green section shows the number of paths that entered the focus zone originated in this zone. Hovering your cursor over a blue section shows the number of paths that originated in the focus zone ended in this zone.

- **Correlation:** This element provides a detailed summary of correlation of client devices between two locations. Correlation data can be used to determine the relation between two zones. Low correlation between zones indicates lack of access between the two zones. For example, you can expect a high correlation between the food court and the cinema in a shopping mall. As the widget is based on the idea of comparison, you can select the zones to compare (they can be what CMX calls "zones," but they can also be entire floors or buildings) and then display the output as a graph or as a table.

Figure 14-1 displays some of the Analytics widgets. As a networking professional, you need to be familiar with the different widget types.

Figure 14-1 *CMX Analytics Widgets*

The widgets are accessible in the CMX dashboard, but they can also be generated as reports. The report can focus on the data of an existing widget, a specific time slice or a subset of SSIDs, or can be completely customized. To generate such custom report from the Analytics dashboard, in the left panel of the dashboard, click the **Add** icon. The **Create New Report** window is displayed. Choose **Customized** from the Report Type widgets row in the right pane and then choose the locations that you want to analyze from the **Focus Area Filter** drop-down list. The location types are Building, Campus, Floor, and Zone. Choose the date and time range you want to run the report for from the **Date & Time filters** drop-down list. You can click the dot at the bottom of the **Add Widget** area to scroll to the next set of options. You can select multiple widgets to combine in one overall widget: in the **Add Widget** area, click the **Add+** icon to include any of the existing widgets in the report. You can select multiple widgets to combine into one overall widget. You can also set a threshold for dwell time. This is the amount of time spent by a client device (visitor) at a given location, which is set by selecting the minimum and maximum times from the drop-down options in the **Advanced Widget Filters** area. Once your selection is made, click **Done** to create the widget. Repeat as many times as you need to add the widget. At the end, click the report title to name your report and click **Save** to validate.

These reports are very useful to watch the evolution of your network over time. They rely on an efficient initial setup, where zones are designed logically and location is provided with an accuracy that matches the zones' definition. If you deployed Presence instead of Location, you will also see the visitor count, dwell time, and dwell time distribution, with the same granularity as with Location about repeat versus first-time visitors. However, the location will be limited to proximity to a site where detecting APs are present. You cannot create subzones.

Implementing DNA Spaces Analytics

CMX supposes that you install a server on premises. This is especially useful if you need to track, in near real time, the location of individual MAC addresses. If you only need analytics, then the WLC can aggregate station counts and locations and then send its observations in batches. In this case, your need for bandwidth decreases, as you do not need an update for each MAC and each movement anymore. DNA Spaces, in the cloud, can then be a good solution, providing the data you need without the need to manage your own appliance.

Initial Setup

The first element needed to efficiently manage Analytics with DNA Spaces is to set up locations and maps. This function is accessible by clicking the lines icon in the upper-left corner of the DNA Spaces dashboard screen and choosing **Setup**. From the Setup menu, you can add wireless networks or maps. A new wireless network is an on-premises CMX, a DNA Spaces Connector, or a WLC with direct connection that has been uploaded to DNA Spaces. Refer to Chapter 13 for the connection details. The map service allows you to define the various campuses, buildings, and floors that you want to manage. You can also upload floor plans, position APs, and create zones, as described in Chapter 13.

Once you have maps and wireless networks, from the main dashboard menu, select the **Location Hierarchy** function, as displayed in Figure 14-2.

Figure 14-2 *DNA Spaces Location Hierarchy Function*

From the Location Hierarchy page, you can visualize all your sites with the root account at the top (called DNACDemo in this section). For each site, you can see the number of locations (represented by a geolocation icon), the number of APs (represented by a WiFi AP icon), the number of BLE beacons (represented with the Bluetooth icon), the number of proximity rules (represented by a document icon), and the number of users (represented by a human figure icon), as shown in Figure 14-3. On the left side of each site, a plus sign can be clicked to expand the site. When you hover your mouse to the right side of the root site beyond the User Count, a **More Actions** icon appears. From this menu, you can rename your root site but also add a new wireless network or create a new group. This way, you can associate wireless networks, maps, and zones to groups, and even group groups together.

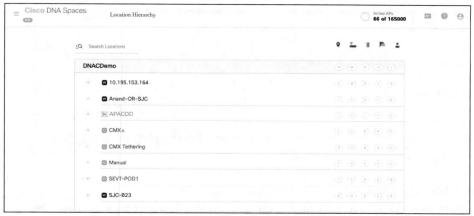

Figure 14-3 *DNA Spaces Location Hierarchy Sites and Options*

Managing DNA Spaces Analytics

Once this setup is complete, the Analytics service is fairly automated. From the main dashboard, by clicking the Location Analytics icon, you can see graphs of the number of visitors and visits, as shown in Figure 14-4, and also dwell time and dwell time breakdown for your network, as displayed in Figure 14-5.

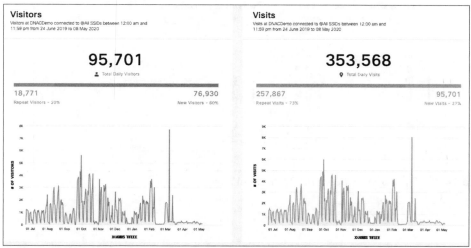

Figure 14-4 *DNA Spaces Location Analytics—Visitors and Visits*

You can choose to visualize the statistics for all SSIDs and networks, or you can filter by locations (groups, then buildings, floors, or zones), dates, and SSIDs.

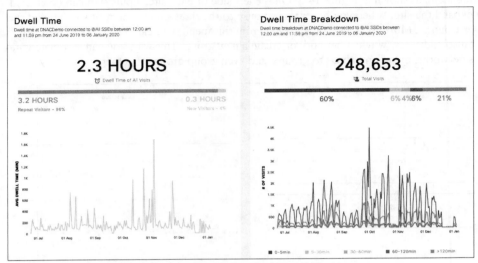

Figure 14-5 *DNA Spaces Location Analytics—Dwell Time*

Similarly, from the main dashboard, you can click the Behavior Metrics widget and obtain metric data complementary to those of location metrics. In this page, you can see not only the visits' duration and frequency, as shown in Figure 14-6, but also the duration of these visits and a distribution of which visitors were detected at more than one location, as shown in Figure 14-7.

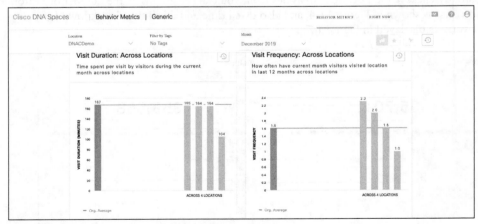

Figure 14-6 *DNA Spaces Behavior Metrics—Visits*

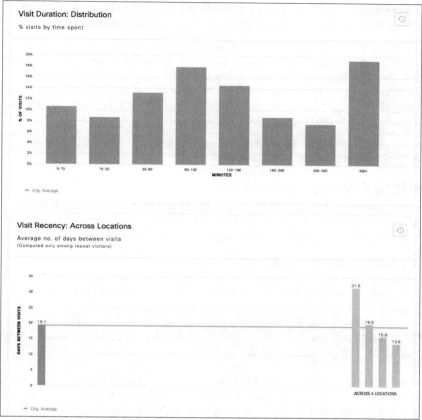

Figure 14-7   *DNA Spaces Behavior Metrics—Visits' Duration and Spread*

At the bottom of the page, you can also see a visit distribution by hour of day and day of the week, as shown in Figure 14-8.

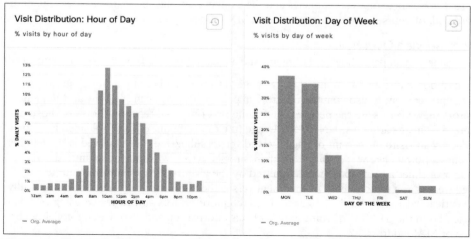

Figure 14-8   *DNA Spaces Behavior Metrics—Distribution by Hour and Day*

For all the elements on this page, you can use the top filter function to focus on a specific location, group of locations (assembled together under the same tag), or time period.

The features listed so far in this section for DNA Spaces are accessible with the See license. When you implement the Act license, you also have access to the Operational Insight function. When you click this widget in the DNA Spaces dashboard, you can monitor specific assets (MAC addresses, BLE, or RFID tags) and get notifications when these assets enter or leave a zone. Just like the equivalent function in CMX, this advanced function is beyond the scope of this book. You can find configuration details here:

https://www.cisco.com/c/en/us/td/docs/wireless/cisco-dna-spaces/operationalinsights/b_operationalinsights/b_operationalinsights_chapter_01.html

Implementing Guest Portals

The other major tool in the administrator toolbelt is the ability to create location-specific portals for guests and visitors connecting to the local Wi-Fi. This function heavily relies on location capabilities and can be implemented both on CMX and DNA Spaces.

Implementing CMX Connect Service

The CMX Connect service is a customizable and location-aware guest captive portal service. You access it by clicking **Connect** in the upper menu of the CMX main window.

NOTE Depending on your version of CMX, the menu may also be called **Connect & Engage.**

The CMX Admin user role can, of course, be used to create anything. This role has access to the Connect dashboard and can configure portals (called Experiences), policies, and the Connect settings, along with all the other CMX services. However, you may also want to create a Connect role, dedicated to Connect management. Such a role is created from **Manage > Users.** The Connect role can also access the Connect dashboard, create Experiences and policies, access the Connect settings, but cannot access other services on CMX. You can also create a ConnectExperience user, who can create portals (Experiences), can see (but not change or create) policies and the Connect settings, but cannot access the dashboard and, of course, cannot manage other CMX services.

Connect Service Overview

The Connect main page shows a dashboard and a location filter, as you can see in Figure 14-9.

The dashboard contains a summary report page with the user count per portal and zone for the present day. It also contains a historical page, where you can see **New and Repeat Visitors** (new visitors are the people seen for the first time, and repeat visitors are those recognized from an earlier visit), **Network Usage** (the total amount of data uploaded and downloaded by all visitors), a count of pages served versus submitted (pages served is the number of times a portal page was displayed to the visitors' devices, while pages submitted is the number of times a portal page was submitted by the visitors), SMS sent versus authenticated (that is, the total number of texts sent versus the number of texts used to successfully authenticate visitors), and the languages used (count of visitors authenticated using each language). From the dashboard, you can export this information and also search for visitors by name or MAC address.

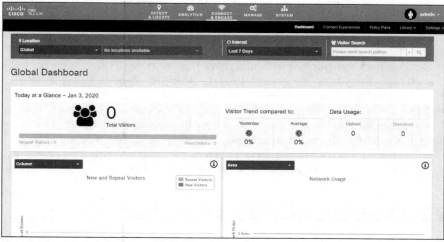

Figure 14-9   *CMX Connect Main Page*

The main element for Connect is the portal (Experiences). When connecting to the guest WLAN, the user is redirected to CMX, where the local portal is displayed or where the request is relayed to Facebook or another social media platform. Therefore, in order to provide the correct Experience, you need to configure the following:

- Your WLC WLAN for WebAuth and redirect to the correct CMX Experience

- Your CMX Experience to define which zone it should apply to and what authentication source it should use

Configuring the WLC for Guest Portal Services

The first step is to configure your WLAN. The process is slightly different depending on whether you will be using your CMX as the web portal or if you want the social media provider (for example, Facebook) to also provide the web interface for your user authentication. If CMX is the web portal, you need to create a preauthentication ACL on your WLC, allowing HTTPS traffic to and from the CMX IP address (in the examples that follow, this is represented as the IPv4 address 10.10.10.124). If your social media provider is also the web portal, you also need to allow HTTPS traffic to and from any source and destination IP address. Setting a permit rule for HTTPS mechanically denies any other traffic. An example of such a rule is displayed in Figure 14-10. In AireOS, this ACL is created from **Security > Access Control List > Access Control Lists > New**. Click **Add New Rule** to insert individual lines and follow the wizard to define the direction and protocol.

Seq	Action	Source IP/Mask		Destination IP/Mask		Protocol	Source Port	Dest Port	DSCP	Direction	Number of Hits	
1	Permit	0.0.0.0	/ 0.0.0.0	0.0.0.0	/ 0.0.0.0	TCP	HTTPS	Any	Any	Any	0	
2	Permit	0.0.0.0	/ 0.0.0.0	0.0.0.0	/ 0.0.0.0	TCP	Any	HTTPS	Any	Any	0	
3	Permit	10.10.10.124	/ 255.255.255.255	0.0.0.0	/ 0.0.0.0	TCP	HTTPS	Any	Any	Any	0	
4	Permit	0.0.0.0	/ 0.0.0.0	10.10.10.124	/ 255.255.255.255	TCP	Any	HTTPS	Any	Any	0	

Figure 14-10   *Preauthentication ACL for CMX Experience with Web Portal on a Social Media Provider Site*

Once the ACL is configured, in your AireOS WLAN configuration, in **Security > Layer 2**, set the security to **None** and click **Apply**. In the **Layer 3** tab, choose **Web Policy**. For web passthrough, choose **Passthrough**. Then choose the preauthentication ACL you created in the previous paragraph. Also override the global authentication and web authentication pages by checking the **Over-ride GlobalConfig** check box. You need to also define the web authentication pages for wireless guest users, from the **Web Auth Type** drop-down list, by choosing **External (Re-direct to external server)**. This redirects clients to an external server for authentication. The server can either be CMX (in the case of a local portal) or the CMX relay page for Facebook or another social media provider (such as Instagram or Foursquare). In the **URL** field, enter the corresponding portal on Cisco CMX, either for a CMX-based portal or for CMX redirection to an external social media portal provider (for example, https://<CMX>/fbwifi/forward). An example is show in Figure 14-11. Click **Apply** to validate.

Figure 14-11 *WLAN Configuration for Guest Portal Using CMX Connect*

The method is slightly different in Catalyst 9800, where you first have to create a parameter map from **Configuration > Security > Web Auth**. Create a new parameter map of type **consent**, as shown in Figure 14-12.

Create Web Auth Parameter	✕
Parameter-map name*	CMX_Connect
Maximum HTTP connections	100
Init-State Timeout(secs)	120
Type	consent ▼
✕ Close	✔ Apply to Device

Figure 14-12 *Parameter Map Definition on C9800*

Once the parameter map is created, click it in the list to edit its settings. Click the **Advanced** tab and enter the portal URL, along with the MSE IP address, as shown in Figure 14-13.

You also need to create an redirection ACL, from **Configuration > Security > ACL**. The ACL is of type IPv4 extended (or IPv6 extended). Deny all HTTPS traffic (if you use Social media authentication) and HTTPS traffic to and from MSE (in all cases). Denied traffic will cause redirection to the Redirect URL. Allow all other traffic. An example is shown in Figure 14-14.

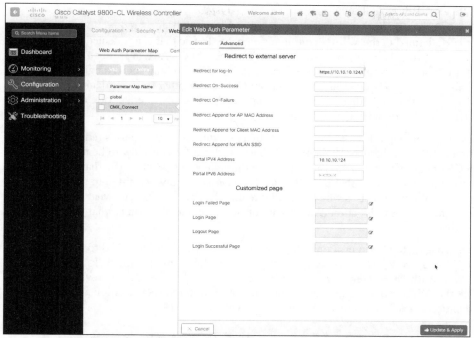

Figure 14-13 *Parameter Map Redirect URL Definition on C9800*

Figure 14-14 *Redirect ACL Creation on C9800*

AireOS vs. C9800 ACLs

On AireOS, traffic denied by this type of redirection ACL triggers redirection to the redirect URL defined in the WLAN configuration page. Traffic that is not denied (that is, traffic that is permitted) is simply permitted. Therefore, the AireOS ACL in Figure 14-10 allows all HTTPS traffic (as this rule is necessary to allow HTTPS to any social media web page) and also allows all HTTPS traffic to and from CMX. Any other traffic is denied (implicitly), which means that any other traffic (including HTTP) will cause a redirection to the Redirect URL (the CMX login page in our case).

On Catalyst 9800, traffic that is permitted by the redirection ACL causes redirection to the redirect URL. In other words, the ACL defines which traffic you allow to be redirected (while AireOS defines which traffic is allowed to go through). On C9800, traffic that is not permitted by the redirect ACL (that is, traffic that is denied) is simply permitted to go through without redirection. This is why the C9800 redirection ACL looks somewhat like the opposite of the AireOS redirection ACL. What you allow on one platform is what you deny on the other.

Then, navigate to **Configuration > Tags & Profiles > WLANs**. Click **Add** to create a new WLAN. In **Layer2**, set the Layer 2 security mode to **None**. In **Layer3**, click **Web policy**. Set the **Web Auth Parameter Map** to the parameter map you created in the previous paragraph. **Click** the **Advanced Settings** link. Enable the **Splash web redirect** function and call the preauthentication ACL you created before, as shown in Figure 14-15.

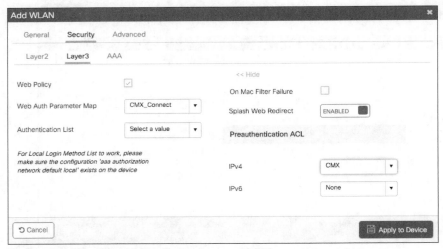

Figure 14-15   *WLAN Configuration on C9800*

Configuring a Portal on CMX

Once your WLC is configured, you can create Experiences (portals) in CMX from **Connect > Library**. There, you can see the portals you already created (**Portals** tab) and create a new Portal by clicking **Create New Portal**, as shown in Figure 14-16.

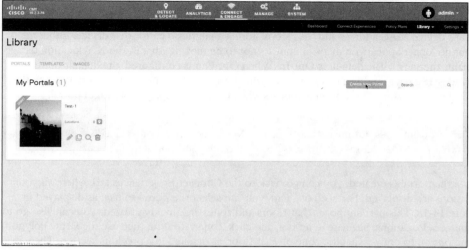

Figure 14-16   *CMX Connect Portals Library*

Clicking **Create New Portal** redirects you to the Templates page, where you can choose from among six types of authentication, as shown in Figure 14-17.

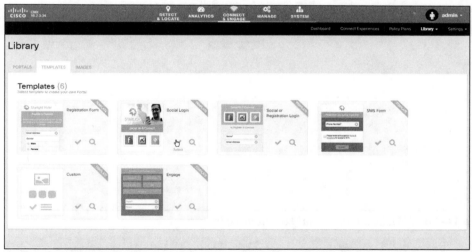

Figure 14-17   *CMX Connect Templates and Supported Authentication Modes*

Selecting an individual template guides you through a portal creation wizard, where you can name your portal and design the login page based on existing and customizable page elements (background, images, and so on). CMX will generate the matching web pages for laptops, tablets, and phones. Each option has design and customization elements for which you can find detailed configuration instructions in the CMX Connect Configuration Guide at https://www.cisco.com/c/en/us/td/docs/wireless/mse/10-6/cmx_config/b_cg_cmx106/the_cisco_cmx_connect_and_engage_service.html. One key element of your portal is the

Opt-Out option, which allows clients to opt out of having their mobile device location history maintained and used by Cisco CMX. When a client opts out, Cisco CMX stops detecting the client's device MAC address and thus stops storing analytics data for that device. Either the client no longer appears on maps or appears not to be moving (that is, the X,Y location data remains the same). The default is **Opt-In**. When Opt-Out is configured, the default opt-out period is 180 days (and can be changed as you configure the option in the portal). When the period ends, the Opt-Out option reappears when the client displays your login portal.

> **NOTE** Opt-out does not mean that the client MAC address is not retained. The option means that the MAC address location is not tracked beyond portal assignment.

Once the portal is created, you can go back to the Connect Experiences tab, where all your locations are displayed. For each of them, you can select the portal to use, as displayed in Figure 14-18. This part supposes that floors and zones are already created. You can also go to **Manage > Locations**, navigate to a floor, and click **Zones**. You can then use the **Draw Polygon Zone** option to draw a specific zone on that floor, as detailed in a previous section. Then, in Connect, you can assign a specific Experience and Policy Plan to each zone on the floor.

Figure 14-18 *CMX Connect Portal Location Assignment*

> **NOTE** At the top of each column, the "i" icon can be used to display the redirect URL that should be entered in your WLAN Redirect URL field.

Once this configuration completes, any new user joining your guest WLAN will be redirected to CMX, where the user will be located and redirected to the matching portal.

You can also create policies associated to Experiences and locations. The **Policy Plans** feature gives you the option to provide your client with different bandwidths as the client moves from one location to the next. For example, the bandwidth provided to clients in a hotel room could be higher than the bandwidth provided in a hotel lobby. From **Connect > Policy Plans**, click **New Policy Plan** and then provide a name and a bandwidth value (in Kbps).

Implementing DNA Spaces Connect Service

The equivalent of CMX Connect on DNA Spaces is called Captive Portals. The WLC configuration is identical to the CMX configuration. Refer to the previous section for details.

Creating a New Portal from Scratch

When you click the Captive Portals widget on DNA Spaces main dashboard, you access a page where all your existing portals are listed, as shown in Figure 14-19.

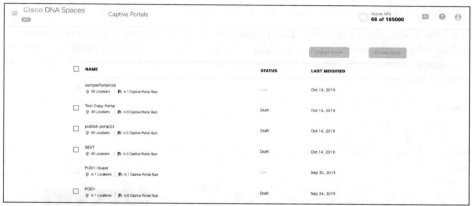

Figure 14-19 *DNA Spaces Captive Portals Page*

To create a new portal from scratch, click **Create New**. The wizard first asks you to enter a name for the new portal and to select which location the portal should be applied to. You can choose to apply the portal to all locations, or you can select one or more locations. Click **Next** to continue. The following page allows you to define how users will be authenticated. You can choose to have a password sent to a phone number of their choice. This option is optimal when the device to connect is not a phone (but the user has access to a phone). Alternatively, the system can send a connection link to a phone number. This option is better, if the device to connect is the phone itself, as shown in Figure 14-20. The authentication step can also take the form of a simple email address, a social media account, or no authentication at all.

Figure 14-20 *DNA Spaces Captive Portals Creation Wizard, Authentication Page*

Regardless of the authentication mode chosen, you can decide if the user agreement should be displayed on the portal home page and if users can be given the choice to opt in (or not) to receive additional messages. Once your authentication choice is made, click **Next** to continue. The next page, Data Capture, allows you to collect more information from the users. You can ask them to enter their title, mobile number, first and last names, gender, a tag (for example, their role), and also their ZIP code (or CPF code in Brazil). Such additional data capture is optional. Click **Next**. The last page of the wizard displays the terms and conditions. You can enable or disable the display of these conditions and then edit them as needed. Click **Save & Configure Portal** to exit this part of the wizard.

A new page opens, shown in Figure 14-21, that allows you to customize your portal page, including different forms for phones, tablets, or laptops, and also different languages. Once your customization is completed, click the back arrow in the upper-left corner of the page to exit the wizard.

Figure 14-21 *DNA Spaces Captive Portals Page Customization*

Your portal now appears in the list. At any point if you hover over the portal line, you can click the pen icon to edit the portal again, the trash can icon to delete the portal, or the copy icon to duplicate the portal.

Creating a New Portal from a Template

Duplicating is a common task, as many enterprises use variations of a main template based on specific location needs. If you do not want to create a portal manually, the bottom of the Captive Portals page also contains various templates you can use, as shown in Figure 14-22.

You can preview each template and also edit it. You can also duplicate the template (and edit the copy if needed). Duplicating the template pushes the copy into the list of available portals. You can then check the box on the left side of a portal in the list and click **Add to**

Location at the bottom of the page. A new page appears that allows you to select the locations where the portal will be valid. Click **Save Changes** to validate.

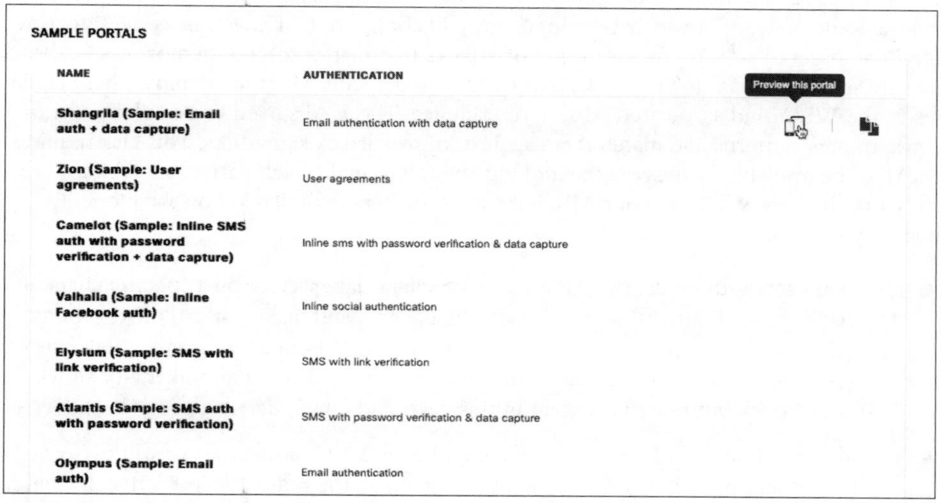

Figure 14-22 *DNA Spaces Captive Portals Templates*

DNA Spaces does not provide bandwidth policies like CMX does. The only accessible filter is to allow direct or indirect connection to the Internet. During the portal customization phase, you can click the **Get Internet** module and configure there whether access will be direct or if users will be redirected to another web server after the login completes.

Implementing WIPS on MSE

Wireless Intrusion Prevention System (WIPS), also called adaptive wireless intrusion prevention system (AWIPS), has a complex history on Cisco systems. You need to keep in mind that wireless intrusion detection relies on the concept of signatures. Each attack leverages specific frames that are sent (or replayed) with an identifiable target source or destination, and at a particular pace, that can be uniquely identified (thus representing the signature of an associated attack). Over the years, as new attacks appeared and were analyzed by Wi-Fi researchers, Cisco implemented their matching signatures in a central database and the most common signatures directly on the WLC. Today, after more than 20 years of Wi-Fi development, the central database includes more than 260 signatures, and the WLC includes 17 signatures. However, many of them match attacks that would not occur on a modern network. For example, some signatures match the detection of WEP 40 implementations. Such a weak protocol has long been considered obsolete and is equivalent to "no protection." The tool to detect this implementation only runs on Windows 2000 and earlier. As such, it is unlikely to occur in today's deployments. In summary, it is time to update these signatures and those that are obsolete. Cisco is working on this update. In between, you can find the full AWIPS on CMX/MSE 8.x but not on the 10.x generation (yet). In parallel, the essential WLC signature set is still present in AireOS WLCs but is not implemented (yet) in the Catalyst 9800. As the new signature set gets finalized, it will be implemented on the new platforms, and the traditional platforms will progressively be updated.

AP Deployment for WIPS

Still, as a networking professional, you may be asked to implement AWIPS, and you need to know that this requirement means deploying CMX 8.0 with AireOS. You also need to understand the logic of WIPS. In such a deployment, you configure CMX, acting as the signature central database, to activate the detection of attacks that matter to you. In most cases, these are a subset of the 261 known attacks that CMX can detect. CMX then deploys these signatures to the WLCs and associated APs of your choice. These APs need to be able to identify specific frames' patterns and match them against known attack signatures. This task requires each AP to be available to observe the air long enough to make such pattern matching. As such, you can apply WIPS on your APs, but their efficiency will depend on the mode in which they operate:

- In Local (standard) mode, the AP focuses on client data service on a specific channel. The AP only has limited time to observe the channel and make pattern observations. The AP scans other channels at intervals as part of RRM but spends only a few tens of milliseconds on each other channel, thus making attack detection unlikely (or slow). WIPS can work but is least efficient in this case, and attack detection may be slow.

- In Enhanced Local mode (ELM), also called Local-WIPS mode, the AP still performs client data servicing, but when scanning off-channel, the radio dwells on the channel for an extended period of time, allowing enhanced attack detection. If you deploy WIPS on some APs, you should prefer ELM to Local mode.

- In Monitor mode with WIPS, the AP is fully dedicated to attack detection and mitigation. This is, of course, the most efficient mode, but the AP does not provide client data service anymore. Note that your AP can be in regular Monitor mode (with "None" as submode) and then only perform RRM-focused monitoring. You need to set the monitor AP to WIPS submode in order to make it a full-time WIPS AP.

- You can also install a radio module on some AP models (Aironet APs 3600 and 3700), called Wireless Security Module (WSM). This module is in Monitor WIPS mode all the time, while the main AP can stay in another mode.

You do not need to apply WIPS mode to all your APs. In a standard deployment, WIPS is treated like any other rogue detection system. You need enough WIPS APs to monitor the entire coverage area, but you also need to keep in mind that most attacks are performed using management frames. These frames are usually sent at the lowest configured mandatory data rate, which is usually 6Mbps. Perform a site survey and ensure that your WIPS APs can detect traffic sent at low data rates (for example, 6Mbps). Such a requirement typically results in fairly large cells, between 10K and 26K square feet each in 2.4GHz (depending on the floor layout and building material) and between 4.5K and 26K square feet in 5GHz (assuming an attacker is sending traffic at 15 dBm). In an office deployment, this size means that you will deploy one WIPS for every five standard (Local mode) APs.

It is clear that the final density will depend on your building layout, and you should survey before making the density decision. You should also keep in mind that some attackers will (purposely) use lower-power devices in order to escape your detection or send their management frames at higher rates (such as 24 or even 54Mbps). You should also consider the location sensitivity and the cost of successful attacks before deciding on a deployment scheme.

CMX WIPS Configuration

WIPS activation is done from Cisco Prime Infrastructure, when you're adding the MSE, in **Services > Mobility Services Engine**. After entering the MSE details (name, IP address, admin username and password), and after adding the WIPS license, in **Select Service**, choose **WIPS**, assign the maps (campus, buildings, and floors) that you want under the WIPS service, and then click **Synchronize** to activate WIPS for these locations.

You also need to decide which APs are set to ELM and Monitor mode. The configuration is individual to each AP. From **Wireless > Select AP**, set the **AP mode** to either **Local** or **Monitor** and set the submode to **WIPS**. The same task can also be done from Cisco Prime Infrastructure.

The next and main task is to configure a WIPS profile from Cisco Prime Infrastructure. In the **Services > Mobility Services > wIPS Profile** page, select **Add Profile** and click **Go**.

Because it is unlikely that all 261 known attacks will be relevant to you, and because the sensitivity of the detection also depends on your environment, PI allows you to choose a template from which to build your WIPS profile, as shown in Figure 14-23.

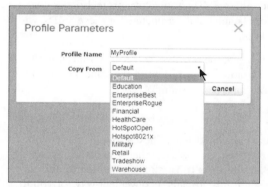

Figure 14-23 *WIPS New Profile Creation*

In most cases, you would use the template that best matches your environment type and then customize it to your needs. Such a course of action saves you time, as customization allows you to change the profile at will, adding, removing, or editing attack parameters as needed. This way, you could conceptually change the content of one profile into another if you decided to do so. In other words, using a template does not constrain your profile but saves you time by presetting it with attacks and parameters that are commonly of concern for the target environment.

Therefore, you should enter a name for your profile in **Profile Name**, select the environment template that best matches your environment description, the choose **Add and Edit** to customize the profile.

The WIPS wizard then displays a list of SSID types. This page is useful to seed WIPS with the names of SSIDs that you know and that have a clear meaning in your environment. For example, if your network includes the Corporate and Research SSIDs, check the box on the left of **MyWLAN**, and in the upper right drop-down list choose **Edit Group** and click **Go**. Then, in the new window, enter your SSID names, one per line, and click **Save** to validate. If your guest SSID is called CompanyGuests, check the box on the left of the **Guest** category and repeat the same process done previously, as displayed in Figure 14-24.

Figure 14-24   *Editing SSIDs with WIPS*

WIPS offers five SSID categories:

- **MyWLAN:** For your corporate SSIDs, typically with encryption (WPA2/WPA3) and authentication (PSK/802.1X).

- **Guest:** For your WebAuth-based SSIDs.

- **Neighbors:** For SSIDs that are known in your environment but do not belong to you. In most cases, you will want to exclude these SSIDs from active protection, as your neighbors may be adding, removing, or changing AP parameters for these SSIDs, without these changes being a cause for alarm.

- **Any:** For SSIDs that you know and for which the previous categorization is not relevant (for example, when guest and corporate users are sent to the same SSID, or in cases where some SSIDs may have more than one meaning).

- **Other:** For all other SSIDs.

You can also create your own group or delete existing groups. These group names are not constraining; they are just suggested categories. In a later phase, when you manage your alarm and the expected intrusion prevention action, you can assign each action to one or more of the SSID types. In other words, these groups are only a convenient way for you to group alike SSIDs in common containers.

Once you have defined your groups and their associated SSIDs, click **Next**. In the new page, all the known attacks are displayed on the left column, organized in categories. You can click each attack to see details on the right part of the screen, including the threshold (how many detections per sampling period would trigger the alarm), the severity, the SSID group to which the alarm applies, and the action to take when the alarm is triggered (notify or contain). An example is shown in Figure 14-25.

In most cases, your initial configuration task would be to click each attack, in turn, carefully read the description in the bottom-right part of the screen, and decide if detection of that attack is relevant in your environment and for which SSID groups the detection is needed. Then you would edit the attack parameters to match your environment detection needs. This initial configuration task is time-consuming but necessary to adapt WIPS to your environment. If you need different thresholds for different SSID categories, you can also add policy rules and their associated SSID groups, detection thresholds, and action.

Figure 14-25 *Editing an Attack Alarm Properties with WIPS*

NOTE   It may be tempting to think that all attacks are relevant and worth detecting. Although this thought is likely true conceptually, you should also keep in mind the outcome of each detection and the likelihood of each attack in your environment. For example, if your corporate WLANs implement WPA3/802.1X on 802.11ax/Wi-Fi 6 and Protected Management Frames (PMF), then a man-in-the-middle attack (as detected by attack ID 64) is simply not possible (as your clients ignore spoofed management frames), and you are wasting detection resources. Similarly, implementing detection of Soft APs (attack ID 99) in an environment where people are allowed to use tethering on their personal devices (for example, a public venue) will generate a large number of alarms with no clear action to take as a result of such detection.

There are two types of monitoring objects: SSID Group and Device Group. Depending on signatures, it can be that neither, one, or both are available to be configured. The Device Group is a list of device MAC addresses that you want to monitor for attacks. You can edit the groups and manually enter the MAC addresses of assets to protect. Alternatively, if your assets are all infrastructure devices, such as APs and their clients, you can use the Internal option as the Device Group to be monitored.

The Severity value represents the classification of the associated alarm. In Cisco Prime Infrastructure, each alarm category matches one or more reporting mechanisms, from simple display in the dashboard to SMS or email alerts. It is expected that alarms with higher severity would need faster reporting, because an immediate action may need to be taken. Besides reporting, an additional option for some alarms is Forensic. When you activate that option, the detecting APs capture, over the air, the packets that trigger the alarm and send it to the MSE, where the capture is saved for troubleshooting and analysis purposes. It is not recommended to enable Forensic for all alarms, because such capture increases the WIPS alarm-related traffic dramatically, especially in case WLC and MSE are separated in different locations and communicate over a WAN link.

Once an attack is detected, the matching alarm is triggered and surfaced in Cisco Prime Infrastructure. The alarm can be configured (beyond its severity) with additional parameters, such as the following:

- **Location:** The location of the attacker is computed by CMX, and this location can be displayed on a floor plan. This is useful in order to physically remove the offender.

- **Auto-Immune:** For some DoS attacks, a potential attacker can use specially crafted packets to mislead WIPS to treat a legitimate client as an attacker. This action may cause the controller to disconnect the legitimate client. The auto-immune feature is designed to ignore the crafted packets from an attacker and protect the legitimate client from loss of connectivity. This protection is valid only for reassociation messages.

- **Blacklist:** Different from the auto-immune, blacklist is a more aggressive mitigation action to de-authenticate the identified attacking device if it is connected first, and then ignore all traffic from it afterward as long as it is on the blacklist. This protection is useful for attacks where an offender starts infrastructure services (for example, a fake DHCP or DNS server).

- **Containment:** The containment action in WIPS attacks is similar to rogue AP containment in the WLC. It is designed to initiate containment on SSID-related attacks to prevent legitimate clients connecting to those SSIDs set up by attackers. The offender MAC address is disconnected and prevented from connecting again to the affected SSIDs.

One you have reviewed and customized the attacks, click **Save** to validate your changes and **Next** to continue. You can then select the MSE(s) and WLCs to which this profile should be applied. Click **Apply** to validate. As the profile is deployed to these WLCs, their internal signature detection, only allowing the detection of the 17 most common attacks, is deactivated and replaced by the WIPS profile. You can see this deactivation in the WLC by navigating to **Security > Wireless Protection Policies > Standard Signatures**. The **Enable Check for all Standard and Custom Signatures** box should be unchecked. Keep in mind that you cannot have both the MSE WIPS profile and the local WLC signature detection mechanism active at the same time. If you enable WIPS, you need to deactivate the WLC local detection tool.

Ensuring Location Operational Efficiency

At the conclusion of this chapter, your MSE and DNA Spaces should provide the components you need to act upon the detection and location of Wi-Fi devices in your environment. Although DNA Spaces does not require optimization, an on-premises MSE implementation is different, as it offers a single point of failure. Therefore, you need to ensure that MSE can continue to provide services, even in the event of failure. This requirement implies deploying high availability. Additionally, the services you will provide are only as efficient as the location you compute is accurate. You also need to make sure that the location technique you use provides the accuracy you expect.

Deploying MSE High Availability

The purpose of MSE HA is to ensure that, in the event of the main MSE failure, a secondary MSE can take over and continue performing CMX tasks. In order to maintain the failover transparent from a network connectivity point of view, the concept of virtual IP (VIP) is used. When both the primary and secondary are in the same subnet, the primary and secondary MSEs are identified as a single VIP. This VIP is mapped to the real IP of the running primary CMX. When failover happens, VIP is remapped to the address of the secondary CMX. It is not mandatory to use a virtual IP. If you are doing CMX Layer 3 high availability (that is, having the two servers in different subnets), you cannot use a virtual IP. The virtual IP provides a unique IP for the IT admin (or Prime Infrastructure / Cisco DNA center) to manage CMX regardless of a failover or failback. The WLCs, however, will have an NMSP tunnel only toward the currently active CMX physical IP address.

To install HA MSEs, start by installing the primary MSE as described in Chapter 13. Once the installation completes, install the second MSE. During the installation process, select the MSE as a secondary server for high availability, as shown in Figure 14-26.

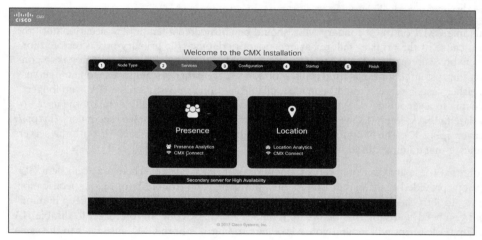

Figure 14-26   *Secondary MSE Installation*

At any point of the installation (on the primary or the secondary server), you can connect to the MSE web interface using https://mse_ip_address:1984/ and follow the installation process. Once the installation completes, you can connect on port 4242 (htttps://mse_ip_address:4242) to access the HA interface. On the primary server, connect using the cmxadmin account and enter the secondary server IP address, along with the virtual IP address that both servers should share, the password for the cmxadmin account on the secondary server, and the failover type. Auto-failover will allow CMX to automatically fail over to the secondary server when a serious issue is detected. Manual failover will require the user to initiate the failover from the web interface or command line. The failure will be reported to the user via notifications, but no action is taken for manual failover.

You can also inform the notification email address—the email address where you send notifications about HA information or issues. The email settings used for HA are the same as CMX. This field is required even though you don't have an email server configured. Feel free to enter a dummy email address and click "enable" if you don't intend to use email notifications.

The initial synchronization of all the data between the primary and secondary server can take a significant amount of time to complete. The user interface will indicate the state as

"Primary Syncing" while the synchronization is being done. When the synchronization has completed successfully, the server on the primary will enter the state "Primary Active." When completed, an information alert will be generated in CMX. In addition, an email alert will be sent that indicates that the system is active and syncing properly.

Your MSE pair is not ready for high availability. When the primary MSE fails, failover occurs and the secondary MSE becomes active. A failover can occur automatically when CMX detects an issue with the primary server. A failover can be done manually by a user in the web user interface or on the command line. The progress of the failover can be monitored based on the current state of each system.

To start the failover manually, log in to the CMX HA web interface on the primary or secondary **(https://server_ip:4242)**. The monitor page will have a button labeled "Failover" if the servers are actively syncing.

Running CMX on the secondary MSE should be considered a temporary situation until the root cause of the primary failure has been identified. Once the primary box is restored (or a new box is provided), the failback process should be initiated. The other option is to convert the system to a primary and replace or convert the other system to a secondary server. In either case, a server should be made available as soon as possible since HA is no longer syncing to a secondary server. The failback process must be manually done by the user. To initiate failback, log in to the CMX HA web interface on the primary or secondary **(https://server_ip:4242)**. The Monitor page will have a button labeled "Failback" if both the servers indicate that a failover is active.

Note that these are your only tools to monitor or manage failover. There are equivalent CLI options provided at the end of this chapter, but there is no troubleshooting or specific monitoring tool to check the synchronization progress between MSE copies. Also keep in mind that you need to disable HA before upgrading your CMX code. If you forget to disable HA, the upgrade script will remind you. Make sure to upgrade both CMX instances to the same code version.

Managing Location Accuracy

Most services examined in this and the previous chapter rely on the fundamental principle that location is performed and is accurate to the level you have configured (Presence, RSSI trilateration with or without FastLocate, and Hyperlocation). At the same time, indoor location does not defy the laws of physics. Accurate location cannot happen if your deployment is subpar. Therefore, you need to make sure you have enough APs, that they are positioned properly, and that the location engine has enough information to compute clients' positions.

Location Requirements

AP position and density are the first elements you should keep in mind when you suspect that location is not optimal. As you'll recall from Chapter 3, "Conducting an Onsite Site Survey," and Chapter 6, "Designing Radio Management," APs should not be set in a straight line but should form a convex hull within which location is possible. At each point of your floor where you want location to be possible, there should be at least four APs, one within each quadrant, as shown in Figure 14-27. Three of these four APs should be within a 70-foot range (the ideal range is 40 to 70 feet).

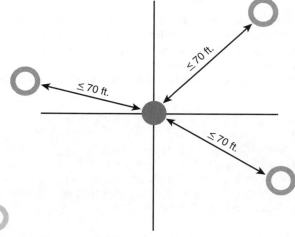

Figure 14-27 *Location Readiness Checklist*

This location readiness can be verified from Cisco Prime Infrastructure. From the PI **Maps > Site Maps (New)** page, click a floor plan of your choice. In the upper-right corner of the page, in the **Tools** menu, select the option **Inspect Location Readiness**. The system will compute, for each point of your floor, the APs' distance and positions and will color green the areas that match the location requirements, as illustrated in Figure 14-28.

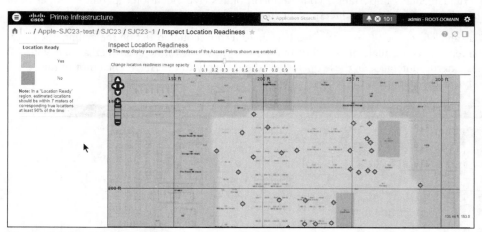

Figure 14-28 *Location Readiness Result in PI*

This test does not guarantee location accuracy within the green zone. It simply displays in red areas where location is unlikely to be possible or provide usable results. In the green zone, you have enough APs to perform location if the area is an open space. PI does not take the walls into account and also does not know if the APs are really where the map reports them.

Verifying AP Settings

Your next step is to examine each AP on the map and verify that it matches the location and position of your APs in the real world. In the upper-right corner of your floorplan view, select the **Edit** button and choose to edit the APs' positions. Carefully verify that each AP icon position matches the real AP position on your floor. Also verify the AP height, keeping in mind that no accurate location will occur if the AP is positioned more than 20 feet above the height of your clients.

NOTE   This requirement is usually simplified as "not higher than 20 feet (approx. 6 meters) above the ground." Most clients are carried at 2 to 3 feet (60 to 90 cm) height, but this detail does not matter. What this rule expresses is that, as the distance from the AP increases, the signal decreases fast at first, then more slowly (it follows a log curve, as seen in Figure 13-1 of Chapter 13). If your AP is too high, then most clients' signals are weak in general without a clear difference as a client moves. This reduces ranging accuracy.

You should also verify the AP orientation, as shown in Figure 14-29. The azimuth represents the horizontal orientation of the AP. Each AP has a Cisco logo with the word "Cisco" printed below the logo. When you hold the AP in front of you and read the word "Cisco" (with the correct orientation), the bottom part of the AP represents the direction of the azimuth arrow in PI. Therefore, if your AP is mounted flat on the ceiling and the "bottom" (now horizontal) points toward the west, then in PI the azimuth arrow should also point toward the west for that AP. Such orientation is not important for indoor APs with omnidirectional antennas, but it is fundamentally important if your AP incorporates Hyperlocation capabilities. An error of a few degrees in the arrow direction may result in poor location accuracy.

You can also set the tilt, or elevation. If your AP is not mounted flat on the ceiling, the elevation represents the angle of that "bottom" part of the AP with the horizontal axis. If your AP uses external antennas, all these operations should apply to the AP antenna (not to the AP body), as the antenna is the RF part of the AP.

Figure 14-29   *Verifying AP Positions in PI*

Once these operations are performed, synchronize your results with MSE (in PI, select **Services > Location Services > Select MSE > Synchronize**).

Verifying Location Accuracy on MSE

You can continue your verifications from CMX. From the CMX activity map, on a floor map, locate and click a client, as shown in Figure 14-30. Then, in the upper-right corner of the screen, click the blue geolocation icon.

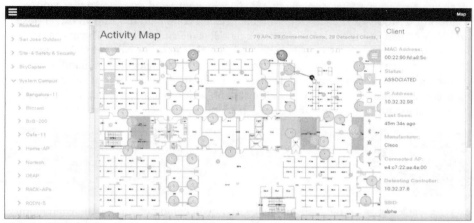

Figure 14-30   *Location Accuracy Test in CMX*

A pop-up window appears, asking you to name the test. Enter a name of your choice in the **Enter the test name** field. Then position the bottom tip of the geolocation icon at the exact location where your client is positioned. Do not move the client, and let the test run for a while. The tool will collect signal samples from the client and perform 20 location computations before displaying a results table that shows, for each location computation result, the interval since the previous computation (called Location Computation Frequency in seconds), the percentage of time that the client was evaluated to be on the correct floor, the percentage of time the computation produced a client location estimation within 30 feet (about 10 meters) of the actual location (the tip of your geolocation icon), the average distance error for that estimation, and then the error for the best 90 percent estimations, the best 75 percent estimations, and the best 50 percent estimations.

If the results do not match your expectations, after having verified again the position and orientation of your APs, you should also verify onsite that, from the target locations, at least four APs are around the client, three of which are at 70 feet (approx. 21 meters) or less apart. You should also verify that the AP signal is at –72 dBm or higher. Too weak a signal reveals a density of obstacles that may prevent proper signal reception on the APs.

NOTE   You will see different values for this signal level. Some references will refer to –75 dBm, and they mean the minimum signal (signal should be at least at –75 dBm). Others will mention –72 dBm as the "preferred" minimum, meaning that –75 dBm is acceptable, but –72 dBm will provide a better location estimation. Also keep in mind that this is the signal of the client on the detecting APs, not the signal of the AP at the target location. So you should make sure to connect the client to an AP and use the WLC GUI or CLI to check the client signal at that AP.

Customizing RF Calibration Model on PI

If the signal is within the appropriate range, then a last task is to refine the RF calibration of your floor. As detailed in Chapter 13, each floor has obstacles (walls and such) that affect signal propagation and that are accounted for when you add a floor map to a building in PI, with an associated RF calibration model. If location is inaccurate, it may be that the RF model you chose does not work for your floor, and you need to create your own. To do so, you need a client that supports Cisco Compatible Extensions, such as an Intel adapter. Then, in PI, navigate to **Map > Site Maps**. From the **Select a command** drop-down list, choose **RF Calibration Models** and click **Go**. From the **Select a command** drop-down list, choose **Create New Model** and then click **Go**. Enter a model name and click **OK**. The new model appears along with the other RF calibration models with a status of **Not Yet Calibrated**. Click the model name to open the model name page. From the **Select a command** drop-down list, choose **Add Data Points** and click **Go**. Enter the MAC address of the device being used to perform the calibration, and then choose the appropriate campus, building, floor, or outdoor area where the calibration is performed. Then click **Next** to start.

> **NOTE** It is best to perform these steps from the laptop you will use for the calibration task. If you are connecting to PI from that laptop, its MAC address will automatically be populated in PI.

Click your real location on the map and click **Go**. PI will compute your location and modify its model to account for your real location. You will need to collect at least 150 points per band for the calibration to complete. The tool offers point calibration options, as described here, or linear options (where you click a starting point and then a stopping point after walking in a straight line).

Once your point collection completes (the point collection status bar next to the floor map appears as filled in green), click the name of the calibration model at the top of the page to return to the main page for that model to calibrate the data points, and then choose **Calibrate** from the **Select a command** drop-down list and click **Go**. The process can take a while. PI will recompute the RF model based on your data collection. At the end of the calibration phase, you can click the **Inspect Location Quality** link to see a map showing the RSSI readings. If there are areas where location accuracy is poor (area shows in red), you need to go back to that location and collect more data points to help PI refine the model. Once all areas are green, to use the newly created calibration model, you must apply the model to the floor on which it was created (and on any other floors with similar attenuation characteristics as well). Choose **Monitor > Site Maps** and find the specific floor to which the model is applied. At the floor map interface, choose **Edit Floor Area** from the drop-down list and click **Go**. From the **Floor Type (RF Model)** drop-down list, choose the newly created calibration model. Click **OK** to apply the model to the floor.

This process can be repeated for as many models and floors as needed. After a model is applied to a floor, all location determination performed on that floor is done using the specific collected attenuation data from the calibration model.

Verifying Hyperlocation Configuration

If you use Hyperlocation (or FastLocate), do not forget to enable that feature. This can be done globally for all APs on the WLC in **Wireless > Global configuration**, per AP group in **WLAN > AP group > Edit**, or per AP in **Wireless > Edit AP > Advanced**. In the WLC, **Packet Detection RSSI Minimum** is set by default to a low value (–100 dBm). It may be worthwhile to increase the value to the threshold where a client should not be in your network anymore (for example, –82 dBm).

On your WLC, you should see that Hyperlocation is enabled by using the command **show advanced hyperlocation summary**, as shown in Example 14-1.

Example 14-1 *Output of the show advanced location summary Command*

```
(Cisco Controller) >show advanced hyperlocation summary

Hyperlocation.................................. UP

Hyperlocation NTP Server......................... 172.31.255.1

Hyperlocation pak-rssi Threshold................ -80

Hyperlocation pak-rssi Trigger-Threshold........ 10

Hyperlocation pak-rssi Reset-Threshold.......... 8

Hyperlocation pak-rssi Timeout.................. 3

AP Name               Ethernet MAC      Slots    Hyperlocation

----------------      ------------------- -------  ------------

AP00aa.bbbb.cccc      00:aa:bb:bb:cc:cc     3            UP
```

On MSE, you should also be able to verify that the Hyperlocation service is running with the command **cmxctl status**. This command produces a long output. Verify that Location and Hyperlocation services are running. If these services are not running, your MSE configuration may need to be verified (and MSE may need to be restarted).

You can also capture on the MSE network interface traffic coming from the WLC and verify that there is traffic sent to port UDP 2003 with the following command:

```
tcpdump -i eth0 dst port 2003 -w test.pcap
```

You can then open the test.pcap file (for example, with Wireshark). You should see traffic sent from your WLC IP address to the MSE IP address on port UDP 2003. You cannot see the content of the packets, as they are encrypted, but their presence shows that AoA information is reaching the MSE.

Also make sure to use NTP time synchronization on the WLC, PI, and MSE. Keep in mind that Hyperlocation only works with on-premises MSE, not with DNA Spaces Cloud without MSE.

Beyond AP placement on PI and synchronization between PI and MSE, the most common issues are Hyperlocation not enabled on the WLC and improper NTP configuration on one of the devices. Check for these elements, and you should be able to face the CCNP Enterprise questions and any location accuracy issue in real deployments.

Summary

This chapter described advanced location services available on CMX and DNA Spaces. In this chapter you have learned the following:

- The main services available in CMX and DNA Spaces

- How to deploy Analytics services

- How to deploy location-specific guest portals

- How to configure AWIPS on the MSE

- How to ensure MSE efficiency and location accuracy

References

For additional information, refer to these resources:

CMX Configuration Guide: https://www.cisco.com/c/en/us/td/docs/wireless/mse/10-6/cmx_config/b_cg_cmx106.html

Guest access configuration in C9800: https://www.cisco.com/c/en/us/td/docs/wireless/controller/9800/config-guide/b_wl_16_10_cg/cisco-guest-foreign.html#concept_e5l_1np_njb

WIPS deployment guide: https://www.cisco.com/c/en/us/td/docs/wireless/technology/wips/deployment/guide/WiPS_deployment_guide.html#pgfId-43454

CMX HA guide: https://www.cisco.com/c/en/us/support/docs/availability/high-availability/213664-configure-cmx-high-availability.html

DNA Spaces Configuration Guide: https://www.cisco.com/c/en/us/td/docs/solutions/Enterprise/Mobility/DNA-Spaces/cisco-dna-spaces-config/dnaspaces-configuration-guide.html

Calibrating RF models: https://www.cisco.com/c/en/us/td/docs/net_mgmt/prime/infrastructure/3-0/user/guide/pi_ug/wireless-maps.html

Exam Preparation Tasks

As mentioned in the section "How to Use This Book" in the Introduction, you have a few choices for exam preparation: the exercises here, Chapter 18, "Final Preparation," and the exam simulation questions in the Pearson Test Prep Software Online.

Review All Key Topics

Review the most important topics in this chapter, noted with the Key Topic icon in the outer margin of the page. Table 14-3 lists these key topics and the page numbers on which each is found.

Key Topic

Table 14-3   Key Topics for Chapter 14

Key Topic Element	Description	Page Number
List	CMX object types	335
List	CMX Connect configuration procedure	343
Paragraph	AireOS vs. C9800 ACLs	346
Paragraph	CMX Portal library	346
Paragraph	DNA Spaces portal creation	349
List	AP modes for WIPS	352
Paragraph	CMX WIPS profiles	353
Note	Limiting attack detection scope	355
Figure 14-27	Location readiness checklist	359

14

Define Key Terms

Define the following key terms from this chapter and check your answers in the glossary:

perimeter, zone, preauthentication ACL, Enhanced Local mode

CHAPTER 15

Security for Wireless Client Connectivity

This chapter discusses the following topics:

Implementing 802.1X and AAA on Wireless Architectures: This section examines how EAP and 802.1X work in a wireless LAN, exploring the various network components involved in end-to-end client security. This section also looks at how ISE is implemented in wireless networks to provide authentication and authorization services.

Implementing Client Profiling: This section examines the wireless client onboarding process and how clients can be profiled based on their authentication credentials, the type of device that is associating, and many other criteria. This section examines how client profiling and policy can be implemented both on the controller and in ISE.

Implementing BYOD and Guest: BYOD and wireless guest access (through portals) are widely used wireless deployments. This section looks at various ways to deploy guest networks with the Cisco wireless controller and ISE. In addition, this section examines how to deploy Bring Your Own Device (BYOD), including how and where authentication of the users should take place, including the differences between local and central web authentication methods.

This chapter covers the following ENWLSI exam topics:

- 6.1 Configure client profiling on WLC and ISE
- 6.2 Implement BYOD and guest
  - 6.2.a CWA using ISE (including self-registration portal)
  - 6.2.b LWA using ISE or WLC
  - 6.2.c Native supplicant provisioning using ISE
  - 6.2.d Certificate provisioning on the controller
- 6.3 Implement 802.1X and AAA on different wireless architectures and ISE
- 6.4 Implement Identity-Based Networking on different wireless architectures (VLANs, QoS, ACLs)

As you begin to deploy a wireless network, no doubt security is top of mind. However, deploying security can be one of the most complex challenges to implement and manage. In addition, over the last 20 years, the IEEE has been continually improving security standards, introducing new frameworks such as Wireless Protected Access version 3 (WPA3). However, best practices for wireless security go far beyond the jurisdiction of WPA. For example, just because a client is able to provide authentication credentials doesn't mean all devices with these credentials should be given the same level of access to a network or to all places in a network. To illustrate, a wireless client that is brought from home and is essentially untrusted should not be given the same level of access to sensitive parts of the network as a fully trusted device. In addition, based on the type of device, different levels of QoS may be warranted, such as devices that require high-definition video. Furthermore, depending on the type of device and the user who authenticates, it may be desirable to associate different security profiles to certain user groups or even assign them to specific VLANs.

Allowing guests to use the wireless network through the use of a portal is another aspect that has become increasingly important in recent years. While an organization may grant access to guest users, ensuring they do not become a security risk and have access to sensitive areas of the network is an important requirement that must be considered. This involves not only how the guest portal is made available to end users but also how the wireless network itself is architected.

BYOD is yet another area that can be challenging to secure. BYOD is becoming commonplace in many corporations where users are encouraged to bring their own mobile devices from home and use them on the corporate network. Not only are these BYOD devices untrusted and in some cases insecure, there is no way to know what software (or malware) may be lurking on such devices. To facilitate the use of BYOD, it has become necessary to provide users a secure way to self-register their devices and then deploy security software to the BYOD devices so that they can be trusted on the corporate network. Over the last several years, Cisco has developed BYOD capabilities on the controller and ISE that facilitate this.

"Do I Know This Already?" Quiz

The "Do I Know This Already?" quiz allows you to assess whether you should read this entire chapter thoroughly or jump to the "Exam Preparation Tasks" section. If you are in doubt about your answers to these questions or your own assessment of your knowledge of the topics, read the entire chapter. Table 15-1 lists the major headings in this chapter and their corresponding "Do I Know This Already?" quiz questions. You can find the answers in Appendix D, "Answers to the 'Do I Know This Already?' Quizzes and Review Questions."

Table 15-1 "Do I Know This Already?" Section-to-Question Mapping

Foundation Topics Section	Questions
Implementing 802.1X and AAA on Wireless Architectures	1–3
Implementing Client Profiling	4, 5
Implementing BYOD and Guest	6–8

1. Which of the following protocols is used between a client and the authentication server?

   a. LDAP

   b. RADIUS

   c. 802.1X

   d. EAP

2. Which of the following EAP methods supports X.509 certificates on client and server?

   a. EAP-FAST

   b. EAP-TLS

   c. EAP-GTC

   d. PEAP

   e. EAP-MSCHAPv2

3. Which EAP method supports fast roaming?

   a. PEAP

   b. EAP-MSCHAPv2

   c. EAP-FAST

   d. EAP-GTC

4. Which of the following local profiling options is not used on the controller?

   a. MAC OUI

   b. Device Type

   c. DHCP

   d. HTTP

   e. NMAP

5. After a client has been profiled, what policy features may be used? (Choose all that apply.)

   a. VLAN ID assignment

   b. Time of day restrictions

   c. QoS profile

   d. ACLs

6. What is a key property of LWA? (Choose two.)

   a. In LWA, the guest/BYOD portal may only be implemented on the controller.

   b. In LWA, the guest/BYOD portal may be implemented on either the controller or another server such as ISE.

   c. In LWA, the redirect URL and ACLs are configured on ISE.

   d. In LWA, the redirect URL and ACLs are configured on the controller.

7. What is are key differences between CWA and LWA? (Choose two.)

   a. LWA uses Layer 2 only, whereas CWA uses Layer 3 only.

   b. LWA uses Layer 3, whereas CWA uses a mixture of Layer 2 and Layer 3.

   c. LWA uses MAC filtering, whereas CWA does not.

   d. CWA uses MAC filtering, whereas LWA does not.

8. After authentication with CWA, how does ISE make security changes to the client on the controller?

   a. RADIUS attributes

   b. SNMPv3

   c. CoA

   d. TACACS+

Foundation Topics

Implementing 802.1X and AAA on Wireless Architectures

Before a wireless client device can communicate, it must first authenticate to the access point and controller using a trusted authentication mechanism that verifies the client's identity and credentials. Using security best practices, once a client has been authenticated, it is provided an encryption key to ensure confidentiality of the data communication. In this section, the security architecture of the wireless network will be discussed, along with the various network elements and methods involved in client authentication. This will include an overview of how the various Extensible Authentication Protocol (EAP) methods work and how they are implemented in Cisco wireless networks.

Wireless Network Authentication Framework

To ensure wireless security, clients must be first authenticated and then use encryption in their communication. Although pre-shared keys are simple to deploy and require minimal authentication infrastructure (you will often see pre-shared keys used in home wireless networks), it is recommended to deploy a more robust and manageable system in corporate wireless networks. For example, if a large network was deployed with pre-shared keys, it would be a trivial matter for any client to decrypt and record any other client's traffic with the same pre-shared key. If one of the clients became compromised, things would be much worse. This would then require the immediate manual rekeying of all devices everywhere—something that is next to impossible to accomplish. In addition, with pre-shared keys, it is not possible to see the unique identity of the users who are associated to the wireless network.

A much better alternative is to use a mechanism based on the EAP authentication framework. EAP is an authentication framework for the communication of identity credentials over a network, either wired or wireless. EAP employs IEEE 802.1X between the client and the wireless controller, as well as RADIUS between the controller and the back-end authentication server. Today, both the IEEE 802.11i standard and the Wi-Fi Alliance Wireless Protected Access (WPA) compatibility standard have adopted 802.1X for authentication on wireless LANs.

NOTE Defined in RFC 3748 (now updated in RFC 5247), EAP is not actually a single security protocol but is rather a framework that provides common security functions and methods to handle authentication credentials over a network. Currently, approximately 40 different EAP authentication methods exist, but only a few are in common use.

Today, EAP is widely deployed in corporate wireless networks worldwide. EAP allows clients to be *authenticated* before they are fully associated to the wireless network, and it allows the wireless infrastructure to *authorize* them for different levels of security, access, and QoS once they have been authenticated. Figure 15-1 illustrates the overall EAP authentication framework and associated components.

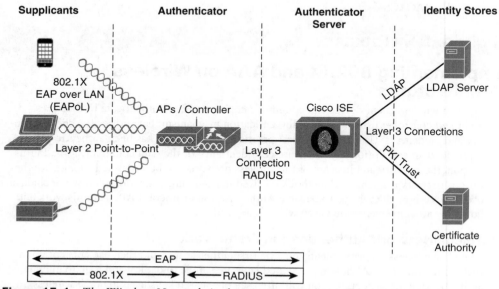

Figure 15-1   *The Wireless Network Authentication Framework*

As illustrated in Figure 15-1, the authentication framework leverages EAP, end to end. Between the client and the AP/controller EAP runs over 802.1X, and between the AP/controller and the Authentication server it runs over RADIUS. The framework includes the following key components:

- **Supplicant:** The supplicant is a piece software that runs on the client device. The supplicant is responsible for providing the identity (the username) and password of the client to the authenticator over EAP. The supplicant is commonly a native part of the mobile device's operating system, or it may be installed separately, such as the Cisco AnyConnect Secure Mobility Client.

- **Authenticator:** The authenticator is the network device that authenticates the client device (such as the AP and/or the controller). In a wired LAN this would be the switch directly connected to the wired client. In a wireless LAN, this is either the access point or the controller, depending on how the APs are deployed. The authenticator is also referred to as a Network Access Device (NAD).

- **Authentication server (AS):** This is the back-end RADIUS component that authenticates the client device via the authenticator. Cisco ISE is an example of an authentication server that is able to apply network policy controls to clients as they connect to the network. The AS is also commonly referred to as the Network Authentication Server (NAS).

■ **Identity store:** The identity store is a directory server that is typically accessed by the authentication server using Lightweight Directory Access Protocol (LDAP). The authentication server may also have an identity store, although this is less common. The identity store may also optionally include a certificate authority. Active Directory is a common example of an identity store.

Extensible Authentication Protocol (EAP)

Authentication begins at the time of association when the supplicant on the wireless client provides its user credentials to the authenticator, which then passes them to the authentication server.

End to end, EAP encapsulates usernames, passwords, certificates, tokens, and other credentials that allow the client to be authenticated. As shown in Figure 15-1, EAP communication is established between the supplicant and the authentication server. However, there are two steps to establish this communication. First, 802.1X using EAP over LAN (EAPoL) is used between the supplicant and the authenticator. Second, RADIUS is used between the authenticator and the authentication server.

Authentication occurs in the following steps:

1. **EAPoL Start:** The supplicant initiates an authentication request to the AP/controller.

2. **EAPoL Request Identity:** The authenticator requests the supplicant to supply credentials to access the network.

3. **EAP Identity Response:** The supplicant supplies its identity to the authenticator. The authenticator (the AP/wireless controller) forwards the identity to the authentication server (ISE).

4. **EAP Request-EAP Type:** The authentication server responds with an EAP type (an EAP method) that it requests the supplicant to use. This is returned to the authenticator using RADIUS AV pairs.

5. **EAP Response-EAP Type:** The supplicant returns confirmation of the EAP method that it will use to communicate with the authentication server.

6. **EAP Success:** The authentication server responds with an EAP Success message that communication has been established and the client may now be authenticated.

This process is illustrated in Figure 15-2.

Figure 15-2 illustrates the overall EAP authentication process; however, this is somewhat generic. In reality, many different implementations of EAP exist (known as EAP methods). The EAP method depends on the software and configuration of the supplicant, as well as which methods are supported by the network. While the overall frameworks of the various EAP methods are similar, implementations of EAP offer different security characteristics that may be required by an organization, such as the use of a public key infrastructure (PKI) and certificates on a supplicant rather than relying on only username and passwords.

15

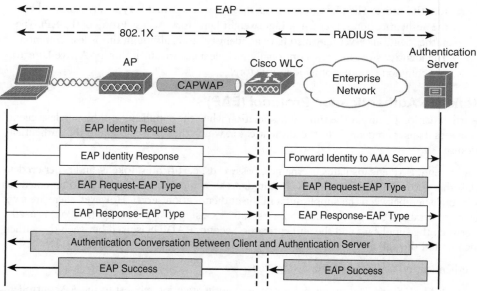

Figure 15-2 *The EAP Authentication Process*

Common EAP types generally fall into one of three classes: inner methods, tunnel methods, and certificate-based methods. These are described as follows:

■ **Inner methods:** Inner methods involve the direct authentication of the user credentials between a supplicant and an authentication server. Common EAP inner methods include the following:

■ **EAP-MSCHAPv2:** Microsoft Challenge-Handshake Authentication Protocol version 2 is one of the most popular inner methods in use today. MSCHAPv2 allows for simple transmission of username and password from a supplicant to the RADIUS server.

■ **EAP-GTC:** EAP Generic Token Card is a method that was created by Cisco as an alternative to MSCHAPv2. It allows integration with a wide variety of identity stores, including one-time password (OTP) token servers, LDAP, and others.

■ **EAP-TLS:** EAP Transport Layer Security (TLS) is an X.509 certificate-based mechanism that employs both client-side and server-side certificates and requires a PKI.

■ **Tunnel methods:** Tunnel methods are typically employed in conjunction with an inner-EAP method, such as EAP-MSCHAPv2. Due to their weaker security, inner methods are often encrypted inside an EAP tunnel to give them an added level of protection (effectively, two tiers of protection). With tunneled EAP methods, authentication occurs in a nested fashion. First, the outer authentication (outside the TLS tunnel) is established, and then inner authentication occurs (inside the TLS tunnel).

Common EAP tunnel methods include the following:

- **PEAP (Protected EAP):** Jointly developed by Cisco, Microsoft, and RSA, PEAP is a tunneled method that requires a certificate on the server but not on the client. PEAP forms an encrypted TLS tunnel between the client and server similar to how an SSL tunnel is used between a browser and a secure website. Once the PEAP tunnel is established, an inner method such as EAP-MSCHAPv2 is used to authenticate the client.

- **EAP-FAST (Flexible Authentication via Secure Tunnels):** EAP-FAST was developed by Cisco and is similar to PEAP in the way it uses a secure TLS tunnel between client and server (however, the server-side certificate is optional with EAP-FAST). The main advantage of EAP-FAST is in how it provisions Protected Access Credentials (PACs) on the client. The PAC can be thought of as a secure token/cookie on the client that validates that it has been correctly authenticated. The benefit of a trusted client-side PAC is that fast roaming between APs can be accomplished, making it a good choice for wireless deployments that use real-time applications.

EAP-FAST occurs in a sequence of three phases:

- **Phase 0:** The PAC is generated or provisioned on the client.

- **Phase 1:** After the supplicant and authentication server have authenticated each other, they negotiate a Transport Layer Security (TLS) tunnel.

- **Phase 2:** The end user can then be authenticated through the TLS tunnel for additional security.

The PAC is made up of three parts:

- **PAC key:** A 32-octet key used to establish the tunnel

- **PAC-Opaque:** A variable-length field that contains the user credentials

- **PAC-Info:** A variable-length field used to pass information about the PAC issuer, PAC key lifetime, and so on

Like other EAP-based methods, a RADIUS server is required. However, the RADIUS server must also be configured for EAP-FAST to be able to generate PACs for each user.

- **Certificated-based EAP methods:** A third EAP class involves certificate-based methods, such as EAP-TLS. These methods offer exceptional security because they require a certificate on both the client and authentication server. While EAP-TLS is an inner method, it rarely needs to be tunneled with PEAP or EAP-FAST due to its inherent security using client and server-side X.509 certificates. Due to its extra overhead requiring a public key infrastructure (PKI), EAP-TLS is not as common as the other methods.

Table 15-2 summarizes the common EAP methods used in wireless networks.

Table 15-2 A Summary of Common EAP Methods

	Tunnel Method	Inner Method	X.509 Certificate Requirements
EAP-PEAP (Protected EAP)	Yes	No	Server-side certificate only
EAP-FAST (Flexible Authentication via Secure Tunnels)	Yes	No	Server-side certificate only (optional)
EAP-GTC (Generic Token Card)	No	Yes	N/A
EAP-MSCHAPv2	No	Yes	N/A
EAP-TLS (Transport Layer Security)	No	Yes	Client- and server-side X.509 certificates required

Implementing Client Security on the Wireless Controller and ISE

To implement wireless security for wireless clients, both the controller (the authenticator) and the authentication server (ISE) infrastructure need to be correctly implemented.

The steps to implement client authentication are as follows:

Step 1. Identify the RADIUS server that will be used on the controller. In AireOS controllers, navigate to **Security > AAA > RADIUS > Authentication**. Here, configure the correct IP address and shared secret that is used with the authentication sever. Figure 15-3 illustrates the configuration of a RADIUS server. The RADIUS server being connected to here is an ISE Policy Services Node (PSN).

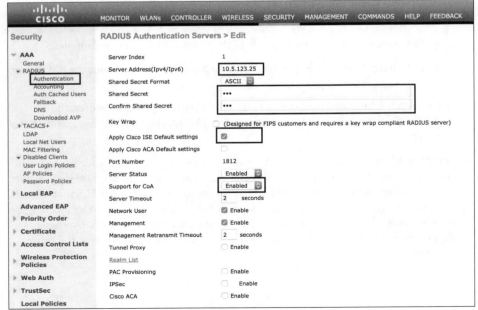

Figure 15-3 *Configuring a RADIUS Authentication Server*

When configuring the RADIUS server, keep in mind that **Support for CoA** (Change of Authority) should be enabled. CoA is an important feature that allows ISE to send network configuration changes to the controller.

In addition, ensure that the **Apply Cisco ISE Default Settings** option is selected, as this will ensure that RADIUS Accounting is also enabled—a required feature for client profiling. If this feature is not used, a RADIUS account should be configured, as this is used to pass attributes back to the controller from ISE. Note that it is possible to configure multiple RADIUS authentication and accounting servers for different purposes—something that will be useful when implementing web authentication for guest and BYOD.

Once the RADIUS Authentication and Accounting servers are configured, be sure to set the **Auth Called Station ID Type** to a value that will send the MAC address of the client in the Calling-Station-Id field of the RADIUS Request packet (it is set to AP MAC Address:SSID in Figure 15-4). This is an important implementation step because it allows profiling of non-802.1X clients and ensures that ISE is able to add the endpoint to the database and associate other profile data based on its MAC address.

Figure 15-4   *Setting the Auth Called Station ID Type*

Step 2.   Navigate to the WLAN where you wish to implement client authentication. This can be done in the **WLANs > WLAN ID > Security > Layer 2** menu. Figure 15-5 illustrates this step.

As shown in Figure 15-5, the key security features to configure are the **Layer 2 Security** and **Security Type** options. **Layer 2 Security** should be set to **WPA2+WPA3** (this is the default) and **Security Type** should be set to **Enterprise** (this is also the default; the other option here is **Personal**, which will change the security profile to use pre-shared keys). The **Enterprise** option ensures that 802.1X is used between the client and the controller.

Correct configuration of the security parameters can be confirmed by clicking the **General** tab under the **Security** menu. Note that the security policies of WPA2 and 802.1X have been correctly implemented, as shown in Figure 15-6.

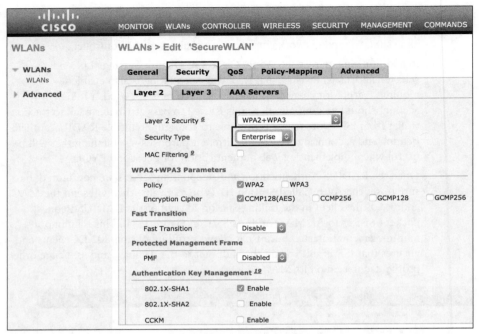

Figure 15-5 *Configuration of the WLAN Security Features*

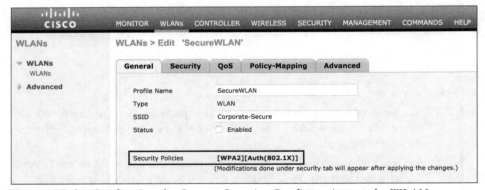

Figure 15-6 *Confirming the Correct Security Configuration on the WLAN*

IOS-XE controllers (such as the Catalyst 9800) can be configured in a similar way by navigating to the **Configuration > AAA** menu. From here, there are two options: (1) directly configure the RADIUS server configuration and (2) launch the **AAA Wizard** option. Figure 15-7 illustrates what is seen after launching the AAA Wizard.

15

Figure 15-7 *Configuring the RADIUS Server Through the AAA Wizard in IOS-XE*

Once the RADIUS server has been defined, click **Next**. On the **Server Group Association** screen, select the **dot1x** type pull-down option, as shown in Figure 15-8.

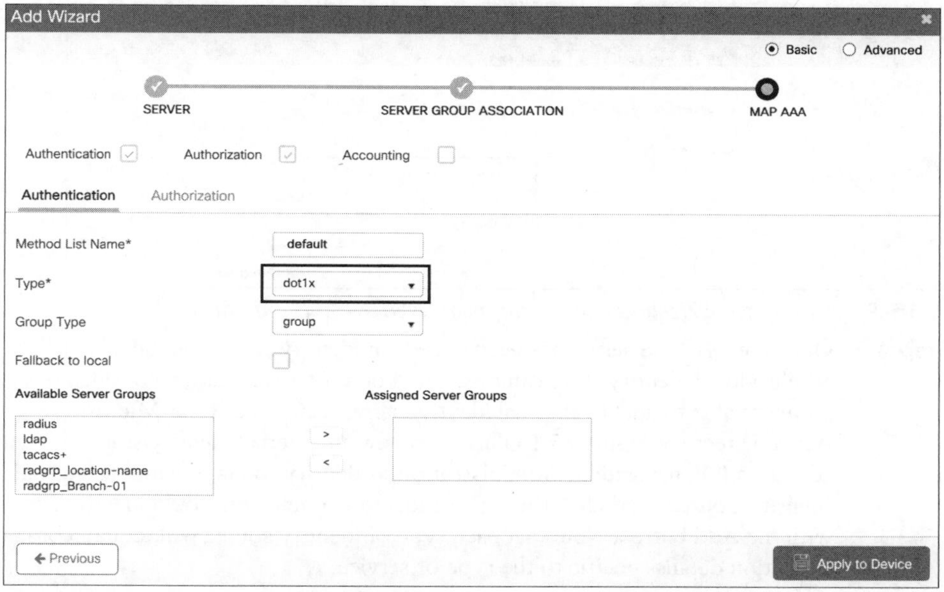

Figure 15-8 *Configuring the Controller to Use a RADIUS for Client Authentication (802.1X)*

The last step is to assign the correct server to **Assigned Server Groups**. The purpose of this step is to allow different RADIUS servers to be used for different purposes, such as wireless client 802.1X authentication versus management login authentication services (discussed in more detail in Chapter 17, "Device Hardening").

Step 3. On the ISE server, the wireless controller must be added as a network device (the controller is the authenticator). Navigate to the **Administration > Network Resources > Network Devices** menu and click **+Add**. Figure 15-9 shows how to add a wireless controller as a RADIUS authenticator (ensure the same shared secret that was configured in the controller is reflected here).

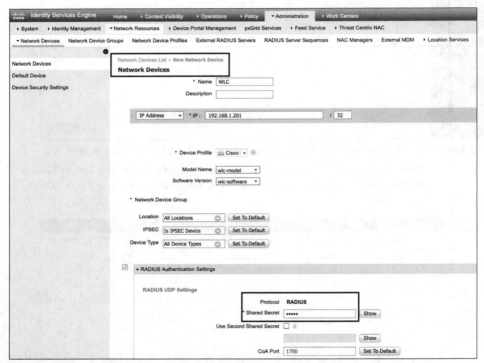

Figure 15-9 *Adding the Wireless Controller as a RADIUS Authenticator*

Step 4. Once the RADIUS server has been added, an identity store must be added. While a local identity store can be created on ISE, it is generally considered more scalable to add an external identity store, such as LDAP or Microsoft Active Directory. Figure 15-10 illustrates how an external identity store may be added. In ISE, navigate to **Administration > Identity Management > External Identity Sources** and click the type of identity source you would like to add with the **Add** button. Note that each type of identity source will require configuration details specific to the type of service.

Step 5. The final step is to configure the appropriate authentication rules. In ISE, this is done with a policy set, found in the **Policy > Policy Sets** menu. Policy sets provide a way to create logical policy rules and conditions for any kind of authentication method. Figure 15-11 illustrates the creation of a policy to allow network access for authenticated users.

Figure 15-10   *Adding an External Identity Store (Active Directory in This Case) to ISE*

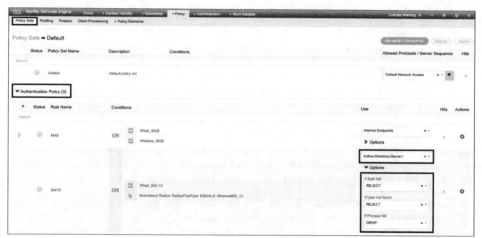

Figure 15-11   *The Default Policy Set to Allow Authenticated Users Access to the Network*

In ISE, policy sets function much like access control lists (ACLs)—they are configured to first match certain conditions and then take an action based on the result. In Figure 15-11, the default policy set condition is configured to match any client trying to authenticate via either MAC Authentication Bypass (MAB) or 802.1X, for both wired and wireless clients. In other words, any client trying to authenticate by one of these means will match the policy statement so that an action can be taken. The action ISE takes is to first confirm the identity of the user by examining one of the available identity sources. In the example in Figure 15-11, the **Active-Directory-Server1** identity source is chosen to authenticate the credentials of the user (note that it is also possible to choose all available identity sources with the **All_User_ID_Stores** option).

If the authentication is successful, an action can be taken, such as accepting the user on the network. If the user is not identified, the default action (shown in Figure 15-11) is to reject the unknown user or just drop the request if the connection to the back-end identity source fails. It is also possible for policy sets to be very granular, both in the conditions that match the rule and in the policy action taken. For example, an option can be added to the policy set condition to look for specific SSIDs or other options.

Implementing Client Profiling

While EAP-based authentication allows the network to validate the user's credentials, it does not inspect the type of device the client is joining from, nor does it have any knowledge of the device's behavior—details that could lead to a policy for the device once network access has been granted. In light of this, once authentication has occurred, the next step is to collect as much information as possible about the device and to use this to further enhance the security policy, such as determining the level of access the client should be given, what VLAN the client should be assigned to, or what QoS profile the client should use. For example, profiling may include device hardware identification, such as validating if it is an Apple iOS device, a Samsung Galaxy device, and so on.

Once a device has been profiled, how are network policy decisions implemented to influence security for the device as well as the wider network? Consider an example where a user with valid credentials attempts to use the credentials on an IoT device the user brought from home. While the IoT device may have a valid username and password from the user, the device itself may be violating the company security policy. In this case, once the IoT device has been profiled and correctly identified by the infrastructure, a policy rule could reject the device, even if the credentials are valid. Consider another situation where a corporate policy has been issued against using certain types of mobile devices on the corporate network. A user may bring a non-standard device from home and use private credentials on this device, thinking this is totally valid. Instead of the device being rejected completely, a policy may be implemented that moves this device to an Internet-facing isolated VLAN where it only has access to the Internet, and access to the corporate network is restricted.

The following section describes the function of client profiling in a wireless LAN and how it can be implemented on both the wireless controller and ISE.

Wireless Client Profiling Principles

Cisco wireless controllers support device sensor functionality, allowing them to become aware of physical and software characteristics of the client device. To do this, the controller collects important information about the device so it can then either make a local policy decision or send the collected information via RADIUS to an ISE server where a policy decision can be made centrally.

On the controller, profiling of devices is based on examining a variety of parameters, including its MAC OUI, DHCP option fields, and application-layer characteristics, such as HTTP headers. Profiling and enforcement of the ensuing policy is done on a per-device basis.

Profiling on the controller can be based on any of the following:

- Device type (MAC OUI), which helps identify the device as a Windows machine, smartphone, iPad, iPhone, Android, and so on.

- Username/password.

- DHCP option fields. This feature allows the controller to locally capture DHCP client attributes and send them to ISE via RADIUS Accounting Updates.

- HTTP fields (for example, the HTTP User Agent field).

- Time of the day, based on what time of the day the endpoint is allowed on the network.

In addition, ISE is able to profile based on additional contextual information from external sources, including the following:

- Role of the user, such as which group the user belongs to (from LDAP or Active Directory)

- NMAP scan information

- NetFlow scans learned from Stealthwatch

- Location context, based on the AP group to which the endpoint is connected

After the client is profiled, policy can be enforced based on the following:

- VLAN assignment

- QoS profile (precious metal profile)

- ACLs

- AVC policy

- Time of day usage

- Session timeout value

Figure 15-12 illustrates the process by which a client is profiled and policy is enforced.

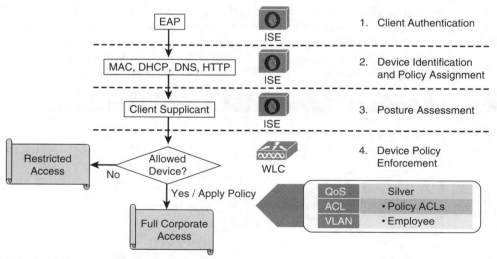

 Figure 15-12 *Client Profiling Process*

As illustrated in Figure 15-12, the client-profiling process uses the following steps:

1. The client authenticates to the network using 802.1X / EAP.

2. The client device is profiled by the controller and AP. The controller can either perform local policy enforcement or forward the information to ISE in RADIUS attributes for central enforcement.

3. If ISE is used, it performs posture assessment of the client. This encompasses much more than the controller can accomplish alone. For example, ISE is able to consolidate information for other external sources, such as Stealthwatch (using PxGrid), NMAP scans, and more. Through the multiple lenses, ISE is able to do a holistic posture assessment of the client with greater context and make a policy decision.

4. In the final stage, policy changes are implemented by the controller (either by ISE or by the controller itself). If the device is permitted on the network, it may be assigned any combination of a VLAN assignment, device-specific ACLs, a QoS profile, a time-of-day usage policy, or an AVC policy. If the device is rejected, access to the network is completely restricted.

Configuring Local Client Profiling on the Wireless Controller

On an AireOS wireless LAN controller, client profiling is configured through the following steps:

1. Enable local client profiling on the WLAN.

2. Configure the profiling policy.

3. Enable the profiling policy on the WLAN.

Figure 15-13 illustrates how client profiling is enabled in the AireOS controller.

Step 1. Navigate to **WLANs > Advanced** and enable the two options under **Local Client Profiling**. Note that the two options are **DHCP Profiling** and **HTTP Profiling**. Enabling these features allows the controller to examine the DHCP option fields and HTTP headers to further refine the client profiling. Notice on the same configuration menu there is an option for **Radius Client Profiling**. This is only used in conjunction with ISE when the profiling is handled centrally.

Figure 15-13 *Enabling Local Client Profiling on the WLAN*

Step 2.   In the second step, a policy is created. This is done by navigating to the **Security > Local Policies** menu. In the example shown in Figure 15-14, a policy is created to identify traffic from video game consoles using the **Device Type** drop-down menu. In this example, two policy identifiers are added—one for SonyPS4 and another for NintendoWII.

With the match criteria enabled, the next step is to define how the controller will handle these clients. The same menu shown in Figure 15-14 lists various options, including assigning ACLs, a VLAN ID, or a QoS profile for matching clients. In this case, the controller will map the clients to VLAN 40 as traffic exits the controller, and traffic will be assigned to the Silver (best effort) QoS class. There are also other options, such as time of day when the policy is active.

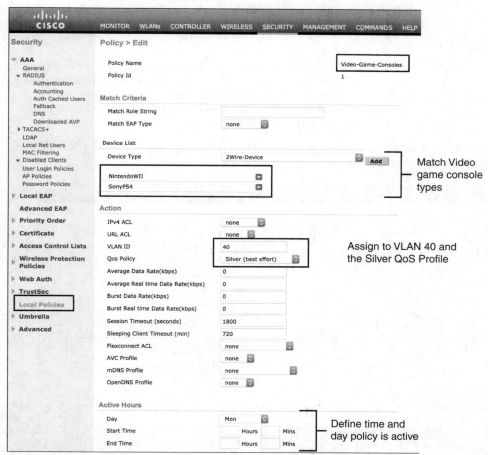

Figure 15-14   *Configuring the Client Profiling Policy*

Step 3.   The final step is to add the newly created policy to the correct WLAN. As shown in Figure 15-15, this can be done on the **WLANs > Policy-Mapping** menu.

15

Here, the policy for Video-Game-Consoles that was just created is added to the correct WLAN.

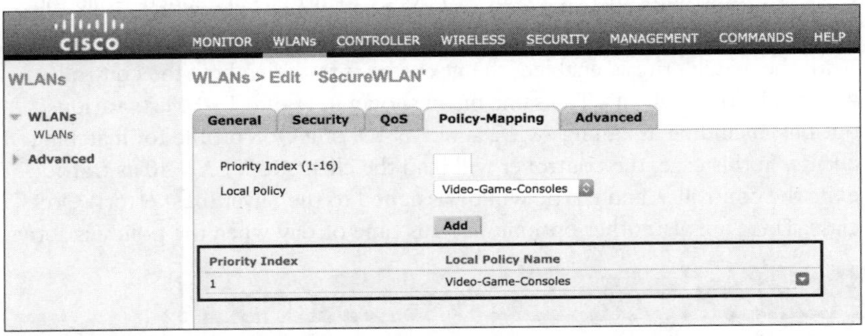

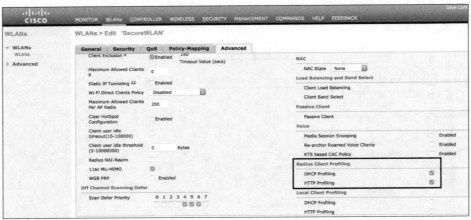

Figure 15-15 *Attaching the Profiling Policy to the WLAN*

The example shown in Figure 15-15 demonstrates how the controller can be used to profile a client locally; however, using ISE for central profiling opens up many new profiling dimensions that a controller on its own does not have. For example, using ISE, it is possible to combine external probe data from multiple sources, including SNMP traps, DNS probes, NetFlow probes, Network Scan probes (NMAP), and others.

To enable ISE profiling, ensure that the **Local Client Profiling** options are disabled and that **Radius Client Profiling** is enabled on the controller (as shown in Figure 15-16).

Figure 15-16 *Configuring the Controller for RADIUS-Based Client Profiling Using ISE*

> **NOTE**   As of AireOS 8.7.x, the WLC sensor is limited to sending only DHCP Option 12 (host-name) and Option 60 (dhcp-class-identifier) to ISE. Therefore, if additional DHCP attributes are required to more fully profile endpoints, it is recommended to use a DHCP probe to capture all required options. The device sensor features in Cisco IOS-based devices do not have this same limitation.

Implementing BYOD and Guest

Bring Your Own Device (BYOD) and guest are popular use cases for wireless networks. When you stop by your favorite coffee shop and open your laptop, you likely expect to be given free wireless access after accepting the disclaimer on the coffee shop's guest portal and be granted unfettered access to the Internet. This service is almost ubiquitous in retail, restaurants, and even in public areas of well-connected cities. While guest deployments are often used in public hotspots, they are also widely deployed by companies to support temporary guests and contractors.

BYOD refers to users who bring their own devices from home. At first, BYOD devices are generally considered untrusted and are given limited network access until they are properly onboarded through a guest portal and certain security measures are implemented, at which point the devices are considered trusted and are given wider network access. From the perspective of the wireless infrastructure, BYOD is simply a method of onboarding untrusted devices through a guest WLAN, allowing them to self-register on a guest portal such as ISE, and then implementing the correct security controls and software on the client.

This section examines how wireless controllers and ISE work together to onboard clients through a guest portal and how supplicants and certificates can be deployed to clients as they join the wireless network.

Implementing BYOD and Guest

Guest wireless connectivity involves providing limited network access privileges to an unknown or untrusted user. One important consideration is to decide what type of security will be implemented for the guest (and by extension the BYOD) network. Clearly, different types of authentication are possible. An EAP/802.1X method may be chosen, but this has a drawback that each user will need to request an account and manually deploy a supplicant before even being connected to the WLAN—something that may not be attractive to an IT department that is trying to simplify and streamline the whole process of supporting devices brought from home.

While an SSID using 802.1X authentication for clients is much more secure than an open SSID (a WLAN without security), an open SSID has the advantage that it can be used in conjunction with other security mechanisms, such as a guest portal or VPN. For BYOD users, the open SSID is typically only used during the initial onboarding process, after which the client is moved to a protected SSID.

NOTE   In some cases, a pre-shared key (PSK) is used for guest networks. This is common at large conferences where all attendees are given the same PSK for the wireless network. Obviously, this doesn't offer much security because everyone with the same encryption key could easily decrypt anyone else's traffic. However, the PSK approach does have the benefit of keeping other devices off the network and exhausting DHCP resources.

One of the most common techniques to handle wireless guests, as well as onboard BYOD clients, is through the use of a guest portal. Using this approach, when users connect to the network, they are immediately redirected to a secure captive portal that asks them to agree to the terms and conditions of use of the network, called the Acceptable Use Policy (AUP), and in some cases, to enter or set up new credentials. Offering free access in this way accomplishes the following benefits for companies:

- Drives customer loyalty and dwell time at the location

- Allows the vendor to be legally compliant through the use of a disclaimer that the user must accept

- Allows the vendor to engage with visitors

The key design consideration when deploying BYOD is to decide how the onboarding guest portal and authentication will be handled. From a high-level perspective, there are two common methods:

- Local web authentication (LWA)

- Central web authentication (CWA)

The following sections examine these two redirection methods.

Local Web Authentication (LWA) with the Wireless Controller

LWA is a guest mechanism that allows a client to be redirected to a web authentication portal directly from the wireless controller. Specifically, LWA requires the controller to (1) enforce ACL match criteria that identify traffic sent to a guest portal and (2) redirect users to the guest portal URL without relying on a central server for this function (which is the main difference with CWA). This doesn't imply that the guest portal must actually be on the controller; rather, the redirect to the guest portal must be on the controller (with LWA the portal can be either on the controller itself or another server).

With LWA, when a BYOD client connects to the WLAN, the controller intercepts the connection and redirects the client's first web URL to either an internal or external portal where the user can be asked either to enter authentication credentials or to accept the AUP. The controller then captures the credentials and authenticates the client either using a local user database or through an external RADIUS server. In the case of a guest user, an external server such as ISE is required because the portal provides options for device registration and self-provisioning.

Note that with LWA, the web portal can reside either directly on the controller itself or on another remote server. As mentioned earlier, the thing that makes LWA "local" is the handling of the ACL that matches traffic to send to the portal and the URL redirect, not the location of the portal.

LWA works as follows:

1. The user is associated with an open SSID that uses web authentication or an AUP.

2. The user opens a browser or is automatically redirected by a pre-WebAuth ACL on the controller. The pre-WebAuth ACL generally matches any web traffic coming from the client's web browser and also permits DNS and DHCP access for the client.

3. When the ACL is matched, the controller redirects the client to either an internal or an external guest portal.

4. The user is asked to enter authentication credentials on the portal or to accept the AUP (or both). The guest portal redirects the user back to the controller, along with the provided credentials (if an external portal is used).

5. The controller authenticates a guest user either through a local database or via RADIUS or LDAP to an authentication server.

6. The controller redirects the client back to the original URL that was entered in the web browser.

Figure 15-17 illustrates LWA with the controller providing the web authentication portal locally (an external guest portal may also be used with LWA, but this is not shown in Figure 15-17).

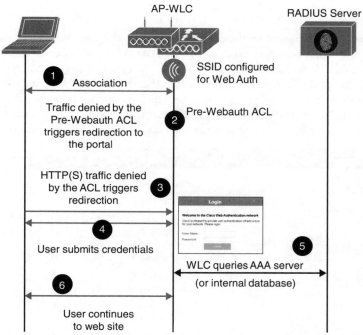

Figure 15-17 *The LWA Redirect and Authentication Process*

To configure LWA on an AireOS controller, use the following steps:

Step 1. Create an Open SSID WLAN that will be used for BYOD clients. This WLAN will employ specific ACLs on the controller that trigger URL redirection of the client toward the authentication portal (which can either be on the controller or a remote portal). In the following example, a WLAN called BYOD has been created.

Step 2. In the next step, Layer 2 security should be set to **None**. This means no 802.1X or PSK will be used on this WLAN. The reason is that BYOD requires open access to the SSID so the client can be onboarded. Figure 15-18 illustrates the Layer 2 security screen. This screen is accessible from **WLAN > Security > Layer 2**.

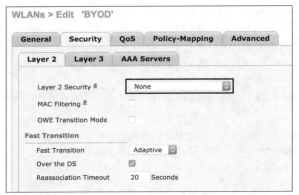

Figure 15-18   *Configuring Layer 2 Security on the LWA BYOD WLAN*

Step 3.   An ACL must be configured on the controller to trigger the URL redirect. With URL redirect, the ACL is designed to trigger when a connection is denied (typically the implicit **deny** statement at the end of the ACL). Other **permit** criteria in the ACL are used to allow DNS and DHCP traffic between the client and network services without causing the client to be redirected to the authentication or AUP portal. Figure 15-19 illustrates an ACL that will be used to redirect traffic. Take note of the **deny** statement at the end that will be used for redirection.

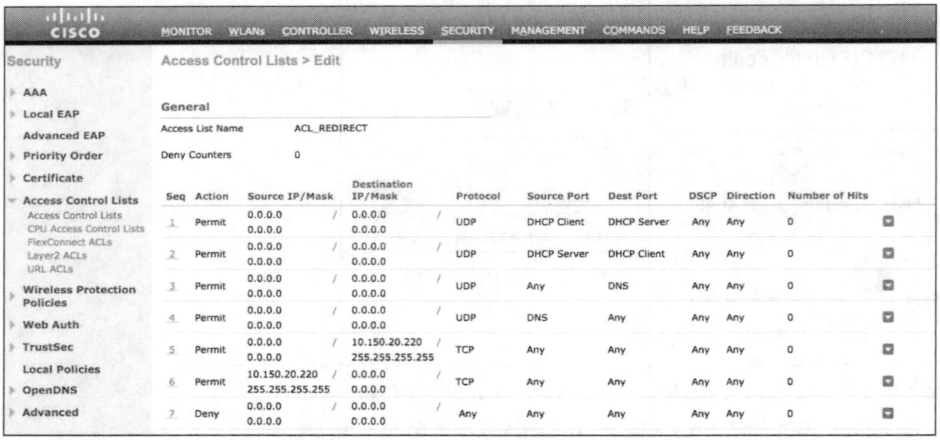

Seq	Action	Source IP/Mask	Destination IP/Mask	Protocol	Source Port	Dest Port	DSCP	Direction	Number of Hits	
1	Permit	0.0.0.0 / 0.0.0.0	0.0.0.0 / 0.0.0.0	UDP	DHCP Client	DHCP Server	Any	Any	0	▾
2	Permit	0.0.0.0 / 0.0.0.0	0.0.0.0 / 0.0.0.0	UDP	DHCP Server	DHCP Client	Any	Any	0	▾
3	Permit	0.0.0.0 / 0.0.0.0	0.0.0.0 / 0.0.0.0	UDP	Any	DNS	Any	Any	0	▾
4	Permit	0.0.0.0 / 0.0.0.0	0.0.0.0 / 0.0.0.0	UDP	DNS	Any	Any	Any	0	▾
5	Permit	0.0.0.0 / 0.0.0.0	10.150.20.220 / 255.255.255.255	TCP	Any	Any	Any	Any	0	▾
6	Permit	10.150.20.220 / 255.255.255.255	0.0.0.0 / 0.0.0.0	TCP	Any	Any	Any	Any	0	▾
7	Deny	0.0.0.0 / 0.0.0.0	0.0.0.0 / 0.0.0.0	Any	Any	Any	Any	Any	0	▾

General — Access List Name: ACL_REDIRECT — Deny Counters: 0

Figure 15-19   *Configuring ACL That Will Be Used to Redirect Clients to the Authentication Portal*

NOTE   One difference to be aware of between AireOS and IOS-XE controllers (such as the Catalyst 9800) is that IOS-XE will trigger the URL redirect based on matching a **permit** statement, whereas AireOS controllers trigger the URL redirect based on matching a **deny** statement.

Step 4.   In this step, the L3 security rules are implemented. Because the redirect happens at Layer 3, this is where the ACL and redirect information must be configured. Under **WLANs > Security > Layer 3**, configure the **Layer 3 Security** policy to be **Web Policy**. This is illustrated in Figure 15-20.

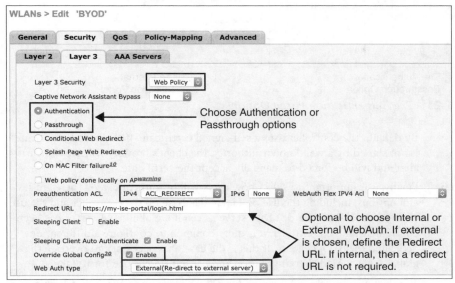

Figure 15-20   *Configuring Layer 3 Security on the LWA BYOD WLAN*

Notice in Figure 15-20, there is a pull-down menu to select the **Preauthentication ACL**. This is the security ACL defined in Step 3. As soon as a client web connection triggers the deny statement matching the ACL, the client will be redirected to the authentication portal.

It is also important to decide where the BYOD portal will be located. LWA supports both an internal portal on the controller itself or an external portal such as ISE. Both have their pros and cons. Implementing LWA using the controller's internal portal is quick, cheap, and easy to deploy, but it's less flexible and less scalable than an external portal such as ISE. Under the **Web Auth type** pull-down shown in Figure 15-20, you can select either **Internal** (which is the default) or **External**. If an external server is chosen, the **Redirect URL** option must be configured. In this example, an external web portal with the URL https://my-ise-portal/login.html is being used.

Also, note there are several portal configuration options available on this menu. The **Authentication** option will present an authentication request to the client, whereas **Passthrough** will simply ask the user to click **Accept** and accept the AUP before proceeding.

Figure 15-21 illustrates how the redirect portal differs for both the **Authentication** and **Passthrough** options.

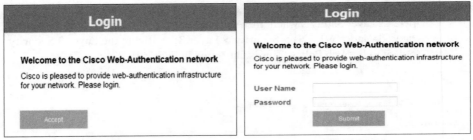

The Authentication
Passthrough Option

The Internal
Authentication Portal

Figure 15-21 *The Authentication Portal Options*

By default, the controller uses a self-signed certificate. If the portal certificate is not signed by a well-known authority, the client's browser will see a security alert and will be forced to manually accept the certificate.

Step 5.   Finally, it is important to select how users will be authenticated. There are several options, including the use of a local database on the controller and the use of an external RADIUS or LDAP server. Even if a global AAA server has been configured on the controller, it is quite common to configure a different one dedicated for BYOD clients. If this is the case, it is necessary to override the global AAA RADIUS configuration and use a different one for BYOD.

To select an alternate AAA server for BYOD, navigate to **WLANs > Security > AAA Servers** and select the RADIUS server that will be used for BYOD. Figure 15-22 illustrates this configuration step.

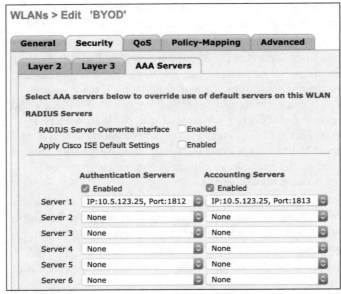

Figure 15-22 *Configuring the AAA Override Settings*

If a dedicated RADIUS server is used for BYOD, the WLAN must be configured to override usage of the global RADIUS server. This is done by navigating to **WLANs > Advanced** and selecting **Allow AAA Override**.

Local Web Authentication on an IOS-XE Controller

Configuration of LWA on an IOS-XE controller is very similar to AireOS, with a few exceptions. To begin configuration, navigate to **Configuration > Security > Web Auth**. Once the **Web Auth Parameter Map** is created, it can be configured with similar features that are used in AireOS, as shown in Figure 15-23.

One interesting difference to be aware of is that the **passthrough** option (where the user only has to accept the AUP) is called **Consent** on the IOS-XE controller. By clicking on the **Advanced** tab, other features, such as the redirect URL and the portal IP address, can be configured.

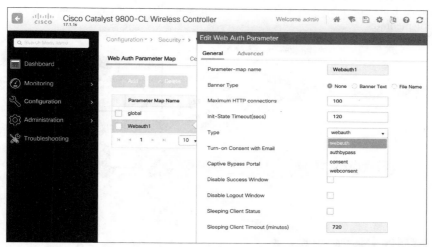

Figure 15-23   *Configuring LWA on an IOS-XE Controller*

Local Web Authentication with an Anchor Controller

An approach commonly used in conjunction with guest and BYOD is the use of anchor controllers. Anchor controllers were first developed to support client roaming between controllers through the use of an inter-controller L2 tunnel that bridges the client's 802.11 traffic back to the initial pre-roam controller. This allows IP continuity between controllers instead of forcing a client to obtain a new IP address from DHCP each time it roams to an AP managed by a different controller. With inter-controller tunnels, if a client roams to an AP connected to a different controller, the Layer 2 tunnel between the two controllers makes it appear as if the client is still Layer 3 connected to the first controller (the anchor controller), while Layer 2 is being serviced by the new controller (the foreign controller). In other words, the tunnel stretches the L2 domain from the anchor to the foreign controller.

Over time, this became an elegant way to isolate all guest traffic. Instead of handling each guest user independently on each controller, through the use of an anchor it became possible to funnel all guest or BYOD traffic over the inter-controller Ethernet over IP (EoIP) or

CAPWAP tunnels into a centrally located guest anchor. Here, they could be redirected to the guest portal by a single controller, and once allowed onto the network traffic could be forwarded through a protected DMZ interface on a central firewall and then sent to the Internet, ensuring these users were isolated from all corporate traffic.

As discussed, anchors have two key components: *foreign* and *anchor* controllers. When a guest or BYOD user connects to a wireless network, the local controller is called the foreign controller, and the one with the guest portal (or redirect to the guest portal) is called the anchor controller.

Figure 15-24 illustrates a general network framework using an anchor controller with LWA.

When anchor controllers for LWA are used, traffic from the users is tunneled through the foreign controller to the anchor, meaning the certificate and the authentication portal the client uses are on the anchor, not the foreign controller.

In LWA, redirection is triggered by the anchor, meaning the Layer 3 security redirection and pre-WebAuth ACL are configured there. On the foreign controller, only Layer 2 security features are implemented.

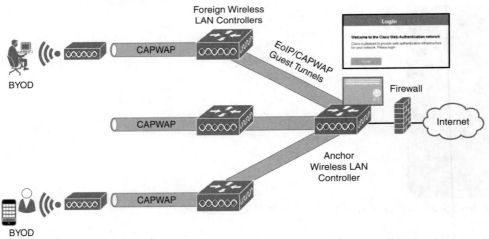

Figure 15-24 *Using an Anchor Controller for LWA*

Certificate Provisioning on the Wireless Controller

One thing that makes LWA somewhat complicated is the number of certificates involved. Regardless of whether you use an internal or an external portal, a certificate of some type is invariably required on the controller. Even if a central portal is used, the redirect function on the controller will use a certificate. In fact, if a central portal is used, two certificates will be used: one for the local controller redirect and the second on the portal.

Generally, self-signed certificates are less effective as they require manual acceptance of the certificate and an override of the client browser's native security policy. This can be especially problematic when a remote portal is used, as the client will be forced to manually accept two certificates.

On the AireOS controller, certificates for LWA can be found in the **Security > Web Auth > Certificate** menu. Here, the default self-signed certificate is identified, as well as an option to import a new trusted SSL certificate (see Figure 15-25).

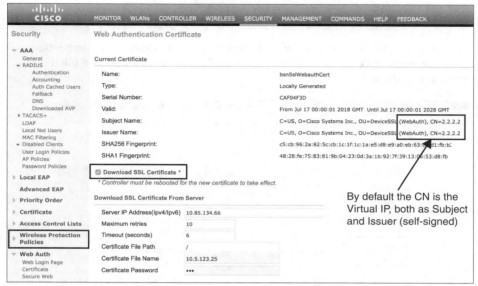

Figure 15-25 *Web Authentication Certificates in AireOS*

In IOS-XE, certificate management can be found in the **Configuration > Security > Web > Certificate** menu (see Figure 15-26).

Figure 15-26 *Web Authentication Certificates in IOS-XE*

LWA and Self-Registration

External centralized BYOD and guest portals offer many advantages over local portals on the controller. For example, ISE offers great flexibility in how portals can be used for different use cases. For example, ISE allows you to create the following types of use-case driven portals:

- Hotspot guest portals

- Self-registration (a self-registered guest portal is typically used for BYOD clients)

- Sponsored guest portals

A self-registration portal is an effective tool for BYOD deployments as it allows users to create their own accounts, which are then added to the ISE identity store.

In ISE, navigate to **Work Centers > Guest Access > Portals & Components** to configure one of these portal options. Figure 15-27 illustrates this configuration page in ISE (ISE version 2.6 is illustrated).

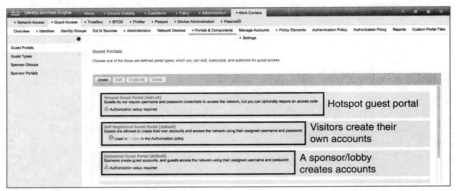

Figure 15-27   *ISE Guest Portal Options*

The ISE self-registration option allows granular configuration of how clients may register with the portal, the AUP they are presented with, and so on. Figure 15-28 illustrates this capability in ISE.

Figure 15-28   *Setting Up an ISE Self-Registration Portal*

Central Web Authentication (CWA) with ISE

Central web authentication is similar to LWA in many respects, with the main differences being that the URL redirect and pre-WebAuth ACLs are centrally located on ISE (instead of on the controller) and authentication instructions are communicated to the controller through

RADIUS. Thus, with CWA, there is no need for a local web-auth certificate on the controller. This obviously makes the controller deployment simpler in many ways but does require an external authentication server and portal. For example, if there are many controllers in a large organization, it is probably impractical to process the BYOD redirects and ACLs on each controller. Additionally, only one certificate is needed on the central web portal instead of two (in LWA there is one certificate on the controller and another on the authentication portal). On the other hand, CWA requires the deployment of a central authentication server, such as ISE.

The CWA process works as follows:

1. A client is associated with an open SSID that is using CWA. MAC filtering is enabled on the controller for this WLAN.

2. The controller forwards the MAC address of the client as an authentication request to ISE.

3. ISE is configured in such a way that even if it doesn't know the MAC address of the client, it sends a redirect URL and an ACL to the controller.

4. The user opens a browser. The URL request hits the ACL on the controller and is denied, triggering a URL redirect to ISE.

5. The user is redirected to the ISE BYOD/guest portal. The user is authenticated and/or is presented with the AUP.

6. ISE sends a RADIUS CoA (Change of Authorization—UDP port 1700) message to the controller, informing it that the user has correctly entered credentials. Other RADIUS attributes are optionally sent to control the client's behavior (such as ACLs).

7. The user is either redirected to the original URL or does this manually.

This process is illustrated in Figure 15-29.

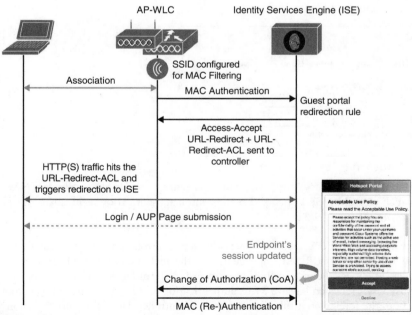

Figure 15-29 *How a Client Authenticates Through CWA Using ISE*

The key difference with LWA is that there is no preconfigured Layer 3 security policy on the controller—both the ACL and the web-preauth configuration are centralized on ISE and are communicated to the controller through RADIUS, with the final security policy being communicated to the controller with a CoA message from ISE.

The following are the steps to configure CWA on an AireOS controller:

Step 1.   On an AireOS controller, CWA is configured similarly to LWA but with some subtle differences. On the **WLANs > Security > Layer 2** menu, enable the **MAC Filtering** option, as shown in Figure 15-30.

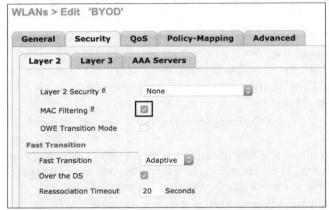

Figure 15-30   *Configuring Layer 2 Security for CWA*

Step 2.   Disable all Layer 3 security (as CWA relies on Layer 2 security, not Layer 3). This is shown in Figure 15-31.

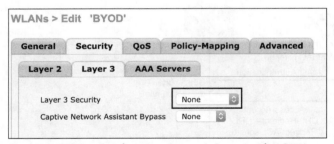

Figure 15-31   *Configuring Layer 3 Security for CWA*

Step 3.   Under the WLANs > Advanced menu, configure the NAC State to be ISE NAC, which will allow ISE to be used as the central authentication mechanism, as shown in Figure 15-32.

You might be wondering how CWA works if anchor/foreign controllers are used. Recall that for LWA, the ACL and redirect URL are implemented on the anchor controller, whereas the foreign controller simply has the responsibility to forward traffic at Layer 2 to the anchor. However, because CWA relies on Layer 2 MAC authentication (not Layer 3), the redirect from ISE must be sent to the foreign controller, not the anchor controller. The foreign controller, in turn, passes these attributes (the pre-WebAuth ACL and the redirect URL) to the anchor controller. At this point, the anchor takes over and manages the redirection to the ISE guest portal.

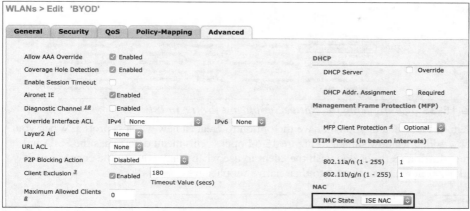

Figure 15-32 *Configuring the NAC State to Use ISE NAC*

It is important to keep in mind that LWA happens purely at Layer 3 whereas CWA happens at both Layer 2 and at Layer 3, with the Layer 3 portion performed by ISE. From a high-availability perspective, LWA is fairly limited, especially if the controller's own portal is used. On the other hand, because CWA uses ISE as its back-end system, it also inherits the natural resiliency capabilities of ISE clustering. For example, if a first ISE Policy Services Node (PSN) doesn't reply, another PSN can be used from the cluster.

LWA has its advantages as well, though. The local guest portal is free and comes included with the controller, whereas CWA requires investment in external portal.

Native Supplicant Provisioning Using ISE

Once a BYOD client has been authenticated through ISE, it is often necessary to provision a properly configured supplicant to the client so it can become part of a secure 802.1X WLAN. Client provisioning is a capability on ISE that allows users to download resources and configure agent profiles. You can configure agent profiles for Windows clients, MacOS clients, as well as native supplicant profiles for personal devices.

Generally speaking, client provisioning resources are downloaded to endpoints after the endpoint is authenticated and connects to the network. Client provisioning resources consist of compliance and posture agents for desktops and native supplicant profiles for phones and tablets. Examples of provisioning resources include Cisco AnyConnect and Advanced Malware Protection (AMP) software.

Native supplicant profiles can be created in ISE that enable users to bring their own devices and maintain an acceptable level of security. When the user signs in, ISE uses the profile you associated with the user's authorization requirements to choose the necessary supplicant provisioning wizard. The wizard then runs and sets up the user's personal device so it can access the network.

To configure a native supplicant profile in ISE, navigate to the **Policy > Policy Elements > Results > Client Provisioning > Resources** menu and choose **+Add**. When the menu opens, choose **Native Supplicant Profile**, as shown in Figure 15-33.

Figure 15-33 *Configuring the Native Supplicant Profile in ISE*

When this is selected, you will have the option to create a new wireless profile. When you click +Add, a window similar to Figure 15-34 opens. This menu determines the SSID and authentication methods you wish the client to use when connecting to the corporate network by programming them into their native supplicant.

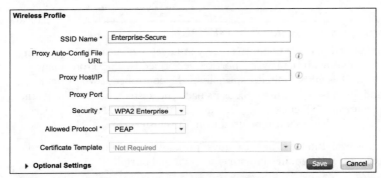

Figure 15-34 *Configuring the Native Supplicant Profile for a Wireless Network*

Summary

This chapter focused on the implementation of security in wireless LANs. In this chapter you have learned the following:

- Implementation options for various EAP types as well as differences between the inner and tunneled EAP methods

- How to implement 802.1X and EAP using a AAA server

- How to profile a client device using the controller and ISE

- How ACL, VLAN, and QoS policies can be implemented on a client after profiling

- Fundamentals of guest and BYOD wireless deployments

- The function of LWA and various implementation options on a wireless network, including certificate management

- The function of CWA and how it is implemented on a wireless network with ISE

- How a client can use the self-provisioning feature of ISE to deploy a native supplicant

References

For additional information, refer to these resources:

Which EAP Types Do You Need for Which Identity Projects? https://www.networkworld.com/article/2223672/which-eap-types-do-you-need-for-which-identity-projects.html

ISE Profiling Design Guide: https://community.cisco.com/t5/security-documents/ise-profiling-design-guide/ta-p/3739456#toc-hId--511047482

SE deployment guide for BYOD: https://community.cisco.com/t5/security-documents/cisco-ise-byod-prescriptive-deployment-guide/ta-p/3641867

Web Authentication on the WLAN Controller: http://www.cisco.com/c/en/us/support/docs/wireless-mobility/wlan-security/115951-web-auth-wlc-guide-00.html

Identity Services Engine Guest Portal Local Web Authentication Configuration Example: http://www.cisco.com/c/en/us/support/docs/security/identity-services-engine/116217-configure-ISE-00.html

Central Web Authentication on the WLC and ISE Configuration Example: http://www.cisco.com/c/en/us/support/docs/security/identity-services-engine/115732-central-web-auth-00.html

Central Web Authentication with FlexConnect APs on a WLC with ISE Configuration Example: http://www.cisco.com/c/en/us/support/docs/security/identity-services-engine/116087-configure-cwa-wlc-ise-00.html

Enterprise Mobility 8.5 Design Guide: https://www.cisco.com/c/en/us/td/docs/wireless/controller/8-5/Enterprise-Mobility-8-5-Design-Guide/Enterprise_Mobility_8-5_Deployment_Guide.html

Catalyst 9800 Technical References: https://www.cisco.com/c/en/us/support/wireless/catalyst-9800-series-wireless-controllers/products-technical-reference-list.html

Catalyst 9800 Configuration Examples and Tech Notes: https://www.cisco.com/c/en/us/support/wireless/catalyst-9800-series-wireless-controllers/products-configuration-examples-list.html

Exam Preparation Tasks

As mentioned in the section "How to Use This Book" in the Introduction, you have a few choices for exam preparation: the exercises here, Chapter 18, "Final Preparation," and the exam simulation questions in the Pearson Test Prep Software Online.

Review All Key Topics

Review the most important topics in this chapter, noted with the Key Topic icon in the outer margin of the page. Table 15-3 lists these key topics and the page numbers on which each is found.

Table 15-3   Key Topics for Chapter 15

Key Topic Element	Description	Page Number
Figure 15-1	The wireless network authentication framework	370
Figure 15-2	The EAP authentication process	372
Table 15-2	A summary of common EAP methods	374
Figure 15-12	Client profiling process	381
Figure 15-17	The LWA redirect and authentication process	387
Figure 15-29	How a client authenticates on a CWA portal using ISE	395

Define Key Terms

Define the following key terms from this chapter and check your answers in the glossary:

EAP (Extensible Authentication Protocol), IEEE 802.1X, Wi-Fi Protected Access (WPA), supplicant, authenticator, authentication server (AS), Lightweight Directory Access Protocol (LDAP), identity store, Remote Authentication Dial-In User Service (RADIUS), Protected EAP (PEAP), Flexible Authentication via Secure Tunnels (EAP-FAST), Transport Layer Security (EAP-TLS), Bring Your Own Device (BYOD), local web authentication (LWA), central web authentication (CWA), Acceptable Use Policy (AUP)

CHAPTER 16

Monitoring and Troubleshooting WLAN Components

This chapter discusses the following topics:

Using Reports on Cisco Prime Infrastructure and DNAC: This section discusses how reports are managed on Cisco PI and DNAC and how you can better understand both your network current state and projected future state by using reports.

Managing Alarms on Cisco Prime Infrastructure and DNAC: This section gives you the tools you need to manage alarms on Cisco PI and DNAC and also to manage rogue clients and APs.

Troubleshooting Client Connectivity: This section helps you troubleshoot client issues, by first providing a method and then pointing to the tools at your disposal to determine the root cause of the client problem.

Troubleshooting and Managing RF Interferences: This section expands troubleshooting to the RF side of your network and helps you assess the effect of non-802.11 interferers on your network efficiency.

This chapter covers the following ENWLSI exam topics:

- 7.1 Utilize reports on PI and Cisco DNAC
- 7.2 Manage alarms and rogues (APs and clients)
    - 7.2.a WLC
    - 7.2.b PI
    - 7.2.c Cisco DNAC
- 7.3 Manage RF interferers
    - 7.3.a WLC
    - 7.3.b PI
    - 7.3.c DNAC
- 7.4 Troubleshoot client connectivity
    - 7.4.a WLC
    - 7.4.b ISE
    - 7.4.c PI
    - 7.4.d DNAC

Once your network has been deployed, you enter what network lifecycle specialists call the monitoring phase. In this phase, you need to evaluate the state of your network to validate its performance levels as well as solve issues ranging from unexpected effects of device configuration changes to client troubleshooting tickets or physical changes (a new wall added, a broken cable, and so on). You also must predict the future changes needed to adapt your network to utilization trends.

These responsibilities cover a vast set of tasks and skills that the CCNP exam will test. An easy way to address these various functions is to separate them into two different functional requirements: monitoring the network, including evaluating its performances and understanding the main trends, and troubleshooting issues, including addressing client problems and the effect of interferers.

Therefore, this chapter starts with reports. On Cisco Prime Infrastructure (PI), reports are a great way of selectively observing key metrics relevant to your network operations. As reports can be run for long periods of time (lasting several months), they can also help you understand trends that, in turn, will help you predict the likely changes needed to your network as it continues to evolve. Moving from Cisco PI to DNAC offers an interesting perspective, because DNAC continuously produces reports, and you can select from their outcomes the elements that should attract your attention.

These elements can be thought of as alarms, which will be the object of our second section. DNAC surfaces elements that affect the performance of your networks, and you need to understand their various levels and categories. On Cisco PI, alarms also match different criticality levels. However, the severity is seen in the event itself, not in the way the event affects your network. Therefore, you may need to refine the way Cisco PI reports events, so as to only concentrate on impactful issues. Out of all issues, rogue APs and clients are central to your RF environment and will be covered in detail in this chapter.

The third section of this chapter focuses on troubleshooting client issues. This activity is, of course, central to your network management. The WLC, Cisco PI, and DNAC record all connection transactions and provide you with all the information you need to understand what affects your clients.

The last section of this chapter focuses on a particular type of issue—that caused by RF interferers. Although their effect on your cells is not very different from any other RF issue, the way they are detected depends on the type of APs you have deployed, so you need to know both the vocabulary and the management process.

"Do I Know This Already?" Quiz

The "Do I Know This Already?" quiz allows you to assess whether you should read this entire chapter thoroughly or jump to the "Exam Preparation Tasks" section. If you are in doubt about your answers to these questions or your own assessment of your knowledge of the topics, read the entire chapter. Table 16-1 lists the major headings in this chapter and their corresponding "Do I Know This Already?" quiz questions. You can find the answers in Appendix D, "Answers to the 'Do I Know This Already?' Quizzes and Review Questions."

Table 16-1 "Do I Know This Already?" Section-to-Question Mapping

Foundation Topics Section	Questions
Using Reports on Cisco Prime Infrastructure and DNAC	1, 2
Managing Alarms on Cisco Prime Infrastructure and DNAC	3, 4
Troubleshooting Client Connectivity	5, 6
Troubleshooting and Managing RF Interferences	7, 8

1. Which of the following best describes a trend report on Cisco Prime Infrastructure?

    a. A projection of AP loads for the next 6 months

    b. An aggregated report of your client protocols over the last 6 months

    c. A report on new AP types adopted by other Cisco customers

    d. A Machine Learning–produced analysis of your network performance

2. You want to configure a new report on your AP loads over the last week from DNAC. Where should you go to configure such report?

    a. Manage > Network > Reports

    b. Settings > Performances > Reports

    c. Dashboards > Health > Network Health

    d. Dashboards > Performance > Network

3. A network associate reports that a rogue was detected at the edge of your network, in one of your multitenant buildings. The associate asks what action should be taken. What would be the best answer?

    a. Set the rogue to Contain on the WLC or Cisco PI.

    b. Set the rogue to Smart Containment on DNAC.

    c. Immediately alert the building security.

    d. Do nothing for now and spend more time evaluating the rogue.

4. Why is a rogue client something you would want to get alarms about?

    a. Because the fact that one of your clients has decided to leave your network for an AP you do not manage is suspicious

    b. Because a rogue client is sending invalid frames to your network and is a likely sign of an ongoing attack

    c. Because a rogue client offers AP service, which is not normal when a wireless infrastructure is available

    d. Because a rogue client establishes direct communication with other clients, thus avoiding the infrastructure, which is suspicious

5. In what state will your WLC CLI report a client with a static IP address that just completed L2 authentication?

    a. Run

    b. Authcheck complete

    c. DHCP_fail

    d. DHCP_reqd

6. Under what conditions will a WLC report a Client Scan report for a client?

    a. If the client is Apple iOS or Samsung and sent an 802.11k report

    b. If the client is CCX and sent a Channel Scan report

    c. If you clicked the "test connectivity" button on the client 360 page

    d. If neighboring APs detected the client before or during the association phase

7. A junior associate wants to use the C9800 Packet Capture function to collect and analyze the 802.11 management frames sent by a particular client. What would you tell the junior associate?

    a. This is the correct function, and you can configure it to only report management frames (no data frames) to limit the capture volume.

    b. This is a waste of time, as clients do not send management frames (management is an AP function).

    c. This is the wrong function, as it will only capture wired frames.

    d. The Packet Capture function only collects management frames if the capture is set to "headers only."

8. Your network uses C1800 APs with Spectrum Intelligence. The network uses a C9800 WLC with default settings. A junior associate complains that the sporadic keepalives sent an inverted waveform by an industrial sensor are not reported. What can you tell the junior associate?

    a. SI does not detect inverted waveform signals.

    b. By default, CleanAir is not enabled on C9800.

    c. The C1800 will only report an interference if it affects the AP radio performance.

    d. CleanAir does not report keepalives because they are short-lived.

Foundation Topics

Using Reports on Cisco Prime Infrastructure and DNAC

The network lifecycle is often summarized using the acronym PPDIOO: Prepare, Plan, Design, Implement, Operate, Optimize (then back to Prepare, for the next phase). The logic behind this cyclic structure is that network deployments are never a one-time effort. A network is like a living organism. Once implemented, your network needs to be maintained, which includes several complementary tasks:

- **Monitoring the network:** This is done to verify that it performs at its expected level. This task includes observing load levels (client counts, interface counters, and other volume-related metrics).

- **Evaluating reported issues:** These issues can be surfaced by customers raising support tickets or by automated mechanisms triggering messages. A key element for this task is to determine if an issue relates to a temporal event, relates to a particular device or user, or if the issue is representative of a deep, more systematic aspect of your deployment.

■ **Troubleshooting discrete issues:** Temporal issues that pertain to a small number of devices need to be addressed to maintain the network quality. Usually, the remedy includes partial configuration changes (on the client or on the network).

■ **Preparing for network evolution:** Issues that appear to be systematic will require deeper changes to your network, including moving, removing, or adding APs, switches, controllers, and so on. At the same time, your client population is also likely to change over time with increased or decreased density in some areas, changes in the way people work or use the network, new devices, and new technologies (for example, Wi-Fi 6, then Wi-Fi 7, and so on.)

The "monitoring" and "preparing" elements are closely related. Although the presence of new technologies may easily be noticed (for example, by reading the specifications of new clients introduced in your network), its impact on your network is often difficult to evaluate. Similarly, changes in density of work behavior are sometimes associated with vast and visible organizational changes but are also often the result of multiple small changes that are hard to track. However, as a networking professional, it is your responsibility to foresee the need for deep network changes before they manifest as the result of massive network outages. Therefore, one of your first tasks after deployment is to take the pulse of your network at regular intervals. In most cases, this job means collecting information from your networking devices, measuring their activity and changes over time. This task is so critical that most network management platforms include report functions that are highly configurable. In a Cisco network, both Cisco Prime Infrastructure (PI) and DNA Center include such reports.

In many networks, Cisco PI is already present as a tool to manage and monitor the network. DNA Center is more recent and might not be available in your network. Because Cisco PI is a well-established tool, you should know its main functions. Because DNA Center is where many new functions are developed, such as issue root cause analysis and network trend prediction through machine learning, you should make sure to be familiar with this tool as well. As DNA Center becomes more common, the reliance on Cisco PI is likely to slowly be reduced, and there will come a time when you will only need to master a single tool. Until then, being familiar with both is required to successfully pass the professional-level exams.

Reports on Cisco Prime Infrastructure

Cisco PI offers more than 120 different report types that can be generated to run on an immediate or scheduled basis. Each report type has a number of user-defined criteria to aid in the defining of the reports. You can use the predefined criteria directly, or you can customize the report to add specific parameters. The reports are formatted in summary, tabular, or graphical layout. When defined, the reports can be saved for future diagnostic use or scheduled to run on a regular basis. Reports are saved in either CSV or PDF format and are either saved to a file on Cisco PI for later download or sent to a specific email address.

The reporting types include the following:

■ **Current:** Provides a snapshot of the data from the last polling cycle without continuously polling. This type or report is useful to understand the current state of your network.

■ **Historical:** Retrieves data from the device periodically and stores it in the Cisco PI database. This type of report is very valuable in understanding what happened in your network.

■ **Trend:** Generates a report using aggregated data. Data can be periodically collected based on devices at user-defined intervals, and a schedule can be established for report generation.

You would use the historical reports to analyze how events or activities in the building correlated with network counter changes. You would use the trend reports to evaluate what deeper changes in network activity mean for the future of your deployment.

With Cisco PI, you also have the ability to export any report that you can view, sort reports into logical groups, and archive reports for long-term storage.

Report Types

Although you do not need to learn by heart the details of each individual report, you should know the general report families and structure. All reports can be accessed from the main menu icon in the upper-right part of Cisco PI window or by choosing **Reports > Report Launch Pad.** Thirteen different report families are available, as illustrated in Figures 16-1 and 16-2 and detailed in the following list:

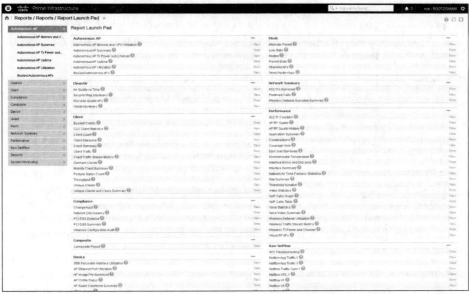

Figure 16-1 *Cisco Prime Infrastructure Report Launch Pad (Upper Part)*

■ **Autonomous APs:** Because these APs are not connected to any WLC, you cannot monitor them centrally. This type of report allows you to collect information on autonomous APs' uptime, memory and CPU utilization, radio channel, power, and utilization. You can also get detailed information on which of these APs is busiest.

Figure 16-2 *Cisco Prime Infrastructure Report Launch Pad (Lower Part)*

- **CleanAir:** RF interferers may be transient and difficult to detect. With this family of reports, you can monitor air quality over time as well as check which APs are most affected by interferers, which detected interferers are most impactful to your network, and which of them provide the highest security risk to your clients.

- **Client:** Clients are obviously at the heart of your network, and this category includes many reports. You can get a client count per protocol (802.11a/b/g/n/ac/ax), per SSID, or per AP as well as measure their traffic volume and throughput over time or per session and monitor dormant clients (clients that became idle beyond the SSID session timeout). You can also measure more specific items, such as real-time voice or video performance indicators (called Traffic Stream Metrics, which are collected by the AP to measure the frame delays to and from voice or video clients), observe client posture (clients whose access to the network is conditioned by complying with configuration or parameter sets enforced by a posture server). You can also get more detailed information from clients that implement Cisco Compatible Extensions (CCX, a set of proprietary parameters that provides additional exchange capabilities to supporting clients).

- **Compliance:** Compliance is critical if your network includes a publicly accessible area where payment is being processed. You may need to comply with the Payment Card Industry (PCI) Data Security Standard (DSS), which includes several requirements for wireless networks. From the compliance menu, you can run a compliance audit. Beyond PCI, this family of reports allows you to check your wireless network configuration for security weaknesses (insecure protocols and such) and also verify what configuration changes have been made on your network and whether these changes result in inconsistent configurations between network elements.

■ **Composite:** Because you might need some elements found in different reports, you can create a composite report, built from subsections of other report types.

■ **Device:** "Device" is a generic term. Here, it is understood to mean a networking device, like an AP or WLC. Here, you can monitor radio or Ethernet interfaces and their associated counters, such as status over time, traffic volume, utilization, client count, and memory or CPU utilization. You can also monitor the devices more globally, checking their status, uptime/downtime, software image, or hardware versions. For APs, you can also review the WLCs they have been associated to over time.

■ **Guest:** Guests are defined as clients that connect to WebAuth WLANs. You can monitor guest session count, duration per SSID, and volume of traffic exchanged, but you can also monitor the guest-related activity on Cisco PI, like the list of accounts created, deleted, or modified and the identity of the account creators, along with the Wi-Fi activity of these accounts (session start/end time and SSID).

■ **Mesh:** Mesh networks have specific constraints, as mesh APs (MAPs) need to use their radio as a backhaul link to connect to root APs (RAPs) that provide the wired connectivity toward the WLC. The MAPs automatically select the best path to the RAP through a series of other MAPs (called parents). You can monitor MAPs changing parents, statistics on the AP radio links (like SNR, hop count to the RAP, traffic volume, and errors), details of the mesh tree (like parent and AP count), observe the traffic over the entire mesh tree, or pay particular attention to APs that failed to reach a RAP (stranded APs) or those that can only reach a RAP through a poor backhaul connection (worse nodes).

■ **Network Summary:** This section contains two types of reports. At the bottom, the Wireless Network Executive summary provides a view of the number of APs, WLCs, and MSEs, along with their status (associated or not), a short view of client count and volume, and a summarized snapshot of the RF network operating conditions (air quality, utilization, client count, and percentage per protocol). From the top part of the Network Summary section, you can run legacy reports about the 802.11n client statistics and about clients that made specific SIP calls. These last two reports are present for backward-compatibility purposes.

■ **Performance:** Just like Client and Device, this segment is critical for your network management. You can look at the network performance of your devices (802.11 counters, RF quality, traffic volume, application types and flows, coverage gaps, interface performances, and utilization) but also focus on specific performance aspects, such as interface errors, temperatures, threshold violations, and voice and video statistics.

■ **Raw NetFlow:** NetFlow is a network protocol developed by Cisco for collecting IP traffic information and monitoring network traffic. Using a NetFlow collector and analyzer, you can see where network traffic is coming from and going to and how much traffic is being generated. Here, you can create NetFlow tests using IP addresses or Fully Qualified Domain Names (FQDN), let them run, and then collect reports on their observed performance. NetFlow has undergone multiple enhancements over time, and some of your network devices may support NetFlow v7, v5, or the older v1.

- **Security:** Beyond a summary of security alarms raised by Cisco PI, security reports are primarily about rogue APs or peer-to-peer (ad hoc) networks. You can monitor their count over time and their detection times, and you can review which APs detect the most rogues. If you implement WIPS in MSE, you can also get reports on WIPS activity. Last, you can monitor wired rogues, if you have configured rules to monitor over the wire any rogue MAC addresses detected over the air.

- **System Monitoring:** "System" in this context represents your network objects, such as APs, WLCs, and switches. You can create specific reports to monitor their CPU, memory, and disk threshold breaches.

Scheduling and Managing Reports

From the Report Launch Pad, all report types are listed. For each type, you can click **New** to directly configure a new report. If you are unsure of a report function or features, you can use the **Verbose** icon to obtain more information about the report.

Clicking the **Report Type** heading in the left menu opens a new page, listing all reports of this type that are available or have been configured on Cisco PI.

Click each report to edit its settings. You can also enable or disable scheduling or run the report immediately. You can also delete a report using the **Delete** button. If you want to run the report at a later time or on a recurring basis, you will need to schedule it. The procedure to schedule a report configuration is the same for all reports. To schedule a report, use the following procedure:

Step 1.   Each report has a Settings and Schedule side of the screen, as illustrated in Figure 16-3. On the Schedule side, check the **Enable** check box.

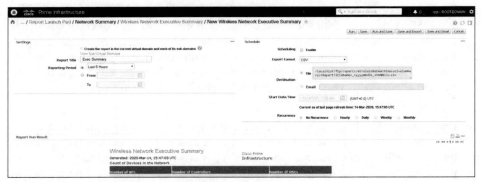

Figure 16-3   *Configuring Cisco PI Reports*

Step 2.   Specify the export format to be either .csv (a file containing the MAC addresses of access points) or .pdf from the **Export Format** drop-down menu.

Step 3.   Choose either the **File** or **Email** option as the **Destination** type.

Step 4.   If you select the **File** option, a destination path must first be defined at the **Administration > Settings > Report** page. Enter the destination path for the files in the **Repository Path** field.

Step 5.   If you select the **Email** option, an SMTP mail server must be defined prior to entry of the target email address. Go to **Administrator > Settings > Mail Server** to enter the appropriate information.

Step 6. Enter a start date/time (MM:DD:YYYY format) in the provided field or click the calendar icon to select a date. The report begins running on this date.

Step 7. Click one of the **Recurrence** buttons to select how often the report is run.

Step 8. When entry is complete, do one of the following:

- Click **Run** if you want to run the report immediately and review the results in the Cisco PI window. The report runs regardless of any scheduled time associated with the report.

- Click **Save** to simply save the entry.

- Click **Run and Save** to save the changes and run the report now. The report is run, and the results are either emailed or saved to a designated file as defined in the Schedule tab. The report runs again at the scheduled time.

- Click **Save and Export** to save the changes and export the report as defined in the **Destination** section (CSV or PDF).

- Click **Save and Email** to save the changes and send the report to the email address specified in the **Destination** section.

> **NOTE**   You can use the **Run** command to check a report scenario before saving it or to run ad hoc reports as necessary.

A report can be customized to meet your specific needs. The **Create Custom Report** page allows you to customize the report results. An example is shown in Figure 16-4.

Figure 16-4   *Customizing Cisco PI Reports*

To customize a report, in the **Settings** section of the report configuration page, click the **Customize** button. A **Create Custom Report** page appears.

From the **Create Custom Report** page, use the **Add >** and **< Remove** buttons to move high-lighted column headings between the two panels (**Available data fields** and **Data fields to include**).

> **NOTE**   Column headings in blue are mandatory in the current subreport. They cannot be removed from the Selected Columns area.

You can also use the **Move Up** and **Move Down** buttons to determine the order of the columns in the results table. The higher the column heading appears in the Selected Columns list, the farther left it appears in the results table. In the **Data field Sorting** section, indicate your sorting preference (ascending or descending). Determine how the report data is sorted. You can select four data fields for which you can specify sorting order. Use the **Sort by** and **Then by** drop-down lists to select each data field for sorting.

> **NOTE**   Only reports in table form (rather than graphs or combined) can be sorted. Only fields that can be sorted appear in the Data field sorting drop-down lists.

Reports on Cisco DNA Center

DNAC is aimed at integrating advanced network monitoring functions grouped under the label "Assurance." As such, the main page of DNAC provides multiple metrics about your network that can be customized. In other words, DNAC Assurance continuously collects information about your network and runs reports that can be visualized directly in the DNAC Assurance interface. The interface is organized into three tabs:

- **Dashboards:** The dashboards include the Health component (Overall/Summary, Network, Client, and Applications), the Issue component (Open, Resolved, and Ignored), and then Wireless Sensors, Rogue Management, and the Dashboard library.

- **Trends and insights:** This section includes Network Insight, Network Heatmap, Peer Comparison, and Site Comparison.

- **Manage:** This section allows you to configure various settings, such as Issue settings (what issue detection is enabled, what priority/severity it should get, and how it is triggered), Health score settings, Sensor settings, and Intelligent Capture settings. Sensors allow you to deploy APs that test your network at regular intervals. Intelligent Capture allows you to capture over-the-air traffic based on specific events or thresholds.

Managing Dashboards

The Dashboards menu is where you will find the equivalent of Cisco PI reports. The concept of *health* in DNAC combines metrics about status (up/down), traffic volume, and also dynamic ratios related to specific elements and their activity. For network elements, the Network Health page displays device counts and status, their health level as a measure of elements that can disrupt normal activity, and a severity level. Heath can be good (green status), fair (orange status), poor (red status), or unmonitored (grey status). For example, for access points, radio health can be impacted by interferers.

For each dashboard, you can have a summarized view (for example, a list of all network element types and their count and health status). The global health status is displayed as the health level of the worst element. An example is displayed in Figure 16-5.

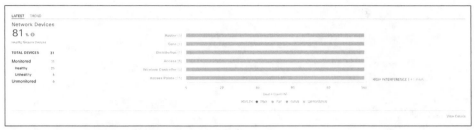

Figure 16-5 *DNAC Global Network Health*

In this case, Access Points shows a health score of 60, which means that at least one AP has a health score of 60, and the worst health score for all APs is 60 (all the others are displaying a score higher than 60). You can then click a particular element (for example, the **Access Points** hyperlink) to display details about this element, as shown in Figure 16-6.

Figure 16-6 *DNAC Access Point Health Detail Page*

In this example, nine APs have a good health score and six APs have a fair health score. The bottom of the page provides individual details.

For each element, the dashboard provides a view of the current state of elements (using the **Latest** option) but also counters for the last 24 hours (using the **Trend** option). At the top of the page, you can use the slider to reduce or extend the computed time window. Alternatively, you can click the **Time Range** hyperlink and configure the interval to display, as illustrated in Figure 16-7.

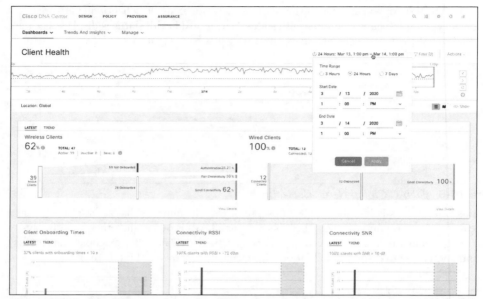

Figure 16-7   *Configuring Reporting Time Range on DNAC—Client Health Example*

Additionally, for each element of interest, you can use the **Filter** option (visible on the bottom left of Figure 16-6) to only display a subset of elements. Each time a set of element health is displayed as a graph, the bottom of the page also displays a table with the details of each component. You can then click the **Export** button (visible at the bottom of Figure 16-6) to export the table in a CSV format.

Wherever needed, you can customize the dashboards and their elements by clicking the **Actions > Edit Dashboard** option in the upper-right part of the page. There, you can reorganize the elements in the page. You can also navigate to **Dashboards > Dashboard Library** to create a new customized dashboard and its customized elements.

Trends and Insights

The dashboards are built by computing performance numbers based on Key Performance Indicators (KPI) collected from the network elements. DNAC also integrates a Machine Learning engine that uses multiple techniques to predict trends or issues. This element is organized around the idea that the first concern of a network administrator is to avoid network issues, the second concern is to understand the network activity, and the third concern is to determine if the level and type of activity are normal.

With this mindset, the first element of **Trends and Insight** is the **Network insight**, which displays the list of events that show abnormal activity. In this context, abnormal represents a metric that shows an important variation over time. For each monitored element in your network and associated counters, DNAC computes the values' averages, standard deviations, and so on, and can alert you when there is a sudden drop or increase. This approach is useful, because a small store's traffic characteristic is unlike a large stadium's, and what is normal here may not be normal there. When you compute your network baseline, the Network Insight element can surface deviations that should alert you, even if the computed numbers would be normal elsewhere. In the Network Insight page, the last detected deviations are listed. Clicking each of them opens a details page, as illustrated in Figure 16-8.

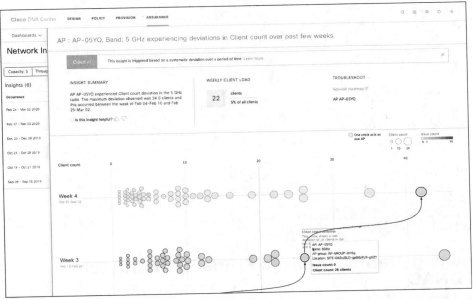

Figure 16-8   *DNAC Network Insight*

In this example, the client count on a particular AP increased dramatically over the last few weeks. With this element of information, you can then check the AP location and verify if this increase is normal (for example, a cafeteria terrace opened when spring arrived).

This notion of counter, baseline, and deviation can be visualized in the Network Heatmap page, where you can choose the KPI (such as client count represented in Figure 16-8, but also AP radio throughput, radio resets, packet failure rate, interference, channel change count, average client RSSI or SNR, traffic volume, channel utilization, or Cloud, Social or media app throughput) and the system will list all network elements, sorted from highest to lowest for the KPI you are monitoring over the last (configurable) 1-month period.

The amount of information provided can be overwhelming. It may be particularly difficult to estimate if a deviation is normal or even if your baseline is normal. To help you further, the **Site Comparison** option in Trends and Insight displays a comparison graph for key counters (such as client onboarding time, average RSSI, and SNR) across all your sites, to help you evaluate if a local deployment would be different from the others.

In the Trends and Insight menu, you can also choose the **Peer Comparison** option. By comparing (locally) your network to the KPIs collected anonymously from tens of thousands of networks with the same type of deployment as yours, the tool can help you understand if what looks normal in your network is really normal, or if you are just got accustomed to seeing these numbers. An example is displayed in Figure 16-9, where the local network provides a much higher throughput than other networks of the same type.

This difference may be caused by a lower client density or smaller cells. Higher performance is usually not much of a concern. The comparison can be done for radio throughput, radio resets, radio packet failure rate, interference, client RSSI, or average cloud-app throughput.

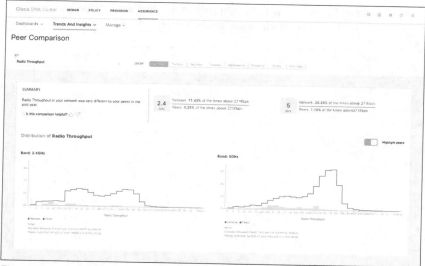

Figure 16-9 *DNAC Peer Comparison*

Managing Alarms on Cisco Prime Infrastructure and DNAC

Both Cisco Prime Infrastructure (PI) and DNAC surface alarms when abnormal events occur. The previous section showed the outcome of these alarms in DNAC, as they are a natural consequence of the way DNAC constantly builds reports. However, you need to know how to configure them. In Cisco PI, alarms are treated independently from reports.

Alarms in Cisco Prime Infrastructure

In Cisco PI terminology, alarms and events are different. An *event* is a distinct incident that occurs at a specific point in time, such as a port status change or a device becoming unreachable. Events can indicate errors, failures, or exceptional conditions in the network. Events can also indicate the *clearing* of those errors, failures, or conditions.

An *alarm* is a Prime Infrastructure response to one or more related events. Only certain events generate alarms. Alarms have a state (cleared or not cleared) and a severity (Critical, Major, Minor, and so forth). An alarm inherits the severity of its most recent event. Alarms remain open until a clearing event is generated (or if the alarm is manually cleared).

You can access the alarms and events from **Monitor > Monitoring Tools > Alarms and Events.**

The alarms are classified into four categories and displayed in separate tabs in the Alarms table:

- **Network Health tab:** Shows the Network Health alarms that are not covered under Rogue AP, Ad-hoc Rogue, Security, and System category alarms

- **Rogue AP:** Shows the Rogue AP and Ad-hoc Rogue category alarms

- **Security:** Shows the security category alarms

- **System:** Shows the system category alarms

Rogues

In the context of Cisco Wireless networks, a rogue is any 802.11 device that is not managed by your organization. For example, if you manage the Wi-Fi service of a department store in a shopping mall, the neighboring stores' Wi-Fi APs are all considered rogues from your network's viewpoint. This does not mean that any action should be taken against them; they are just not APs managed by your systems.

Rogue APs are detected because of their beacons, sent from a MAC address that your WLC (or Cisco PI or DNAC) does not recognize as one of your APs. All three systems will alert you about these rogues. They are by default unclassified. You can then manually classify them as friendly (internal if they belong to your organization but are not managed by your WLCs and external if they are neighbors) or malicious (you have identified them as posing a threat).

Rogue clients are any of your clients (a client that was associated to one of your APs in the past) that is now associated to a rogue AP (your clients should have no reason to decide to jump off your networks and prefer an AP that is not managed by your system).

Ad hoc rogues are clients of your network that establish a peer-to-peer connection (that is, they decide to avoid going through the infrastructure in order to communicate with each other).

The count next to each tab name indicates the total number of alarms in that specific alarm category. The alarm severity can be one of the following:

- Critical (red cross)

- Major (orange warning sign)

- Minor (yellow warning sign)

- Warning alarm (light blue warning sign)

- Alarm cleared, back to normal (green checkmark)

- Informational alarm (blue Information icon)

- Underdetermined alarm (blue icon with white question mark)

For each alarm, you can click the "i:" icon on the right to get additional details.

The page (columns order and content) can be customized by clicking the wheel icon in the top-right part of the page. The alarm status can be modified, and you need to clearly understand the different states:

- When it appears, an alarm is "Not Acknowledged," which means the problem is not being worked on. It could indicate a new fault condition in the network or a cleared fault condition that has recurred. Not Acknowledged alarms are not removed from the Alarms and Events tables until they are either acknowledged or cleared.

- "Acknowledged" means a fault condition has either been recognized and is being worked on, or it can be ignored. Moving an alarm to the Acknowledged status is a manual operation and changes the alarm's status. An Acknowledged event is still considered to be open (that is, not cleared), so if any related events recur, the events are added to the alarm. Acknowledged alarms can be moved back to the Not Acknowledged status (for example, if you acknowledged the wrong alarm).

> **NOTE**   By default, acknowledged alarms are not removed from the Alarms list. This behavior depends on the Hide Acknowledge Alarms setting that is controlled by the administrator.

■ "Cleared" means the fault condition no longer exists. If an alarm is cleared but an associated event recurs, Prime Infrastructure opens a new alarm. By default, cleared alarms will not be shown in the Alarms and Events page. To view the cleared alarms in the Alarms History table in the Alarms and Events page, under **Alarm Display Options**, uncheck the **Hide Cleared Alarms** box.

You can also customize how often information is gathered (polling interval), the threshold value that indicates a problem, and whether Prime Infrastructure should generate an informational event or an alarm (of severity) when a problem is detected. Not all policies have all of these settings; for example, a policy may only collect statistics, so it would not have any thresholds or alarms associated with it.

To customize an alarm, use the following steps:

Step 1   Choose **Monitor > Monitoring Tools > Monitoring Policies > My Policies** and select the policy you want to edit.

Step 2   Locate the parameter you want to change. You can search for the parameter by entering a string in the **Parameter** text box.

Step 3   To adjust the polling interval, select the new interval from the **Polling Frequency** drop-down list. To disable polling, choose **No Polling**. Note that some polling frequencies are applied to groups of parameters. Changing the group interval will change the polling for all settings in the group. If a policy does not have any thresholds or events associated with it, Prime Infrastructure prompts you to save the changes.

Step 4   To change a threshold value, expand the parameter and choose a value from the parameter's drop-down list.

Step 5   To specify what Prime Infrastructure should do when the threshold is surpassed, choose an alarm value from the parameter's drop-down list. You can configure Prime Infrastructure to generate an alarm of a specified severity, generate an informational event, or do nothing (if no reaction is configured).

Step 6   Click **Save** and **Activate** to save and activate the policy immediately on the selected devices. Click **Save** and **Close** to save the policy and activate it at a later time.

A special treatment needs to be made for rogue management. From the **Monitor > Monitoring Tools > Alarms and Events**, and from the **Dashboard > Wireless > Security** pages, you can select a rogue and change its default classification from **Unclassified** to **Friendly** (**Internal**, if it is one of your APs, or **External**, if it is a known neighbor). Doing so and acknowledging the rogue will prevent it from being reported in future alarms, unless its parameters change. You can also classify the rogue as malicious to maintain it in an alarm state. From within this classification, you can also choose to contain the rogue. In this case, your APs in range of the rogue will start sending deauthentication messages to any detected client of the rogue.

> **NOTE** Be careful with this feature! In most countries, deauthenticating clients of a legitimate Wi-Fi network is considered an attack and is illegal. Make sure that the rogue you are containing is within the physical venue under your control, is not legitimate, and is posing a threat to your network. If you are in doubt, do not contain the rogue and investigate locally.

16

You can also configure larger rogue policies, from **Security > Wireless Protection Policies > Rogue Policies**. From this page, you can refine how alarms about rogues are triggered:

- **Rogue Location Discovery Protocol:** RLDP determines whether or not the rogue is connected to the enterprise wired network. It does so by using one of the neighboring APs that pretends to be a client and associates to the rogue. That pretend client then attempts to contact its WLC, through the rogue, on UDP port 6352 (RLDP port). If the message reaches the WLC, then the WLC signals to Cisco PI that the rogue is effectively connected to your wired infrastructure. Obviously, this attack only works if the SSID on the rogue is open (your AP will not be able to connect to an SSID protected by WPA/WPA2/WPA3) and if no firewall between the rogue and your WLC blocks UDP 6352. If you decide to enable RLDP, you can choose one of the following options:

  - **Disable:** Disables RLDP on all access points. This is the default value.

  - **All APs:** Enables RLDP on all access points.

  - **Monitor Mode APs:** Enables RLDP only on access points in Monitor mode.

- **Rogue APs Policies:** You can configure the parameters upon which a rogue should be reported:

  - **Expiration Timeout for Rogue AP and Rogue Client Entries (seconds):** Enter the number of seconds after which the rogue access point and client entries expire and are removed from the list. The valid range is 240 to 3600 seconds, and the default value is 1200 seconds. If a rogue access point or client entry times out, it is removed from the controller only if its rogue state is Alert or Threat for any classification type.

  - **Rogue Detection Report Interval:** Enter the time interval in seconds at which the APs should send the rogue detection report to the controller. The valid range is 10 seconds to 300 seconds, and the default value is 10 seconds. This feature is applicable to APs that are in Monitor mode only.

  - **Rogue Detection Minimum RSSI:** Enter the minimum RSSI value that a rogue should have for the APs to detect and for the rogue entry to be created in the controller. The valid range is −70 dBm to −128 dBm, and the default value is

-128 dBm. This feature is applicable to all the AP modes. There can be many rogues with very weak RSSI values that do not provide any valuable information in the rogue analysis. Therefore, you can use this option to filter the rogues by specifying the minimum RSSI value at which the APs should detect rogues.

- **Rogue Detection Transient Interval:** Enter the time interval at which a rogue has to be consistently scanned for by the AP after the first time the rogue is scanned. By entering the transient interval, you can control the time interval at which the AP should scan for rogues. The APs can filter the rogues based on their transient interval values. A valid range is between 120 seconds and 1800 seconds, and the default value is 0. This feature is applicable to APs that are in Monitor mode only.

- Rogue Clients parameters:

  - **Validate rogue clients against AAA:** Select the check box to use the AAA server or local database to validate if rogue clients are valid clients. The default value is unselected.

  - **Detect and report ad hoc networks:** Select the check box to enable ad hoc rogue detection and reporting. The default value is selected.

Alarms in DNAC

Alarms in DNAC are called "issues" and are found at the bottom of most dashboard pages. Behind the scenes, DNAC distinguishes global issues from device issues. The boundary between both is malleable. A device issue is, as the name indicates, an issue that affects a single device (for example, an STA failing to obtain an IP address). When the device is a networking device, the local issue may affect many users and may become global by nature (for example, a WLC crashing). An issue affecting a single device may also be reflective of a global issue. For example, an STA may fail to obtain an IP address because of local RF issues at the station level (local issue) or because the DHCP server stopped responding (global issue). This classification is not directly visible in DNAC, but you need to keep it in mind. Cisco PI directly reports the events and alarms as they are configured. By contrast, DNAC also attempts to analyze the events and alarms to determine their most likely root cause. And it is the root cause that will drive the classification of the alarm. Therefore, you may see a similar event (an STA failing to get an IP address) be classified differently in DNAC, depending on what might have caused the issue.

Additionally, with a focus on network performance (not general data collection), rogues are not reported in DNAC by default, unless they effectively affect your network performance. If you want to surface rogues that are detected but have no effect on your network, you need to download a special DNAC add-on called Cisco DNA Center Rogue Management Application. Refer to this page for more details on this package:

https://www.cisco.com/c/en/us/td/docs/cloud-systems-management/network-automation-and-management/dna-center-rogue-management-application/1-3-3-0/quick-start-guide/b_rogue_management_qsg_1_3_3_0.html

As you navigate to the main issues page, in **Assurance > Dashboards > Issues > Open**, you will see at the bottom the top 10 issues. They are classified by severity (global impact first). You can click the various columns (Priority, Issue Type, Device Role, Category, Issue Count, Site Count, Device Count, and Last Occurred Time) to change the way the issues are sorted. DNAC recognizes eight categories:

- **Onboarding:** Displays the wireless and wired client onboarding issues

- **Connectivity:** Displays network connectivity issues, such as OSPF, BGP tunnels, and so on

- **Connected:** Displays client issues

- **Device:** Displays device-related issues, such as CPU, memory, fan, and so on

- **Availability:** Displays device availability issues for APs, wireless controllers, and so on

- **Utilization:** Displays utilization issues of APs, wireless controllers, radios, and so on

- **Application:** Displays application experience issues

- **Sensor Test:** Displays sensor global issues

You can also click **View All Open Issues** to expand the view beyond the top 10. You can click each issue to get more details. You can then use the Actions drop-down list to move the issue from the **Open** status to **Resolved** or **Ignored**. The classification has no direct effect on the issue, but is an easy way for you to separate issues that matter for your network from issues that are not important.

For each type of issue, DNAC offers a preset series of possible remediation actions, as shown in Figure 16-10.

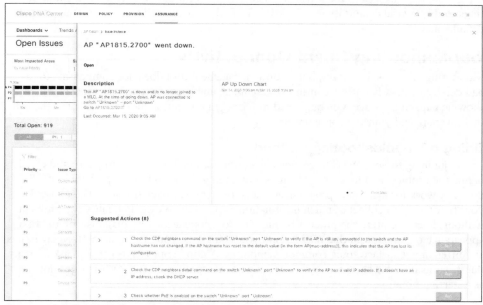

Figure 16-10   *DNAC Issue Remediation Page*

These actions can be used to verify that the issue is still occurring. They can also be used as a step-by-step process to validate the root cause of the issue. When the action is a command that can be sent to a particular device, a Run button is available for DNAC to issue the correct command, on the correct device, for you.

An issue may not have the same severity in all networks. You can manage the issues that are relevant to your network by navigating to **Manage > Issue Settings**. As DNAC lists close to 200 different issues, you can use the filters at the top of the page to only display issues relevant to a particular device type (router, core/distribution and access switches, WLCs, access points, wired clients, wireless clients, applications, or servers) and only one of the eight categories listed previously.

You can then click each issue to open a slide-in pane with the settings. Click the **Enabled** toggle to enable or disable the issue. To set the issue priority, click the **Priority** drop-down list and select from the following priority options:

- **P1**: Indicates a critical issue that needs immediate attention that can result in wider impact on network operations

- **P2**: Indicates a major issue that can potentially impact multiple devices or clients

- **P3**: Indicates a minor issue that has a localized or minimal impact

- **P4**: Indicates a warning issue that may not be an immediate problem but addressing it can optimize the network performance

In the **Trigger Condition** area, you can change the threshold value for when the issue is reported.

If there are any changes to the settings, you can hover your cursor over **View Default Settings** to display the default issues. Click **Use Default** to restore all the issue settings to the default values.

Troubleshooting Client Connectivity

Monitoring alarms is important, but a good management tool does not compensate for a bad deployment. When users continue to complain about connectivity or when alarms keep showing gaps in coverage, you may need to focus your attention more closely onto the cells, their overlap, and your AP configurations.

Building a Troubleshooting Method

Before jumping to your WLC to change any configuration, it is critical to pause and clearly define the problem and its scope. The most commonly reported issue is probably "Wi-Fi does not work for me." Such pronouncement is too vague to be actionable. Therefore, your first task is to collect as much information as possible to exactly qualify the problem, without short-circuiting the process by jumping to a conclusion or a diagnosis on the first appearance of a symptom that may remind you of an issue you saw in the past. Many issues are different yet surface some common symptoms. A good approach is often to ask as many questions as possible so as to reduce the scope of the problem, using "Wi-Fi does not work" as a starting point:

- Can the user connect to Wi-Fi, but not use it, or is connection itself impossible? Although this narrowing down does not tell you at what Open System Interconnection (OSI) layer the issue is occurring (the problem may be occurring at Layer 2, after association), it still helps narrow down the phase you should focus on. If association itself is an issue, then checking the state at which the client stops, as detailed in the following list, will also help you focus. In most cases, the client utility cannot provide these details, but the WLC exposes the client state, if it is detected as attempting to connect through one AP. Here again, do not jump to conclusions. For example, a client stuck in *DHCP-required* state does not directly point to a DHCP server problem. An RF issue, too many collisions, and a VLAN misconfiguration are all causes that may prevent the client from completing the DHCP process.

- Is the problem permanent or temporary? A temporary issue will conduct you to look into environmental conditions, while a permanent issue will drive you toward systemic configurations.

- Is the problem affecting all traffic or only some of the traffic? This approach is called "top-down." If all applications are affected, then the Application layer is likely not at fault, and something in a lower layer is likely at fault. A next step in this case could be to go down in the OSI layer logic and check if DNS resolution works, then if a particular server IP address can be reached (ping), thus testing Layer 3 connectivity, then if the gateway can be reached (both the gateway IP address on the client side and the IP address on the other side of the router), thus testing both IP connectivity and routing, and then, of course, if the client obtained an IP address (and in the right scope). If only some applications are affected, then the lower layers are likely to perform normally, and the issue may be related to the application itself.

In order to effectively solve connection issues, you need to clearly understand the client association phases and how they are labeled on the WLC:

1. The client first has to discover the network, by sending probe requests (or listening to the AP beacons). As this component does not mean that the client will want to effectively join the network (it may just be collecting information about APs but failing to find an SSID matching one of its profiles), the client may simply be labeled as *Probing* on the WLC, if the client is known, but may also simply not be reported (if the client has never joined the network in the past).

2. The client really begins the join process with an 802.11 authentication. This initial phase is labeled as *Start* on the WLC. In the early days of 802.1, this phase had a real (security) authentication component. Today, this phase simply authenticates the client as a valid 802.11 device.

3. The client continues with an 802.11 association, which is a simple obtention of an association identifier (AID) on the AP SSID.

4. At the conclusion of the 802.11 association phase, the client status moves from *Start* to another state that depends on the WLAN security. For Open and WebAuth SSID, the client moves to *L2authcomplete*. For PSK/802.1X WLANs, the client moves to *Authcheck*. A PSK network will display this state while the AP and the client verify that they both have the same key (4-way handshake). An 802.1x network will immediately switch to *802.1X_reqd* while the client RADIUS exchanges occur. For both authentication methods (PSK/802.1X), *auth failure* shows an issue, and *L2authcomplete* is the expected successful outcome.

5. Once the authentication phase completes, the client will need an IP address and will therefore switch to the *DHCP_reqd* state. *DHCP failure* will obviously display a problem for this phase.

6. Once an IP address is obtained, the WebAuth client will still need an extra step (web authentication) and will therefore switch to *Webauth_reqd*. Here, *Auth failure* will point you to credential issues.

7. The client then moves to fully authenticated—a fully associated and functional state, labeled on the WLC CLI as the *Run* state. This state is also called *Active* in the WLC web interface.

These states are visible on the WLC by navigating in AireOS to **Advanced > Monitor > Clients > Client Details** and on C9800 to **Monitoring > Wireless > Clients > Select Client > General**.

Once you have validated the conditions of the issues mentioned and the client state, you can focus your attention on the wired side of the network if the issue is associated with a wired service (DNS, DHCP, server reachability, and so on.) However, keep in mind that if some clients in a cell successfully obtain a service but others do not, then the issue may either come from the clients themselves or from the cell.

RF Coverage Validation

One common cause of connectivity or service completion issue is a lack of good RF coverage. Before the deployment, you should have performed a site survey. After the deployment, you should have performed a verification survey. However, over time, APs get moved, their power gets changed, and furniture and walls may change the RF environments. Therefore, a common task associated with a rise of client support tickets is to verify the RF coverage again:

■ Conduct a verification survey of the entire affected environment (divided into several shorter surveys, if necessary) and compare the results to those generated during the planning stage of the pre-deployment process.

■ Make any required adjustments that were not accounted for in the preinstallation portion in order to make the network meet user and throughput requirements.

■ Conduct a separate verification site survey for each protocol supported (802.11a/b/g/n/ac/ax). Check for co-channel interference by standing near an access point on one channel and watch for other access points that are on the same channel. Check to see if the signal level on other access points that are heard on the same channel is at least 19 dBm weaker than the access point you are next to. For example, if the local AP signal is –67 dBm, the signal from the next AP on the next channel should not be stronger than –86 dBm (86 – 67 = 19).

■ Validate performances by testing a client against each AP. This process also allows you to verify that the real-world network traffic (for example, physical data rate, packet loss or packet retry, and uplink or downlink data) meets user requirements.

A key component of this phase is roaming verification. As part of your initial survey, you should have identified roaming paths (that is, the path users take when they move around) and therefore roaming points. It is common to observe that support ticket locations match roaming points between APs. If this case is observed in your network, focus your attention on the area between cells:

■ Take some time to walk back and forth at the edge of each cell to precisely determine where roaming occurs in each direction. At each point, verify that a standard user device has the time to discover the next AP and then roam to it.

■ Also verify that the next AP the client roams to is the one intended in your AP layout (that is, the view from the ground should be the same as the view from the ceiling, as explained in Chapter 3, "Conducting an Onsite Site Survey").

■ Make sure to use the client whose technical specifications are closest to the one your users are reporting about in their support tickets. Your network probably has a large variety of clients types. When you tested those clients in the early phase of your site survey, you probably determined "good" and "poor" clients. The qualification of "good" and "poor" may not have any absolute meaning but may be a client-to-client comparison. Good clients are those that offer a good RSSI, good SNR (as reported by a client utility and the AP), and good throughput at a location position, whereas poor clients, at the exact same physical location, would offer a lower RSSI, lower SNR, and/or lower throughput. In your client test, you want to select the poor client. The assumption is that if performance is satisfactory for poor clients, it will be acceptable for good clients as well.

NOTE   Keep in mind that the RSSI alone is not enough to compare clients, as the RSSI is a vendor-specific value expressing the client's ability to transform an RF signal into usable information. The RSSI can usually not be compared between two clients from two different vendors. Throughput is therefore a good additional metric.

■ Be sure to survey from all edges of the cell; do not assume that coverage on one side of the access points will be identical to coverage on the opposite side. The edge of the cell is not only the point where you expect your client to roam but also the (farther) point where the AP signal gets lost in the noise (typically by −94 dBm).

■ Your body may interfere with the signal. Other users will also experience this issue, and the opposite effect is true. If there is no obstacle between your wireless device and the AP, you will get a better signal than if your body is in the way. You need to take this fact in consideration when verifying the coverage. If you walk down a corridor in one direction with your laptop in front of you, make sure to also walk the same corridor in the other direction (still with your laptop in front of you) to test various body positions in the same environment.

■ Moving too quickly can result in insufficient data collected; however, moving too slowly results in longer processing times due to an excess of information.

As you review coverage, remember that channels play an important role. Many clients do not support the U-NII-2 extended (Band 3) channels 100 through 140 (5.470 to 5.725GHz). Most supporting clients take longer to discover APs in these channels than in other channels. Account for this added delay in roaming. Some clients support ISM channel 165; some others stop at the edge of the band that is defined for U-NII-3 (Band 4) channel 161. Ensure that only channels enabled on the controller or access points are supported by all wireless clients on the network. Failure to do so can cause coverage holes for clients that do not support certain channels.

After having verified the channels supported by all clients that are expected on your network, you can choose the list of channels that should be enabled and those that should be disabled. Keep in mind that channel support is not just related to the client hardware (the physical capacity of the radio installed on each client) but also to the client firmware. Channel support may change when upgrading or downgrading client firmware.

The network is also not ready until all applications have been tested on the wireless network Layers 1 through 7. You should perform density testing and roam testing while using the target applications that are reported in your support tickets. In density testing, you should ensure that each client gets the level of service it needs when peak activity levels are reached. In roam testing, you should verify that mobile clients can roam without losing their application session and that handoffs are smooth between access points (no freezes or losses).

WLC, PI, and DNAC Client Troubleshooting Tools

Once the RF conditions have been validated, it may be time to go back to individual client troubleshooting. The WLC is a network management tool, and one of its functions is to provide visibility into your network and its conditions.

Client Troubleshooting on the WLC

In AireOS, the **Home > Monitoring > Clients** page should be your first stop to monitor your associated clients and their state. The **Client Detail** page provides a lot of information about the client connection, such as connected AP, SSID, authentication and encryption mechanisms, QoS values, and so on. An example is provided in Figure 16-11.

Figure 16-11 *AireOS Client Detail Page*

A Samsung (S9 or later) or Apple iOS client will also display its details (hardware and OS version).

The Performance and Connection Score sections provide more information about the client RF characteristics, as detected by the AP. The connection score is 100% if the client connects at the maximum MCS/data rate it supports. In most cases, clients may not be close enough to the AP to connect at max MCS, and a lower connection score may not be of concern.

If the client implements Cisco Compatible Extensions (CCX), it is labeled "Cisco Compatible."

On the right side, the WLC monitored the client onboarding and colored green all steps that completed as expected. Steps that got a warning (long delay and so on) are colored yellow, and steps that failed are colored red.

In the lower part of the page, you can see the connection path for this client, including the SSID and the AP names, but also the AP path to the WLC (switches and their ports). This information can help you evaluate the path taken by the client traffic through the network.

At the very bottom of the page, you can test the client connection by running a ping test. You can also navigate to the **Connection** tab and click **Start**. Then, on the client, attempt a connection. Then click **Stop** on the **WLC Connection** tab. The WLC will log and display each phase on the client association. Clicking each phase (802.11 association, Security Policy, Network Membership, IP addressing, or IP Addressing Options) will expand the relevant section to provide a list of frames and their content and outcome. The same logic applies to the **Event Log** tab, where you start logging each event relevant to the target client.

If AVC is enabled on your WLC, the **Top Application** section shows the main applications used by the client, along with volume (in MB) and proportion of the client total traffic.

If your client runs Apple iOS 11 or later, you will also see the **Client Scan** report section in the page. Right after (re)association, the iOS client sends an unsolicited 802.11k neighbor report to its connecting AP, listing all the other APs it detected (for the target SSID) while scanning before joining the local AP.

NOTE Do not be alarmed if the client does not list all APs. When an AP signal is strong, the client may stop scanning and directly join that AP.

Lower down in the page, you can see the client network, QoS, and security policies. This section is very useful to verify, from all policies configured on the WLC (and possible AAA), which one was applied to this client.

The same type of information is available in the **Monitoring > Clients >Details** page in the C9800 WLC, as shown in Figure 16-12.

You will note that the page is organized slightly differently compared to AireOS. The 360 View includes the client general information (the AireOS equivalent is shown in Figure 16-11) along with the top applications list. The General tab includes five subtabs: Client Properties, AP Properties (client), Security Information (client policy), Client Statistics, and QoS Properties (QoS policies applied to the client). In AireOS, the Client Statistics, along with the equivalent to the C9800 QoS Statistics, ATF (Air Time Fairness) Statistics, Mobility History, and Call Statistics tabs are not accessible from the home page but from the **Advanced > Monitor > Client > Details** page.

Figure 16-12   *C9800 Client Detail Page*

The C9800 also includes a Troubleshooting menu, intended to help you troubleshoot most client and network issues, as illustrated in Figure 16-13.

Figure 16-13   *C9800 Troubleshooting Page*

Most of the menus are self-explanatory. Keep in mind that the logs can provide a view of past client issues (in AireOS, logs are accessible from **Management > Logs**). With the Radioactive Trace function, you can enter a client MAC and let the system collect in a single file all the subsequent logs relevant to this client. The Core Dump and System Report and Debug Bundle menus are used to troubleshoot the WLC platform. The Packet Capture menu only applies to wired capture (physical or VLAN interfaces). Therefore, you should only use it if you suspect that the client issue you are troubleshooting has a strong wired component.

If you suspect a wireless component, you can use the AP Packet Capture function. The function only works if you have defined how and where the capture should be stored. This is done from **Configuration > Tags & Profiles > AP joint**. Add or edit a profile and then navigate to the **AP** tab. Within this tab, click the **Packet Capture** tab. At this location, you can create a capture profile that defines what frames are to be captured (802.11 control, 802.11 management, 802.11 Data, Dot1x, ARP, IAPP, IP, Broadcast, Multicast, and TCP/UDP with target ports). You can also define the maximum capture size (in KB) and duration (in minutes) and also decide if you only want to capture the header of the frames (using the Truncate option, where you define the number of bytes of the frame to capture). You can then define the FTP server address and credentials to use for the capture. Save the capture profile by clicking **Update** and **Apply to Device**. You can then go to **Configuration > Wireless Setup > Advanced > AP Join Profile** to select the profile you created and then **Tag APs** to apply that profile to your APs. They will then be able to capture over-the-air traffic.

Navigate back to **Troubleshooting** and click **AP Packet Capture**. A new page appears. You can enter the target client to monitor in the **Client MAC Address** field. The Capture mode is by default set to **Auto**, which means that the system will automatically capture the channel on the AP to which the client is associated. You can also set the mode to **Static** (for example, if the client is not associated or if you want to verify how a neighboring AP detects the client). In Static mode, you can manually enter the AP name. Once you click **Start**, the AP will capture the client traffic and send it to storage upon completion. You can stop the capture manually by clicking **Stop**, or you can wait for the maximum duration or maximum size to be reached.

In some cases, you will conclude that the issue occurs during the 802.1X/EAP authentication phase and that the AAA server is either rejecting the authentication or simply not responding. In the first case, the WLC will display an authentication failure message. In the second case, the WLC will display a AAA timeout message. In both cases, you may need to go to the Identity Services Engine (ISE) interface to investigate further. In many networks, a different team manages the AAA server, and this access may not be available to you. Additionally, the CCNP exam does not expect you to be a security expert. However, you should be aware that you can verify connectivity with the WLC, in ISE, from **Administration > Network Resources >Network Devices**. If the WLC considers a Network Access Device (NAD) to be misconfigured, you will see the issue in its status. Make sure you correctly configure the IP addresses and keys, both in ISE and in the WLC, as explained in the Chapter 15, "Security for Wireless Client Connectivity."

Additionally, you can also monitor the authentication and authorization dialogs in **Monitor > Authentication**. For each user and attempt, you can click the attempt and get details on what message was received and what ISE's answer was. Because the details of the authentication dialogs are usually encrypted, they are not visible to the WLC. Therefore, ISE is the best place to investigate AAA issues. Refer to Chapter 15 and the ISE troubleshooting guide at the end of this chapter for more details on troubleshooting functions in ISE.

16

For most nonsecurity issues, the WLC likely provides all the information you need to troubleshoot your clients. However, your efforts might lead you to Cisco PI (or DNAC) for two reasons:

- Some network management teams only use central management tools, such as PI or DNAC. Therefore, the tools that exist on the WLC are also available on PI and DNAC. In most cases, the functions are the same. The difference only lies in the troubleshooting preferences of the support team.

- However, the WLC does not store historical information and therefore can only provide a live snapshot of the network conditions. By contrast, Cisco PI and DNAC can be configured to store historical information and can be preferred if you need to look at past events, either in search of a particular point in time when an issue occurred or because you need to compare past states or conditions to the present.

Client Troubleshooting in Cisco Prime Infrastructure

There are multiple ways in which you can view the list of clients connected to your network in Cisco PI. One of them is to navigate to **Dashboard > Network Summary**, where a dashlet represents graphically the number of wireless clients connected over time.

At the top of any page in the dashboard, you can also look for a particular client by using the Search field and entering a client MAC address, IP address, or username.

To get information about more than one client, you can use the **Dashboard > Overview > Client** page. There, you will see dashlets representing the client distribution by RSSI, by SNR, by 802.11 protocol (802.11a/n/ac/ax), or by type (iPhone and so on, when available). To get a list of clients, instead of a graphical split by type, navigate to **Monitor > Monitoring Tools > Clients and Users**. You will see all the clients, with the MAC address, IP address and type (9IPv4/IPv6), username, device type and vendor, location (if you use MSE/DNA Spaces), WLC and its interface, the client VLAN, 802.11 protocol, and status (associated and so on). You can sort or filter the view by using the **Show** drop-down list and selecting only a subcategory of clients. You can also click the filter icon and select the filter criteria. When you click the icon next to each client username, a client 360 pop-up appears that shows similar information as what you had in the WLC client 360 view.

You can click a single client and click **Troubleshoot**. This action opens a new page where you will see several tabs. The default tab is **Troubleshoot and Debug**. In the upper part of the page, you will see client general information (username, IP address, MAC, vendor, and so on), session details (WLC and AP details, SSID, protocol, state, and VLAN), and security details (EAP-type ACLs and so on.). The **Overview** tab will also show the client path (AP and WLC).

At the bottom of the **Overview** section, the **Association History** segment is where Cisco PI diverges from the WLC. Here, you can see each past session for this client, along with association time and session duration, AP, WLC, IP address, and so on. This part is very useful to understand the client behavior over time and identify sporadic disconnection issues.

In the **Troubleshoot and Debug** tab, you can push your investigations further by looking at the **Troubleshoot** section at the bottom of the page. There, you will see tabs for each client association phase (802.11 Association, Open Authentication, IP Address Assignment, and Successful Association) and a status indicator (green checkmark for pass, red X for failed). Clicking each tab provides more details on the frames exchanged for this phase and the outcome. On the right side, the **Debug and Analysis** section allows you to trigger log captures from the WLC. You can select the types of messages to log (All or a subset, like 802.1X authentication or DHCP messages). In case of troubleshooting, **All** is likely a good choice. You can click **Start**, ask your client to attempt to connect to the network, and then click **Stop** when the experiment completes. The page will display the details of the frames received and sent (802.11 association, 802.1X authentication, and so on) along with their outcome.

Client Troubleshooting in Cisco DNA Center

DNAC offers similar functions as Cisco PI. When you navigate to **Dashboards > Health > Client Health**, you will see global statistical graphs at the top and then the list of all clients in the **Client Devices** section. For each client, you can see the username, IP address, device type, traffic volume, AP name, band RSSI location (and then time where the client was last reported). You can also see a composite health index for the client. This index is a simple composite indicator of the client status. DNAC defines "good RSSI" as –72 dBm and above, and it defines "good SNR" as 9 dB and above. The client will display a health index of 1 if it failed to complete association, 4 if it connected but has both poor RSSI and poor SNR, 7 if RSSI or SNR gets above the threshold, and 10 if both RSSI and SNR get above the threshold for the connected client.

At the top of the section, you can use **Type** selection buttons to reduce the display list to only wireless clients or wired clients, only inactive clients, or only clients with poor (4 or less), fair (7 or less), or good health (more than 7). You can also refine the display with the Data button to only show the clients whose onboarding times exceed key values (more than 10 seconds for total onboarding time, more than 5 seconds for association, more than 5 seconds for DHCP, more than 5 seconds for authentication [Webauth, 802.1X, PSK], less than –72 dBm RSSI, and less than 9 dB SNR). You can also use the Filter button and enter a particular client MAC address, IP address, username, or any other criterion present for a client (health score, RSSI, connected AP, and so on) to focus your attention on a particular case.

The client's **Details** page is organized around the idea of performance monitoring and issue root cause analysis. The top of the page shows a graph of the client health over time. You can use the date on the upper-right part of the screen, or the sliders on each side of the graph, to change the monitored interval. The default is a sliding 24-hour window.

Below the graph is a list of issues (if any) for the same period. The lower part of the page displays the elements you are now familiar with from the other interfaces we covered in this chapter, an onboarding section showing the various steps (association, AAA, DHCP) and their status (green or red), a list of frames for each of these events, and a graph of the client connection (SSID, AP, WLC). However, you will notice that DNAC provides more information than the other interfaces (for example, the count of other clients on the same AP or the WLC, the IP address of the AAA authentication server, and so on).

Lower in the page, the **Application Experience** section shows the applications used by that client. Instead of providing a list sorted by default by volume, DNAC organizes applications based on their policy classification: Business Relevant, Business Irrelevant, or Default (that is, either business relevant or not, depending on what payload that application carries). In the **DNAC Policy** menu, you can change this classification.

The very bottom of the page provides additional information about the client, such as device type, operating system (when known), MAC address, IP address, and so on. A **Connectivity** tab shows graphs for transmission elements, such as Tx and Rx bytes over the monitored period, DNS requests and responses, and overall data rate. An **RF** tab shows the client RSSI and SNR over the period. If the client is Apple iOS, an **iOS Analytics** tab is visible that displays the 802.11k neighbor report that the client provided at association time. If the client is a Samsung Galaxy S9 or later, a **Samsung Analytics** tab is visible that displays more details about the client (SP or manufacturer build, detailed reasons for client de-association, and so on).

Although DNAC does not give you access to the raw logs like Cisco PI does, you can access the same content. It is simply preorganized into relevant phases. DNAC also includes two additional client troubleshooting tools that are specific and often seen as very valuable:

- **Path Trace:** Start by clicking the icon by the middle of the client details page. Path Trace allows you to configure a starting and terminating point as well as a traffic type (protocol and ports) and to evaluate what would happen if that traffic were to run. This function is very useful for troubleshooting specific applications and their path through the network as well as networking device issues on the path. For example, in Figure 16-14, the Cat93200-2 outbound interface is dropping packets for the target traffic. You then know exactly where to focus your troubleshooting efforts.

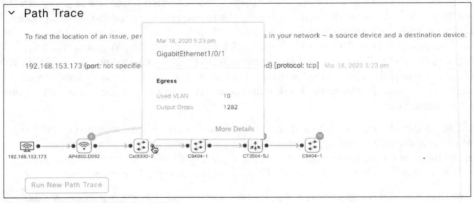

Figure 16-14 *DNAC Path Trace*

- **Intelligent Capture:** Start by clicking the name in the upper-right part of the client details page. DNAC then sends an instruction to the AP to which the client is associated to start a live capture and return the flow to DNAC, where you can see near-real-time (about 3-minute delay) information about the client, including location on a map, RF statistics (RSSI, SNR, Rx data rate, Tx/Rx packets, and retries) and the management frames exchanged with the clients (authentication, key exchanges, and so on). When an exchanged has failed, you can click the flagged frame. An Auto Packet Analyzer will display the packet details and the reasons for the failures, as shown in Figure 16-15.

You can also download the full PCAP capture, if you want to leverage the capture on another tool. Intelligent Capture is very useful either to troubleshoot clients in near real time, to continuously monitor the performance of key devices (for example, your boss crossing the floor), or to run what-if scenarios (during AP or new client device deployment, walk target areas with a few test clients and monitor the outcome).

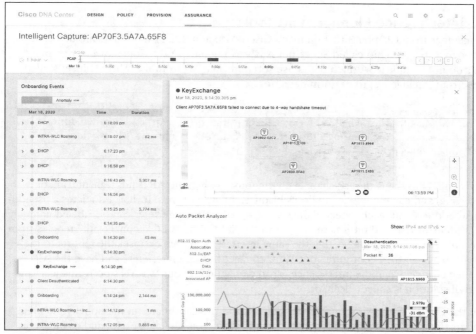

Figure 16-15   *DNAC Intelligent Capture*

> **NOTE**   Intelligent Capture is also its own menu, accessible from **Assurance > Manage > Intelligent Capture**, where you can schedule a client capture (immediately or with a delayed start) with the same logic detailed previously in the C9800 section, and also review and manage the list of clients currently monitored with Intelligent Capture. Therefore, clicking Intelligent Capture from the client details page automatically starts Intelligent Capture for that client, but you can manage Intelligent Capture outside of the client details page.

For all cases where you cannot directly test with a client, DNAC allows you install sensors—access points with a small form factor that are installed where clients would be placed (that is, connected to a power socket near ground level). These sensors can then be configured to test your RF environment, along with target applications. For more details, refer to the sensor deployment guide at https://www.cisco.com/c/dam/en/us/td/docs/cloud-systems-management/network-automation-and-management/dna-center/deploy-guide/Cisco_1800S_Sensor_Deployment_Guide_133.pdf.

Troubleshooting and Managing RF Interferences

In your client troubleshooting efforts, you will have encountered many scenarios where the issue comes from the RF environment. As such, this section does not need to be long. However, the CCNP exams expect you to be able to manage RF interferers, regardless of their effect on your clients, so you need to make sure you know what tools are available and where to find them.

WLC Interference Management Tools

Remember from Chapter 3 that on many Cisco APs, non-802.11 interferers are detected through a specific chip called Spectrum Analysis Engine (SAgE). Some lower-price-point APs do not include a SAgE chip and use software analysis from the Wi-Fi chipset (called Spectrum Intelligence) to perform detection.

> **NOTE**   SI is a subset of what SAgE does. Refer to this document for a detailed comparison: https://www.cisco.com/c/en/us/td/docs/wireless/controller/technotes/8-6/b_wlc_8_6_spectrum_intelligence_on_cisco_wave_2_aps.html.

The SAgE chip scans the AP channel continuously (when the AP is not transmitting or receiving) and can recognize hundreds of different signal types. It then associates a pseudo-MAC address with each detected non-Wi-Fi signal (so the interferer can be labeled uniquely with an identifier) and returns the report to the WLC. The WLC reconciles the reports from multiple APs that may be hearing the same interferer and then exposes the reports to the admin. You can then configure your WLC to react to these interferers and have the APs change channel when the interference is too damaging to your WLAN's performance. This overall solution is called CleanAir.

On the C9800, CleanAir is enabled by default, and the dashboard (in the upper-right area) counts the interferers detected in 2.4GHz and 5GHz. You can click each band or interferer count to get more details. This action redirects you to the **Monitoring > Wireless > CleanAir Statistics** page, where the interferers are listed, along with their type, the affected channel, the reporting AP, the severity, duty cycle, RSSI, and allocated unique identifier (pseudo-MAC).

> **NOTE**   The severity is an index from 1 to 100 that reflects how badly the interferer affects your channel. At 100, the channel is completely unusable.

> **NOTE**   The duty cycle represents the percentage of time, each second, the interferer transmits energy.

You can click each interferer to get a graphical view of the channel Air Quality and interferer RSSI (its transmission strength).

As more than one interferer can affect each channel, the WLC also outputs a channel Air Quality report, available in the **Air Quality Report** tab, that provides for each channel an

Air Quality Index (AQI), which is a composite measure of the effect of all interferers on that channel. An AQI of 100 means "no interferer."

> **NOTE**   Although there is a direct relationship between each interferer severity and the AQI for that channel, the relationship is not linear. In other words, a single interferer with a severity of 35 does not cause the AQI to be exactly 65 (100 – 35), as the AQI factors multiple components to provide the index value.

To help you better visualize your environment, a **Worst Air Quality Report** tab also shows which AP has the worst AQI, along with the number of detected interferers.

Although CleanAir is enabled by default, you can configure it from the **Configuration > Radio Configuration CleanAir** page. From that page, you can enable or disable CleanAir and SI and also decide which interferer to detect and report (and which to ignore, because they may be expected and unavoidable in your network). You can also decide which detected interferer is reported via SNMP (to Cisco PI or DNAC). You can also disable CleanAir for each individual AP (in **Configuration > Wireless > Access Points > [5GHz | 2.4GHz] Radios > Configure > CleanAir Admin Status**).

Last, from the **Configuration > Radio Configurations > RRM > Band > DCA** page, you can enable or disable several functions related to interferers:

- **Avoid non-5GHz noise:** This is a Wi-Fi chipset-based detection of energy that the chipset does not recognize. It is enabled by default and causes the AP to attempt to change channel on the next RRM cycle.

- **Avoid persistent non-Wi-Fi interference:** This is a CleanAir function that analyzes interferers and identifies those that will affect the channel continuously (for example, a camera feed). It is disabled by default. When enabled, it causes the AP to attempt to change channels on the next RRM if a detected interferer on the channel is persistent.

- **Event-Driven RRM (EDRRM):** This is a CleanAir function that reacts to severe interferers. If these interferers are present for more than 30 minutes, this feature triggers RRM instead of waiting for the next RRM cycle. The feature is disabled by default. When it is enabled, you can also configure the sensitivity threshold: high (AQI of 60), medium (AQI of 50), or low (AQI of 35), at which point the RRM event would be triggered.

On AireOS, the same functions are of course available. In the **Home > Monitoring > Interferers** page, you will find the list of interferers per band, along with their type, the detecting AP, device type, affected channel, severity and duty cycle, RSSI, and pseudo-MAC address. Clicking an interferer sends you to **Advanced > Monitor > Cisco CleanAir > [802.11a/n/ac/ax | 802.11b/g/n/ax] > Interference Devices**. In the same Cisco CleanAir umbrella, you will find Air Quality reports for each band and the **Worst Air Quality Report** option.

In **Wireless > [802.11a/n/ac/ax | 802.11b/g/n/ax] > CleanAir**, you can enable CleanAir. In AireOS, the feature is disabled by default (recall that it is enabled by default in C9800). You can also enable SI, choose what interferers to detect and report in the WLC, and from those, which ones to report via SNMP (to Cisco PI or DNAC).

In **Wireless > [802.11a/n/ac/ax | 802.11b/g/n/ax] > RRM > DCA**, you can configure **Avoid non-802.11a noise** (enabled by default and called in C9800 "non-5GHz noise"), configure **Avoid Persistent non-Wi-Fi Interference**, and configure EDRRM. For each individual AP, you can disable CleanAir (if CleanAir is enabled globally) from **Wireless > Access Points > [802.11a/n/ac/ax | 802.11b/g/n/ax] Configure CleanAir Status**.

Interferers on Cisco PI and DNAC

Naturally, interferers on Cisco PI are only reported if CleanAir or SI SNMP reporting is enabled on the WLC. Then, you will see CleanAir and SI interferers in the alarms, along with severity and reporting AP and WLC. You can also use the Search function to look for interferers by severity, type, or reporting AP.

For each AP listed in Cisco PI, a column mentions if CleanAir is enabled for this AP on the WLC.

The situation is even simpler on DNAC. The Health and Issues pages focus on the consequences of interferers (that is, high radio utilization or poor RF). Interferers are not reported as individual objects but as a possible root cause of detected issues. As such, interferers with little to no impact do not clog the interface and are not mentioned.

However, for each AP, in the AP 360 page, on the RF tab, you can see a graph with the Air Quality reported by this AP for each radio over the monitored period. When the AQI is less than 100, you can hover over the affected time interval to see the details of the associated interferer.

Summary

This chapter addressed the management of reports and alarms in Cisco Prime Infrastructure and DNA Center. It also pointed to tools and resources to help you troubleshoot issues related to client connectivity and RF interferences. In this chapter you have learned the following:

- How to configure reports on Cisco Prime Infrastructure

- How DNAC continuously produces reports, and how to tailor these reports to your needs

- A step-by-step methodology to analyze client connectivity issues

- How to use the WLC, Cisco PI, and DNAC tools to evaluate client issues, and how to perform dynamic air captures

- How to visualize reports and alarms about RF interferers on the WLC, Cisco PI, and DNAC

- How to configure your system to integrate RF interferences into the global RRM scheme

References

For additional information, refer to these resources:

Cisco Prime Infrastructure User Guide, Managing Reports: https://www.cisco.com/c/en/us/td/docs/net_mgmt/prime/infrastructure/3-6/user/guide/bk_CiscoPrimeInfrastructure_3_6_0_UserGuide/bk_CiscoPrimeInfrastructure_3_6_0_UserGuide_chapter_010111.html

Cisco DNAC, Managing Client Health: https://www.cisco.com/c/en/us/td/docs/cloud-systems-management/network-automation-and-management/dna-center-assurance/1-3-1-0/b_cisco_dna_assurance_1_3_1_0_ug/b_cisco_dna_assurance_1_3_1_0_chapter_0111.html

Cisco DNAC Path Trace: https://www.cisco.com/c/en/us/td/docs/cloud-systems-management/network-automation-and-management/dna-center-assurance/1-3-1-0/b_cisco_dna_assurance_1_3_1_0_ug/b_cisco_dna_assurance_1_3_1_0_chapter_01000.html

Cisco DNAC Intelligent Capture: https://www.cisco.com/c/en/us/td/docs/cloud-systems-management/network-automation-and-management/dna-center-assurance/1-3-1-0/b_cisco_dna_assurance_1_3_1_0_ug/b_cisco_dna_assurance_1_3_1_0_chapter_01100.html

Cisco DNAC Sensors and Sensor-Driven Tests: https://www.cisco.com/c/en/us/td/docs/cloud-systems-management/network-automation-and-management/dna-center-assurance/1-3-1-0/b_cisco_dna_assurance_1_3_1_0_ug/b_cisco_dna_assurance_1_3_1_0_chapter_01010.html

Cisco Prime Infrastructure, Troubleshooting Clients: https://www.cisco.com/c/en/us/td/docs/net_mgmt/prime/infrastructure/3-6/user/guide/bk_CiscoPrimeInfrastructure_3_6_0_UserGuide/bk_CiscoPrimeInfrastructure_3_6_0_UserGuide_chapter_010100.html#task_1082131

Cisco C9800, Client Troubleshooting: https://www.cisco.com/c/en/us/support/docs/wireless/catalyst-9800-series-wireless-controllers/213949-wireless-debugging-and-log-collection-on.html

Cisco CleanAir on C9800: https://www.cisco.com/c/en/us/td/docs/wireless/controller/9800/config-guide/b_wl_16_10_cg/cisco-cleanair.html

AireOS Configuration and Troubleshooting Guide: https://www.cisco.com/c/en/us/td/docs/wireless/controller/8-8/config-guide/b_cg88.html

Cisco Identity Solution Engine (ISE) Troubleshooting Client Guide: https://www.cisco.com/c/en/us/td/docs/security/ise/1-2/troubleshooting_guide/ise_tsg.html#pgfId-193059

Exam Preparation Tasks

As mentioned in the section "How to Use This Book" in the Introduction, you have a few choices for exam preparation: the exercises here, Chapter 18, "Final Preparation," and the exam simulation questions in the Pearson Test Prep Software Online.

Review All Key Topics

Review the most important topics in this chapter, noted with the Key Topic icon in the outer margin of the page. Table 16-2 lists these key topics and the page numbers on which each is found.

Table 16-2   Key Topics for Chapter 16

Key Topic Element	Description	Page Number
List	Report types on Prime Infrastructure	407
Paragraph	Reports on DNA Center	412
Paragraph	Rogues	417
List	Alarm types on PI	417
Paragraph	Good management vs. bad design	422

Define Key Terms

Define the following key terms from this chapter and check your answers in the glossary:

rogue AP, rogue client, ad hoc rogue, Probing state, L2authcomplete state, 802.1X_reqd, DHCP_reqd, Webauth_reqd, Run, Health, Path Trace, Intelligent Capture, SAgE, SI, CleanAir, severity, pseudo-MAC, AQI, EDRRM

CHAPTER 17

Device Hardening

This chapter covers the following topics:

> **Implementing Device Access Controls:** This section examines how remote network management through AAA systems, such as RADIUS and TACACS+, can be used to control management access to the controller and restrict certain functions on a per-user basis. This section also examines the steps involved in setting up device-level authorization using the Cisco Identity Services Engine (ISE).

> **Implementing Access Point Authentication:** This section examines how to enable authentication on the AP using 802.1X and RADIUS so it can gain access to the network as a client.

> **Implementing CPU ACLs on the Wireless Controller:** CPU ACLs are a method to limit access to services that involve the wireless controller's CPU. This section discusses how this can be implemented as well as best practices to be aware of when using this feature.

This chapter covers the following ENWLSI exam topics:

- 8.1 Implement device access controls (including RADIUS and TACACS+)

- 8.2 Implement access point authentication (including 802.1X)

- 8.3 Implement CPU ACLs on the controller

Like other elements of a network, both physical and virtual wireless devices are susceptible to attack and need to be protected against potential vulnerabilities. One common strategy in protecting network devices is to reduce the attack surface as much as possible, thereby limiting the scope and domain of potential threats. One way to do this is to have central control of not only who can administer the controllers but what levels of access they are allowed to have. This type of granular and centrally controlled access is accomplished through AAA services using protocols such as RADIUS and TACACS+.

This chapter presents an examination of how RADIUS and TACACS+ are configured on the controller. In addition to implementation of security on the controller, this section reviews how AAA services can be implemented on ISE, allowing granular command-level administration for different user groups.

This chapter also examines how APs can be deployed in a campus where they themselves are authenticated as clients against LAN switches.

Finally, this chapter discusses how CPU ACLs can be used to harden wireless infrastructure devices. CPU access control lists (ACLs) are a method to protect the controller from attacks that could ultimately harm management functions on the controller, causing serious degradation of all wireless services. This feature does not come without risk, so the final section of this chapter discusses best practices to be aware of when deploying this capability.

"Do I Know This Already?" Quiz

The "Do I Know This Already?" quiz allows you to assess whether you should read this entire chapter thoroughly or jump to the "Exam Preparation Tasks" section. If you are in doubt about your answers to these questions or your own assessment of your knowledge of the topics, read the entire chapter. Table 17-1 lists the major headings in this chapter and their corresponding "Do I Know This Already?" quiz questions. You can find the answers in Appendix D, "Answers to the 'Do I Know This Already?' Quizzes and Review Questions."

Table 17-1 "Do I Know This Already?" Section-to-Question Mapping

Foundation Topics Section	Questions
Implementing Device Access Controls	1, 2
Implementing Access Point Authentication	3, 4
Implementing CPU ACLs on the Wireless Controller	5

1. Why would someone prefer to use TACACS+ over RADIUS for management of users on a wireless controller?

   a. TACACS+ is considered more secure due to its encryption capabilities.

   b. RADIUS support has been deprecated.

   c. TACACS+ offers granular levels of command authorization.

   d. TACACS+ would not be preferred. They are essentially the same except that RADIUS is an open standard allowing support by third-party AAA servers.

2. In ISE, what is the role of the Device Admin Policy Sets?

   a. This is where the TACACS+ profiles are defined.

   b. This is where the controller is given command-level authorization control from ISE.

   c. This is where specific aspects of command-level access is defined.

   d. This is where user groups are mapped to the TACACS+ profiles according to the policy rules.

3. What is the purpose of enabling an access point with an 802.1X supplicant?

   a. This feature forces all user traffic to be authenticated against a back-end RADIUS or TACACS+ server, such as ISE.

   b. This feature is used when the AP is not able to challenge the users for 802.1X credentials, so the switch performs this feature instead.

   c. This feature enables authorization of which commands the controller is able to execute on the AP.

   d. This feature is used in NAC deployments where the AP itself must be authenticated to gain access to the network.

4. What is required on ISE to implement 802.1X for access points?

   a. Radius attributes specific for Cisco APs

   b. Policy sets

   c. Policy groups

   d. TACACS+ with CoA

5. When deploying CPU ACLs, what is one consideration that should be addressed?

   a. The final policy rule of the ACL should be an explicit "deny any" in most cases.

   b. The final policy rule of the ACL should be an explicit "permit any" in most cases.

   c. The CPU ACL must allow control plane functions originating from the controller itself, such as intercontroller, RRM, and DHCP communication.

   d. The CPU ACL should also have Control Plane Policing enabled.

Foundation Topics

Implementing Device Access Controls

Controlling management access to a wireless LAN controller can be implemented either using local accounts directly on the controller or through an AAA server using RADIUS or TACACS+.

Using an AAA server for management-level access, whether it is for CLI or GUI access, has several operational and security advantages:

- **Centralized password and user management:** If an administrator were to change a password, or if an administrator leaves the organization, centralized authentication means it is only necessary to make the change on the AAA server rather than on each device individually. Consider an organization that may have tens or even hundreds of wireless LAN controllers distributed around the world. If the local usernames and passwords were maintained on each device, modifying a user account would require significant effort whenever a change is required.

- **Centralized permission and command-level authorization to devices:** Using an AAA server, granular permission rules and policy can be implemented in one central place rather than in many. Using TACACS+, the AAA server can also provide granular levels of access to functions of the controller for different administrators or groups. For example, the AAA server may have a policy rule that grants certain users read-only access, while other administrators may have full access to all configuration options.

- **Accounting:** AAA servers support centralized accounting services, allowing each command that is executed on the wireless controller to be recorded for later review. This may be used as forensic evidence if the device is incorrectly configured or is maliciously tampered with.

- **Device Control:** A particular device can be centrally deauthorized or deactivated from the network if an administrator wishes to remove it. This may be useful if a device has gone missing or if it is older and needs to be deprecated.

NOTE RADIUS servers only offer two types of authorization to the controller: read-write or read-only access. TACACS+ supports more granular command-level authorization of the configuration, both through the CLI and the web interface.

AAA Design Overview

When an administrator logs in to the controller, the controller can provide authentication services based on local credentials (stored directly on the controller) or it can authenticate using a remote AAA server that is accessible by the controller. Cisco wireless LAN controllers support both RADIUS and TACACS+ authentication methods.

The AAA authentication process works as follows:

1. A management user logs in to the controller (either through the management GUI or through SSH). The controller responds, asking for the user to provide credentials (the username and password).

2. Once the user provides login credentials to the controller, the controller sends these to the RADIUS or TACACS+ AAA server (such as ISE) and asks the user to be authenticated and authorized. The AAA server first authenticates the user (based on supplying the correct username and password) and then provides an authorization level for this user, such as read-only or read-write privilege, or in the case of TACACS+, which functions of the controller the user is allowed to access.

3. The user is then granted or declined access based on the response from the AAA server. If the user is granted access, the user is only allowed to access specific aspects of the controller configuration that have been authorized by the AAA server.

Figure 17-1 illustrates this process.

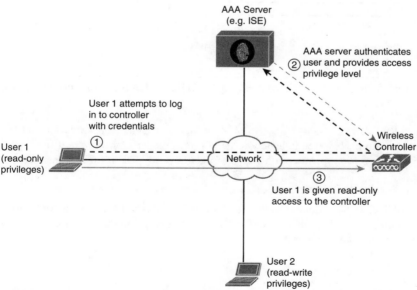

Figure 17-1 *Using a Remote AAA Server to Authenticate a Management User on the Wireless Controller*

AAA Configuration Overview on the Wireless Controller

This section examines how to implement centralized RADIUS authentication for administrators of a wireless LAN controller.

In an AireOS controller, navigate to **Security > AAA > RADIUS > Authentication** to configure the AAA server. In this configuration page, select the **Management** radio button to enable the RADIUS server function to authenticate administrators who log in to the WLC (without this enabled, the RADIUS server can only be used for wireless client authentication). Once this option is enabled, the AAA server will be used as a RADIUS authentication server for administrators, and all controller user-management authentication requests will go to the RADIUS server. This will be used for administrators who attempt to log in to either the web interface or the command line via SSH.

Figure 17-2 illustrates this configuration page.

Figure 17-2   *Configuring an AireOS Controller for RADIUS Management Authentication*

> **NOTE**   Modern RADIUS servers use UDP 1812 for authentication and authorization and UDP 1813 for accounting. However, in legacy RADIUS versions these ports were different: UDP 1645 was used for authentication and authorization and UDP 1646 was used for accounting.

Configuration of TACACS+ is done through the **Security > AAA > TACACS+ > Authentication** menu. Configuration is similar to RADIUS, with the exception that it is not necessary to explicitly select the **management** option.

On the Catalyst 9800, configuration of AAA for management users is accomplished by navigating to **Configuration > AAA** in the web interface. From here, there are two options: directly configure the RADIUS/TACACS+ servers manually or launch the **AAA Wizard** option. Figure 17-3 illustrates what is seen after launching the AAA Wizard.

Figure 17-3 *Configuring a RADIUS Server Through the AAA Wizard*

Once the RADIUS server has been defined, click **Next**. To enable administrative management authentication services, select the **login** pull-down option on the **Server Group Association** screen, as shown in Figure 17-4.

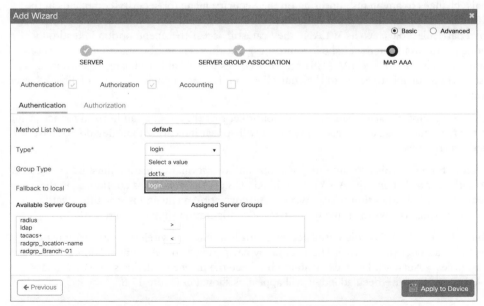

Figure 17-4 *Configuring the Controller to Use a RADIUS Server for Management (Login) Authentication*

The last step is to assign the RADIUS or TACACS+ server to the **Assigned Server Group**. The purpose of this step is to allow different AAA servers to be used for wireless client 802.1X authentication versus management authentication services (only enable this if a separate AAA server is used for management authentication purposes; if not, just use the same AAA server).

Implementing TACACS+ Profiles and Command Authorization

Terminal Access Controller Access Control System Plus (TACACS+) is a client/server protocol that provides centralized security for users attempting to gain management access to a networking device. It serves as a centralized authentication system similar to RADIUS; however, one key difference is that RADIUS provides only authentication support with limited authorization (users can only be authorized as read-only or read-write), whereas TACACS+ provides authentication, granular authorization, and accounting services. TACACS+ also uses TCP port 49, making it a reliable protocol for communications (RADIUS uses UDP).

For TACACS+, authorization is based on a privilege level (or role) that grants the administrator access to different configuration aspects of the controller. For AireOS controllers, the available roles correspond to the seven configuration menu options on the controller's web interface: **MONITOR, WLAN, CONTROLLER, WIRELESS, SECURITY, MANAGEMENT,** and **COMMANDS**. An additional role, **LOBBY**, is available for administrators who require only lobby ambassador privileges. The roles to which users are assigned are configurable in the AAA TACACS+ server (that is, ISE). Users can be authorized for one or more roles, giving far more flexibility than a RADIUS server's read-only or read-write options.

The minimum TACACS+ authorization level is **MONITOR** only, which is equivalent to read-only access in RADIUS. The maximum level is **ALL**, which authorizes an administrator with super-user privileges to execute configuration changes across the entire controller (both at the CLI and web interface). For example, a user who is assigned the role of **SECURITY** can make changes to any items appearing on the **Security** menu (or security commands in the CLI) but will be restricted from the other configuration options. If users are not authorized for a particular role (such as **WLAN**), they can still access that menu option in read-only mode (or the associated CLI **show** commands), but they will not be able to make any configuration changes. If the TACACS+ server becomes unreachable or unable to authorize, users will be unable to log in to the controller, so it is generally wise to have a fallback server available.

If users attempt to make changes on the controller that they are not authorized for according to their assigned role, a message on the GUI will appear indicating that they do not have sufficient privileges.

In order for a controller to support TACACS+ authorization, this feature must be enabled on both the controller and the AAA server. In AireOS controllers, this is configured in the **Security > Authentication > TACACS+ > Authorization** menu and is straightforward to configure (this follows the same web interface configuration shown in Figure 17-3).

To configure TACACS+ role-based access controls in ISE, the wireless controller must first be added as a network device. This is done by navigating to the **Administration > Network Resources > Network Devices** menu in ISE. Once the device credentials for the wireless LAN controller have been added, it will appear as shown in Figure 17-5.

Figure 17-5 *Adding the Wireless LAN Controller as a Network Device in ISE (Note: ISE Version 2.6 Used Here)*

Once the network device has been added, the next step is to ensure that the ISE server is itself enabled to authorize administrative control for network devices. This is done by navigating to **Administration > System > Deployment** and clicking the name of the ISE server (shown as **"iceman"** in the example in Figure 17-6).

Figure 17-6 *Navigating to the ISE Deployment Settings*

From this screen, ensure that **Enable Device Admin Service** is correctly checked, as shown in Figure 17-7.

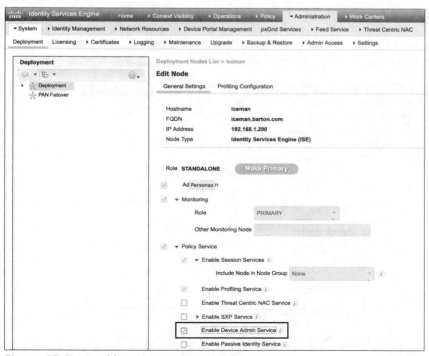

Figure 17-7 *Enabling the ISE Server Admin Service*

The next step is to define the TACACS+ profiles that will be used to grant specific levels of access to different groups of administrators.

> **NOTE**   An assumption is made that an LDAP directory service such as Active Directory has been configured on the ISE server and will return group identifiers that can be used for TACACS authorization. If an LDAP server is not in use, it is also possible to use locally defined users in ISE.

Navigate to the **Work Centers > Device Administration > Policy Elements** menu in ISE and expand the **Results** tab on the left. Clicking **TACACS Profiles** causes certain default profiles to be displayed. Figure 17-8 illustrates this step.

Figure 17-8   *Navigating to the TACACS Profiles in the Policy Elements Page of ISE*

TACACS Profiles allow granular privileges to be created, giving different administrators access to selected portions of the controller's web interface and CLI. For example, clicking the **+Add** button causes a screen similar to Figure 17-9 to be displayed.

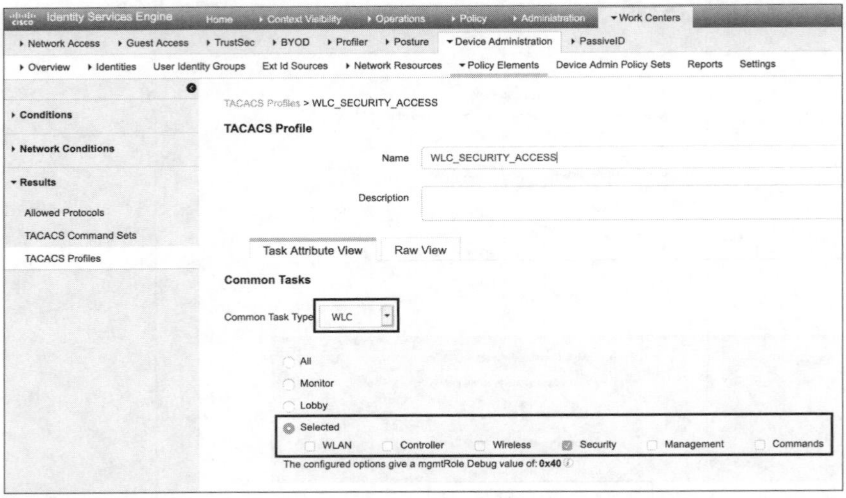

Figure 17-9   *Configuring a Policy to Only Allow Access to the Security Configuration Area of the Controller*

Figure 17-9 shows the various command-level authorization profiles available. Here, the **Security** option is selected. This specifically relates to the AireOS class of controllers. If the Catalyst 9800 is in use, the **Shell** option can be selected, which equates to the 0–15 privilege levels commonly used in IOS and IOS-XE.

This example demonstrates the creation of a TACACS profile that will grant an administrator access to only the Security tab of the controller. As such, the name of the profile in Figure 17-9 is called **WLC_SECURITY_ACCESS**, and only **Security** is selected in the profile option table.

As different profiles are created, any combination of the options shown in Figure 17-9 may be selected, and as many different profiles as are required may be defined (although it is reasonable to keep the number of profiles small for administrative simplicity).

Once the TACACS profiles have been configured, the last step is to create a policy that maps user groups to these policies. To do this, navigate to the **Work Centers > Device Administration > Device Admin Policy Sets** menu in ISE, as shown in Figure 17-10.

Figure 17-10 *Navigating to the Device Admin Policy Sets Page Where the TACACS Profile Will Be Applied to User Groups*

As shown in Figure 17-10, a new policy has been created called **Wireless Controller Policy**. Although the device admin policy can be extremely granular if needed, in this case the policy is wide open and will be triggered when the device location matches **All Locations**, meaning all network devices defined in ISE will use this rule.

By clicking the arrow at the far right of the policy, it is possible to configure the authorization policy where specific user groups are mapped and actions can be taken. Figure 17-11 shows four entries for this policy. The Authorization Policy rules first match against a condition. Note that there are names assigned to these conditions. These are simply rules that identify which user groups will match the policy (for example, the condition may match which Active Directory group they are part of). For each rule, the result will be an assignment to one of the previously defined profiles, shown in this example as **WLC MONITOR, WLC_SECURITY_ACCESS, WLC ALL**, followed by an implicit deny all profiles at the end of the rule set (meaning if they don't fall into one of the prior groups, the user is declined access).

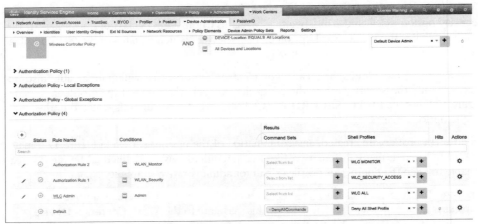

Figure 17-11 *Configuring the ISE Authorization Policy*

Implementing Access Point Authentication

When networks are widely deployed with Network Admission Control (NAC), client devices must support some method of authentication to gain access to the network. Most commonly, 802.1X supplicants are used on client devices so they can be authenticated through a local switch and the backend AAA server (that is, ISE). While support for 802.1X supplicants in most computers and mobile devices is expected, other network devices such as IP phones, printers, IoT devices, and wireless APs may require specific configuration if network-wide 802.1X is implemented.

In this regard, this section explores how to implement an 802.1X supplicant on a Cisco AP. Once a switch port is configured as an 802.1X authenticator, the switch will restrict the AP's traffic until it authenticates successfully with 802.1X. Thus, only after the AP is configured to act as an 802.1X supplicant will it be authenticated and given access to the network.

On Cisco controllers, EAP-FAST is used with anonymous Protected Access Credentials (PAC) provisioning to enable 802.1X authentication of access points.

Implementation of 802.1X on the access point requires the three following steps:

1. Enable the 802.1X supplicant on the AP (either globally or on a per-AP basis).

2. Configure the local switch port with 802.1X and the backend ISE server as the authentication server.

3. Configure ISE with the correct security policies to authenticate and authorize traffic from the AP.

Figure 17-12 illustrates how the 802.1X supplicant may be configured on an AP. In an AireOS controller, this is configured in the **Wireless > Access Points** menu. Note that the 802.1X supplicant configuration may be implemented either locally on a per-AP basis or globally for all APs. In this configuration step, the 802.1X credentials must be entered and the **EAP-FAST** method must be selected. In the example shown here, the AP username **maverick** is used.

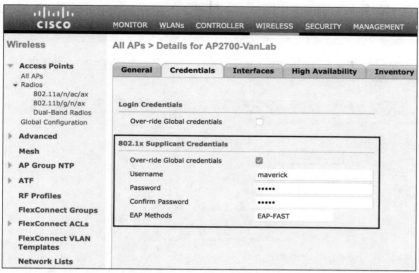

Figure 17-12 *Configuring the AP with 802.1X Supplicant Credentials*

Once the APs have been configured with 802.1X supplicants, the local switch must be configured to authenticate devices with 802.1X on a per-interface basis and the AAA server must be defined in the global configuration of the switch.

Example 17-1 illustrates a sample configuration on a Cisco Catalyst switch.

Example 17-1 *Configuring the Switch for 802.1X Authentication*

```
! enable dot1x on the switch globally and add the ISE server to the switch

aaa new-model
!
aaa authentication dot1x default group radius
!
dot1x system-auth-control
!
radius server ISE
address ipv4 10.48.39.161 auth-port 1645 acct-port 1646
  key 7 123A0C0411045D5679

! next configure AP switch port for dot1x
interface GigabitEthernet0/15
 switchport access vlan 123
 switchport mode access
 authentication order dot1x
 authentication port-control auto
 dot1x pae authenticator
 spanning-tree portfast edge
```

In the final step, ISE must be configured to authenticate the AP and authorize it for access to the network. After logging in to ISE, the first step is to ensure that EAP-FAST is allowed in the **Allowed Protocols** for default network access.

Figure 17-13 shows how this is configured under the **Policy > Policy Elements > Results > Default Network Access** tab.

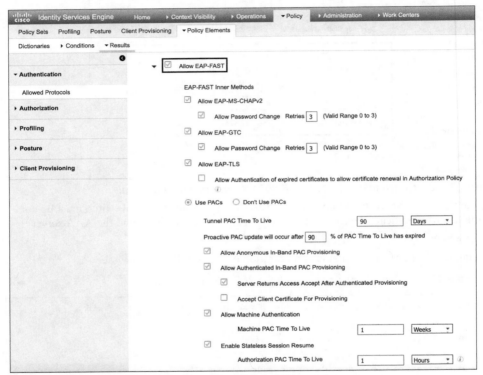

Figure 17-13 *Enable EAP-FAST in the Allowed Protocols*

Similar to users who are authenticating to gain network access, the device's username and password credentials must also be added to ISE; however, in this case there must be a special group defined for these types of users (this will be used later when authorizing the AP for access to the network).

Figure 17-14 illustrates the creation of a new user group called **APs** and adding the user credentials for **maverick** to this group (the username of the AP that is to be authenticated). This is added in the **Administration > Identity Management > Groups > User Identity Groups** menu. Note that the AP's user identity can be stored either locally or in a remote directory store such as Active Directory.

Once the user is defined, the final step is to create the authentication and authorization policies for the AP. ISE uses the concept of policy sets to apply customized policy rules to different kinds of users or devices. Policy sets are really just an ordered list of rules that first match a set of authentication criteria and then apply different policies based on the outcome of the rule.

Figure 17-14 *Configure the AP Authentication Credentials*

Once a new policy set has been created and named, the next step is to identify the conditions that will trigger the policy set. This simply means that if there is an event that matches these conditions, the subsequent authentication and authorization policy rules will be invoked. For example, Figure 17-15 illustrates a new policy called **dot1x Policy Set**. In order to invoke the authentication or authorization policies, an authentication method of either **Wired_802.1X** or **Wireless_802.1X** must have been used. Obviously, this covers a pretty wide array of authentication possibilities, but it is used here to illustrate the purpose of a policy set (meaning the rule will be used for either wired or wireless 802.1X access attempts). Note also a default policy set is defined if none of the earlier ones are matched.

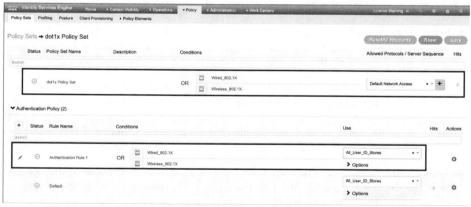

Figure 17-15 *Configure the ISE Policy Set and Authentication Rule*

Once the policy set has been set up, it is now possible to configure the authentication and authorization policies below it. Clicking the right-pointing arrow on the policy set causes the suboptions menu to open, which includes the authentication and authorization submenus. As shown in Figure 17-15, an authentication rule can be configured. In this case, a simple rule is implemented that matches on either the Wired or Wireless 802.1X authentication method, and All_User_ID_Stores is used to authenticate the user. Note that the default rule would have also worked in this case, as it will attempt to authenticate users against all known ID stores (it could also be more granular if desired).

The final step is to configure the authorization policy. This is a key configuration step, as it allows the AP and all traffic it passes to have access to the network. In this case, a new rule is created called Port_AuthZ. The conditions of the rule are that the user must be part of the Identity Group name APs and that the user must be authenticating through the Wired_802.X method. The result of a successful match is that the AP is permitted access to the network. Note in Figure 17-16 how this authorization rule has been created and how the default rule below it is an explicit deny if authentication fails.

Figure 17-16   *Configure the ISE Authorization Rule to Allow Network Access*

Implementing CPU ACLs on the Wireless Controller

Another method to harden and protect the wireless controller is to implement CPU access control lists (ACLs). CPU ACLs are used to restrict what kind of traffic is allowed and which devices can communicate with the controller's control plane functions governed by the CPU. This includes SSH, ICMP, and other management functions that are processed by the CPU.

It is important to mention a few key characteristics of CPU ACLs:

- For AireOS controllers using versions 6.0 and later, CPU ACLs are applicable for traffic originating both to and from the controller. Thus, when you're creating the ACLs and attaching them to the CPU, the ACL direction fields do not have any relevance.

- By default, CPU ACLs use an implicit deny rule at the end of the ACL, meaning once the ACL is implemented, critical management and control functions may be restricted if they are not explicitly permitted. Since this can cause unexpected problems, if CPU ACLs are used, it is generally recommended to use an explicit **permit all** statement at the end of the ACL.

- The controller has a set of filtering rules for internal processes that can be checked with the **sh rules** command. ACLs do not affect these rules, nor can these rules be modified on the fly. However, CPU ACLs take precedence over these internal rules.

One of the main challenges to be considered when deploying a strict CPU ACL is the possible impact it may have on critical management and control functions that are not explicitly permitted by the ACL. For example, the implicit "deny any" statement at the end of the ACL policy may impact communications between controllers on the same mobility group, DHCP functions, and many critical activities of the controller. Thus, it is highly recommended to limit the rules of the CPU ACL to only what must be absolutely restricted and permit everything else. In fact, if CPU ACLs are incorrectly implemented on the controller, the administrator could be locked out of the controller with no way back in other than through physical access to the console.

In many situations, CPU ACLs can be risky, so the general guideline is to only use them to restrict remote access methods, such as SSH, Telnet, HTTP, HTTPS, and ICMP from specific risky locations, and then use a "permit any" statement at the end. Note that it is also possible to implement these kinds of rules on a firewall or aggregation router in front of the controller, so a controller CPU ACL may not be necessary.

Figure 17-17 illustrates the creation of sample CPU ACL on an AireOS controller that restricts HTTP and ICMP traffic from various parts of the network. Note the "permit any" rule at the end of the policy.

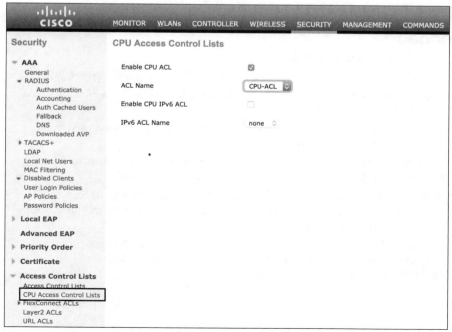

Figure 17-17 *Configuring a CPU Access Control List*

Once the ACL has been defined, the final step is to attach it to the CPU ACL policy. This can be configured in the **Security > Access Control Lists > CPU ACLs** menu. Figure 17-18 illustrates this configuration step.

Figure 17-18 *Implementing the CPU Access Control List*

NOTE   One aspect of protecting a network device is to make sure that the control plane and CPU are not overwhelmed with more management traffic than they can process. This is commonly referred to as *control plane policing*. On all Cisco controllers (after AireOS 4.1), control plane policing is enabled by default. This function is enabled if control plane traffic directed toward the CPU exceeds 2Mbps. It is possible to enable or disable this feature but not to set trigger data rates against which traffic it will act. In normal operations, it is recommended this feature be left enabled.

Summary

This chapter focused on methods of hardening devices in the wireless LAN deployments. In this chapter you have learned the following:

- How to set up the wireless controller to be managed through AAA services such as RADIUS and TACACS+

- How ISE can be used to control privilege levels of management access to the wireless controller

- How to configure the AP as an 802.1X supplicant such that it can gain network access to a secured switch

- How to configure the ISE policy to authenticate and authorize an AP onto the network

- How to implement CPU ACLs on the controller and when this should be done

References

For additional information, refer to these resources:

How to implement access to the wireless controller management with RADIUS and TACACS+: https://www.cisco.com/c/en/us/td/docs/wireless/controller/8-5/config-guide/b_cg85/aaa_administration.html

Configuring the AP as an 802.1X supplicant: https://www.cisco.com/c/en/us/support/docs/wireless-mobility/wireless-fixed/107946-LAP-802-1x.html

Implementing CPU ACLs on the controller: https://www.cisco.com/c/en/us/td/docs/wireless/controller/8-5/config-guide/b_cg85/access_control_lists.html

Configuring an external RADIUS server in the Identity Services Engine (ISE): https://www.cisco.com/c/en/us/support/security/identity-services-engine/products-installation-and-configuration-guides-list.html

ISE and Catalyst 9800 Integration Guide: https://community.cisco.com/t5/security-documents/ise-and-catalyst-9800-series-integration-guide/ta-p/3753060#toc-hId--389699194

Exam Preparation Tasks

As mentioned in the section "How to Use This Book" in the Introduction, you have a few choices for exam preparation: the exercises here, Chapter 18, "Final Preparation," and the exam simulation questions in the Pearson Test Prep Software Online.

Review All Key Topics

Review the most important topics in this chapter, noted with the Key Topic icon in the outer margin of the page. Table 17-2 lists these key topics and the page numbers on which each is found.

Table 17-2   Key Topics for Chapter 17

Key Topic Element	Description	Page Number
Figure 17-1	Using a remote AAA server to authenticate a management user on the wireless controller	443
Figure 17-2	Configuring an AireOS controller for RADIUS management authentication	444
Figure 7-11	Configuring the ISE authorization policy	450
Example 17-1	Configuring the switch for 802.1X authentication	451
Figure 17-15	Configuring the ISE policy set and authentication rule	453
Figure 17-17	Configuring a CPU access control list	455

Define Key Terms

Define the following key terms from this chapter and check your answers in the glossary:

Remote Authentication Dial-In User Service (RADIUS), Terminal Access Controller Access-Control System+ (TACACS+), Network Admission Control (NAC), policy set, CPU ACL

CHAPTER 18

Final Preparation

The first 17 chapters of this book cover the technologies, protocols, design concepts, and considerations required to be prepared to pass the CCNP Designing Cisco Enterprise Wireless Networks (ENWLSD) 300-425 and Implementing Cisco Enterprise Wireless Networks (ENWLSI) 300-430 exams. While these chapters supply the detailed information, most people need more preparation than simply reading the first 17 chapters of this book. This chapter details a set of tools and a study plan to help you complete your preparation for the exams.

This short chapter has two main sections. The first section lists the exam preparation tools useful at this point in the study process. The second section lists a suggested study plan now that you have completed all the earlier chapters in this book.

Getting Ready

Here are some important tips to keep in mind to ensure you are ready for these rewarding exams!

- **Build and use a study tracker:** Consider taking the exam objectives shown in each chapter and build yourself a study tracker. This will help ensure you have not missed anything and that you are confident for your exam! As a matter of fact, this book offers a sample Study Planner as a website supplement.

- **Think about your time budget for questions in the exam:** When you do the math, you realize that on average you have one minute per question. While this does not sound like enough time, realize that many of the questions will be very straightforward, and you will take 15 to 30 seconds on those. This builds time for other questions as you take your exam.

- **Watch the clock:** Check in on the time remaining periodically as you are taking the exam. You might even find that you can slow down pretty dramatically as you have built up a nice block of extra time.

- **Get some ear plugs:** The testing center might provide ear plugs, but get some just in case and bring them along. There might be other test takers in the center with you and you do not want to be distracted by their noise.

- **Plan your travel time:** Give yourself extra time to find the center and get checked in. Be sure to arrive early. As you test more at that center, you can certainly start cutting it closer time-wise.

- **Get rest:** Most students report success with getting plenty of rest the night before the exam. All-night cram sessions are not typically successful.

- **Bring in valuables but get ready to lock them up:** The testing center will take your phone, your smart watch, your wallet, and other such items. They will provide a secure place for them.

- **Take notes:** You will be given note-taking implements, so do not be afraid to use them. Consider jotting down any questions you struggled with during the exam. Memorize these at the end of the test by reading your notes over and over again. Make sure you have a pen and paper in the car so you can write the issues down in there just after the exam, while the exam questions are still fresh on your mind. Then when you get home, with either a pass or fail, you can research those items.

Tools for Final Preparation

This section lists some information about the available tools and how to access them.

Pearson Cert Practice Test Engine and Questions on the Website

Register this book to get access to the Pearson IT Certification test engine (software that displays and grades a set of exam-realistic, multiple-choice questions). Using the Pearson Cert Practice Test Engine, you can either study by going through the questions in Study mode or take a simulated (timed) CCNP wireless specialization exam.

The Pearson Test Prep practice test software comes with two full practice exams. These practice tests are available to you either online or as an offline Windows application. To access the practice exams that were developed with this book, please see the instructions in the card inserted in the sleeve in the back of the book. This card includes a unique access code that enables you to activate your exams in the Pearson Test Prep software.

Accessing the Pearson Test Prep Software Online

The online version of this software can be used on any device with a browser and connectivity to the Internet, including desktop machines, tablets, and smartphones. To start using your practice exams online, simply follow these steps:

Step 1. Go to: http://www.PearsonTestPrep.com.

Step 2. Select **Pearson IT Certification** as your product group.

Step 3. Enter your email/password for your account. If you don't have an account on PearsonITCertification.com or CiscoPress.com, you will need to establish one by going to PearsonITCertification.com/join.

Step 4. In the **My Products** tab, click the **Activate New Product** button.

Step 5. Enter the access code printed on the insert card in the back of your book to activate your product.

Step 6. The product will now be listed in your My Products page. Click the **Exams** button to launch the exam settings screen and start your exam.

Accessing the Pearson Test Prep Software Offline

If you wish to study offline, you can download and install the Windows version of the Pearson Test Prep software. There is a download link for this software on the book's companion website, or you can just enter this link in your browser:

http://www.pearsonitcertification.com/content/downloads/pcpt/engine.zip

To access the book's companion website and the software, simply follow these steps:

Step 1.   Register your book by going to PearsonITCertification.com/register and entering the ISBN 9780136600954.

Step 2.   Respond to the challenge questions.

Step 3.   Go to your account page and select the **Registered Products** tab.

Step 4.   Click the **Access Bonus Content** link under the product listing.

Step 5.   Click the **Install Pearson Test Prep Desktop Version** link under the Practice Exams section of the page to download the software.

Step 6.   Once the software finishes downloading, unzip all the files on your computer.

Step 7.   Double-click the application file to start the installation, and follow the on-screen instructions to complete the registration.

Step 8.   Once the installation is complete, launch the application and select **Activate Exam** button on the My Products tab.

Step 9.   Click the **Activate a Product** button in the Activate Product Wizard.

Step 10. Enter the unique access code found on the card in the sleeve in the back of your book and click the **Activate** button.

Step 11. Click **Next** and then the **Finish** button to download the exam data to your application.

Step 12. You can now start using the practice exams by selecting the product and clicking the **Open Exam** button to open the exam settings screen.

Note that the offline and online versions will synch together, so saved exams and grade results recorded on one version will be available to you on the other as well.

Customizing Your Exams

Once you are in the exam settings screen, you can choose to take exams in one of three modes:

- Study Mode
- Practice Exam Mode
- Flash Card Mode

Study Mode allows you to fully customize your exams and review answers as you are taking the exam. This is typically the mode you would use first to assess your knowledge and identify information gaps. Practice Exam Mode locks certain customization options, as it is presenting a realistic exam experience. Use this mode when you are preparing to test your exam readiness. Flash Card Mode strips out the answers and presents you with only the question stem. This mode is great for late-stage preparation when you really want to challenge yourself to provide answers without the benefit of seeing multiple-choice options. This mode will not provide the detailed score reports that the other two modes will, so it should not be used if you are trying to identify knowledge gaps.

In addition to these three modes, you will be able to select the source of your questions. You can choose to take exams that cover all of the chapters or you can narrow your selection to just a single chapter or the chapters that make up specific parts in the book. All chapters are selected by default. If you want to narrow your focus to individual chapters, simply deselect all the chapters and then select only those on which you wish to focus in the Objectives area.

You can also select the exam banks on which to focus. Each exam bank comes complete with a full exam of questions that cover topics in every chapter. The two exams printed in the book are available to you as well as two additional exams of unique questions. You can have the test engine serve up exams from all four banks or just from one individual bank by selecting the desired banks in the exam bank area.

There are several other customizations you can make to your exam from the exam settings screen, such as the time of the exam, the number of questions served up, whether to randomize questions and answers, whether to show the number of correct answers for multiple answer questions, or whether to serve up only specific types of questions. You can also create custom test banks by selecting only questions that you have marked or questions on which you have added notes.

Updating Your Exams

If you are using the online version of the Pearson Test Prep software, you should always have access to the latest version of the software as well as the exam data. If you are using the Windows desktop version, every time you launch the software, it will check to see if there are any updates to your exam data and automatically download any changes that were made since the last time you used the software. This requires that you are connected to the Internet at the time you launch the software.

Sometimes, due to many factors, the exam data may not fully download when you activate your exam. If you find that figures or exhibits are missing, you may need to manually update your exams.

To update a particular exam you have already activated and downloaded, simply select the **Tools** tab and select the **Update Products** button. Again, this is only an issue with the desktop Windows application.

If you wish to check for updates to the Pearson Test Prep exam engine software, Windows desktop version, simply select the **Tools** tab and select the **Update Application** button. This will ensure you are running the latest version of the software engine.

Premium Edition

In addition to the free practice exam provided on the website, you can purchase additional exams with expanded functionality directly from Pearson IT Certification. The Premium Edition of this title contains an additional two full practice exams and an eBook (in both PDF and ePub format). In addition, the Premium Edition title also has remediation for each question to the specific part of the eBook that relates to that question.

Because you have purchased the print version of this title, you can purchase the Premium Edition at a deep discount. There is a coupon code in the book sleeve that contains a one-time-use code and instructions for where you can purchase the Premium Edition.

To view the Premium Edition product page, go to www.informit.com/title/9780136590866.

Chapter-Ending Review Tools

Chapters 1 through 17 have several features in the "Exam Preparation Tasks" section at the end of the chapters. You might have already worked through these in each chapter. It can also be useful to use these tools again as you make your final preparations for the exam.

Suggested Plan for Final Review/Study

This section lists a suggested study plan from the point at which you finish reading through Chapter 17, until you take the 300-425 ENWLSD exam or 300-430 ENWLSI exam. Certainly, you can ignore this plan, use it as is, or just take suggestions from it.

The plan uses two steps:

Step 1. **Review key topics and DIKTA? questions:** You can use the table that lists the key topics in each chapter or just flip the pages looking for key topics. Also, reviewing the DIKTA? questions from the beginning of the chapter can be helpful for review.

Step 2. **Use the Pearson Cert Practice Test engine to practice:** The Pearson Cert Practice Test engine can be used to study using a bank of unique exam-realistic questions available only with this book.

Summary

The tools and suggestions listed in this chapter have been designed with one goal in mind: to help you develop the skills required to pass the CCNP 300-425 ENWLSD and 300-430 ENWLSI wireless specialization exams. This book has been developed from the beginning to not just tell you the facts but to also help you learn how to apply the facts. No matter what your experience level leading up to when you take the exams, it is our hope that the broad range of preparation tools, and even the structure of the book, help you pass the exam with ease. We hope you do well on the exam.

APPENDIX A

802.11ax

Although not called out directly in the first version of the CCNP exam blueprint, 802.11ax is at the heart of Wi-Fi innovations for the first half of the 2020 decade. If you work in Wi-Fi, having some knowledge of the protocol, and of what it changes, will go a long way in helping you assess why Wi-Fi 6 deeply changes Wi-Fi.

In fact, you will often hear Wi-Fi 6 and 5G compared. 5G, a cellular technology developed by 3GPP, has been designed and thought of throughout the 2010 decade as the next generation of radio interface standards for mobile systems. The goal was to prepare the cellular world for massive machine-type communications as well as and ultra-reliable and low-latency communications. The ability to communicate over higher frequencies (suitable only for medium-range communications, a few hundred meters at most) and in unlicensed bands (the same bands that Wi-Fi uses today) was added. This fifth generation of cellular standards release started being published and implemented in 2018 and 2019. Its characteristics brought some actors to claim that 5G would be sufficient for all needs and that soon Wi-Fi would no longer be needed.

However, this rather partisan view tended to compare 5G to older Wi-Fi technologies, like 802.11a and 802.11n. Just like their cellular counterparts, the 802.11 experts at the IEEE were also designing the next generation of Wi-Fi protocols with similar concerns: addressing super-high density and low-latency communications (like AR/VR), for which delay, jitter, or loss can be highly destructive of the user quality of experience. The outcome is 802.11ax. Just like for 802.11ac and 802.11n, the industry excitement was so high that the Wi-Fi Alliance (WFA) decided to design a first 802.11ax certification based on a stable 802.11ax from 2018 (draft 3.0). Also recognizing that certifications bearing code names (like "802.11ac wave 1" or similar) could cause confusion for the general public, the WFA decided to adopt a consistent naming convention for all certifications relative to what we call PHY technologies. These are technologies that implement new modulations, new data rates, and so on, while the WFA also publishes many new MAC-based certifications that implement new features (for example, around security, quality of service [QoS], and so on).

Figure A-1 represents these Wi-Fi generations, following the WFA's new naming convention.

You will hear many experts say that Wi-Fi 6 brings to 802.11 technologies the same ground-breaking improvements that 5G did for cellular. In essence, these improvements can be placed in three groups: efficiency (much in the same line as 802.11ac and previous generations), a new scheduling method, and Internet of Things (IoT).

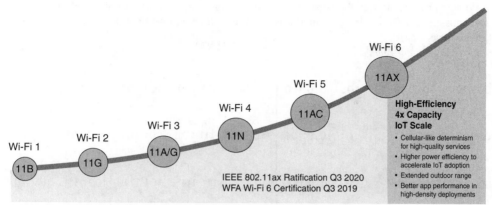

Figure A-1 *The WFA 6 Generations of Wi-Fi PHY-Based Certifications*

Efficiency

Until 2009, 802.11 channels were 20MHz wide and sending a single signal at any given time. 802.11n introduced the idea of grouping two adjacent channels in a single transmission, thus allowing 40MHz transmissions. With the OFDM modulations and its 64 subcarriers, this transmission more than doubled the potential throughput by allowing the reuse of subcarriers that were at the edge of the channel. These subcarriers were flat in 20MHz transmissions to create a margin at the edge of the channel. With 40MHz, the upper part of the lower channel and the lower part of the upper channel could now also actively send data, thus only keeping flat the subcarriers at the bottom of the lower channel and at the top of the upper channel.

802.11n also allowed up to four concurrent transmissions (from a single transmitter), called spatial streams. Via careful coordination between these streams, 802.11n allowed for increased range or increased throughput. In theory, if you send four signals at the same time, you can send four times as many bits in the same time window. This technology was called Multiple Input, Multiple Output (MIMO).

Finally, as chipsets became more efficient, allowing a receiver to differentiate between two or more concurrent streams, 802.11n also improved OFDM modulations. In its higher data rates, 802.11 OFDM uses a quadrature amplitude modulation (QAM) transmission technique, where each subcarrier varies its intensity and transmission direction so that the peak of the signal matches a target position. Although the process occurs in the time and space domains, an easy way to represent it is to imagine a target with a vertical and a horizontal line passing through the center, with four quadrants, as represented in Figure A-2.

Each target position represents a specific code (for example, 45 degrees up and left, a mid-intensity represents 001 101). To limit losses, a percentage of the signal is repeated (for example, 25% repeats, coded as "3/4 of new symbols in all transmissions"). Naturally, more repeats decrease the risk of losses but also reduce the amount of new information transmitted. Thus, lower repeat schemes are adapted for transmissions in quieter RF conditions. Similarly, with RF noise, the various targets in each quadrant are never reached exactly. Therefore, a system with more targets in each quadrant will require chipsets of better quality and a quieter RF channel. 802.11a and 802.11g allowed for up to 64-QAM 3/4, which means 64 different possible signal positions (16 in each quadrant), and 3/4 of new symbols in all transmissions. 802.11n also extended this scheme, still using 64-QAM, but allowing for the 5/6 scheme.

64-QAM

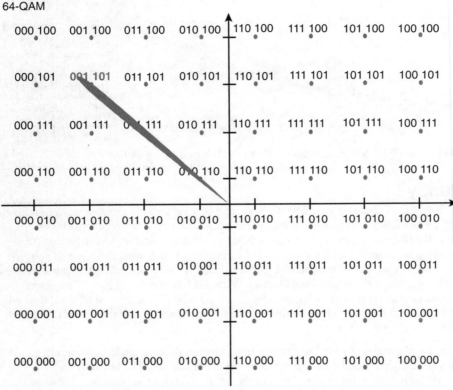

Figure A-2 *OFDM QAM Transmissions*

802.11ac continued this trend, allowing 80MHz and even 160MHz transmissions, 256-QAM 8/9, and up to eight spatial streams (SS). Practically, though, no vendor implemented more than four SS (because it's complicated), and the WFA did not certify beyond four SS. 802.11ac also allowed Multi-User MIMO (MU-MIMO), by which an Access Point (AP) could send spatial streams to different users (up to four SS = up to four stations receiving the AP transmission at the same time, with each station receiving its own data in its own stream).

802.11ax continued that same trend, still allowing 160MHz transmissions, eight SS, but also allowing 1024-QAM 5/6. 802.11ax allows upstream MU-MIMO (UL MU-MIMO). This new mode became possible by improving the clocks on the 802.11ax chipset, thus enabling the stations (STA) to carefully coordinate their upstream transmissions (upon trigger from the AP) so their signal would combine (and not collide randomly with one another). The result of these improvements is a theoretical 9.6Gbps throughput per radio, up to four times more than 802.11ac.

802.11ax also introduced the concept of Basic Service Set (BSS) coloring. In high-density environments, you can expect that two neighboring APs will be on the same channel, especially in settings where large channels (80MHz or 160MHz) are used. APs may not hear one another, especially if they use directional antennas (for example, in a stadium) or if an obstacle is placed between them. However, clients positioned between these APs will suffer (collision with traffic from the neighboring cell may happen while the client is attempting to send to or receive traffic from its AP). With 802.11ax, such clients can send a Basic Service Set (remember, this means the AP cell) collision report. At that time, the AP marks, and asks its clients to mark, all the frames with a specific series of bits (a sort of cell-specific label, called the "color," although it really has no relationship with a color). The clients will also reduce their sensitivity (so as to ignore a bit more of the noise coming from the neighboring cell, where clients will also proceed with the same logic). Then, with the assumption that the neighboring cell is "farther away" than the local cell, the clients will detect if transmissions have their cell color (in which case, a client or the AP in their cell is transmitting, and they should stay quiet to avoid collisions) or another cell color (in which case, the transmission is just noise from the neighbors and can be ignored; the station can send if it needs to, knowing that stations in the neighboring cells have reduced their sensitivity and will ignore that STA signal). This mechanism allows for higher cell density and better coexistence for OBSS (Overlapping BSS, on the same channel) scenarios.

New Scheduling Method

The major revolution in 802.11ax is undoubtedly OFDMA (Orthogonal Frequency Division Multiple Access), a new modulation technique to complement the regular OFDM (Orthogonal Frequency Division Multiplexing) leveraged in 802.11g/a/n/ac. OFDMA brings multiple major enhancements to improve operations in high-density environments but also for IoT. Of course, 802.11ax transmitters can still use OFDM, but the implementation of the OFDMA scheme dramatically changes the channel efficiency.

The first major improvement is a change in the subcarrier structure. With OFDM under 802.11a/g/n/ac, a 20MHz channel is split into 64 subcarriers (or tones). Each subcarrier center frequency is 312.5kHz away from the next subcarrier center frequency (312.5 * 64 = 20,000). Each subcarrier transmits bits organized in what is called a symbol. With legacy OFDM, the transmission of a symbol takes 3.2 microseconds. There is then 0.8 microsecond, with the standard "guard interval," or 0.4 microsecond with the "short" guard interval, of meaningless signal (giving a space where echoes and reflections can come back to the main signal without affecting the transmitted message) before the next symbol.

With 802.11ax, the space between channels is 78.125kHz, thus allowing for 256 subcarriers in a 20MHz channel. However, the symbol duration was extended to 12.8 microseconds (with 0.8, 1.6, or 3.2 microsecond guards between symbols). This change means that more symbols can be sent in parallel, but they are sent at a slower pace, thus better resisting interferences. Four times more tones, but four times slower signal, may give the impression that both models provide the same overall throughput. This is "almost" true. With OFDMA, more of these subcarriers are actively carrying data (instead of being used as references), thus allowing for a 10 to 20% throughput increase (depending on the mode), with the benefit of a much better resistance to interferences. This model is very useful in the outdoors or in indoor noisy environments.

Another improvement with the carrier structure is that subcarriers can be accessed, or addressed, *almost* individually. Tones are grouped in Resource Units (RUs) of various sizes: 26, 52, 106, 242, 484, or 996 tones. Obviously, the last two are only possible in 40MHz and 80MHz transmissions, respectively. A 26-tone RU occupies about 2MHz. These numbers also account for side-tones that are left unused at the edge of each RU and at the edge of the channel.

This change is the one that is seen as revolutionary. With OFDM, only one station can send at a time. With standard contention methods (CSMA/CA), a station gains access to the medium and sends a frame. With large channels (80MHz, for example), it may be that the sender does not really need to full channel and may simply send over 20 or 40MHz. As the AP has the entire 80MHz, the other 40 or 60MHz are simply not used if the transmission is narrower. This is a clear waste of resources. In an ideal world where each station sends one after the other, you get the scheme illustrated on the left side of Figure A-3, where each station has to wait on average seven contention cycles before being able to transmit, while there is still space available on the channel during these other seven cycles.

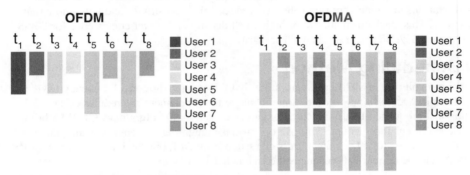

Figure A-3   *OFDM vs. OFDMA Transmissions*

In this scheme, as more stations join the cell, latency and jitter increase accordingly.

OFDMA changes everything. With the concept of RU, several stations can send at the same time, as illustrated on the right side of Figure A-3, making transmissions much more deterministic.

This transmission scheme works as follows:

1. At regular intervals, the AP performs sounding. This technique has existed since 802.11n and MIMO. It allows the AP to group stations that are "RF-compatible" (that is, the transmission from one would not be destructive to the transmissions of the others).

2. At regular intervals, or upon AP trigger, each station sends to the AP a Buffer Status Report (BSR). This report lists, for each 802.11 access category (AC_VO, AC_VI, AC_BE, AC_BK), the buffer depth and characteristics of the station. In other words, the station is able to say, for example, "I have a lot of voice packets ready to send" or "I have a few best-effort and a few background bytes to send."

3. Based on these BSRs and its own scheduling algorithm, the AP switches to OFDMA trigger-based mode. In this mode, the AP defines a transmission opportunity period (TXOP, typically around 2.5 milliseconds) and allocates to each station in a given group a number of RUs.

4. Starting at the exact same time, the stations send symbols only in the RUs they were allocated. This allows the transmission to occupy the full channel, permits multiple stations to send at the same time, and maximizes the overall system efficiency.

The AP can then switch back to the standard contention-based CSMA/CA (unscheduled) method before going back to scheduled periods. This method is revolutionary not only because it increases the efficiency of the channel, but also because this scheduling allows the AP to provide a very deterministic access to the medium for stations that need it. For example, if your voice application needs to send one frame of about one RU per 20 ms, the AP can allocate exactly that amount, at exactly that interval, removing the uncertainties from contention and collisions in multistation environments. This process opens the door to the support of applications that need high reliability and very low latency or jitter. And with multiple RUs, 1024 QAM, and the other improvements, massive machine-type communications (with low tolerance for losses and retries) also become possible. As you can see, 802.11ax, pursuing similar goals as 5G, at about the same time, developed solutions providing comparable efficiency. This is not entirely surprising, as designers for both groups worked in the same general cultural and technical contexts. The main difference is that Wi-Fi does not require a user to pay a monthly (or per GB) fee to access the RF channel.

IoT Improvements

We place the next set of improvements in the Internet of Things (IoT) category because they were designed with IoT in mind. However, keep in mind that these improvements also benefit regular stations. Also keep in mind that Wi-Fi is not alone in this effort. LTE (4G) and 5G also brought radio efficiency improvements targeted to IoT devices.

IoT stations tend to have power and CPU constraints, so they need to minimize the cost of modulating and transmitting a signal (or receiving it). With narrower subcarriers and longer symbols, transmission in OFDMA is simpler than with OFDM. A narrow tone means that transmission costs less energy. A longer symbol means that the computation and the modulation of the symbol take less processing. Even if the transmission duration is longer, the overall result is that a simpler, cheaper Wi-Fi module can be implemented in IoT devices and can transmit with less energy consumption than with OFDM.

A major roadblock in Wi-Fi adoption for IoT devices was indeed related to energy. 802.11 was initially designed with laptops in mind. It was extended, of course, to phones and tablets, but these devices have batteries that can be charged daily. Their requirements are very different from those of a battery-operated sensor, which has a battery the size of a coin, and whose lifetime needs to be 5 years or more. Such characteristics were not compatible with Wi-Fi. With 802.11, a station would need to associate and end keepalives at regular intervals, even if it had nothing to send. Each AP has a session timeout that would cause the station to be removed from the list of associated clients, if the station failed to exchange data with the AP for too long. The initial 802.11 did not even bother create a way for the AP to tell the station what the timeout would be. 802.11 introduced some enhancements over the years, and 802.11ax introduced a radical improvement: the Target Wake Time (TWT).

With TWT, the station can tell the AP how often it would wake up (the AP can negotiate or override this interval). Then, the station can sleep for a long time, without sending anything and without losing its association from the AP. The AP keeps any incoming traffic for the station. Then, at the time the station is supposed to wake up, the AP can send that traffic directly, without waiting for the station to signal its return (because the AP knows that the station must be back, as scheduled). This process allows battery-operated devices to appear in Wi-Fi networks. The longest possible sleeping period is also gigantic (5 years!), allowing applications like rust sensors in walls (sending updates only every few months) to become possible. Additionally, as the AP can override the schedule, super-high density becomes possible, where the AP can organize a large number of clients in smaller groups that wake up and communicate at rotating intervals.

This concern for low power and IoT is pervasive in OFDMA, and the main IoT-friendly features are represented in Figure A-4. By allowing a station to send only over a single RU, power is also saved (as the station does not need to modulate an 80MHz-wide signal beyond the preamble and can just send a 2MHz-wide signal). In fact, it can even only send a 20MHz preamble. This is also useful because most IoT objects do not need to send a lot of data— they do not need 1Gbps! With such a small transmission and using a simple (and power-efficient) modulation (like Binary Phase Shift Keying [BPSK]), the IoT object can send traffic at 375Kbps, which is more than enough.

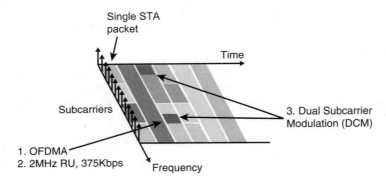

Figure A-4   *802.11ax OFDMA Improvements for IoT*

A last improvement of 802.11ax for IoT solves the IoT nightmare of retries. Being highly battery-sensitive, IoT objects are very vulnerable to the cost of retries. If a transmission is not received (not acknowledged), the IoT object has to wait (a duration called the extended interframe space, or EIFS) and then attempt to resend, thus incurring again the entire cost of computing the modulation and sending the preamble and the symbols. In most cases, the transmission failed because of a narrow interference that affected a few symbols of the transmission.

To save on this cost, 802.11ax allows a mode called dual subcarrier modulation (DCM). With this technique, the IoT object can send its frame in a redundant mode, over two RUs, far apart from each other. This is economical, because the station only needs to modulate a single preamble and only needs to compute the modulation once. The station does spend twice the energy at the time of the symbol transmission, but this is (from a power standpoint) cheaper than waiting for an EIFS and then retransmitting everything, if the first transmission fails. DCM is optional but can be useful in noisy environments where a high level of retries are measured. A last important detail is that 802.11ax is allowed in the 2.4GHz band and the 5GHz band (while 8023.11ac is only allowed in the 5GHz band), which is great, as many simple Wi-Fi chipsets (targets for IoT) were designed to operate in 2.4GHz.

All these features make 802.11ax ready for high-density, real-time, and IoT environments. The Wi-Fi Alliance certifies 20, 40, 80, or 160MHz channels, 1024 QAM, downlink MU-MIMO, BSS coloring, TWT, and OFDMA with Wi-Fi 6.

At the same time, operations in 6GHz are envisioned for a second certification phase. This is likely to introduce major changes for your networks as well, because operations in 6GHz will not have to coexist with legacy systems (like operations in 5GHz or 2.4GHz do). This will allow these operations to be "pure 802.11ax," directly with high efficiency and without the need to implement any overhead to avoid collisions with stations running older technologies.

Meanwhile, the IEEE 802.11be working group is designing the next generation of Wi-Fi, with in mind the possibility for a station to communicate with several APs at the same time (thus ensuring maximum throughput and zero delay or drop when roaming), as well as the possibility for several APs to communicate with a target station at the same time (thus ensuring hyper-high throughput as the station moves). The future of Wi-Fi looks bright.

Software-Defined Access with Wireless

Campus networks have traditionally been built upon the three-layer architecture of access, distribution, and core. Over time, many large campus networks have added virtualization, employing technologies such as Multiprotocol Label Switching (MPLS), Generic Routing Encapsulation (GRE), and others that allow overlay segmentation of traffic into virtual private networks (VPNs).

Software-Defined Access (SDA) is a Cisco technology that is an evolution of the traditional campus network that delivers intent-based networking (IBN) and central policy control using Software-Defined Networking (SDN) components.

SD-Access is built upon the following three network-centric pillars:

1. **A network fabric:** The network fabric is an abstraction of the network itself, supporting programmable overlays and virtualization. The network fabric supports both wired and wireless access and allows it to host multiple logical networks that are segmented from one other and are defined by business intent.

2. **Orchestration:** DNA Center is the orchestrator engine of SDA and functions much like an SDN controller, implementing policy and configuration changes in the fabric. DNA Center also incorporates a tool supporting network design and supports real-time network telemetry operations and performance analytics through DNA Assurance. In summary, the role of DNA Center is to orchestrate the network fabric to deliver policy changes and network intent for security, quality of service (QoS), and microsegmentation.

3. **Policy:** Identity Services Engine (ISE) is the tool that defines network policy, which organizes how devices and nodes are segmented into virtual networks. While ISE defines the policy, the orchestration of the policy, including segmentation, is implemented in the network fabric by DNA Center. ISE also defines scalable group tags (SGTs) that are used by access devices to segment user traffic as it enters the fabric. SGTs are responsible for enforcing the microsegmentation policy defined by ISE.

Figure B-1 illustrates the three pillars of Cisco SDA.

Network fabrics have been around for many years. For example, it is common to see campus networks using GRE or MPLS supporting multiple VPNs. The challenge is that overlay fabrics tend to be complex and require a significant amount of administrator overhead when deploying new virtual networks or implementing security policies for existing ones. Other network fabrics such as DMVPN, FlexVPN, VXLAN, and many others have also been popular; however, they also suffer from the same challenges and limitations as MPLS or GRE. While the fabric implementations just mentioned do not require centralized orchestration, SDA is built up on it. For SDA, the combination of DNA Center as the programmable orchestration engine, ISE as the policy engine, and a new generation of programmable switches makes it a much more flexible and manageable fabric system than anything that has come before.

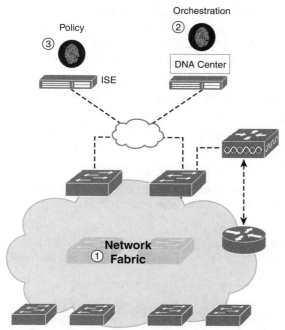

Figure B-1 *Core SDA Components*

The network fabric is composed of the following elements (see Figure B-2):

■ **Control plane (CP) node / mapping server:** This is the location mapping system that is part of the Location Identifier Separator Protocol (LISP) control plane, managing endpoint identity (EID) to location relationships. Either the CP node can be a dedicated router that provides control plane functions (similar to a route reflector in a BGP deployment) or it can coexist with other fabric network elements (it is preferable to use a dedicated router for this purpose, especially in large or mission-critical SDA deployments). The CP is a critical infrastructure piece of the SDA architecture, so it is recommended to be deployed in a resilient way.

■ **Fabric border nodes:** A fabric border node is typically a router that functions at the border between external networks and the SDA fabric, providing routing services to the virtual networks in the fabric. The fabric border node is responsible for internetworking between the internal SDA virtual networks and the networks on the outside of the fabric. The border node can be thought of as an exit point from the SDA virtual networks as they send traffic to outside segments, such as to a firewall, a guest network, or to the Internet.

■ **Fabric edge nodes:** A fabric edge node is a device within the fabric that connects non-fabric devices, such as switches, wireless access points (APs), and routers to the SDA fabric. These are the nodes that create the virtual overlay tunnels and virtual networks (VNs) with Virtual eXtensible LAN (VXLAN) and impose the SGTs on fabric-bound traffic. The fabric nodes are similar to border nodes in that they sit on the edge of the fabric, with a key difference being that the networks on both sides of the fabric edge are inside the SDA network. The networks on the non-fabric side are where the virtual networks live. When they enter the fabric, they must go through a fabric edge node where they are encapsulated in VXLAN as they are sent over the SDA core fabric. The fabric edge and border nodes participate in the fabric control plane using LISP.

■ **Extended nodes:** These are network elements not directly part of the fabric (they do not participate in LISP and their traffic is not encapsulated in VXLAN) but are connected to the fabric edge nodes. The extended nodes may be managed by DNA Center.

■ **Intermediate nodes:** These nodes are inside the core of the SDA fabric and connect to either edge or border nodes. The intermediate nodes simply forward SDA traffic as IP packets, unaware that there are multiple virtual networks involved.

■ **Fabric wireless controller:** This is a wireless controller that is fabric-enabled and participates in the SDA control plane (similar to a fabric edge node) but does not process the CAPWAP data plane.

■ **Fabric mode APs:** These access points are fabric-enabled. Wireless traffic is VXLAN-encapsulated at the AP, which allows it to be sent into the fabric through an edge node.

Figure B-2 illustrates the various components of the SDA network fabric.

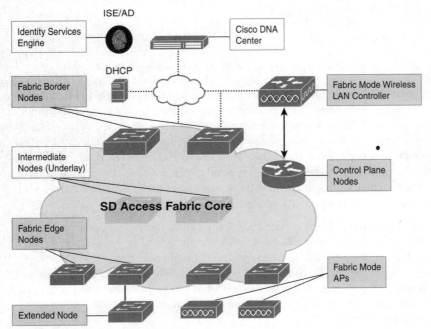

Figure B-2 *Cisco SDA Fabric Components*

SDA Network Architecture—Underlay and Overlay Networks

The SDA architecture utilizes fabric technology that supports programmable virtual networks (overlay networks) that run on a physical network (an underlay network).

The fabric underlay network is defined by the physical nodes, including switches, routers, and wireless access points that are used in the SDA network. All network elements of the underlay must have IP connectivity and use an IP routing protocol. In the case of SDA, IS-IS is the underlay routing protocol of choice. While the underlay network is not likely to use the traditional access, distribution, core model, it must use a well-designed Layer 3 foundation that delivers robust performance, scalability, and high availability. In SDA, the underlay switches support the transport of physical endpoints connected to extended nodes and beyond. The end-user subnets and endpoints are not part of the underlay fabric network core routing table, as these subnets are routed through the overlay (this is similar to MPLS, where the backbone P and PE routers do not carry virtual network subnets—these are part of the VPN routing tables in the overlay). In SDA, the user subnets are part of a programmable overlay network that may run at Layer 2 or Layer 3. SDA supports IPv4 in the underlay network and IPv4 and/or IPv6 in overlay networks.

An overlay network is created on top of the underlay to create one or more virtualized and segmented networks. Due to the software-defined nature of overlays, it is possible to connect them in very flexible ways without the constraints of physical connectivity. For example, if you wanted to connect two accounting offices in a campus network that were physically separated, it would be possible to connect these two sites through a fabric overlay and make them appear as if they were part of the same physical network. In this way, network overlays offer natural segmentation that is not possible on physical networks. They also provide an easy way to enforce security policies because the overlay can be programmed to have a single physical exit point (the fabric border node), and thus one firewall can be used to protect the networks behind it, wherever they may be located.

Data plane traffic and control plane signaling (routing updates) for the overlays are independent of each other within each virtualized network. The SDA fabric implements virtualization of the overlays by encapsulating user traffic in VXLAN tunnels that connect through the underlay. These tunnels are sourced and terminated at the boundaries of the fabric (the fabric edge and border nodes).

The fabric is designed to carry multiple overlays at the same time supporting multitenancy and segmentation between networks. For example, one overlay may be created for IoT devices, such as digital ceiling lights, whereas another may be created for contractors who are working at the office. Through the fabric, the devices and subnets used on each overlay are completely separated from each other, no matter where the devices are physically located.

At the fabric edge, each overlay network appears as a virtual routing and forwarding (VRF) instance, similar to MPLS. In order to preserve extension of the overlay separation outside of the network, VRF-Lite is used (VRFs are used in combination with 802.1q tunnels between non-fabric switching nodes to securely extend the fabric). Overlays also support the flexibility of Layer 2 or Layer 3, depending on the requirement of the overlay.

When Layer 2 is used across overlays, an important point is that SDA supports MAC learning without the use of flooding. Flooding on traditional Layer 2 networks can easily overwhelm resources on a router and cause performance issues, thus limiting the feasible size of the network; however, with SDA, MAC learning removes this restriction and supports the creation of large Layer 2 domains.

Figure B-3 illustrates a comparison between underlay and overlay networks.

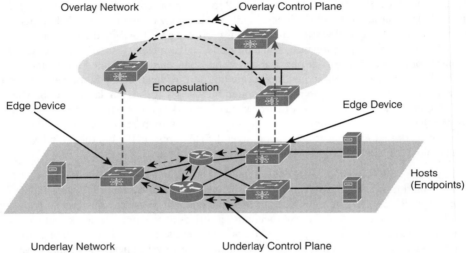

Figure B-3   *Comparing the Fabric Underlay and Overlay*

Fabric Control, Data, and Security Planes

The function of SDA incorporates three separate "planes": the control, data, and security planes. These are summarized as follows:

- **Control plane:** Based on LISP, functions in the underlay

- **Data plane:** Based on VXLAN, encapsulates the overlay traffic

- **Security plane:** Utilizes SGTs to securely identify users and devices and put them into the correct overlay

The function of mapping and resolving endpoint addresses requires a control plane protocol. For the control plane, SDA uses LISP. LISP brings the advantage of routing based not only on the IP or MAC address as the endpoint identifier (EID) of a device but also routing based on an additional IP address that it provides as a routing locator (RLOC) to represent the network location of that device. This has the advantage of allowing the IP addresses of a device to move from one location to another location without having to readdress through DHCP. In this way, the EID and RLOC work very similarly to DNS—instead of finding exactly where a node is by looking up its IP address in a routing table, the RLOC allows LISP to check with the control plane node (the LISP mapping server) to find the current location of an IP address, and it reroutes the overlay tunnel to the EID of this location, allowing the fabric to follow a user wherever a device may go. Note that the control plane (CP) is key in this capability—the CP is signaled in real time as a node moves, providing updated routing information via LISP so connectivity can be maintained. In this way, the CP is the authoritative trust point to find a node—any user who wants to send a packet to another node inside the fabric will use the CP to find the node's current location, similar to how a DNS server resolves a host name to find a current IP address for a certain domain.

Thus, the EID and RLOC combination provides the necessary information for traffic forwarding, even if an endpoint continues to use the same IP address as it moves to a different network location. Simultaneously, the decoupling of the endpoint identity from its location allows addresses in the same IP subnet to be available behind multiple Layer 3 gateways, versus a one-to-one coupling of IP subnets with a network gateway, as is used in a traditional network. Figure B-4 illustrates how the LISP control plane functions in an SDA network.

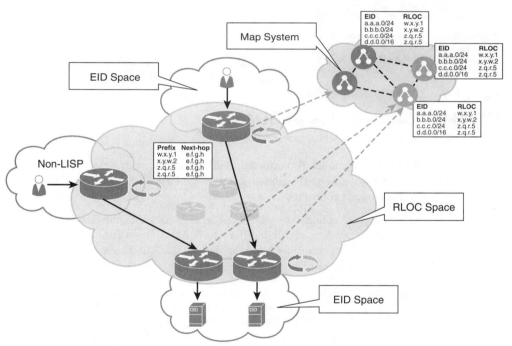

Figure B-4   *The VXLAN-GPE Header*

The SDA overlay encapsulates traffic using VXLAN. VXLAN encapsulates complete Layer 2 frames for transport across the underlay with each overlay network identified by a VXLAN network identifier (VNI). The VXLAN Generic Protocol Extension (GPE) header also carries the SGTs that are defined by ISE and allow for microsegmentation of traffic. Figure B-5 illustrates the entire VXLAN header format, including the RLOC source and destination address.

As noted in Figure B-5, the 16-bit SGT is embedded directly into the VXLAN header. The SGT is assigned from ISE during the authentication of the user or the device during the onboarding phase to indicate the security policy. The SGT is used to identify what virtual network (VN) overlay the traffic should be assigned to. The SGTs can also be used at firewalls for filtering purposes.

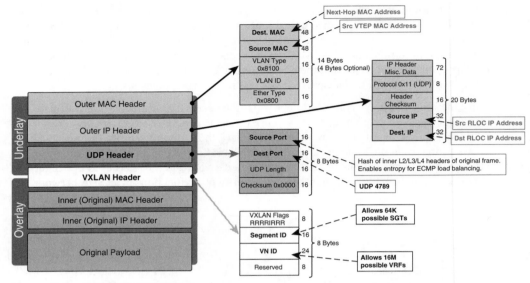

Figure B-5   *The VXLAN-GPE Header*

Wireless Capabilities of SDA

SDA supports two wireless deployment models:

- **Over the top (OTT) model:** A traditional CAPWAP deployment connected on top of a fabric wired network. The SDA fabric transports the CAPWAP control and data plane traffic to the wireless controller.

- **Fully integrated SDA model:** The wireless network is fully integrated to the fabric and participates in overlays, allowing different WLANs to be part of different VNs. In this model, the wireless controller only manages the CAPWAP control plane, and the CAPWAP data plane does not come to the controller.

In the OTT model, the SDA fabric is simply a transport network for wireless traffic—a model often deployed in migrations. In this model, the AP works very similarly to classic Local mode, where both the CAPWAP control and data planes terminate on the controller, meaning the controller does not directly participate in the fabric. This model is often used when wired switches are first migrated to the SDA fabric but the wireless network is not yet ready for full fabric overlay integration. Figure B-6 illustrates the OTT model.

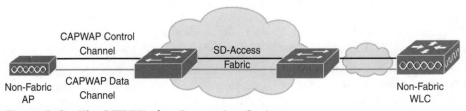

Figure B-6   *The OTT Wireless Integration Option*

The second deployment option is to fully integrate wireless into the SDA fabric, extending the SDA benefits to include wireless users where endpoints and users are part of VN overlays. There are significant advantages to be gained by integrating wireless into the SDA fabric, such as allowing wired and wireless networks to be part of the same VN, as well as unification of the security policy. Figure B-7 illustrates a fully integrated wireless fabric.

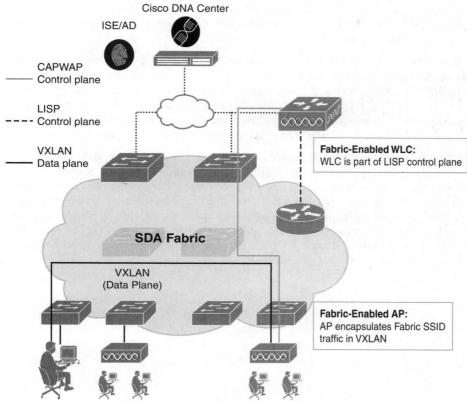

Figure B-7 *Wireless Fully Integrated SDA Fabric*

Fully integrated SDA involves the wireless controller using the CAPWAP control plane to manage APs, while the data plane does not go to the controller. In this case, the wireless data plane is handled similarly to wired switches—each AP encapsulates data in VXLAN and sends it to a fabric edge node where it is then sent across the fabric to another edge node. In this mode, the wireless controllers must be configured as fabric controllers—a modification from their normal operation. Fabric-enabled controllers communicate with the fabric control plane, registering Layer 2 client MAC addresses, SGTs, and Layer 2 Virtual Network Identifier (VNI) information. The APs are responsible for communication with wireless endpoints, and in the wired domain, the APs assist the VXLAN data plane by encapsulating and de-encapsulating traffic.

From a CAPWAP control perspective, the wireless LAN controllers manage and control the fabric mode APs in the same way as APs running in classic Local or FlexConnect mode. The controller continues to perform Radio Resource Management (RRM), mobility control, authentication of clients, and other functions that use the CAPWAP control function. A significant difference is that wireless client data from fabric-enabled SSIDs does not use CAPWAP encapsulation and forwarding from the APs to the controller. Instead, communication from wireless clients is VXLAN-encapsulated by fabric-attached APs and uses the LISP control plane to communicate with other fabric endpoints or outside of the fabric. This difference enables the wireless network to take advantage of the integrated policy elements of SDA, such as using SGTs. When this is deployed, traffic forwarding takes the optimum path through the SD-Access fabric to the destination with consistent policy, regardless of wired or wireless endpoint connectivity.

The SDA control plane inherently supports roaming by updating the host-tracking database on the control plane node (the mapping server), updating any changes to a wireless client's EID-to-RLOC mapping. Although fabric mode APs are used for VXLAN traffic encapsulation of wireless traffic, they are not considered edge nodes. Instead, APs are connected to edge node switches using VXLAN encapsulation and rely on those switches to provide fabric services. APs can be physically connected to either an edge or extended node switch.

Integrating wireless into the fabric leads to several advantages for the wireless network, including addressing simplification, mobility with stretched subnets across physical locations, and microsegmentation with centralized policy that is consistent across both of the wired and wireless domains. Another significant advantage of wireless fabric integration is that it enables the controller to shed data plane forwarding duties while continuing to function as the centralized services and control plane for the wireless network. In this way, wireless controller scalability is actually increased because it no longer needs to process data plane traffic, similar to the FlexConnect model.

RRM TPC Algorithm Example

Chapter 6, "Designing Radio Management," explained how the transmit power control (TPC) algorithm automatically adjusts the transmit power level of access points (APs) in a radio frequency (RF) group. If you decide to enable TPC in a wireless network, you might like to have a better understanding of how TPC chooses the values it assigns to the APs. This appendix presents a real-world example that you can follow as TPC does its job.

The example scenario is one of a large classroom where a high density of users normally exists. There are ten APs in the room, each mounted on the ceiling and connected to a directional antenna pointing downward. The design goal was to create relatively small cells to constrain the number of users and maximize performance. Figure C-1 shows the layout of the room and its APs.

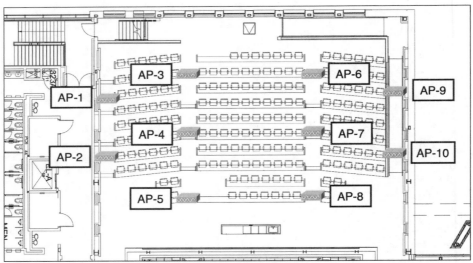

Figure C-1 *Example Scenario of a Large Classroom with Ten APs*

Viewing an NDP Neighbor List

As you have learned in the "Discovering the RF Neighborhood with NDP" section in Chapter 6, each AP periodically transmits a Neighbor Discovery Protocol (NDP) message frame on each channel that it supports. Each AP also records any NDP messages it receives from other APs, forming a list of up to 34 neighboring APs that have the strongest received signal strength indicator (RSSI) values. This gives each AP a concept of its neighbors and their spacing, at least in terms of RF proximity. A stronger received signal strength correlates with a shorter distance through space (and objects). The neighbor lists get sent up to the wireless LAN controller (WLC) for processing by the radio resource management (RRM) algorithms.

To understand how RRM's TPC algorithm works, you need to start by displaying a typical neighbor list and collecting the same data that the controller does. You can use the controller GUI to see a list of neighbors on 5GHz by selecting **Monitor > Access Points > Radios > 802.11a/n/ac**, as shown in Figure C-2. Notice that it lists the MAC address of the neighboring AP (ending in hex digit F, rather than the base radio MAC address ending in 0) and the channel number and width. However, the RSSI value is shown as a bar graph, which is not very useful for this TPC exercise. Numerical values would be much easier to compare and compute.

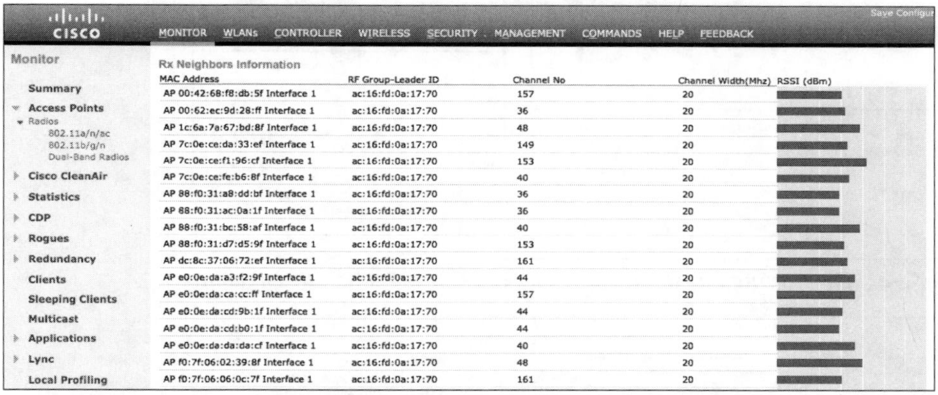

Figure C-2 *Displaying an AP Neighbor List in the Controller GUI*

Cisco Prime Infrastructure (PI) is better suited to display the neighbor list data. First, go to **Maps > Site Maps** and select the building and floor where the APs are located. Select one AP on the map to examine. Red circles will be shown around the AP, while its interface information will be listed in a side panel. Select the tab for the band (802.11b/g/n or 802.11a/n/ac) you are interested in seeing.

To access the AP page containing the neighbor list, you will need to select the middle dot, as shown in Figure C-3. The neighboring AP names and their MAC addresses will be listed. To add the RSSI values to the list, select the drop-down menu triangle, as shown, and then select RSSI from the list of parameters to view.

The neighbor list, complete with RSSI values, will be displayed, as shown in Figure C-4. You can click the "RSSI" column heading to sort the RSSI values in increasing order, which is quite handy when you need to look for the third strongest signal in the list. In a highly dense wireless network, the neighbor list can be quite long—up to 34 entries per AP. If you want to collect all of the data for further analysis, you can select and copy the entire list and then paste it into a spreadsheet or other application.

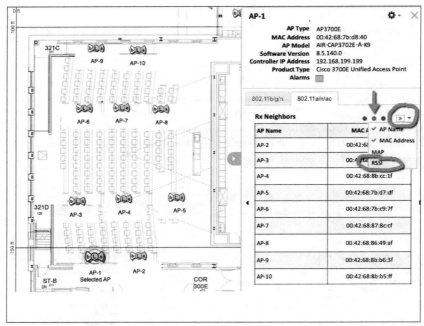

Figure C-3   *Displaying an AP Neighbor List in Cisco Prime Infrastructure*

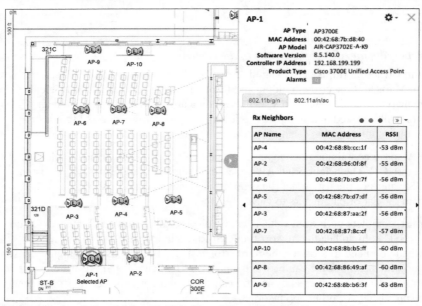

Figure C-4   *A Complete AP Neighbor List with RSSI Data Added*

Keep in mind that the neighbor list is relevant for only one AP. You will need to gather the neighbor data from one AP at a time until all of the neighbors have been examined, and then work with all of the collected data as explained in the remainder of this appendix.

Neighbor Lists for the Example Scenario

This section brings together the neighbor lists of each of the ten APs in the large classroom example scenario, presented in Tables C-1 through C-10. Each AP has received NDP messages from its nine neighbors and has recorded the RSSI value that each message had. Notice that the lists are sorted by RSSI and not necessarily by AP name. The third strongest RSSI entry has been highlighted for quick reference.

Table C-1   NDP Neighbors Received by AP-1

AP Name	MAC Address	RSSI
AP-4	00:42:68:8b:cc:1f	−53 dBm
AP-2	00:42:68:96:0f:8f	−55 dBm
AP-6	00:42:68:7b:c9:7f	−56 dBm
AP-5	00:42:68:7b:d7:df	−56 dBm
AP-3	00:42:68:87:aa:2f	−56 dBm
AP-7	00:42:68:87:8c:cf	−57 dBm
AP-10	00:42:68:8b:b5:ff	−60 dBm
AP-8	00:42:68:86:49:af	−60 dBm
AP-9	00:42:68:8b:b6:3f	−63 dBm

Table C-2   NDP Neighbors Received by AP-2

AP Name	MAC Address	RSSI
AP-1	00:42:68:7b:d8:4f	−38 dBm
AP-4	00:42:68:8b:cc:1f	−43 dBm
AP-5	00:42:68:7b:d7:df	−44 dBm
AP-6	00:42:68:7b:c9:7f	−47 dBm
AP-8	00:42:68:86:49:af	−52 dBm
AP-7	00:42:68:87:8c:cf	−52 dBm
AP-9	00:42:68:8b:b6:3f	−53 dBm
AP-10	00:42:68:8b:b5:ff	−54 dBm
AP-3	00:42:68:87:aa:2f	−54 dBm

Table C-3   NDP Neighbors Received by AP-3

AP Name	MAC Address	RSSI
AP-4	00:42:68:8b:cc:1f	−47 dBm
AP-6	00:42:68:7b:c9:7f	−55 dBm
AP-5	00:42:68:7b:d7:df	−55 dBm
AP-1	00:42:68:7b:d8:4f	−55 dBm
AP-8	00:42:68:86:49:af	−59 dBm
AP-9	00:42:68:8b:b6:3f	−60 dBm
AP-2	00:42:68:96:0f:8f	−60 dBm
AP-10	00:42:68:8b:b5:ff	−63 dBm
AP-7	00:42:68:87:8c:cf	−64 dBm

Table C-4   NDP Neighbors Received by AP-4

AP Name	MAC Address	RSSI
AP-1	00:42:68:7b:d8:4f	–54 dBm
AP-7	00:42:68:87:8c:cf	–55 dBm
AP-5	00:42:68:7b:d7:df	–55 dBm
AP-3	00:42:68:87:aa:2f	–56 dBm
AP-10	00:42:68:8b:b5:ff	–57 dBm
AP-6	00:42:68:7b:c9:7f	–57 dBm
AP-8	00:42:68:86:49:af	–58 dBm
AP-2	00:42:68:96:0f:8f	–59 dBm
AP-9	00:42:68:8b:b6:3f	–61 dBm

Table C-5   NDP Neighbors Received by AP-5

AP Name	MAC Address	RSSI
AP-4	00:42:68:8b:cc:1f	–54 dBm
AP-2	00:42:68:96:0f:8f	–54 dBm
AP-1	00:42:68:7b:d8:4f	–56 dBm
AP-10	00:42:68:8b:b5:ff	–60 dBm
AP-8	00:42:68:86:49:af	–60 dBm
AP-3	00:42:68:87:aa:2f	–61 dBm
AP-7	00:42:68:87:8c:cf	–63 dBm
AP-6	00:42:68:7b:c9:7f	–65 dBm
AP-9	00:42:68:8b:b6:3f	–68 dBm

Table C-6   NDP Neighbors Received by AP-6

AP Name	MAC Address	RSSI
AP-3	00:42:68:87:aa:2f	–51 dBm
AP-4	00:42:68:8b:cc:1f	–56 dBm
AP-1	00:42:68:7b:d8:4f	–58 dBm
AP-9	00:42:68:8b:b6:3f	–60 dBm
AP-7	00:42:68:87:8c:cf	–60 dBm
AP-10	00:42:68:8b:b5:ff	–63 dBm
AP-8	00:42:68:86:49:af	–64 dBm
AP-5	00:42:68:7b:d7:df	–64 dBm
AP-2	00:42:68:96:0f:8f	–64 dBm

Table C-7   NDP Neighbors Received by AP-7

AP Name	MAC Address	RSSI
AP-6	00:42:68:7b:c9:7f	–43 dBm
AP-8	00:42:68:86:49:af	–47 dBm
AP-5	00:42:68:7b:d7:df	–47 dBm

AP Name	MAC Address	RSSI
AP-4	00:42:68:8b:cc:1f	–47 dBm
AP-9	00:42:68:8b:b6:3f	–48 dBm
AP-10	00:42:68:8b:b5:ff	–49 dBm
AP-3	00:42:68:87:aa:2f	–50 dBm
AP-1	00:42:68:7b:d8:4f	–51 dBm
AP-2	00:42:68:96:0f:8f	–57 dBm

Table C-8   NDP Neighbors Received by AP-8

AP Name	MAC Address	RSSI
AP-10	00:42:68:8b:b5:ff	–51 dBm
AP-9	00:42:68:8b:b6:3f	–53 dBm
AP-7	00:42:68:87:8c:cf	–53 dBm
AP-6	00:42:68:7b:c9:7f	–53 dBm
AP-5	00:42:68:7b:d7:df	–53 dBm
AP-4	00:42:68:8b:cc:1f	–53 dBm
AP-3	00:42:68:87:aa:2f	–55 dBm
AP-1	00:42:68:7b:d8:4f	–56 dBm
AP-2	00:42:68:96:0f:8f	–61 dBm

Table C-9   NDP Neighbors Received by AP-9

AP Name	MAC Address	RSSI
AP-7	00:42:68:87:8c:cf	–51 dBm
AP-4	00:42:68:8b:cc:1f	–52 dBm
AP-6	00:42:68:7b:c9:7f	–54 dBm
AP-10	00:42:68:8b:b5:ff	–56 dBm
AP-1	00:42:68:7b:d8:4f	–60 dBm
AP-5	00:42:68:7b:d7:df	–61 dBm
AP-8	00:42:68:86:49:af	–62 dBm
AP-3	00:42:68:87:aa:2f	–65 dBm
AP-2	00:42:68:96:0f:8f	–65 dBm

Table C-10   NDP Neighbors Received by AP-10

AP Name	MAC Address	RSSI
AP-8	00:42:68:86:49:af	–51 dBm
AP-9	00:42:68:8b:b6:3f	–53 dBm
AP-4	00:42:68:8b:cc:1f	–56 dBm
AP-6	00:42:68:7b:c9:7f	–58 dBm
AP-7	00:42:68:87:8c:cf	–59 dBm
AP-1	00:42:68:7b:d8:4f	–59 dBm

AP Name	MAC Address	RSSI
AP-5	00:42:68:7b:d7:df	–60 dBm
AP-3	00:42:68:87:aa:2f	–61 dBm
AP-2	00:42:68:96:0f:8f	–66 dBm

Performing the TPC Algorithm

TPC calculates an ideal transmit power level in dBm for each AP in the RF neighborhood or RF group using the following equation:

$Tx\_Ideal = Tx\_Max + (Threshold - RSSI\_3rd)$

Tx_Max is the AP's maximum supported transmit power in dBm. Each AP model has a maximum transmit power level, but the actual maximum that can be used is determined by the channel and band the AP is currently using, according to the limits imposed by the regulatory domain. Table C-11 lists the *Tx_Max* values according to frequency band and channel number. The transmit power level is set as a value from 1 to 8; level 1 is always the maximum supported level, with each successive level being about 3 dBm less until the physical minimum is reached. Therefore, when APs are operating in the U-NII-1, U-NII-2, and U-NII-2 Extended bands, they may not support all eight levels.

Table C-11   Example Cisco AP Transmit Power Level Value Correlation

Power Level	2.4GHz Ch 1–13	U-NII-1 Ch 36–48	U-NII-2 Ch 52–64	U-NII-2 Ext Ch 100–140	U-NII-3 Ch 149–161
1 (max)	23 dBm	15 dBm	17 dBm	17 dBm	23 dBm
2	20 dBm	12 dBm	14 dBm	14 dBm	20 dBm
3	17 dBm	9 dBm	11 dBm	11 dBm	17 dBm
4	14 dBm	6 dBm	8 dBm	8 dBm	14 dBm
5	11 dBm	3 dBm	5 dBm	5 dBm	11 dBm
6	8 dBm	—	2 dBm	2 dBm	8 dBm
7	5 dBm	—	—	—	5 dBm
8	2 dBm	—	—	—	2 dBm

The value of *Threshold* is set by default to –70 dBm. This parameter gives TPC a baseline to work toward. You can think of it as a gauge to limit an AP's cell size from extending too far outward and into the cells of other APs that might be using the same channel. Unless you have a good reason to change the threshold, you should leave it at the default value.

RSSI_3rd is the third strongest RSSI value for the AP as recorded by neighboring APs. Remember that NDP messages are sent at maximum transmit power, and the goal is to get the AP's messages received at the –70 dBm threshold at the neighboring AP where the third strongest RSSI is found.

Because you will need to find the AP's maximum transmit power level based on which channel it is currently serving, Figure C-5 shows the channel number for each of the ten APs. In this example, the RRM DCA algorithm has selected and assigned the AP channels.

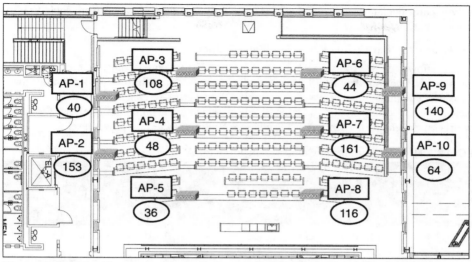

Figure C-5   *The Classroom Example Scenario with Channel Numbers Added*

Begin with a single AP, filling in the parameters of the equation to find the *Tx_Ideal* value. You can use Table C-12 as a guide, where AP-1 is the AP that is transmitting NDP messages. From Figure C-5, you know that AP-1 is using channel 40. Then, from Table C-11, you know that *Tx_Max*, the maximum power possible (power level 1), on channel 40 is 15 dBm.

Now you need to find the AP neighbor that has received the third strongest NDP message from AP-1. You could search through the neighbor lists from every possible AP (Tables C-1 through C-10 for the example scenario) to find entries for AP-1, then sort them and choose the third strongest. Instead, the TPC algorithm takes a novel approach to simplify the process.

When an AP transmits an NDP message, it always uses the maximum power level that is supported on its normal operating channel. It also uses that same maximum power level when it tunes off-channel to send NDP messages on every other supported channel. That means the sending AP might use a maximum power level that is higher or lower than the maximum normally used on other channels. To compensate, each receiving AP normalizes the RSSI value of incoming NDP messages to correlate with its own operating channel and maximum transmit power level expected there.

Because the RSSI values are normalized by every AP according to its own operating channel, TPC can assume that NDP messages sent between two APs in one direction are received with the same RSSI as NDP messages sent in the other direction. In other words, the RSSI values contained in an AP's neighbor list also reflect how those neighbors have received that AP's NDP messages. Finding the neighbor that has received the third strongest NDP message becomes a simple matter of finding the third strongest value in an AP's own neighbor list.

For example, you can find a good estimate for the AP that has received the third strongest NDP message from AP-1 by looking in AP-1's neighbor list from Table C-1. It is true that the message from AP-6 was the third strongest neighbor received by AP-1. TPC can also assume that AP-1's NDP message was the third strongest received by AP-6. Indeed, Table C-6 lists AP-1 as the third strongest. Even though the RSSI values are different in each direction, they are very close to the same value.

Now you can calculate the *Tx_Ideal* value for AP-1 by substituting values from Table C-1 into the equation, as follows:

$$Tx\_Ideal = 15 \text{ dBm} + (-70 \text{ dBm} - -56 \text{ dBm}) = 1 \text{ dBm}$$

You now know the ideal transmit power level in dBm, but Cisco APs must be configured using a power level value of 1 to 8, corresponding to the desired dBm value. Remember that AP-1 is using channel 40 and then refer to Table C-11 to cross-reference the dBm value. The closest value to 1 dBm listed in the table is 3 dBm, which is the minimum level that the AP supports on the channel. Therefore, TPC will use 3 dBm, selected by power level 5.

Table C-12   TPC Parameters to Calculate Tx_Ideal for AP-1

Tx Neighbor	Channel	Tx Max	Strongest Neighbor (dBm)			Tx Ideal	Tx Actual	Tx Power Level
			#1	#2	#3			
AP-1	40	15 dBm	−53 AP-4	−55 AP-2	−56 AP-6	1 dBm	3 dBm	5

The same process is repeated for all ten APs, as listed in Table C-13. Keep in mind that TPC also constrains the *Tx_Ideal* dBm values within a minimum and maximum limit. By default, TPC uses a minimum of −10 dBm and a maximum of 30 dBm, which are well outside the range of an AP's capabilities, imposing no limit at all.

Table C-13   TPC Parameters for AP-1 Through AP-10

Tx Neighbor	Channel	Tx Max	Strongest Neighbor (dBm)			Tx Ideal	Tx Actual	Tx Power Level
			#1	#2	#3			
AP-1	40	15 dBm	−53 AP-4	−55 AP-2	−56 AP-6	1 dBm	3 dBm	5
AP-2	153	23 dBm	−38 AP-1	−43 AP-4	−44 AP-5	−3 dBm	2 dBm	8
AP-3	108	17 dBm	−47 AP-4	−55 AP-6	−55 AP-5	2 dBm	2 dBm	6
AP-4	48	15 dBm	−54 AP-1	−55 AP-7	−55 AP-5	0 dBm	3 dBm	5
AP-5	31	15 dBm	−54 AP-4	−54 AP-2	−56 AP-1	1 dBm	3 dBm	5
AP-6	44	15 dBm	−51 AP-3	−56 AP-4	−58 AP-1	3 dBm	3 dBm	5
AP-7	161	23 dBm	−43 AP-6	−47 AP-8	−47 AP-4	0 dBm	2 dBm	8
AP-8	116	17 dBm	−51 AP-10	−53 AP-9	−53 AP-7	0 dBm	2 dBm	6

Tx Neighbor	Channel	Tx Max	Strongest Neighbor (dBm)			Tx Ideal	Tx Actual	Tx Power Level
			#1	#2	#3			
AP-9	140	17 dBm	–51 AP-7	–52 AP-4	–54 AP-6	1 dBm	2 dBm	6
AP-10	64	17 dBm	–51 AP-8	–53 AP-9	–56 AP-4	3 dBm	2 dBm	6

Keep in mind that the Tx Actual and Tx Power Level columns of Table C-13 list the end goal of the TPC algorithm, based on the neighbor data presented in this appendix. As long as the neighboring APs and RF conditions remain stable, TPC should also reach a steady state. TPC does not change transmit power levels abruptly. Instead, it makes changes incrementally and periodically, changing the power levels 3 dB at a time until the end goal or a limit is reached.

To get an idea of the TPC process and how it automatically handles transmit power settings as a whole over time, refer to Figures C-6 through C-13. Each figure represents a snapshot of the AP cell sizes at each TPC iteration. The process begins in Figure C-6 with all APs powering up and using the maximum transmit power level allowed on their respective channels. The circles represent the approximate cell boundary of –67 dBm.

By the time the final iteration is reached, as shown in Figure C-13, all of the AP cells have been reduced to an appropriate size with a decent overlap. Without any manual configuration, TPC has automatically adjusted the entire high-density classroom based on dynamic data from the RF environment!

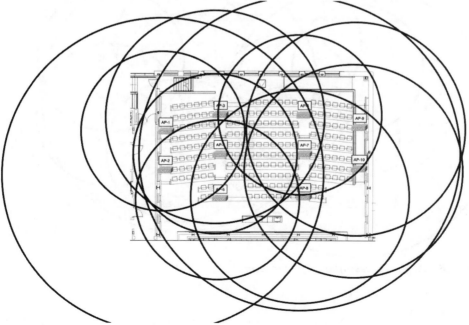

Figure C-6 *Initial AP Cell Sizes at Maximum Power Level*

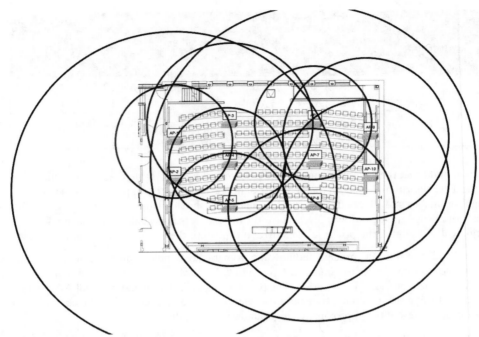

Figure C-7   *AP Cell Sizes After TPC Iteration 1*

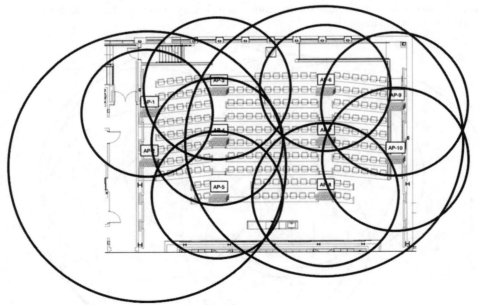

Figure C-8   *AP Cell Sizes After TPC Iteration 2*

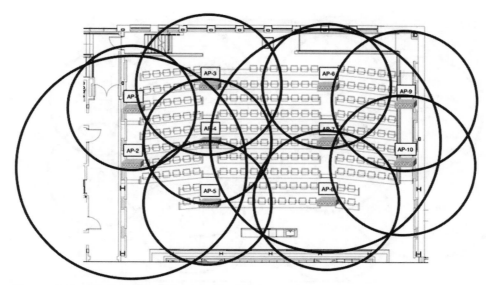

Figure C-9 *AP Cell Sizes After TPC Iteration 3*

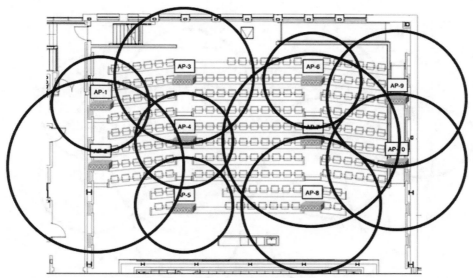

Figure C-10 *AP Cell Sizes After TPC Iteration 4*

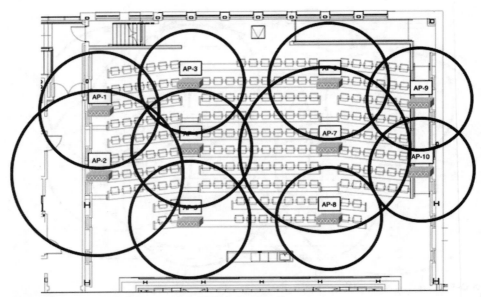

Figure C-11   *AP Cell Sizes After TPC Iteration 5*

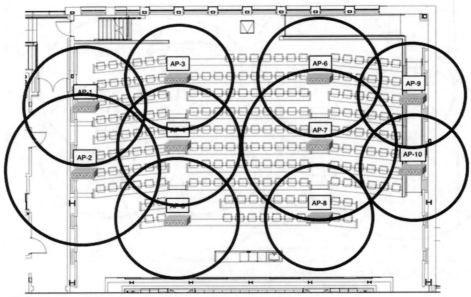

Figure C-12   *AP Cell Sizes After TPC Iteration 6*

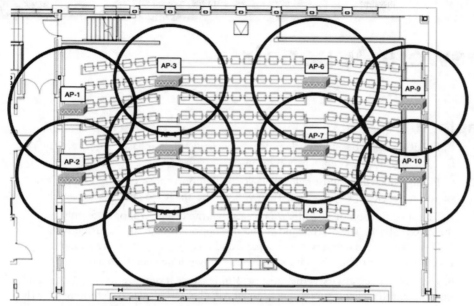

Figure C-13 *Final AP Cell Sizes After TPC Iteration 7*

Answers Appendix

Chapter 1

1. C. PPDIOO describes a lifecycle process consisting of six phases: Prepare, Plan, Design, Implement, Operate, and Optimize.

2. C. Floor plans will be most helpful, as you will import those directly into the site survey or wireless planning tool. Then you will be able to locate APs accurately.

3. A. The specification of 802.11b/g/n reveals that the device will operate only on the 2.4GHz band. The 5GHz band would be supported with the inclusion of "a," "ac," or "ax." The data rates, antenna gain, and receiver sensitivity are all important specifications, too, but they are not given as shown for a specific band.

4. B. The receiver sensitivity is the most helpful because it defines the minimum usable signal strength a client can receive from an AP. The AP cell size is determined by the distance a client can be located from the AP before the AP's signal falls below the receiver sensitivity.

5. C. High density in a wireless design is determined by the number of clients per AP in an area. If the user population is high in a small area, all of the users might end up joining a single AP. The goal of a good wireless design would be to add additional APs and distribute the clients across them, maintaining an adequate level of performance for each AP.

6. A. APs with internal or integrated antennas usually use omnidirectional antennas. Therefore, those APs are most useful in locations that need a broad coverage pattern. Otherwise, an AP with external antenna connectors would be more appropriate.

7. A, B, C. The customer is wanting user authentication, so you could leverage RADIUS, AAA, or ISE servers to meet that need. AES cannot be used to authenticate users because it is an encryption standard.

8. D. A data AP deployment model is usually used when clients use normal applications that have no specific performance requirements.

9. B. A voice deployment model is indicated because of the strict jitter requirement given. Jitter implies network performance that is necessary for real-time applications such as voice and video.

10. D. A client's location is estimated by calculating its distance from the APs that have received its signal. The client's received signal strength (RSSI) is collected from each AP and then sent to an application that computes the location based on the free space path loss and some assumptions about signal attenuation in the area.

Chapter 2

1. **B.** The attenuation depends on the wall structure, but 3 dB is a commonly accepted value.

2. **B.** Attenuation tables are only intended to reflect common values; they are not absolute references. Attenuation would be worse close to the wall (because it would measure near field attenuation instead of far field). Attenuation reflects the signal loss between a transmitter and a receiver; the fact that communication could be unidirectional or bidirectional is irrelevant.

3. **E.** Although the usages listed are common in healthcare, you cannot guess why coverage is needed and should start by asking your customer for input on the WLAN intent.

4. **D.** The EIRP can be expressed in mW or dBm. The maximum limit for U-NII-3 in the FCC domain is 30 dBm, or 1W.

5. **A.** A predictive survey uses a floor plan to predict the number of APs needed. In most cases, the predictive survey is used to estimate the duration of the onsite site survey (knowing how many AP locations can be surveyed per day).

6. **B.** Chanalyzer provides a view of the raw RF on the band, allowing you to detect non-802.11 interferers. Such a process is called a Layer 1 sweep.

7. **D.** A predictive site survey does not account for the RF environment; it is not sufficient to decide the AP placement.

Chapter 3

1. **C.** The goal of the walkthrough is to identify, with a professional eye, the areas that are likely to be problematic for the survey and the deployment. It is a mandatory phase, especially in buildings (like this factory example), where metal, hazardous, and restricted areas are expected.

2. **D.** Spikes are typical of a frequency hopper, which is Bluetooth (BT) transmission mode. BT headsets are also usually low power. A wireless security camera would show a stable trace (no spikes). A microwave oven would show a large transmission in the upper part of the spectrum. An 802.11b AP would show a round shape and no spike.

3. **A.** DECT keepalives may use a single frequency, but the protocol allows for frequency jumps, making it likely to affect any channel in 2.4GHz. Although the transmitter is on channels 4–5, it overlaps with any AP on channel 6, as Wi-Fi channel 6 spans from channel 4 to channel 9. Putting an AP on channel 6 would cause increased noise and losses.

4. **A.** Starting from a strong obstacle is typically the easiest way to go. Any other starting point will cause more trial and error before finding the right position and overlap.

5. **D.** Surveying for voice support implies designing efficiency cells, which are usually smaller than data cells, with APs at lower power and higher minimum data rate. You cannot design for data and then add a voice component: voice has to be designed from the very beginning. In most cases, the network is not operational at survey time, and you cannot test it.

6. **B.** A 50 ms gap while roaming between APs is likely to be small enough to be invisible to the application and the user. This interval has to be measured for the data traffic, not for management frames, as these constitute an overhead that is not relevant for the application experience. Channel scans should happen before the roaming decision, and their number has no direct influence on the roaming phase duration. Ten percent packet loss is likely to be disruptive for most applications and is not the sign of efficient roaming.

Chapter 4

1. **C.** UPOE is capable of 60W per port, with a maximum of 51W to the PD. PoE+ is limited to 30W per port and only 25.5W maximum to the PD.

2. **D.** Wi-Fi 6 / 802.11ax will likely drive more traffic than older generations of APs can accommodate—pushing throughput beyond 1Gbps per AP. Thus, the switch will need to be upgraded to support the higher data rates delivered by mGig.

3. **C.** This is a supported configuration, but specialized mounting brackets will be required.

4. **E.** Each of these aspects can be a possible congestion point and will need to be analyzed for possible oversubscription concerns.

5. **B** and **E.** In newer versions of AireOS, the Management Interface is used for all service communication and also functions as the CAPWAP channel termination interface. In older versions, the AP-Manager interface was used for this purpose.

6. **E.** Smart Licensing allows for the pooling of licenses into a Smart Account that can be used by all controllers in the organization.

Chapter 5

1. **A.** The receiver's sensitivity level defines the threshold between intelligible and unintelligible signals. As long as the received signal strength is greater than the sensitivity level, the receiver can likely interpret the signal correctly.

2. **C.** The AP's signal strength is measured according to the received signal strength indicator (RSSI) of a client device and compared against the design criteria. The cell boundary is then defined by the points surrounding the AP where the RSSI is equal to the design threshold.

3. **E.** The commonly used best-practice value for the AP's RSSI at the cell boundary is −67 dBm. To eliminate some of the potential answers, remember that due to free space path loss, the cell boundary would never have a positive dBm value.

4. **D.** The SNR is defined as the received signal strength minus the noise floor, in dB.

5. **D.** The closer a client is located in relation to an AP, the stronger the AP's signal will be. With a stronger received signal, and constant or increasing SNR, the client will likely try to use a faster data rate.

6. **A.** At its cell boundary, an AP should have a signal strength that is at least 19 dB greater than any of its neighbors on the same channel. Ideally, no other AP should be heard above −82 dBm at an AP's cell boundary; otherwise, the CCA mechanism can trigger and flag the channel as busy based on transmissions from neighboring APs.

7. **B.** The cell boundary should be defined where the RSSI of the AP is –67 dBm when the lowest mandatory or supported data rate is used. The SNR should be 25 dB at any point within the cell area. The RSSI of the AP will eventually equal the noise floor as the signal is attenuated due to free space path loss over a much greater distance than the optimal cell boundary.

8. **B.** If the AP is already at its lowest transmit power level setting, your next strategy should be to connect an external directional antenna to the AP. The patch antenna will focus the AP's RF energy into a smaller area and will help reduce the AP's cell size.

9. **A, B, D.** Voice designs should use a minimum data rate of 12Mbps. It is important to consider the number of simultaneous calls that each AP can support, based on the minimum data rate. As a general guideline, you should leverage the many 5GHz channels, but carefully validate that you can use each DFS channel, only if radar signals have not been detected on them.

10. **C.** Multiple APs (at least three, preferably four or more) must be able to receive the tracked device's signal at a minimum level of –72 dBm. The device does not have to receive the AP signals at all; it can simply send periodic probe requests that are received by any neighboring APs. That also means the device does not have to associate with any AP.

Chapter 6

1. **B.** Cisco APs send Neighbor Discovery Protocol (NDP) messages to advertise their presence on every supported channel. APs can receive these messages to learn of the presence of other neighboring APs.

2. **B, D.** Cisco APs transmit their NDP advertisements on each supported channel, using the maximum supported transmit power level.

3. **B.** Two neighboring APs must have an RSSI of greater than –80 dBm to be considered close enough to influence each other as neighbors in a neighborhood.

4. **D.** The transmit power control (TPC) algorithm adjusts the power level used by each AP in an RF group.

5. **B.** The TPC algorithm automatically controls AP transmit power levels. If a change is needed, TPC raises or lowers the AP's transmit power level by one 3 dB increment each time it runs until the power level gets as close as possible to the desired value.

6. **C.** The goal of DCA is to maintain an efficient channel layout and avoid interference and noise. Therefore, DCA might choose to move the AP to a different channel.

7. **A.** TPC and DCA are RRM algorithms that run on a per-RF group basis. Therefore, the controller that is currently the RF group leader runs the algorithms.

8. **D.** A failed radio will probably cause a hole or weakness in the RF coverage around the AP. Coverage hole detection can detect the failure based on the weak signal clients in that area are experiencing. The algorithm can also boost the transmit power level in neighboring APs to help heal the coverage hole or other coverage gaps that are detected.

9.   **A, C.** The Flexible Radio Assignment (FRA) algorithm computes a Coverage Overlap Factor (COF) value for each AP. If the COF exceeds a threshold, the AP is considered to be providing redundant coverage. FRA can only reassign a flexible (XOR) radio from 2.4GHz to the 5GHz band, so 2.4GHz coverage overlap is also an FRA criteria.

10.   **B.** You can customize RF-related settings by creating an RF group that will be applied to APs in the one unique building. The APs in that building must be mapped to an AP group and then the RF profile must be applied to that AP group.

11.   **D.** You can use RxSOP to filter out weak signals from neighboring APs using the same channel. However, you should carefully choose the RxSOP threshold so that you do not end up creating coverage holes and stranding wireless clients. You should not raise the TPC maximum limit because that might allow TPC to increase the transmit power level of some APs, which would only make the problem worse. You should not disable any 5GHz channels and lose the advantage of a greater number of available channels. With a reduced set of channels, more APs will have to reuse the same channel numbers, increasing the possibility of co-channel interference.

Chapter 7

1.   **C.** The root access point (RAP) is the root of a Wi-Fi mesh network and provides backhaul to the child MAPs, as well providing connection back to the wired network that links to the controller.

2.   **C.** There are two 160GHz channels available in the 5GHz spectrum. It is generally recommended to use wider channels when possible to support better performance; however, interference and increased contention are considerations to be aware of when using wider channels.

3.   **D.** MAPs and RAPs have an Ethernet interface that allows wired clients to be connected. These are switches natively through a mesh header, but they exit the mesh through the RAP natively to the switched network on the correct VLAN. The wired traffic does not use CAPWAP and does not terminate on the controller.

4.   **B and C.** To configure an AP as a mesh device (a MAP or a RAP), it must be either in Bridge mode or Flex+Bridge mode.

5.   **B and C.** Many mesh APs have only a single 5GHz radio for backhaul. This means that all APs in a mesh tree must operate on the same channel, which causes interference and increases contention. To overcome this issue, multiple APs may be daisy chained, allowing the creation of different cells on non-overlapping channels. This allows the mesh tree to be larger and to perform better.

6.   **C.** WGBs function as wireless clients to the mesh network.

Chapter 8

1.   **D.** A reassociation request frame signals that a client is wanting to move its existing association to the target AP. An authentication request is used to initiate 802.11 authentication (open or WEP) before a client begins an association. An association request is used to begin an initial association with an AP. There is no valid roam request frame in 802.11.

2.   **B.** The client undergoes inter-controller roaming at Layer 2 both times, because the APs are joined to different controllers. Because the same IP subnet exists on each AP, the roam was at Layer 2.

3.   **C.** AP-2 is joined to WLC-2. The client initially associated with AP-1, so WLC-1 is the anchor controller and WLC-2 is the foreign controller. The client is currently associated with AP-2, so WLC-2 is its point of attachment (POA). WLC-1 would be the client's point of presence (POP), marking the location where the client appears to be connected.

4.   **B.** A single mobility group can have a maximum of 24 controllers.

5.   **D.** A single mobility domain can consist of a maximum of three mobility groups (up to 24 controllers each), or a total of 72 controllers in the mobility domain.

6.   **C.** CAPWAP tunnel testing uses the **cping** command. EoIP tunnel testing uses **eping**, and mobility control messaging uses the **mping** command. The familiar **ping** command is used to test generic IP connectivity through ICMP echo requests and replies.

7.   **B.** A client uses active scanning to actively discover any neighboring APs. The client tunes its radio to various channels and transmits 802.11 probe requests, then waits a short time to see if it receives any probe response frames from live APs.

8.   **A, D.** The 802.11k and 802.11v amendments are useful to help roaming clients find candidate APs more efficiently. The 802.11r amendment is useful in roaming scenarios, too, but it focuses on making the roaming process itself more efficient rather than helping clients find APs.

9.   **C.** 802.11r is known as Fast BSS Transition, or FT. The term "fast secure roaming" does not refer to a specific technique; rather, it is a general term used to describe any method of making roaming more efficient in a secure WLAN.

10. **B.** The FT 4-way handshake occurs during the client's 802.11 authentication and reassociation frame exchange with the AP. The PTK and GTK keys are generated then, even before the client is fully reassociated and joined to the target AP. With an 802.11r roam, the 802.1X/EAP authentication, PMK generation, and normal 4-way handshake steps are not needed.

Chapter 9

1.   **C, D.** The LAG (link aggregation group) bundles multiple physical ports into a single logical one. This is done to add redundancy, in case one or more distribution port links fail, as well as to load-balance traffic across the multiple links.

2.   **B.** Bundling multiple physical ports into a single logical one forms a LAG (link aggregation group). The LAG connects to an EtherChannel or port-channel on a switch.

3.   **D.** The switch must be configured to form an EtherChannel or port-channel unconditionally because the WLC does not support any negotiation protocol for its LAG.

4.   **C.** The APs must first detect that their original working controller has failed. Then they must decide on a new controller to try to join.

5.   **B.** The AP priority determines which APs can join a controller when the controller fills with APs.

6.   **A.** Every AP begins with the default Low priority value.

7.   **D.** APs use CAPWAP keepalive messages that are sent to the controller every 30 seconds.

8.   **D.** The AP Fallback feature allows APs to fall back or revert to a primary controller at any time.

9.   **C.** N+N redundancy is being used because there are two active controllers and no standby or backup controllers.

10. **D.** Stateful switchover (SSO) keeps the AP and client states synchronized between the active and hot standby controllers, which minimizes any disruption. The other redundancy methods are more disruptive as APs take time to detect a failure and move to another controller.

Chapter 10

1.   **B.** Only Mobility Express does not require a centralized controller.

2.   **A, B.** RRM and WIPS will be lost, but roaming will continue to work.

3.   **B.** In this case, only RRM is lost. Clients may still roam within the FlexConnect group while in standalone mode, and only central authentication will be lost. Local authentication is still possible if it has been configured.

4.   **C.** Because the application includes only wireless data applications, and because 10 APs are in use, the minimal bandwidth requirement is 128Kbps with a minimum of 300 ms latency between the FlexConnect APs and the controller.

5.   **C.** The missing step is to configure the WLAN for local switching. Without doing this from the WLAN configuration, all WLANs will be centrally switched.

6.   **D.** FlexConnect groups are required to cache the keys locally, thus allowing fast roaming between APs.

7.   **B, D.** CAPWAP message aggregation should be turned on to improve the performance of the CAPWAP control messages, and local authentication will use a local RADIUS server instead of relying on the central RADIUS server located over the WAN.

8.   **C.** An ACL is required to identify which centrally switched traffic should have access to the local LAN. Answer A is incorrect because this changes the behavior of the centrally switched WLAN to be locally switched. Answer B is incorrect because NAT/PAT is automatically enabled by the split tunneling feature. Answer D is incorrect because split tunneling may be configured at either the AP or the FlexConnect group level.

9.   **B.** Smart AP image upgrades will still function without a predefined master, but the master will be automatically selected based on the lowest MAC address from the APs in the FlexConnect group.

10. **B.** Office Extend APs use DTLS to secure communications between the AP and controller.

11. **A, B, D.** IOS-XE controllers use Site, RF, and Policy tags for configuration.

12. **A.** For an AP to be put into OEAP mode, it must first be converted to FlexConnect mode.

Chapter 11

1. **D.** In CSMA/CA, every frame must be acknowledged by the receiving station; otherwise, it would be impossible to know if a collision occurred.

2. **B.** EDCA specifies exactly four Access Categories (ACs) for Wi-Fi. Any WMM-compliant device must support the four well-defined ACs.

3. **D.** The TXOP (Transmission Opportunity) is the metric defined that allows a station to continually transmit until the timer expires. The TXOP interval is unique per AC.

4. **D.** Although it can do other things, the primary role of the AireOS QoS profile is to set the maximum DSCP value on the CAPWAP header, and thus the downstream UP value.

5. **C.** The Silver profile will limit the DSCP marking on the CAPWAP tunnel to zero, which will also translate to an UP value of 0 on the 802.11 header.

6. **A, B, C.** For Microsoft environments, Group Policy may be used. For Apple environments, Apple Configurator may be used. Meraki MDM may be used for most mobile devices; however, DNA-Center does not have this capability.

7. **B.** AVC is capable of remarking DSCP, dropping traffic, and rate limiting but not Weighted Tail Drop.

Chapter 12

1. **B, D.** Multicast frames are not required to be acknowledged like unicast frames are. They must be transmitted at the highest mandatory configured data rate, rather than the rate in use for unicast traffic to the client. The frame must be sent on a 20MHz channel or on the primary 20MHz channel of a wider channel.

2. **C.** The recipient must first send an IGMP membership report packet upstream to the local router. The router will then add the ingress interface to its multicast routing table and will inform other routers. Multicast traffic can reach all hosts if it is flooded on switches and into AP cells, but not always—especially if IGMP snooping is enabled.

3. **B.** By using the multicast-multicast mode, a WLC and its APs will first build a multicast group for CAPWAP traffic. Then the underlying wired infrastructure can deliver multicast CAPWAP packets from the WLC to all of its APs simultaneously, rather than force the WLC to replicate the CAPWAP traffic to each AP with individual unicast streams.

4. **C.** Each AP must learn the CAPWAP multicast group address from the WLC as it joins. Then the AP must send an IGMP Membership Report packet to the upstream router and ask to join the multicast group. From then on, the WLC can send multicast traffic to its CAPWAP group address to reach all APs simultaneously.

5. **B.** Through IGMP snooping, the controller can eavesdrop and learn about multicast groups that wireless clients have joined. The WLC will also know which APs those clients are associated with.

6. **D.** The MGID is a unique identifier or index into a table of multicast groups and the wireless client recipients that have registered to receive group traffic.

7. **A, D.** Controllers in the same mobility group can send mobility event messages to each other over multicast. All of the controllers must be configured to use the same multicast mobility group address. Mobility multicast messaging operates independently of the CAPWAP multicast group.

8. **C.** The Bonjour protocol uses mDNS to discover resources that are available on a network. However, the discovery requests and advertisements must stay within the same IP subnet. You should configure mDNS snooping to enable a controller to intercept Bonjour messages and relay them across subnets and VLANs when necessary.

9. **B.** Location Specific Services (LSS) narrows the list of specific resources down to only the ones learned from the list of APs that neighbor the requesting client.

10. **B.** Multicast Direct (also called VideoStream or Media Stream) allows a WLC to take incoming multicast video streams and redirect them as unicast streams to individual recipient wireless clients. The goal is to improve the quality of video delivery over the wireless medium.

Chapter 13

1. **B.** Accuracy measures how close to the actual location (ground truth) the location estimation is. High accuracy is highly desirable. Precision measures how close each location estimate is to the others. Precision is useful but not critical. The RSSI threshold is configurable. SNR is usually not configured for location.

2. **C.** AoA typically provides an accuracy down to 1 to 2 meters. FastLocate augments RSSI trilateration by bringing the expected accuracy from 7 to 9 meters to 5 to 7 meters. Cell of origin may provide inaccurate location, with possibly errors of hundreds of meters.

3. **C.** AireOS 8.8 MR2 and later, along with C9800/eWLC, can be configured to connect to DNA Spaces directly. These and older code releases can be configured to connect through a DNA Spaces connector virtual appliance. APs cannot connect to DNA Spaces without a WLC. MSE is not required.

4. **A.** Maps can be automatically exported from Cisco Prime Infrastructure into MSE. They can also be exported and imported manually when Cisco Prime Infrastructure and MSE are not connected. WLCs do not include maps. Maps cannot be configured on the MSE directly. There is no option to import a map from DNA Spaces.

5. **D.** On the activity map, the heat map represents the density of users in various areas: red for more users; green then blue for fewer users.

6. **B.** A single map cannot display the location of more than 2,000 devices. When more than 2,000 devices are present, CMX will display the associated clients in priority. If your map consistently has more than 2,000 devices, you should divide it into submaps.

Chapter 14

1. **A.** MSE comes with a 120-day trial license and 100 APs for all services. This allows customers to try its functionalities in a lab or a test site. This capability is likely one of the reasons why networking professionals are expected to be familiar with the tool.

2. **B.** You need the Act license in order to access the Location Analytics feature in DNA Spaces, while the See license restricts your access to business insight. The other license names do not exist for DNA Spaces.

3. **D.** A zone is defined manually on a map and assigned a label. Although the zone may have a meaning for the facility or network owner, it does not map specifically to any associated RF element.

4. **B.** In C9800 redirect ACLs, traffic denied by the ACL rule is redirected. In AireOS, traffic allowed by the rule is redirected.

5. **B.** An AP in Monitor mode needs to stay on each channel long enough to detect frames and their repeat pattern. The WIPS submode is designed around this need. WIPS is a submode available for APs in Local mode and Monitor mode. CMX does not implement the concept of WIPS zone.

6. **C.** The WLC receives the AoA messages from the AP and relays them immediately to the MSE, on port UDP 2003. TCP 16113 is used by other Network Mobility Services Protocol (NMSP) messages.

Chapter 15

1. **D.** EAP is the protocol used between a supplicant on the client and the authentication server. It employs EAPoL using 802.1X between the client and the authenticator (the controller), and uses EAP over RADIUS between the authenticator and the authentication server.

2. **B.** EAP-TLS is the EAP method that supports PKI and X.509 certificates. Some EAP methods, such as PEAP, only require a certificate on the server.

3. **C.** EAP-FAST uses Protected Access Credentials (PACs) on the client, which functions as a cookie/token to validate that the client has been authenticated and thus improves roaming performance.

4. **E.** The controller can profile a client based on MAC OUI (which identifies the device type), DHCP options, and HTTP headers. Incorporating NMAP information as part of the profile scan is possible with ISE but is not natively possible on the controller.

5. **A, B, C, D.** The controller can enforce policy based on all of these.

6. **B, D.** In LWA, the guest/BYOD portal may be on either the controller or another external portal server; however, the redirect URL and ACL are only configured on the controller.

7. **B, D.** LWA is based on Layer 3 (the redirect URL is configured on the controller), whereas CWA uses MAC filtering first (Layer 2) and then ISE pushes down the redirect URL and ACL to the controller (Layer 3).

8. **C.** ISE uses Change of Authority (CoA) using RADIUS accounting to make security changes on the controller after authentication.

Chapter 16

1. **B.** A trend report uses aggregated data to output an analysis over a past chosen period for particular sets of metrics. Cisco PI does not make future projections and does not use Machine Learning techniques. Cisco network management tools do not produce industry analysis.

2. **C.** DNAC continuously produces reports, so you do not need to configure them specifically. AP loads are visible from the Dashboard on Network Health. From there, you can customize the period you want to review and then export the results.

3. **D.** A rogue is an AP not managed by your system and may be a perfectly valid AP operated by one of your neighbors. Containing a valid AP is illegal in most countries. Therefore, you should investigate very carefully before making any containment decision. DNAC does not have a Smart Containment option.

4. **A.** A rogue client is one of your clients that is connecting to a rogue AP instead of your wireless infrastructure. The reason why one of your clients made this decision might need to be investigated. A rogue client does not offer AP services (otherwise, it would be classified as a rogue AP) and does not send invalid frames (it just associates to a rogue). A client that establishes direct connection to other clients is called an ad hoc rogue.

5. **D.** By default, a client that completes L2 authentication moves to the DHCP_reqd state. It is only after the WLC detects that the client uses a static IP address (seeing client data traffic) that the WLC understands that no DHCP phase is required, and the client is moved to Run state. Authcheck appears during the L2 authentication phase, and the end of the L2 authentication phase is labeled L2authcomplete. DHCP_fail is not a valid message.

6 **A.** An Apple iOS client will send an unsolicited 802.11k neighbor report at (re)association time, and a Samsung client will send the report upon query from the AP (at [re]association and various intervals). The report shows how the client hears the surrounding APs (which APs and at what RSSI level). The report does not show how the APs hear the client. There is no "test connectivity" button in the Client 360 page, and the WLC does not query the clients for CCX scan reports.

7. **C.** On C9800, Packet Capture enables capture over the wired interfaces (physical interfaces and VLAN). AP Packet Capture enables capture over the air. When this function is activated, you can capture headers (to limit the volume) or the whole frames, and you can select which types of 802.11 frames you want to capture: data, management, or control. Both clients and APs send all three types.

8. **A.** SI is a subset of CleanAir and only reports some interferers. Inverted waveforms are not detected by this system. The C1800 AP includes SI functionality, but not the SAgE chip needed to activate full CleanAir. By default, CleanAir is enabled on the C9800 and reports all interferers (from supporting APs), both short- and long-lived.

Chapter 17

1. C. The key advantage of TACACS+ over RADIUS is the support for granular levels of authorization, whereas RADIUS only supports read-only or read-write access.

2. D. The Device Admin Policy Set menu allows the administrator to create rules that map user groups (for example, defined by Active Directory) to the TACACS+ profiles. The TACACS+ profiles define the specific levels of management access to a controller.

3. D. The 802.1X supplicant is used in NAC implementations where all devices must authenticate to the switch to gain access to the network.

4. B. Policy sets are required to enable authentication and authorization of an AP with an 802.1X supplicant.

5. B. Because the CPU ACL will restrict all communication to and from the CPU (the management control plane), the recommended method is to explicitly deny certain traffic types that you wish to restrict but permit all others.

D

CCNP Enterprise Wireless Design ENWLSD 300-425 and Implementation ENWLSI 300-430 Exam Updates

Over time, reader feedback allows Pearson to gauge which topics give our readers the most problems when taking the exams. To assist readers with those topics, the authors create new materials clarifying and expanding on those troublesome exam topics. As mentioned in the Introduction, the additional content about the exam is contained in a PDF on this book's companion website, at http://www.ciscopress.com/title/9780136600954.

This appendix is intended to provide you with updated information if Cisco makes minor modifications to the exam upon which this book is based. When Cisco releases an entirely new exam, the changes are usually too extensive to provide in a simple updated appendix. In those cases, you might need to consult the new edition of the book for the updated content. This appendix attempts to fill the void that occurs with any print book. In particular, this appendix does the following:

- Mentions technical items that might not have been mentioned elsewhere in the book

- Covers new topics if Cisco adds new content to the exam over time

- Provides a way to get up-to-the-minute current information about content for the exam

Always Get the Latest at the Book's Product Page

You are reading the version of this appendix that was available when your book was printed. However, given that the main purpose of this appendix is to be a living, changing document, it is important that you look for the latest version online at the book's companion website. To do so, follow these steps:

Step 1. Browse to www.ciscopress.com/title/9780136600954.

Step 2. Click the Updates tab.

Step 3. If there is a new Appendix E document on the page, download the latest Appendix E document.

> **NOTE** The downloaded document has a version number. Comparing the version of the print Appendix E (Version 1.0) with the latest online version of this appendix, you should do the following:
>
> - **Same version:** Ignore the PDF that you downloaded from the companion website.
>
> - **Website has a later version:** Ignore this Appendix E in your book and read only the latest version that you downloaded from the companion website.

Technical Content

The current Version 1.0 of this appendix does not contain additional technical coverage.

GLOSSARY

Numerics

802.11k An amendment to the 802.11 standard that defines a method of assisted roaming, as part of "Radio Resource Management."

802.11r An amendment to the 802.11 standard that defines a method of fast BSS transition (FT). Clients capable of FT associate normally and then can reassociate very quickly by using a special FT 4-way handshake during the authentication and reassociation exchanges with subsequent APs.

802.11v An amendment to the 802.11 standard that defines methods of BSS transition, as part of "Wireless Network Management."

802.1X_reqd The state on the WLC of a Wi-Fi client that successfully completed 802.11 authentication and 802.11 association and has now moved to the 802.1X/EAP authentication state.

A

Acceptable Use Policy (AUP) An agreement that a guest or BYOD user must accept before gaining access to a network. The AUP typically contains legal disclaimers and an agreement on how the client may use the network.

Access Category (AC) Introduced as part of EDCA, there are four Access Categories: Voice, Video, Best Effort, and Background. Each AC is given different access rules to prefer higher- over lower-priority traffic.

Adaptive Wireless Path Protocol (AWPP) AWPP is a mechanism used by MAPs to dynamically find the best parent link in a mesh network. AWPP uses the ease metric in its selection of the MAP.

ad hoc rogue One of your clients that establishes a peer-to-peer Wi-Fi connection to another Wi-Fi client, instead of going through the wireless infrastructure connection.

anchor controller The original controller a client was associated with before a Layer 3 inter-controller roam occurs. An anchor controller can also be used for tunneling clients on a guest WLAN or with a static anchor. Traffic is tunneled from the client's current controller, the foreign controller, back to the anchor.

AP Fallback An AP can try to rejoin its primary controller at any time it becomes available, rather than staying with the secondary or tertiary controller after a controller failure.

AP on a stick (APoS) A survey mode where APs are tentatively positioned on a tripod, so as to determine the best position for intended APs in this area.

AP prioritization   An AP can be assigned a priority value (low, medium, high, critical) to be used when joining a controller. Higher-priority APs are admitted to the controller ahead of ones with lower priorities.

AP-COS   A controller-based operating system used on 802.11ac Wave 2 and later APs.

Application Visibility and Control (AVC)   A method used on the wireless controller to inspect the payload of the traffic. Once AVC identifies the type of application in use, it has the ability to change the DSCP markings, rate limit, or drop the traffic.

AQI   Air Quality Index, a measure of how each channel is affected by all detected interferers. The scale is from 1 to 100, with 100 representing no interference detected, and 1 representing an unusable channel.

Arbitrated Interframe Space Number (AIFSN)   A mandatory wait timer that must be observed by stations before transmitting onto the medium. There are different AIFSNs for each Access Category.

association   A fresh wireless connection between a client and an AP.

asymmetric transmit power levels   The condition where an AP and a client device use different transmit power level values, resulting in one of them not receiving the other.

authentication server (AS)   The authentication server looks up the identity of the authentication request (either from a local store or from a distributed identity store) and authenticates them for access to the network. The authentication server can also provide policy for how new clients should be handled. The AS is sometimes referred to as a Network Authentication Server (NAS).

authenticator   A network device that communicates with the supplicant to receive the username and password from the client. The authenticator communicates with the authentication server over RADIUS to authenticate the user and apply policy as they are connected to the network. In a wireless LAN, the authenticator is either the access point or the controller. The authenticator is sometimes referred to as the Network Access Device (NAD).

B

Bring Your Own Device (BYOD)   A common modality used in wireless networks where the users bring their own mobile devices and gain access to the network through an onboarding process. BYOD is typically deployed in conjunction with LWA or CWA on the wireless infrastructure.

C

CAPWAP Message Aggregation   A method where multiple CAPWAP control messages are sent to an AP, and then the AP responds with a bulk acknowledgment. This is a method used to improve the performance of CAPWAP control over the WAN.

Carrier Sense Multiple Access / Collision Avoidance (CSMA/CA)   A "listen before you talk" method of transmitting a frame onto the wireless medium. In CSMA/CA, each frame must be acknowledged by the receiving station.

CCKM   Cisco Centralized Key Management is a proprietary fast secure roaming method. A client's PMK is cached for future roams, shortening the time needed for reassociation. CCKM requires a CCX-capable client.

cell   The RF coverage area of a wireless access point; also called the basic service area (BSA).

central switching   In FlexConnect, this refers to SSIDs that are centrally switched on a controller.

central web authentication (CWA)   A method of redirecting BYOD and guest users where the redirection URL and the pre-WebAuth ACL are centrally configured on ISE and communicated to the controller via RADIUS.

CHDM   See coverage hole detection mitigation (CHDM).

Cisco MultiGigabit   Also known as Cisco mGig, this is a technology based on NBASE-T providing up to 5Gbps on standard Cat 5e cabling and up to 10Gbps on Cat 6a cabling.

CleanAir   The Cisco solution to detect and report interferers and manage WLAN channels based on detected interferers' characteristics.

client (location context)   Any 802.11 device, with the exclusion of rogue APs, their clients, and RFID tags.

client density   The relative number of wireless clients located in proximity to each other, requiring special consideration.

CM   See cost metric (CM).

CMX   Connected Mobile Experience is the location-based services engine software that runs on Cisco MSE appliances.

COF   See coverage overlap factor (COF).

connected mode   This is a FlexConnect mode when the controller is reachable from the AP.

Contention   The phenomenon that occurs when multiple stations must compete for access to a wireless medium. In Wi-Fi, only one station may transmit at a given time. If more than one station wishes to transmit, it creates contention for the medium.

Contention Window (CW)   A period that a station must wait before transmitting a frame. The CW comes after the DIFS/AIFSN. The CW is a random number that is generated by the station between 0 and CWmin on the first attempt. The CW doubles in size after each retry, until a maximum of CWmax is achieved.

cost metric (CM)   A metric computed and used by the DCA algorithm to determine the potential performance that is possible on each channel that APs are using, as well as channels that they potentially could use.

coverage hole An area that is left without good RF coverage. A coverage hole can be caused by a radio failure or a weak signal in an area.

coverage hole detection mitigation (CHDM) An RRM algorithm that can automatically detect areas of weak RF coverage and compensate by increasing AP transmit power levels.

coverage overlap factor (COF) A metric computed by the RRM FRA algorithm that indicates the percentage of an AP's cell area that has overlapping coverage from other neighboring APs.

CPU ACL A type of ACL that can be implemented on the controller to restrict stations and traffic types from accessing functions of the controller that impact the controller, such as SSH, HTTP, ICMP, and others.

D

daisy chaining A method of increasing the size of a mesh by connecting two mesh segments back-to-back using a wired connection.

DBS See dynamic bandwidth selection (DBS).

DCA See dynamic channel assignment (DCA).

decibel (dB) A logarithmic scale measuring an increase or decrease in power.

decibel milliwatt (dBm) A measure of power relative to a reference value of 1 milliwatt.

DHCP_reqd The state on the WLC of a Wi-Fi client that successfully completed the L2 authentication phase and is in process of obtaining an IP address through DHCP. A client with a static IP address may stay in this state until the WLC detects the static IP address.

Diffserv Code Point (DSCP) An IP marking scheme that uses 6 bits in the IP packet header. DSCP allows for 64 possible levels of service.

Distributed Coordination Function (DCF) The rules of how a frame is transmitted onto the wireless medium. DCF leverages CSMA/CA and was the primary media access algorithm used by 802.11a/b/g.

DNA Spaces Cisco cloud-based location solution that can work in combination with WLCs, connecting directly to or through DNA Spaces Connector, or can work in combination with on-premises MSE appliances.

dynamic bandwidth selection (DBS) A criteria used by the DCA algorithm to maximize throughput by changing an AP's channel width in a dynamic fashion.

dynamic channel assignment (DCA) An RRM algorithm that monitors APs in an RF group and adjusts their channel assignment based on poor RF conditions.

Dynamic Frequency Selection (DFS) A mechanism where the AP can scan and avoid RF channels used by radar stations.

dynamic rate shifting (DRS) The process of dynamically changing the data rate used in a wireless transmission based on the RF conditions affecting the signal.

E

EAP (Extensible Authentication Protocol)   EAP is an authentication framework used extensively in wireless networks for the handling of access credentials between a client device and an authentication server. The EAP framework defines common authentication functions. There are numerous available EAP methods that can be used between a client and the authentication server.

EAP-FAST (Flexible Authentication via Secure Tunnels)   Similar to PEAP, a tunneled EAP method. EAP-FAST uses Protected Access Credentials (PACs) on the client to help improve fast roaming in wireless environments.

EAP-MSCHAPv2 (Microsoft Challenge-Handshake Authentication Protocol version 2)   A popular EAP inner-method. MSCHAPv2 allows for simple transmission of username and password from a supplicant to the RADIUS server.

EAP-TLS (Transport Layer Security)   An EAP inner-method that utilizes X.509 certificates on both the client and authentication server.

ease   A metric used by a MAP in the AWPP mechanism as it tries to join the optimal parent.

EDRRM   Event-Driven RRM, a mechanism to trigger an RRM channel recomputation when a severe interferer has been reported on a channel for more than 30 minutes.

ED-RRM   See event-driven RRM (ED-RRM).

end user license agreement (EULA)   A license agreement on the controller that, once accepted, allows the controller to manage AireOS access points.

Enhanced Distributed Channel Access (EDCA)   An improvement over DCF that was introduced as part of 802.11e and provides QoS handling through different media access rules for each class of service.

Enhanced Local mode   An AP mode where the AP performs data service and WIPS detection (solely on its active channel).

European Telecommunication Standards Institute (ETSI)   The regulatory body in charge of wireless communications for the European Union. Its rules are followed by several non-European countries.

Event-driven RRM (ED-RRM)   Normal RRM algorithms that are triggered by an event such as detecting a source of interference or a rogue device, rather than running periodically.

F-G

fast BSS transition (FT)   See 802.11r.

Fastlane   An AutoQoS macro that is supported on both AireOS and IOS-XE controllers as a way to implement a wide array of QoS features in best-practice approach.

FastLocate   A location accuracy augmentation technique where a connected client's unicast frames complement broadcast management frames to compute the client's most probable location.

Federal Communications Commission (FCC)   The regulatory body in charge of wireless communications for the United States. Its rules are also followed by several other countries.

FlexConnect   An access point mode used in remote branch office scenarios where the AP is managed by a central controller but has the ability to switch traffic locally without sending it back to the controller over a CAPWAP tunnel.

FlexConnect groups   A logical grouping of Flex Connect APs that allows local authentication key caching allowing high-speed roaming as well as roaming while in standalone mode.

Flexible Radio Architecture (FRA)   A Cisco innovation that allows one AP radio to be configured to switch bands and switch between a macro and micro antenna pattern, either as a static configuration or a dynamic operation.

flexible radio assignment (FRA)   An RRM algorithm that can automatically detect an AP that is providing redundant 2.4GHz coverage and can reassign that AP to offer added coverage in the 5GHz band or monitor RF conditions.

foreign controller   The current controller a client is associated with after a Layer 3 inter-controller roam occurs. Traffic is tunneled from the foreign controller back to an anchor controller so that the client retains connectivity to its original VLAN and subnet.

FRA   See flexible radio assignment.

FT   See fast BSS transition.

H

Health   On DNAC, Health refers to a number of KPIs combined to surface a connectivity and performance evaluation level for an infrastructure or client device.

Hyperlocation   An Angle of Arrival (AoA) technique that can help bring location accuracy down to a meter level.

I

identity store   The identity store is the place where the client credentials are stored. The identity store is typically kept in an LDAP server.

IEEE 802.1X   A standard for port-based network access control (NAC). 802.1X provides a method for authentication of devices connecting to a network. 802.1X defines encapsulation of EAP over Layer 2 protocols. This is commonly known as EAPoL (EAP over LAN).

IGMP   See Internet Group Management Report (IGMP).

IGMP Snooping   A feature that allows a network device, such as a switch or WLC, to eavesdrop on IGMP packets in transit and make multicast delivery decisions based on the group membership contents.

Intelligent Capture   On C9800 and DNAC, Intelligent Capture (sometimes abbreviated as iCap) is a dynamic over-the-air capture tool that analyzes the exchanges between a client and the infrastructure to surface anomalies. The tool can also export the capture in .pcap format.

inter-controller roaming   Client roaming that occurs between two APs that are joined to two different controllers.

Internet Group Management Protocol (IGMP)   A protocol used to control membership in a multicast group.

intra-controller roaming   Client roaming that occurs between two APs joined to the same controller.

J-K

jitter   The variance of the end-to-end latency experienced as consecutive packets arrive at a receiver.

L

L2authcomplete state   The state on the WLC of a Wi-Fi client having successfully completed Layer 2 authentication (PSK handshakes or 802.1X/EAP authentication).

latency   The amount of time required to deliver a packet or frame from a transmitter to a receiver.

Layer 1 sweep   A site survey process aiming at discovering non-802.11 transmitters on the bands intended for the WLAN deployment.

Layer 1 sweep   A survey mode intended to detect (and locate) non-802.11 interferers.

Layer 2 roam   An inter-controller roam where the WLANs of the two controllers are configured for the same IP subnet.

Layer 3 roam   An inter-controller roam where the WLANs of the two controllers are configured for different IP subnets. To support the roaming client, a tunnel is built between the controllers so that client data can pass between the client's current controller and its original controller.

Lightweight Directory Access Protocol (LDAP)   An open, standards-based protocol used by the authentication server to access device and user identity stores. Microsoft Active Directory (AD) is an example of a popular LDAP server used by many companies.

local switching   In FlexConnect, this refers to SSIDs that are locally switched on the AP itself and do not transit to the controller.

local web authentication (LWA)   A method of redirecting BYOD or guest users to a portal directly from the wireless controller. The redirection and pre-WebAuth ACL are locally configured on the controller, not an external server.

location accuracy   The measure of how close to the client's actual location (ground truth) the location estimation is.

location precision   The measure of how consecutive location evaluations are close to one another.

Location Specific Services (LSS)   A WLC feature that works with mDNS to respond to resource queries with only the resources learned from AP neighbors nearest the requesting client.

LSS   See Location Specific Services (LSS).

M

mDNS   See multicast DNS (mDNS).

mesh access point (MAP)   The MAP is an access point that forms a wireless link to either the RAP or another MAP.

MGID   See multicast group ID (MGID).

mobility domain   A logical grouping of all mobility groups within an enterprise.

Mobility Express   An access point mode where the AP supports controller capabilities directly on the AP, without the need for an external controller. Mobility Express is often used in remote branch settings.

mobility group   A logical grouping of one or more controllers between which efficient roaming is expected.

MSE   Mobility Services Engine is an appliance, typically on premises, where the CMX services run.

multicast   A type of packet delivery where one packet is sent to multiple recipients over a network.

Multicast Direct   A WLC feature that can redirect incoming multicast video streams into unicast streams directed toward each individual recipient on a wireless network. By doing so, the WLC can maximize the quality and delivery of the multicast video stream.

multicast DNS (mDNS)   The multicast domain name system uses IP multicast to discover online resources dynamically. mDNS is used by Apple Bonjour and Google Chromecast and can work over wired and wireless networks.

multicast group   A destination IP address from a special range of addresses used only for multicast traffic.

multicast group ID (MGID)   An arbitrary index into a table of multicast groups and their registered recipients, as defined and used by a WLC.

Multicast Listener Discovery (MLD)   A feature that eavesdrops on traffic to learn of IPv6 multicast recipients, much the same way IGMP snooping does for IPv4 multicast.

N

N+1 redundancy   High availability offered by N number of active controllers plus one idle standby controller.

N+N redundancy   High availability offered by N number of active controllers. The AP load is distributed across the active controllers, removing the need for an additional backup controller.

N+N+1 redundancy   High availability offered by N number of active controllers plus one idle standby controller.

NDP   See neighbor discovery protocol (NDP).

neighbor discovery protocol (NDP)   A Cisco proprietary protocol used by APs to advertise their presence, allowing other neighboring APs to discover them. Many of the RRM algorithms use the data collected from NDP advertisements to compute their results.

Network Admission Control (NAC)   A technology used to challenge all access to the network to ensure the device or user is trusted and is allowed to connect. Typically, NAC employs IEEE 802.1X as a challenge-response system to first identify the user or device and then grants access with a certain privilege level.

noise floor   The level of ambient noise present in the environment at a particular frequency.

O

OEAP   An Office Extend Access Point. This is an AP mode used in remote office scenarios where the AP uses a VPN tunnel to connect over the Internet back to a central controller, in effect extending the corporate network to a remote office location.

OKC   See Opportunistic Key Caching.

omnidirectional antenna   An antenna that directs RF energy in all directions, resulting in a low antenna gain.

Opportunistic Key Caching (OKC)   A fast, secure roaming method that caches the PMK for the lifetime of the client and shares it across all APs on the same controller. OKC is not defined in the 802.11 standard.

P-Q

packet loss   The percentage of packets sent that does not arrive at the receiver.

patch antenna   An antenna that directs RF energy toward a specific direction, usually perpendicular to the antenna's flat area, resulting in a higher antenna gain.

Path Trace   On DNAC, Path Trace is a function by which you can test the communication between two points on a particular set of ports. Path Trace is not only useful for troubleshooting application performances but also to evaluate the effect of the configuration ofnetworking devices on endpoints' communication.

PBM   A lifecycle process that includes three phases: Plan, Build, and Manage.

perimeter   In CMX, a perimeter is the area where location will be performed.

PIM   See Protocol Independent Multicast (PIM).

PMKID Caching   A fast, secure roaming method introduced in 802.11i that caches the pairwise master key (PMK) identifier to improve roaming efficiency.

POA   See point of attachment.

PoE (Power over Ethernet)   Based on the IEEE 802.3af standard; provides up to 15.4W of power to a device.

PoE+   PoE+ is based on the IEEE 802.3at standard and provides up to 30W of power to a device.

point of attachment (POA)   The controller that anchors a client's IP address for Layer 3 roaming.

point of presence (POP)   The controller where a client is currently associated.

policy set   A mechanism in ISE used to create policy rules for authentication and authorization of users to the network.

POP   See point of presence.

power injector   A network device that is externally connected to a power source and injects electrical power into the cable to power an end device.

power sourcing equipment (PSE)   The PSE is the networking hardware (such as a switch) that delivers PoE to an end device.

powered device (PD)   The PD is the end device that is powered by either the PSE or a power injector over twisted pair copper cable.

PPDIOO   A Cisco lifecycle process that includes six phases: Prepare, Plan, Design, Implement, Operate, and Optimize.

preauthentication   A fast, secure roaming method introduced in 802.11i that preauthenticates a client by sharing its PMK across neighboring APs after it associates with one. Cisco WLCs and APs do not support preauthentication.

preauthentication access control list   For guest portals, a preauthentication ACL is created on the WLC for a target WLAN to ensure that all traffic prior to guest authentication is directed to the portal.

predictive survey   A survey mode where the number of APs is estimated offsite, from a scaled floor plan.

proactive key caching (PKC)   See opportunistic key caching (OKC).

Probing state   The state on the WLC of a Wi-Fi device from which probe requests have been received. That device may or may not decide to continue to the association phase.

Protected EAP (PEAP)   PEAP is a tunneled EAP method that protects inner EAP methods, such as MSCHAPv5 or EAP-GTC. PEAP requires a server certificate on the authentication server.

Protocol Independent Multicast (PIM)   A multicast routing protocol used between routers.

pseudo-MAC   A virtual MAC address allocated to an interferer by a detecting SAgE chipset, so as to be able to allocate a unique identifier to each detected interferer.

R

radio resource management (RRM)   The set of Cisco proprietary algorithms used to automatically control and tune a wireless network and its AP radios.

real-time location services (RTLS)   The process of automatically determining the location of wireless devices.

reassociation   A roaming action, where a wireless client moves its association from one AP to another.

received signal strength indicator   The measured signal strength of a received signal, normally expressed in dBm.

receiver start of packet threshold detection (RxSOP)   A Cisco proprietary feature that can apply a threshold to APs such that received signals with an RSSI lower than the threshold will be ignored.

Remote Authentication Dial-In User Service (RADIUS)   A UDP-based networking protocol that provides centralized authentication, authorization, and accounting (AAA) management for users connecting to a network service.

RF group   A logical grouping of wireless LAN controllers that operates as a single RF domain. RRM algorithms run on a per-RF group basis.

RF group leader   A controller that is elected to handle all of the RRM algorithms for the entire RF group on a single frequency band.

RF neighborhood   A logical set of APs that are in close RF proximity to each other.

RF profile   A policy of RRM-related RF parameters that can be applied to a logical grouping of APs in an RF group.

Right-to-Use (RTU)   An honor-based licensing system that requires the user to accept an EULA on the controller.

rogue AP   An access point that is not managed by your WLCs. A rogue can be an access point from your organization, managed by another system (friendly, internal rogue), a valid neighboring AP (friendly, external rogue), or an attacker AP posing a threat to your network (malicious rogue).

rogue client   One of your clients that disconnected from your network to attach to a rogue AP.

root access point (RAP)   This is the root of any mesh tree and is a mandatory requirement for any mesh. The RAP connects to the wired network.

RRM   See radio resource management (RRM).

RSSI trilateration   A location technique where the signals (RSSI) from mobile device broadcast management frames (for example, probe requests) received at several APs are compared to compute the device's most probable location.

Run   The state on the WLC of a client that successfully completed all onboarding phases and can exchange data through the Wi-Fi infrastructure.

RxSOP   See receiver start of packet threshold detection (RxSOP).

S

SAgE   Spectrum Analysis Engine, a specialized chip on most Cisco APs that can read, demodulate, and interpret non-802.11 signals to report interferers.

sensitivity level   The received signal strength threshold that divides intelligible, useful signals from unintelligible ones.

severity   For an interferer, this is the measure of the effect of the interference on your network performance. The scale is from 1 to 100, with 100 representing an unusable channel.

SI   Spectrum Intelligence, a software-based non-802.11 interferer-detection mechanism implemented on lower-end Cisco APs that do not include a SAgE chipset. SI typically detects a subset of the interferers that SAgE detects.

signal-to-noise ratio (SNR)   The difference between a received signal's strength and the noise floor.

SKC Caching   See PMKID Caching.

Smart Image upgrade   A feature where a FlexConnect master AP is used as a proxy to upgrade the image of other APs in the FlexConnect group.

Smart Licensing   A newer method of managing Cisco software licenses that allows central pooling of licenses in a Smart Account. This approach negates the need to license each controller for the APs it is managing.

split tunneling   The ability for a centrally switched WLAN client to access resources directly on the local LAN.

SSO   High availability offered by two controllers configured as a failover pair. One controller is active and supports the AP and client load, while the other controller is a hot standby. Stateful information about APs and clients in the RUN state is synchronized between the active and hot standby units for efficient failover.

standalone mode   A fallback mode for the FlexConnect AP when the controller is no longer reachable. The AP still functions but with fewer services.

supplicant   The supplicant is a piece of software running on the client device that provides the username and password to the authenticator over EAP.

T

Telecom Engineering Center (Telec)   The regulatory body in charge of wireless communications for Japan.

Terminal Access Controller Access-Control System + (TACACS+)   A TCP-based client/server protocol that provides centralized AAA security controls for users attempting to gain management access to a controller.

TPC   See transmit power control (TPC).

Transmission Opportunity (TXOP)   A time period given for a station to continually transmit frames once it has won the EDCA contention algorithm.

Transmission Specification (TSpec)   A method of Call Admission Control that is used in 802.11e to reserve bandwidth on an AP, allowing a client to transmit high-priority traffic.

transmit power control (TPC)   An RRM algorithm that automatically adjusts the transmit power level of APs to minimize cell overlap and interference.

U

UPOE   Universal PoE is a Cisco proprietary standard that delivers up to 60W of power to a device.

UPOE+   Universal POE+ is a Cisco proprietary standard that delivers up to 90W of power to a device.

User Priority (UP)   A 3-bit field in the 802.11 frame header that identifies the QoS class of the frame. The UP field allows for eight levels of service, although there are only four available Access Categories.

V

validation survey   Also sometimes called passive survey, this is a survey mode where an application associates a floor plan to detected APs.

W-X-Y

Webauth_reqd   The state on the WLC of a client of a WebAuth WLAN that successfully associated and authenticated, obtained an IP, and moved to the WebAuth authentication phase. As this phase is manual while the previous phases of the association are usually automatic, some clients may stay in this state for a long time (until the user notices the authentication requirement on the device screen).

Wi-Fi Protected Access (WPA)   WPA, WPA2, and WPA3 are security compatibility standards used by the Wi-Fi Alliance, which leverage EAP. The WPA standards were developed in response to vulnerabilities discovered in WEP.

Wireless Multimedia (WMM)   The QoS compatibility standard used by the Wi-Fi Alliance (WFA). WMM leverages the recommendations in the 802.11e specification.

Workgroup Bridge (WGB)   A device that provides switching services that are backhauled over the wireless link.

Z

zone   In CMX and DNA Spaces, a zone is an area defined by the operator to which a label was applied.

Index

B

T

X-Y-Z

CCNP Enterprise Wireless Design ENWLSD 300-425 and Implementation ENWLSI 300-430
Official Cert Guide
Companion Website

Access interactive study tools on this book's companion website, including practice test software, review exercises, Key Term flash card application, study planner, and more!

To access the companion website, simply follow these steps:

1. Go to **www.ciscopress.com/register**.
2. Enter the print book ISBN: **9780136600954**.
3. Answer the security question to validate your purchase.
4. Go to your account page.
5. Click on the **Registered Products** tab.
6. Under the book listing, click on the **Access Bonus Content** link.

If you have any issues accessing the companion website, you can contact our support team by going to **pearsonitp.echelp.org**.